FOSTERING A GLOBAL COMMUNITY
OF SHARED FUTURE:
CONTEMPORARY SIGNIFICANCE
AND TANGIBLE ACHIEVEMENTS

构建人类命运共同体的
时代价值和实践成就

（中文版）

新华社国家高端智库课题组　著

新 华 出 版 社

图书在版编目（CIP）数据

构建人类命运共同体的时代价值和实践成就 / 新华社国家高端智库课题组著 .
北京 : 新华出版社 , 2025. 6.
ISBN 978-7-5166-8006-3

Ⅰ . D81

中国国家版本馆 CIP 数据核字第 2025Y54Z33 号

构建人类命运共同体的时代价值和实践成就（中文版）

著者： 新华社国家高端智库课题组
出版发行： 新华出版社有限责任公司

（北京市石景山区京原路 8 号　邮编：100040）

印刷： 捷鹰印刷（天津）有限公司

成品尺寸： 170mm×240mm 1/16　　　　**印张：** 16.5　**字数：** 220 千字
版次： 2025 年 6 月第 1 版　　　　　　　**印次：** 2025 年 6 月第 1 次印刷
书号： ISBN 978-7-5166-8006-3　　　　　**定价：** 98.00 元（中英文版）

微店

视频号小店

抖店

京东旗舰店

微信公众号

喜马拉雅

小红书

淘宝旗舰店

扫码添加专属客服

目录
Contents

构建人类命运共同体的时代价值和实践成就 [①]

人类社会在发展进步中，孕育出不同的文明和制度。同处人类唯一的地球家园，我们该如何共存，如何并行向前？

2013年3月，中国国家主席习近平提出推动构建人类命运共同体。[②]中国共产党的二十大报告鲜明指出："构建人类命运共同体是世界各国人民前途所在。万物并育而不相害，道并行而不相悖。只有各国行天下之大道，和睦相处、合作共赢，繁荣才能持久，安全才有保障。"[③]

11年来，人类命运共同体理念不断丰富、发展，理论体系不断完备，时代价值日益凸显，真理光芒穿越时代风云，成为引领时代前进的不竭思想动力。

11年来，构建人类命运共同体从中国倡议发展为国际共识。越来越多的国家和人民认识到，这一理念符合全人类共同价值和共同利益，汇聚了各国人民共建美好世界、共创美好未来的最大公约数。构建人类

---

① 2024年4月30日发布于贝尔格莱德，中塞媒体智库研讨会

② https://www.gov.cn/ldhd/2013-03/24/content_2360829.htm

③ https://www.gov.cn/xinwen/2022-10/25/content_5721685.htm

命运共同体因而多次被写入联合国等国际组织文件，受到众多国家和国际组织领导人高度赞赏和支持。

11 年来，推动构建人类命运共同体从美好愿景转化为丰富实践，取得丰硕成果。共建"一带一路"等国际合作蓬勃展开，双多边命运共同体建设不断推进，人类卫生健康共同体、网络空间命运共同体、核安全命运共同体、海洋命运共同体、人与自然生命共同体、地球生命共同体、全球发展共同体、人类安全共同体等多领域建设，使推动构建人类命运共同体有了多维架构和切实抓手。

推动构建人类命运共同体，是习近平外交思想的核心理念，体现了中国共产党人的世界观、秩序观、价值观，指明了世界文明进步的方向。它既是马克思主义"真正的共同体"（die wirkli - che Gemeinschaft）思想的发展运用，也是对中华优秀传统文化的传承弘扬，回响着世界不同文明中古老智慧和共同追求的历史共鸣。

推动构建人类命运共同体，是中国式现代化的本质要求之一。作为拥有世界近五分之一人口、与世界紧密联系的大国，中国通过自身现代化发展，助力世界迈向持久和平、普遍安全、共同繁荣、开放包容、清洁美丽的未来。"世界好，中国才会好；中国好，世界会更好。"[1] 推动构建人类命运共同体，既体现了中国在当今世界实现自身发展的要求，也体现了中国的大国责任与担当。

"这个世界，各国相互联系、相互依存的程度空前加深，人类生活在同一个地球村里，生活在历史和现实交汇的同一个时空里，越来越成为你中有我、我中有你的命运共同体。"[2] 推动构建人类命运共同体，与每一个民族、每一个国家、每一个人的前途与命运紧密相连，是着眼

---

[1] http://www.beltandroadforum.org/n101/2023/1018/c132-1174.html

[2] https://www.gov.cn/ldhd/2013-03-24/content_2360829.htm

人类命运终极关怀的具象操作，是人类文明赓续传承的精神指引。

一、治世之道——应对共同挑战的中国方案

当今世界，人类社会不仅面临沉重的历史欠债，也面临严峻的现实考验。推动构建人类命运共同体是各国应对挑战、解决纷争、弥合分歧的治世之道，是推动人类社会迈向持久和平、普遍安全、共同繁荣、开放包容、清洁美丽世界的中国良方。

（一）直面共同挑战的时代强音

15 世纪的地理大发现以来，西方发达国家依靠武力征服和全球掠夺逐步建立起不平等的国际产业分工体系和不公正的国际政治经济秩序，导致多数发展中国家至今无法彻底摆脱跨国资本的枷锁和意识形态操控，始终在发展困境中挣扎。与此同时，西方发达国家一味逐利的资本主义体系也面临过度金融化、产业空心化、社会两极化、政治极端化等一系列问题，政坛纷乱、经济滞缓、社会撕裂，民众困惑迷茫愤懑。

长期以来特别是 18 世纪工业革命以来，人类向大自然索取了太多，构成了严重破坏，也影响到人类社会的可持续发展。地球升温、气候变化造成极端天气频发、农作物减产和一些疾病流行，人类生命财产损失巨大，经济社会可持续发展挑战巨大。

新技术革命速度不断加快，由此引发的社会变革势头迅猛，考验各国的适应能力和治理能力。新技术带来新的不平等，技术差异、数字鸿沟形成新的割裂分化，出现技术寡头垄断与恶意操控等新的不公正现象，人类不仅要应对技术霸权带来的新危害，还要面对不可预知的技术风险。

在非传统威胁日益突出的同时，各种传统威胁并未减少。俄乌冲突硝烟未止，中东地区纷争再起。局部安全形势恶化，负面影响外溢全球。

一些大国缺少合作共识，阵营对抗氛围再度弥漫。世界经济复苏乏力，保护主义、零和思维搅乱全球产业链、供应链。当今世界的和平赤字、发展赤字、安全赤字、治理赤字并存，多边治理体系面临严峻挑战。

新老问题叠加碰撞，复杂矛盾交织发酵，世界的不稳定、不确定成为常态。正如联合国秘书长古特雷斯 2023 年 8 月在金砖国家同非洲国家及其他新兴市场和发展中国家领导人对话会上发表讲话时所说："我们无法承受一个全球经济和金融体系分裂、人工智能等技术战略各行其是、安全框架相互冲突的世界。"① 何去何从，人类又一次站在十字路口。

面对当今世界各种风险挑战，面对"建设一个什么样的世界，如何建设这个世界"这一关乎人类命运的重大课题，中国提出了鲜明方案——推动构建人类命运共同体。

（二）共创美好未来的世界愿望

人类社会在漫长的发展过程中，自然形成了不同的族群、不同的历史、不同的文化。在中国人看来，世界是个百花园，不同社会制度、不同历史文化的国家各美其美。虽然走过的路不同，但各国人民对美好未来的向往是一样的，追求和平与繁荣的目标是一致的。推动构建人类命运共同体，汇聚了各国人民共建美好世界的最大公约数。

推动构建人类命运共同体，强调"共"——不是以一种制度代替另一种制度，不是以一种文明代替另一种文明，而是不同社会制度、不同意识形态、不同历史文化、不同发展水平的国家在国际事务中利益共生、权利共享、责任共担。

推动构建人类命运共同体，促进"融"——即便在交通工具极不发

---

① https://news.un.org/zh/story/2023/08/1120907

达的古代，丝绸之路上的驼队、漂洋过海的商船、游历广泛的旅行家、无所不至的探险家，都为人类文明交流互鉴、进步发展发挥了作用。地理大发现加速全球资源流动，科学技术发展拓宽人类认知，全球化的壮丽画卷徐徐铺开，人类日益成为一个"你中有我、我中有你"、命运交融、密不可分的共同体。

推动构建人类命运共同体，主张"合"——习近平主席强调："在人类追求幸福的道路上，一个国家、一个民族都不能少。"[①] 推动构建人类命运共同体符合全人类的共同利益，反映了世界人民追求和平、发展、公平、正义、民主、自由的心声，昭示了历史演进的正确方向，因而得到越来越多国家和人民的认同，汇聚起强大的文明合力。

自习近平主席2013年提出构建人类命运共同体理念至今，其思想内涵不断丰富发展，具体实践稳健推进。推动构建人类命运共同体，已成为中国在世界历史演变重要关头，为共同应对全球挑战、共创美好未来提供的中国方案，为动荡变革的世界廓清迷雾，为全球发展指明前行方向。

（三）中国式现代化的本质要求

以中国式现代化全面推进中华民族伟大复兴是新时代中国共产党的历史使命。在实现中国式现代化的历史进程中，推动构建人类命运共同体是其有机组成部分，也是其本质要求之一。

中国从来不以孤立割裂的视角看待自身与世界的关系。习近平主席在第三届"一带一路"国际合作高峰论坛的主旨演讲中这样讲述中国与世界的关系："世界好，中国才会好；中国好，世界会更好。"[②]

---

① http://www.xinhuanet.com/politics/leaders/2021-07/07/c_1127628998.htm
② http://www.beltandroadforum.org/n101/2023/1018/c132-1174.html

"中国的发展离不开世界，世界的繁荣也需要中国。"① 中国从世界多国进口先进设备、原材料和重要物资，进口来源覆盖全球六大洲200多个国家和地区，中国庞大的市场需求为各国企业提供了巨大的合作机遇。② 中国广泛学习世界各国优秀文明成果和先进经验，在交流借鉴中激发思想火花，形成具有中国特色的智慧结晶。作为世界第二大经济体、制造业第一大国、货物贸易第一大国，中国积极为世界和平稳定和经济发展贡献力量。中国是联合国预算第二大出资国③，成为"维和行动的关键因素和关键力量"。④ 过去十年，中国对世界经济增长的贡献超过三分之一。中国从世界汲取发展动力，也让中国的发展更好地惠及世界。

构建人类命运共同体是建设中国式现代化的逻辑必然。中国式现代化是人口规模巨大的现代化，是全体人民共同富裕的现代化，是物质文明和精神文明相协调的现代化，是人与自然和谐共生的现代化，是走和平发展道路的现代化。中国不仅走和平发展道路，同时也是维护世界和平的坚定力量，致力于推动"建设一个持久和平的世界"；中国秉持共同、综合、合作、可持续的安全观，致力于推动"建设一个普遍安全的世界"；中国追求全体人民共同富裕，也希望通过合作共赢，推动"建设一个共同繁荣的世界"；中国坚持物质文明和精神文明相协调，主张坚持交流互鉴，"建设一个开放包容的世界"；中国加强生态文明建设，努力实现人与自然和谐共生，致力于推动"建设一个清洁美丽的世界"。中国式现代化的五个"中国特色"同构建人类命运共同体的"建设五个世界"

---

① http://www.xinhuanet.com/politics/2020-11/10/c_1126723118.htm
② https://www.gov.cn/lianbo/fabu/202401/content_6925700.htm
③ https://www.gov.cn/xinwen/2018-12/24/content_5351537.htm
④ http://www.mod.gov.cn/gfbw/jsxd/wh/4839681.html

一脉相通，均体现了中国经济、政治、文化、社会、生态"五位一体"的全方位发展理念，体现了对个体的尊重、对公平的坚守、对和平的崇尚、对发展的追求、对自然的敬畏，体现了中国妥处人与人、人与自然两对关系的智慧和努力。

实现中国式现代化与推动构建人类命运共同体有机联系、密不可分。中国式现代化将为推动构建人类命运共同体提供坚实基础。占世界人口近五分之一的中国实现现代化，本身就是对人类社会现代化的巨大贡献。中国式现代化的成功也将为其他发展中国家的现代化提供借鉴和新的路径选择，助力全球共同发展，推动全人类的现代化，使构建人类命运共同体具备更有利的现实条件。构建人类命运共同体是中国式现代化的本质要求之一。这既源于中国共产党内在的历史使命，也源于实现中国式现代化所需的外在环境。中国共产党不仅要为中国人民谋幸福，也立志为人类谋进步、为世界谋大同。人类共同和平发展的良好外部环境，无疑是中国实现现代化的有利条件。

坚持在推进中国式现代化过程中推动构建人类命运共同体，使中国式现代化进程有别于西方现代化。西方的现代化伴随着侵略、掠夺、血腥和不平等。中国不走西方现代化的老路，发展过程中不危害他国利益，而是秉持人类命运与共的理念，坚持平等协商、合作共赢、共同发展，以自身的发展为他国发展提供机遇，让各国人民都从中国发展中受益。

"立己达人"，在实现中国式现代化的过程中推动构建人类命运共同体，中国人民将与世界人民携手共创美好未来。

二、美美与共——激发世界共鸣的中国主张

人类命运共同体，就是每个国家的前途命运都紧密相连，不同群体风雨同舟、和谐共生、合作共赢。这一理念道出了国与国交往的人间正道，

激发国际社会的共鸣和期盼，也展现中国的大国责任和担当。

（一）人类命运共同体理念的思想内涵

人类命运共同体理念，蕴含有开放包容、公平正义、和谐共处、多元互鉴、团结协作的丰富内涵：

开放包容——不以意识形态划线，不针对特定的对象，不拉帮结派，不搞排他的"小圈子"，海纳百川，有容乃大；

公平正义——维护以国际法为基础的国际秩序，维护国际法治权威，确保国际法平等统一适用，不搞双重标准，不搞"合则用、不合则弃"；

和谐共处——各国在求同存异的前提下实现和平共处、共同发展，世界发展的活力恰恰在于多样性的共存；

多元互鉴——人类文明多样性是世界基本特征，不同文明交流互鉴是推动人类进步的重要动力；

团结协作——"计利当计天下利"，单打独斗无法应对全球性的发展难题，各国通力合作才是唯一选择。

2013 年 3 月，习近平主席在访问俄罗斯期间首次提出人类命运共同体理念，呼吁国际社会树立"你中有我、我中有你" 的命运共同体意识。[①]

2015 年 9 月，在世界反法西斯战争胜利和联合国成立 70 周年这一重要节点，习近平主席在联合国倡议构建以合作共赢为核心的新型国际关系，阐述构建人类命运共同体"五位一体"的总体框架：建立平等相待、互商互谅的伙伴关系；营造公道正义、共建共享的安全格局；谋求开放创新、包容互惠的发展前景；促进和而不同、兼收并蓄的文明交流；

---

① https://www.gov.cn/ldhd/2013-03/24/content_2360829.htm

构筑尊崇自然、绿色发展的生态体系。[①]

2017 年 1 月，习近平主席在联合国日内瓦总部发表主旨演讲，提出推动建设持久和平、普遍安全、共同繁荣、开放包容、清洁美丽的世界。[②] "五个世界"总目标是人类命运共同体理念的深化拓展，为人类未来描绘了更清晰的图景：坚持对话协商，建设一个持久和平的世界；坚持共建共享，建设一个普遍安全的世界；坚持合作共赢，建设一个共同繁荣的世界；坚持交流互鉴，建设一个开放包容的世界；坚持绿色低碳，建设一个清洁美丽的世界。

"五位一体"的总体框架和"五个世界"的总目标，使人类命运共同体理念更加立体而丰富，为人类政治、安全、经济、文化、生态发展提供了重要遵循。

在人类命运共同体理念指引下，中国提出构建新型国际关系，走出一条相互尊重、公平正义、合作共赢的国与国交往新道路。中国践行真正的多边主义，呼吁各国成为世界和平与发展的参与者、贡献者、受益者。中国提出和平、发展、公平、正义、民主、自由的全人类共同价值，体现人类命运共同体理念的价值追求。

（二）人类命运共同体理念的文化渊源

构建人类命运共同体理念是极富科学性的思想体系。它是对马克思主义思想精髓的科学运用，是对中华优秀传统文化的传承发扬，是马克思主义和中华优秀传统文化贯通结合的智慧结晶，同时也反映了人类不同民族长期形成的文明成果和价值认同。

人类命运共同体理念是马克思主义中国化时代化的重要理论成果，

---

① http://www.xinhuanet.com/world/2015-09/29/c_1116703645.htm
② http://www.xinhuanet.com/world/2017-01/19/c_1120340081.htm

它的理念基础和内在逻辑与马克思主义思想精髓一脉相承。

马克思在《1844年经济学哲学手稿》中写道，"人是类存在物"。他在《关于费尔巴哈的提纲》这篇论著中也指出，"人的本质并不是单个人所固有的抽象物，在其现实性上，它是一切社会关系的总和"。人类生命的绽放，只有在共同体中才能完成。马克思和恩格斯在《德意志意识形态》中指出："只有在共同体中，个人才能获得全面发展其才能的手段，也就是说，只有在共同体中才可能有个人自由。"共同体符合人类本质的内在要求，是人类本质的必然显现。

马克思主义认为，人类共同体的演进经历了这样一个历史过程：前资本主义阶段，人类社会形态以血缘、亲属关系为纽带，构成一种"自然的共同体"。进入资本主义阶段后，人类社会形成"虚幻的共同体"，人的个体有能力进行生产和交换，看似获得自由，实则开始从依赖共同体转变为依赖于以财产或货币形式存在的"物"。"虚幻的共同体"不能真正代表绝大多数人民的实际利益，未来必定被"真正的共同体"取代，每个人终将成为自身的主宰，是处于一定社会关系并自由自觉地从事生产生活的人，每一个自由发展的人以个体身份参与联合，并在联合中真正获得自由发展。

构建人类命运共同体理念是新的时代条件下对马克思主义"共同体"理论的创新与发展，开创了科学社会主义理论的新天地新境界。

人类命运共同体理念体现中华优秀传统文化的思想，如"协和万邦""万国咸宁"的世界观、天下观，"以和为贵""和合共生"的价值观、文明观，"天下为公""义利并举"的道义观、利益观，"天人合一""道法自然"的生态观、自然观。

"协和万邦""万国咸宁"的当代内涵意味着平等相待、和平合作。习近平主席2013年在二十国集团领导人第八次峰会第一阶段会议上就指出，各国要树立命运共同体意识，真正认清"一荣俱荣、一损俱损"

的连带效应，在竞争中合作，在合作中共赢。在追求本国利益时兼顾别国利益，在寻求自身发展时兼顾别国发展。让每个国家的发展都能同其他国家的增长形成联动效应，相互带来正面而非负面的外溢效应。①

"以和为贵""和合共生"意味着彼此尊重，美美与共。正如《中庸》所说："万物并育而不相害，道并行而不相悖。"中国始终主张以平和的态度看待不同文明和国家的差异，以包容的心胸理解不同政治制度和价值观念的差别，"万物并育""道并行"的当代诠释，就是构建人类命运共同体理念所强调的，尊重文明多样性，尊重各国人民自主决定本国发展道路的权利。

"天下为公""义利并举"奠定了构建人类命运共同体理念追求公平正义、互利共赢的思想底色。习近平主席 2015 年在第七十届联合国大会一般性辩论时的讲话中，全面阐述人类命运共同体的核心思想内涵时指出："我们要在国际和区域层面建设全球伙伴关系，走出一条'对话而不对抗，结伴而不结盟'的国与国交往新路。大国之间相处，要不冲突、不对抗、相互尊重、合作共赢。大国与小国相处，要平等相待，践行正确义利观，义利相兼，义重于利。"②

"天人合一""道法自然"蕴含着尊重自然、顺应自然、保护自然的系统思想，体现了中华文明关于人与自然和谐相处的理念与追求。习近平主席多次强调，自然是生命之母，人与自然是生命共同体，人类要像保护眼睛一样保护生态环境，像对待生命一样对待生态环境，解决好人与自然和谐共生问题。

构建人类命运共同体理念关怀的是全人类的共同命运，倡导的是全球各方互利共赢的价值导向，追求的是建设更加公平正义、团结合作

---

① http://www.xinhuanet.com//politics/2013-09/06/c_117249618.htm

② http://www.xinhuanet.com/world/2015-09/29/c_1116703645.htm

的美好世界，彰显中国共产党人矢志不渝推动人类和平与发展的天下情怀，也给予全世界所有抱持同样美好愿望和理想信念的民族和群体以崇高回应。

人类命运共同体理念体现人类文明的共同智慧和人类社会的共同追求。人类在历史长河中创造了多元共生的文明。尽管不同文明的语言载体不同，思维框架不一，信仰基础有异，但追求和平与发展的目标是共同的，建立公平、正义秩序的愿望是共同的，实现民主、自由权利的追求是共同的。

人类很多文明都存在与人类命运共同体理念共通的文化基因。瑞士联邦议会的联邦官圆顶中央，铭刻着一句格言——"我为人人，人人为我"（Unusproomnibus，omnesprouno）。① 古印度经典哲学文献《奥义书》提出"世界是一个大家庭"（Vasudhaiva Kutumbakam）。② 非洲很多地区信奉"乌班图"思想，其核心观念是"我们在故我在"。在美国犹他州费舍湖畔，一株地表以上有4万多棵枝干、地表下却共享同一根系的8万年巨树被命名为"潘多"，拉丁语含义是"我延伸"。"潘多"精神感召人们，看似毫不相干的独立个体，其实彼此存在深层联系。正因为每个个体都为整体提供养分，这个8万年的生命才能抵御洪水、干旱、山火、虫害等各种灾难，顽强地存活下来。

人类命运共同体理念是极具包容性的思想体系。它汲取世界多元文明相融相通的优秀成果，反映全人类的普遍愿望和共同心声，凝聚不同民族、不同信仰、不同文化的价值共识，体现了不同地区、不同国家、不同族群的治理经验和思想智慧。

---

① https://blog.nationalmuseum.ch/en/2020/04/one-for-all-all-for-one/
② https://pib.gov.in/PressReleasePage.aspx?PRID=1591742

（三）推动构建人类命运共同体的时代价值

凡益之道，与时偕行。人类命运共同体理念，汇聚各国人民求和平谋发展盼稳定的最大公约数，画出不同文化背景和发展程度国家之间的最大同心圆，超越零和博弈、强权政治、冷战对抗的陈旧思维，成为引领时代潮流和人类前进方向的鲜明旗帜。推动构建人类命运共同体，是中国在国际格局演变转折关头，为共同应对全球挑战、共创人类美好未来提供的中国方案。

推动构建人类命运共同体有助于建立更加公平公正的国际治理体系。国际社会普遍认为，世界不能走弱肉强食、零和博弈的老路，但对于如何进一步完善国际治理体系，使其向更加公平公正的方向发展，各国如何参与和推动这一进程，尚未形成共识。在人类历史的转折关头，推动构建人类命运共同体为世界治理体系的公平化民主化指明方向。

推动构建人类命运共同体，意味着坚持大小国家一律平等，反对霸权主义和强权政治，反对少数国家垄断国际事务，意味着尊重各国自主选择社会制度和发展道路的权利，全球事务应该由各国共同商量。任何国家都没有包揽国际事务、主宰他国命运、垄断发展优势的权力。

推动构建人类命运共同体，顺应经济全球化的时代潮流。从历史的眼光看，当今人类经济交往比过去任何时候都更深入广泛，各国相互联系和彼此依存比过去任何时候都更频繁紧密，各国走向开放、融合是时代大势。

推动构建人类命运共同体，意味着坚持经济全球化正确方向，反对任何人搞技术封锁、发展脱钩，共同将全球经济的蛋糕做大，同时秉承合作共赢的精神，将经济发展的蛋糕分好，让发展成果更多更公平地惠及各国人民，不让任何一个国家、任何一个人掉队。

推动构建人类命运共同体，契合世界对持久和平与普遍安全的追求。当今世界变乱交织，一些国家为追求自身绝对安全，在全球范围内挑动冲突对抗。

推动构建人类命运共同体，就是推动人类社会永铸和平之犁，坚持通过对话协商解决国家间分歧和争端，重视彼此合理安全关切，共同防范各类安全风险，反对肆意扩大军事同盟、挤压别国的安全空间，努力构建不冲突不对抗、相互尊重、合作共赢的新型国际关系。

推动构建人类命运共同体为人类文明进步揭示开放包容、交流互鉴的新愿景。推动构建人类命运共同体，意味着以文明交流超越文明隔阂、文明互鉴超越文明冲突、文明包容超越文明优越，追求各美其美、美美与共；意味着认同各国现代化道路的多样性，鼓励各国探索适合本国国情的发展模式；意味着推动各国优秀传统文化在现代化进程中实现创造性转化、创新性发展，促进各国人民相知相亲。

文明没有高下、优劣之分，只有特色、地域之别。文明差异不应成为世界冲突的根源。推动构建人类命运共同体，蕴含着对人类文明形态的前瞻性思考和对人类发展进步大势的准确把握，指明了不同国家、不同民族、不同文明的共同奋斗方向，必将凝聚越来越多的共识，推动人类社会迈向光明前程。

推动构建人类命运共同体将助力人类更好地面对生态挑战，实现永续发展。地球是全人类赖以生存的唯一家园。建设美丽家园是人类的共同梦想。面对生态环境危机，人类一荣俱荣、一损俱损，没有哪个国家能独善其身。

推动构建人类命运共同体，意味着共同建设更紧密的绿色发展伙伴关系，共同建设人与自然和谐共生的现代化，共同应对气候变化，共同守护人类栖息的蓝色星球。

三、惠益世界——造福全人类的中国实践

2013 年以来，在中国的不断推动下，构建人类命运共同体的实践

稳步推进，实现从"一方领唱"到"众声合唱"的多重跨越。构建人类命运共同体理念日益深入人心，日益受到国际社会广泛欢迎和支持，给世界带来巨大红利，为各国人民创造实实在在的福祉。

（一）不同层面、多个领域的命运共同体建设稳步推进

中国在多边与双边合作中，从不同层面、多个领域推动构建命运共同体，为全球和平与发展发挥建设性作用。

在多边层面，中非命运共同体是最早提出的区域命运共同体。世界上最大的发展中国家与发展中国家最集中的大陆命运紧紧相连。2013 年 3 月，习近平主席就任国家主席后不久就出访非洲，面向世界首次提出真实亲诚对非政策理念和正确义利观，郑重宣告中非永远做可靠朋友和真诚伙伴，强调"中非从来都是命运共同体"。10 余年来，在中非领导人引领和顶层设计下，中非在共建"一带一路"倡议和中非合作论坛等机制平台上不断深化合作，成果涵盖经贸、基建、民生等多个领域，新时代中非命运共同体建设持续造福双方民众，成为中国与地区国家构建命运共同体的成功范例。

此后，中阿、中拉、中国－太平洋岛国、中国－东盟、上海合作组织、中国－中亚等命运共同体建设稳步推进，相关国家团结共进、合作共赢，推动人类命运共同体理念获得更广泛国际认同，命运共同体建设不断走深走实。

在双边层面，中国同老挝、柬埔寨、缅甸、印度尼西亚、泰国、马来西亚、巴基斯坦、蒙古国、古巴、南非、越南等国，就构建双边命运共同体发表行动计划、联合声明或达成重要共识，同中亚五国双边层面践行人类命运共同体全覆盖，打造了新时代国家间关系的典范。

在不同领域，中国积极推动相关议题下的国际合作，将人类命运共同体理念转化为具体实践，以应对各种全球挑战。面对肆虐的新冠疫情，

中国提出构建人类卫生健康共同体；面对失序的网络空间治理，中国提出构建网络空间命运共同体；面对不断上升的核安全风险，中国提出打造核安全命运共同体；面对日益复杂的海上问题，中国提出构建海洋命运共同体；面对日趋严峻的气候变化挑战，中国先后提出构建人与自然生命共同体、地球生命共同体等重要理念……

人类命运共同体理念不仅是多元立体的，而且是生动鲜活的，它既解决当前世界面临的紧迫问题，也解决未来人类社会可持续发展的长远问题。

（二）"一带一路"合作有力践行人类命运共同体理念

"一带一路"倡议是中国为世界提供的重要国际公共产品和国际合作平台。它以互联互通为主线，坚持共商共建共享原则，秉持开放、绿色、廉洁理念，以高标准、可持续、惠民生为目标，沿着高质量发展方向不断前进，推动基础设施"硬联通"、规则标准"软联通"、共建国家人民"心联通"，使共建国家在政策、设施、贸易、资金乃至民心上产生更加紧密的连接，促进协同联动发展，实现共同繁荣。11 年来，共建"一带一路"从亚欧大陆延伸至非洲、拉美，150 多个国家、30 多个国际组织签署共建"一带一路"合作文件，举办 3 届"一带一路"国际合作高峰论坛，成立了 20 多个专业领域多边合作平台。

"一带一路"成为中国与共建国家携手发展的合作之路、机遇之路、繁荣之路。2013—2022 年，中国与共建国家进出口总额累计 19.1 万亿美元，年均增长 6.4%；与共建国家双向投资累计超过 3800 亿美元。[1]2023年，中国与共建国家进出口规模和占中国外贸总值的比例再创新高。[2]

---

① http:/www.scio.gov.cn/zfbps/zfbps_2279/202310/t20231010_773682.html

② https://www.gov.cn/lianbo/fabu/202401/content_6925700.htm

经济走廊和国际通道建设卓有成效，共建国家港口航运、"空中丝绸之路"建设、国际多式联运大通道持续拓展。共建"一带一路"有力提高共建国家的减贫能力。据世界银行预测，到 2030 年，共建"一带一路"相关投资有望使共建国家 760 万人摆脱极端贫困，3200 万人摆脱中度贫困。此外，中国与共建国家积极扩展在文化旅游、教育、媒体和智库等领域合作，搭好"民心相通"的社会根基。"一带一路"合作在健康、绿色、创新、数字丝绸之路建设等方面也取得积极进展，国际合作空间更加广阔。①

"一带一路"合作开创 21 世纪人类大合作、大发展的新格局，成为构建人类命运共同体的重要实践。共建国家致力于协同发展、互利共赢，有力推动各国产业结构升级、产业链优化布局。陆海空网大建设改善了许多国家的基础设施，平等协商对话打通共建国家之间的政策堵点，贸易往来蓬勃开展促进国际商品交易，各种便利化措施加速共建国家之间资金流动，合作共赢的经济交流带动各国人文交流促进民心相通。人类历史上从未有过涉及国家如此之多、涉及人口如此之众、涉及领域如此广泛、涉及内容如此丰富的"大合作"。"一带一路"合作给 21 世纪的世界带来巨大发展空间，成为推动人类社会共同发展和构建人类命运共同体的重要实践，具有重要历史意义。

（三）落实三大倡议成为构建人类命运共同体的战略引领

2021 年以来，习近平主席陆续提出全球发展倡议、全球安全倡议、全球文明倡议，引领中国扎扎实实维护全球和平、促进全球发展、推动文明交流互鉴。

---

① http://www.scio.gov.cn/zfbps/zfbps_2279/202310/t20231010_773682.html

全球发展倡议有效回应了国际社会特别是广大发展中国家加快经济发展、实现可持续发展的强烈愿望和迫切需求，着眼破解国家间和各国内部发展不平衡、不充分问题，为推动世界以合作促发展指明了方向，得到国际社会广泛响应。

2021年9月，习近平主席在第七十六届联合国大会一般性辩论上的讲话中首次提出全球发展倡议，呼吁国际社会加快落实联合国2030年可持续发展议程，构建全球发展命运共同体。[①] 全球发展倡议，最核心的要求是坚持以人民为中心；最重要的理念是倡导共建团结、平等、均衡、普惠的全球发展伙伴关系；最关键的举措在于坚持行动导向，推动实现更加强劲、绿色、健康的全球发展。

如今，全球发展促进中心顺利运转，全球发展倡议项目库不断扩大，超过200个合作项目开花结果，100多个国家和国际组织支持全球发展倡议，70多个国家参与在联合国成立的"全球发展倡议之友小组"。

中国始终是全球发展的贡献者。中国坚定推动建设开放型世界经济，已成为140多个国家和地区的主要贸易伙伴，同28个国家和地区签署了20多个自贸协定。作为世界上最大的发展中国家和"全球南方"的一员，中国力所能及地为其他发展中国家提供援助，帮助受援国提高发展能力。中国同世界粮食计划署等近20个国际组织开展合作，在埃塞俄比亚、巴基斯坦、尼日利亚等近60个国家实施了130多个项目，涵盖减贫、粮食安全、抗疫、气候变化等领域，受益人数超过3000万人。中国帮助非洲减缓债务压力，积极推动并全面落实二十国集团缓债倡议，同19个非洲国家签署缓债协议或达成缓债共识，在二十国集团缓债倡议中贡献最大。[②]

---

① https://www.gov.cn/xinwen/2021-09/22/content_5638597.htm

② https://www.gov.cn/zhengce/202309/content_6906335.htm

全球安全倡议倡导自身安全与共同安全不可分割、传统安全与非传统安全不可分割、安全权利与安全义务不可分割、安全与发展不可分割，主张国际社会成员以更加全面综合的视角审视全球安全问题，以更强烈的责任感使命感守护国际共同安全，为解决国际纷争、维护共同安全指明了方向。

2022年4月，习近平主席在博鳌亚洲论坛年会上提出全球安全倡议，强调安全是发展的前提，人类是不可分割的安全共同体。[①]2023年2月，中国发布《全球安全倡议概念文件》，提出"六个坚持"，进一步阐释了倡议的核心理念与原则、重点合作方向及合作平台和机制。文件指出，坚持共同、综合、合作、可持续的安全观是理念指引，坚持尊重各国主权、领土完整是基本前提，坚持遵守联合国宪章宗旨和原则是根本遵循，坚持重视各国合理安全关切是重要原则，坚持通过对话协商以和平方式解决国家间的分歧和争端是必由之路，坚持统筹维护传统领域和非传统领域安全是应有之义。[②]

全球安全倡议自提出以来受到国际社会广泛欢迎和积极响应，目前已得到100多个国家和国际组织支持、赞赏，写入中国与其他国家、国际组织交往合作的众多双多边文件，一些合作行动稳步推进。倡议框架下提出20个重点合作方向，涵盖国际和地区热点问题、维和行动等传统军事安全领域和气候变化、信息、生物、外空、人工智能、公共卫生等非传统安全领域，直面当前国际社会最突出的安全关切。

长久以来，中国始终致力于成为维护世界和平安宁不可或缺的建设性力量。从持之以恒推动政治解决朝鲜半岛以及伊朗核问题，到成功斡旋沙特阿拉伯和伊朗复交，并围绕乌克兰危机和巴以新一轮冲突发布代

---

① https://www.gov.cn/xinwen/2022-04/21/content_5686424.htm

② https://www.fmprc.gov.cn/wjbxw_new/202302/t20230221_11028322.shtml

表中方立场的文件、积极促和止战，中国守护全球安全的诚意和担当始终如一。

全球文明倡议展现中国对人类文明多元平等的高度尊重和致力于推动中外文明交流互鉴、共同繁荣的宽广胸怀。

2023年3月，习近平在中国共产党与世界政党高层对话会上提出全球文明倡议，强调不同文明包容共存、交流互鉴，在推动人类社会现代化进程、繁荣世界文明百花园中具有不可替代的作用。[①] 文明因交流而多彩，因互鉴而丰富。在中国看来，文明没有高下、优劣之分，只有特色、地域之别。文明差异不应该成为世界冲突的根源，而应该成为人类共同进步的动力。全球文明倡议既强调遵循人类文明发展的客观规律，又指出处理不同文明之间关系的正确态度和方法；既要让本国文明充满勃勃生机，又要为他国文明发展创造条件，是推动不同文明和衷共济、和谐共生、互尊互敬、互谅互让的重要遵循。

中国主持召开中国共产党与世界政党高层对话会、中国共产党与世界政党领导人峰会、亚洲文明对话大会等，广泛开展双多边政党交流合作，推进形式多样的民间外交、城市外交、公共外交，与多国共办文化旅游年、国际艺术节等双多边文化交流活动，推动建立发展友好城市（省州）关系，为促进各国文明交流发展搭建新平台，汇聚新力量，促进新共识，有力推进全球文明交流互鉴，受到国际社会普遍欢迎。

今天，世界之变、时代之变、历史之变正以前所未有的方式展开。和平、发展、合作、共赢的历史潮流不可阻挡。站在充满挑战的十字路口，中国鲜明提出推动构建人类命运共同体，让人类共识的理性光辉照耀未来，推动人类社会在风雨考验中携手前行！

---

① https://www.gov.cn/xinwen/2023-03/15/content_5746950.htm

中国提出构建人类命运共同体，是站在历史正确的一边，站在绝大多数国家的共同利益一边，站在人类进步的一边。中国始终致力于做世界和平的建设者、全球发展的贡献者、国际秩序的维护者。

构建人类命运共同体，正在得到越来越多国家和人民的认同与支持。这是世界迈向可持续发展的正确路径，也是人类在这个星球上的共同未来。

编写说明

《构建人类命运共同体的时代价值和实践成就》智库报告课题组由新华通讯社社长、新华社国家高端智库学术委员会主任傅华任组长，总编辑吕岩松任副组长，副总编辑任卫东任执行副组长，课题组成员包括倪四义、刘刚、班玮、薛颖、尚军、邓玉山、杨晴川、徐海静、刘畅、刘华、韩冰、陈健、黄尹甲子、刘晨、贾金明、靳博文、李晨曦、王佳琳、王雪飞、马震、何毅等。

携手推动高质量发展共筑亚太命运共同体 ①
——面向未来的 APEC 发展成效与中国行动

前　言

　　400 多年前，中国商人在浩瀚的太平洋上开启了与秘鲁之间的贸易航线，建立连接亚洲、太平洋岛屿与美洲之间的一条海上丝绸之路，为跨越太平洋的友好交往奠定了历史基础。几百年来，海上丝绸之路精神在太平洋的浩渺烟波之上闪耀，照亮了人类克服一切阻碍、彼此文明交流互鉴的历史进程。

　　35 年前，亚太地区领导人顺应和平与发展的时代潮流，一致同意超越集团对抗、零和博弈的旧思维，成立亚太经合组织。自此以来，亚太区域合作推动地区发展进入快车道，助力亚太成为世界经济增长中心，成为全球发展稳定之锚与合作高地，成为推动全球高质量、可持续发展

---

① 2024 年 11 月 8 日发布于秘鲁利马。

的关键力量。

连接东西方的海上丝绸之路，是开放包容的象征，也是合作共赢的象征。它与亚太经合组织成立初心相契合，是人类共同的宝贵财富。它将使 21 世纪的亚太地区继续成为创新合作的典范，助力全球共同应对重大挑战；它激励我们携手合作，共同推动高质量发展，形成彼此互助的亚太命运共同体。

一、聚焦发展：共创举世瞩目的"亚太奇迹"

"发展是亚太地区永恒的主题。我们始终聚焦发展，不断深化经济技术合作，增强发展中成员自主发展能力。我们共同开创了自主自愿、协商一致、循序渐进的'亚太经合组织方式'，尊重各成员发展权。"①

——中国国家主席习近平

自 1989 年成立以来，亚太经合组织（APEC）始终秉持开放合作、互利共赢的原则，致力于推动亚太地区经济一体化和贸易自由化。

APEC 的价值在于其秉持的"开放的地区主义"理念和成员的"跨太平洋的广泛地域性"，推动了亚太地区 35 年的和平与发展。APEC 在促进地区经济增长、深化区域合作方面取得辉煌成就，有力提升了亚太地区贸易投资自由化便利化水平，使亚太地区成为全球最活跃、最具增长潜力的地缘经济板块。

---

① 习近平在亚太经合组织工商领导人峰会上发表《同心协力 共迎挑战 谱写亚太合作新篇章》书面演讲，2023 年 11 月 16 日。

（一）世界经济增长的"火车头"

APEC 为世界经济发展做出巨大贡献。通过加强多边合作和互联互通，APEC 经济体的总体经济增长势头保持长期稳定，成为推动世界经济增长的重要力量。

2023 年，21 个 APEC 经济体 GDP 总量达到 64.45 万亿美元，占全球 GDP 的 60% 以上。GDP 增速达 3.5%，超过 3.2% 的全球平均增长率[①]。亚太地区极端贫困人口由 1990 年的 15 亿下降到 2015 年的 2.6 亿[②]。根据国际货币基金组织的预测，2024 年，亚太地区的经济增长率将达到 4.2%，高于预期为 2.9% 的全球经济增长率。这些数据充分说明，亚太是全球极具经济活力和发展韧性的地区。

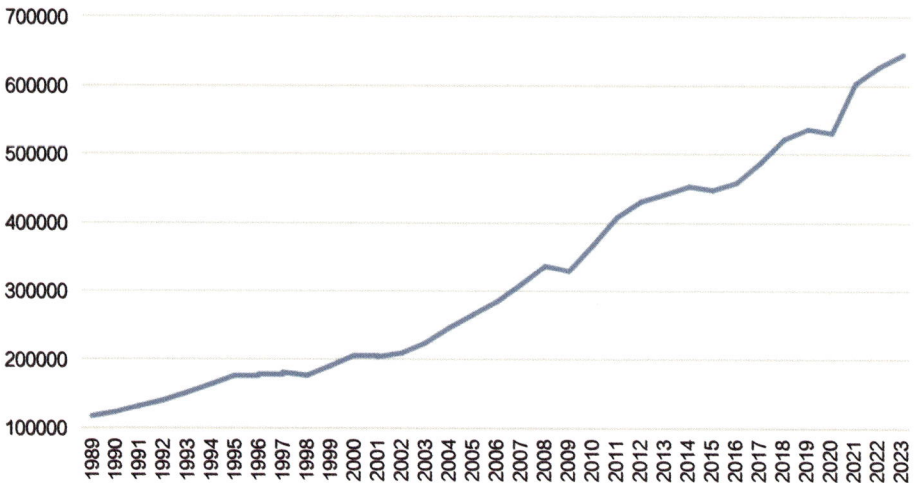

图 1 APEC 经济体 GDP 总量（单位：亿美元）
数据来源：世界银行、国际货币基金组织、经济合作与发展组织

---

① 数据来源：国际货币基金组织
② 数据来源：亚洲开发银行

APEC 经济体较高的经济增长率主要来自各自内部需求的增加和相互贸易的拉动。2023 年，APEC 经济体消费占 GDP 比重的平均值达到 65.6%，APEC 经济体服务业增加值占 GDP 的比重超过 62%，服务业的增长给地区经济复苏注入新的动力。APEC 经济体内外商品贸易占 GDP 的比重一直处于 70% 以上的高位，2018 年以来在 90% 上下波动①。亚太地区各经济体在经济发展水平、要素禀赋及政策法规方面存在更显著的互补性，这使亚太地区内部的增加值贸易联系和价值链联系更为密切，具备优势互补、包容共赢的发展基础。

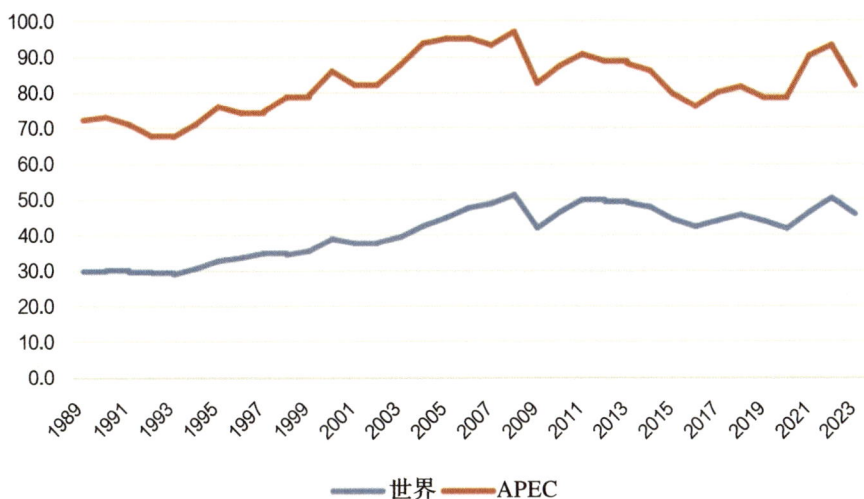

图 2 商品贸易占 GDP 比重年度变化（单位：%）
数据来源：世界银行、世界贸易组织

强劲的贸易需求和安全稳定的环境促进了亚太地区国际航运、贸易、金融快速发展。新华·波罗的海国际航运中心发展指数（2023）显示，在全球航运中心城市综合实力前 20 席中，有 13 个城市来自 APEC 经

---

① 数据来源：亚洲开发银行、经济合作与发展组织

济体。新加坡、上海分列第一和第三位，领衔全球航运发展。世界金融重心也向亚太地区偏移。国际金融中心发展指数（2023）显示，排名前10位的国际金融中心城市中，亚洲占6席，上海、香港、新加坡、东京、北京、深圳等城市带动了亚洲金融快速发展。

中国在APEC经济合作中持续发挥"推进器"作用。中国经济韧性强、潜力大、活力足，有利于推动亚太持续发展繁荣。中国已成为13个APEC经济体的第一大贸易伙伴[①]。2022年，中国与APEC成员进出口总额为37390.8亿美元，占中国进出口总额的59.7%。利用APEC经济体投资占中国实际利用外资总额的86.6%，而中国对外投资的73.3%流向了APEC经济体[②]。中国前十大外资来源地和前十大对外直接投资目的地中，有半数为APEC成员。

（二）贸易投资自由化的推动者

APEC框架下的贸易投资自由化便利化使亚太地区成为地区经济一体化的优秀范例。秉持APEC大家庭精神，相关经济体合力推动贸易投资自由化便利化，促进经济技术合作，倡导"开放的地区主义"，采取自主自愿、协商一致、灵活务实、循序渐进的APEC方式，为促进亚太区域经济一体化做出了重要贡献，也为推动构建亚太命运共同体注入了不竭动能。

1994年，APEC在印尼制定了茂物目标（Bogor Goals），即APEC发达成员与发展中成员分别于2010年前和2020年前实现贸易投资自由化，这成为APEC合作进程的"灯塔"。APEC进程的两个核心是贸易投资自由化便利化（TILF）和经济技术合作（ECOTECH），

---

① 此处及本报告提到的中国统计数据，均不含中国香港、中国台北数据。

② 数据来源：中国商务部

被称作 APEC 之"两轮"。在贸易投资自由化便利化方面，茂物目标基本上得到了实现；在经济技术合作方面，《马尼拉框架》（Manila Framework）制定的合作内容，基本上均得到开展。

关税与非关税壁垒极大降低。过去 30 年，亚太地区平均关税水平从 17% 下降至 5%[1]，对世界经济增长的贡献达到七成。同时，1989 至 2022 年，APEC 地区的货物和服务贸易总额由 3.1 万亿美元增长到 30 万亿美元，年平均增长率约为 7.4%，远高于世界其他地区的贸易增长速度。2001 年至 2010 年实施的《APEC 贸易便利化行动计划》和 2009 年实施的《APEC 营商便利化行动计划》成为贸易便利化措施的代表。通过在海关措施、标准和一致化、电子商务和商务人员流动等优先领域所开展的形式多样的合作，APEC 有效降低了各成员之间的交易成本，改善了亚太地区的营商环境。在 APEC 推动下，亚太地区的投资环境不断改善，对外国直接投资（FDI）的流入产生了显著激励作用。

自由贸易协定有效拓展合作网络。通过实施集体行动计划（CAPs）和单边行动计划（IAPs），APEC 持续推动成员在贸易和投资自由化方面采取实际措施。这种方式不仅尊重了各成员的自主权，也促进了区域内贸易和投资的便利化。

截至 2022 年 7 月，APEC 成员共签署了 207 项自由贸易协定，其中 196 项已经生效。这些自由贸易协定的签署与生效，进一步促进了成员之间的贸易和投资自由化，为推进区域经济一体化提供了制度保障。

2020 年 11 月 15 日，《区域全面经济伙伴关系协定》（RCEP）签署。历经 8 年谈判后，全球最大的自由贸易区宣告诞生、正式启航。随着 RCEP 的落地生效，贸易政策红利不断释放，区域间经贸往来显著提升。

---

[1] APEC 官网 https://www.apec.org/About-Us/About-APEC/ Achievements-and-Benefits

《2024RCEP 区域合作发展》报告显示，2022 年，全球外国直接投资流量下降了 12.4%，而 RCEP 区域吸引外国直接投资流量达到 5311.1 亿美元，逆势增长 13.9%，占全球的比重达到 41.0%，较 2021 年提高了 9.5 个百分点[①]。RCEP 为亚太自由贸易区（FTA-AP）进程提供了重要的实现路径，进一步提升亚太地区未来在全球发展格局中的分量。

倡导多边主义，坚持开放的区域主义，中国理念、中国方案得到亚太经合组织成员广泛认可。作为亚太地区重要经济体，中国一直积极参与亚太经合组织合作。从高质量实施《区域全面经济伙伴关系协定》（RCEP）、开展中国－东盟自贸区 3.0 版谈判，到积极推进加入《全面与进步跨太平洋伙伴关系协定》（CPTPP）《数字经济伙伴关系协定》（DEPA），中国践行开放的区域主义，推动形成更高水平开放型经济新体制。

（三）创新性合作的典范

发展理念创新引领。为应对 2008 年国际金融危机，APEC 在 2009 年和 2010 年先后通过《新的增长模式——为了 21 世纪联通的亚太地区》和《APEC 领导人增长战略》。领导人声明指出，亚太地区需要新的增长模式和实现这些战略的具体行动计划。这种新增长模式以创新和知识为支撑，其特征可归纳为"平衡、包容、可持续"。这种新增长模式可称为"APEC 的新发展观"，区别于以强调降低关税、扩大贸易、促进增长为特征的传统发展观。

近年来，面对新一轮科技革命和产业变革浪潮，APEC 不断扩大了"新发展观"方面的讨论和合作。以科技创新合作推动亚太区域"创新性增长"

---

① 数据来源：联合国贸易和发展会议《2023 年世界投资报告》。

成为 APEC 关注的重点议题。亚太各经济体将数字经济合作、智能化转型发展作为创新性合作的重点。2020 年 APEC 吉隆坡会议通过的《2040 年亚太经合组织布特拉加亚愿景》强调"利用数字经济和技术促进经济包容性""推动创新型可持续发展",以实现 APEC 在"后茂物时代"的发展。

互联互通推动区域协调发展。在亚太地区制定互联互通蓝图,适应了域内经济体加强经贸往来、推进工业化以及深化国际合作的需要,有助于亚太地区扩大投资和内需,增加就业,减少贫困,抑制极端主义,为亚太乃至世界经济增长注入新的动力。

早在 2014 年,在北京举行的亚太经合组织第二十二次领导人非正式会议上,各成员批准了《亚太经合组织互联互通蓝图(2015—2025)》,并决定在 2025 年前完成各方共同确立的倡议和指标。在互联互通蓝图的指引下,APEC 框架下的机制互联互通合作在海关和边境管理措施、供应链、贸易便利化、结构改革、规制合作等重点领域均取得了不同程度的进展和成效。

以海关和边境管理措施领域为例,通过简化手续和推广应用新科技,部分成员已实现海关和边境管理机构的现代化,提高通关效率,最具代表性的措施包括海关电子单一窗口系统和"经认证经营者(AEO)"制度等。在此推动下,贸易便利化和物流效率逐步提升。2020 年世界银行物流绩效指数(Logistics Performance Index,LPI)显示,2015—2017 年 APEC 地区的出口前置时间由平均 2.4 天下降为 2.3 天,已低于经济合作与发展组织(OECD)国家的平均水平。

数字经济引领未来方向。加强数字基础设施和能力建设,努力消弭数字鸿沟,已经成为 APEC 各方的共识和重点合作领域。2014 年和 2017 年,APEC 分别通过《APEC 促进互联网经济合作倡议》和《APEC 互联网和数字经济路线图》。2018 年,在巴布亚新几内亚举行的亚太经合组织第二十六次领导人非正式会议，以"把握包容性机遇，拥抱数字化未来"为主题，得到了各方的积极支持。

以项目建设为抓手，APEC 区域经济体在"智慧城市""智慧医院""智能基建"等重大领域扎实推进合作，助力区域经济体智能化转型发展。在此过程中，中国发挥了积极作用。截至目前，中国已与 80 多个共建国家签署了政府间科技合作协定，支持联合研究项目 1100 余项，共建 50 多家"一带一路"联合实验室和 70 余个海外产业园区[①]。面向东盟、南亚、拉美等 APEC 区域经济体建设多个跨国技术转移平台，有效促进 APEC 经济体间科技合作创新。中国还与 23 个国家建立"丝路电商"双边合作机制[②]，并加深同新加坡、印度尼西亚、马来西亚等国的跨境电商项目与电子商务合作，成为 APEC 区域经济体共享数字经济红利的合作典范。

（四）绿色发展的倡导者

绿色发展是 APEC 未来发展合作的重要领域之一。早在 2010 年与 2011 年，APEC 领导人非正式会议主题均强调了绿色增长的重要性，"包容性增长""可持续增长"是近十年来 APEC 各类场合讨论的核心议题。APEC 各成员携手合作，共同探索实践绿色发展之路，协同推进降碳、减污、扩绿、增长，不仅有效保护生态环境，助力应对气候变化，还推动绿色经济成为突出增长点，为亚太地区乃至全球发展贡献重要力量。

多维度森林保护与创新，森林保护成绩亮眼。作为基于 APEC 机制发起成立的区域性国际组织，亚太森林组织（全称为亚太森林恢复与可持续管理组织，APFNet）十余年来，开展了多层次、多类型的合作

---

① 数据来源：中国科技部
② 数据来源：中国商务部

项目，共筑亚太生态屏障。截至 2023 年 8 月，共资助开展各类森林可持续管理和恢复项目 53 个，资助金额约 4300 万美元[①]。根据联合国粮农组织的数据，全球在近十年内森林面积下降了 1.2%，然而亚太地区森林面积却实现明显增长[②]，主要贡献来自中国、越南以及智利，其中中国森林面积提升了 9.53%。过去十年，中国为全球贡献约四分之一的新增绿化面积，居世界首位[③]，作为全球森林资源增长最快的国家，创造了令人刮目相看的绿色奇迹。

合力推进海洋保护，共促海洋可持续发展。近年来，APEC 各经济体积极落实海洋垃圾防治路线图（2019）、打击非法、未报告和无管制（illegal, unreported and unregulated，简称 IUU）捕捞路线图（2019）及小规模渔业和水产养殖路线图（2022）。2011 年，APEC 海洋可持续发展中心在中国厦门成立，APEC 蓝色经济论坛作为 APEC 海洋可持续发展中心常态化推进的项目，截至 2023 年 12 月已成功举办七届，为各经济体代表提供了分享蓝色经济实践经验与合作框架建议的平台。2024 年 2 月，第 22 届 APEC 海洋与渔业工作组（OFWG）会议在秘鲁利马举办，各经济体在会议中对各路线图的完成情况进行了通报，对未来海洋与渔业的规划进行了展望。

亚太新能源汽车市场表现强劲，增长趋势明显。近年来，亚太地区大力发展绿色经济，既实现应对气候变化的减碳目标，又能够以新兴产业助力经济发展。其中，新能源汽车行业成为典型案例。2012 年至 2022 年，亚太地区各经济体积极推进新能源汽车的应用，地区纯电动汽车年销量增长了 142 倍，并有力带动了相关产业发展。

---

① 《中国绿色时报》，2023 年 10 月。
② 数据来源：世界银行数据库（联合国粮农组织），2024。
③ 《美丽中国建设最新成果》，国家林草局，2023 年 8 月。

随着全球范围内低碳出行趋势进一步加强，新能源汽车领域合作将成为亚太绿色经济发展的重要方向。例如，中国上海汽车集团股份有限公司与泰国正大集团合资车企的两款纯电动汽车的市场份额在泰国居领先地位，比亚迪在泰国已开设超过 100 家门店。

图 3　2012-2022 年亚太地区电动汽车销售情况（千辆）[①]

图表来源：亚太经合组织官方报告

能源合作前景看好，结构优化转型升级。APEC 各经济体致力于推动能源结构的优化调整，大力发展风能、太阳能等可再生能源，减少化石能源依赖，加快能源转型步伐。亚太经合组织可再生能源发电量从 2000 年的 1384 太瓦时（TWh）增加到 2021 年的 4709 太瓦时，年均增速为 6%。可再生能源发电占比从 2010 年的 16% 提高到 2021 年的 25%，其中水电占 2021 年亚太经合组织可再生能源发电量的一半以上，其次为风能（25%）和太阳能（15%）。2010 年至 2021 年期间，风力发电平均每年增长 19.2%，太阳能发电平均每年增长 47.3%[②]。

---

① 《2023 年 APEC 图表》，亚太经合组织政策支持小组，2023 年 11 月。
② 《2023 年 APEC 图表》，亚太经合组织政策支持小组，2023 年 11 月。

中国为亚太区域的绿色转型提供了强有力的引领和支持。中国风电、光伏发电装机容量分别连续 14 年、9 年处于世界第一，截至 2023 年底累计装机突破 10 亿千瓦。2023 年，中国对世界可再生能源新增装机容量贡献超过一半。2024 年 7 月，由中国电力建设集团承建的智利最大单体光伏项目 CEME1 项目正式启动商业运营，该项目能为约 50 万户家庭提供清洁能源，每年可减少二氧化碳排放约 28 万吨。智利能源部副部长路易斯·费利佩·拉莫斯表示，该项目将帮助智利提高清洁能源发电占比，向实现脱碳目标迈出重要一步。

绿色"一带一路"建设与亚太绿色发展同频共振。绿色是亚太合作与共建"一带一路"的共同底色。APEC 与"一带一路"互融互促、同频共振，绿色发展合作机制逐步健全，合作成效日益显现。

截至 2023 年 8 月，中国与 30 多个国家及国际组织签署环保合作协议，与超过 40 个国家的 150 余家合作伙伴建立"一带一路"绿色发展国际联盟，与 32 个国家建立"一带一路"能源合作伙伴关系[①]。2018 年，中国金融学会绿色金融专业委员会和伦敦金融城共同发起"一带一路"绿色投资原则（GIP），鼓励"一带一路"地区大力发展绿色金融合作。截至 2024 年 9 月，已有来自 17 个国家和地区的 49 家签署机构、20 家支持机构以及 2 家观察机构[②]。

"一带一路"绿色发展国际联盟大力支持各成员开展可再生能源投资。2023 年 10 月，第三届"一带一路"国际合作高峰论坛上，印尼国家电力公司（PLN）与中国合作伙伴达成了价值超过 540 亿美元的交易。天合光能作为中国企业代表与印度尼西亚签署中国—印度尼西亚合作文

---

① 数据来源：国务院新闻办《共建"一带一路"：构建人类命运共同体的重大实践》白皮书。

b 数据来源：中国金融学会绿色金融专业委员会 2023/24 年度工作报告与 2024/25 年度工作展望。

件，为印度尼西亚建设第一个光伏电池和组件生产基地。中国愿与广大合作伙伴一道，共建"绿色丝绸之路"，共促亚太地区绿色发展道路行稳致远。

二、应对挑战：肩负时代重任搏击风雨

"亚太繁荣发展的历程表明，唯有合作才能发展，不合作是最大的风险，搞'脱钩断链'对谁都没好处。"[①]

——中国国家主席习近平

发展与安全犹如车之两轮、鸟之两翼，相互依存、相互促进，缺一不可。安全是发展的前提，发展是安全的保障。

当今世界正经历百年未有之大变局，大国博弈、地缘冲突、阵营对抗阻碍国际合作与互信，使亚太地区发展的安全环境面临内外冲击。一些国家在经济领域泛化国家安全概念，大搞保护主义、"脱钩断链"和"小院高墙"，使本已复苏乏力的世界经济雪上加霜，也给亚太地区带来负面影响。地区各经济体发展不平衡、经济体内部贫富差距加大，均对区域合作构成挑战。气候变化导致极端天气和自然灾害频发，严重危害亚太人民生产生活安全与福祉。

（一）地缘政治风险带来多重冲击

当前，某些国家固守"冷战思维"，执着于"零和博弈"，拉拢盟友搞阵营对抗，导致地缘政治形势趋紧，对亚太地区构成多重冲击。

---

① 习近平在亚太经合组织工商领导人峰会上发表《同心协力 共迎挑战 谱写亚太合作新篇章》书面演讲，2023 年 11 月 16 日。

地缘形势紧张冲突影响亚太地区内外安全环境。区域合作与发展不可避免会受到地区安全形势的影响。当前全球地缘形势的动荡与冲突，不仅威胁亚太地区安全稳定，也对地区贸易和投资活动造成不利影响，对区域经济合作构成挑战。

从外部看，地缘冲突加剧了欧洲和中东等地区的紧张局势，受此影响，从亚太通往欧洲的交通运输受阻。连接亚太到欧洲的不少航班因相关国家关闭领空被迫停航或绕飞；已成为连接中国和欧洲运输大动脉的"中欧班列"部分线路因相关制裁措施被迫停运或改道；红海到苏伊士运河的海上航线因冲突外溢效应而安全风险增加，很多船只被迫绕行。

欧盟分管经济事务的委员真蒂洛尼今年 2 月表示，由于原本通过红海的航运改变了路线，欧亚海上航线的航运时间增加了 10 至 15 天，运输成本增加大约 400%。运输效率的降低和成本的提高，对于经济对外依存度普遍较高的亚太经济体造成不利影响。

从内部看，有的国家为谋取地缘战略私利，鼓吹"大国竞争"，利用地区国家间分歧挑拨矛盾，拉拢部分国家共同打压、遏制竞争对手，大搞阵营对抗，不仅损害地区国家对话合作的政治基础，而且令个别地区热点问题升温，不利于整个亚太地区和平稳定，恶化亚太各经济体安全环境。

地缘冲突引发粮食与能源危机，连锁反应冲击亚太地区经济社会安全。在粮食方面，亚太地区原本就属于对于风险高度敏感的区域。联合国粮农组织的报告显示，亚太地区营养不足者占全球一半，女性的粮食不安全状况更为严重[①]。尽管亚太经合组织各经济体的营养不良发生率在 2010—2023 年间从 3.6% 降到了 2.3%[②]，但粮食安全依然是制约亚

① 《2023 年亚洲及太平洋区域粮食安全与营养状况》，联合国粮食及农业组织，2023 年 12 月 11 日。

② 《2023 年 APEC 图表》，亚太经合组织政策支持小组，2023 年 11 月。

太地区发展水平的一大因素。

在能源方面，亚太地区能源消耗近年来迅速增长。《2024 年亚太经合组织能源展望报告》显示，在能源产品最终能耗中，电力增长最快，达到 7.2%，占最终能耗比重的 33.6%。石油在最终能源消费中的比重占第二大份额，为 32.9%，增速为 6.2%；天然气的增速为 3%，在最终能源消费中的比重达到 18%[①]。

在此背景下，地缘冲突导致的国际能源和粮食市场动荡、能源和粮食价格飙升，对于亚太地区经济体特别是发展中经济体的经济社会稳定造成明显冲击。能源和粮食价格上涨还推升部分经济体通胀，对其外汇等金融市场造成影响，甚至在一些国家导致经济社会动荡。

（二）贸易保护主义危及产供链安全

近年来，随着逆全球化思潮泛起，区域内个别国家将贸易投资泛安全化，以维护国家安全之名行贸易保护主义之实，阻碍国际经济合作，扰乱全球产业链、供应链，对亚太地区合作亦造成明显冲击。

跨国投资势头下降，发展中经济体受到更大冲击。联合国贸易和发展组织发布的《2024 年世界投资报告》显示，2023 年全球范围内的外国直接投资规模为 1.3 万亿美元，同比下降 2%，流向发展中经济体的投资下降了 7%。其中，亚洲发展中经济体获得的外国直接投资下降了约 8.4%，大洋洲发展中经济体获得的外国直接投资降幅则高达约 64%。过去数十年间，制造业领域的外国直接投资一直是亚太地区诸多发展中经济体的重要经济推动力，也是构建地区甚至全球产业链、供应链的重要资金来源。但是，当前这一投资下降趋势，将明显迟滞部分亚

---

① 《2024 年亚太经合组织能源展望报告》，亚太经合组织，2024 年 8 月

太地区发展中经济体的工业化升级进度，削弱地区产供链安全的基础。

部分国家大搞"脱钩断链"、"小院高墙"，危害地区产业发展。一些国家出于政治原因和贸易保护动机，试图将其认为的"竞争对手"剔除出产业链供应链，这种做法不仅违背 APEC 的初衷和目标，而且也严重阻碍国际经济科技合作，大幅增加生产成本，危害地区产业发展。

例如，区域内个别国家为制裁别国通讯科技企业，以技术设备存在"安全风险"为由，强行禁止在本国网络建设中使用上述企业设备。这种单边制裁措施对其本国电信企业造成巨额经济损失，拖延了其通讯行业的升级换代进程，只会"反噬其身"。

再如，个别国家出台大规模排他性歧视性产业政策，破坏全球产业的合理分工格局，试图强行推动制造业"回流"本土。结果是其制造业未见起色，"脱钩断链"反作用却日益显现，导致自身经历近年来最严重的通胀，其国内民众尤其是低收入人群生活受到明显冲击。

（三）发展失衡制约经济长期增长

亚太地区是全球最具活力和经济增长潜力的地区，但仍面临着显著的发展不平衡问题。国家间的两极分化、群体间贫富差距扩大，成为制约亚太地区经济长期增长的重要因素。

亚太地区经济体间的经济发展水平差异显著，形成了鲜明的两极分化现象。亚太地区既有高度发达的经济体如日本、韩国、新加坡，也有一些位于太平洋岛屿和内陆的经济体。由于地理位置偏远、资源匮乏、经济基础薄弱等原因，该地区长期处于发展滞后状态。这种两极分化的趋势在近年来有所加剧。根据国际货币基金组织（IMF）数据，亚太地区内最高与最低人均 GDP 经济体之间的差距已超过数十倍①，悬殊的经济差距不仅限制区域整体发展潜力，也加剧了地区内部的不稳定。

不同群体间贫富差距持续扩大。在亚太地区的部分经济体，伴随快速的城市化和工业化进程，部分群体受益显著，而其他一些群体，特别是农村和偏远地区居民，却未能充分享受经济发展成果。世界银行发布的数据显示，一些亚太地区经济体的基尼系数长期居高不下，甚至有所上升。在经济增长的同时，社会财富并未得到合理分配，大量人口仍生活在贫困线以下。贫富差距的扩大不仅影响社会稳定，也削弱了经济增长的可持续性。

《2023 年亚太地区人口和发展报告》指出，2023 年，亚太区域的青年人口（15—24 岁）占全世界青年人口的 56%，总人数突破 7 亿。在亚太区域中，有 24.8% 的青年人没有接受过教育，也没有就业或参加培训，妇女在这一群体中的比例明显高于男性。

发展失衡问题是亚太经济合作面临的重要挑战。APEC 各成员经济体应加强沟通与协作，共同制定和实施促进区域平衡发展和缩小社会贫富差距的政策措施，通过共同努力，推动亚太地区实现全面、均衡的长期发展。

（四）气候变化危及可持续安全

亚太地区经济体自然条件多样，但多受气候变化进程影响。气候变化导致极端天气加剧，自然灾害频发，给地区可持续发展带来日益严峻的挑战。

自然灾害频发造成严重经济损失。2023 年，亚太地区因自然灾害

---

① 《世界经济展望》，国际货币基金组织，2024 年 4 月 16 日。

造成的经济损失达到 650 亿美元。发生与水文气象危害事件相关的灾害共 79 起，其中 80% 以上与洪水和风暴事件有关，造成 2000 多人死亡，900 万人直接受灾[1]。

美国国家航空航天局（NASA）通过海平面变化科学团队的分析显示，在未来的 30 年里，图瓦卢、基里巴斯和斐济等太平洋岛国的海平面将至少上升约 15 厘米，未来几十年太平洋岛国沿海区域的洪灾频率和严重程度可能均会加剧[2]。

由于经济体系相对较弱，亚太地区的部分发展中经济体防灾减灾能力不足，受到自然灾害影响较为显著。特别是太平洋小岛屿发展中国家，自然灾害造成的损失接近 GDP 的 8%，几乎是地区其他经济体这一比例的两倍。东南亚国家的这一损失则至少达到国内生产总值的 5%[3]。

亚太地区仍面临日益严重的环境污染问题。亚太地区的部分发展中经济体在工业化、城市化进程中，往往无力顾及环境保护，导致环境污染问题日益严重，碳排放幅度亦难以控制。在 2020 年全球空气污染最为严重的城市中，前 148 个城市全部位于亚太地区。到 2050 年，亚太地区约有 70% 的人口将生活在城市，要满足新市民需求，需要对基础设施进行大量投资，而这将进一步加深对清洁水和能源的依赖，并可能产生更多的温室气体[4]。

海洋污染威胁也同样严重。由于人口密集、垃圾处理能力相对落后等原因，亚太地区面临诸多类型的海洋污染威胁。以海洋塑料污染问题

---

[1] 数据来源：联合国亚洲及太平洋经济社会委员会《亚太灾难 2023》报告

[2] 《美国宇航局分析显示太平洋岛屿的海平面上升是不可逆转的》，NASA，2024 年 9 月 27 日。

[3] 《2023 年亚太灾害报告》，联合国亚洲及太平洋经济社会委员会，2023 年 7 月 25 日。

[4] 《2040 年亚太地区的未来：树立健康环境的宏伟目标》，联合国亚太经社会，2021 年 9 月 26 日。

为例，2022 年，亚太地区海洋塑料污染对渔业和航运业等造成的直接经济损失总额达到 108 亿美元，较 2009 年增加了近 10 倍，亚太地区海洋塑料垃圾的管控已成为全球海洋塑料污染治理的关键一环①。

土地荒漠化加剧可持续发展压力。亚太地区荒漠化问题日益严峻，尤其是在内陆和干旱半干旱地区。《联合国防治荒漠化公约》报告显示，截至 2019 年，由于气温上升等因素影响，在该地区部分国家，已经出现向沙漠气候转变的情况。除此之外，气候变化导致的降水模式变化、水资源短缺以及不合理的土地利用方式，如过度放牧、乱砍滥伐和农业活动，加速了土壤侵蚀和土地退化，使得原本脆弱的生态系统进一步恶化，荒漠化面积不断扩大，不仅直接威胁到当地的农业生产和居民生计，还影响食物安全、水资源供给和社会稳定，对可持续发展构成长远挑战。

此外，在全球气候变化背景下，亚太地区遭受的热浪、干旱、洪水、台风等极端天气事件日益频繁和剧烈。极端高温加剧了地表水分的蒸发，减少了土壤湿度，从而加剧了荒漠化进程；而极端降水事件，尤其是短时间内的强降雨，可能引发严重的水土流失和土壤侵蚀，进一步破坏土地资源。

三、续写辉煌：在共创共享中实现共同繁荣

"我们要牢固树立亚太命运共同体意识，以自身发展带动他人发展，以协调联动最大限度发挥各自优势，传导正能量，形成各经济体良性互

---

① 《从污染到解决方案：海洋垃圾和塑料污染全球评估》，联合国环境署，2021 年 10 月 21 日。

动、协调发展的格局。"①

——中国国家主席习近平

当前，世界百年变局加速演进，世界经济面临多重风险挑战，亚太作为全球增长引擎，肩负更大的时代责任。亚太合作未来的路怎么走，关乎地区发展，关乎人民福祉，关乎全球未来。

在这一背景下，构建开放包容、创新增长、互联互通、合作共赢的亚太命运共同体是大势所趋，也理应成为 APEC 成员的共同目标。APEC 各成员应秉持合作初心，再倡 APEC 精神，携手推动区域高质量发展，努力共建开放、活力、强韧、和平的亚太共同体，共创共享亚太发展的下一个"黄金三十年"。

（一）携手共进，合作发展仍是亚太主旋律

31 年前，面对冷战结束后"人类向何处去"的世界之问、历史之问、时代之问，亚太地区领导人顺应和平与发展的时代潮流，召开了首次亚太经合组织领导人非正式会议，一致同意超越集团对抗、零和博弈的旧思维，深化区域经济合作和一体化，致力于共建一个活力、和谐、繁荣的亚太大家庭。这一重大决定推动亚太发展和经济全球化进入快车道，助力亚太成为世界经济增长中心、全球发展的稳定之锚和合作高地。

如今，尽管亚太地区因各种因素面临新的纷争和摩擦，单边主义、阵营对抗等苗头在个别国家区域出现，但毋庸置疑的是，亚太经济合作从来不是零和博弈、你输我赢的政治游戏，而是相互成就、互利共赢的发展平台。求同存异促合作、齐心协力谋发展仍是亚太地区的主旋律。

---

① 2013 年 10 月 7 日，中华人民共和国主席习近平在亚太经合组织工商领导人峰会上发表的题为《深化改革开放　共创美好亚太》的演讲。

正如新西兰国际贸易专家克里斯·利普斯科姆所言，亚太地区实践证明，通过合作而非对立，国家和经济体可以获得更多收益。正如一句新西兰谚语："你的菜篮子满了，我的菜篮子满了，人民就会茁壮成长。"

在进一步深化区域合作中，可进一步发挥 APEC 主渠道作用，其中应当充分发挥 APEC 经济体的多样性特点。APEC 成员既包括发达经济体，也包括发展中经济体，各经济体在地缘、产业、社会、文化等方面各有特色，这种多样性带来良好的互补性，进一步提升了开展合作的意义和潜力。

原亚太经合组织工商咨询理事会（ABAC）执行主任杰柯陛说，不论各成员经济体量如何、地缘或政治上有什么不同，APEC 都应让本地区各经济体携手，一起寻找解决方案。

未来，APEC 应继续聚焦发展，继续发扬和而不同、和衷共济的伙伴精神，继续遵循自主自愿、协商一致、灵活务实、循序渐进的"APEC 方式"，尊重各成员的发展权和发展道路选择，着力提升发展中成员的自主发展能力，不断将成员多样性转化为合作推动力。

（二）和谐包容，共同构建亚太命运共同体

再倡 APEC 精神，APEC 将继续在区域合作中发挥主要机制作用。亚太大家庭各成员发展高度互补、利益深度融合，本就是命运与共的整体。再倡"亚太大家庭"精神，更好发挥 APEC 在区域合作中的主要机制作用，对于亚太地区的可持续发展具有不可忽视的意义。

布特加拉亚愿景设定，到 2040 年建成一个开放、活力、强韧、和平的亚太共同体。APEC 既包括发达经济体，也包括发展中经济体，多样性增强了开展合作的意义和潜力。为避免在解决绿色技术和数字技术等方面出现阻碍，APEC 应贯彻"开放的区域主义"，积极促进合作创新，成为推动技术发展的重要平台。

　　未来，各成员经济体应聚焦发展命题，增强"亚太大家庭"成员的自主发展能力，尊重自主自愿、协商一致、循序渐进的"亚太经合组织方式"；通过加强互联互通和互利合作，弘扬和而不同、和衷共济的伙伴精神，不断将成员的多样性转化为长期合作的动力源泉。

　　和谐包容是亚太命运与共的矢志追求。正如联合国秘书长古特雷斯所说："如果没有不让任何人掉队的包容性和可持续发展，就无法确保真正的和平。"①

　　应对亚太各经济体依然存在发展不平衡问题，特别是在减贫、粮食安全、工业化、发展筹资等关键领域，需要以积极的多边合作解决全球发展赤字，确保所有成员经济体，特别是发展中经济体，能够公平参与和受益。无论经济体量大小、人口多少，地缘特点或政治体制有何异同，在 APEC 的初心之下，各成员体都可以携手探讨应对方案，找到解决之道。

　　发展与合作依旧是亚太地区永恒的主题，建设亚太命运共同体符合时代潮流。在构建亚太命运共同体的大背景下，无论是"一带一路"倡议，还是《区域全面经济伙伴关系协定》（RCEP）、《全面与进步跨太平洋伙伴关系协定》（CPTPP），都能够找到新的发力点。要推动亚太 发展进入新阶段，还需加速《2040 年 APEC 布特拉加亚愿景》的落实，并以此推动全球经济复苏，维系整个世界的稳定发展。

　　随着多边贸易体制得到加强，各成员应坚定不移推进亚太自贸区进程，尊重经济规律，发挥各自比较优势，促进各成员经济联动融通，加强相关区域经贸协定和发展战略对接，促进贸易和投资自由化，提高贸易便利化水平，带动各成员之间的供应链整合，进而提高 APEC 各成员

---

① 联合国秘书长古特雷斯 2023 年 11 月在联合国安理会以"共同发展促进持久和平"为主题的公开辩论会上发表的讲话。

的供应链上下游的多元化水平。同时，应加强项目引导，加强合作机制与行动计划的阶段性实施评估，吸引工商界和社会群体的更多参与。

（三）充满活力，"中国行动"赋能亚太发展

展望 2035 年，中国将基本实现社会主义现代化，中国式现代化也为推动亚太高质量发展提供新机遇。

中国经济仍然是全球增长最大引擎，更是亚太腾飞的最大动力。中国拥有超大规模市场的需求优势、产业体系配套完整的供给优势、大量高素质劳动者和企业家的人才优势，中国经济发展具备强劲的内生动力，也为亚太经济发展带来动力。

"中国经济体量大，5% 的增量相当于一个欧洲小国的经济总量。"美中贸易全国委员会会长克雷格·艾伦表示，2024 年中国将贡献全球GDP 增长的 30% 左右，预计这种情况在 2025 年和 2026 年也会持续。

秘鲁 APEC 高官雷纳托·雷耶斯表示，中国作为 APEC 重要成员，在推动区域经济合作、引领亚太经济增长持续发挥着积极作用，某种程度上是决定性的作用，对带动出口具有重大战略作用，符合秘鲁经济战略发展要求。

中国高度重视发展中拉关系，将拉美和加勒比国家视为团结发展中国家、推动南南合作的重要伙伴。截至 2023 年 12 月，中国已同 22 个拉美和加勒比国家签署共建"一带一路"谅解备忘录，同 5 个拉美国家签署自由贸易协定①，在拉美地区累计实施超过 200 个基建项目。

直面共同挑战，"中国行动"不断赋能亚太发展。中国是亚太区域合作的积极倡导者、推动者和弘扬者，中国人民的梦想同各国人民的梦

---

① 《国家发展改革委：中拉共建"一带一路"合作展现强劲发展势头》，中国一带一路网 2023 年 12 月 15 日。

想息息相通。

中国式现代化是走和平发展道路的现代化。中国坚定奉行独立自主的和平外交政策，也倡导各方推动构建人类命运共同体，践行全人类共同价值，落实全球发展倡议、全球安全倡议、全球文明倡议，倡导平等有序的世界多极化，坚持共同、综合、合作、可持续的安全观，契合亚太的发展大势。

坚持人与自然和谐共生，中国正加快推动和引领发展方式绿色低碳转型。中国协同各方推进降碳、减污、扩绿、增长，落实好《生物循环绿色经济曼谷目标》，厚植亚太增长的绿色底色。同时，中国新能源汽车、锂电池、光伏产品出口快速增长，有助于地区成员体进一步实现减排目标；即将启动的中国温室气体自愿减排交易市场也将创造巨大的绿色市场机遇。

强化科技创新和成果转化，中国推进数字经济和实体经济深度融合向亚太释放活力。中国致力于共同落实《互联网和数字经济路线图》，加强数字基础设施建设，促进新技术传播和运用，努力构建开放、公平、非歧视的数字营商环境。完善全球科技治理，强化科技创新对绿色化数字化转型和可持续发展的支撑，营造开放、公平、公正、非歧视的科技发展环境。

推动高水平对外开放，中国激发贸易活力，为亚太伙伴造就更多新机遇。中国通过优化贸易和投资便利化政策，扩大服务业对外开放，保障外商投资合法权益；打造市场化、法制化、国际化营商环境，为外商投资提供优质服务，完善外商投资权益保护机制，缩减外商投资准入负面清单，保障外商投资企业国民待遇，持续加强知识产权保护；打破制约创新要素流动的壁垒，促进数据依法有序自由流动。中国实现更大范围、更高层次、更宽领域的对外开放必将惠及整个亚太地区。

中国是亚太互联互通、联动发展的积极倡导者和推动者。"一带一路"倡议包含的"共商、共建、共享"原则及"五通"等理念与亚太经济合作的需求及目标高度契合。2023 年 10 月，习近平主席在第三届"一带一路"国际合作高峰论坛开幕式上宣布：丝路基金新增资金 800 亿元人民币，以市场化、商业化方式支持共建"一带一路"项目。增资完成后，丝路基金资金规模将达到 400 亿美元 +1800 亿元人民币。[①] 共建"一带一路"的持续推进，也必将有助于亚太地区的互联互通建设稳步前行。

未来，亚太经济将继续引领世界经济，也必将助力全球共同应对重大挑战，实现人类社会可持续发展。亚太合作再出发，让高质量发展惠及所有亚太人民，将继续成为 APEC 各个成员的共同目标。让我们秉持亚太合作初心，积极回应时代呼唤，携手应对全球性挑战，建设开放、活力、强韧、和平的亚太共同体，实现亚太人民和子孙后代的共同繁荣。

结 语

秘鲁谚语说："人民的声音就是上天的声音。"

亚太地区的交往历史证明，对真诚合作的伙伴而言，茫茫大洋不是阻隔，而是联结。正是因为这一联结，亚太地区各经济体组成利益交融、命运与共的大家庭。

亚太经合组织 （APEC）建立领导人定期会议机制以来，始终走在全球开放发展的前沿。在"亚太大家庭"精神驱动下，通过"一带一路"倡议、RCEP 等多边框架深化合作，亚太地区国际航运、贸易、金融快速发展，贸易投资自由化 便利化成为地区经济一体化的优秀范例，以科技创新合作推动"创新性增长"，携手发展绿色经济，为世界可持续发

---

① 数据来源：中国一带一路网

展贡献重要力量，多方面合作 取得丰硕成果，创造了举世瞩目的"亚太奇迹"。

与此同时，世界百年变局加速演进，世界经济面临多种风险挑战，大国博弈、地缘冲突、阵营对抗阻碍国际间合作与互信，使亚太地区发展的安全环境面临内外冲击。作为全球增长引擎，亚太肩负着更大的时代责任。

从亚太合作的非凡历程中展望未来，我们认为，再倡 APEC 精神，构建开放包容、创新增长、互联互通、合作共赢的亚太命运共同体是大势所趋，也理应成为 APEC 成员的共同目标。

面向未来的亚太发展，给人以深刻启迪，同时也指引着一条生动的实践路径：合作发展是亚太地区主旋律，创新是引领发展的重要动力，开放是迈向共同繁荣的必由之路，绿色是亚太增长的鲜明底色，普惠是弥合发展鸿沟的关键之举。

未来，面对充满不确定性的世界，亚太大家庭唯有继续秉持开放包容、务实合作、互利共赢的 APEC 精神，发挥 APEC 平等沟通、协商合作的功能，携手共建创新、开放、绿色、共享的区域合作发展格局，才能实现大家庭所有成员及子孙后代的共同繁荣，共创全球和平、稳定和发展的美好未来，以更好地建设亚太命运共同体，推动构建人类命运共同体。

参考文献

[1]李向阳等，《2023～2024 年亚太地区形势分析与展望》// 中国社会科学院国际研究学部．中国社会科学院国际形势报告（2024），北京：社会科学文献出版社，2024 年 3 月

[2]杨泽瑞，《APEC30 年：机制·进程·前景研究》，世界知识出版社，2021 年

5 月

[3]孙壮志等，《"一带一路"高质量发展：认识、实践与前景》，人民出版社，
    2023 年 12 月

[4]苏格等，《亚太互联互通现状与未来》，世界知识出版社，2021 年 11 月

[5]王镭，《全球发展倡议：以人民为中心推动落实 2030 年议程》，中国社会科
    学出版社，2023 年 6 月

[6]姜凌等，《国际区域经济一体化与当代南北经济关系研究》，人民出版社，
    2019 年 12 月

[7]林雪萍，《供应链攻防战：从企业到国家的实力之争》，中信出版社，2023 年
    12 月

[8]王微、李汉卿，《超级链接：高质量共建"一带一路"贸易大通道》，机械工
    业出版社，2023 年 6 月

[9]张蕴岭、李雪威，《命运共同体构建与东北亚和平发展》，世界知识出版社，
    2019 年 12 月

[10] 王世渝，《第三次全球化浪潮》，中国民主法治出版社，2020 年 2 月

[11]王辉耀，《全球化：站在新的十字路口》，生活·读书·新知三联书店，
     2021 年 4 月

[12] 王义桅，《人类命运共同体：新型全球化的价值观》，外文出版社，2021 年
    12 月

[13] 张志明，《亚太价值链中的中国》，人民出版社，2021 年 2 月

[14] 亚太经合组织政策支持小组，《2023 年 APEC 图表》，2023 年 11 月

[15] 《2023 亚洲气候状况》，世界气象组织，2024 年 4 月 23 日

编写说明与致谢

《携手推动高质量发展 共筑亚太命运共同体》智库报告课题组由
新华通讯社社长、新华社国家高端智库学术委员会主任傅华任组长，新
华通讯社总编辑吕岩松任副组长，新华通讯社副总编辑任卫东任执行副
组长。课题组成员包括刘刚、潘海平、曹文忠、薛颖、崔峰、李月、杨茜、
陈小彬、曹占忠、张文娟、徐海静、刘华、李慧敏、李桃、刘赞、郐捷、

亓芳芳、李志兰、常嘉路、周晓苗、黄芯、石昂、潘宇昕、靳萱、常旭蝉、赵熠煊、梁洽闻、朱雨博、郝云甫、欧阳迪娜、李亭、李晓渝、卢怀谦等。

课题自2024年上半年启动以来，历时半年多采访、调研、撰写、修改、审校完成。

在报告写作和发布过程中，中国社科院学部委员、亚太与全球战略研究院院长李向阳，中国现代国际关系研究院副院长王鸿刚，南开大学APEC研究中心主任刘晨阳，商务部国际贸易经济合作研究院亚洲研究所原所长宋志勇，中国现代国际关系研究院全球化研究中心原主任刘军红，中国社科院世界经济与政治研究所国际投资室主任高凌云，中国社科院亚太与全球战略研究院"一带一路"研究室执行主任谢来辉，对外经贸大学国际贸易学系主任荆然，中国海洋大学经济学院副教授黄友星，厦门大学南洋研究院国际关系学院助理教授金向东等专家学者给予了多方面的帮助和指导，在此一并表示诚挚谢意。

全球发展倡议实践成就与世界贡献 ^①

前　言

发展是人类社会的永恒追求。对各国人民而言，发展寄托着生存和希望，象征着尊严和权利。

已通过 37 年的联合国《发展权利宣言》始终强调，每个人和所有各国人民均有权参与、促进并享受经济、社会与文化和政治发展。

但是进入 21 世纪第三个十年，百年变局和世纪疫情交织叠加，给人类社会带来深刻变化，世界进入新的动荡变革期。站在人类前途命运的十字路口，中国国家主席习近平在 2021 年 9 月 21 日第 76 届联合国大会上提出全球发展倡议。这是新时代中国向国际社会提供的又一重要公共产品，是人类命运共同体理念在全球发展领域的重要实践。

全球发展倡议坚持发展优先，紧扣落实联合国 2030 年可持续发展议程（以下简称"2030 年议程"）这个中心任务深化合作，以具体项目推进政策对话、经验分享、能力建设及各领域务实合作，推动各方参与。

---

① 2023 年 9 月 19 日发布纽约联合国总部，全球发展倡议合作成果展示高级别会议期间。

全球发展倡议表达了当前国际社会特别是广大发展中国家对推进全球发展事业的殷切期盼，为全球共同发展指明方向，倡议提出两年来，得到国际社会广泛响应，取得积极进展和多项早期收获。

日前发布的《全球发展倡议落实进展报告》显示，倡议理念内涵不断丰富，落实机制不断健全，推进路径更加清晰，务实合作逐步落地，有效推动国际社会重新聚焦发展问题，加强国际发展合作，共同破解发展难题，为加快落实 2030 年议程注入了新的动力。

本报告围绕全球发展倡议提出两年来的实践成就进行梳理。两年来，中国携手各方合作伙伴，推动全球发展倡议走深走实，给各国带来实实在在的好处：守护脆弱人群，让世界更有爱；营建温馨家园，让世界更宜居；应对共同危机，让世界更安全；助力可持续发展，让世界更绿色；创造强劲增长，让世界更繁荣。

本报告认为，全球发展倡议引领推动了国际发展合作新格局，其特点为：以更具包容力的合作理念，构筑共享型发展空间；以更加多元化的合作渠道，聚合高质量发展资源；以更可持续的合作方式，培育内生式发展动能。本报告呼吁，通过科技变革提振经济复苏活力、完善全球治理建设公正合理秩序、采取集体行动构建人类发展命运共同体，将全球发展倡议与 2030 年议程更有机地结合起来，与发展中国家的发展战略更紧密对接起来，共创普惠平衡、协调包容、合作共赢、共同繁荣的全球发展新时代，共建人类发展命运共同体。

一、推动全球发展的中国倡议

全球发展遭遇逆风逆流之际，中国国家主席习近平提出全球发展倡议，有力回应了全球性挑战和广大发展中国家的发展需求，得到各方积极响应，倡议提出两年来取得积极进展。

（一）全球发展倡议的缘起和目标

进入 21 世纪第三个十年，世界百年变局加速演进，全球经济复苏乏力，特别是在新冠疫情影响下，全球南北鸿沟持续拉大，地缘冲突、气候变化、粮食能源危机等多重挑战交织，近 8 亿人生活在饥饿之中，人类发展指数连续两年下滑，全球发展进程面临前所未有的严峻考验。联合国 2030 年可持续发展议程落实进度落后于预期。

同时，一些国家漠视发展中国家最紧迫需求，具体体现在：不兑现发展领域资金承诺；挑起意识形态斗争；用人权、民主等议题边缘化发展议题；拉小圈子、企图搞"脱钩"，投入大量人力、财力进行地缘政治博弈。

联合国秘书长古特雷斯警告：全球发展已到"决定性时刻"。

与此同时，作为世界上最大的发展中国家，中国始终把自身发展置于人类发展的坐标系中。特别是进入新时代的十年多来，中国取得了举世瞩目的发展成就。在促进自身发展的同时，中国始终心系广大发展中国家，尽己所能通过贸易、投资、援助和发展知识分享等多种方式帮助其他发展中国家实现共同发展。

在这样的背景下，2021 年 9 月，第 76 届联合国大会一般性辩论上，习近平主席提出全球发展倡议，旨在推动全球发展迈向平衡协调包容新阶段。

全球发展倡议以减贫、粮食安全、抗疫和疫苗、发展筹资、气候变化和绿色发展、工业化、数字经济、数字时代互联互通等为重点合作领域，同联合国 2030 年可持续发展议程高度契合，是为了推动实现更加强劲、绿色、健康的全球发展。

2022 年 6 月，习近平主席主持召开全球发展高层对话会，18 个主要发展中国家和新兴市场国家领导人"云聚首"，对话会还发布了一份包含 32 项举措的成果清单，覆盖倡议八大重点合作领域，为全球发展倡议落地生根指明方向。

全球发展倡议吹响了聚焦发展的"集结号"，铺设了促进发展的"快车道"，有助于推动发展问题回归国际核心议程，为各方对接发展政策和深化务实合作搭建有效平台。

（二）全球发展倡议的理念和原则

习近平主席指出，各国一起发展才是真发展，大家共同富裕才是真富裕。全球发展倡议最核心的理念是坚持以人民为中心，最主要的目的是克服疫情带来的挑战，加快落实联合国 2030 年可持续发展议程，最根本的追求是满足全世界人民对美好生活的向往，实现全人类共同价值。这样的价值追求决定了全球发展倡议独有的核心理念与价值原则。

全球发展倡议呼吁坚持发展优先，以人民为中心，不让任何一国、任何一人掉队，人与自然和谐共生，创新驱动，全球发展伙伴关系，行动导向，协同增效等理念与原则。秉持这样的原则与价值理念，倡议作为国际公共产品，其自身具有的开放属性，以及注重"小而美、惠民生"等特质愈发凸显。

打造全球开放平台。倡议由中国提出，属于整个国际社会。从参与国家看，中方在联合国发起成立的"全球发展倡议之友小组"已有 70 多个国家参与，向发达国家开放；从合作方式看，既有通过联合国系统发起的合作，也有中方直接参与的三方合作；从对接平台看，倡导同非盟《2063 议程》、非洲发展新伙伴计划、支持非洲发展伙伴倡议等同 2030 年议程充分对接，推动联合国、二十国集团、亚太经合组织、金砖国家、中国—东盟（10+1）等多边合作进程汇聚共谋发展的强大合力。

提供国际公共产品。习近平主席指出，全球发展倡议是"向全世界开放的公共产品"。从思想层面看，全球发展倡议秉持以人民为中心的核心理念和绿色与创新原则，为全球发展事业谋定前行航向，注入思想动力；

从行动层面看，全球发展倡议明确重点领域，为推进全球发展进程指明优先选项，增添物质力量。全球发展倡议作为理念、原则与行动相统一的国际公共产品，为破解全球发展难题提供了系统化、整体性方案。

注重"小而美、惠民生"。全球发展倡议框架下，一批"小而美"的项目落地生根，如尼泊尔实施微笑儿童（粮食发放）项目，塞拉利昂宫颈癌筛查防治项目等。

根植于中华优秀传统文化。中华民族追求"大道之行、天下为公"、崇尚"亲仁善邻、协和万邦"、倡导"和衷共济、守望相助"，"天下为公"，这些精神与文化基因，是当代中国国际发展合作的传统渊源，也是中国开展全球发展合作始终不变的坚守。

（三）全球发展倡议的早期收获

两年来，全球发展倡议得到国际社会广泛积极响应，在各方共同努力下，倡议合作路径更加明确，合作机制日臻完善，八大重点领域合作有序推进，项目库不断充实，发展资源逐步汇集，呈现重点突出、全面推进的良好态势，有效凝聚国际发展共识，动员发展合作行动，取得多项早期收获。

全球发展倡议和可持续发展目标关系

GDI 核心理念和重点领域	对应可持续发展目标
减贫（包容发展）	直接对应目标1，涉及目标2、3、4、5、6、7、8、9、10、11、16、17
粮食安全	直接对应目标2，涉及目标3、4、6、9、10、11、12、13、16、17
抗疫和疫苗	重点对应目标1，涉及目标4、5、6、10、16、17
发展筹资	该领域是实现可持续发展目标的基础，对应所有17个可持续发展目标
气候变化和绿色发展	直接对应目标13，涉及目标1、3、5、7、8、9、11、12、14、15、17

GDI 核心理念和重点领域	对应可持续发展目标
工业化	对应目标 1、4、5、8、9、10、11、12、13、17
数字经济	对应目标 1、3、4、5、8、9、10、11、13、14、15、16、17
数字时代互联互通	对应目标 1、2、5、6、7、8、9、10、11、17

【注：2030 年议程 17 项目标：目标 1 无贫穷，目标 2 零饥饿，目标 3 良好健康与福祉，目标 4 优质教育，目标 5 性别平等，目标 6 清洁饮用水和卫生设施，目标 7 经济适用的清洁能源，目标 8 体面工作和经济增长，目标 9 产业、创新和基础设施，目标 10 减少不平等，目标 11 可持续城市和社区，目标 12 负责任消费和生产，目标 13 气候行动，目标 14 水下生物，目标 15 陆地生物，目标 16 和平、正义与强大机构，目标 17 促进目标实现的伙伴关系】

重振了国际发展议程。中方召开了全球发展高层对话会和"全球发展倡议之友小组"部长级会议，推动发展议题重回国际议程中心位置；倡议八大重点领域务实合作全面覆盖所有 17 项可持续发展目标，为 2030 年议程落实作出积极贡献。

开展了众多合作项目。中方就落实全球发展倡议宣布的 32 项务实举措目前已完成过半，成立全球发展促进中心、全球发展促进中心网络，30 多个国家和区域组织对口部门正式加入，为发展合作理念交流、规划对接、资源统筹等提供平台和支持。

2022 年 9 月，中国设立全球发展倡议项目库并公布首批项目清单。首批 50 个务实合作项目清单，涉及减贫、粮食安全、工业化等多个领域，其中 10 多个项目已经实施完毕，剩余项目正积极推进，此外，项目库还在不断扩大，目前项目总数已经接近 200 个。

促进筹集发展资源。中方整合组建全球发展和南南合作基金，并增资至 40 亿美元，中方还积极参与国际开发协会、全球环境基金增资，正式启动中国－联合国粮农组织第三期南南合作信托基金。

促进建立广泛合作网络。目前已有 100 多个国家和国际组织支持全球发展倡议，70 多个国家加入"全球发展倡议之友小组"，中方还同

20多个国家和国际机构签署了合作谅解备忘录。团结、平等、均衡、普惠的全球发展伙伴关系正在加快形成。

促进改善各国人民生活。为南太平洋岛国巴布亚新几内亚东高地省开展菌草和旱稻技术援助，在老挝、缅甸、柬埔寨的6个贫困村实施的"东亚减贫示范合作项目"，向尼泊尔贫困社区儿童发放粮食包……从抗疫"健康爱心包"到白内障患者复明手术，从建设中小学校到科研技术合作，全球发展倡议正在为各国人民带来实实在在的变化，触手可及的希望。

全球发展倡议顺应历史潮流，有效凝聚起国际社会团结合作、加快发展的共识，提高了发展议题在国际上的关注度，得到了国际社会，特别是广大发展中国家的广泛支持和响应。

联合国秘书长古特雷斯说，中方提出的全球发展倡议同联合国2030年可持续发展议程相契合，在帮助发展中国家共同发展方面，中国所作努力无可比拟。

巴基斯坦总理夏巴兹认为，全球发展倡议呼吁国际社会将发展置于优先位置，回应了国际社会对民生发展的关切，为各国和谐共存、共谋发展提供了现实路径。

泰国副总理兼外长敦表示，中方提出的全球发展倡议，旨在建立发展的全球共同体，也为加速实现联合国可持续发展议程提供了绝佳机会。

当前，全球发展倡议已实现从"打基础""搭框架"到"强合作""显实效"的跨越。中方积极团结国际社会，脚踏实地推进倡议重要举措，取得重要早期收获，全球发展倡议呈现多国、多部门、多领域共同参与的良好局面。

二、全球发展倡议的实践成就

自习近平主席提出全球发展倡议以来，两年间围绕八个重点合作领域——减贫、粮食安全、抗疫和疫苗、发展筹资、气候变化和绿色发展、工业化、数字经济、数字时代互联互通，各方通过双边、多边机制，表达对倡议的支持和认同。

更引人注目的是全球发展倡议框架下不断加快推进的合作实践和显著成效。从个体的人，到家庭、社区，推及自然和人文环境，全球发展倡议正在从一幅幅规划蓝图，化为一项项"小而美、惠民生"的务实合作成果。

（一）守护脆弱人群，让世界更有爱

为脆弱人群筑起"后盾"是全球发展倡议的重要使命之一。为此，倡议的视野深入到全球最不发达的偏远乡村，倡议的实践走进区域动荡之地，为贫困儿童送上营养餐食，为困难妇女提供技能培训，为战争难民和流离失所者提供人道主义救济和生活物资援助，改善他们的生存状况和生活条件，并为他们创造接受教育、参与经济活动的可能性。

柬埔寨首都金边以南 60 公里处的茶胶省巴提县达弄村是中柬友好扶贫示范村。2022 年 8 月，中柬"健康爱心包"项目在这里正式启动。口罩、餐盒、水壶、大米、罐头……昂坎拿小学的 257 名学生率先收到来自中国的礼物。六年级的塞索格纳兴奋之情溢于言表："这个爱心包太有用了，衷心感谢中国的慷慨捐助，我们将永远铭记这份善意。"作为联合国公布的全球最不发达国家之一，柬埔寨深受新冠疫情之苦，失业和贫困人口增加，部分儿童面临失学辍学风险。"健康爱心包"为柬贫困地区 10000 名孩子提供了基本的餐食和抗疫保障，也让他们的家庭减少了后顾之忧，更加安心地复工复产。

尼泊尔微笑儿童供餐项目和老挝学校粮食援助项目同样得到了全球发展和南南合作基金的大力支持。截至目前，已为 3000 多名尼泊尔儿童提供了装有大米、豆类、食用油的粮食包，并助力老挝政府延续为偏

远地区 1400 多所学校超过 13 万名学生提供营养餐的国家校餐计划。学校供餐被视为社会保障网的必要一环，也是对未来一代的合理投资。这些项目降低了贫困学生营养不良状况的发生率，从长远看，更是推动贫穷国家迈向可持续发展的人力资源积累。根据联合国世界粮食计划署的一项成本收益分析，在老挝每向学校午餐计划投入 1 美元，可帮助每位受益人在一生中多带来 5 美元收入。

世界上最贫穷和最脆弱的群体正经历前所未有的全球性挑战的最严重冲击，应给予特别保护的还有妇女、难民以及在贫困线上挣扎的人群。无法无视的严峻现实是：根据联合国数据，全球饥饿水平已达 2005 年以来的高位，约 6.7 亿人处于极端贫困状态；若使妇女在工作场所的权力和领导职位上有平等的代表仍需 140 年的时间；而全球被迫流离失所者在 2022 年年底已升至 1.084 亿人，是 10 年前的 2.5 倍。

国际社会亟需采取务实行动——哪怕只是带来点滴改变或局部变化。在全球发展倡议框架下，中国继续与吉尔吉斯斯坦妇女大会合作举办"知识女性，知识国家"培训班项目，为当地妇女开设信息技术、缝纫技术、演讲培训、商业规划、网络营销等课程，帮助她们提高职业技能，增加就业机会；与联合国开发计划署合作，向莫桑比克德尔加杜角省流离失所的 5300 户家庭发放了防护物资、家庭应急包、生计工具包和屋顶搭建包，帮助难民安置和恢复生产生活。南太平洋岛国巴布亚新几内亚东高地省菲尼图古村的村民成为菌草和旱稻技术合作项目的受益者。在很长一段时间，他们曾深陷部落纷争，深受贫困之苦，如今，在中国专家手把手的教授下，学习平整地块、种植水稻，尝到了丰收的滋味。菲尼图古村长托尼感叹道："种植旱稻让大家看到了经济发展的希望，促使大家放下了纷争，给村子带来了和平与安宁。"

2022 年 11 月 15 日，全球人口总数创造了 80 亿的新纪录。这是人类发展史上的新里程碑，也是国际社会思考对地球负起共同责任的新时刻。人口增长越来越集中在贫穷国家。比如，在世界人口从 70 亿增长至 80 亿的过程中，约 70% 新增人口出现在低收入和中低收入国家；根据预测，未来在 80 亿至 90 亿的增长区间，这两个组别的国家将占到新增人口九成以上。能否帮助数量庞大的脆弱群体和边缘化人群摆脱战乱、饥饿、疾病、贫困，让他们过上稳定温饱的生活，考验着人类的良心。聚焦全世界每一个活生生的人，全球发展倡议所展开的行动，具有重要意义。

（二）营建温馨家园，让世界更宜居

"安得广厦千万间，大庇天下寒士俱欢颜。"1200 多年前中国唐代诗人杜甫所描摹的宏愿，也是当今中国所提全球发展倡议正在践行的国际合作。

倡议旨在为个体和家庭提供更加安全稳定的庇佑，其所聚焦的减贫、工业化等重点合作领域，一些合作项目致力于为全球 80 亿人口营造更温馨、宜居的家园。

8 幢住宅楼、共计 1008 套住宅，正在蒙古国乌兰巴托市苏赫巴托区加紧建设。这一棚户区改造项目由中国政府资助，中国北部的包头市对接承建。2024 年建成后，受益群体将覆盖乌兰巴托市 700 余户拆迁家庭和 200 余户在棚区周转的家庭，总计约 5000 人。相关项目有助于改善棚户区居民居住环境，助力当地实现可持续发展目标。

营建温馨家园，不仅体现在居住条件改善上。全球发展倡议所追求的是人类生存环境的普遍改善。通过全球各方和衷共济，尽可能改善发展中国家每个家庭的生活质量，包括提供清洁的水源和经济适用的清洁能源、可持续的社区保障等。这些细节与联合国 2030 年可持续发展议程清晰对应，亦是践行倡议的具体行动。

从修建水井到开辟水源，从建设供水系统，到设立全新污水处理厂，从东南亚地区，到非洲多国，中国政府、企业及社会组织等，协调各国合作方等，走进当地社区，开辟清洁水源并提供相关技术，造福一方。

埃及锡瓦地区居民及灌溉用水全依靠地下水，之前该地区所钻的水井，基本以 500 米以内的浅井为主，长期取水后水质变硬，口感苦涩。在当地政府和居民的支持下，中方专家团队参与调研，启动钻探超过 800 米深的新水井。这些深水井大大缓解了锡瓦地区用水难及灌溉不足的问题。

从水井项目，到道路照明工程，再到部分地区的风电项目等，中国以其丰富的基础设施建设经验，通过这类"小而美"的合作品牌项目，为当地带来更优质、可持续、清洁的能源，同时创造了新增就业。

单是哈萨克斯坦 Abay 风电项目就可提供年预期发电量 5.1 亿千瓦时，能满足 140 万户家庭日常用电需求。项目建设还为当地提供了超过 500 个临时就业岗位和 50 个长期岗位，培养超过 20 名新能源工程建设及运维紧缺技术人员。

这是对当地人权的充分尊重，也有助于让共同发展的红利在全球范围覆盖更加均衡、更加普惠，有助于相关可持续发展目标的加速实现。

（三）应对共同危机，让世界更安全

当今世界，来自非传统安全领域的威胁和挑战日益增多，重大传染性疾病、粮食和能源危机、突发自然灾害等，都威胁着人类生存和发展。

在全球发展倡议框架下，各方共同努力，携手应对危机与挑战。新冠疫情肆虐，全球疫苗供应紧张，约旦、叙利亚、黎巴嫩境内数十万巴勒斯坦难民迫切需要疫苗应对，中国政府分批向联合国近东巴勒斯坦难民救济和工程处交付 20 万剂新冠疫苗，用于援助在约旦、叙利亚和黎巴嫩的巴勒斯坦难民。

新冠疫情严重冲击广大发展中国家的医疗卫生体系。伊斯兰合作组

织的很多非洲成员国普遍面临医疗设施、人员和物资匮乏等问题。对此，中国支持该组织在其"非洲计划"下开展项目，提高其最不发达非洲成员国公共卫生能力水平，包括开展卫生知识宣传和意识培养； 加强重点领域医疗水平和公共卫生体系建设； 为医疗条件欠缺国家提供集中救助服务，提升疾病控制和预防能力等。

新冠疫情不会是人类面临的最后一次公共卫生危机，全球性危机需要各国携手应对。坦桑尼亚是非洲疟疾流行最严重的国家之一。为帮助该国控制和消除这一传染性疾病，中国、瑞士、坦桑尼亚正在探讨开展三方合作项目，发挥各自优势和经验，探索新的合作模式，推进坦桑尼亚疟疾控制和消除进程。

粮食安全是世界面对的又一重大挑战。根据 《2023 年世界粮食安全和营养状况》 报告，目前全球约有 7.35 亿饥饿人口，较 2019 年新增 1.22 多亿，如果放任态势发展，到 2030 年，世界各国无法如期实现消除饥饿的可持续发展目标。

在东非国家布隆迪，当地农业人口占比超 90%，农业在国民经济中起决定作用。中国水稻专家在这里普及杂交水稻技术，帮助当地人实现"人人有所食、人人有储蓄" 的目标。"在中国农业专家组的支持和帮助下，我们种植杂交水稻获得了丰收，现在生活有很大改善，盖了新房子，还抚养 7 个孩子。" 来自布隆迪吉汉加县宁加 4 村的 43 岁农民夏尔说。

2023 年 7 月，由中国乡村发展基金会和中国高级农业专家组联合发起的"布隆迪杂交水稻技术减贫示范项目"在班扎省吉汉加县正式启动，该项目旨在支持当地农户采购杂交水稻种植所需的种子、化肥、农药等原料，并通过资金的回收滚动机制，不断增加受益农户数量； 该项目还将与当地合作社合作，提升其管理能力，共同助力当地村民摆脱贫困。

新冠肺炎疫情冲击、地缘政治安全冲突、单边主义保护主义抬头等，严重阻碍全球发展进程，更加凸显践行全球发展倡议、深化务实合作的重要性、迫切性。

（四）助力可持续发展，让世界更绿色

近年来，南半球的多个太平洋岛国正遭遇海上漂浮巨量塑料垃圾的威胁。岛国无法处理这些塑料垃圾，它们堆成的小山甚至成为岛屿上"海拔最高的山峰"，南太平洋区域环境署反复表达了担忧。

"以竹代塑"——一项面向全球的环保倡议及行动计划，由中国和国际竹藤组织于 2022 年共同发起。倡议呼吁，深化全球合作，更好地发挥竹子在减少塑料污染、代替塑料产品方面的作用，为高能耗、难降解的塑料制品提供基于自然的解决方案。

在多国专家看来，竹藤制品具有巨大的潜力，有望替代大量塑料制品，从而更好地发展绿色经济，营造一个更健康的世界。巴西经济学家罗尼·林斯认为，践行"以竹代塑"倡议，将有助于推动塑料产业投资创新，减少塑料污染对环境的影响。

减塑和节水是世界共同面临的两大难题。在课堂上热烈讨论水知识，动手制作污水过滤器，走进街巷收集本地用水情况和挑战……经过生动直观的学习，肯尼亚内罗毕布鲁克希尔学院的师生们对生活中的水有了更深刻的认识，也对自己生活的社区和自然有了更科学的了解。

2022 年，中国水科院在与联合国教科文组织联合编译出版的《水知识读本》英文版成功发布的基础上，逐步开展了水科普教育走进非洲校园的系列活动。肯尼亚内罗毕布鲁克希尔学院、瑞莱区和平皇后教育中心、伊弗汀小学肯尼亚学校的师生们都参与其中。

对于生活在广大发展中国家，特别是最不发达国家的民众而言，改善生活水平的同时，又要尽可能让生活方式更为"绿色"，统筹好经济发展和生态环境保护的关系，更加需要来自国际社会的支持与帮助。

西非国家马里电力资源紧缺，农村通电率不足 20%。2023 年，中国援助马里太阳能示范村项目在马里科纽布拉村和卡朗村通过竣工验收。项目共安装 1195 套离网太阳能户用系统、200 套太阳能路灯系统、17 套太阳能水泵系统以及 2 套集中太阳能供电系统，当地直接受益民众达上万人。

如今，晚间漆黑的村落不仅有了路灯，村民还用上了免费的太阳能自动抽水水塔。"如果没有中国慷慨援助，我们无法想象什么时候才能为家里配备这么先进的新能源设备。"村民迪奥普说。

类似的项目，向"全球南方"国家倾斜，还深入到太平洋岛国斐济等地。一年多来，斐济逾 3 万村民开始使用太阳能照明系统。不仅夜间出行安全得到保障，还能为孩子的夜间学习提供充足的照明及网络互联互通保障。同时，该项目利用太阳能，减少了化石燃料的使用，有助于碳减排，为共同应对气候变化问题作出了积极贡献。

这是全球发展倡议框架下，在民生领域分享清洁能源、分享绿色发展经验的一系列务实举措。小而美、惠民生的合作项目，不仅契合斐济、马里等国完善农村配套设施建设的现实需要，也顺应了当地百姓长期渴求幸福生活的热切期盼。

灼热、干旱、野火、暴雨、洪水……今天我们生活的世界，与气候变化紧密相关的极端天气正在全球多地更加频繁出现，对人类健康、生态系统、经济、农业、能源和水供应等各个方面产生重大影响甚至持续威胁。

近年来，世界各地极端天气伴随着前所未有的高温，让人们对全球气候变化的累积效应有了更直接可感的认知。"全球变暖时代已经结束，全球'沸腾时代'到来。"古特雷斯秘书长以"沸腾时代"就全球气候危机再次发出警告。

全球极端气候导致的自然灾害频发，生物多样性丧失速度加快，人与自然和谐相处面临严峻挑战。如何提升相关发展中国家应对气候变化的能力？如何推动形成保护自然环境和生物多样性的国际共识？

全球发展倡议坚持人与自然和谐共生、行动导向的理念，推动加强国际合作、搭建交流对话平台、促进生产生活方式改变，推动实现更加强劲、绿色、健康的全球发展。

（五）创造强劲增长，让世界更繁荣

近年来，全球产业链、供应链正加快变革重组。发展中国家各自所处的发展阶段和具体国情不同，需要结合自身实际，发展具备比较优势的产业，更好地嵌入全球和区域产业链、供应链，获得更多发展机会和动能；同时，随着更多发展中国家的加入，全球和区域产业链、供应链发展将获得更强韧性，增强世界经济的稳定性和可持续发展水平。

全球发展倡议提出后，中国作为表率积极助力发展中国家工业化进程。2021 年 12 月，在中非合作论坛第八届部长级会议上，中国宣布未来 3 年将推动企业对非洲投资总额不少于 100 亿美元，设立"中非民间投资促进平台"，帮助非洲实施 10 个工业化和就业促进项目。在《中国—拉共体成员国重点领域合作共同行动计划（2022—2024）》中，中拉同意将加强工业政策交流，深化在原材料、装备制造、绿色低碳产业、产业链供应链等领域的合作，推动中拉产业智能化、数字化、绿色化发展。

如何为全球增长注入更多新动能？响应倡议的各方认为，这离不开多边协同配合，采取切实行动，才能提升产业链供应链韧性、促进直接投资、弥合"数字鸿沟"等。

联合国工业发展组织、德国国际合作机构、中国纺织工业联合会和埃塞俄比亚纺织服装行业研究与发展中心共同合作，帮助埃塞俄比亚纺织服装行业通过能力建设提高应对市场准入环境、社会和治理（ESG）相关标准，并提高当地纺织服装企业的 ESG 意识，促进商业伙伴关系。相关

经验已在非洲和亚洲其他地方进行推广复制。该项目被联合国南南合作办公室评选为 2022 年"可持续发展南南合作与三方合作良好实践"案例。

当前巨大的"数字鸿沟"仍在不断拉大南北差距，全球发展倡议积极搭建交流平台、支持发展中国家的数字能力建设。

中国联合部分区域性国际组织，努力拆除数字"高墙"，将"数字＋"的概念推广到诸多"全球南方"国家和地区，覆盖精准农业、智慧渔业、电子商务和在线技能培训等，将数字化红利直接赋能"全球南方"经济发展。单以咖啡豆为例，近年来中国通过向非洲和中南美洲市场进口咖啡豆，再依托国内强大的电商网络进行分销，为卢旺达、东帝汶、哥斯达黎加等地的咖农带来国际大订单，也直接改善了咖农的工作和生活质量。

又如以各经济体瞩目的"跨境电商"能力培训为例，中国政府、联合国南南合作办公室等合作推出的在线培训项目——发展中国家青年跨境电商扶贫和可持续发展能力建设系列合作项目，吸引了 93 个国家 1090 名学员积极参与，培训期间每天有上千人同时在线学习。这类培训不仅介绍全球相关行业最新动态，还分享中国经验和其他发展中国家经验，将电子商务助力减贫的好办法带给更多迫切需要提升数字能力的各国青年。

又比如华为埃及公司与埃及通讯和信息技术部及高等教育和科学研究部合作，开展持续性能力建设工程——ITB 人才培养项目 (ICT Talent Bank Program)，聚焦人工智能、云、物联网、大数据和 5G 等前沿科技领域，为埃及培训专业人才，助力当地数字化转型。通过设立学院、开设技术课程，华为已为当地培训超过 3.5 万名大学生，超 8000 名学生获得认证，培训还促进了青年就业，形成良性循环。埃及通信部、高教部、劳工部等高度评价与华为开展 ITB 项目合作情况，赞赏该项目为"数字埃及"建设作出的贡献。

全球发展倡议框架下，多方通过搭建交流平台，推动数字技术应用全球合作；加强数字能力建设，弥合"数字鸿沟"；顺应数字化潮流，促进大数据应用。这都将促进2030年议程的相关愿景加快实现，同时也将赋能发展中国家，获得更多从"跟跑"到"并跑"的信息技术红利，促进世界共同繁荣。

三、全球发展倡议的世界贡献

坚持将发展作为"第一要务"，中国创造了令世人惊叹的发展奇迹，迈入了中国发展与世界发展相互交融相互成就的新时代。在这一新时代，中国既矢志于在国内推进共同富裕，又致力于在世界范围促进共同发展；既坚定地以中国式现代化全面推进中华民族伟大复兴，也以大国责任担当为全球发展事业不断作出新的更大贡献。全球发展倡议的提出、落实和推进是新时代的生动篇章。

全球发展倡议是2030年议程遇阻之时中国提供的兼具思想力和行动力的国际公共产品。两年来，它为无数个体和家庭创造了切实的福祉，为一系列国家带来了实现稳定与增长的希望，也向国际社会展现了一种更具包容力、更加多元化、更可持续的国际发展合作新模式，为人类携手走出发展困局、奔赴共同发展的美好前程开辟了新路径,提供了新启迪。

（一）再塑造：开创国际发展合作新模式

我们认为，全球发展倡议所引领推动的新型国际发展合作，具有以下鲜明特征：

天下一家：以更具包容力的合作理念构筑共享型发展空间

全球发展倡议面向全球，不分南北，不讲集团政治，不以意识形态划线。它在坚持南北合作主渠道的原则下，不断开拓南南合作新场域新方式，重振全球发展伙伴关系，携手各方打造开放联动的全球发展环境，让各国和各国人民共享发展机遇、发展成果。它不干涉他国内政、不附加任何政治条件，坚定支持各国走自己的路。它坚持共商共建共享，欢迎世界各国和所有致力于全球发展的积极力量贡献智慧和力量。目前，已有 100 多个国家和国际组织支持全球发展倡议，70 多个国家加入"全球发展倡议之友小组"，中方还同 20 多个国家和国际机构签署了合作谅解备忘录。在今年 7 月举行的全球共享发展行动论坛首届高级别会议上，中方宣布同瑞士在坦桑尼亚开展疟疾防控合作，同德国在尼日利亚开展农业合作，成为全球发展倡议开放性、包容力的新例证。

众行致远：以更加多元化的合作渠道聚合高质量发展资源

全球发展倡议强调充分发挥各国政府、民营部门、社会组织、国际机构的作用，积极调动各国工商界、学术界、民间社会力量，建立广泛的合作网络，聚合资金、技术、人才、数据等发展要素和发展资源，将其用到最急需领域以实现最大化效益。在全球发展和南南合作基金支持下，联合国粮农组织、世界粮食计划署等实施了近 50 个三方合作项目，助力相关发展中国家提升粮食安全水平和农业综合生产能力。中方还与盖茨基金会签署谅解备忘录，在卫生健康、能力建设、发展融资等领域开展务实合作，共同推进落实全球发展倡议，加速落实 2030 年议程。

授人以渔：以更可持续的合作方式，培育内生式发展动能

全球发展倡议注重硬援助与软援助相结合，发展援助与互利合作相结合，既授人以鱼，也授人以渔。在授人以渔的过程中，超越狭隘经济理性认知，倡导坚守正确义利观，义利相兼，以义为先，推动各方通过多种方式毫无保留地将发展经验和行业技术分享给发展中国家，帮助他们培育"造血"机能，提升自主发展能力。中国积极推进全球发展知识网络建设，搭建综合性合作网络平台，推动国际发展经验交流分享。"中国—东盟知识网络秘书处"已经成立，未来中国还将探索设立"中国—中亚发展知识网络""中国—非洲发展知识网络"等区域支柱网络和减贫、清洁能源发展等专题性网络建设。

（二）再出发：开启迈向可持续发展目标新里程

2015 年 9 月 25 日，纽约联合国总部，联合国 193 个会员国在具有历史意义的发展峰会上共同启动了 2030 年议程。落实议程的时间框架过半，只有约 12% 的可持续发展目标有望按期实现。根据联合国今年 7 月发布的《2023 年可持续发展目标报告：特别版》，在可评估的约 140 个具体目标中，有半数出现中度或严重偏离预期，其中超过 30% 的具体目标与 2015 年的基准相比毫无进展，甚至出现倒退。

尽管现实令人忧虑甚至沮丧，2030 年议程仍是当前国际社会对发展问题的最广泛共识，是人类愿景的最清晰蓝图。正如"特别版报告"所指出的，"当历史学家撰写 21 世纪时，他们将以我们是否成功地将这一蓝图变为现实作为标准来评判我们这个时代"。当下，最紧迫的是采取行动创造更有希望的新现实。在这个意义上，全球发展倡议指明了行动方向：

拥抱科技变革，提振经济复苏活力

全球通电人口比例 2015 年为 87%，2021 年增至 91%；全球网民人数自 2015 年以来增长 65%，2022 年达到 53 亿；虽然全球制造业增长放缓，但中高端和高端技术产业表现出强劲增长势头……全球发展事业在数字经济和中高端制造业等领域取得的重要进展表明，国际社会仍可能通过抓住新一轮科技革命和产业变革的历史机遇，为所有人创造更美好未来取得实质突破。

绿色转型和数字转型可以成为摆脱发展困境的新出路。比如，在提供高质量互联网服务的地区，44% 的企业是出口商，而在互联网服务较弱的地区，只有 19% 的企业是出口商。这也是全球发展倡议为何将创新驱动作为基本原则之一，同各方在互联网、大数据、5G、人工智能等领域展开积极合作。

完善全球治理，建设公正合理秩序

更鼓舞人心的是"全球南方"国家在世界瞩目中的崛起，全球发展倡议所发出的"将发展议题重置国际核心议程"的强烈呼声，在推进落实议程进程中所展现的高涨合作热情和团结协同行动，为国际发展合作注入了强劲动力。

当前，国家之间的贫富分化正在加剧，一个根本性原因是全球经济治理体系没有公平对待"全球南方"的发展诉求。比如，新冠疫情期间，被视为发达国家代表的七国集团从国际货币基金组织获得总计 2800 亿美元资金，而一些最不发达国家获得的资助只有约 80 亿美元；七国集团总人口约 7.7 亿，而上述最不发达国家人口合计约 11 亿。因此，联合国秘书长古特雷斯强烈呼吁，改变"根植于现有国际金融架构中的偏见和不公"，对国际货币基金组织和世界银行进行彻底改革。

通过一系列务实行动和大胆改革构建更加公正合理的全球发展治理体系和制度环境成为当务之急。这意味着，要坚持真正的多边主义，支持联合国发挥统筹协调作用；要建设开放型世界经济，建立安全稳定、开放包容的产供链；要推动多边发展机构改革，提升新兴市场国家和发展中国家代表性和发言权；要构建团结、平等、均衡、普惠的全球发展伙伴关系，敦促发达国家按时足额履行向发展中国家提供资金、技术和能力建设等官方发展援助承诺。

中国是世界上最大的发展中国家，是"全球南方"的当然成员。中国将同广大新兴市场国家和发展中国家一道，在新一轮全球治理体系变革中推动扩大"全球南方"国家的话语权和代表性，维护好共同利益，携手捍卫发展权利。

采取集体行动，构建人类发展命运共同体

当今世界，如果说不发展是最大的不安全，那么不合作是最大的风险，不团结是最大的挑战。国际货币基金组织的经济学家警告说，"一个分裂的世界可能会更穷"。他们特别提到"友岸外包"的兴起对欠发达市场可能造成的"最大伤害",因为"他们更为依赖在地缘政治上较远的国家提供的投资"。

国际社会的强烈共识是,应避免将发展议程政治化,以地缘冲突和集团对抗带偏世界前进方向,这将对全球发展事业造成无法估量的巨大损失。发展是解决人类一切问题的关键和基础,发展问题是全球所有国家和地区都面临的问题。包括联合国、南方国家、北方国家、穷人、富翁、区域和次区域组织在内的各方,都应团结起来,承担共同责任、采取共同行动。

在这方面,各国国家元首和政府首脑应展现担当,在国家和国际层面采取 7 年加速、持续和变革性行动。联合国各会员国应以此次可持续发展目标峰会为契机,凝聚发展共识,汇集发展资源,将全球发展倡议与 2030 年议程更有机地结合起来,与发展中国家的发展战略更紧密对接起来,与联合国发展机构和多边开发机构的工作联系起来,共创普惠平衡、协调包容、合作共赢、共同繁荣的全球发展新时代。

展望未来,共同构建人类命运共同体,各国一道努力消除冲突,共建和平;重振活力,共促发展;开放包容,共谋进步;团结一致,共商合作。

作为"全球南方"大家庭成员和负责任的"地球村"成员,中国主张要坚持把发展置于国际议程中心位置,进一步凝聚促发展的国际共识,维护发展中国家正当发展权利。重振全球发展伙伴关系,培育全球发展新动能。推动发达国家切实履行援助承诺,让发展成果更多惠及各国人民。

正如习近平主席所指出的,发展是人类社会的永恒主题,共享发展是建设美好世界的重要路径。全球发展倡议不是中方的独奏曲,而是各方的交响乐。全球发展事业,应当由各国人民一起努力,一同分享,不把任何一个国家、任何一个人落下。

将蓝图变为现实,就从现在开始。

编写说明与致谢

《全球发展倡议实践成就与世界贡献》智库报告于 2023 年 9 月 19 日在纽约联合国总部举行的"全球发展倡议合作成果展示高级别会议"期间发布。国家副主席韩正出席会议，并在致辞中推介了《全球发展倡议实践成就与世界贡献》智库报告。

该智库报告在外交部国际经济司指导下展开调研，课题组由新华通讯社社长、新华社国家高端智库学术委员会主任傅华任组长，新华通讯社总编辑吕岩松任副组长，课题组成员包括任卫东、刘刚、班玮、崔峰、郝薇薇、刘华、杨柳、郑明达、许晓青、刘明霞等。课题自 2023 年 3 月启动以来，历时半年多采访、调研、撰写、修改、审校完成。

课题组认真学习习近平外交思想相关重要论述，调研国家国际发展合作署、中国国际知识发展中心、中国联合国协会等机构，召开多场专家研讨会；深入国家电力、国家能源、招商局、中国海洋石油等 20 多个央企实地调研；通过外交部多个驻外使领馆收集"全球发展倡议"在各国的进展案例，与华中科技大学国家治理研究院合作整理出 50 多个国家 130 余个"全球发展倡议优秀案例集"，其中 30 多个典型合作项目在报告中展现，有力彰显倡议对国际发展事业的贡献。

人工智能时代新闻媒体的责任与使命①

从全球范围看，媒体智能化进入快速发展阶段。我们要增强紧迫感和使命感，推动关键核心技术自主创新不断实现突破，探索将人工智能运用在新闻采集、生产、分发、接收、反馈中，用主流价值导向驾驭"算法"，全面提高舆论引导能力。②

——习近平

前　言

生成式人工智能技术的快速发展及广泛应用，引发席卷全球的人工智能热潮，新闻媒体也再一次迎来变革发展的机遇。科幻小说中那个神秘的"技术奇点"正从想象走入现实，带领人类进入一个充满未知的崭新时空。"智媒"时代正向我们走来。

人工智能为新闻媒体行业带来无限可能性，但正如之前历次传播技

---

① 2024年10月14日发布于在新疆乌鲁木齐举行的第六届世界媒体峰会
② 习近平在十九届中央政治局第十二次集体学习时的讲话（2019年1月25日）。

术革命一样，人工智能的发展也无法摆脱"科林格里奇困境"，新兴技术的利弊在得到实践检验之前，仍处于"黑箱"之中。

构建有效的治理机制，促进人工智能造福人类，已经成为国际社会的广泛共识。2023 年 10 月，中国国家主席习近平在第三届"一带一路"国际合作高峰论坛上提出《全球人工智能治理倡议》。《倡议》指出，人工智能治理攸关全人类命运，是世界各国面临的共同课题。在世界和平与发展面临多元挑战的背景下，各国应坚持发展和安全并重的原则，通过对话与合作凝聚共识，构建开放、公正、有效的治理机制，促进人工智能技术造福人类，推动构建人类命运共同体。围绕人工智能发展、安全、治理等问题，《倡议》提出了"以人为本""智能向善"等基本原则，为解决人工智能治理难题贡献了中国方案。

人工智能时代，新闻媒体面临哪些机遇与挑战？推动智能向善，新闻媒体应该如何履行职责使命？围绕这些问题，新华社国家高端智库课题组以中、英、法三种语言面向全球新闻媒体机构开展问卷调查，最终得到有效问卷 1094 份，受访者来自 53 个国家和地区，包括报刊、广电、通讯社、网站、移动应用服务商等。与此同时，课题组还广泛走访全球各大主流媒体、科技公司与科研院所，聚焦人工智能时代新闻媒体的机遇与挑战、责任与使命开展深入调研。基于调研数据及访谈结果，课题组进行了科学的定性和定量分析，经过深入研究、反复研讨，最终形成《人工智能时代新闻媒体的责任与使命》研究报告。

报告发现，全球新闻媒体整体上（66.0%）对生成式人工智能对行业的影响持积极态度，多数媒体（67.6%）已切身感受到人工智能带来的变化，超半数媒体（51.2%）已开始应用人工智能。媒体对生成式人工智能的期待主要聚焦于提高新闻报道的时效性（74.6%）与生产效率（74.4%）等，同时警惕人工智能带来的"新闻线索和素材失真失准"（76.4%）等可信度风险。多数新闻媒体（85.6%）认为需要对生成式人工智能的应用加强监管。

报告认为，人工智能给新闻媒体的发展带来产能新驱动，从内容的采集、生产、分发、评估等环节促生了媒体新质生产力；赋予媒体及其消费者超越时空、虚实融合、人机交流的体验新升级；开创了万物媒介化、媒体平台化、产业数智化的新兴业态。

报告提出，人工智能的不确定因素及其滥用、恶用，催生了多重风险挑战。虚假信息在规模、形态和传播路径上不断升级，引发了全球范围内的真实性危机；技术的自身局限与使用者的私利诉求产生"合谋"，污染了舆论生态，对个体认知和社会舆论造成负面影响，并加重了国际层面的信息对抗；广泛存在的价值争议和伦理困境，令人工智能在发展与治理中陷入"两难"；"智能鸿沟"或将进一步拉大人际、城乡和南北差距，助长技术霸权，加剧全球发展失衡。

报告提议，新闻媒体需肩负社会责任使命，坚持"以人为本"，推动"智能向善"，从加快智能驱动、提升媒体价值，立足善意使用、健全伦理规范，加强对话合作、完善全球治理等方面坚守人工智能时代下的责任与使命，为构建人类命运共同体，建设更加美好的世界汇聚强大的媒体力量。

一、机遇：人工智能赋能传媒发展

把握数字化、网络化、智能化融合发展契机，在质量变革、效率变革、动力变革中发挥人工智能作用，提高全要素生产率。[①]

——习近平

新一代人工智能正在全球范围内蓬勃兴起，为经济社会发展注入了

---

① 习近平在十九届中央政治局第九次集体学习时的讲话（2018 年 10 月 31 日）。

新动能,正在深刻改变人们的生产生活方式。①在新闻媒体领域,智能"涌现"与5G、大数据、云计算、物联网、区块链等技术共同点燃了新一轮媒介革命的引擎。透过徐徐拉开的人工智能变革大幕,我们看到,新闻媒体正迎来产能新驱动、体验新升级、业态新前景的良好机遇。

(一)产能新驱动

当今,人工智能迎来爆发式增长,算法推荐、语音交互、知识问答、图像生成等技术应用不断突破,生成式人工智能的热潮蔓延全球。2022年底,美国OpenAI公司研发的生成式人工智能ChatGPT横空出世;2024年,文生视频大模型Sora再度惊艳世界;近来,OpenAI推出最新o1模型、快手"可灵"入局文生视频赛道、Kimi大模型助手更新支持到200万字超长文本分析……多模态及垂直领域大模型不断在世界各地涌现,人工智能技术在全球呈现加速发展的趋势。

人工智能技术"井喷式"发展为新闻媒体提供了新的产能驱动。众多媒体纷纷把握这一技术先机,争做人工智能"早鸟"。新华社课题组调查显示,目前全球已有10.2%的媒体机构全面拥抱人工智能,在机构层面设立了相应机制,由上而下地将人工智能引入生产流程;41.0%的媒体机构正在积极探索人工智能技术应用,鼓励和支持部分新闻业务板块试用人工智能技术。人工智能正在成为新闻媒体催生新质生产力、实现高质量发展的重要增量。

---

① 习近平致二〇一八世界人工智能大会的贺信(2018年9月17日)。

受访媒体机构对生成式人工智能（大语言模型）的应用程度：

■ 全面拥抱，机构层面设有相应机制，由上而下地将之引入生产流程
■ 机构层面正在积极探索，鼓励和支持部分新闻业务板块试用
■ 仅编辑记者个人层面尝鲜，机构层面不反对
■ 极少有人使用或机构禁止使用

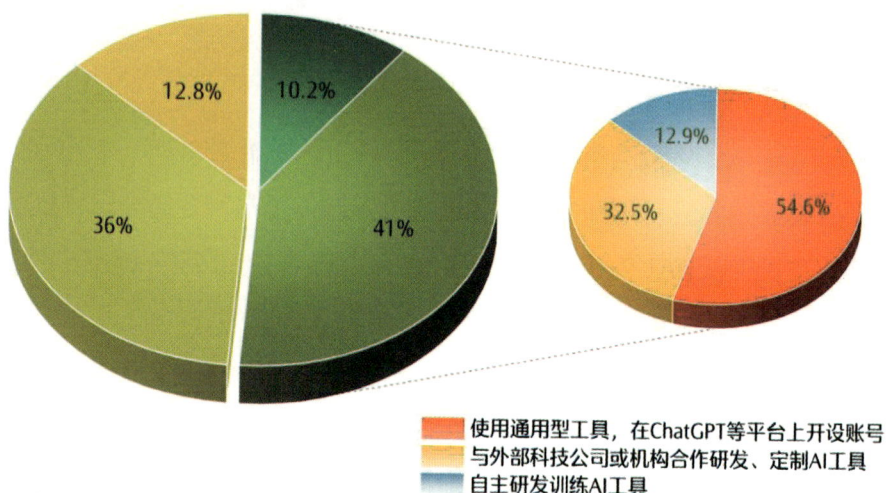

■ 使用通用型工具，在ChatGPT等平台上开设账号
■ 与外部科技公司或机构合作研发、定制AI工具
■ 自主研发训练AI工具

1. 聚合信息，丰富来源

新一代人工智能技术通过精准的搜索引擎、分析引擎和可视化组件，自动收集背景信息，推荐消息来源和线人，进行消息源验证和核查，为采编人员提供更具价值的新闻线索和多元观察视角。

新华社研发的"新闻雷达（NewsRadar）"，能够自动预警突发事件，并根据事件性质和规模预测事件热度；BBC研发的新闻聚合和内容抽取系统"榨汁机（Juicer）"，能够自动抓取全球免费新闻网站的内容，利用人工智能将新闻分类、贴标签，为记者提供新闻素材和选题参考；《纽约时报》开发的数据分析机器人"Blossomblot"，通过对社交平台上推送文章的分析，预测适宜在社交平台上传播的信息，帮助打造"爆款"内容；美联社推出由人工智能驱动的多模态搜索平台，用户可以通过语义搜索更容易地找到符合条件的照片和视频，为丰富新闻媒体的信息来源提供帮助。

2. 辅助生产，优化品质

在新闻生产环节，智能创作平台以"知识服务+AI"的方式，为媒体从业者提供更多的知识辅助与支撑；写作机器人、AI创作助手等技术应用，能完成语音转文字、自动剪辑、字幕生成、智能配乐、自动翻译、文本图片转视频等一系列工作任务。人工智能的深度应用，让媒体人从大量重复琐碎的人工劳动中解放出来，专注于内容创新创意。

新华社自主打造的可控、可靠、多智能体融合生产引擎"新华新语"，在内容核查、虚假信息鉴别、智能态势分析、知识增强的智能策划、视觉增强的智能创作等方面表现突出。人民日报推出的"创作大脑AI+"平台，集纳了近20款智能工具，可及时制作、快速生成多模态新媒体产品，一站式完成采访、拍摄、直播、剪辑、发布等全流程工作；全息采录眼镜支持实时人脸识别、AI语音互动、实时直播流发起等多种功能。在垂直报道领域，针对各类细分行业的专业模型也不断涌现。彭博社是人工智能、机器学习和自然语言处理在金融领域应用的开拓者，其开发的Bloomberg GPT TM语言模型专门针对各种金融数据进行训练，为进一步优化金融信息服务打开了新空间。

课题组调查显示，在应用场景上，媒体机构有组织探索较多的前三个方向是：

1. 辅助编辑，如事实核查、语音转文字、配字幕、翻译等；

2. 创作内容，如生成摘要、制作图表海报、数字主播配音等；

3. 策划选题或草拟提纲。

在机构层面应用生成式人工智能（大语言模型）的受访媒体机构已探索或有意探索的应用场景：

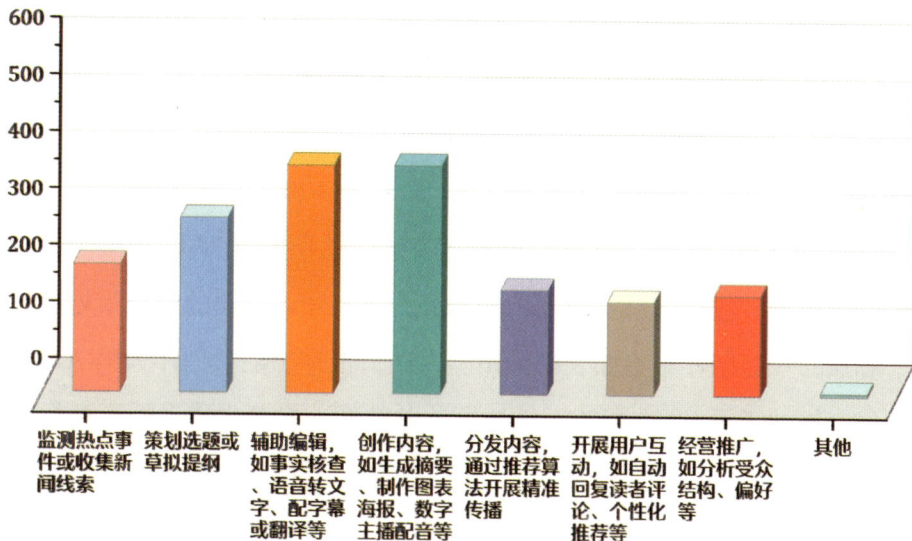

3. 精准画像，个性分发

在内容分发环节，人工智能依托广泛串联的数据信息，帮助媒体开启深度洞察，勾勒用户画像，与用户建立深度联接，更好实现精准推送。

今天，借助人工智能技术，个性化推荐已经成为新闻分发的主流方式。媒体的推荐逻辑不仅基于历史浏览记录，还将更多精细化的数据纳入考量。美国新闻聚合网站 BuzzFeed、风靡全球的短视频平台 TikTok 都将用户数据分析做到极致，根据用户点击的频次、停留的时间、喜好的内容等做出综合分析，指导内容策划、运营和推广。

不仅如此，生成式人工智能还赋能"点对点"信息传播，这意味着，用户能够通过嵌入在各种搜索引擎和应用程序里、专属于自己的"信息管家"，获得特定场景下所需要的内容。借助"点对点"传播，智能分发甚至不必通过集中性的平台就能实现。目前，微软、谷歌、百度等均已在搜索引擎中部署了生成式人工智能程序，大型语言模型与搜索引擎的融合，或将成为新的流量入口和新闻分发渠道。

4. 科学评价，高效管理

人工智能技术能精准实现传播效果评估与数据考核，帮助媒体进一步提升管理效率。如通过分析用户观看时长、点击率以及分享次数等数据来量化评估内容的吸引力；通过情感分析工具捕捉受众在观看过程中的情感变化和社交媒体上的讨论，判断传播内容的感染力；通过观察用户的互动行为，如评论数量、点赞、踩、举报等，来评估用户的参与热情。

在《华盛顿邮报》"中央厨房"编辑室的屏幕上，可视化数据图表同步显示网站的登录人数、每篇文章的阅读数排名、用户喜欢作者排名以及读者喜欢阅读的文章类型百分比等数据。英国《金融时报》会用机器人检查报道中引用的信源是否过多地来自特定人群。

课题组调查显示，有74.6%的受访媒体预期，生成式人工智能有助于提高新闻报道的时效性；有74.4%的受访对象认为，生成式人工智能有助于提高新闻生产效率；预期生成式人工智能对提升新闻分发精准度和作品呈现创造性有帮助的媒体占比分别达到66.7%和63.3%。

受访媒体机构对生成式人工智能在新闻报道中的效用预估：

■ 大有助益　■ 有一定帮助　■ 不好说　■ 有些破坏性　■ 破坏性极大

新闻报道的时效性

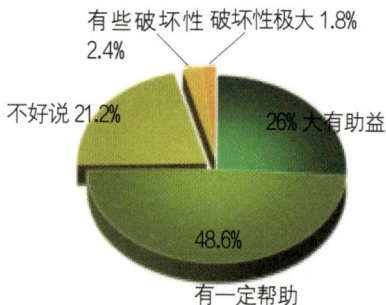

有些破坏性 2.4%　破坏性极大 1.8%
不好说 21.2%
26% 大有助益
48.6%
有一定帮助

新闻生产效率

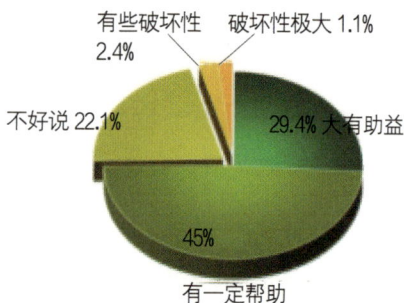

有些破坏性 2.4%　破坏性极大 1.1%
不好说 22.1%
29.4% 大有助益
45%
有一定帮助

新闻分发的精准度

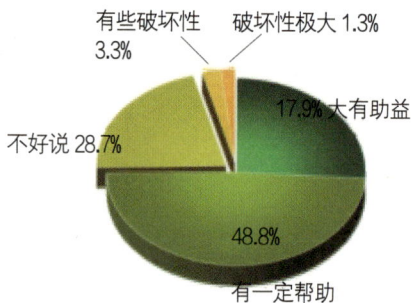

有些破坏性 3.3%　破坏性极大 1.3%
不好说 28.7%
17.9% 大有助益
48.8%
有一定帮助

作品呈现的创造性

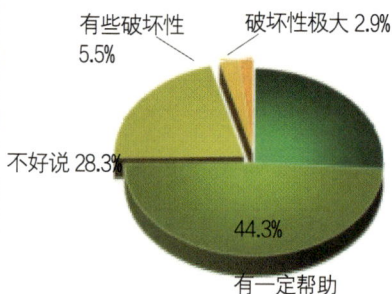

有些破坏性 5.5%　破坏性极大 2.9%
不好说 28.3%
44.3%
有一定帮助

（二）体验新升级

人工智能技术与新闻媒体的深度结合，不仅强力赋能新闻信息生产，而且为新闻信息的消费者带来充满惊喜的新变化。人工智能时代的媒介消费，将是一种以人为本、联通万物的全新体验，"四全媒体"（全程媒体、全息媒体、全员媒体、全效媒体）的发展图景更加清晰、机遇空间更加广阔。

1.超越时空，随时触达

人工智能技术的广泛应用，让传播超越时空限制，在任何时间、任何空间、任何场景都能到达用户。

媒体智能系统能够根据用户行为、立场、兴趣偏好的动态变化，第一时间捕捉用户的即时需求，在重大新闻事件爆发时，迅速识别并推送相关资讯。大模型还可以根据已知信息进行信息补全，模拟事件发生经过和还原新闻现场，用具象化的方式解释新闻事件，确保用户在"黄金时间"获取真实、全面的信息。

智能驱动的场景感知贴身服务，能够识别用户的地理位置信息，推送与其生活紧密关联的内容。NBC 环球在巴黎奥运会期间新推出电子商务广告工具"虚拟售货亭"，结合受众观看节目时的消费习惯，推出不同类型的广告服务。未来，越来越复杂的算法总能随时随地感知用户对于信息获取、商品交易、享受服务等多元需求，用户到哪里，服务就延伸到哪里，并以合适的方式呈现出来。

2. 虚实融合，身临其境

人工智能与虚拟现实（VR）、增强现实（AR）、混合现实（MR）等技术结合，搭建起全方位、多感官、多维度的传播场景，为沉浸式体验增添智能维度。

全息通讯叠加强大的算法、算力，让高保真的数字化影像实时呈现，用户可化身为与自己等比的虚拟形象，在虚拟世界中通过"数字分身"实现实时互动，不仅可在人与人之间创建更真实的情感联结，更能够使用户"亲身"体验难以获得的现实经历。中央广播电视总台利用"虚幻引擎 +XR+ 虚拟演播室技术"，在台风"摩羯"等相关报道中实现室内与户外多场景的丝滑转场，不仅显著增强了信息传递的有效性，也提升了报道的艺术表现力；《纽约时报》《泰晤士报》《时代周刊》等也利用 AR 技术还原 NASA 火星任务、重温阿波罗 11 号执行任务全程、呈现亚马逊热带雨林变迁，给用户带来更真实、直观的感受。

人工智能与多模态技术的融合，还将实现文化、地域、传统、美学的数字化跃迁，广泛应用于历史文化艺术的传播。用户可以用手代槌敲响虚拟国家一级文物——曾侯乙编钟，亲身体验国宝魅力；用户可以深入一砖一瓦、每一幅壁画、每一处雕刻都被精准还原的巴黎圣母院，以全息全感的方式领略这座世界级文化遗产的历史回响与艺术精髓。

3. 人机交流，达意传情

媒体利用大模型技术，采用人性化的对话方式提供信息内容，打破传统媒体与受众间的单向传播模式，实现双向交流和互动，使用户在信息获取过程中有更多的参与感。随着机器对人类心理洞察、情绪感知能力的不断增强，人工智能还将推动媒体从"物理性媒介"向"心理性媒介"过渡，使用户在信息接收过程中，得到内心抚慰和情感满足。

当前，生成式人工智能在新闻活动中已有一定的"主体性人格"，借助人工智能开发的"新闻管家""信息伴侣"等垂直化应用，将具有更强的社交智能，能根据其所定位的角色、个体信息和个性化需求来定制功能。随着聊天的不断深入，用户会发现，这些人工智能在交互中越来越主动，会自行引入新的话题、提供意想不到的额外信息和情感支持，用户也可以对人工智能的回答进行反驳、质疑，促使其不断提高回答质量。在互动中，人工智能已逐步从"工具"发展成为"伙伴"。

（三）业态新前景

人工智能是引领这一轮科技革命和产业变革的战略性技术，具有溢出带动性很强的"头雁"效应。[1] 在人工智能驱动下，一些国家和地区的传媒业态正从简单的"+AI"（将人工智能作为辅助工具）逐步提质升级到"AI+"（人工智能成为核心驱动力）的新高度。展望未来，在

---

[1] 习近平在十九届中央政治局第九次集体学习时的讲话（2018年10月31日）。

人工智能技术的加持下，传媒业态或将加速呈现万物媒介化、媒体平台化、产业数智化的新前景。

1. 万物媒介化

以信息技术、人工智能为代表的新兴科技快速发展，大大拓展了时间、空间和人们认知的范围，人类正在进入一个"人机物"三元融合的万物智能互联时代。[①] 人工智能，正携手 5G、物联网、大数据、云计算等技术，让"万物皆媒"成为现实。

在人工智能的赋能下，信息传播将突破人的限制，实现人与人、人与物、物与物的泛在化连接。如无人机、摄像头、传感器等应用，延伸了人的"感官"，可触达远距离、多维度的信息。生成式人工智能则更像"人脑"，具有归纳总结、推理演绎、内容生成等功能。这些具备了泛媒介化媒体属性的"智能体"，与人协同融合、自我进化。

在"万物皆媒"的时代，几乎任何智能终端都不仅是内容分发接收终端，也是人机互动、协同、陪伴的能动主体。智能家居、智能汽车、智能音箱、智能手表等终端的传播潜能日渐凸显，对智能终端及其采集数据的控制和利用，也将成为传媒业及媒介生态中的新竞争力。新闻媒体积极适应智能网联汽车发展趋势，面向高速移动环境下的媒体应用场景，基于人工智能、生物传感、情感计算等技术进行个性化音频内容推送，拓展新闻信息传播应用场景，打造传感器技术与新闻传媒融合新模式。未来，人体终端化、脑机接口技术等，更将不断扩展人类信息传播和精神交往的广度和深度。

2. 媒体平台化

平台作为数字基础设施，具有强大的技术、庞大的用户群以及将不

---

① 习近平在中国科学院第二十次院士大会、中国工程院第十五次院士大会和中国科学技术协会第十次全国代表大会上的讲话（2021 年 5 月 28 日）。

同群体相连接的能力，成为"重构传播权力"的重要力量。在人工智能技术的驱动支撑下，"媒体平台化"的现实可能和未来空间将进一步被拓展。

媒体平台化意味着，通过技术创新和用户参与，新闻媒体实现了信息的快速传播、个性化推送和多样化表达，增强了信息传播的便捷性和互动性，并整合传统媒体和新媒体的优势，通过多渠道传播提供综合服务，实现对传播触角、内容生态、商业模式、运营机制的全新塑造。新华社客户端不断优化提升算法，升级智能推荐、精准推送能力，将用户阅读习惯、专业新闻判断与前沿计算机技术结合，突出主流价值导向，探索打造移动互联网时代的新型消息总汇和主流传播平台。

在媒体平台化的过程中，新闻媒体既是传播媒介，即内容生产机构和运营机构；又是技术载体，即利用数据、算法、人工智能技术等对社会关系产生影响；同时具有商业资本的属性，通过聚合连接，实现对市场资源的匹配和再分配。由此，智能化的媒体平台在新传播场景中可以占据更多主动，成为社会信息传播的主要场景和容纳各类社群的服务载体。

3.产业数智化

人工智能带来了巨大的产业机遇和广阔的市场前景。中国《新一代人工智能发展规划》提出，到2030年，中国人工智能核心产业规模超过1万亿元，带动相关产业规模超过10万亿元。越来越多的新闻媒体率先接纳、坚持、寻求数字化和智能化技术带来的转型与突破，从传统媒体向智能媒体不断迈进。

数智化转型意味着传媒产业从内容驱动向技术、资本和内容等多重驱动的转变，这种转型升级不仅体现在内容与技术的紧密结合，更涉及整个产业链的深度融合与重构。在人工智能的推动下，传媒产业链上下游及其关系发生深刻变化：上游内容创作者与技术专家更紧密地合作，共同参与内容创作全过程，使得内容创作更加便捷和高效；中游媒体平台加强与技术公司合作，建立"智能中台"，在提升全要素生产效率的同时连接更广泛的社会资源，为传媒产品的创意策划、内容审核等提供科学、高效的技术解决方案；下游终端渠道重视内容分发和推广策略制定，精准推送内容给目标用户，增强传播效果和用户黏性。

传媒产业链的升级演变，将推动传媒产业结构进一步调整和优化，为传统传媒业突破发展瓶颈、实现更高质量发展提供更多可能性。新京报依托空间漫游技术，推出《沉浸中轴 (AR+VR)：全景穿越京城脊梁》视觉产品，立体形象地重现了北京中轴线上的 15 个申遗遗产点位，助力文化传承与申遗保护工作，探索挖掘衍生文创产品等商业价值。齐鲁晚报基于虚拟设计、AI 数字人、光学动捕拍摄等技术打造了元宇宙平台"壹点天元"，推出"云祭孔"元宇宙发布会、齐鲁国际车展元宇宙展厅、元宇宙医院，建设元宇宙文化综合社区，探索新型商业模式。未来，人工智能技术将为媒体的多元化跨界"淘金"，实现"增产增收"带来更多可能。

二、挑战：人工智能催生多重风险

> 人工智能技术发展和其他技术进步一样，是一把"双刃剑"。[①]
>
> ——习近平

一切技术发展，都具有"福祸相依"的两面性。著名物理学家霍金曾发出警告，强大人工智能的崛起对人类来说，可能是最好的事情，也可能是最糟糕的事情。由于人工智能技术自身的不确定性和应用的广泛

---

① 习近平在十九届中央政治局第九次集体学习时的讲话（2018 年 10 月 31 日）。

性，人工智能发展在赋能新闻媒体的同时，也催生出种种风险。

（一）虚假信息引发信任危机

真实性是新闻的生命，事实是新闻的本源，虚假是新闻的天敌。[①]人工智能技术的滥用恶用使得虚假信息生产及传播呈现大规模、多样化、病毒式等特点，不仅侵蚀着新闻媒体的社会信任基础，还引发了全球信息环境的真实性危机。

1."无限量产"更具灾难性

人工智能的介入从技术上降低了虚假信息生产传播的门槛和成本，大幅提升了正常信息环境中虚假信息的数量级，为人类正确认知社会制造出层层"信息迷雾"。

在一项针对人工智能大模型的测试中，研究人员向 ChatGPT 提出充满阴谋论和虚假叙述的问题，结果它以新闻、散文和电视脚本等形式，在几秒钟内编成大量看似令人信服却毫无信源的内容。业内人士感叹，"这个工具将成为互联网上有史以来最强大的传播错误信息的工具。"

课题组调查显示，生成式人工智能在传媒领域已引发行业变局，不过不同媒体机构的感知存在"温差"。有 32.4% 的受访媒体表示生成式人工智能对他们的影响"尚不明显"，67.6% 的受访对象则明显觉察到近在眼前的变局，共鸣较多的三个侧面是：

1. 生产流程需要改造，编辑记者工作方式面临转变；

2. 媒体之间，尤其是来自自媒体的竞争更激烈；

3. 需抽出更多精力来分辨虚假新闻、虚假照片等。

---

① 习近平在党的新闻舆论工作座谈会上的讲话（2016 年 2 月 19 日）。

生成式人工智能对受访媒体机构的影响

影响尚不明显
32.4%

有某些影响
67.6%

尚不明显
（与其余选项互斥）

需抽出更多精力
来分辨虚假新闻
虚假照片等

媒体之间、尤其是
来自自媒体的竞争
更激烈

生产流程需要改
造，编辑记者工
作方式面临转变

内容生产效率提升，
人力需求减少，组织
架构面临调整或精简

内容分发机制经历迭
代，传播效益得
以提高

技术投入成本学
习成本增加，但
收益未能跟上

其他

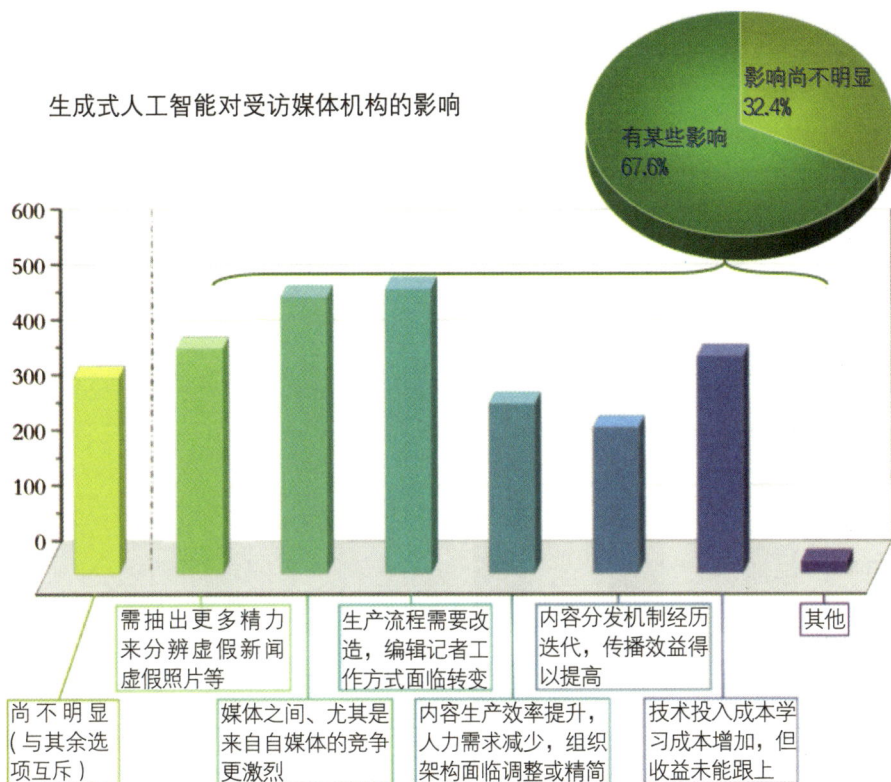

不同国家的调查数据都表明，人工智能在虚假信息传播中起到强力推动作用。清华大学新闻与传播学院新媒体研究中心 2024 年 4 月发布的报告《揭秘 AI 谣言：传播路径与治理策略全解析》指出，人工智能工具的不当使用使得 AI 谣言量高速增长，近半年信息量增长 65%，其中经济与企业类 AI 谣言量增速甚至高达 99.91%。美国新闻可信度评估与研究机构在 2023 年底发布的一份报告称，利用人工智能代理创建的假新闻网站在 7 个月内从 49 个激增至 600 多个，"人工智能正在成为下一个'错误信息超级传播者'"。

课题组调查显示，多数媒体机构对生成式人工智能的应用较为审慎，担心被其拉低可信度。对于"您所在媒体机构遇到过或预期会遇到哪些生成式人工智能带来的问题"这一提问，高达 76.4% 的受访对象表示，担心出现"新闻线索和素材失真失准"的情况，明显超过回答数量排在第二位的"版权及权责归属问题"（占比为 61.1%）。

受访媒体机构运用生成式人工智能时遇到过或预期会遇到的问题：

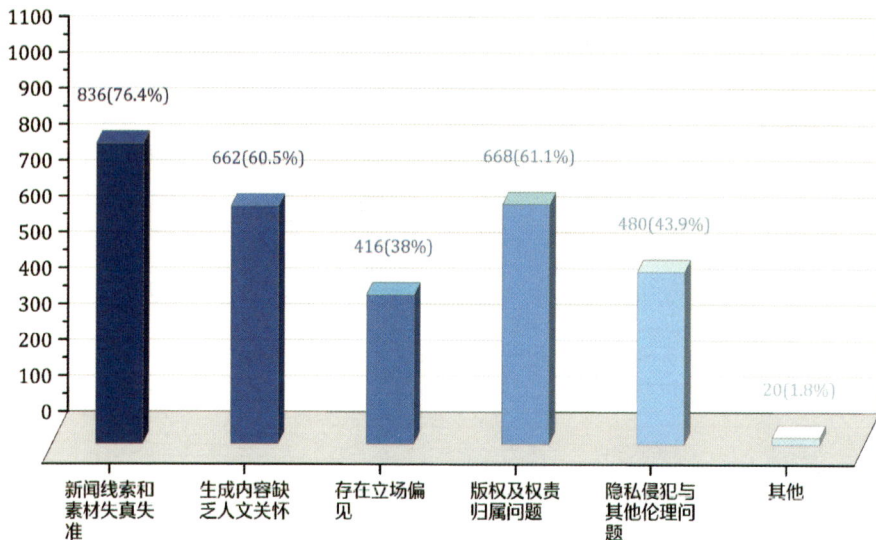

人工智能助长虚假信息泛滥已经引起全球范围内的警惕与担忧。韦氏词典、剑桥词典分别选择"Authentic（真实）""Hallucinate（幻觉）"为 2023 年度词汇，均是对人工智能引发真实性危机的回应。在世界经济论坛 2024 年年初公布的《全球风险报告》中，人工智能生成的错误信息和虚假信息也被排在气候变化、战争和经济疲软等问题之前，成为人类世界在短期内要面对的头号风险。

对于未来 3 至 5 年生成式人工智能与传媒行业融合会否提升信息环境可信度可靠性的问题，有 36.4% 的受访对象持悲观预期，比持乐观预期者（24.1%）高出 12.3 个百分点，另有 39.5% 的受访对象持中性预期。

> 真实可信是新闻报道的生命。由此推测，多数媒体机构短期内或许只会让生成式人工智能在内容生产环节扮演有限的辅助角色。

随着生成式人工智能与传媒行业融合，受访媒体机构对未来 3 至 5 年信息环境可信度可靠性的预判：

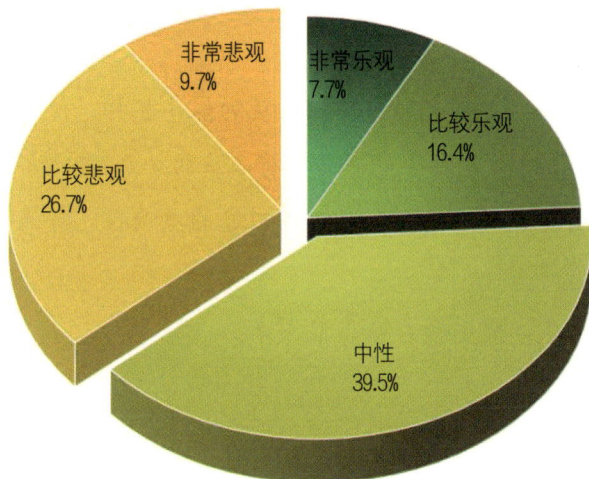

2."深度伪造"更具迷惑性

人工智能的多模态功能拓展，使得虚假信息的内容形态更加多元，也更加难以被普通人所辨别。以"深度伪造"为代表的前沿技术突破文字限制，可以通过对图像、声音、视频的篡改或伪造，产生高度逼真且难以甄别的多媒体信息。

随着深度伪造技术的成熟和普及，过去只有在影视大片中才能出现的虚构场景，如今只需一个软件就能一键生成。有些伪造内容不仅仅是"张冠李戴""捕风捉影"，甚至还可以"无中生有"。这种迷惑性极强的技术应用大大助长了电信诈骗、色情视频合成等社会性犯罪活动，也令新闻信息更加真假难辨。近年来，各种针对公众人物的深度伪造视频屡次掀起舆论风波。2023 年底，不法分子利用深度伪造技术，篡改了新加坡前总理李显龙在国庆群众大会上的讲话和接受 CGTN 主持人访谈时的录像，用以宣传加密货币的投资骗局，相关视频在网络上广泛流传。李显龙在社交媒体发文进行澄清，"利用深伪技术传播虚假信息的现象将继续增加，我们须保持警惕，学会保护自己和亲人免受这类骗局的侵害。"

课题组调查显示，对于那些尚在观望的媒体机构，阻碍其成建制应用生成式人工智能的众多因素中，排在前三位的分别是：

1. 人工智能自身还不完善，如生成内容的准确性、可靠性等达不到预期和要求；

2. 人机协作难，缺乏相应融合型人才；

3. 技术投入成本高。

尚未在机构层面应用生成式人工智能的受访媒体机构驻足观望的主要原因：

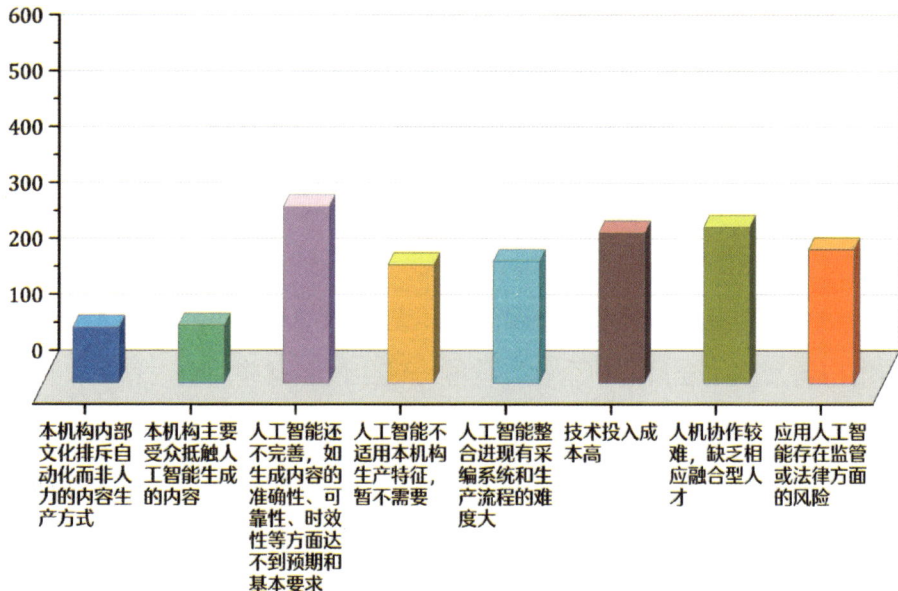

基于对深度伪造技术的担忧，公众对虚假信息的风险感知意识也在不断加深，对任何信息来源，包括新闻媒体等传统信源也逐渐产生警惕和怀疑，社会整体信任无疑遭到严重侵蚀。路透社发布的《2023年数字新闻报告》称，受深度伪造等技术影响，只有40%的受访者表示信任媒体报道的新闻。

3. "仿真传播"更具隐蔽性

人工智能不仅在生产层面助推了虚假信息的泛滥，还在传播层面为其提供了更加强大的工具。以"社交机器人"为代表的新一代"网络水军"散布在全球各大社交媒体上，成为无孔不入的"网络隐形病毒"。

"在互联网上，没有人知道你是一条狗"，多年前美国杂志《纽约客》上的这句话随着互联网的普及而被世人熟知。在人工智能时代，越来越多的智能大模型通过了用以检验机器人类特征的"图灵测试"，人们愈发难以判断互联网的另一端是人还是机器，也无从知晓每一条信息背后的真正主体和行为动机。

作为一种运行在社交媒体平台上的智能代理，"社交机器人"能够根据操控人的意愿自动生成内容，并模仿人类真实用户的状态和行为参与互动交流，制造各种"虚假热度""虚假共识"。相比于"人工操作＋匿名账号"的传统"网络水军"，由"社交机器人"构成的"机器人水军"可以输出个性化观点，并24小时不间断工作，持续打造自身的"人设形象"，使得虚假信息的传播更加隐蔽和难以察觉。2022年8月底，美国斯坦福大学网络观察室（Stanford Internet Observatory，简称SIO）和社交平台分析公司Graphika联合发布报告，披露美国利用社交媒体操纵全球涉疆舆论，"社交机器人"就在其中扮演了重要角色，其操作套路包括用人工智能生成照片当头像、冒充"独立"新闻机构、制造热门标签引起话题讨论等。

（二）技术滥用破坏舆论生态

营造良好的舆论环境，是治国理政、定国安邦的大事。[①]安全、和平、清朗的国际舆论空间，也对全球合作与发展意义重大。人工智能在信息传播领域的广泛应用，为全球舆论生态注入新变量，在个体、社会和国际等多个层面形成新的风险挑战。

1. 算法偏见诱导个体认知

人是舆论的主体，也是舆论环境的关键构成要素。人工智能难以摆脱内嵌于数据和算法中的偏见，以及定制化内容的"茧房"效应，对独立、理性、健康的个体认知与价值塑造带来挑战。

由于机器深度学习的特点，大型语言模型无可避免地会继承数据语料库和人类设计师的刻板印象或价值偏见。这些或明或暗的立场、偏见如果不加以限制，机器控制人类的场景很有可能成为现实。在刘慈欣的科幻小说《三体》中，高级文明可以通过技术手段将某种思想或信念刻印在个体意识中，书中称之为"思想钢印"。人工智能目前虽然无法直接作用于人的大脑，但已经深入参与到社会信息流动的各个环节中，可以凭借"量"的碾压和"时间"的积累逐渐占领社会意识生产领域，最终实现对用户的价值传导甚至是认知侵蚀。

即使人工智能始终秉持"为人类服务"的宗旨，其所遵循的个性化生产和精准化推送的算法逻辑，也可能会限制用户的信息认知范围，使认知窄化、思维固化、群体极化等问题更加突出。尤其是在传媒领域的注意力争夺中，用户往往偏好那些具有强烈视觉冲击力、故事性和情感化的信息内容，人工智能可能会为了满足大众喜好，予以相关内容更高的权重和更多的曝光，而有深度有价值的内容则面临被不断边缘化的风险。

[①] 习近平同志在会见中国记协第九届理事会全体代表和中国新闻奖、长江韬奋奖获奖者代表时讲话（2016 年 11 月 7 日）。

2. 机器水军操控社会舆论

在人工智能技术的加持下，舆论操纵的手法不断翻新、工具持续升级，舆论生态进一步复杂化与浑浊化，极大增加了社会意见分裂、秩序混乱、心理动荡的现实风险，对社会的正常稳定运行构成严重威胁。

"舆论是社会的皮肤"，公众围绕公共事务形成敏锐、理性的舆论，社会肌体也就有了能够感知民意的健康皮肤。舆论是现代民主社会持续稳定运行的重要基石，但其强大的社会影响力也令各方"虎视眈眈"。高级人工智能的出现为影响甚至控制舆论提供了便利，为社会舆论应有的透明性、公正性蒙上阴影。

在政治领域，人工智能很早即被用于影响目标对象的价值判断和政治立场，或破坏敌对势力的舆论环境和社会形象。2016 年，剑桥分析公司未经同意收集脸书数千万用户的个人信息进行选民分析，为唐纳德·特朗普的总统竞选活动投放政治广告，成为技术干预政治选举的一大标志性事件。随着人工智能技术的升级迭代，各种"操纵工具"更加唾手可得，隐蔽性和欺骗性大幅提升。2024 年，各方对利用人工智能干扰选民、操纵选举、破坏稳定的担忧愈加强烈。在社会领域，恶意操控者还利用人工智能工具发布大量情绪化内容，在种族、移民、贫富差距等社会敏感议题上激化社会矛盾、影响舆论走向。在商业领域，人工智能也被广泛用于"刷数据""刷评分""刷销量"等，以达到歪曲和屏蔽真实评价、促销商品或诋毁竞争对手的目的，对市场秩序造成严重破坏。

3. 智能武器加重信息对抗

在社会矛盾多发、地缘政治紧张的国际局势下，人工智能被广泛应用于"情报战""舆论战""认知战"中，使国际舆论关系更加紧张，对抗升级、冲突爆发的风险大大增加。

人工智能为广泛开展网络入侵、情报搜集、舆论攻击等提供了极大便利。通过数据差异化投送，人工智能可以瞬时制造舆论潮流，影响群体认知。通过数据跟踪和算法策略，人工智能可以预判不同地域、群体的认知态势，辅助规划、推动实施核心叙事和议题。

在社交媒体上，利用人工智能捏造虚假信息、煽动群体对立、开展意识形态渗透的行为也已司空见惯。2022年，关于乌克兰总统泽连斯基要求其军队投降与俄罗斯总统普京宣布战争结束的伪造视频广泛流传。本轮巴以冲突以来，社交媒体上也产生了大量虚假内容，如将效果逼真的游戏视频篡改成哈马斯发动袭击的录像，伪造国际知名人物挥舞巴勒斯坦国旗的照片等。在人工智能技术散布的战争信息迷雾中，真与假混淆，猜疑与分歧滋长，人工智能改变了现代战争的性质、手段、方式。

（三）快速发展加剧治理忧虑

随着新型人工智能的密集涌现，对于未来技术颠覆人类价值可能性的讨论不断升温，引发不同程度担忧，人工智能带来的价值争议和治理难题也已成为全球焦点。

1. 发展路径之争

人工智能具有基于程序自我学习控制等特点，即使是人工智能算法的设计者，也难以完全预测其经过自我优化学习后的数据处理方式，这种"技术黑箱"令人工智能的"未知"远大于"已知"，引发了对其发展路径的广泛争议。

"加速"还是"价值对齐"？围绕人工智能的未来发展方向，研发人员逐渐分化为两个阵营。支持"加速"的一方认为，社会进步依赖技术创新，推动人工智能发展是人们不断追求的目标。而"价值对齐"派则主张首先考虑人工智能的伦理影响和社会后果，确保技术沿着符合人类价值的轨道前进。2023年3月，包括图灵奖得主约书亚·本吉奥（Yoshua Bengio）、特斯拉 CEO 埃隆·马斯克（Elon Musk）等在内的数千名 AI 领域企业家、学者、高管发出了一封题为《暂停大型人工智能研究》的公开信，集中表达了人类社会对超级人工智能的种种担忧，并强烈呼吁共同制定和实施一套全人类共享的安全协议。但与此同时，全球各大科技公司都在加紧部署研发，各类新产品、新应用层出不穷。

在未来很长一段时间内，人工智能的发展仍将处于两种理念的博弈之下。面对人工智能这一未来核心战略资源，利益相关方可能产生更大分歧。技术伦理问题被政治化、商业巨头间的"科技竞赛"、国家间的"军备竞赛"等，无疑将为后续全球立法和治理带来更多阻碍。

课题组调查显示，大部分观望中的媒体机构并不排斥或轻视生成式人工智能，而是计划在相关条件成熟时再入局，他们优先考虑的前三个条件是：

1. 确定可用人工智能来显著提升生产力、节省人力的业务板块；

2. 人工智能的性能跃升，准确性、可靠性等大幅改善；

3. 确保不会陷入新闻伦理争议、监管麻烦或法律纠纷。

仅有 6.4% 的受访媒体表示，无论如何都暂不考虑采用生成式人工智能工具。

尚未在机构层面应用生成式人工智能的受访媒体机构改弦易辙的前景：

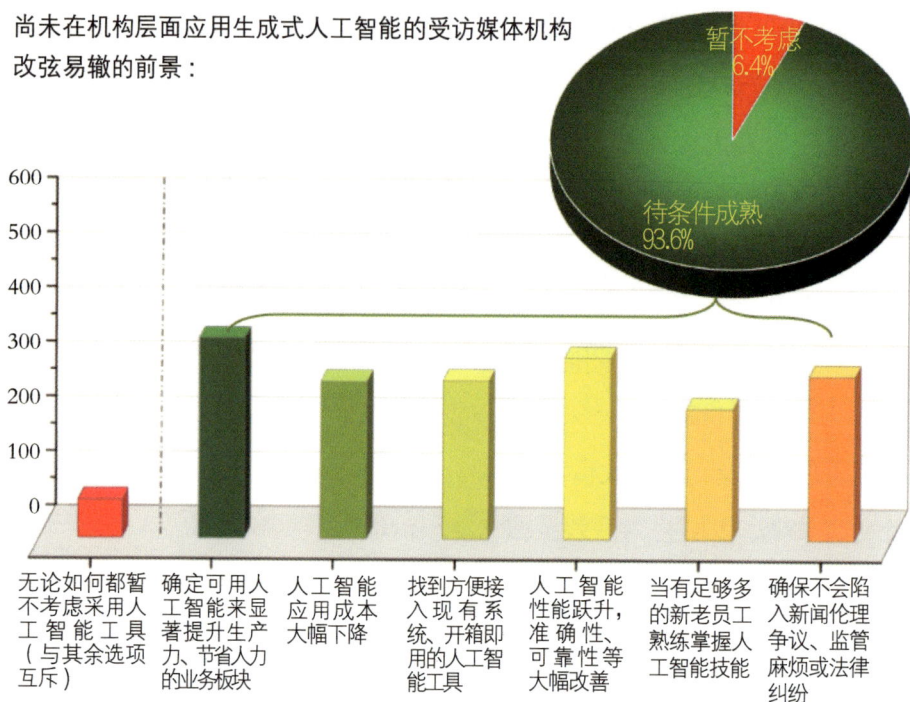

2.价值对齐之困

随着"人工智能威胁论"的声量日渐扩大，"价值对齐"已经成为人工智能治理领域最根本也最具挑战性的概念之一。但在实际操作中，价值对齐面临多方面挑战。

价值对齐旨在让人工智能在道德原则、伦理规范和价值观上与人类保持一致，以确保其能以对社会无害的方式运转。但在全球多元文化背景下，"向谁对齐""如何对齐"的问题依然难以解决。在媒体领域，不同国家的媒体人在新闻价值判断、职业身份认同和采编操作惯例上都存在差异，很难对人工智能技术的媒体应用标准进行对齐。哪怕是"真实""公正""非歧视"等原则性的新闻理念，通过技术路径进行抽象、量化和对齐也存在失灵风险。例如，当亚马逊公司尝试利用人工智能筛选求职履历时，人们很快就发现算法在大量"过滤"女性申请人，类似的性别偏见、种族歧视等在新闻编辑部的人工智能应用中同样难以避免。

更值得注意的是，人工智能与新闻生产紧密结合，其操作规范和运行逻辑会影响编辑记者对什么是新闻、什么是好新闻、什么是有价值的新闻的评价标准，新闻价值体系面临新的调整与更迭。而如果新闻生产过度强调以技术规则限定记者行为、以流量数据评估新闻质量、以程序规范衡量新闻价值，将可能导致工具理性偏离价值理性、新闻价值偏离公共价值、新闻媒体偏离社会主流，影响其正向社会功能的发挥。

3. 监管制度之失

人工智能等新技术新应用快速发展，催生一系列新业态新模式，但相关法律制度还存在时间差、空白区。① 尤其在隐私、版权等具体问题上，相关共识达成和制度建设仍需加快步伐。

隐私数据保护与人工智能发展之间存在着天然矛盾。海量的人类行为和知识数据是人工智能升级迭代的关键要素，其各种应用场景同样基于大量个人数据，人工智能对数据的高度依赖令隐私"无处遁形"。2023 年，意大利就曾因隐私数据问题一度禁用 ChatGPT，并限制OpenAI 公司处理意大利用户的相关信息，英国、爱尔兰等国也启动了针对人工智能大模型违规收集数据隐私的调查。在媒体领域，用户数据虽然有助于新闻媒体提供更加便捷、精准、高效的信息服务，但也让隐私泄露风险进一步加剧。作为社会公共利益的守卫者，媒体在划定隐私边界、化解隐私悖论中面临更为苛刻的伦理期待，人工智能则进一步提高了这一问题的广泛性与敏感性。

随着信息生产权、加工权、发布权和转载权不断下放，人工智能带来的版权争议也日益凸显。对媒体而言，专业、优质的新闻报道是人工智能的重要学习数据集，但其生成内容不可避免地带有原始数据的影子，

---

① 习近平在中央全面依法治国工作会议上讲话（2020 年 11 月 16 日）。

容易对部分专业媒体的内容版权构成侵犯。2023年12月，纽约时报正式向OpenAI及其投资人微软公司提起侵犯版权诉讼，指控这两家机构未经许可就采集该报数百万篇文章以训练人工智能。这是全世界首个人工智能公司被大型媒体机构起诉侵犯版权的案例，也成了媒体在人工智能时代面临版权问题的一个缩影。此外，人工智能辅助生产的新闻产品的版权归属与利益分配问题，同样处于悬而未决的状态。如何保障各方合法权益，建立公正透明的版权机制，对各国立法者提出了迫切要求。

（四）智能应用加大发展鸿沟

和其他影响深远的技术突破一样，新一代人工智能技术的广泛应用必然会带来社会财富和权力的转移，引发一系列社会、政治和经济问题，带来关于贫富差异、城乡差别、南北差距等问题的讨论。这些问题的核心，是如何公平分享技术发展带来的红利，让技术成果惠及全人类。

1. 个体差异与"弱势群体"

拥有人工智能技术的人在未来将更具竞争力和优势毋庸置疑。但由于认知能力、资源占有、人工智能素养的差异，老年人群体、低学历群体、低收入群体等在人工智能应用发展演进的过程中不断被边缘化，成为人工智能时代新型的"弱势群体"。

以老年群体为例，《数字化生存》的作者尼古拉斯·尼葛洛庞帝曾断言，"人类的每一代都会比上一代更加数字化"，在全球老龄化程度日益加深与人工智能技术高速发展的双重作用下，老年群体往往因信息技能水平不高、学习能力下降、身体机能退化等，无法获取人工智能所带来的"红利"，走向"抵制"与"沉迷"两种极端。一方面，大多数老年人对新技术新事物更容易产生抵触心理，很难接受并掌握新的技术应用；另一方面，部分老年群体则极易陷入"数字沉迷"，更易遭受虚假信息、算法欺骗、信息茧房等带来的伤害。

2. 城乡差别与"智能洼地"

全球范围内普遍存在的城市和乡村间的"智能鸿沟"不仅是一个技术问题，更是一个社会和经济问题。这种差距不仅存在于社会发展、要素配置、教育水平、基础设施等方面，还存在于个体收入、文化素养、信息技术能力、知识观念等方面。

在中国，城市用户多已接入 5G 和千兆光网，而农村网络服务在速度和稳定性方面跟城市相比仍存在不小差距。人工智能新技术公司也大多集中在北京、长三角和珠三角地区，西部地区寥寥无几。在美国，人工智能"洼地"甚至"荒漠"也大范围存在。《华盛顿邮报》在 2024 年 6 月的一篇报道中指出，"美国农村地区对宽带服务的等待已久，多数地方仍依赖通过铜线传输速度较慢的互联网，无法传输大量数据，一些地区甚至根本没联网"。在少数族裔和原住民居住的广大乡村地带，"断网"问题尤为突出。

人工智能时代的教育资源失衡等问题也愈加突出。生活在城市的孩子从小有机会亲身体验科技的魅力，感受人工智能所带来的新奇与便捷，了解人工智能背后的科学逻辑；而对大多数乡村孩子而言，"人工智能"只是一个抽象的词语、模糊的概念，他们对此缺乏具体感受和理性认知。显然，人工智能"洼地"的普遍存在将在一定程度上加大社会的分化与撕裂，技术发展的"红利共享"仍任重道远。

3. 南北差距与"智能鸿沟"

中国驻联合国大使傅聪在联大介绍《加强人工智能能力建设国际合作决议》草案的发言中提到"当前全球人工智能技术飞速发展，对各国经济社会发展和人类文明进步产生深远影响。但大多数国家特别是发展中国家人民尚未能真正接触、使用人工智能并从中受益，全球数字鸿沟仍有扩大之势。"随着全球经济加速向人工智能驱动转型，欠发达国家面临着被更远落下的局面，与发达国家间经济和社会发展鸿沟正不断加剧。人工智能技术的不平衡应用正成为远超经济增速本身的关键性问题。

目前，人工智能的经济和社会效益在地理上主要集中在全球北方。英国媒体 Tortoise 于 2023 年发布第四版《全球 AI 指数》，根据投资、创新、实施三个维度对全球 62 个国家和地区进行排名，其中美国排名第一，中国、新加坡分列第二、三位，在前二十的国家中，有 11 个欧洲国家。在 ChatGPT、Sora、工业机器人已经在领先国家广泛使用之际，非洲、拉美等国家还有不少人口只能用 2G 网络打电话、发短信，甚至处于完全"断联"状态。随着未来社会生产方式进一步向智能化转型，南北方之间的全要素生产率、经济增长、教育水平、数字素养与研发能力的分化趋势或将更加严重。特别是大语言模型的训练与开发、顶尖人才的培养与招募，以及通信网络、大数据平台、算力中心、算法库等人工智能基础设施建设都离不开巨额资本投入，这将成为发展中国家短期内难以逾越的"智能鸿沟"。

国际劳工组织 2024 年《注意人工智能鸿沟：塑造关于未来工作的全球视野》报告指出，人工智能技术在为创新和发展带来巨大机遇的同时，其在各国之间不均衡的投资建设和部署应用极有可能加剧收入水平和生活质量的不平衡。当前，"智能鸿沟"正在形成，高收入国家在有关技术发展和应用中获益，而以非洲为代表的中低收入国家则较为落后。具体到人工智能技术对劳动市场的冲击上，不同国家和地区也是处境各异。发达国家的各类工作更多处在智能化、自动化大潮之下，但这些国家同时也能更好地利用人工智能技术，以此提高生产力。相比之下，发展中国家虽然因为缺乏数字基础设施建设，在短期内不会受自动化替代风险影响，但长期来看将面临生产力瓶颈。报告警告称，若不采取措施加强国际合作帮助发展中国家，这一鸿沟将进一步扩大，甚至抵消掉人工智能技术本身对社会经济发展的促进作用。

人们还注意到，当前，一些发达国家还凭借人工智能技术的"先发优势"，试图谋求科技霸权，构建排他性小圈子，阻挠他国技术发展，人为制造科技壁垒，恶意阻断全球人工智能供应链。种种形式的"小院高墙"势必进一步加深全球南北方之间人工智能的发展鸿沟，导致"强者恒强、弱者恒弱"。

三、使命：坚持以人为本 推动智能向善

如何正确回答时代课题，广泛凝聚世界共识，媒体肩负着重要社会责任。①

——习近平

今天，加强人工智能监管，已经成为世界各国的共识。中国国家主席习近平在《全球人工智能治理倡议》中提出了"以人为本""智能向善"等基本原则，为解决人工智能治理难题贡献了中国方案。在人工智能掀起的时代浪潮下，世界各国媒体需要机遇共享、风险共担，以专业优势营造良好的信息环境和舆论生态，为构筑开放、公正、有效的人工智能全球治理机制，构建人类命运共同体，建设更加美好的世界汇聚强大的媒体力量。

（一）加快智能驱动，提升媒体价值

新闻媒体要充分发挥人工智能的工具价值，探索将人工智能运用在新闻采集、生产、分发、接收、反馈全流程、全要素中，以人工智能打造媒体新质生产力，为人们提供更好的新闻产品和新闻服务。

---

① 习近平致第四届世界媒体峰会的贺信（2021 年 11 月 22 日）。

1. 以智能化提升系统效能

为应对万众皆媒、去中心化的挑战，新闻媒体要更注重自我技术赋能，从传统"信息加工者"转型为"智能信息生产者"。构建人工智能支撑和驱动的生产传播体系、数据技术体系、组织管理体系、效果反馈体系，着力提升新闻媒体的传播力、引导力、影响力、公信力。以智能技术为依托，提升新闻传播的速度、深度、广度和准度，增强新闻媒体连接社会、凝聚共识的作用。

课题组调查显示，多数媒体机构认识到，生成式人工智能正以不可阻挡之势渗入传媒行业，无论现在是下场共舞还是静观其变，媒体都面临自我变革的压力以适应行业变局。

对于如何自我变革来应对变局，受访媒体机构认可度较高的三个路径是：

1. 增强采编队伍的适应能力；

2. 增加技术投入；

3. 改造采编发业务流程。

受访媒体机构认可的自我变革路径：

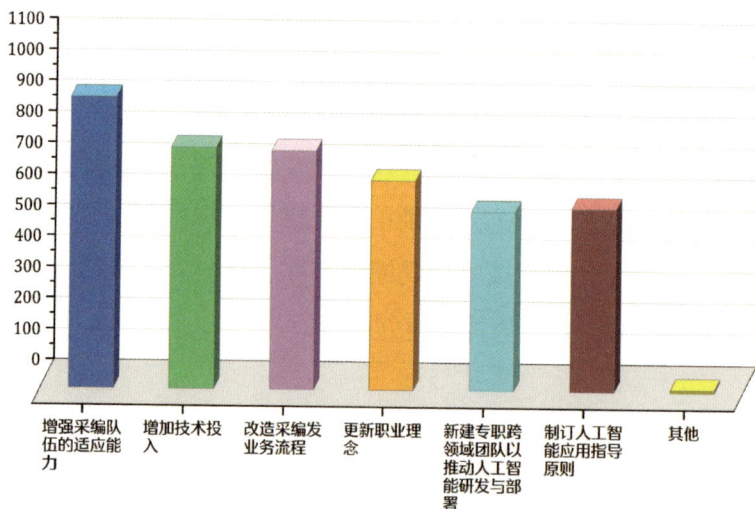

2. 以标准化确保安全可靠

针对人工智能时代业态变化特点，媒体应不断改进升级新闻生产与传播标准，在采集、生产、发布和传播等各个环节，既充分运用人工智能技术赋能，又尽力规避人工智能技术风险，在媒体领域建立人工智能风险测试评估和防范保障体系。针对深度伪造内容、自动写作内容和各类算法推荐内容，新闻媒体要进一步完善新闻内容真实性审核机制，运用人工智能技术，对线索、素材进行严格的验证，确保向公众提供的信息可信可靠。加大事实核查技术研发和专业人才培养投入，并鼓励公众积极参与事实核查。

3. 以专业化升维新闻品质

在"信息过载"和"信息茧房"并行的背景下，报道的深度与专业性具有更加宝贵的价值，是媒体履行社会责任、彰显自身公信力的重要体现。一方面应加强采编团队在细分领域的专业能力，另一方面可充分利用人工智能技术对信息进行挖掘、筛选、鉴别、关联、分析，延伸报道触角，以更有深度更有品质的新闻产品，满足受众需求，推动社会进步。

（二）立足善意使用，健全伦理规范

人工智能时代，媒体不仅是新闻信息传播的桥梁和纽带，更是社会价值观的塑造者和守护者。全球媒体在强化技术应用的同时，要坚守新闻伦理、践行社会责任，以人类主流价值驾驭"机器算法"，将新闻伦理贯穿于媒体人工智能应用的全流程、全要素，健全以人为本的伦理规范体系。

课题组调查显示，针对生成式人工智能在传媒行业的应用可能产生的负面效果，只有14.4%的受访对象认为"现有规则框架具有足够约束力"，85.6%的受访对象都支持以某种形式加强规范与治理。

是否有必要采取以下措施来规范和治理
传媒行业对生成式人工智能的使用：

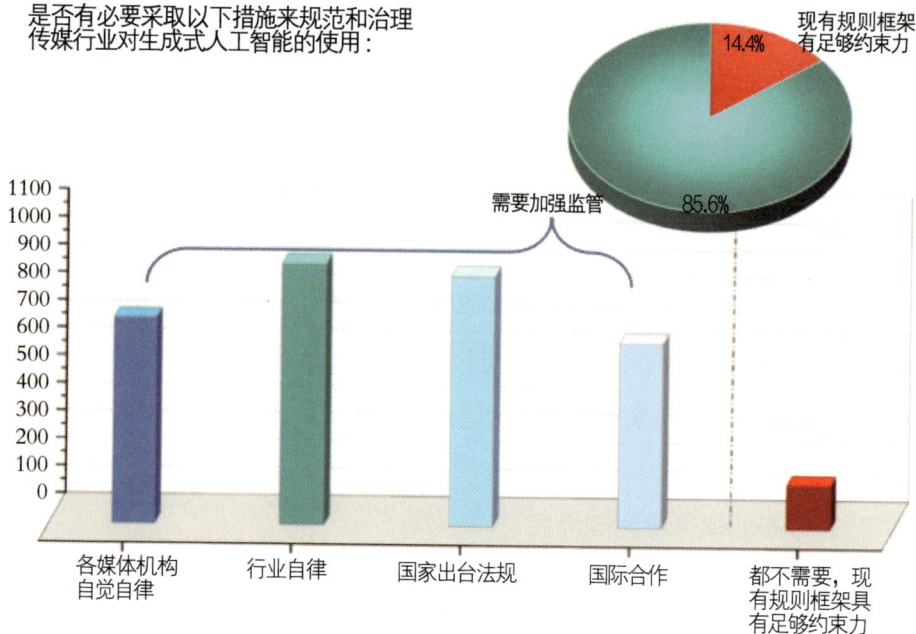

现有规则框架
有足够约束力
14.4%

85.6%

需要加强监管

各媒体机构
自觉自律　　行业自律　　国家出台法规　　国际合作

都不需要，现
有规则框架具
有足够约束力

1. 以新闻真实破除信息迷雾

新闻真实是媒体维系公信力和影响力的基石所在，脱离新闻真实性的技术创新都是舍本逐末。新闻媒体要以新闻真实性作为应用人工智能技术的最终标准，用真实报道构建公众可信赖的基础认知空间。要把新闻媒体专业优势和人工智能技术优势相结合，向受众提供真实、公正、全面、及时的信息，破除信息失真、信息污染、信息孤岛、信息误导。各国媒体应发挥示范效应，不制造虚假信息，不操纵舆论干涉他国内政，不充当、不沦为"认知战"工具，努力成为防御虚假信息传播的"守夜人"和"防波堤"。

2. 以新闻伦理驾驭工具理性

媒体从业者是人工智能应用的直接使用者，其伦理意识水平将直接影响技术应用的社会效果。媒体应加强对从业者的人工智能伦理教育，通过持续的培训和学习，提升其伦理意识和技术素养，确保人工智能在实际操作中的规范合理应用。媒体在利用人工智能技术进行数据获取、算法设计、技术和产品研发运用的过程中，应特别关注产品中可能存在的失真与偏见，确保信息的多样性、公正性和包容性，主动识别并消除可能有悖于公平性和非歧视性原则的因素，减少公众误解、分歧与敌视。媒体应以全人类共同价值为基准，做好新闻信息把关人和社会价值引领者，主动消除对冲网络极端信息和有害信息，共同阻遏极端思想和恐怖主义内容扩散。媒体应坚持新闻伦理，强化社会责任，努力营造"真实为本、理性沟通、多元包容、健康积极"的认知环境和舆论生态，推动知识有效传播和技术红利普惠，为增进人类福祉和推动社会进步注入积极动力。

3. 以规范机制保护数据隐私

媒体要更加关注人工智能潜在的技术安全风险、网络安全风险和经济社会风险，监督反映人工智能模型算法"黑箱"带来的个人隐私和国家机密泄露、深度伪造风险、版权归属问题。媒体应深刻认识数据安全、用户保护尤其是未成年人保护的重要性，建立健全机制，确保用户信息在采集、存储、处理和传输过程中得到充分保护。遵循"数据最小化"原则，尽量减少对个人信息的采集和存储。在使用人工智能技术分析数据时，应严格控制数据的访问权限。媒体在设计和使用人工智能算法时，应遵循适度透明化算法的运行机制，确保用户知情权，形成行业自律机制，提升整个行业的运行规范水平。媒体还应通过加密技术和安全协议等手段，防范数据泄露和网络攻击等风险，通过风险监测、事实核查等方式，维护各国认知域空间安全，增进国际间沟通互信。

（三）加强对话合作，完善全球治理

各国媒体应通过对话与合作凝聚共识，构建开放、有效、公正的人工智能全球治理机制，促进人工智能技术造福人类。

1. 弥合智能鸿沟，实现公平普惠

各国媒体应当共同致力于弥合不同社会群体、不同地区国家之间存在的数字鸿沟、智能鸿沟，充分运用人工智能技术，通过多语种、多形式的内容生产，确保知识传播能够覆盖到社会各个群体，推动社会整体认知水平提升。高度重视人工智能应用的南北差距，在技术研发、内容生产、数据分析、规则制定、人才培养等领域分享经验、共享资源、协同共进，反对人工智能领域的"小院高墙"、技术霸权。全球南方国家媒体应积极参与全球媒体领域各类人工智能规则标准的制定，增强自身在国际规则制定中的代表性和发言权，以实际行动争取各国人工智能发展与治理的权利平等、机会平等、规则平等。

2. 加强共享共建，推动务实合作

各国媒体要联合专业机构，加强信息交流和技术合作，共享最新动态和知识成果，鼓励技术开源，探索人工智能媒体运用标准。在共识度较高的领域，如自然语言处理、图像识别、用户行为分析等方面，可考虑共同开发人工智能工具和系统，减少重复研发、避免资源浪费；针对"黑箱效应""信息茧房"等突出问题，可联合开展风险测试评估，分享实践经验。要提升人工智能在虚假信息甄别和应对中的应用水平，整合各方资源，设立长期运行的联合核查项目或机制。探索多边媒体对话机制，搭建长期化、常态化交流平台，为联合传播、合作研究奠定基础。

3. 寻求价值对齐，改进全球治理

各国媒体不仅是信息传递的媒介，也是文化传承、文明交流的重要力量。和平、发展、公平、正义、民主、自由等全人类共同价值，是全球不同文明之间能够达成共识的基础，是推动全球治理的重要思想源泉，也是摆脱人工智能价值对齐之困的"金钥匙"。各国媒体应围绕全球人工智能治理议题，开展多层次、多形式的议题传播，引导理性讨论，倡导共同价值，推动公众关注、认识和参与治理进程，为形成国际共识营造良好社会环境；基于广泛参与、协商一致、循序渐进的原则，在充分尊重各国政策法规和实践差异的基础上深化对话交流，促进各国法律法规和行业规范的对接；坚持以人为本，推动智能向善，致力于构建基于共同价值的人工智能伦理准则和全球治理范式，使人工智能朝着有利于构建人类命运共同体的方向发展。各国媒体应借助"文化＋科技"的双向赋能，提高不同文明在国际传播中的话语权和影响力，打造国际社会的"网络大外交"平台，深化文明交流互鉴，消除隔阂误解，促进民心相知相通，推动构建人工智能时代的人类命运共同体。

四、调查：全球新闻媒体人工智能认知及应用现状

围绕全球新闻媒体对人工智能的认知态度与应用情况，新华社国家高端智库于 2024 年 7 月至 8 月启动一项面向全球新闻媒体机构的问卷调查。问卷以中、英、法三种语言发放，受访者来自 53 个国家和地区的新闻媒体机构，包括报刊、广电、通讯社、网站、移动应用服务商等。调查共收回 1207 份答卷，其中有效答卷 1094 份。

受访媒体机构类型：

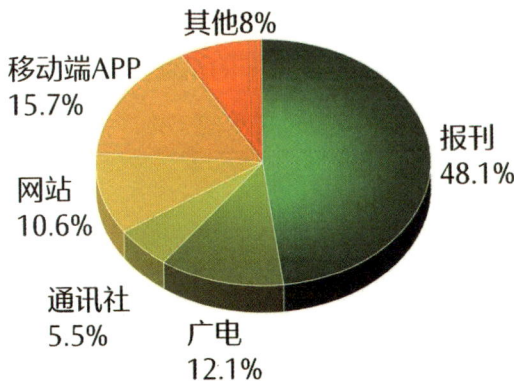

- 其他 8%
- 移动端APP 15.7%
- 网站 10.6%
- 通讯社 5.5%
- 广电 12.1%
- 报刊 48.1%

受访媒体机构规模：

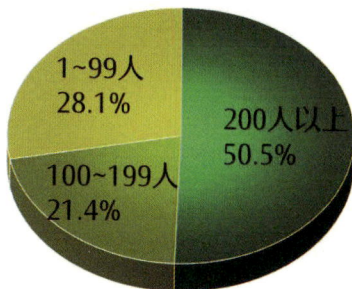

对于以生产文图视等内容为主业的新闻媒体机构而言，以ChatGPT 为代表的生成式人工智能带来的影响和冲击较大，故本次问卷调查以此为焦点，力求透视人工智能引发的传媒新变局、新图景。对有效答卷的分析发现：

（一）多数新闻媒体（66.0%）对生成式人工智能持积极态度

新事物的出现一般都会伴随争议与疑虑，生成式人工智能亦然，它既被视作一种新质生产力而备受推崇，又因幻觉、偏见、思维定势、"政治正确"等问题而屡遭质疑。本次调查结果显示，媒体机构整体上对生成式人工智能对行业的影响持积极态度。

数据显示，分别有 20.3% 和 45.7% 的受访媒体高度认同和基本认同"生成式人工智能给传媒行业带来的机遇大于挑战、益处大于弊端"，不认同和极不认同者分别只占 2.8% 和 1.6%，另有 29.6% 的受访机构认为生成式人工智能的利弊尚无定论。

对于"生成式人工智能（大语言模型）给传媒行业带来的机遇大于挑战、益处大于弊端"这一论述，受访媒体机构的态度：

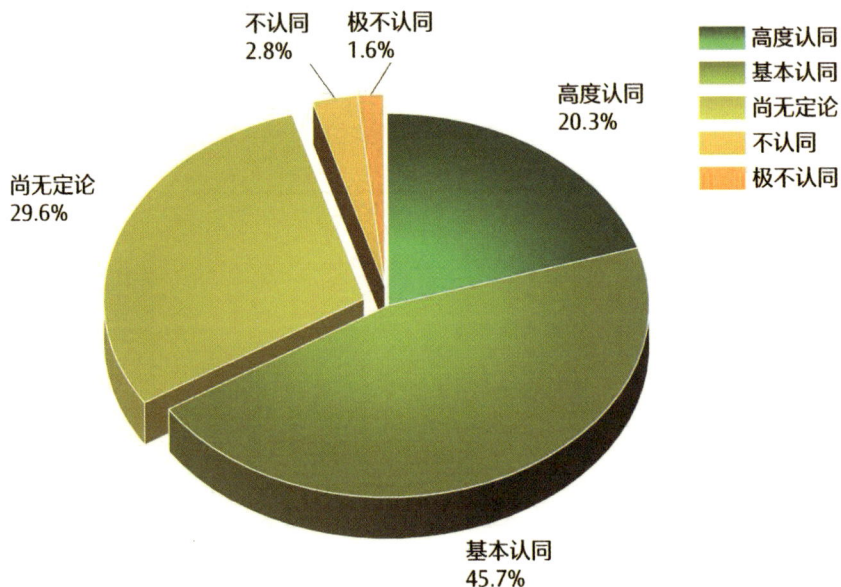

这组数据在较大程度上表明，整体而言，全球媒体机构对事关全行业共同命运的科技变革保持高度关注，乐见生成式人工智能成为传媒行业的"游戏规则改变者"。

（二）多数新闻媒体（67.6%）已切身感受到生成式人工智能带来的变化

生成式人工智能在传媒领域已引发行业变局，不过不同媒体机构的感知存在"温差"。有 32.4% 的受访媒体表示生成式人工智能对他们的影响"尚不明显"，67.6% 的受访对象则明显觉察到近在眼前的变局，共鸣较多的三个侧面是：

1. 生产流程需要改造，编辑记者工作方式面临转变；

2. 媒体之间，尤其是来自自媒体的竞争更激烈；

3. 需抽出更多精力来分辨虚假新闻、虚假照片等。

生成式人工智能（大语言模型）对受访媒体机构的影响

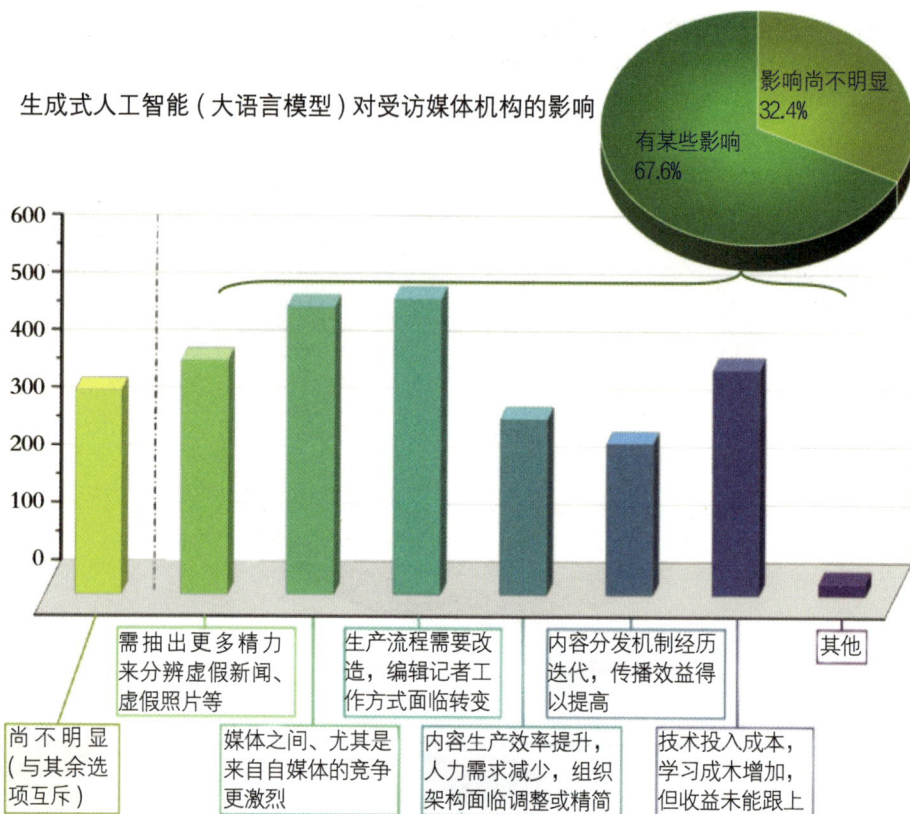

饼图：
影响尚不明显 32.4%
有某些影响 67.6%

柱状图横轴标注：

需抽出更多精力来分辨虚假新闻、虚假照片等

生产流程需要改造，编辑记者工作方式面临转变

内容分发机制经历迭代，传播效益得以提高

其他

尚不明显（与其余选项互斥）

媒体之间、尤其是来自自媒体的竞争更激烈

内容生产效率提升，人力需求减少，组织架构面临调整或精简

技术投入成本，学习成本增加，但收益未能跟上

从中可以看出，多数媒体机构认识到，生成式人工智能正以不可阻挡之势渗入传媒行业，无论现在是下场共舞还是静观其变，媒体都面临自我变革的压力。

对于如何应对变局，受访媒体机构认可度较高的三个路径是：

1.增强采编队伍的适应能力；

2.增加技术投入；

3.改造采编发业务流程。

受访媒体机构认可的自我变革路径：

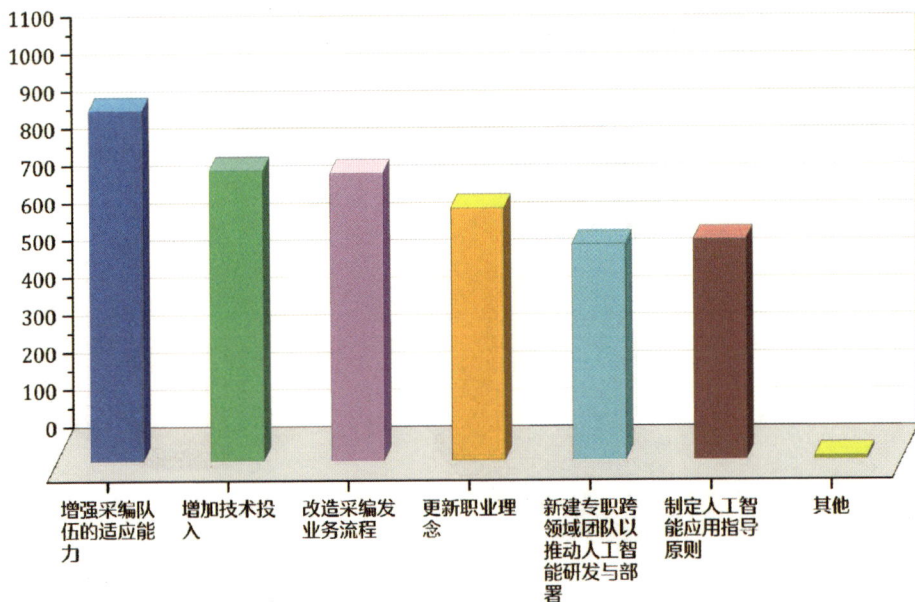

（三）超半数新闻媒体（51.2%）已开始应用生成式人工智能

2024 年是生成式人工智能大规模应用元年，作为内容生产引领者，众多媒体争做"早鸟"。目前全球已有 10.2% 的媒体机构全面拥抱人工智能，在机构层面设立了相应机制，由上而下地将人工智能引入生产流程；41.0% 的媒体机构正在积极探索人工智能技术应用，鼓励和支持部分新闻业务板块试用人工智能技术；36% 的受访媒体虽然未由机构管理层牵头由上而下地把生成式人工智能融入生产，但其内部员工已开始在机构默许的情况下在个人层面试水；12.8% 的受访媒体表示，本机构内极少有人使用或机构禁止使用。

受访媒体机构对生成式人工智能（大语言模型）的应用程度：

- 全面拥抱，机构层面设有相应机制，由上而下地将之引入生产流程
- 机构层面正在积极探索，鼓励和支持部分新闻业务板块试用
- 仅编辑记者个人层面尝鲜，机构层面不反对
- 极少有人使用或机构禁止使用

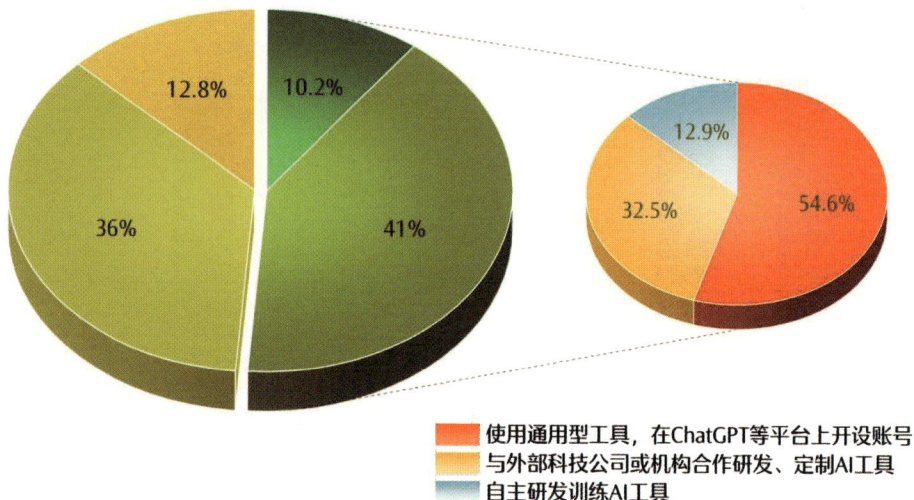

- 使用通用型工具，在ChatGPT等平台上开设账号
- 与外部科技公司或机构合作研发、定制AI工具
- 自主研发训练AI工具

在机构层面推动生成式人工智能应用的受访对象中，其应用路径主要为采用 ChatGPT 等市面上对公众开放的通用型工具，选择这一路径的媒体占比达 54.6%。有 32.5% 的媒体选择的应用路径是与第三方合作研发、定制生成式人工智能工具，另有 12.9% 的媒体选择自主研发与训练。由此来看，私有化部署的新闻领域垂类大语言模型仍有较大发展空间。

在应用场景上，媒体机构有组织探索较多的前三个方向是：

1. 辅助编辑，如事实核查、语音转文字、配字幕、翻译等；

2. 创作内容，如生成摘要、制作图表海报、数字主播配音等；

3. 策划选题或草拟提纲。

在机构层面应用生成式人工智能（大语言模型）的受访媒体机构已探索或有意探索的应用场景：

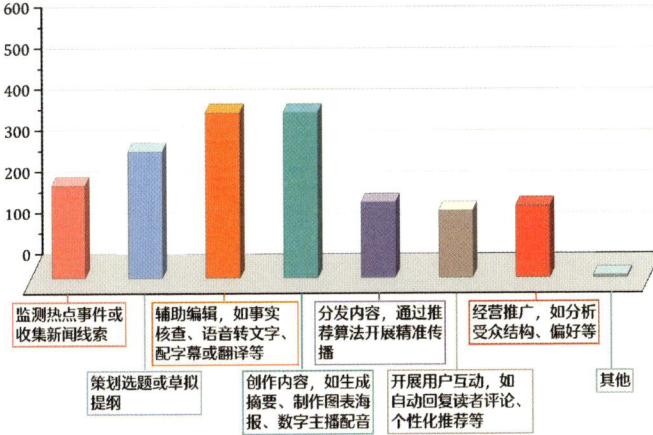

对于那些尚在观望的媒体机构，阻碍其成建制应用生成式人工智能的众多因素中，排在前三位的分别是：

1. 人工智能自身还不完善，如生成内容的准确性、可靠性等达不到预期和要求；

2. 人机协作难，缺乏相应融合型人才；

3. 技术投入成本高。

尚未在机构层面应用生成式人工智能的受访媒体机构驻足观望的主要原因：

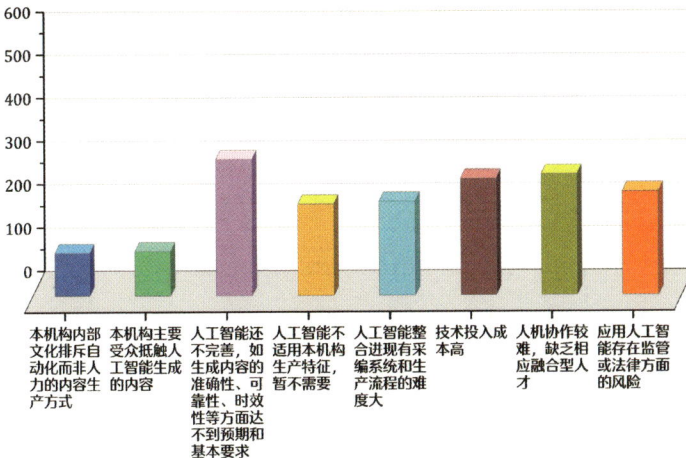

不过，大部分观望中的媒体机构并不排斥或轻视生成式人工智能，而是计划在相关条件成熟时再入局，他们优先考虑的前三个条件是：

1. 确定可用人工智能来显著提升生产力、节省人力的业务板块；

2. 人工智能的性能跃升，准确性、可靠性等大幅改善；

3. 确保不会陷入新闻伦理争议、监管麻烦或法律纠纷。

仅有 6.4% 的受访媒体表示，无论如何都暂不考虑采用生成式人工智能工具。

尚未在机构层面应用生成式人工智能的受访媒体机构改弦易辙的前景：

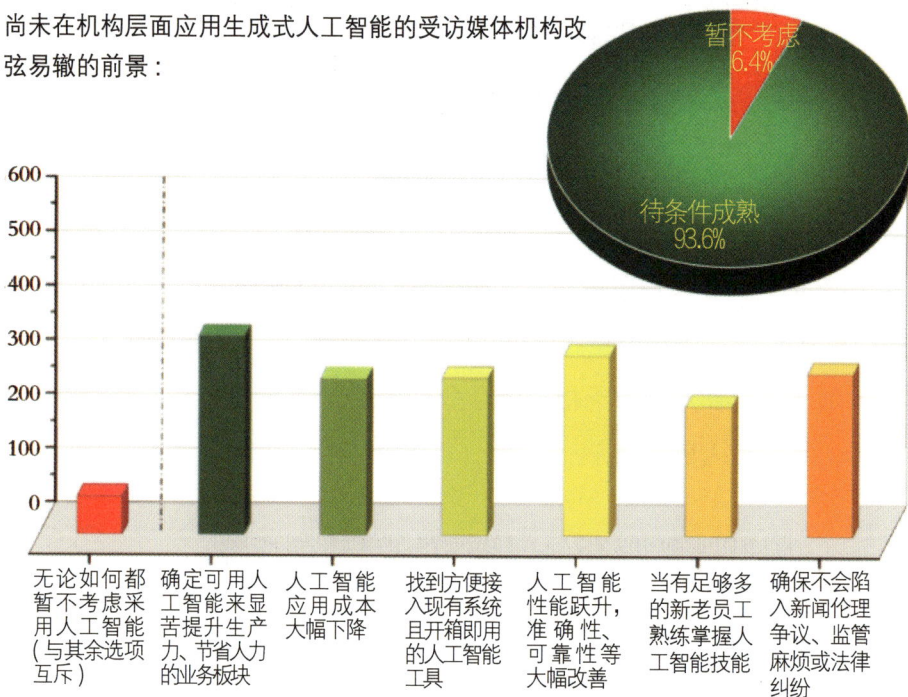

（四）新闻媒体对生成式人工智能的期待聚焦于时与效

无论是否已在机构层面应用生成式人工智能，受访媒体普遍对这种新技术助力传媒行业的潜力抱有一定期待。受访媒体希冀生成式人工智能重点在"时"与"效"上推动新闻报道再上新台阶。

有 74.6% 的受访媒体预期，生成式人工智能有助于提高新闻报道的时效性；有 74.4% 的受访对象认为，生成式人工智能有助于提高新闻生产效率；预期生成式人工智能对提升新闻分发精准度和作品呈现创造性有帮助的媒体占比分别达到 66.7% 和 63.3%。

受访媒体机构对生成式人工智能在新闻报道冲大的效用预估：

■ 大有助益　　■ 有一定帮助　　■ 不好说　　■ 有些破坏性　　■ 破坏性极大

新闻报道的时效性

有些破坏性 2.4%　破坏性极大 1.8%
不好说 21.2%
26% 大有助益
48.6% 有一定帮助

新闻生产效率

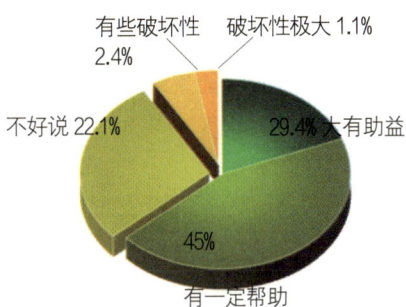

有些破坏性 2.4%　破坏性极大 1.1%
不好说 22.1%
29.4% 大有助益
45% 有一定帮助

新闻分发的精准度

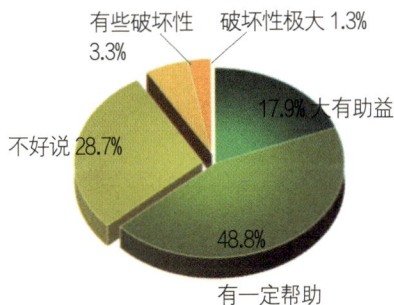

有些破坏性 3.3%　破坏性极大 1.3%
不好说 28.7%
17.9% 大有助益
48.8% 有一定帮助

作品呈现的创造性

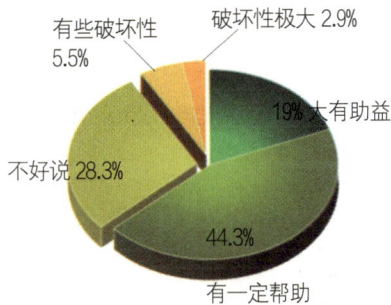

有些破坏性 5.5%　破坏性极大 2.9%
不好说 28.3%
19% 大有助益
44.3% 有一定帮助

媒体机构看重的生成式人工智能赋能排名前三的领域分别为：

1. 智能检校及智能事实核查；

2. 智能创作图表、视频及音乐；

3. 文字生成 / 机器人写稿 / 翻译。

受访媒体机构看重的生成式人工智能赋能领域：

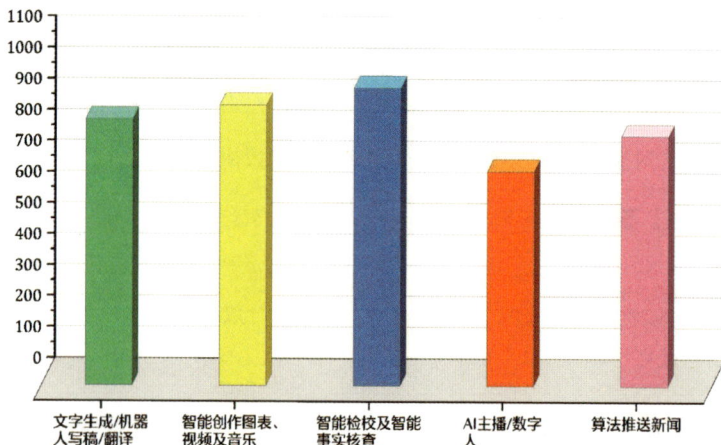

（五）新闻媒体对生成式人工智能的警惕集中在可信度

多数媒体机构对生成式人工智能的应用较为审慎。对于"您所在媒体机构遇到过或预期会遇到哪些生成式人工智能带来的问题"这一提问，高达 76.4% 的受访对象表示，担心出现"新闻线索和素材失真失准"的情况，明显超过回答数量排在第二位的"版权及权责归属问题"（占比为 61.1%）。

受访媒体机构运用生成式人工智能时遇到过或预期会遇到的问题：

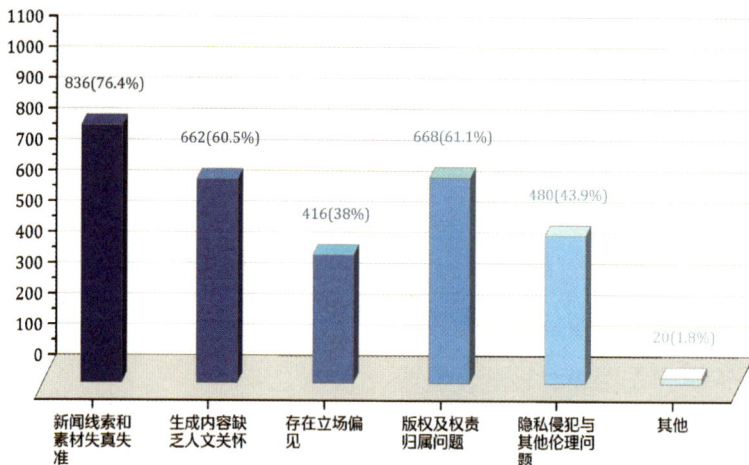

另外，对于未来 3 至 5 年生成式人工智能与传媒行业融合会否提升信息环境可信度可靠性的问题，有 36.4% 的受访对象持悲观预期，比持乐观预期者（24.1%）高出 12.3 个百分点，另有 39.5% 的受访对象持中性预期。

真实可信是新闻报道的生命。由此推测，多数媒体机构短期内或许只会让生成式人工智能在内容生产环节扮演有限的辅助角色。

随着生成式人工智能与传媒行业融合，受访媒体机构对未来 3 至 5 年信息环境可信度可靠性的预判：

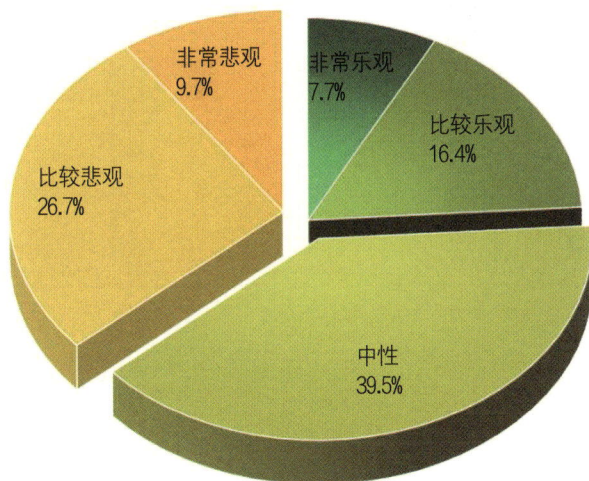

（六）多数新闻媒体（85.6%）认为需要对生成式人工智能的应用加强监管

针对生成式人工智能在传媒行业的应用可能产生的负面效果，只有 14.4% 的受访对象认为"现有规则框架具有足够约束力"。85.6% 的受访对象都支持以某种形式加强规范与治理，认同度较高的治理形式包括"行业自律""国家出台法规""各媒体机构自律"等。

这反映出，生成式人工智能除了技术本身内生性的缺陷引发媒体机构警觉之外，其被无意错用、有意滥用而导致错误信息、虚假信息流传的风险也使得媒体机构心存防范，而这类风险难以仅靠"各扫自家门前雪"的方式得到遏止。

是否有必要采取以下措施来规范和治理
传媒行业对生成式人工智能的使用：

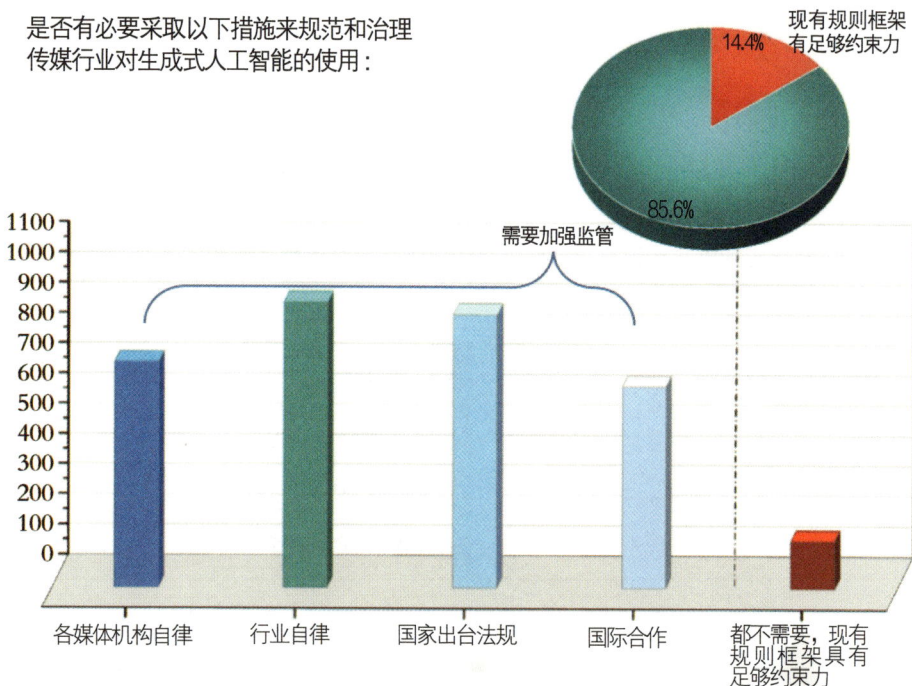

调研说明：本次问卷调查采取在线问答和当面访谈相结合的方式进行。其中，在线答卷者均为受邀参与的机构代表，大多为新华社的全球媒体用户，受访对象全都是机构型媒体且一家媒体只提交一份答卷。从最终回收的有效答卷来看，受访对象在类型、规模、国别分布、受众群体等方面具有广泛代表性，他们对生成式人工智能的认知和应对能够大致反映全球传媒行业的整体情况。

本次问卷调查在对回收数据进行分析和解读的部分环节，用到了生成式人工智能作为辅助，吸纳到本报告中的机器生成内容均经过人工溯源和确认。

结　语

人类的一切都正在被人工智能重塑。经过多年演进，人工智能如今进入爆发期，成为科技革命、产业变革乃至社会变革的重要驱动力量。近两年以 ChatGPT、Sora 等为代表的生成式人工智能技术正引发全球人工智能技术与产业的新一轮浪潮。

未来已来，但未知大于已知。人工智能正不断挑战着人们的认知边界和伦理边界。人类对自己创造出的"新物种"有点措手不及。人们甚至不知道，是自己创造了人工智能这一"工具"，还是人类不过是在人工智能演进中"充当了历史的不自觉的工具"？

人们惊叹着、欣喜着、焦虑着、忧愁着，处于人工智能带来的"文化震惊"中。

幸运的是，人类的理性也在同步觉醒，开始思考探索人机融合的新形态。面对人工智能发展在监管、法律、安全、道德伦理、就业等方面面临的一系列新课题，国际组织和世界多国已开始探索人工智能治理的可行路径并达成一些共识，努力在发展和安全之间寻求平衡。目前，有关国家和地区发布的关于人工智能治理的法律法规、行政指令、伦理规范已达数百项。

人工智能时代的信息环境正在发生重要变化。在虚拟与现实边界消融、线上与线下高度统合的媒介生态中，信息传播营造的"拟态环境"在构建人类认知、影响主体决策、引导文明走向等方面，变得更具有决定性意义。人工智能从"工具"向"主体"的演化，无疑让信息环境变得更为复杂。

在此背景下，新闻媒体塑造信息环境和认知环境的传统社会角色被重新构建。全球新闻媒体应站在人类文明的高度，共同思考人工智能时代的新角色、新使命、新责任，更好地捍卫全人类共同价值，为推动构建人类命运共同体注入更多正能量。

编写说明与致谢

　　《人工智能时代新闻媒体的责任与使命》智库报告由新华通讯社社长、新华社国家高端智库学术委员会主任傅华任组长，新华通讯社副总编辑任卫东任副组长，课题组成员包括刘刚、文建、刘华、陈怡、李飞虎、何慧媛、李成、陈谊娜、何小凡、李桃、申丽、赵熠煊、窦书棋、周瑜、李利军、刘蓉蓉、郭信峰、李雪笛、朱俊清、黄鑫川、王仲豪、陈国权、梁洽闻等。

　　课题立项启动后，课题组广泛走访媒体、科技公司与科研院所，并以中文、英文、法文三种语言面向全球媒体发放调查问卷，最终完成撰写、修改、审校、翻译等工作。

　　在报告写作过程中，中国社会科学院教授胡正荣、清华大学教授沈阳、中央民族大学教授郭全中，以及中国网络空间研究院、赛迪研究院、腾讯、百度、阿里巴巴等机构的专家给予了多方面的帮助和指导，调查问卷得到 53 个国家和地区包括报刊、广电、通讯社、网站等上千家媒体机构的反馈支持，在此一并表示诚挚谢意。

　　由于课题组所掌握的材料和作者水平有限，错漏之处在所难免，敬请批评指正。

更好赋能中国繁荣世界 ①
——新质生产力的理论贡献和实践价值

2023 年，习近平总书记在地方考察期间首次提出"新质生产力"这一重大概念。此后，在中央经济工作会议、中央政治局集体学习、全国两会和赴地方考察中，习近平总书记对新质生产力作出系统阐释和重大部署，深刻回答了"什么是新质生产力、为什么要发展新质生产力、怎样发展新质生产力"的重大问题。

习近平总书记关于发展新质生产力的一系列重要论述，是对马克思主义生产力理论的创新和发展，进一步丰富了习近平经济思想的内涵，为中国在新时代新征程上进一步解放和发展生产力、实现高质量发展、推进和拓展中国式现代化提供了根本遵循和行动指南，也将为中国和世界的繁荣发展注入新的智慧和动力。

---

① 2024 年 6 月 19 日发布于比利时布鲁塞尔。

一、马克思主义生产力理论的创新发展

"概括地说，新质生产力是创新起主导作用，摆脱传统经济增长方式、生产力发展路径，具有高科技、高效能、高质量特征，符合新发展理念的先进生产力质态。"①

——习近平

（一）新质生产力的理论贡献

1. 新质生产力的基本内涵

2024 年 1 月 31 日，中共中央政治局就扎实推进高质量发展进行集体学习，习近平总书记发表重要讲话，对新质生产力这一全新概念进行深入阐释——

"概括地说，新质生产力是创新起主导作用，摆脱传统经济增长方式、生产力发展路径，具有高科技、高效能、高质量特征，符合新发展理念的先进生产力质态。它由技术革命性突破、生产要素创新性配置、产业深度转型升级而催生，以劳动者、劳动资料、劳动对象及其优化组合的跃升为基本内涵，以全要素生产率大幅提升为核心标志，特点是创新，关键在质优，本质是先进生产力。"

高质量发展是新时代的硬道理。中国进入新时代以来，中共中央作出一系列重大决策部署，推动高质量发展成为全党全社会的共识和自觉行动，成为经济社会发展的主旋律。近年来，科技创新成果丰硕，创新驱动发展成效日益显现；城乡区域发展协调性、平衡性明显增强；改革开放全面深化，发展动力活力竞相迸发；绿色低碳转型成效显著，发展

---

① 《习近平在中共中央政治局第十一次集体学习时强调加快发展新质生产力扎实推进高质量发展》，新华社，2024 年 2 月 1 日

方式转变步伐加快，高质量发展取得明显成效。同时，制约高质量发展因素还大量存在，要高度重视，切实解决。

习近平总书记指出，高质量发展需要新的生产力理论来指导，而新质生产力已经在实践中形成并展示出对高质量发展的强劲推动力、支撑力，需要我们从理论上进行总结、概括，用以指导新的发展实践。[①]

新质生产力是创新驱动主导的生产力。创新特别是原创性、颠覆性科技创新，在发展新质生产力中发挥关键作用。回顾历次产业革命，都是以新的科学理论作为基础，由此带来新生产工具的出现、经济结构和发展方式的重大调整、社会生产生活方式的重要变革。技术革命性突破将推动劳动者、劳动资料、劳动对象及其优化组合的跃升，进而实现生产力的大幅跃升。

新质生产力是变革增长方式的生产力。传统生产力推动的经济增长普遍依靠劳动资料、劳动对象和劳动者大量投入的水平型、复制型扩张，严重依赖要素投入。新质生产力致力于提高劳动者的素质与劳动效率、改进生产方式和生产工具，犹如建立一种新的"生产函数"，改变"自变量"要素投入与"因变量"产出之间的对应法则，带动全要素生产率大幅提升。

新质生产力是应用于产业的生产力。新质生产力以高质量供给满足和创造新需求，又通过新需求催生新产品、新服务、新产业，带来产业结构的变革。从产业发展梯次看，科技创新成果应用到具体产业和产业链上后，能够改造提升传统产业，培育壮大新兴产业，催生构建未来产业，推动产业的不断迭代升级。

新质生产力是实现绿色发展的生产力。新质生产力摆脱传统经济增

---

① 《习近平在中共中央政治局第十一次集体学习时强调加快发展新质生产力扎实推进高质量发展》，新华社，2024 年 2 月 1 日

长方式对传统资源、能源的过度依赖，是体现绿色发展理念的先进生产力质态，本身就是绿色生产力、可持续发展的环境友好型生产力。发展新质生产力意味着必须加快发展方式绿色转型，走生态优先、绿色发展之路。

2.对马克思主义生产力理论的创新和发展

生产力是人们改造自然、利用自然的能力，是推动社会进步最活跃、最革命的因素。

在马克思主义生产力理论产生前，亚当·斯密、大卫·李嘉图、弗里德里希·李斯特等西方经济学家，已经对生产力进行了研究和论述。

马克思、恩格斯对生产力进行了系统分析和深刻阐释。马克思在《资本论》中指出，"生产力，即生产能力及其要素的发展"[①] "劳动生产力是由多种情况决定的，其中包括：工人的平均熟练程度，科学的发展水平和它在工艺上应用的程度，生产过程的社会结合，生产资料的规模和效能，以及自然条件"。[②] 恩格斯认为，生产力的本原是具有劳动能力的人和生产资料相结合而形成的改造自然的能力。[③] 在《共产党宣言》中，马克思和恩格斯指出，无产阶级取得政权后，要"尽可能快地增加生产力的总量"[④]。

生产力理论是马克思主义经典理论。中国共产党始终坚持运用并结合自身实践不断发展马克思主义生产力理论。毛泽东同志明确指出，"社会主义革命的目的是为了解放生产力"。[⑤] 邓小平同志提出，"社会主

---

① 《马克思恩格斯文集》第 7 卷，人民出版社，2009 年 12 月

② 《资本论：第一卷》，人民出版社，2018 年 4 月

③ 《当代中国马克思主义评论（第 2 辑）》，社会科学文献出版社，2018 年 4 月

④ 《共产党宣言》，人民出版社，2015 年 1 月

⑤ 《毛泽东文集》第 7 卷，人民出版社，1999 年 6 月

义的任务很多，但根本一条就是发展生产力"。①

中共十八大以来，习近平总书记高度重视生产力的作用，作出一系列重要论述，强调"全面建成小康社会，实现社会主义现代化，实现中华民族伟大复兴，最根本最紧迫的任务还是进一步解放和发展社会生产力"②"必须坚持科技是第一生产力、人才是第一资源、创新是第一动力，深入实施科教兴国战略、人才强国战略、创新驱动发展战略，开辟发展新领域新赛道，不断塑造发展新动能新优势"③"坚持和发展中国特色社会主义，必须不断适应社会生产力发展调整生产关系"。④

面对快速变化的世界和中国，如果墨守成规、思想僵化，没有理论创新的勇气，就不能科学回答中国之问、世界之问、人民之问、时代之问。习近平总书记统筹中华民族伟大复兴战略全局和世界百年未有之大变局，准确洞察和把握世界科技和经济发展趋势，创造性地提出发展新质生产力这一重大理论。习近平总书记指出，"发展新质生产力是推动高质量发展的内在要求和重要着力点，必须继续做好创新这篇大文章，推动新质生产力加快发展"⑤。习近平总书记的一系列重要论述，系统阐明新质生产力的丰富内涵、核心要义、实践路径和科学方法，深刻回答了"什么是新质生产力、为什么要发展新质生产力、怎样发展新质生产力"等重大理论和实践问题，丰富和发展了马克思主义生产力理论，

① 《邓小平文选第三卷》，人民出版社，2001年4月

② 《习近平：切实把思想统一到党的十八届三中全会精神上来》，新华社，2013年12月31日

③ 《习近平强调，坚持科技是第一生产力人才是第一资源创新是第一动力》，新华社，2022年10月16日

④ 《习近平在中共中央政治局第十一次集体学习时强调推动全党学习和掌握历史唯物主义更好认识规律更加能动地推进工作》，新华社，2013年12月4日

⑤ 《习近平在中共中央政治局第十一次集体学习时强调加快发展新质生产力扎实推进高质量发展》，新华社，2024年2月1日

标志着中国共产党对生产力发展规律的认识达到新境界。

3. 进一步丰富了习近平经济思想

马克思指出："理论在一个国家实现的程度，总是取决于理论满足这个国家的需要的程度。"①

习近平经济思想植根中国发展的时空方位，在中国式现代化伟大实践中不断丰富发展，为中国经济高质量发展指明正确方向、提供根本遵循。习近平总书记关于新质生产力的重要论述，是习近平经济思想的最新成果，对新时代新征程推动高质量发展、推进中国式现代化具有重大现实意义和深远历史意义。

中共十八大以来，习近平总书记围绕中国经济发展提出一系列新理念新思想新战略，其中蕴含着内在统一的逻辑性。"经济发展新常态"构成了中国经济发展的基本语境，"高质量发展"提出了塑造中国未来发展的大逻辑，"新发展阶段""新发展理念""新发展格局"明确了中国发展的历史方位、现代化建设的指导原则和中国经济现代化的路径选择。"新质生产力"揭示了生产力演变规律，体现了生产力升级方向，旨在释放驱动高质量发展的新动力。

当前，全球科技创新进入空前密集活跃的时期。习近平总书记始终把握生产力发展大势，指引中国抓住新一轮科技革命和产业变革的机遇，不断推动生产关系变革适应生产力发展要求，确保中国经济巨轮乘风破浪、不断向前。

新质生产力理论的提出为习近平经济思想提供了重要的底层逻辑。习近平总书记强调"创新是引领发展的第一动力"，开宗明义、一语道破，指明经济社会发展的"牛鼻子"就是创新。"深化供给侧结构性改革"

---

① 《马克思恩格斯全集（第三卷）》，人民出版社，2002年10月

方面，当前改革的核心目标就是实现以科技创新推动产业创新。通过科技创新不断增加产品和服务的技术含量，更能适应人的物质需要和心理需要，让供给与需求出现一个新的更高水平的匹配度。习近平总书记强调推进"高质量发展"，明确建设"现代化经济体系"，提出加快建设"现代化产业体系"。创新发展依靠新质生产力来引领，现代化产业体系的根本特征在于形成新质生产力，现代化经济体系的核心竞争力体现为发展新质生产力。可以说，新质生产力的提出为这些重要概念提供了创新引领发展、以先进生产力赋能发展的底层逻辑，标志着习近平经济思想的进一步丰富和发展，进一步回答了新时代中国特色社会主义经济建设一系列重大问题，具有丰富的理论内涵和重要的实践价值，不断开拓着马克思主义政治经济学新境界。

发展新质生产力，根植于中国式现代化和社会主义经济建设的生动实践，反映了中国特色社会主义制度的巨大优势与生机活力，是社会主义根本任务在新时代新征程的具体体现，是以更先进的生产力推进高质量发展的必然选择。这也意味着中国将以更大决心走创新驱动发展之路，构筑新竞争优势、赢得发展主动权。

（二）理解新质生产力需要把握的几对关系

1. 生产力与生产关系

马克思主义政治经济学认为，生产力发展到一定阶段便与其现存的生产关系发生矛盾，当现有生产关系构成生产力发展的制约时，生产关系的变革成为必然，这种变革又反过来促进生产力的发展。

习近平总书记在纪念马克思诞辰200周年大会上发表重要讲话时指出，"学习马克思，就要学习和实践马克思主义关于生产力和生产关系的思想""我们要勇于全面深化改革，自觉通过调整生产关系激发社会生产力发展活力，自觉通过完善上层建筑适应经济基础发展要求，让中国特色社会主义更加符合规律地向前发展"。①

中共十八大以来，中国在生产资料所有制、收入分配制度、社会主义市场经济体制等方面进行了一系列探索和实践，拓展了马克思主义政治经济学关于生产关系的理论，有力推动生产力发展。

发展新质生产力同样需要构建与之相适应的新型生产关系。这是一个推动新时代高质量发展的紧迫命题，需要在经济体制、科技体制等领域不断深化改革，着力打通束缚新质生产力发展的堵点卡点，让各类先进优质生产要素向发展新质生产力顺畅流动和高效配置。

2. 供给与需求

新质生产力以平衡供给和需求为目标导向。供给和需求是经济发展的一体两面，两者之间的平衡是相对的，不平衡是绝对的。以优质供给满足人民日益增长的美好生活需要，是发展新质生产力的题中必有之义。

中共二十大报告提出，"把实施扩大内需战略同深化供给侧结构性改革有机结合起来"。②新质生产力形成的新产品、新服务、新产业，不断满足人民日益增长的美好生活需要，将主动创造、激发并满足新的需求。与此同时，生产力不能脱离需求而单独存在，企业的产品或服务供给，必须通过交换转化为消费才具有意义。发展新质生产力必须以满足人的全面发展需要为导向，充分发挥需求对生产力发展的牵引功能。

当前和今后一个时期，制约中国经济发展的因素，供给和需求两侧都有，但矛盾的主要方面在供给侧。发展新质生产力，就是要发挥创新

---

① 《习近平：在纪念马克思诞辰 200 周年大会上的讲话》，新华社，2018 年 5 月 4 日
② 《习近平：高举中国特色社会主义伟大旗帜为全面建设社会主义现代化国家而团结奋斗——在中国共产党第二十次全国代表大会上的报告》，新华社，2022 年 10 月 25 日

第一动力作用，着力突破供给约束堵点，以优质有效的供给满足和创造需求。在持续扩大内需、不断满足人民美好生活需要的过程中，要促进供给侧不断升级创新，推动新产业、新技术、新产品、新业态不断涌现，形成需求牵引供给、供给创造需求的更高水平动态平衡。

3. 传承与创新

马克思主义认为，世界上的一切事物都处于运动和变化之中，劳动生产力总是在不断地变化。新质生产力也并非固定不变，而是动态生成、不断发展的。

苟日新，日日新，又日新。科技的不断进步，将推动新的生产力质态、产业业态次第产生。掌握发展新质生产力的主动权，必须密切跟踪科技前沿动态，把握科技发展趋势，推动原创性、颠覆性科技创新成果竞相涌现，持续形成发展新质生产力的新动能。

发展新质生产力要坚持从实际出发，先立后破、因地制宜。在科技创新上，要以形成现实生产力为基本导向，避免不切实际、"邯郸学步"；在产业发展上，要防止一哄而上、泡沫化，也要避免"黄钟毁弃，瓦釜雷鸣"。习近平总书记有一句形象生动的比喻："不能把手里吃饭的家伙先扔了，结果新的吃饭家伙还没拿到手，这不行。"各地在积极培育战略性新兴产业、发展未来产业的同时，不能忽视、放弃传统产业。要将改造提升传统产业、培育壮大新兴产业、布局发展未来产业有机统一起来，科学统筹推进。当前，既要支持战略性新兴产业和未来产业发展，也要用新技术改造提升传统产业，向高端化、智能化、绿色化迈进。

4. 物质与文明

社会经济形态及文明的跃迁，生产力和生产工具都是重要标志。从人类历史看，从石器时代、青铜时代、铁器时代到钢器时代，从蒸汽时代、电气时代到信息时代，既反映出工具的变迁，又反映出生产力发展带来的文化发展、文明进步。

新质生产力的培育生成是文化发展、文明进步的重要力量、重要标志。文化是活跃着的文明，文明是沉淀下来的文化。文明的本质是一种进步状态，不断掌握新的科技手段，才能推动文明的不断发展。当前，世界正处于以信息化全面引领创新、以信息化为基础重构国家核心竞争力的新阶段。谁能更好认识和把握这一大势，更好适应和引领新生产力发展方向、推动生产关系和上层建筑变革，谁就能全方位提升综合国力。新质生产力是在移动互联网、大数据、人工智能日益生成、不断演进的时代提出的。要看到颠覆性创新及其应用的无限可能性，从这个角度来思考文明的发展、时代的进步。

（三）发展新质生产力的时代意义

1. 强国建设、民族复兴的实践要求

发展新质生产力是推进中国式现代化、实现中华民族伟大复兴的必然选择，是推动高质量发展的内在要求和重要着力点，也是不断实现人民群众对美好生活向往的现实需要。

当下，世界百年未有之大变局加速演进。如何应变局、育先机、开新局，牢牢把握发展主动和历史主动？发展新质生产力，是时代所需、发展所急、大势所趋。

经过新中国成立 75 年特别是改革开放 40 多年来的快速发展，中国经济总量稳居世界第二，但在科技创新、产业核心竞争力等方面与世界先进水平还有不小的差距。到 2035 年基本实现社会主义现代化，到本世纪中叶把中国建成富强民主文明和谐美丽的社会主义现代化强国，客观上要求推动经济发展质量变革、效率变革、动力变革，提高全要素生产率，加快形成新质生产力。中国用几十年的时间走完了西方发达国家几百年走过的工业化历程，建成全球最完整、规模最大的工业体系，进入创新型国家的行列，为发展新质生产力奠定坚实基础。踏上新征程，扭住创

新"牛鼻子"，厚植发展"绿底色"，下好改革"先手棋"，打造人才"强引擎"，中国将不断开辟新赛道、增强新动能、塑造新优势、拓展新空间，推动高质量发展不断迈上新台阶。

2. 全球可持续发展的时代呼唤

当前，世界经济仍在艰难复苏中，尚未找到有效的新增长动能。根据国际货币基金组织（IMF）2024年4月的预测，2024年全球经济增速为3.2%，相比2023年10月的预测值上调了0.3个百分点，但仍远低于3.8%的历史（2000—2019年）平均水平。

多年来，中国一直是全球增长的动力源，对全球经济增长的年均贡献约30%。中国加快形成以科技创新支撑引领的新质生产力，将为全球经济发展注入强劲动力。

中国发展新质生产力将有力助推全球技术变革。2023年，中国全年研究与试验发展经费支出3.3万亿元，比上年增长8.1%，[①]研发支出绝对额居世界第二位；截至2023年年底，中国国内（不含港澳台）发明专利拥有量达401.5万件，同比增长22.4%，成为首个国内有效发明专利数量突破400万件的国家。中国已成为名副其实的知识产权大国，持续为全球创新发展贡献重要力量。

中国新质生产力走向世界，将助推全球经济发展。中国的5G技术为多国通信与移动互联网提供支撑。中国的台式计算机、笔记本电脑、手机等产品长期保持世界第一。新模式也在走出国门，来自中国的Temu等多款软件成为全球市场下载量增速最快的购物应用，越来越多人开始享受由中国企业提供的高性价比商品与服务。

中国正在为全球绿色低碳发展提供重要支持。中国建立起高效的太

---

① 国家统计局：《中华人民共和国2023年国民经济和社会发展统计公报》，2024年2月

阳能装备、电动汽车等生产制造体系，有效降低了世界绿色低碳转型的成本。2023 年，中国以新能源汽车、锂离子蓄电池和太阳能电池为代表的"新三样"产品出口在全球贸易疲软的大背景下逆势增长，突破万亿元大关，同比增长 29.9%。

中国秉持人类命运共同体理念，持续扩大高水平对外开放，推动共建"一带一路"高质量发展，为其他国家提供更多参与新兴产业的机遇，共享新质生产力发展红利，这将对推进国际经济合作、促进地区可持续发展起到重要作用。

二、以科技创新为核心要素发展新质生产力

"科技创新能够催生新产业、新模式、新动能，是发展新质生产力的核心要素。"[1]

——习近平

（一）加强科技创新特别是原创性、颠覆性科技创新

科技创新是推动生产力发展的重要力量。从"生产力中也包括科学"[2] 到"科学技术是第一生产力"[3] 再到"科技创新是发展新质生产力的核心要素"[4]，马克思主义者对科学技术之于发展生产力核心关键作用的认识，在理论和实践探索中不断发展演进。

---

[1] 《习近平在中共中央政治局第十一次集体学习时强调加快发展新质生产力扎实推进高质量发展》，新华社，2024 年 2 月 1 日
[2] 《马克思恩格斯文集》，人民出版社，2009 年
[3] 《邓小平文选（全三卷）》，人民出版社，1994 年
[4] 《习近平在湖南考察时强调坚持改革创新求真务实奋力谱写中国式现代化湖南篇章蔡奇陪同考察》，新华社，2024 年 3 月 21 日

科技成果转化为现实生产力，表现形式为催生新产业、推动产业深度转型升级。当前，科技创新以无处不在的渗透性、扩散性、带动性，广泛赋能经济社会发展。发展新质生产力，中国具有得天独厚的优势。近年来，中国科技创新整体实力稳步提升，基础研究能力不断增强，2023 年基础研究经费占全社会研发投入比重提高到 6.65%；中高端人才数量红利逐步显现；国内市场规模巨大，应用场景丰富；产业链结构全、链条长，制造业规模连续 14 年位居全球第一。

新质生产力的提出，意味着中国将以更大决心和力度推动科技创新，加快实现高水平科技自立自强，打好关键核心技术攻坚战，产出更多原创性、颠覆性科技创新成果，为经济社会发展注入新动能。

1. 牢牢掌握关键核心技术

关键核心技术在产业技术生态体系中居于核心地位，是增强科技创新引领作用的重要抓手，也是实现高水平科技自立自强的保证。

习近平总书记强调："关键核心技术是要不来、买不来、讨不来的。"[①]只有加快突破关键核心技术，才能把创新主动权、发展主动权牢牢掌握在自己手中。

打好关键核心技术攻坚战，必须聚力突破重点难点。要从国家急迫需要和长远需求出发，在基础原材料、高端芯片、工业软件等领域全力攻坚。要以关键共性技术、前沿引领技术、现代工程技术、颠覆性技术为突破口，前瞻部署一批战略性、储备性技术研发项目，实施好国家重大科学计划和科学工程。要优化财政科技投入，引导企业和社会增加研发投入，加强知识产权保护，完善推动企业技术创新的税收政策，加大资本市场对科技型企业的支持力度，积极发展风险投资，壮大耐心

---

① 《习近平：在中国科学院第十九次院士大会、中国工程院第十四次院士大会上的讲话》，新华社，2018 年 5 月 28 日

资本。

打好关键核心技术攻坚战，要发挥社会主义制度集中力量办大事的显著优势，强化党和国家对重大科技创新的领导，健全新型举国体制。围绕国家战略需求，完善顶层设计，科学配置创新资源，优化国家科研机构、高水平研究型大学、科技领军企业定位和布局，把政府、市场、社会等各方面力量拧成一股绳，形成科技攻关的强大合力。

2. 持之以恒加强基础研究

基础研究处于从研究到应用再到生产的科研链条起始端，地基打得牢，科技事业大厦才能建得高。当前，科学研究范式发生深刻变革，全球基础研究转化周期明显缩短，迫切需要加强基础研究，从源头和底层解决关键技术问题。

2023年2月21日，中共中央政治局就加强基础研究进行集体学习。习近平总书记强调，加强基础研究，是实现高水平科技自立自强的迫切要求，是建设世界科技强国的必由之路。[①]

近年来，中国"从0到1"的原始创新能力不断提升，取得一批有国际影响力的重大原创成果：建成"中国天眼"FAST、稳态强磁场、散裂中子源等一批国之重器，在量子计算、人工合成淀粉、纳米限域催化等方面实现突破。

基础研究是实现科技自立自强的源头。通过基础研究才能变不确定性为确定性，变未知为已知。世界已经进入大科学时代，基础研究组织化程度越来越高，制度保障和政策引导对基础研究产出的影响越来越大。

一方面，要优化基础学科建设布局，支持重点学科、新兴学科、冷

---

① 《习近平在中共中央政治局第三次集体学习时强调切实加强基础研究夯实科技自立自强根基》，新华社，2023年2月22日

门学科和薄弱学科发展，以高质量学科体系支撑基础研究和原始创新。另一方面，要增加基础研究多元投入，满足不同类型基础研究的需求，为基础前沿方向重大原创成果的持续涌现提供资金支持。

对重大科学问题和重大战略需求，必须系统谋划、前瞻布局，统筹部署战略导向的体系化基础研究、前沿导向的探索性基础研究、市场导向的应用性基础研究，以占据前沿技术制高点为目标，以体制机制创新为保障，加强从基础研究、关键技术、装备研制到成果转化的全链条设计、一体化部署。

3. 强化企业创新主体地位

企业是科技创新活动的主要组织者和参与者，也是发展新质生产力的重要支撑。强化企业科技创新主体地位，是推动实现高水平科技自立自强的关键。

数据显示，截至 2023 年底，中国拥有有效发明专利的企业达 42.7 万家，较上年增加 7.2 万家，企业拥有有效发明专利 290.9 万件，占比增至 71.2%，首次超过七成。企业研发投入占全社会研发投入的比重连续多年超过 75%，企业创新主体地位进一步凸显。

在加快发展新质生产力的背景下，中国多措并举进一步强化企业科技创新主体地位——

强化企业在科技创新决策方面的主体地位，支持企业在更大范围、更深程度参与国家科技创新决策；强化企业在研发投入中的主体地位，加大企业研发费用加计扣除等政策落实力度，打通科技、产业、金融的链条；强化企业在科研组织中的主体地位，在重大专项、重点工程等关键技术攻关项目中，让企业唱主角。

打通科技成果转化的"最后一公里"，关键在企业。中国将继续完善科技成果转化法律法规，破除科技成果使用、处置和收益权等政策障碍；健全产学研成果对接和产业化机制，支持企业建设中试验证平台，提升企业科技成果转化的能力；发挥领军企业的牵引推动作用、中小企业的配套支撑作用，促进全产业链上下联动、融合发展，形成完善的产业生态。

发展新质生产力需要一大批高素质复合型科技企业家。他们不仅要具备创新精神，还要具有科学素质，能够洞察科学新发现的重要价值，并具有围绕创新组合生产要素、协调产学研各方的能力。中国正在创造良好环境，让通晓科技创新、商业模式和管理方法的企业家脱颖而出。

（二）以科技创新引领产业创新

人类近现代史上历次生产力的跨越式进步都伴随着科技革命和产业革命的发生，但科技革命只有在适宜的经济条件与社会体制下才能催生产业变革。

当前，以人工智能、清洁能源、生物技术等为重点的新一轮科技浪潮扑面而来，各国纷纷加快实施推动新产业革命的国家战略，比如美国的"先进制造业伙伴计划"、德国的"工业4.0"、日本的"再兴战略"、法国的"新工业法国"、英国的"高价值制造战略"等。

在中国式现代化进程中，现代化产业体系建设成为加快培育新质生产力的必然要求。

1.改造提升传统产业

中国产业体系较为完备，在全球分工体系和产业链供应链体系中具有举足轻重的地位，一些产业在国际上处于领先地位，必须把这个优势巩固好、发挥好。

传统制造业是支撑国民经济发展和满足人民生活需要的重要基础。为传统产业赋予"新"和"质"，就是要以高端化、智能化、绿色化为方向，加快结构体系升级、技术路径创新、发展模式优化，促进实现质的有效提升和量的合理增长。

加装"高端"引擎。加快先进适用技术推广应用，推动传统制造业优势领域锻长板，推进强链延链补链，支持传统制造业深耕细分领域，孵化新技术、开拓新赛道、培育新产业。深入实施产业基础再造工程，强化传统制造业基础支撑体系。

加装"智能"引擎。加快数字技术赋能，大力推进企业智改数转网联，加快人工智能、大数据、云计算、5G、物联网等信息技术与制造全过程、全要素深度融合。促进产业链供应链网络 化协同，推动产业园区和集群整体改造升级。

加装"绿色"引擎。加快绿色科技创新和先进绿色技术推广应用，做强绿色制造业，发展绿色服务业，壮大绿色能源产业，发展绿色低碳产业和供应链，构建绿色低碳循环经济体系，以产业含"绿"量提升发展含"新"量。

根据工业和信息化部、国家发展改革委等八部门联合印发的指导意见提出的目标，到 2027 年，传统制造业高端化、智能化、绿色化、融合化发展水平明显提升，有效支撑制造业比重保持基本稳定，在全球产业分工中的地位和竞争力进一步巩固增强。工业企业数字化研发设计工具普及率、关键工序数控化率分别超过 90%、70%，工业能耗强度和二氧化碳排放强度持续下降，万元工业增加值用水量较 2023 年下降 13% 左右，大宗工业固体废物综合利用率超过 57%。

当前，中国正在推进新一轮大规模设备更新和消费品以旧换新。根据国务院印发的行动方案，中国将聚焦石化化工、钢铁、有色、建材、机械、汽车、轻工、纺织、电子等重点行业，开展先进设备更新、数字化转型、绿色装备推广、安全水平提升四大行动，全面推动设备更新和技术改造，为改造提升传统产业奠定坚实基础。

2. 培育壮大新兴产业

战略性新兴产业处在科技和经济发展前沿，对经济社会的长远发展具有重大引领作用，在很大程度上决定着一个国家或地区的综合实力，特别是核心竞争力。

战略性新兴产业是新质生产力的重要载体。2023 年 9 月，习近平总书记在新时代推动东北全面振兴座谈会上指出，"积极培育新能源、新材料、先进制造、电子信息等战略性新兴产业，积极培育未来产业，加快形成新质生产力，增强发展新动能。"①

战略性新兴产业具有先导性，融合化、集群化是产业发展的新模式。战略性新兴产业集群通过产业在一定地理空间的集聚，实现人才、技术、资金的有机结合和效益最大化，已成为中国产业发展的重要趋势。

2024 年 3 月，南京发布 18 个人工智能应用场景，聚焦"AI + 工业""AI + 电力""AI + 交通""AI + 医疗""AI + 信息消费"五大领域，打造底层技术和应用协同的"试验场"，探索落地更具前景的人工智能创新模式和产品方向。

当前，中国把握战略性新兴产业发展机遇，在新一代信息技术、人工智能、生物技术、新能源、新材料、高端装备、绿色环保等领域打造一批具有国际竞争力的先进产业集群，构建一批各具特色、优势互补、结构合理的新增长点。

推动战略性新兴产业融合集群发展，还需在围绕产业链部署创新链、完善生态构建和场景应用、加强数字平台建设等方面持续发力。

要围绕产业链部署创新链，充分发挥龙头企业链主优势、平台效应和示范引领作用，促进创新链与产业链的共融和产业链上下游协同发展。要完善生态构建和场景应用，强化政府投资对全社会投资的引导带动，支持各地围绕禀赋优势、着眼未来发展，打造细分领域的标志性产业，

---

① 《习近平主持召开新时代推动东北全面振兴座谈会强调：牢牢把握东北的重要使命奋力谱写东北全面振兴新篇章蔡奇丁薛祥出席》，新华社，2023 年 9 月 9 日

以产业需求牵引教育、科技、人才发展。

要以数字平台建设促进数实融合，以数字化为基础，集合行业上下游相关企业、行业科研机构和政府公共部门等创新力量，实现系统集成、资源共享。

3. 布局发展未来产业

未来产业是重塑全球创新版图与经济格局的前沿力量，是牢牢把握未来发展主动权的关键所在。

习近平总书记高度重视发展未来产业，作出一系列重要指示和决策部署。《中华人民共和国国民经济和社会发展第十四个五年规划和2035年远景目标纲要》明确，"在类脑智能、量子信息、基因技术、未来网络、深海空天开发、氢能与储能等前沿科技和产业变革领域，组织实施未来产业孵化与加速计划，谋划布局一批未来产业"。中国未来产业发展思路不断明晰，重点领域发展蓝图逐渐展开。

当前，未来产业已成为从中央到地方打造新增长引擎的关键领域，发展未来产业不仅有望培育形成一批千亿级甚至万亿级新支柱产业与产业集群，还能通过广泛赋能推动传统优势产业转型升级，在强链补链延链上发挥更大作用。

2022年11月，科学技术部、教育部批复《未来产业科技园试点及培育名单》，北京市、上海市、江苏省、湖北省、广东省、四川省、陕西省、黑龙江省等8省市的10家未来产业科技园成为首批未来产业科技园建设试点。2023年8月，工业和信息化部办公厅印发《关于组织开展2023年未来产业创新任务揭榜挂帅工作的通知》，面向元宇宙、人形机器人、脑机接口、通用人工智能四个重点方向，加速新技术、新产品落地应用。

各地结合科技与产业基础竞相"落子"未来产业。北京、上海、浙江、广东深圳等地率先出台关于未来产业的发展规划、行动计划、实施方案与配套政策，把前瞻布局未来产业作为拼经济谋长远的重头戏。

中国未来产业正处于创新活力、辐射能力、综合实力实现大跨越的关键时期，要不断创新适应产业发展的思路和举措，前瞻谋划未来产业时空布局。由于未来产业的技术路线有待清晰、商业模式亟需成熟，培育未来产业不能简单使用大水漫灌式支持，需要精细的温光水气调控式支持，其支持导向要更加突出厚植发展土壤、更加突出扶小扶新扶幼、更加突出强化原始创新、更加突出场景市场支持，创新监管模式，加大制度供给，营造鼓励创新、宽容失败、敢闯敢试的创新氛围和发展空间。

（三）因地制宜发展新质生产力

不论是科技创新还是产业创新，关键都是从实际出发，都要立足科技基础，用好用足自身优势。

2024年全国两会期间，习近平总书记在参加江苏代表团审议时强调，"要牢牢把握高质量发展这个首要任务，因地制宜发展新质生产力""发展新质生产力不是忽视、放弃传统产业，要防止一哄而上、泡沫化，也不要搞一种模式"。[①] 习近平总书记强调的"因地制宜"，体现了马克思主义的认识论和方法论，为中国不同地区结合自身优势发展新质生产力指明了方向。

"因地制宜"，既是对中国国情的准确把握，也是对创新规律的深刻理解。发展新质生产力涉及科技创新、产业升级、组织管理、人才引育等多个层面，各地资源禀赋、主体功能、产业基础、科研条件等存在差异，发展新质生产力的打法也会不尽相同。不能忽视创新规律、产业

---

① 《习近平在参加江苏代表团审议时强调：因地制宜发展新质生产力》，新华社，2024年3月5日

规律和自身条件盲目行动，要坚持一切从实际出发，实事求是，探索符合自身实际的新质生产力发展之路。

发展新质生产力要谋"新"，更要重"质"。从以科技创新推动产业创新的历史经验和现实情况看，从来没有相同的发展路径，也没有可以简单照搬照抄的发展模式。要着眼国家区域创新布局，立足各地特色优势和基层探索实践，找到科学合理的创新发展路径，避免千篇一律、搞一种模式。

发展新质生产力，要注重创新成果的落地应用和价值转化。创新成果不能只停留在实验室，更要成为生产线上的产品、大市场里的商品。在加快科技创新成果转化应用过程中，要更加注重解决本地经济社会发展实际问题，围绕产业链部署创新链，围绕创新链布局产业链，加快转化为现实生产力，增强地方发展内生动力。

发展新质生产力，要防止"内卷式"同质化竞争。在谋划和推进产业转型升级时，不必一味追求大而全，不能只盯着某些领域、某些产品，而要发挥比较优势，形成错落有致、互嵌互补、各有千秋的整体格局。

发展新质生产力，要加强跨部门协调合作，打通科技链、产业链、政策链、人才链、资金链，避免各地区各部门"各播各的种，各撒各的肥"，坚持"全国一盘棋"统筹优化，从彰显国家整体优势的角度科学布局、各展其长。

科技创新等不得，也急不得。做好创新发展这篇大文章，必须坚持以科技创新为核心要素，坚持以产业创新为有力支撑，坚持统筹兼顾，才能让科技创新成果迸发涌流，使发展新质生产力的步伐更稳健、动力更强劲。

三、塑造适应新质生产力的新型生产关系

"生产关系必须与生产力发展要求相适应。发展新质生产力，必须进一步全面深化改革，形成与之相适应的新型生产关系。"①

——习近平

发展新质生产力，既是发展命题，也是改革命题。

习近平总书记指出，"改革是解放和发展社会生产力的关键，是推动国家发展的根本动力"②"发展新质生产力，必须进一步全面深化改革，形成与之相适应的新型生产关系"。

从人类工业发展的历史来看，任何一个能够引领全球科技浪潮和工业革命的国家，一定是构建了新的、相对于其他国家能够更有效激励创新、保护创新的制度体系，这正是国家核心竞争力的重要载体。因此，新质生产力的国家间竞争表面上是新技术和新产业的竞争，本质上则是国家间的制度竞争，谁能率先提供与新科技浪潮和产业变革匹配的市场机制、产业监管、金融制度、产业政策，谁就能够在国家间的新质生产力竞争中胜出。

（一）进一步全面深化改革，促进新质生产力诸要素实现高效协同匹配

新质生产力既需要政府超前规划引导、科学政策支持，也需要市场机制调节、企业等微观主体不断创新，是政府"有形之手"和市场"无

---

① 《习近平在中共中央政治局第十一次集体学习时强调加快发展新质生产力扎实推进高质量发展》，新华社，2024 年 2 月 1 日

② 《习近平：在经济社会领域专家座谈会上的讲话》，新华社，2020 年 8 月 24 日

形之手"共同培育和驱动形成的。

改革开放以来，中国共产党经过持续探索和实践，创造性地提出在社会主义条件下发展市场经济，建立并完善了社会主义市场经济体制。中共十八大以来，中国围绕构建高水平社会主义市场经济体制，加快完善产权保护、市场准入、公平竞争、社会信用等市场经济基础制度，完善落实"两个毫不动摇"的体制机制，为各类生产要素高效协同匹配奠定制度基础。

1. 把握新质生产力要素的"新"特征

与传统生产力相比，新质生产力是包容了全新质态要素的生产力。在新技术革命浪潮推动下，劳动者、劳动工具、劳动对象实现总体跃升、优化组合、创新性配置，必须准确把握新质生产力要素的新特征。

更高素质的劳动者是新质生产力的第一要素。新型劳动者是新质生产力中最活跃、最具决定意义的因素。不同于传统以简单重复劳动为主的普通技术工人，新型劳动者代表现代劳动力的转变，是能够创造新质生产力的创新型战略人才和能够熟练掌握新质生产资料的应用型人才，拥有更高的教育水平、更强的学习能力，不仅掌握传统职业技能，更能适应数字化、智能化的工作环境，具备跨界融合的综合能力。

新型劳动者，包括引领世界科技前沿、创新创造新型生产工具，特别是在颠覆性科学认识和技术创造方面做出重大突破的顶尖科技人才，在基础研究和关键核心技术领域作出突出贡献的一流科技领军人才；以卓越工程师为代表的工程技术人才和以大国工匠为代表的技术工人；敢闯敢干，拥有战略思维，能够敏锐把握科技前沿技术和产业趋势，持续投入创新、能够以科技创新推动产业创新的优秀企业家。

更为高精尖的劳动工具是新质生产力的动力源泉。新一代信息技术、先进制造技术、新材料技术等融合应用，孕育出一大批更智能、更高效、更低碳、更安全的新型生产工具。传统机械为主的生产工具发生颠覆性变化，工业互联网、工业软件等广泛应用，极大丰富了生产工具的表现形态。劳动过程向平台化、生态化、共享化、远程化生产协作转变，促进数字经济与实体经济有机融合，极大提高了生产率和经济效益。

作为劳动工具的重要方面，新型基础设施是新质生产力的基础支撑。新型基础设施以信息网络基础设施为核心，以数字化、网络化和智能化为特征，包括高速网络、大数据中心、智能物流系统等。中国正在加快构建系统完备、高效实用、智能绿色、安全可靠的现代化基础设施体系，这将为新型劳动对象的生成和新型劳动工具的应用提供必要条件。

更广泛的劳动对象是新质生产力的物质基础。得益于科技创新，人类劳动对象发生极大变化。一方面，人类从自然界获取物质和能量的手段更加先进，利用和改造自然的范围扩展至深空、深海、深地等；另一方面，人类通过劳动不断创造新的物质资料，并转化为劳动对象，大幅提高了生产率。数据等新型劳动对象在各行各业中广泛渗透，将释放出巨大的生产力效能。

在新一轮科技革命和产业变革驱动下，劳动者、劳动工具、劳动对象和生产方式实现变革调整，推动劳动力、资本、土地、知识、技术、管理、数据等要素便捷化流动、网络化共享、系统化整合、协作化开发和高效化利用，促进新质生产力加快形成。

2.创新生产要素配置方式

2024年1月31日，习近平总书记在主持中共中央政治局集体学习时强调，着力打通束缚新质生产力发展的堵点卡点，建立高标准市场体系，创新生产要素配置方式，让各类先进优质生产要素向发展新质生产力顺畅流动。[①]

[①]《习近平在中共中央政治局第十一次集体学习时强调加快发展新质生产力扎实推进高质量发展》，新华社，2024年2月1日

实现生产要素的创新性配置，核心还是靠深化改革。

——持续深化要素市场化改革。

中共十九大明确将要素市场化配置作为经济体制改革的重点之一。中共十九届四中全会进一步强调，推进要素市场制度建设，实现要素价格市场决定、流动自主有序、配置高效公平。2020 年，《中共中央国务院关于构建更加完善的要素市场化配置体制机制的意见》出台，分类提出土地、劳动力、资本、技术、数据五个要素领域的改革方向。

中国要素市场化改革正持续向深入推进。2024 年开年，中国发布《"数据要素 x"三年行动计划（2024—2026 年）》，明确提出"发挥数据要素的放大、叠加、倍增作用"。与前期"互联网＋"行动相比，"数据要素 x"行动充分体现了生产要素创新性配置的考量。

——加快建设全国统一大市场。

市场，当今世界最稀缺的资源。中国超大规模市场具有丰富应用场景和放大创新收益的优势。加快建设全国统一大市场，可以促进创新要素有序流动和合理配置，支撑科技创新加快向产业创新转变；可以更好发挥规模经济优势和集聚效应，进一步降低市场交易成本；可以让更高质量的商品和服务在市场竞争中脱颖而出，为新质生产力持续迸发创造有利条件。

近年来，中国加快建设全国统一大市场取得积极进展，包括全面实行股票发行注册制改革，全面启动深化农村集体经营性建设用地入市试点，推进全国统一电力市场体系和碳市场等。同时，废止、修订和纠正了一批妨碍统一市场和公平竞争的政策措施，在完善产权、市场准入、公平竞争、信用等方面出台了一批配套政策。

下一步，中国将持续破除地方保护和区域壁垒，为经营主体构建良好环境；优化创新资源布局和产业布局，构建省级—国家级—世界级集群梯次培育发展体系，推动制造业在国内有序转移。

——建设高标准市场体系。

着力打通束缚新质生产力发展的堵点卡点，要从制度上为创新资源优化配置提供基础支撑。

中国正在建设的高标准市场体系是一项基础性改革，其特征是统一开放、竞争有序、制度完备、治理完善，内容涵盖高标准的市场体系基础制度、高标准的要素市场体系、高标准的市场环境和质量、高标准的市场基础设施、高标准的市场开放、高标准的现代市场监管机制。

就高标准的市场体系基础制度而言，严格的产权保护，是激发各类经营主体活力的原始动力；实施全国统一的市场准入负面清单制度，是形成全国统一市场的前提条件；公平竞争是有效的市场运行机制，可以促进经营主体充分竞争、优胜劣汰。

建设高标准的市场体系更加强调制度的完备性、更加强调公平竞争、更加强调政府维护市场秩序和弥补市场失灵的重要性。总而言之，要充分发挥市场在资源配置中的决定性作用，更好发挥政府作用，推动有效市场和有为政府更好结合。

3. 健全要素参与收入分配机制

健全要素参与收入分配机制，对于调动各类生产要素参与生产的积极性、主动性、创造性，

让各类生产要素的活力竞相迸发，具有重要的理论意义和实践价值。

新质生产力条件下，对土地、资本、劳动力等传统数量型要素的创新性配置提出更高要求，人工智能、绿色能源、数据、空天、深海、频率等新型要素形态加快涌现，知识、技术、管理等质量型要素发挥着更为重要的作用。健全要素参与收入分配机制是塑造适应新质生产力的生产关系的题中之义。

中共十九届四中全会把"按劳分配为主体、多种分配方式并存"作为社会主义基本经济制度的重要组成部分。中共二十大强调，完善按要

素分配政策制度。

当前，中国正在完善劳动参与分配的机制，提高劳动报酬在初次分配中的比重，巩固按劳分配的主体地位；完善资本参与分配的机制，推进资本市场改革，完善收益与风险匹配机制；完善土地参与分配的机制，提高土地要素配置精准性和利用效率，建立健全土地增值收益分配机制；完善知识参与分配的机制，在全社会形成知识创造价值、价值创造者得到合理回报的良性循环；完善技术参与分配的机制，建立健全对科研人员实施股权、期权和分红激励的机制；完善管理参与分配的机制，统筹用好员工持股、股权激励、股权分红等中长期激励措施；完善数据参与分配的机制，建立健全数据权属、公开、共享、交易规则，让数据所有者能够从数据使用中获得应有收益。

4. 畅通教育、科技、人才的良性循环

习近平总书记强调，"要按照发展新质生产力要求，畅通教育、科技、人才的良性循环"[①] "深化科技体制、教育体制、人才体制等改革"[②]

教育是发展新质生产力的重要基础，科技是发展新质生产力的核心要素，人才是发展新质生产力的第一资源。中国坚持教育优先发展、科技自立自强、人才引领驱动，进一步强化资源协同配置的坚实基础，激活塑造新动能新优势的重要引擎。

必须在深化科技体制改革上下功夫。要深化科技管理体制改革，给予科研单位更多自主权，赋予科学家更大技术路线决定权和经费使

---

① 《习近平在中共中央政治局第十一次集体学习时强调加快发展新质生产力扎实推进高质量发展》，新华社，2024 年 2 月 1 日

② 《习近平在中共中央政治局第十一次集体学习时强调加快发展新质生产力扎实推进高质量发展》，新华社，2024 年 2 月 1 日

用权。要围绕"为谁创新、谁来创新、创新什么、如何创新",对技术创新决策、研发投入、科研组织、成果转化全链条整体部署,对政策、资金、项目、平台、人才等关键创新资源系统布局。要健全科技成果使用、处置和收益管理制度,不断提高科技成果转化和产业化水平。

必须在深化教育体制改革上持久发力。要围绕人力资源深度开发和创新驱动发展,统筹职业教育、高等教育、继续教育协同创新,推进职普融通、产教融合、科教融汇。要紧紧围绕国家战略和行业需求,调整优化高校学科布局、学科结构、专业设置。无论是基础教育、高等教育还是职业教育,都要注重激发人才的创新性思维和创造性能力。

必须推动人才体制机制改革持续突破。要加快形成有利于人才成长的培养机制、有利于人尽其才的使用机制、有利于人才各展其能的激励机制、有利于人才脱颖而出的竞争机制。要杜绝"一把尺子量到底",加快构建以创新价值、能力、贡献为导向的人才评价体系。要积极为人才"减负松绑",给予人才充分的信任、宽松的成长环境,特别是对于一些研发周期很长的基础科研和技术应用,要保持战略耐心。要落实好"揭榜挂帅"和"赛马"等制度。要实施更加开放包容的国际科技合作战略,畅通教育、科技、人才要素的跨区域循环通道,聚天下英才而用之。

（二）坚持高水平开放,打造一流营商环境

中国取得的经济发展成就是在开放条件下取得的。发展新质生产力、实现高质量发展,也必须在高水平开放的条件下进行。

习近平总书记强调:"要扩大高水平对外开放,为发展新质生产力营造良好国际环境。"[①]面对日趋复杂的国际形势和日益增多的不确定

---

① 《习近平在中共中央政治局第十一次集体学习时强调加快发展新质生产力扎实推进高质量发展》,新华社,2024年2月1日

因素，中国坚持高水平对外开放，持续建设市场化、法治化、国际化一流营商环境，为发展新质生产力构筑重要支撑。

1. 在全球范围内优化资源配置

优质资本、关键资源、先进技术、拔尖人才等是发展新质生产力的关键。当前，全球资源配置呈现新的发展态势。中国推进高水平对外开放，依托超大规模市场优势，以国内大循环吸引全球资源要素，增强国内国际两个市场两种资源联动效应，营造具有全球竞争力的创新生态。

改革开放以来，中国在经济全球化进程中承担了三个重要角色，深度参与者深度参与全球制造业价值链分工，积极促进者为促进全球经济增长作出巨大贡献，合作创新者共同推进全球新一轮科技革命和产业变革。

外媒称，中国正在推动形成一个全球性技术生态系统，逐步成长为国际科技合作不可忽视的参与者、全球创新资源要素重要的引力场。

中国在全球产业链分工中的位势稳步提升，为在更高层次融入国际循环、吸引全球资源要素奠定坚实基础。面对复杂的外部环境，中国以一系列有力措施释放更加鲜明的开放信号一

中国宣布在增值电信等领域开展准入试点，全面取消制造业领域外资准入限制措施；出台扎实推进高水平对外开放更大力度吸引和利用外资行动方案，公布全国版和自贸试验区版跨境服务贸易负面清单、《促进和规范数据跨境流动规定》等；《浦东新区综合改革试点实施方案（2023—2027年）》提出探索资本项目可兑换实施路径，在贸易结算、电商支付、碳交易、绿色电力交易等领域试点使用数字人民币等举措；举办进博会、广交会、服贸会、数贸会、消博会等重大展会，打造双向开放平台……

中国开放的大门正越开越大，促进在全球范围内优化资源要素配置，为发展新质生产力创造更好的环境和条件。

2. 进一步扩大制度型开放

同商品和要素流动型开放相比,制度型开放是一种更高层次的开放。通过打通制度、规则等层面存在的各种壁垒,能够有效增强国内国际两个市场两种资源的联动效应,进一步发挥对全球优质创新要素资源的集聚作用。

习近平总书记强调,要围绕服务构建新发展格局,以制度型开放为重点,聚焦投资、贸易、金融、创新等对外交流合作的重点领域深化体制机制改革,完善配套政策措施,积极主动把我国对外开放提高到新水平[①]。

围绕进一步扩大制度型开放,在开放布局上,中国坚持沿海开放与内陆沿边开放更好结合,探索适应沿海内地联动发展的开放制度规则;在开放方式上,坚持"引进来"和"走出去"更好结合,打造国际合作新平台;在开放水平上,坚持制造领域开放与服务领域开放更好结合,构建推动教育、医疗、金融等开放的新规则新标准;在治理机制上,坚持多边开放与区域开放更好结合,参与推动全球制度型开放,做开放型世界经济的建设者、贡献者。

当前,中国加快推动规则、规制、管理和标准等制度型开放:自贸试验区提质扩围至 22 个,率先在上海、广东、天津、福建、北京等具备条件的自由贸易试验区和海南自由贸易港,试点对接相关国际高标准经贸规则;加大现代服务业领域开放力度,服务业扩大开放综合试点增至 11 个;全面高质量实施《区域全面经济伙伴关系协定》(RCEP),积极推动加入《全面与进步跨太平洋伙伴关系协定》(CPTPP)和《数字经济伙伴关系协定》(DEPA),为加快形成具有全球竞争力的开放

---

① 《习近平主持召开中央全面深化改革委员会第二次会议强调建设更高水平开放型经济新体制推动能耗双控逐步转向碳排放双控》,新华社,2023 年 7 月 11 日

创新生态作出中国贡献。

3. 待续深化国际合作

发展新质生产力，符合中国实现高质量发展的愿景，也符合世界对中国提供"动能变瞿"的预期。尤其是在绿色环保、数字革命等领域，中国与国际合作伙伴存在巨大的合作空间。在新质生产力领域持续深化国际合作，不仅有助于全球产业链、供应链能级提升，也将进一步优化全球资源配置，让各个合作国共享产业升级和高质量发展机遇。

中国正努力深化国际合作，为培育新质生产力夯实基础，具体措施包括：继续推动共建"一带一路"高质量发展，在共商共建共享原则基础上实现合作共赢；加快建设中欧班列、西部陆海新通道等国际贸易和物流大通道，进一步提升互联互通水平；坚定支持多边贸易体制，积极参与并推动（WTO）进行必要改革，进一步完善面向全球的高标准自由贸易区网络等。

2023 年，中国对外非金融类直接投资 1301 亿美元，同比增长 11.4%，连续 11 年稳居世界前三。对外投资存量 2.8 万亿美元，遍布全球 190 多个国家和地区，连续 6 年保持世界前三。截至 2023 年底，中国对"一带一路"共建国家直接投资存量超 3000 亿美元，境外经贸合作区超过 100 家，在共建国家承包工程完成额近 2 万亿美元，"一带一路"投资合作走深走实。中国持续深化绿色发展、数字经济和蓝色经济合作，与 38 个国家签署相关领域投资合作备忘录 64 份；与 60 个国家建立 70 个双边投资合作工作组；在 120 多个国家和地区建立了 150 多个境外中资企业商协会。

习近平总书记指出，世界好，中国才会好；中国好，世界会更好①。

---

① 《习近平在第三届"一带一路"国际合作高峰论坛开幕式上的主旨演讲》，新华社，2023 年 10 月 18 日

在开放中创造机遇、在合作中破解难题，这是中国在扩大开放过程中形成的宝贵经验。以新质生产力发展为重要牵引的国际合作，将有更广阔的空间和更生动的实践。

四、新质生产力的世界意义

"当今世界并不太平，中国一如既往，以人类前途为怀、以人民福祉为念，努力为人类和平和发展事业贡献中国智慧、中国方案，倡导平等有序的世界多极化和普惠包容的经济全球化。"①

——习近平

生产力的发展是各国实现现代化的共同特征。工业革命迄今 200 多年来，少数已经实现现代化的国家均在不同程度上实现了生产力的跃迁。然而总体来看，世界现代化的进程并非一帆风顺，仍然面对诸多挑战，包括经济复苏乏力、地缘政治形势严峻、贸易保护主义和全球化逆流等。

在此背景下，中国发展新质生产力，既是着眼于中华民族伟大复兴的主动作为之举，也是以自身现代化实践推动世界和平发展、互利合作、共同繁荣的担当之举。

（一）为世界经济复苏注入新动力，分享发展机遇

在全球经济版图中，中国发挥的"引擎"和"压舱石"作用越来越突出。彭博社援引国际货币基金组织最新经济预测数据，预计 2024 年到 2029 年，全球经济增长的 75% 将集中在 20 个国家，中国的贡献最大。

---

① 《习近平接受外国新任驻华大使递交国书》，新华社，2024 年 1 月 30 日

同期，全球新增经济活动中，中国占比将达到 21% 左右，高于七国集团的 20%。[①]

1. 发挥经济引擎新作用

为什么中国能在世界经济艰难转型的过程中持续发挥引擎作用？

一个重要因素就在于中国积极拥抱新一轮科技革命和产业变革，以发展新质生产力为牵引，努力通过技术革命性突破、生产要素创新配置来推动产业创新，不断开拓新领域、新优势、新赛道，培育发展新动能。

当前，新质生产力正在激发中国市场的活力和潜力，增强了中国作为世界经济引擎的韧实力。2023 年，中国生物医药、人工智能和纳米技术应用三大产业产值超 550 亿美元；预计到 2027 年，数字经济规模有望达到 15.7 万亿美元。中国推动碳达峰碳中和的努力正在引领构建全新的零碳产业体系，引发海量投资与产业机遇。在可再生能源领域，中国已成为名副其实的全球领导者。根据全球风能理事会发布的《2024 年全球风能报告》，2023 年，全球新增风力发电装机容量达到创纪录的 117 吉瓦，比 2022 年增长 50%，但如果将中国排除在外的话，全球风能产业的增长实际已陷入停滞[②]。

国际货币基金组织的研究表明，中国经济增长对世界其他地区具有积极的溢出效应，中国经济每增长 1 个百分点，将使其他经济体的产出水平平均提高 0.3 个百分点[③]。随着传统产业转型升级、新兴产业蓬勃兴起，新质生产力将为中国经济高质量发展持续注入新动力，带来中等收入群体的不断扩大和消费市场的持续增长升级。届时，中国经济引擎

---

① 《彭博社：中国将是未来 5 年全球经济增长最大贡献者贡献率超七国集团》，新华社，2024 年 4 月 20 日

② 《外媒：渲染中国"绿色产能过剩"危及全球能源转型》，新华社，2024 年 4 月 22 日

③ 《世界坐标中的中国经济基本面》，新华社，2024 年 2 月 8 日

给世界带来的利好将更为可期。

2. 创造共赢发展新机遇

加快发展新质生产力将进一步放大中国市场的独特优势，为国际合作伙伴创造更多发展机遇。

首先，新质生产力的发展将会带来劳动生产率、产业附加值水平、劳动者收入和福利水平的提高。到 2035 年，中国中等收入人群预计会达到 8 亿，形成更为强劲的购买力。随着新质生产力不断发展，消费场景也将不断拓展，中国人的生产生活方式迅速向数字化、绿色化转型，激发出多样化、高端化的消费新需求。在购买力和需求的双重推动下，中国的进口规模会随之扩大，中国的贸易伙伴将在更深、更广的层次上分享中国大市场的发展机遇。

加快发展新质生产力也将使中国成为全球创新链中更重要的环节。越来越多外资企业正在参与到中国先进产业链的打造和创新链的升级，把在华投资的更多精力放在创新赛道上，更加注重研发和开拓具有高附加值的创新技术和服务。对很多跨国公司来说，中国已不仅是一个重要的市场，还是创新收益的"放大器"。

不少跨国公司都用追加投资的方式对中国的创新发展投下"信任票"。扎根中国 30 多年的阿斯利康将投资 4.75 亿美元在无锡新建小分子药厂，投资 7 亿美元在青岛建立吸入气雾剂生产供应基地；法雷奥在上海建立"舒适驾驶辅助系统"生产研发基地；GE 医疗（中国）未来三来年在中国的研发投入将再翻一番。放眼世界，很难找到像中国这样规模巨大、空间广阔的投资高地，新质生产力的加快发展将进一步巩固外国企业界对"下一个中国，还是中国"的认同。

中国的不可替代，可从跨国公司财报中管窥一二。2023 财年，博世集团在华销售额增长超过 5%，其中智能出行是其在华业务的主要增长动力。苹果公司大中华区营收约占公司总营收的五分之一。上海超级工厂已成为特斯拉在全球主要的出口中心，效率稳居同业前列。2024年4月下旬，特斯拉首席执行官马斯克时隔不到一年再度访华。一大批有远见的外国企业家已敏锐感知到中国发展新质生产力带来的新机遇。

（二）探索新型生产关系，拓展经济治理新实践

新质生产力，是中国共产党对马克思主义政治经济学的发展和创新，其中蕴含着巨大的变革力量，也对中国经济治理能力提出了新考验。

当前，中国着力完善自身经济制度、提升经济治理能力。这种战略主动性彰显了中国的制度自信，也为其他发展中国家提供了经济治理的宝贵经验和实践范例。

1. 以战略主动应对全球前沿挑战

当前，中国正在跨越后发国家普遍遭遇的"比较优势陷阱"，在许多新领域的技术研发和应用上处于领先地位，与发达国家同时面临技术发展带来的挑战。为此，中国积极完善政策规划、填补制度空白、挖掘体制机制优势，在变局中开新局，积极把握战略主动。

中国在发展数字经济方面的制度探索令人瞩目。中共十八大以来，以习近平同志为核心的党中央对发展数字经济高度重视，数据成为国家基础性战略资源。2020年4月，中共中央、国务院发布《关于构建更加完善的要素市场化配置体制机制的意见》，数据作为一种新生产要素首次写入中央文件。中国成为全球第一个在国家政策层面将数据确立为生产要素的国家。

2022年以来，中国数据要素市场发展进入快车道。2022年12月，中共中央、国务院印发《关于构建数据基础制度更好发挥数据要素作用的意见》，擘画数据要素市场发展蓝图。2023年2月，中共中央、国务院发布《数字中国建设整体布局规划》，分阶段制定目标任务，提出"到2035年数字化发展水平进入世界前列"。同年3月，中共中央、

国务院发布《党和国家机构改革方案》，提出组建国家数据局。

中国将数据提升到新型生产要素的地位，顺应了数字经济发展潮流。中国努力夯实数据要素驱动基础，维护数据主权、促进数字经济发展，积极构筑数据竞争新优势；同时，积极参与数字经济国际合作及相关规则制定，让中国数据要素发展的成果和经验惠及更多国家和人民。

在应对当前全球数字治理赤字和新兴数字领域的治理挑战上，中国走在前列。2020年，中国提出的《全球数据安全倡议》，明确政府行为规范，推动企业共担责任、合作应对安全风险。

2023年，中国发布的《生成式人工智能服务管理暂行办法》，是全球首部针对生成式人工智能的专门立法。同年，中国还向联合国提交了《中国关于全球数字治理有关问题的立场》，呼吁消除数字鸿沟、反对技术垄断。

围绕新型生产要素，积极主动开展各种探索与应对，展现了中国提升经济治理能力的决心和实干精神，将推动全球经济治理变革，有助于进一步激发全球经济潜能和活力。

2.经济治理新实践激发世界回响

中国发展新质生产力，推动制度创新和生产关系变革，在国际上引发强烈共鸣。

处理好政府和市场关系是中国经济体制改革的核心问题。习近平总书记提出"使市场在资源配置中起决定性作用、更好发挥政府作用"，引领社会主义市场经济理论和实践不断创新突破。在基础研究和关键核心技术攻坚等领域，中国着力完善党中央对科技工作统一领导的体制，健全新型举国体制，强化国家战略科技力量，优化配置创新资源；在科技成果落地转化方面，更加强调市场作用，强化企业创新主体地位，这为用好"看不见的手"和"看得见的手"带来有益启示。

在全面深化改革、完善经济治理的过程中，习近平经济思想中蕴含的"先立后破""稳中求进""以进促稳"等方法论，受到国际社会越来越多的关注。

菲律宾"亚洲世纪"战略研究所副所长安娜·马林博格－乌伊对习近平主席谈到的"积极促进产业高端化、智能化、绿色化"给予高度评价。她认为，这一部署具有前瞻性，既强调以科技、数字经济、绿色技术等赋能经济发展，又强调平衡经济增长、科技进步与可持续发展的关系①。

国际社会评价认为，中国把形成与新质生产力相适应的新型生产关系摆在重要位置，是经济治理日益走向成熟的体现。新质生产力在中国的形成和发展，反映了中国特色社会主义制度的巨大优势与生机活力，将为人类探索更好的经济治理方式提供中国方案。

（三）赋能中国式现代化，开拓人类文明新形态

人类文明的每一次演进都离不开生产力跃迁的推动。在以中国式现代化全面推进中华民族伟大复兴的新征程上，中国发展新质生产力将推动文化发展、文明进步。

1. 深刻践行"人与自然是生命共同体"

工业化创造了前所未有的物质财富，也造成了难以弥补的生态创伤，资源有限和人类需求无限的矛盾凸显，气候变化已成为人类面临的最严峻的挑战之一。依赖要素投入驱动，以低效率、高污染、粗放式增长方式为特征的传统生产力难以支持经济可持续发展。

相较于传统生产力，新质生产力重在以创新驱动实现生产力内涵型增长。其中一个维度就是以知识和信息、数据和算力为基础来推动产业

---

① 《打造中国经济向"新"力共建繁荣美好世界习近平总书记关于发展新质生产力重要论述引发海外人士热议》，新华社，2024 年 3 月 6 日

迭代升级，从而克服自然物质资源的排他性和消耗性，摆脱对资源的过度依赖。推动新一轮生产力跃迁，并不只在于科技创新本身，更在于对"人与自然是生命共同体"的深刻认知。

生态兴则文明兴、生态衰则文明衰，这一理念已在中国成为广泛共识。中国式现代化的特征之一就是人与自然和谐共生的现代化。新质生产力有利于促进绿色低碳产业形成，推动经济社会发展全面绿色转型。"先污染、后治理""控制自然、掠夺自然"的发展模式正在成为过去，以人与自然和谐共生为特征、追求永续发展的文明之路正在开启。

2. 增强现代化进程的人本主义关怀

中国式现代化是以人为本、着眼未来的新型现代化。正如习近平总书记所说："现代化的最终目标是实现人自由而全面的发展。现代化道路最终能否走得通、行得稳，关键要看是否坚持以人民为中心。"[①]

中国发展新质生产力，是为了让现代化的成果更多更公平地惠及全体人民，推动、促进人的全面发展。因此，发展新质生产力是中国发展和改善人权的一部分。

新质生产力更加重视提高劳动者素质和培育新型劳动者，使经济发展方式由投资于物向投资于人转变。中国认为，只有在更高水平、更大范围实现人口高质量发展，才能为持续培育新质生产力提供更深厚的基础。

中国式现代化是全体人民共同富裕的现代化。中国人口规模庞大，必须创造出同人口规模相匹配的社会财富。发展新质生产力有助于培育新的经济增长点和经济增长极，进而保障持续性增长，扩大社会财富总量。中国围绕发展新质生产力健全收入分配机制，有助于缩小贫富差距，

---

① 《习近平在中国共产党与世界政党高层对话会上的主旨讲话》，新华社，2023年3月15日

为实现共同富裕提供有力支撑。

新质生产力的发展还将使人类社会迎来新的经济形态，更多服务于"人的现代化"，这意味着人在现代化的生产生活中展现出更强的主体性、创造性和文明性。新质生产力的发展为实现人的全面发展提供了更大可能，也为人类的现代化增添了更强的人本主义关怀。

3. 提振全球南方的发展自信推动文明互鉴

科学技术是时代的，也是世界的。新质生产力赋能下的中国式现代化实践对全球南方来说是个好消息。中国的技术创新、产业升级和变革经验将为后发国家的现代化开拓新的现实路径，还将推动世界经济走向更加多元平衡的未来。

中国追求的不是独善其身的现代化，而是期待同包括广大发展中国家在内的各国一道，共同实现现代化。这一愿景令人向往，也充满挑战。一方面，以资本为主宰、从产业扩张走向金融扩张，已导致一些国家经济脱实向虚，贫富差距拉大。个别国家制约知识、技术、人才等创新要素流动，打压别国具有竞争力的产业，阻碍世界发展。另一方面，后发国家长期处在"比较优势陷阱"之中，难以突破"依附式现代化"的瓶颈，在生产力发展上无法实现平等自主的跃升。

如果不能在新一轮全球经济治理体系和国际经贸规则调整过程中成为重要的参与者和贡献者，就会在全球经济和产业发展的新赛道上丧失话语权和主动权，这一点对发展中国家来说尤为迫切。在国际创新生态塑造上，中国坚持为后发国家鼓与呼，共同促进创新要素全球流动，挖掘经济增长动力，主张科技成果应该造福全人类，而不应该成为限制、遏制其他国家发展的手段。中国发布《国际科技合作倡议》，倡导践行开放、公平、公正、非歧视的国际科技合作理念，促进建设全球科技共同体；提出《全球人工智能治理倡议》，呼吁各国加强信息交流和技术合作，形成具有广泛共识的人工智能框架和标准规范。

中国还致力于把"一带一路"建成创新之路，合作建设面向共建国家的科技创新联盟和科技创新基地，为各国共同发展创造机遇和平台；主张积极用好亚太经合组织中小企业机制，办好亚太经合组织专精特新中小企业国际合作论坛，不断凝聚中小企业专精特新发展共识。

面对去全球化、逆全球化的政治逆流，中国一直坚持推进高水平制度型开放，坚持推进科技创新，倡导以更深层次的大开放、大交流、大融合来实现生产力的集体跃迁。站在人类发展新的十字路口，面对世界百年变局的风云际会，中国是经济全球化的积极参与者、坚定支持者，中国发展新质生产力将为世界带来广阔的新机遇。在同心打造人类命运共同体的过程中，坚信国际社会能走出一条合作共赢的生产力跃迁之路，开启持续繁荣、和谐共生的文明新篇章。

五、各地发展新质生产力的探索实践

"各地要坚持从实际出发，先立后破、因地制宜、分类指导，根据本地的资源禀赋、产业基础、科研条件等，有选择地推动新产业、新模式、新动能发展，用新技术改造提升传统产业，积极促进产业高端化、智能化、绿色化。"[①]

——习近平

按照习近平总书记关于发展新质生产力的重要指示和党中央决策部署，中国各地立足全国发展大局，坚持从实际出发、因地制宜，在加快培育和形成新质生产力上勇于创新探索，不断取得进展，涌现出一批典

---

① 《习近平在参加江苏代表团审议时强调因地制宜发展新质生产力》，新华社，2024年3月5日

型案例和经验做法，为高质量发展提供新启示、打开新空间。

（一）摘取造船工业"皇冠上的明珠"

造船工业"皇冠上的明珠"大型邮轮建造又传来好消息。第二艘国产大型邮轮开始总装搭载，建造进入加速期。

2024年4月20日，长341米、宽37.2米、总吨位超14万吨的国产大型邮轮"2号船"，进入中国船舶集团上海外高桥造船有限公司的2号船坞，这标志着中国邮轮批量化设计建造能力基本形成。

2023年11月，首艘国产大型邮轮"爱达·魔都号"命名交付，让中国在全球大型邮轮设计建造领域有了一席之地。2024年1月，"爱达·魔都号"开启商业首航，驶入百姓生活。

放眼全球，国产大型邮轮打破了欧美国家的长期垄断；回看当下，中国巨大的消费市场和丰富的应用场景，让这些大国重器的产业化发展天高海阔。

"重器"自有乾坤大。这不仅在千百万级、千万级零部件的体量之大，更在于综合研制、集成创新的难度之大，还在于关键攻关、产业升级的带动之大。

大型邮轮、大型LNG船、航空母舰，造船工业的"三颗明珠"已经全部集齐，从这些先进制造高端装备、科技创新标志性成果中，可以梳理出中国高端制造业拾级而上、勇攀高峰的内在逻辑。

一看实践力。从国产大型邮轮的建造基地中国船舶集团上海外高桥造船有限公司，驶向全球航运市场的大型船舶数以百计，无论是超大型集装箱船，还是海洋石油钻井平台都被一一攻克，这些都是中国新型工业化发展的引领性工程，设计建造大型邮轮，代表着中国造船工业实力再上新台阶。国产大型邮轮集纳了全球1500家供应商，形成的邮轮供应链"图谱"，为大型邮轮批量化建造打下坚实基础。

二看创新力。高端装备本身就是创新能力的"试炼场"。通过大型邮轮项目，中国建立了首支邮轮设计国家队，培养了一批大型邮轮研发设计的核心骨干人才，通过基础科研与实船工程的交叉验证，攻克了邮轮总体布置、美学设计、安全返港、替代设计等多项关键技术。

一艘船就是一个创新平台、一条产业链、一扇开放窗口。2023年，中国三大造船指标实现全面增长，国际市场份额首次全部超过50%。统计数据显示，全球18种主要船型中，中国共有14种船型新接订单量位列全球第一。

三看带动力。大型邮轮以其"巨系统"工程的复杂集成和精益工艺成为造船工业高端装备的巅峰产品。高端装备本身就是创新能力的试炼场。随着批量化生产的实现，国产大型邮轮越来越本土化。上海外高桥造船有限公司在持续加强国际合作的同时不断提升本土配套率，推动建设本土邮轮配套产业集群，打造完备的邮轮产业链条。

当前，除了国产大型邮轮"2号船"，上海外高桥造船还在加快研究超大型、中小型邮轮的设计研发，以期形成邮轮产品的谱系化、规模化发展，形成一支国产大型邮轮船队。通过邮轮项目，有助于构建起集技术需求、产品开发、技术创新、技术验证、产业化于一体的工业创新体系。

（二）安徽打造量子科创高地

近年来，量子科技发展突飞猛进。在致力于打造量子信息科创高地的安徽，量子产业正在蓬勃而起，目前已集聚量子科技产业链企业60余家，居全国前列。

在中科大先进技术研究院所在的合肥高新区，云飞路因遍布着数十家量子科技产业链企业，已成为国内知名的"量子大街"。世界首条千公里级量子保密通信"京沪干线"、全球首颗量子科学实验卫星"墨子号"、实现"量子计算优越性"里程碑的"九章"量子计算原型机等均诞生于这里及附近。

2023 年，首个国家级"量子信息未来产业科技园"在合肥高新区揭牌运行。从实验室成果，迈向"量子大街"应用，再到科技园聚链成势，量子通信、量子计算、最子精密测量产业链三大方向正步入科技产业化"快车道"，提高应用领域生产力水平。

一个中部省份，如何能在量子信息新赛道上一路疾驰？

技术创新是关键。安徽已经形成包括多个研究机构的量子信息基础研究体系，近年成功构建 255 个光子的量子计算原型机"九章三号"、66 比特可编程超导量子计算原型机"祖冲之二号"等。同时，逐渐建立前沿科研"沿途下蛋"机制，布局一批科技成果转化平台，承接高校、科研院所的科技成果就地转化孵化，让量子技术得到更快发展。

场景创新是缩短基础创新和应用端距离的重要探索。安徽通过开放企业生产、政府应用等各领域的场景，为科技企业新技术、新产品和创新解决方案提供真实的应用示范机会，加速科技成果应用和迭代。

得益于政务场景的开放，2012 年，科大国盾量子在企业起步阶段，完成了合肥城域量子通信试验示范网建设。这是全球首个规模化量子通信网络，也是科大国盾量子的量子通信技术从实验室走向工程化的重要节点。如今合肥数字城域网已经建成运行，铺设网络光纤 1147 公里，覆盖 8 个核心站点、159 个用户节点，提供量子安全接入服务和数据传输服务。

企业是创新的主体，创新是企业生命活力的源泉。通过实施科技重大专项、建设创新平台、企业人才引进等方式支持量子企业发展，合肥目前的量子专利累计申请量居全国城市首位。

在国仪量子，2023 年企业研发投入占比近 30%，600 多名员工中，研发人员占比近 70%。正是有了重点研发项目、人才政策等各类支持，国仪量子坚持原始创新，突破一批关键核心技术。如今，其量子测量技术已应用至石油勘探、生命科学、航天航空等诸多领域，去年公司成交订单额超过5亿元。

（三）杭州城西科创大走廊培育增长新引擎

打开杭州地图，东起浙江大学紫金港校区，经过紫金港科技城、未来科技城、青山湖科技城，西至浙江农林大学，绵延39公里、面积约416平方公里，形成了一条宽阔的"大走廊"，这就是杭州城西科创大走廊。

通过无人机视角俯瞰大走廊，这里颇具未来感。"国之重器"超重力实验场犹如展翼的宇宙飞船，之江实验室、西湖实验室等5个浙江省实验室环绕分布，鳞次栉比的高楼里有3354家国家级高新技术企业、91个国家级科创平台、58万名专业技术人才。2023年起，这里每个工作日都能新增80家企业，为经济高质量发展提供源源不断的动力。

杭州亚残运会开幕式上点燃主火炬的"仿生手"、在亚运村地下8米深处默默巡检的四足机器狗，这些"火爆出圈"的高科技产品都来自大走廊。

走进大走廊，来到国内唯一一家脑机接口领域独角兽企业浙江强脑科技有限公司的展厅，"吉祥如意！"失去双手的强脑科技产品体验官倪敏成靠一双智能仿生手，写出了让人赞叹的毛笔字。

目前，大走廊正在致力于打造世界级数字科技产业集群与战略性新兴产业集群。在业内专家看来，多年来大走廊通过相关政策，鼓励人才引入、技术研发与引导市场应用，为产业发展积累了深厚的市场基础，已经构建了优势明显的产业环境。

"大走廊最大的特点，在于打造一个创新创业生态系统，聚齐了5大要素，有为政府、知名高校、头部领军企业、多元多层次的投资人和创业者。"每日互动董事长方毅说，这五大要素保证了产业发展的政策支持、人才输出、技术创新、资本支撑、创业项目等能够长期持续。

为更好服务企业、促进高质量发展，杭州出台了城西科创大走廊产业、人才、科技专项政策，去年以来，30 余个市直部门先后赴大走廊对接服务，在人才"蓄水池"打造、公共设施建设、整体智治方面均取得亮眼成效。

2023 年 4 月，从斩获高规格网络安全大赛一等奖，到带领团队把初创公司落户千大走廊的梦想小镇，26 岁的母浩文只用了 3 天。在母浩文看来，大走廊对他们团队项目的了解令人吃惊，这里的创业氛围、产业配套、热情服务都令他们无法拒绝。

目前，大走廊正依托创新基础优势，加速培育经济增长新引擎。2023 年，大走廊实现产业增加值 3500 亿元，其中高新技术产业增加值贡献率占比超过 85%。

（四）北京"星谷"助力航天强国梦

北京中关村，后厂村以北、东玉河以南的北清路沿线，多家商业卫星及产业链企业星罗棋布，聚集在一片叫作"星谷"的热土上。一批商业卫星从这里飞出，飞向太空，创造了商业航天多个高光时刻。

"3,2,1,点火！"2024 年 4 月 28 日，位于北京"星谷"的邀天科技公司，专门为太空卫星量身打造的氪气电推进发动机正在智能制造车间开展点火试验。

邀天科技研发总监刘同波说，这款自主研发的专用于卫星的新能源发动机，能节省 90% 推进剂、降低 40% 卫星质量，高可靠、高效率、低成本地助推卫星快速入轨。

邀天科技，这项技术背后的科技企业仅成立 6 年，已实现在轨订单、产品交付、应用数量、技术成熟度等多项领先。而这仅是北京"星谷"逐梦太空的一个缩影。

北京是中国航天事业的发源地之一。"星谷"所在的北京海淀，航天科技、航天科工、中国科学院等机构聚集，是北京"南箭北星"产业布局中"北星"的主要承载地。这里坐拥商业航天产业链企业及机构近200家，初步形成了涵盖卫星研制、卫星测控、卫星运营等卫星相关的全产业链生态。

向着最前沿的技术执着攻关，瞄准"卡脖子"领域与行业空白，以技术创新力铸就核心竞争力，塑造了"星谷"的独特优势。

"星谷"运营方中关村意谷（北京）科技服务有限公司董事长姜珂说，"星谷"的企业成立时间不长，但不少企业"小步快跑"，短短几年就完成了从"村高新"到"国高新"的跨越。

业绩节节攀升、年营业收入已突破5亿元的国科天成尝到了自主研发的甜头。不久前，其自主研发的红外组件因极高的性价比，让海外市场加急增派订单。

产品的抢手，与企业深耕光电领域、注重自主研发密不可分。国科天成董事长罗旺典感慨，创新之路是一场没有终点的马拉松。一步一个脚印向前，才能赢得一个接一个突破。

先行先试的机制创新、向前一步的主动服务，更让创新主体心无旁骛、放心发展。2024年，北京市印发《加快商业航天创新发展行动方案(2024-2028年)》，海淀区发布《建设商业航天创新高地行动计划(2024-2028年)》，统筹市区两级资源，推动产业链条提质、应用场景开放、创新生态优化。

瞄准卫星组网与通信、宇航遥感与监测等关键核心领域，北京设立北京市自然科学基金商业航天领域联合基金，支持原始创新，基金规模累计高达3.8亿元，目前北京已有7个区39家企业参与。

"星谷"的辐射力日益扩大，巩固了区域发展新优势。如今，北京海淀正向着"双百双千"的新目标进发，力争到2028年建成100万平方米产业空间，培育 100 家专精特新企业，在轨运行卫星数量超 1000 颗，商业航天产业规模超 1000 亿元，为加快实现空天信息科技领域的创新突破、托起航天强国梦贡献新力量。

（五）在光电子信息产业领域独树一帜的"中国光谷"

成立于 1988 年的武汉东湖高新区，是中国第一根光纤的诞生地、国家光电子信息产业基地，其规模和创新实力突出，被誉为"中国光谷"。目前，这里已聚集 1.6 万家光电子信息企业，涵盖光纤应用延伸的光芯屏端网全产业链，地区生产总值超 2700 亿元。

一个个"首创""第一"在此诞生。例如，全国首个 400G 相干商用硅光收发芯片、世界领先的 232 层三维闪存存储芯片、全国首台最大功率 10 万瓦的工业光纤激光器等。

一根光纤拉出世界级光电子信息产业基地。"中国光谷"聚焦"光"引领、矢志"芯"突破、推动"屏"崛起、促进"端"成长、强化"网"赋能，深入实施建链补链延链计划，打造具有国际竞争力的产业集群。

瞄准核心技术，一批位于"中国光谷"的光电子信息企业强化自主创新意识，以标准开路，不仅引领中国市场，还成功进入海外市场，牢牢掌握产业发展主导权。

武汉光迅科技股份有限公司，是中国最大的光通信器件供货商之一，也是一家专注光电子器件系统性、战略性研发的高科技企业。该企业研发人员抓住光纤通信带宽向 C＋＋波段演进的趋势，于 2020 年研制出光纤放大器产品，树立了这一领域的国际标准。

中国信科集团，通过坚持自主研发，拥有专利超 2 万件，90％为发明专利，主导制定 80 余项相关国际标准，培育了一批具备国际视野、技术精专的标准人才队伍。

"中国光谷"致力于打造一批科学研究基础设施，聚集世界各地才智、建立创新生态系统、打造开放共享的科研中心。湖北九峰山实验室便是其中之一。

"科技创新要'从 0 到 1'，更要实现'从 1 到 10'的突破。"湖北九峰山实验室主任丁琪超介绍，实验室已建成业界领先的化合物半导体基础设施，包括 9000 平方米洁净室以及一流的化合物半导体工艺、检测、材料平台等。

当前，上百个项目同时在此运转，不仅注重联合学界、产业界围绕共性关键技术的堵点进行前沿探索和技术攻关，也注重打通全产业链条中的断点，推动产学研融合发展。

在这里，孵化加速及制造基地也应运而生。在湖北九峰山实验室南面，研发办公楼、中试车间、洁净厂房、会议中心、人才公寓等设施已经启动建设，"政产学研金服用"创新共同体有望再结硕果。

（六）中国西部科技创新港打造"没有围墙的大学"

在西安交通大学的中国西部科技创新港，新型储能与能量转换纳米材料研究中心的研发平台正对多种储能与能量转换材料展开试验。这一共享技术平台成立至今，不仅取得多项技术突破，而且已孵化出 5 家新能源领域企业，涉及锂电池、钠电池、制氢、储氢等领域。

西安一九零八新能源科技有限公司就是其中之一。这家依托西安交通大学原创性科技成果转化成立的高新技术企业，为解决氢能储运行业痛点，开发出系列新型高密度固态储氢材料，可满足氢气的长期存储、长途运输等需求，并能广泛用于工业供氢、电力能源、移动应用等场景，技术已处于国际前列。

"新兴领域企业在发展初期不可能离开高校的滋养。"公司创始人、西安交通大学教授成永红表示，在中试平台建成投用之前，企业一直在与创新港一墙之隔的小区里办公，就是为了人员、信息等要素无缝对接。

在这些方面，西安交通大学发挥着重要的支撑作用。

中国西部科技创新港是陕西省和西安交通大学积极融入共建"一带一路"倡议，以及落实创新驱动发展，推动西部大开发的重要平台，位于西安西咸新区的一期，由平台区、学院区及孵化区构成，其中平台区已在理、工、医、文四大方向建立了8大平台、30个研究院和300多个科研平台，汇聚3万名科技人才。

作为西安交通大学"打破围墙办大学"理念探索的有力载体，中国西部科技创新港积极探索"一中心、一孵化、两围绕、一共享"产学研深度融合新模式，着力汇聚全球创新资源、聚焦国家发展战略、对接地方产业需求、引入各类金融资本、培育良好创新生态、培养卓越创新人才，截至目前已与170多家领军企业、科研院所开展务实合作。

更多探索在推进：强调体系化、任务型的创新联合体，描定重大目标，让学术界与产业界的联结更为紧密。通过引入金融资本，建立大企业承载的技术成果转化孵化器，做到"成熟一批、孵化一批"。发挥"双一流"大学的吸引力，建立起校企联合的海外高端人才引进、培养和使用机制，努力实现学校招、企业供、政府助、多方赢。

"在创新联合体中，校企双方通过组建'科学家＋工程师'团队，打破传统的'甲乙双方、一个项目、一纸合同、一笔经费'合作模式，加快企业主导的产学研深度融合。"西安交通大学党委书记卢建军介绍。

2021年以来，西安交通大学从3万余项存量技术成果中梳理1300项易于转化的成果推送给企业，学校转让、许可专利1000余件，已实现转化科技型企业204家。

（七）山东加速数实融合推动产业数字化

位于潍坊高新技术产业开发区的潍柴集团一号工厂总装车间内，一台台工业机器人快速"飞舞"，一辆辆自动导向车(AGV) 忙碌奔走，从物料投放到在线检测，再到生产节拍提升，实时监测、动态调整，设备的自动化率达到 99%。随处可见的电子显示屏上，反映生产进度的数字持续跳动，平均每 85 秒就有一台柴油发动机下线。作为国家首批智能制造试点示范项目，潍柴加速推进新一代信息技术与制造融合应用。视觉识别、在线检测、机器人等诸多智能制造技术被广泛应用于生产过程；信息化支撑平台犹如"数字大脑"，覆盖产品全生命周期，不仅推动生产的智能化、自动化、数字化，还延展至整个企业运营。

潍柴是山东加速数实融合、推动传统制造业改造升级发展新质生产力的一个典型代表。

近年来，山东出台《关于加快数字经济高质量发展的意见》《山东省制造业数字化转型行动方案 (2022-2025 年)》等一系列政策，创建全国首个中小企业数字化转型促进中心，推出数字产业化"十大工程"和产业数字化"八大行动"，加强数字人才队伍建设，省级层面启动设立 100 亿元专项基金，国家级工业互联网平台数量、产业数字化指数、制造业数字化转型指数、数实融合指数均居全国前列。

建设工业互联网平台，是推动产业数字化的重要抓手。山东持续开展"工赋山东"专项行动，加快工业互联网规模化应用，着力打造一批典型场景，带动企业批量数字化转型。

在有"中国轴承之乡"之称的聊城临清市，依托工业互联网平台，全市轴承产业已上"云"企业超过 400 家、设备 5000 余台套，相关企业平均用工、能耗减少 20%，竞争力大大增强。

目前，山东拥有 47 个国家级工业互联网平台，省级以上平台累计接入工业设备超 1000 万台，服务全国企业 300 余万家。

为实现政府、行业及企业间的数据聚、通、用，山东大力推进"产业大脑"建设。目前，山东已先后培育 32 个省级"产业大脑"。"产业大脑"省级能力中心已汇聚"小快轻准"产品和解决方案 957 个，服务中小微企业 49500 家。浪潮云洲参与打造的山东专用车整车"产业大脑",降低行业原材料供需匹配时间 70%,多款专用车零部件生产成本下降近四分之一。

同时,山东持续推进数字基建。截至 2023 年底,山东累计建成开通 SG 基站 20.2 万个、确定性网络 1.18 万公里,接入工业互联网标识解析国家顶级节点 29 个,注册在用物联网终端数达 2.3 亿个。

2023 年,山东全省规模以上工业企业数字化转型覆盖率达到 87.3%,中小企业特色产业集群工业互联网应用普及率达到 so%。山东规划,2024 年全省规模以上工业企业数字化转型覆盖率达到 90% 左右,到 2025 年数字经济总量占全省生产总值比重超过 50%。

(八)新能源汽车产业的重庆实践

2024 年 4 月中旬,德国总理朔尔茨访问中国,首站便来到位于中国西南的直辖市重庆,并携奔驰、宝马等汽车企业高管一起参观了博世氢动力系统(重庆)有限公司。

作为中国汽车工业重镇,重庆近年来抢抓新能源汽车产业风口,着力打造新能源汽车创新高地,形成了以 16 家新能源整车企业、约 200 家规模以上配套企业为基础,涵盖纯电、增程、混合动力、氢动力等全技术路线,融合智能网联、自动驾驶等技术的全产业链"图谱"。

2023 年,博世氢动力系统(重庆)有限公司氢动力总成产品出货量超过 1000 台,位居国内前列。基于这些成果,其母公司之一的庆铃汽车,相继推出从 4.5 吨至 18 吨不同规格的氢动力商用车,在推进前沿技术产业化方面走在前列。走进长安汽车全球研发中心,一辆辆兼具科技感与高颜值的新能源汽车依次排列,全电数字平台、高算力中央计算平台等最新科技成果也集中展示。长安汽车董事长朱华荣说,多年来公司持续加码研发,已掌握 600 余项智能互联、智能驾驶等领域技术。

在打造新能源汽车创新高地的过程中，重庆意识到这不仅需要整车及配套企业精耕细作、换道超车，还需要ICT及互联网企业的加持。瞄准产业跨界合作发展趋势，重庆近年来引入华为、百度等企业，推动前沿技术先行先试、试点示范，有力驱动了产业发展。

打开手机App一键"召唤"，一辆无人驾驶汽车旋即驶来，将乘客送达目的地后自行离去……这样的智慧出行场景，每天在重庆永川区上演。2022年，百度公司在永川率先开展全无人化自动驾驶商业运营，并以场景应用带动产业落地，陆续吸引了酷哇科技、聚速毫米波雷达等10余家企业聚集成势。

技术创新带来产品竞争力的提升。2024年一季度，重庆新能源汽车产量同比增速超过100%，预计全年产量将达到100万辆。其中，重庆赛力斯汽车首次实现季度盈利2.2亿元。得益于与华为公司联合打造问界（AITO）这一高端品牌，华为公司的汽车软硬件技术在赛力斯汽车全面开花，问界品牌累计销量接近30万辆，其中问界新M7车型累计交付超12万辆。

"当前，重庆正从整车研发制造、关键零部件配套及应用场景搭建、充换电基础设施建设等多方面持续发力，打造万亿元级智能网联新能源汽车产业集群。"重庆市经济和信息化委员会有关负责人说，重庆也正在积极推进自动驾驶及车联网创新应用，加快软件、人工智能与汽车产业深度融合，为汽车行业未来发展蓄力。

（九）粤港澳大湾区建设活跃科技集群

得益于广州"天河二号"超级计算机以及高效高精算法技术分析，香港大学副教授林赞育能更加便捷地在海蜇的病原体基因数据以及其他流行病学和生态学数据中，追踪重要病原体的起源、传播和进化。

同样在广州超算的助力下，香港科技大学海洋动力和模拟研究组甘剑平教授团队开发了新的三维、高分辨率中国海多尺度海洋环流模型，其科研成果取得了重大突破。

"过去 5 年，港科大共有超过 200 位教师使用广州超算。广州超算中心提供的平台，让我们可以做一些原来做不了的事情。"香港科技大学霍英东研究院院长高民说。

粤港澳大湾区科创资源密集、创新创业活跃。近年来，三地携手推进大湾区国际科技创新中心和综合性国家科学中心建设，促进创新要素高效联通、创新效能持续增强、创新产业蓬勃发展，不断释放科技创新的"湾区力量"。

在南方海洋科学与工程广东省实验室（广州），大湾区海洋科技力量正在展开合作。这家实验室把总部设在广州南沙，并在香港、深圳分别设立了分部，向香港分部拨付 3800 万元人民币。

"香港和内地科技交流不断扩大，各方面正在创造条件，鼓励香港科技工作者参与内地科技计划。"该实验室香港分部主任、香港科技大学海洋科学系创系主任钱培元说。

协同引才也按下"快进键"。横琴粤澳深度合作区发挥琴澳两地制度和资源叠加优势，探索琴澳协同引才新模式，充分利用澳门大学、澳门科技大学人才"蓄水池"作用，引进集聚一批具备较高专业素养、熟悉国际市场运作、有志于创新创业的人才。

粤港澳大湾区内的城市，具有各自的突出优势。广州高校和科研院所云集，基础科研能力突出，拥有国家实验室、综合类国家技术创新中心、国家重大科技基础设施等国家级重大平台。深圳企业力最优势突出，全社会研发投入的 94% 都来自企业。香港拥有世界百强大学中的 5 所，特区政府公布了《香港创新科技发展蓝图》，并在过去几年投入超 2000 亿港元，加速创新生态的蓬勃发展。

得益于城市之间优势互补，粤港澳大湾区不断激发科技集群发展的巨大潜力。世界知识产权组织 2023 年 9 月发布的 2023 年版全球创新指数 (GIi) "科技集群" 排名显示，深圳—香港—广州集群位列第二，这也是该科技集群连续 4 年排名高居全球第二位。

目前，粤港澳科技创新规则衔接、机制对接正在进一步深化，积极推动钱过境、人往来、税平衡、物流通，更好地集聚创新要素。这也意味着，在 "一国两制" 下，推动不同制度和体系之间的互动、开放，进而产生更多化学反应，让大湾区在基础科研、应用技术等方面实现更好的融合发展。

（十）成渝共建西部科学城努力形成创新高地

"目前，平台已上线仪器设备 272 台（套）、发布技术服务清单 232 项，为来自成渝及全国 100 余家集成电路设计企业提供数千次的专业服务。"天府新区集成电路设计创新公共平台企业经营发展中心负责人说。

这家位于西部（成都）科学城的公共平台，有 "芯片医院" 之称，能为企业解决概念验证、产品研发、中试生产中的技术难题，让成渝两地芯片企业大幅降低研发成本、研发周期也大大缩短。

成渝地区双城经济圈建设提出 4 年来，两地围绕建设具有全国影响力的科技创新中心，高水平共建西部科学城。

近年来，西部（成都）科学城构建形成 "一核四区多基地" 空间布局，构建 "国家实验室 + 省级实验室 + 重点实验室" 的高水平实验室体系，加快建设西部首个国家实验室，构筑学科方向关联、功能互相支撑的大装置集群。西部（重庆）科学城通过聚力打造数智科技、生命健康、新材料、绿色低碳 4 大科创高地，在人工智能、区块链、云计算、大数据等 16 个重要领域深耕发展。

围绕共建西部科学城，成渝两地相向而行，突出做优做强创新策源转化核心功能、培育壮大现代产业体系，创新资源不断汇聚、创新活力积极迸发的新格局初步成型。

一是协同布局，重大创新平台。截至今年 3 月底，川渝全国重点实验室数量已达 27 个，重大科技平台 319 个，新建国家科技创新基地 22 个，建成国家级创新平台 316 个。目前，西部科学城上万台（套）大型仪器设备已经实现开放共享，川渝联合实施的核心技术攻关项目超过 160 项，攻克了一批难题。

二是优势互补，深化产研合作。四川天府新区企业联合重庆科研院所开展科研项目 9 个，其中航天科工大数据、远望探测公司获得成都市区域合作科技项目支持；成都超算中心已与中科院重庆绿色智能研究院、重庆塞力斯汽车等 50 余家用户建立了合作关系。

三是突出特色，发力科技服务。成渝两地将科技服务作为推动技术创新和成果转化的重要抓手。例如，天府国际技术转移中心与两江新区明月湖协同创新研究院合作，在链接两地资源、推动要素互通上进一步创新探索。

以共建西部科学城为牵引，川渝科技成果转化能量正充分释放，两地汇聚科技型企业近 7 万家、高新技术企业 2.1 万家，技术合同登记成交额突破 2800 亿元。

结　语

中国共产党从诞生之日起就代表中国先进生产力的发展要求，肩负变革旧的生产关系、建立新的生产关系的历史使命。

发展新质生产力是推动高质量发展的内在要求和重要着力点。中共十八大以来，以习近平同志为核心的党中央把进一步解放和发展社会生产力作为实现中华民族伟大复兴最根本和最紧迫的任务，指引中国经济进入高质量发展阶段。在发展新质生产力、实现高质量发展、建设社会主义现代化国家这一必然的逻辑推进中，新质生产力的形成和发展将为中国顺应新一轮科技革命和产业变革趋势，努力实现社会生产力可持续跨越式发展，以高质量发展推进中国式现代化、全面建成社会主义现代化强国提供重要支撑。

生产力是人类社会发展的根本动力。面对全球发展面临的共同挑战，新质生产力将为人类社会生产力发展打开新思路新空间，不仅能够推动中国自身的现代化建设，也将惠及广大发展中国家乃至整个人类社会的现代化进程。

名词解释

1. 国家实验室体系

是指以国家实验室为核心，全国重点实验室为支撑，各类科技创新基地协同合作、良性互动的平台体系。建设结构合理、运行高效的国家实验室体系，一方面要以国家目标和战略需求为导向，加速推进国家实验室建设，建立跨学科、大协同科研组织模式；另一方面要优化整合现有国家重点实验室，通过调整、充实、整合、撤销等方式，提升创新链和产业链支撑能力。

2. 未来产业

是指由前沿科技创新驱动，当前处于萌芽阶段或产业化初期，具备成长为先导产业和支柱产业的巨大发展潜力，对未来经济社会发展具有重大引领和变革作用的前瞻性新兴产业。

3. 现代化基础设施体系

是指围绕推进中国式现代化、保障总体国家安全、构筑国际竞争新优势，在各领域基础设施发展基础之上，通过完善布局、优化结构、拓展功能和系统集成，形成的设施网络完备、枢纽节点支撑有力、装备技术先进、管理服务高效的有机整体，主要包括交通、能源、水利、信息（数字）以及生态、环境、科技、金融等基础设施。

4. 新型基础设施

是以信息网络为基础，以技术创新为驱动，提供数字转型、智能升级、融合创新等方面的基础性、公共性服务，其内涵随着新技术的成熟应用而不断拓展。当前主要包括三类：一是信息基础设施。主要是指基于新一代信息技术演化生成的基础设施，包括5G网络、数据中心等基础设施。二是融合基础设施。主要是指深度应用信息技术，促进传统基础设施转型升级，进而形成的基础设施新形态，包括智能交通物流设施等。三是创新基础设施。主要是指支撑科学研究、技术开发、产品及服务研制的基础设施，包括科学研究设施等。

5. 产业创新工程

是指推动新兴产业、未来产业发展的重要抓手，围绕重大工程项目建设、战略性产品开发、应用场景拓展等实际需求，组织实施关键核心技术攻关、中试验证能力建设、自主创新产品应用示范，一体化配置项目、基地、人才、资金等创新资源，推动产业链上中下游、大中小企业融通创新，打造具有全球竞争力的新兴产业集群，真正把创新落实到创造新的增长点上。

6. 国家战略性新兴产业集群发展工程

是指为抢抓新一轮科技革命和产业变革制高点、构建国际竞争新优势，国家部署推进的一项系统性工程。通过培育若干具有全球影响力的战略性新兴产业基地、布局一批具备国际竞争力的战略性新兴产业集群、引导地方建设和发展各具特色的战略性新兴产业生态，推动战略性新兴产业融合化、集群化、生态化发展，培育壮大新的增长点增长极，构建各具特色、优势互补、结构合理的战略性新兴产业集群梯次发展体系。

7."人工智能+"行动

"人工智能+"行动推动人工智能技术与经济社会各领域深度融合，支撑各行业应用创新，赋能百业智能化转型升级，提高生产效率，激发创新活力，重塑产业生态，培育经济发展新动能，形成更广泛的以人工智能为创新要素的经济社会发展新形态。

8.东数西算

2022 年，按照中共中央、国务院部署，围绕落实国家重大区域发展战略，根据能源结构、产业布局、市场发展、气候环境等情况，在京津冀、长三角、粤港澳大湾区、成渝，以及内蒙古、贵州、甘肃、宁夏等地布局建设国家算力枢纽节点，发展数据中心集群，引导数据中心集约化、规模化、绿色化发展。"东数西算"工程是在全国一体化统筹布局算力基础设施建设，有利于充分发挥体制机制优势，优化算力资源配置，深化东西部算力协同。

9."数据要素 X"行动

是指聚焦重点行业和领域，推动数据要素与劳动力、资本、技术等要素协同，促进数据多场景应用、多主体复用，加快多元数据融合，提高全要素生产率，开辟经济增长新空间，培育经济发展新动能。

10. 海陆空全空间无人体系市场准入建设

海陆空全空间无人体系是通过对无人机、无人车、无人船、电动垂直起降飞行器等海陆空多种无人装备及其配套基础设施一体运行和监管的新型物流运输体系。完善市场准入规则，系统性构建无人体系政策法规、标准检测认证、数据管理、运行监管等体制机制，优化空域资源、数据算力、通信频率、路权分配、国土空间等要素资源的配置方式，形成低空经济、物流交通、车路协同等领域融合发展的新动能。2022 年 1 月，经中共中央、国务院同意，国家发展改革委以市场准入特别措施的形式推动开展海陆空全空间无人体系建设。2023 年 9 月，安徽省合肥市建成全球首个全空间无人体系城市级应用示范项目。按照有关工作安排，2024 年将发布一批海陆空全空间无人体系技术标准，建设检测认证平台，在横琴粤澳深度合作区、广州市南沙新区等地推广示范经验。

参考文献

1. 韩文秀，《巩固和增强经济回升向好态势》，人民日报，2024 年 1 月

2. 国家发展改革委，《加快建设全国统一大市场为构建新发展格局提供坚强支撑》，求是，2022 年 6 月

3. 怀进鹏，《加快建设教育强国》，人民日报，2022 年 12 月

4. 习近平经济思想研究中心，《新质生产力的内涵特征和发展重点》，人民日报，2024 年 3 月

5. 孙学工、荣晨，《中国新质生产力为全球发展注入新动能，光明日报，2024 年 3 月

6. 卢延纯，《夯实数据要素驱动基础培育数据资产价格链》，价格理论与实践，2023 年第 3 期

7. 胡拥军，《前瞻布局未来产业：优势条件、实践探索与政策取向》，《改革》，2023 年第 9 期

8. 张于桔，《加快战略性新兴产业融合集群发展》，经济日报，2024 年 6 月

9. 贺俊，《新质生产力的经济学本质与核心命题》，人民论坛杂志，2024 年

10. 燕连福，《统筹教育科技人才工作推动新质生产力发展》，光明日报，2024年 4 月

11. 陈启清，《健全和完善生产要素参与分配机制》，人民网，2020 年 3 月

12. 刘志彪，《发展新质生产力为世界经济注入新活力》，光明日报，2024 年 4月

13. 吴文，《加快形成新质生产力事关中国现代化全局》，北京日报，2023 年 10月

14. 席伟健，《新质生产力将改变地缘政治格局》，环球网，2023 年 12 月

编写说明

　　《更好赋能中国繁荣世界—新质生产力的理论贡献和实践价值》智库报告课题组由新华通讯社社长、新华社国家高端智库学术委员会主任傅华任组长，新华通讯社总编辑吕岩松任副组长，新华通讯社副总编辑任卫东任执行副组长。课题组成员包括刘刚、张旭东、邹伟、安倍、傅垸、程云杰、袁军宝、商意盈、张紫赞、胡品、张辛欣、戴小河、陈炸伟、李延霞、何慧媛、梁劲、陈雍容、贾远琨、张漫子、马晓澄、王自宸、郑昕、黄兴、杨思琪、李力可等。课题组成员从新华社总社多个部门和国内分社抽调，均为从事新闻报道及研究工作的骨干力量。

　　课题自 2023 年 9 月立项启动以来，历时 9 个月学习、调研、撰写、修改、审校。课题组全体成员认真学习习近平总书记关于新质生产力系列重要论述，广泛采访权威部门和机构、专家学者、企业界人士、科研工作者等，梳理新质生产力的理论脉络和实践路径，挖掘典型案例和生动故事，精心研究写作，历经多版本修改，并征求权威部门和有关专家学者意见，最终形成此报告。

为了全人类共同的价值和尊严[①]
——中国参与全球人权治理的实践与贡献

前　言

　　人权是人类文明进步的成果和标志，尊重和保障人权是现代文明的基本精神。75年前，二战废墟中诞生的《世界人权宣言》申明对基本人权的尊重和保护。30年前，《维也纳宣言和行动纲领》明确各类人权紧密关联，发展促人权、合作促人权的理念日益深入人心。

　　新中国成立以来，特别是中共十八大以来，在习近平新时代中国特色社会主义思想指引下，中国不断总结人类社会发展经验，在建设中国特色社会主义的伟大实践中，奉行以人民为中心的人权理念，坚持将人权普遍性原则同中国实际相结合，在中国共产党的坚强领导下，成功走出了一条顺应时代潮流、适合本国国情的人权发展道路。中国历史性地

---

① 2023年9月19日发布于北京。

解决了绝对贫困问题，全面建成小康社会，建成了世界上规模最大的教育体系、社会保障体系、医疗卫生体系，少数民族、妇女、儿童、老年人、残疾人等特定群体权利得到充分保障。中国人民的人权得到前所未有的保障，中国为世界人权事业发展作出了巨大贡献。中国在不断推进自身人权事业的同时，积极支持广大发展中国家摆脱殖民统治、实现民族独立、消除种族隔离的正义事业，努力帮助发展中国家发展，进行人道主义援助，在维护世界和平与发展、推动国际人权事业发展进步等方面作出了重要贡献。中国始终坚持平等互信、包容互鉴、合作共赢、共同发展的理念，积极参与联合国人权事务，认真履行国际人权义务，广泛开展国际人权合作，以实际行动推动全球人权治理朝着更加公平公正合理包容的方向发展，为全球人权治理提供中国智慧、中国方案。

当前，人类又一次站在历史的十字路口，全球人权治理面临严峻挑战。中国主张以安全守护人权，尊重各国主权和领土完整，同走和平发展道路，践行全球安全倡议，为实现人权创造安宁的环境；以发展促进人权，践行全球发展倡议，提高发展的包容性、普惠性和可持续性，以各具特色的现代化之路保障各国人民公平享有人权；以合作推进人权，相互尊重，平等相待，践行全球文明倡议，加强文明交流互鉴，通过对话凝聚共识，共同推动人权文明发展进步。

中国践行真正的多边主义，弘扬和平、发展、公平、正义、民主、自由的全人类共同价值，推动构建人类命运共同体，为包括人权治理在内的全球治理提供了新思路、新方案、新机遇，彰显了负责任大国担当。

一、参与全球人权治理的中国实践

中国多次当选人权理事会成员国，一直以负责任的态度参与联合国人权事务，积极参与全球人权治理，努力促进国际人权事业的健康发展，其参与的程度日趋深入，参与的广度不断拓展，影响力不断扩大。

2023 年 3 月，中国在联合国人权理事会第 52 届会议上先是代表 70 多个国家就《世界人权宣言》通过 75 周年作共同发言，就落实该宣言提出明确主张；不久又代表巴西、南非等近 80 个国家就《维也纳宣言和行动纲领》通过 30 周年作共同发言，呼吁加强国际合作，重振《宣言》精神，推动实现高质量发展。全球人权治理的舞台上，中国正发挥着越来越重要的作用，作出越来越大的贡献，得到越来越多的国际认同。

（一）国际机制的"深度参与者"

早在 20 世纪 50 年代，中国提出了和平共处五项原则，并推动万隆会议在和平共处五项原则基础上通过了和平共处十项原则。1955 年 5 月，周恩来总理在全国人民代表大会常务委员会扩大会议上指出，《万隆宣言》的十项原则中也规定了尊重基本人权、尊重《联合国宪章》的宗旨和原则……这些都是中国人民的一贯主张，也是中国一贯遵守的原则。

人权是中国积极参与联合国事务和全球治理的重要领域。恢复联合国合法席位后，中国开始参与联合国人权机构的工作，包括派代表团出席相关会议，参加有关人权议题的审议，与联合国人权机构保持建设性合作关系等。改革开放以来，中国在人权领域呈现出更为积极的姿态。

自 1979 年起，中国连续 3 年作为观察员出席联合国人权委员会会议。1981 年，中国当选为人权委员会成员国。2006 年，新成立的联合国人权理事会取代人权委员会，中国即获选首届人权理事会成员，此后一直积极参选，每次参选均顺利当选，成为联合国人权理事会成立以来为数不多的五度当选的国家。

中国以建设性姿态参与人权理事会等联合国人权机制的工作，中国身影越来越多地出现在联合国各人权机构中。多名中国籍专家担任联合国经社文权利委员会、禁止酷刑委员会、消除种族歧视委员会、消除对妇女歧视委员会、残疾人权利委员会等多个人权条约机构的委员。

中国恪守国际法原则，认真履行国际人权义务。截至 2022 年 7 月，中国先后批准或加入了 29 项国际人权文书，包括 6 项联合国核心人权条约。中国全面履行条约义务，及时提交履约报告，参加各条约机构的审议，展现了在人权议题上的开放和自信。

2009 年 2 月，中国首次参加联合国人权理事会国别人权审议。在审议会上，中国代表首先介绍了中国人权事业发展的状况，在随后的互动对话中，60 个国家代表相继发言，多数国家代表认为，中国的人权报告具有"建设性"，"透明、公开"，称赞中国在人权领域取得了"巨大的、令人震惊的"成就。截至目前，中国已顺利完成联合国人权理事会三轮国别人权审议。

中国还同联合国人权事务高级专员及其办公室、人权理事会特别机制等积极拓展合作，推动其公正、客观地开展工作，与各国进行建设性对话。近年来，中国邀请一些国家驻日内瓦使节、联合国官员参访新疆，通过会见会谈、座谈交流、实地走访等多种方式，全面加深了对中国人权发展道路的理解和认同，亲身感受了一个社会安全稳定、发展持续向好、人民安居乐业的真实新疆。

（二）治理规则的"共同建设者"

人权理念和规范是当代全人类共同价值的重要表达方式，世界各国对人权条约的接受和实施是促进和保护人权的重要手段。中国为促进当代人权理念和规范，推动完善人权治理规则体系，弘扬全人类共同价值作出了持续努力。

中国多次派代表参与国际人权法律文书的起草工作。先后参与了《禁止酷刑和其他残忍、不人道或有辱人格的待遇或处罚公约》《儿童权利公约》《残疾人权利公约》等重要国际人权文书的制定，中国提出的意见和修正案受到各方重视，为这些规则的起草、修改和完善作出重要贡献。作为世界上最大的发展中国家，中国坚持把生存权、发展权作为首要的基本人权，在国际舞台上反映广大发展中国家最根本的人权需求。作为主要推动者之一，中国参与了《发展权利宣言》的起草工作，先后推动联合国人权委员会和人权理事会就实现发展权问题进行磋商，致力于推动落实发展权的机制。

1993 年，中国代表参加维也纳世界人权大会，并参加了《维也纳宣言和行动纲领》的讨论和起草，提出许多建设性意见，为《维也纳宣言和行动纲领》的起草和通过作出贡献。中国积极参与劳工保护等人权相关领域国际文书的制定。

（三）交流合作的"积极倡导者"

长期以来，中国积极倡导、大力推进人权领域对外交流交往合作，致力于在平等和相互尊重的基础上开展人权交流与合作。自 20 世纪 90 年代起，中国陆续与 20 多个国家建立人权对话或磋商机制，同德国、瑞士、匈牙利、希腊、欧盟等西方国家和地区组织进行人权对话或交流，同俄罗斯、埃及、南非、巴西、马来西亚、巴基斯坦、白俄罗斯、古巴、非盟等发展中国家和地区组织开展人权磋商。中国人权研究会等人权领域非政府组织在国际舞台愈发活跃，组团赴海外交流访问，邀请多国人权领域官员和专家学者来华交流访问。2023 年 3 月至 4 月，在联合国人权理事会第 52 届会议期间，中国多家社会组织通过线上线下方式积极参会发言，举办了"新时代的少数民族权利保障""可持续发展视角下的女性赋能""中国的人权理念与实践"等主题边会，宣介中国人权观、具体实践与成就，揭批美西方严重侵犯人权问题，在人权理事会积极发出中国民间声音。

中国积极创设平台、搭建载体，促进人权领域交流合作，先后多次举办"北京人权论坛""南南人权论坛""中欧人权研讨会""国际人权文博会",以及"纪念《发展权利宣言》通过 30 周年国际研讨会"等国际会议,推动各方在人权问题上扩大共识、减少分歧,增进相互了解与理解。这些对外交流交往与合作开辟、拓展了交流渠道,推动中国与相关国家在人权议题上相互交流借鉴。

2023 年 6 月 14 日至 15 日,全球人权治理高端论坛在北京举行,来自近百个国家和包括联合国机构在内的国际组织的 300 余名中外嘉宾出席论坛。

与会外宾参访了北京市东城区前门三里河公园、颜料会馆等地,对三里河地区的历史文脉保护、环境整治和人居环境改善赞不绝口,了解到东城区会馆活化利用等文化创新举措,观看了京剧表演。"人们不仅享有公民权利和政治权利,同时也享有经济、社会和文化权利。中国对历史文化的保护和传承令我印象非常深刻,"塞拉利昂人权委员会主席帕特里西亚·纳尔苏·恩达内玛说,"除了文化保护外,还有一点让我印象深刻,那就是这里很干净。享有清洁、健康和可持续的环境是一项基本人权。"

与会嘉宾在高端论坛上畅谈对全球人权治理的看法,充分肯定中国在人权实践和推动世界人权事业发展方面取得的成就。联合国经济、社会及文化权利委员会副主席兼报告员阿巴希泽表示,中国在保护人权方面取得诸多成就,例如减贫,"这不仅仅是中国的重大成就,也代表了人类的重大胜利"。美国《全球策略信息》杂志社华盛顿分社社长威廉·琼斯说,中国在保护公民人权方面发挥的作用值得高度赞扬。更重要的是,中国呼吁将发展作为一项人权,受到了国际社会的广泛欢迎。美国库恩基金会主席罗伯特·库恩称赞道:"这是一场切中肯綮、与时俱进的盛会。"

（四）治理变革的"重要推动者"

2017 年 3 月，中国代表在联合国人权理事会第 34 次会议上代表 140 个国家发表题为"促进和保护人权，共建人类命运共同体"的联合声明，引发在场外交官的广泛共鸣。巴基斯坦常驻联合国副代表阿夫塔卜·库雷希说："在当前全球面临诸多挑战的情况下，我们尤其应该感谢中国为我们这个'地球村'所提供的这一理念。"

中国在推进自身人权发展的同时，始终重视参与全球人权治理体系变革，推动全球人权治理朝着更加公平、公正、合理、包容的方向发展。

中国积极参与联合国人权机构的改革工作，在设立联合国人权理事会的磋商和最后表决过程中发挥了积极作用，提出的一系列主张得到绝大多数国家认同。中国还支持联合国人权理事会设立发展权、粮食权、单边强制措施问题等专题性特别机制；倡导召开关于粮食安全、国际金融危机的特别会议，积极推动完善国际人权机制。

日内瓦时间 2007 年 6 月 18 日晚上 12 点，人权理事会就关于人权理事会建章立制问题的一揽子方案达成一致，中国代表团一直以建设性姿态积极参与有关谈判磋商，特别在涉及发展中国家重大利益的问题上坚持原则，敢于仗义执言，得到广大发展中国家的广泛赞誉。舆论普遍认为，中国代表团在谈判中展示出大国风范，表现灵活，促成各方达成一致，彰显了负责任的大国形象。

多年来，中国立足自身人权实践，提出了一系列符合时代潮流、呼应国际社会关切的建设性理念和倡议，被广为接受。

针对全球人权保障水平提升困境、人权合作困境、疫后复苏中经社文权利保障面临困难等现实挑战，中国多次推动联合国人权理事会通过"在人权领域促进合作共赢"决议，呼吁各方开展建设性对话与合作，加强人权技术援助；多次推动通过"发展对享有所有人权的贡献"决议，呼吁各国实现以人民为中心的发展；推动通过"殖民主义遗留问题对享有人权的负面影响"决议，呼吁消除任何形式的殖民主义，解决殖民主义遗留问题；推动通过"疫情背景下促进和保护经社文权利、消除不平等"决议，呼吁各国促进和保护经社文权利，采取包容性措施应对疫情并推进疫后复苏。

自 2017 年以来，在中国推动下，构建人类命运共同体理念被十余次纳入联合国人权理事会决议，成为国际人权话语体系的重要组成部分。

二、推动世界人权事业发展的中国贡献

人权是具体的、历史的、现实的。尊重和保障人权需要主动创造实现的条件。安全和平的环境、发展进步的动力以及公平正义的秩序等是人权事业得以可持续推进的重要前提。中国积极弘扬和平、发展、公平、正义、民主、自由的全人类共同价值，推动本国人权事业发展的同时，以立己达人、兼济天下的情怀为世界人权事业贡献中国力量，始终做世界和平的建设者、全球发展的贡献者、国际秩序的维护者、人类文明进步的促进者。

（一）夯实全球人权保障的发展基础

发展是解决一切问题的总钥匙，是人权保障的基础，是实现人民幸福的关键。长期以来，中国注重推动广大发展中国家人民生存权、发展权的实现，在基础设施及教育、卫生、农业等领域向发展中国家和地区提供支援和帮助，通过"一带一路"国际合作，为推进联合国 2030 年可持续发展议程助力加速，为进一步夯实全球人权保障的发展基础贡献力量。

所罗门群岛首都霍尼亚拉，国家转诊医院理疗室外经常排起长队，患者是来找中国援助所罗门群岛医疗队针灸大夫的。常常来看病的当地

居民雷克斯·福科纳说，他之前头疼得厉害，一疼就是几个小时，只能靠吃药缓解。针灸大夫给他开了一个疗程十次治疗，他做完六次已感觉缓解了不少。

所罗门群岛是最不发达国家之一，医疗卫生条件较为落后，基层诊所或地区诊所往往只有护士和护士助理提供医疗服务，只有省级以上医院才有医生。中国自 2019 年同所罗门群岛建交之后，于 2022 年初开始向所罗门群岛派出援助医疗队，目前是第二批共 8 名队员在当地工作。在中国医疗队的帮助下，当地医院实现了多个第一次——第一次双镜联合尿道断裂修复术、第一次输尿管镜下碎石取石术、第一次尿道内切开联合前列腺电切术、第一次开展三代药物溶栓治疗、第一次临时起搏器植入……

2023 年是中国援外医疗队派遣 60 周年，自 1963 年向阿尔及利亚派出第一支医疗队以来，中国已累计向全球 76 个国家和地区派遣医疗队员 3 万人次，诊治患者 2.9 亿人次。今年，几内亚比绍总统恩巴洛向中国援几比医疗队集体授予"合作与发展国家荣誉勋章"，老挝国防部授予中国军队第八批援老医疗专家组"老挝人民军英勇勋章"，柬埔寨卫生部向中国援柬中医抗疫医疗队授予"柬埔寨王国骑士勋章"。

新中国成立伊始，在国家百废待兴、财力紧张的情况下，中国即开始向有关国家提供援助，为发展中国家争取民族独立和人民解放、促进经济社会发展提供有力支持。坦桑尼亚和赞比亚人民至今无法忘记，二十世纪六七十年代，正值两国独立后致力于发展民族经济和支持本地区国家民族解放运动之时，是中国克服重重困难，提供无息贷款、派遣数万名专家和铁路工人奔赴非洲，援建坦赞铁路。这条贯通东非和中南非的"自由之路"，有力推动了当地经济社会发展，改善了民生。

改革开放以来，中国对外援助内容更加丰富、形式更加多样。新时代中国对外援助资金规模稳步增长，进一步扩大援助范围，并更多向亚洲、非洲地区最不发达国家和发展中国家倾斜。中国提供的对外援助资金形式多样，包括提供无偿援助、无息贷款、优惠贷款、成套设备等。多年来，中国设立并通过"全球发展和南南合作基金""中国—联合国和平与发展基金"等渠道与联合国开发计划署、世界粮食计划署、世界卫生组织、联合国儿童基金会等近 20 个国际组织和国际非政府组织联合实施援助项目，惠及亚洲、非洲、拉丁美洲等地区一百多个国家的数千万民众。

中国授人以鱼，也授人以渔。

从非洲到大洋洲，菌草技术发明人林占熺教授带领团队将中国菌草技术带到斐济、莱索托、尼日利亚、卢旺达、厄立特里亚等国家，积极开展国际扶贫合作，帮助当地人脱贫致富。在巴布亚新几内亚，它被称作"林草"，以表达对中国扶贫专家的感激。莱索托的民歌这样唱："有人说，它是野草；有人说，它是生命；它，是食物，也是药物；它，是希望的象征……"菌草帮助一些国家突破了多年的农业发展瓶颈，为全球 100 多个国家创造绿色就业机会，得到第 73 届联合国大会主席埃斯皮诺萨的赞许。

中国救急，也救穷。

中国不断加大技术和人力资源开发合作等方面的援助力度，为发展中国家能力建设贡献中国经验和中国方案，帮助提升治理能力、规划水平和行业发展能力，为发展中国家的发展事业培养治理人才和技术力量。例如，中国帮助格林纳达制定国家发展战略规划；与古巴共同开展工业中长期发展规划建议联合编制；为津巴布韦提供经济特区、国企改革等政策咨询；帮助柬埔寨制定国家路网规划和现代农业发展规划等。与卢旺达、吉尔吉斯斯坦、萨尔瓦多、巴布亚新几内亚、特立尼达和多巴哥等 36 国签署了人力资源开发合作谅解备忘录，根据不同国家的实际需求，有针对性地提供能力建设支持。同联合国设立统计能力开发信托基金，为 59 个发展中国家的近 900 名政府统计人员提供培训等。

中国通过共享科技成果、推动技术转移、提升职业技能等，帮助发展中国家提升科技创新能力和产业职业技能。例如，实施千余项政府间科技交流项目，通过国际杰出青年计划，邀请埃及、巴基斯坦、缅甸、印度等国 755 名青年科学家来华开展科研工作，培训来自 100 多个发展中国家和地区的学员 7700 余人。中国的菌草技术在全球 100 多个国家落地生根，为当地创造了数十万个绿色就业机会。在全球发展和南南合作基金支持下，联合国粮农组织、世界粮食计划署等实施了近 50 个三方合作项目，助力相关发展中国家提升粮食安全水平和农业综合生产能力。中国作为负责任大国，就全球发展事业和国际发展合作，向世界提供重要公共产品，为各国聚焦发展、团结发展、共同发展提供了行动指南。2013 年，习近平主席提出"一带一路"倡议，将中国的发展融入全球发展，带动世界各国共同发展，推进各国人民发展权的实现。

2021 年 12 月，"一带一路"标志性工程中老铁路正式开通运营，老挝人民变"陆锁国"为"陆联国"的梦想终成现实。通车仪式上，曾担任公共工程与运输部部长的老挝国会副主席宋玛·奔舍那感慨万千："中国不是第一个说要来老挝修铁路的，但却是唯一实实在在来老挝修好了铁路的。"在"一带一路"沿线，类似合作项目还有很多。从马尔代夫中马友谊大桥、克罗地亚佩列沙茨大桥到莫桑比克马普托跨海大桥，从蒙内铁路、亚吉铁路到雅万高铁……一个个"国家地标""民生工程""合作丰碑"，铺就了共同发展的康庄大道。日本前首相鸠山由纪夫认为，共建"一带一路"能够通过促进周边地区经济发展，防范纷争于未然。

十年来，"一带一路"倡议已成为深受欢迎的国际公共产品和国际合作平台，迄今已吸引了世界上超过四分之三的国家参与其中。十年来，"一带一路"倡议拉动了近万亿美元的投资，形成了 3000 多个合作项目，为共建国家创造了 42 万个工作岗位。

2021年9月，习近平主席提出全球发展倡议，强调坚持发展优先、坚持以人民为中心、坚持普惠包容、坚持创新驱动、坚持人与自然和谐共生、坚持行动导向，倡导构建全球发展共同体，成为中国向世界提供的又一重要公共产品。联合国秘书长古特雷斯点赞：全球发展倡议对促进全球平等和平衡可持续发展具有重要积极意义。

这一重大倡议回应了世界人民对和平发展、公平正义、合作共赢的现实需求，一经提出就得到联合国等国际组织和众多国家的响应，目前已经取得一系列早期收获：一是广泛凝聚了推进倡议合作、加快落实联合国2030年议程的国际共识。目前已有包括联合国在内的100多个国家和国际组织支持倡议，70多个国家参与在联合国平台成立的"全球发展倡议之友小组"，倡议写入中国同东盟、中亚、非洲、拉美、太平洋岛国等合作文件。二是资金举措逐步落地。总额40亿美元的"全球发展和南南合作基金"已落地实施，中国—联合国粮农组织第三期南南合作信托基金正式启动。三是成立了全球发展促进中心网络、世界职业技术教育发展联盟、国际民间减贫合作网络等合作平台，打造各方在农业、教育、抗疫、应对气候变化等领域的合作网络，推进各领域合作机制建设。

目前，全球发展倡议项目库建设正在有序推进，首批清单中50个务实合作及1000期能力建设项目进展积极，涵盖减贫、粮食安全、工业化等领域。四是发展知识分享不断加强。中方发布《全球发展报告》，正加快建设全球发展知识网络，积极开展各国间治国理政和发展经验交流。

（二）守护全球人权保障的安全环境

人人有权享有和平，从而使所有人权得到促进和保护，使发展得以充分实现——2016年第71届联合国大会通过《和平权利宣言》，庄严宣布人人有权享有和平，进一步确认和发展了和平权。

中国始终是维护世界和平的坚定力量。

2016 年 5 月 31 日晚，第四批马里维和工兵分队所在的加奥任务区营地突然遭到满载炸药的汽车炸弹袭击。当时，正在执勤的申亮亮迅速报告敌情，鸣枪示警，生死瞬间他将战友推开，自己却壮烈牺牲，年仅 29 岁。

2015 年 1 月，中国军队向联合国南苏丹特派团派遣一支 700 人的步兵营，这是中国军队首次成建制派遣步兵营赴海外执行维和任务。

2016 年 7 月的一天，南苏丹爆发激烈交火，导致中国第二批维和步兵营失去了两名战士：33 岁的四级军士长杨树朋和 22 岁的下士李磊……

中国自 1990 年起参加联合国维和行动，30 多年来，中国军队已派出官兵 5 万余人次，赴 20 多个国家和地区参加联合国维和行动，先后有 25 名维和人员献出宝贵生命。

目前，中国已经是联合国安理会常任理事国中派出维和人员最多的国家，也是联合国维和行动第二大出资国。2023 年 5 月 29 日是联合国维和人员国际日，也是联合国开展维和行动 75 周年。联合国负责维和事务的副秘书长让－皮埃尔·拉克鲁瓦盛赞中国为联合国维和事业发挥了重要作用，认为中国坚定不移地支持联合国维和事业，作出了"极其宝贵的贡献"。

2023 年"六一"国际儿童节前夕，孟加拉国 12 岁女孩阿里法·沁收到了一份极为特殊的节日礼物。习近平主席复信阿里法·沁，鼓励她努力学习、追求梦想，传承好中孟传统友谊。

时间回拨到 2010 年 11 月 9 日，中国海军"和平方舟"号医院船抵达孟加拉国东南部港口城市吉大港，开始对孟展开为期一周的医疗服务。

当时，当地一位孕妇分娩在即，却因长期患有心脏病而生命垂危。

孟方紧急向"和平方舟"求助，中国医生顶着巨大压力为孕妇实施剖腹产手术。孩子出生后，中国医生在病房又守护了两天，直到母女情况平稳才离开。父亲安瓦尔·霍森给孩子取名为沁（Chin），在孟加拉语中是"中国"的意思，就是希望女儿记住中国。

2013 年，"和平方舟"号医院船第二次到访孟加拉国，医生为沁做了全面体检；2017 年，当年手术的麻醉医师盛睿方随中国海军远航访问编队对孟加拉国进行友好访问，在码头见到了沁，沁第一次叫盛睿方"中国妈妈"；2019 年 12 月，沁及家人来到中国，登上了靠泊在舟山某军港的"和平方舟"号……自沁出生后，来自中国的关怀从未间断，她与中国的故事也越写越长。

截至 2023 年 6 月，中国海军"和平方舟"号医院船已先后 10 次走出国门，航行 26 万余海里，服务 43 个国家和地区，为 25 万余人次提供医疗服务，实施手术 1400 余例。如今，这艘满载着国际人道主义精神的"大白船"，将和平和友谊的种子撒向世界各地，早已成为名副其实的生命之舟、和平之舟、友谊之舟。

中华民族是爱好和平的民族，中国人民是爱好和平的人民，走和平发展道路的自信与自觉，来源于中国自身独特的和平基因。早在 20 世纪 50 年代，中国就与印度、缅甸共同倡导和平共处五项原则。近年来，中国在朝核、伊朗核、叙利亚问题解决进程中贡献中国智慧，提出中国方案，发挥着建设性作用。中国积极奉行和平外交思想，注重与各国和平共处，积极倡导共同、综合、合作、可持续的安全观，致力于推动南南合作和南北对话，努力缩小南北差距，提出全球安全倡议，为世界持久和平与发展、为维护全世界人民的和平权不断贡献中国力量。

中国积极参与国际执法安全合作，在联合国、国际刑警组织、上海合作组织等国际和地区组织框架下加强合作，打击一切恐怖主义、分裂主义、极端主义犯罪和毒品犯罪。中国还积极参与国际军控与裁军进程，加入《不扩散核武器条约》等数十个国际军控条约和机制；在乌克兰危机问题上，中国始终根据事情本身的是非曲直独立自主决定立场，积极劝和促谈。

和平是人权事业发展的重要前提，一个不断发展壮大的中国始终是世界和平的重要守护力量。2022 年 4 月，习近平主席在博鳌亚洲论坛上郑重提出全球安全倡议，系统阐述了中方促进世界安危与共、维护世界和平安宁的立场主张，强调人类是不可分割的安全共同体，倡导以共同、综合、合作、可持续的安全观为理念指引，以相互尊重为基本遵循，以安全不可分割为重要原则，以构建安全共同体为长远目标，走出一条对话而不对抗、结伴而不结盟、共赢而非零和的新型安全之路。斯洛文尼亚前总统图尔克认为，全球安全倡议的提出恰逢其时，为全球安全对话与合作提供了强有力的理念框架。

一年来，全球安全倡议的内涵不断丰富，得到越来越多国际社会成员的认同和接受，为弥补人类和平赤字、应对国际安全挑战贡献了中国智慧、中国方案。2023 年 2 月，中国发布《全球安全倡议概念文件》，进一步阐释了倡议的核心理念与原则、重点合作方向及合作平台和机制。中国积极开展斡旋外交，相继发布了《关于政治解决乌克兰危机的中国立场》《关于阿富汗问题的中国立场》等文件，坚定站在和平一边。2023 年 3 月 10 日，中国、沙特、伊朗三方签署并发表联合声明，宣布沙伊双方同意恢复外交关系。这是中国有力践行全球安全倡议的一次成功实践，为地区国家通过对话协商化解矛盾分歧、实现睦邻友好树立了典范。由此，中东掀起一轮"和解潮"。阿拉伯国家联盟助理秘书长赛义德·阿布·阿里说，阿拉伯国家期待中国在维护中东地区及全球和平中发挥重要作用。

中国还积极推进国际安全对话交流，如推动非洲地区国家举办首届非洲之角和平会议，成功主办两届中东安全论坛，还在上海合作组织、亚洲相互协作与信任措施会议、东亚合作机制等多边平台积极推动各方开展安全领域交流合作等。

中国积极致力于同各方开展抗疫、反恐、生物、网络、粮食、气候变化等非传统安全领域合作。在二十国集团框架下提出国际粮食安全合作倡议，推动通过《金砖国家粮食安全合作战略》；中国—太平洋岛国防灾减灾合作中心已于 2023 年 2 月正式启用，成为中国在全球安全倡议框架下帮助发展中国家应对非传统安全挑战的又一有力行动。白俄罗斯总统卢卡申科评价说，"中国是维护世界和平的中流砥柱"。

（三）捍卫全球人权治理的公道正义

当今世界，发展中国家人口占 80% 以上，全球人权事业发展离不开广大发展中国家的共同努力。冷战结束后，面对西方国家以人权为幌子干涉别国内政，发展中国家积极参与国际人权对话，希望通过国际合作消除国际人权活动中的对抗。

发展中国家强调人权的普遍性、客观性和非选择性，主张通过合作与协商的方式促进人权，在推进人权治理的时候考虑现实世界在政治、经济、社会和文化上的多样性，认为人权不可分割，既包括公民权利和政治权利，也包括经济、社会、文化权利；既包括个人权利，也包括集体权利……1993 年第二次世界人权大会通过《维也纳宣言和行动纲领》，在一定程度上反映了广大发展中国家的人权观和人权主张，是包括中国在内的发展中国家不断为公平正义作斗争的结果。

2023 年 6 月 14 日，到访的巴勒斯坦总统阿巴斯在与习近平主席会谈时说："我谨代表巴勒斯坦人民衷心感谢中方长期以来为巴勒斯坦人民恢复民族合法权利正义事业提供的大力支持和无私帮助。"阿巴斯总统一句"中国是巴方信赖的朋友和伙伴"，表达了对中方长期在多边场合为巴方仗义执言、主持公道的深切认同。

历史上，中国与广大发展中国家有着相似的命运和经历。现如今，在发展经济、改善民生、提高生存权发展权等各项基本人权保障上又有着共同的要求，这些都决定了中国与广大发展中国家在人权问题上有许多相同或相似的理念和主张。中国一贯主持正义，在捍卫第三世界国家的民族自决权和制止大规模侵犯人权方面作出了不懈的努力。在公正合理地解决柬埔寨问题、阿富汗问题、巴勒斯坦和阿拉伯被占领土问题等问题上，中国多年来坚持不懈的努力是众所周知的。2023 年 7 月 5 日，中国代表在联合国人权理事会第 53 届会议就叙利亚问题发言，表示和平与安宁是人权的最大保障，推进政治解决是叙利亚问题的唯一出路。中国代表强调，人权理事会讨论叙利亚问题时，不能忘记美国、英国等对叙人民所受苦难应负的责任。中方敦促上述国家停止在叙境内非法驻扎、非法开展军事行动，停止对叙单边制裁，还叙人民以真正的人权、财富、自由和尊严。作为安理会常任理事国，中国在安理会相关表决中使用的否决权中，大多与叙利亚问题有关。中国始终根据是非曲直，从维护叙利亚人民利益出发，说公道话，办公道事，捍卫了国际公平正义。

主权平等是全球人权治理的基础。在全球人权治理中，要维护人权，必须尊重主权、反对霸权，要坚决反对人权政治化倾向，坚持各国不分大小、强弱、贫富一律平等，以平等伙伴的姿态参与全球的人权交流与对话，努力实现合作共赢，共同为全球人权治理作出贡献。作为国际社会重要一员，中国主持公道正义，多次代表观点相近国家在联合国人权理事会上作共同发言；针对西方国家的无端抹黑，勇于回击，讲述真实的中国人权故事；揭露西方国家种族主义、枪支暴力、强迫劳动、侵犯土著人权利等人权劣迹；坚决反对一些国家动辄对他国采取单边制裁、封锁的霸凌行径……这些实实在在的行动，不仅坚定捍卫了国际公平正义，维护了发展中国家主权和尊严，也有力推动了国际人权交流合作和全球人权治理健康有序发展。

（四）促进不同人权文明的交流互鉴

人权是人类文明进步的成果和标志，尊重和保障人权是现代文明的基本精神。经过长期艰苦奋斗，中国成功走出了一条顺应时代潮流、适合本国国情的人权发展道路。中国人权发展道路，是中国特色社会主义道路在人权领域的重要体现，丰富发展了人类人权文明，为人类进步事业贡献了中国力量、中国智慧、中国方案。

中国式现代化深深植根于中华优秀传统文化，澎湃着中华文明的蓬勃生命力，其实践路径以实现人的自由全面发展为依归，蕴含着深刻而丰富的人权思想，为世界人权事业发展和理念创新注入了中华文明的力量。在"人口规模巨大"的现代化实践中，可以感知"民惟邦本，本固邦宁"的民本思想；在"全体人民共同富裕"的不懈追求中，可以发现"国之称富者，在乎丰民"的治理理念；在"物质文明和精神文明相协调"的统筹兼顾中，可以体会厚德载物、自强不息的风范品格；在"人与自然和谐共生"的扎实行动中，可以感悟道法自然、天人合一的发展理念；在"走和平发展道路"的坚定抉择中，可以读懂讲信修睦、天下大同的社会理想。博大精深的中华文明，既造福中国人民，又为世界提供借鉴。

在大航海时代所开启的"世界历史"进程中，关于现代化道路、文明形态多样性与单一性的思辨从未停止。不同于"文明优越论""文明冲突论"，中国始终从全世界人民的真正福祉出发，主张不同文明包容共存、交流互鉴。"一个国家、一个民族对世界和人类作出的贡献，不仅在于创造了多少物质，还在于提出了什么理念。"希腊前总统帕夫洛普洛斯由衷赞赏中国的文明观。

2014年3月27日，习近平主席在联合国教科文组织总部发表演讲，鲜明阐释新时代中国的文明观，深刻指出："文明交流互鉴，是推动人类文明进步和世界和平发展的重要动力。"赢得现场热烈掌声和深切认同。"中国领导人的远见与联合国教科文组织的使命不谋而合。"时任联合国教科文组织总干事博科娃评论说。

2019年5月，由中国倡导举办的亚洲文明对话大会在北京举行。"以多样共存超越文明优越，以和谐共生超越文明冲突，以交融共享超越文明隔阂，以繁荣共进超越文明固化……"写入亚洲47个国家和世界其他国家及国际组织1000多名与会代表发表的成果文件。中国始终致力于为不同文明平等对话、包容互鉴提供平台。

2023年3月，习近平主席首提全球文明倡议，对世界各国发出殷切呼吁，"充分挖掘各国历史文化的时代价值，推动各国优秀传统文化在现代化进程中实现创造性转化、创新性发展"。全球文明倡议着眼于推动文明交流互鉴、促进人类文明进步，是中国为完善全球治理、推动构建人类命运共同体作出的新的重要贡献，体现了中国维护世界持久和平发展、促进人类文明不断进步的坚定追求。

三、丰富人类人权文明形态的中国智慧

尊重和保障好本国人权，是中国参与全球人权治理的基础。党的十八大以来，中国政府把尊重和保障人权作为治国理政的一项重要工作，推动人权事业取得历史性成就，实现了第一个百年奋斗目标，全面建成小康社会，历史性地解决了绝对贫困问题，对全球减贫贡献率超过70%，提前10年完成联合国2030年可持续发展议程减贫目标，直接加速了国际减贫进程，对世界人权进步事业作出重要贡献，为中国人权事业发展打下了更为坚实的物质基础。

中国不断发展全过程人民民主，推进人权法治保障，坚决维护社会公平正义，人民享有更加广泛、更加充分、更加全面的民主权利；中国推动实现更加充分、更高质量的就业，建成了世界上规模最大的教育体系、社会保障体系、医疗卫生体系，大力改善人民生活环境质量，在幼

有所育、学有所教、劳有所得、病有所医、老有所养、住有所居、弱有所扶等各方面不断取得新进展；中国坚持人民至上、生命至上，有力应对新冠疫情，最大限度保护了人民生命安全和身体健康……自主探索实现路径的中国人权实践取得巨大成功，其成功的底层逻辑来自人民至上的价值坚守、求真务实的实践理性和开放包容的人权自信。

从道义层面看，人是人权发展事业的核心关切。以人民对美好生活的向往为奋斗目标，坚持把实现好、维护好、发展好最广大人民的根本利益作为发展的出发点和落脚点，不断增强人民群众获得感、幸福感、安全感，是中国共产党执政的核心价值所在。坚持人民在人权事业中的主体地位，把人民利益摆在至高无上的位置，让人民过上好日子，使发展成果更多更公平地惠及全体人民，让每个人更好地发展自我、幸福生活，是中国实现人人享有更加充分人权的真谛所在。中华人民共和国成立70多年来，中国的人权事业发展取得巨大成就，生动诠释了以人民为中心的人权理念，这是中国人权道路道义精髓之所在。从实践层面看，人权是一定历史条件下的产物，也会随着历史的发展呈现出渐进性和多样性。各国发展阶段、经济发展水平、文化传统、社会结构不同，所面临的人权发展任务和应采取的人权保障方式也会有所不同。中国人没有照搬别国的做法，而是基于自身实践提出生存权、发展权是首要的基本人权，坚持把人权的普遍性原则同本国实际相结合，走符合自身国情的人权发展道路。

从开放维度看，中国基于70多年人权发展成就形成了系统的以人民为中心的人权理念，也与世界各国开展人权合作交流，相互借鉴，互通有无，在强调和平、发展、公平、正义、民主、自由的全人类共同价值的基础上，汇聚国际人权合作的最大公约数，提出构建人类命运共同体等重大理念，向国际人权事业发展贡献中国智慧和中国方案，为推动全球人权治理向着更加公平公正合理包容的方向发展发挥了重要作用。

（一）人权事业的人民性

人民性是中国人权发展道路最显著的特征。"一国人权状况好不好，关键看本国人民利益是否得到维护，人民的获得感、幸福感、安全感是否得到增强，这是检验一国人权状况的最重要标准。"中国保障人民民主权利，充分激发广大人民群众积极性、主动性、创造性，让人民成为人权事业发展的主要参与者、促进者、受益者，切实推动人的全面发展、全体人民共同富裕取得更为明显的实质性进展。中国要实现的人权，不是抽象的概念，而是实实在在的幸福生活；不是一部分人或少数人享有的特权，而是广大人民群众享有的普惠性人权。多年来，中国坚持以人民为中心的发展思想，把增进人民福祉、保障人民当家作主、促进人的全面发展作为发展的出发点和落脚点，有效保障了人民发展权益。中国把人民幸福作为最大的人权，使人权建设更加具体可感，形成的"目标—实践"逻辑清晰可循，是一种符合新时代发展、崭新的人权观。

（二）人权实践的自主性

中国人权实践的自主性体现在坚持从实际出发，把人权普遍性原则同中国实际结合起来，从中国国情和人民要求出发推动人权事业发展，确保人民依法享有广泛充分、真实具体、有效管用的人权。各国国情不同，历史文化、社会制度、经济社会发展水平存在差异，必须也只能从本国实际和人民需求出发，探索适合自己的人权发展道路。鞋子合不合脚，穿的人最清楚。脱离实际、全盘照搬别国制度模式，不仅会水土不服，而且会带来灾难性后果，最终受害的还是广大人民群众。一国的人权建设，选择权在该国人民，评判者也只能是该国人民。多年来，中国坚持将人权的普遍性原则与本国实际相结合，全面推进人权事业发展，自主探索出适合自己的人权发展路径，开辟了一条有着 14 亿人口的发展中国家依靠本国资源和力量尊重人权、保障人权、发展人权的新道路，树立了新时代增益人权事业的典范，丰富人类文明多样性的同时，也为其他发展中国家自主探索人权道路提供了有益镜鉴。中国的实践表明，走符合国情、自主建设的人权道路才能行得通、走得顺，为人民所满意。

（三）人权推进的全面性

长期以来，中国坚持把人权的普遍性原则同中国实际相结合，不断推动经济社会发展，增进人民福祉，促进社会公平正义，加强人权法治保障，努力促进经济、社会、文化权利和公民、政治权利全面协调发展，显著提高了人民生存权、发展权的保障水平，走出了一条适合中国国情的人权发展道路。人权涉及范围广泛，各类人权相互依存，经济、社会、文化权利与公民、政治权利是人权体系中不可分割的组成部分。《维也纳宣言和行动纲领》再次确认和重申了"一切人权均为普遍、不可分割、相互依存、相互联系"的基本观点和立场。人权内涵是全面的、丰富的，必须综合施策，系统推进。中国基于自身历史传统、具体国情和制度特点，以系统思维规划人权发展目标，既认识到人权事业的渐进性，又认识到人权建设的全面性和协调性。对一个拥有14亿人口的超大型社会来说，中国秉持"民以食为天"理念，着力破除贫困这一"实现人权的最大障碍"，保障人民的生存权和发展权，同时顺应人民对高品质美好生活的期待，不断满足人民日益增长的多方面的权利需求，统筹推进经济发展、民主法治、思想文化、公平正义、社会治理、环境保护等建设，全面做好就业、收入分配、教育、社保、医疗、住房、养老、扶幼等各方面工作，在物质文明、政治文明、精神文明、社会文明、生态文明协调发展中全方位提升各项人权保障水平，走出一条渐进的、协调的、全面的人权发展道路，使每个人更加充分地享有人权，创造了尊重和保障人权的中国模式。

（四）人权发展的可持续性

可持续的人权发展，意味着不仅要为人权发展提供永续的发展动力和物质基础，还要将人权进步的成功经验进行制度化、法治化，形成尊重和保障人权的稳固机制。中国高度重视人权发展的可持续性，坚持以民生为本，以发展为要，为推动人权可持续发展打造坚实基础。中国完整、准确、全面贯彻新发展理念，坚持以人民为中心的发展思想，坚持发展为了人民、发展依靠人民、发展成果由人民共享，着力解决人民群众最关心最直接最现实的利益问题，着力解决发展不平衡不充分问题，努力实现更高质量、更有效率、更加公平、更可持续、更为安全的发展，在发展中使广大人民的获得感、幸福感、安全感更加充实、更有保障、更可持续。与此同时，中国坚持依法治国，建设法治国家，为推动人权可持续发展提供制度保障。"法治是人权最有效的保障"。在推进全面依法治国的进程中，中国将人权保障贯穿于科学立法、严格执法、公正司法、全民守法等各个环节：尊重和保障人权成为立法的一项重要原则，以宪法为核心的中国特色社会主义法律体系不断完善；依法行政深入推进，行政权力运行更加规范；深化司法改革，努力让人民群众在每一个司法案件中感受到公平正义；法治社会建设向纵深发展，全社会法治观念和人权法治保障意识显著增强。党的十八大以来，以习近平为核心的党中央从推进国家治理体系和治理能力现代化的高度，作出全面依法治国的重大战略部署，将尊重和保障人权置于社会主义法治国家建设更加突出的位置，开启了中国人权法治化建设的新时代。从编纂民法典，到全面实施《法治政府建设实施纲要（2015—2020年）》，从坚定不移推进司法体制改革，到全面推进法治社会建设……中国的人权法治化保障取得巨大成就，中国人民的各项基本权利和自由得到切实保障，中国人权可持续发展的基础更加坚实。

四、完善全球人权治理的中国方案

人类人权文明不断发展演进，从时间的纵向看，人类对人权认知的广度和深度随着技术革新、经济发展和社会进步不断拓展，从空间的分布看，历史文化、社会制度、发展阶段等差异让不同国家的人权形态各具特点，人类人权文明的多样性不断丰富。

当今世界，经济全球化深入发展，虽逆风不断但历史趋势无法逆转，人类越来越成为你中有我、我中有你的命运共同体。发展中国家的群体崛起和政治觉醒推动全球力量结构和政治格局朝着多极化演变，谋求自主发展和提升全球治理话语权的诉求不断增加。这种历史潮流对全球人权治理产生重要影响并提出了新的时代要求：人类社会的整体性特征日益凸显，亟需以人类整体主义关照全球人权治理，发展驱动人权进步契合发展中国家的现实诉求，受到越来越多的重视，而提升发展中国家的人权话语权，践行真正的多边主义，成为构建新时代背景下全球人权治理新愿景的迫切任务。中国人权实践取得巨大历史性成就，开辟了中国特色人权发展道路，同时也为推动全球人权事业发展，完善全球人权治理贡献了中国理念、中国方案。

（一）团结合作

共同居住在地球上，人类命运与共，基于人类整体性的全球人权治理是人类人权文明演进的正确方向。从文艺复兴、启蒙运动以及资产阶级革命，到二战结束后民族独立和解放运动，再到全球化高歌猛进让"地球村"融为一体，集体人权在全球人权治理结构中的重要性日益凸显，民族、一国人民或全人类等集体人权的主体形态也在国际人权领域中占据更加重要的地位。当今世界，百年变局加速演进，世界进入动荡变革期，传统风险与现代化风险、外部风险与内生风险叠加，对各国人权保障和全球人权治理形成深度挑战。饥饿、贫困、战乱、恐怖主义、环境污染、气候变化以及互联网新兴领域等挑战交织叠加，特别是新冠疫情全球暴发以及各国的应对理念与策略，在显示现代化风险全球性的同时，也呼唤着应对共同挑战的整体主义与合作思维，以整体性思维推进全球人权治理已经成为全球化背景下人类人权文明演化的必然趋势。

中国传统文化的"入世"哲学中，人不是抽象的、孤立的"自在"，而是基于互动关系的"共在"；唯有存在于与他人的"共在"关系之中，人才生成存在的价值和意义。这种"共在共享"思维决定了中国人看待群己关系的方式，同时也深刻影响着中国与世界的互动关系。

2017年1月18日，习近平主席在日内瓦出席"共商共筑人类命运共同体"高级别会议时，发表题为《共同构建人类命运共同体》的主旨演讲，向全球阐释了人类命运共同体理念。用人类命运共同体理念阐释中国的人权治理观，就是要以全球人权治理主体的多元性和利益诉求的多样性为实践语境，以"这个世界，各国相互联系、相互依存的程度空前加深"的客观事实为逻辑起点，以全球化进程中风险共担和"人类命运与共"为基本意识，以全人类的合作发展和权利保障为指向，呈现出一种显著的整体主义特征。这一重大理念指导下的中国的人权治理观突出共荣共惠、共建共享、平衡包容、和平共生的时代追求，既蕴含着和平、发展、公平、正义、民主、自由的全人类共同价值，又强调了全球人权保障事业的整体性，是对既往人权理念的重大超越，极大丰富了新时代人权内涵，对构建公正合理的国际人权治理体系具有重要指导意义。

2017年3月1日，中国代表140个国家在联合国人权理事会第34届会议上发表题为"促进和保护人权，共建人类命运共同体"的联合声明，阐述人类命运共同体重大理念及其对推动国际人权事业发展的重要意义，受到各方认同和支持。此次会议通过的关于"经济、社会、文化权利"和"粮食权"两个决议，明确表示要"构建人类命运共同体"。

此后，构建人类命运共同体理念被写入多个联合国人权文件，成为国际人权话语体系的重要组成部分。正是在这一理念的指引下，中国主张全球人权治理要由各国共商，人权发展成果要由各国人民共享，推动全球人权治理朝着更加公平、公正、合理、包容的方向发展。

（二）发展驱动

拥有平等的发展机会，共享发展成果，使每个人都得到全面发展，实现充分的发展权，是人类社会的理想追求。发展权与生存权作为首要基本人权，是中国基于自身人权实践得出的成功经验，代表着广大发展中国家自主探索人权道路的现实诉求，符合当前推动完善全球人权治理的时代需要。

发展中国家多历经被长期殖民或半殖民的历史，处于帝国主义殖民体系中的被支配地位，长期遭受经济盘剥和政治奴役。"二战"后亚非拉独立解放运动蓬勃发展，广大发展中国家获得主权独立，但依然受到饥馑贫困、教育落后、发展停滞、治理失效等社会问题的深度困扰，特定政治经历和社会记忆不断塑造的国民集体心理感受，往往使得消除饥馑和贫困、在保障人民生存权的基础上逐步实现发展权，成为发展中国家最紧迫的人权需求。随着发展中国家自主发展的意识不断增强，"基于发展的人权路径"获得越来越多国家的重视和支持。1986年联合国大会第41/128号决议通过《发展权利宣言》，正式将发展权确认为"一项不可剥夺的人权"，这是全球人权治理顺应时代发展的必然。

改革开放以来，中国人权事业不断发展进步的一条根本经验便是坚持发展是硬道理，始终立足自身实际，坚定不移在发展中夯实各项人权全面发展的根基。进入新时代，中国共产党立足新发展阶段，贯彻新发展理念，构建新发展格局，推动高质量发展，领导人民全面建成小康社会，实现了第一个百年奋斗目标，踏上全面建设社会主义现代化国家、向第二个百年奋斗目标进军的新征程。中国的发展与人权事业的进步相互促进、相辅相成，呈现出一种清晰的逻辑关系，即"生存权利的有效保障是享有和发展其他人权的前提和基础"，而"唯有发展，才能消除全球性挑战的根源；唯有发展，才能保障人民的基本权利；唯有发展，才能推动人类社会进步"。正如 2022 年 5 月习近平主席在会见时任联合国人权事务高级专员巴切莱特时指出："对于发展中国家来说，生存权、发展权是首要人权。要努力实现更高质量、更有效率、更加公平、更可持续、更为安全的发展，为人权事业发展提供坚强保障。"

当今世界经济正面临通胀高企、需求转弱、地缘冲突以及能源粮食安全等挑战，各国尤其是发展中国家面临多重发展困境，发展权受阻成为全球人权治理面临的巨大障碍。联合国秘书长古特雷斯在 2023 年发展筹资论坛开幕式上发出警告，联合国 2030 年可持续发展议程正在变成一座"海市蜃楼"。中国基于发展驱动的人权实现路径，倡导"以合作促发展，以发展促人权"理念，并提出全球发展倡议，这在全球发展进程遇阻的当下尤具深意。各国要全面保障本国人权，便无法脱离相互联系的共同发展，各国以合作发展促人权发展，不仅要在经济环节形成发展共同体，而且要以开放的态度互相学习发展经验。对于发展困难的国家，各国当守望相助，积极伸出援手。中国提出的全球发展倡议主张以行动为导向，紧扣发展中国家最迫切的民生需要，在减贫、粮食安全、大流行病应对、发展融资、气候变化以及数字经济等重点领域推进务实合作，致力于以共同发展促进人权共同进步，得到国际社会成员的积极响应。

（三）多边共治

全球力量对比变化必然推动国际关系民主化，发展中国家积极参与全球人权治理，提升人权治理代表性和话语权的诉求显著增强。在此背景下，践行真正的多边主义，推动联合国主导的多边共治，才是全球人权治理的未来。

公平赤字是当前全球人权治理面临的一个重要问题。长期以来，西方国家在全球治理机制中占控制地位，时常根据国家利益在全球治理过程中采取双重标准，国际权力体系"中心—边缘"结构依然明晰，单边主义、霸权主义不断侵蚀着全球人权治理体系的效力和公正。在此背景下，发展中国家难言平等参与全球人权治理，无法享有与其不断上升的国际影响力相匹配的话语权。

近年来，国际社会要求改变西方国家对全球治理机制垄断操纵的呼声不断增强。在此背景下，中国主张全球人权治理结构要反映国际政治的多极化、世界经济的全球化、国际关系的民主化、世界文明的多样性的趋势特点。为此，中国支持发展中国家共同参与全球人权治理的结构改造，不断提升国际人权机构参与主体的民主性和广泛性，坚持文化多样性原则，进一步强化国际人权机构成员参与的地域公平分布原则，提升发展中国家在全球人权治理中的代表权和话语权，使全球人权治理带来的利益由所有国家共同分享，使全球人权秩序建立在公正合理的基础之上。

多边主义是促进世界人权事业发展的重要基础，联合国是全球人权多边合作治理的主导性力量。习近平主席指出："世界只有一个体系，就是以联合国为核心的国际体系。只有一个秩序，就是以国际法为基础的国际秩序。只有一套规则，就是以联合国宪章宗旨和原则为基础的国际关系基本准则。"全球人权治理体系和治理秩序，必须以坚决维护联合国权威和地位为必要条件。中国的主张是，高举多边主义旗帜，坚持真正的多边主义，捍卫国际法和国际关系准则，践行共商共建共享的全球治理观，弘扬全人类共同价值，以公正、客观和非选择性方式处理人权问题，通过平等的对话来化解人权分歧，倡导联合国主导的多边共治，推动全球人权治理朝着更加公正合理的方向演进，携手构建人类命运共同体。

完善全球人权治理离不开民间力量的积极参与，应在不降低甚至加强国家责任的同时，将市场与社会的其他主体纳入共同推进全球人权治理的视野。民间组织也是推动人权与发展的重要力量，在推动共同发展、人权进步，促进对话交流、文明互鉴等方面正发挥着越来越重要的作用。例如，联合国人权理事会第 47 届会议期间，中国民间组织国际交流促进会举办"大变局下民间力量对发展权的贡献"主题视频边会，来自中国、巴基斯坦、印度、保加利亚、斯里兰卡、哈萨克斯坦等国的专家学者和社会组织负责人参与研讨。联合国人权理事会第 49 届会议期间，中国人权研究会、中国民间组织国际交流促进会、中国联合国协会等社会组织和人权研究机构主办了多场云上边会，来自中国、巴基斯坦、柬埔寨、阿根廷、英国等国的社会组织负责人、专家学者等围绕"新疆的人权进步与各族人民的幸福生活""全过程人民民主和发展经验交流""美式人权观及其对全球人权治理的危害"等 12 个主题进行了广泛深入研讨交流。

（四）包容互鉴

无论概念理念还是具体内容实践，人类人权文明都是一个持续开放发展的体系，人权发展的历史轨迹也充分印证了这一点。从范围上看，人权覆盖面逐步扩大，不断向全世界延伸，最终成为国际主流话语，人权的普遍性得到广泛承认。此外，随着越来越多的发展中国家基于具体国情，将人权的普遍性与特殊性结合起来，自主探索适合自身的人权发展道路，人权的多样性也不断得到丰富，展现出各自独立的人权文明价值。由此可见，人权的发展过程随着人类社会的发展进步而进步，具有无限的发展性和丰富的多样性，以西方中心主义观点看待人权只会阻碍人类人权文明进步，以开放演进的思维看待人权发展，以包容互鉴的精神推动人权进步，以发展创新的态度完善全球人权治理，才是人类人权文明的前进方向。

人权事业是各国经济社会发展的重要组成部分，必须根据各国国情和人民需求加以推进。各国人权发展理念和实践的丰富多彩，应该成为国际人权事业欣欣向荣的源泉，而不应成为各方对抗的根源。《世界人权宣言》提倡文明之间的开放包容、互学互鉴，国际人权领域的重要原则之一就是"非歧视原则"。个别国家不承认文明多样性，不尊重各国人民选择自身发展道路的权利，打着人权和人道的旗号，四处策动颜色革命，强推政权更迭，造成冲突动荡，引发一个个人道危机，成为当今世界乱局的重要根源。

人权文明的现代化并不必然是西方中心论的普世化；全球人权治理的现代化，也并不必然意味着全球人权治理的西方化。正如有西方学者所指出的："现代化有别于西方化，它既未产生任何有意义的普世文明，也未产生非西方社会的西方化。"习近平主席强调，世界上没有放之四海而皆准的人权发展道路。"在人权问题上不存在十全十美的'理想国'，不需要对别国颐指气使的'教师爷'，更不能把人权问题政治化、工具化，搞双重标准，以人权为借口干涉别国内政。"

包容互鉴是促进和保护人权的动力。中国人权观以人权文明多元论为理论语境，主张人权理论体系与人权发展道路的多样性，反对国际人权治理的单边主义与霸权主义，归根到底是因为，人权理论体系、话语体系与人权道路的多样性是人类文明多样性的重要组成部分，尊重多样性是人类文明永续发展、永葆活力的根基。人权有"单薄""厚实"之分，所谓"单薄的人权"是指以抽象概念表达的、各个国家都可能会赞同的人权观，简单地讲人权有没有、好不好；而"厚实的人权"则是指根植于每个社会历史文化与具体环境中的丰富人权。各个国家在"单薄的人权"上达成共识比较容易，而在"厚实的人权"上，需要的不是强行千篇一律，而是相互借鉴，美人之美。躲在"单薄的人权"观念里，就不会发现"厚实的人权"丰富多元，也不会找到世界人权文明前行的道路。"文明只有姹紫嫣红之别，但绝无高低优劣之分。认为自己的人种和文明高人一等，执意改造甚至取代其他文明，在认识上是愚蠢的，在做法上是灾难性的！"不同国家、文明和族群之间应平等交流，相互借鉴，取长补短，共同进步。

结　语：完善全球人权治理，构建人类命运共同体

"人人得享人权"是人类孜孜以求的崇高目标，在"人类两度身历惨不堪言之战祸"后，人类社会痛定思痛，成立了联合国，以"促成大自由中之社会进步和民生改善"，国际人权事业自此掀开新篇章。70多年来，世界相对和平与安宁，大多数国家和地区的人民免受战争和冲突影响，和平权和生命权总体得到保障，生存权和发展权取得巨大成就，人权主流化趋势深入发展，国际人权合作蓬勃发展，公正、客观、非选择性原则成为联合国人权工作的基础和遵循。与此同时，世界不公正、不容忍、不安宁依然存在，发展不平衡、不协调、不可持续问题依旧突出，特别是饥饿、贫困、难民、疫情以及恐怖主义、种族歧视、保护主义、气候变化等问题依然存在，严重困扰人类社会发展，人权政治化倾向和双重标准仍大行其道，国际人权领域的"治理赤字"依然严重。

尊重和保障人权，反映了人类在长期的历史进程中反对专制压迫、争取自由平等、爱好和平幸福的正义追求，折射出人类对自身存在的意义与价值认识的日益深化以及对未来的美好憧憬。中国的人权梦是国家富强、人民幸福之梦，也是促进世界和平发展、合作共赢之梦。在推进世界人权事业发展的进程中，中国不是局外人，而是不断参与其中的行

动派，在推动构建人类命运共同体的进程中发挥着越来越重要的作用，成为影响和推进世界人权事业发展的重要力量，为推动世界人权事业发展贡献了中国智慧，提供了中国方案。

当前，在中国共产党的坚强领导下，中国人民正踔厉奋发迈上全面建设社会主义现代化国家新征程，向着第二个百年奋斗目标进军。在新的伟大征程上，中国将坚持人民至上，坚持走顺应时代潮流、适合本国国情的人权发展道路，在推进中国式现代化的进程中不断提升人权保障水平，促进人的自由全面发展。中国愿同国际社会一道，践行《世界人权宣言》和《维也纳宣言和行动纲领》精神，推动全球人权治理朝着更加公平公正合理包容的方向发展，推动构建人类命运共同体，共建更加美好的世界。

编写说明与致谢

《为了全人类共同的价值和尊严——中国参与全球人权治理的实践与贡献》智库报告于 2023 年 9 月 19 日，由中国人权研究会和新华社国家高端智库共同发布。课题组由新华通讯社社长、新华社国家高端智库学术委员会主任傅华任组长，新华通讯社总编辑吕岩松任副组长，课题组成员包括袁炳忠、倪四义、薛颖、叶书宏、乔继红、谢彬彬、李洁等。

课题自 2023 年 4 月启动以来，历时半年多采访、调研、撰写、修改、审校完成。

在报告写作和发布过程中，中国社会科学院国际法研究所副所长柳华文、南开大学人权研究中心主任常健、中南大学人权研究中心执行主任毛俊响、北京师范大学经济与工商管理学院教授贺力平、西南政法大学人权研究院副教授尚海明等专家学者给予了多方面的帮助和指导，在此一并表示诚挚谢意。

中国视力残疾人文化权利保障的实践与启示[①]
——从"光明影院"公益项目谈起

　　新中国成立以来，特别是党的十八大以来，在以习近平同志为核心的党中央坚强领导下，中国残疾人事业取得历史性成就，广大残疾人生存权得到稳定保障，发展权得以更好实现，获得感、幸福感、安全感显著提升。

　　随着经济社会快速发展，不断满足残疾人日益增长的精神文化需求，充分保障残疾人文化权利，对于残疾人体验生命意义、提升生活质量，促进社会的平等、正义、融合、和谐具有重要意义。

　　在残疾人群体中，视力残疾人由于其残疾特点，相应文化产品供给种类少、渠道窄，精神文化生活较为匮乏，需给予特别保障。世界卫生组织 2019 年发布的《世界视力报告》显示，

　　全世界视力损伤或失明人数高达 22 亿人以上。中国是世界上视力

---

① 2024 年 12 月 3 日发布于北京。

残疾人最多的国家之一，数据显示，该群体人数达1731万。感知丰富世界、追求美好人生，是视力残疾人的重要现实需求。

为保障视力残疾人平等享有文化权利，中国健全保障体系，广泛动员社会力量参与，取得显著成效。其中，中国传媒大学倾力打造的"光明影院"公益项目，通过制作推广无障碍影视作品、建设无障碍影院等，推动文化共享、缩小文化落差，为视力残疾人平等参与社会文化生活贡献社会力量，成为中国积极保障残疾人文化权利的生动案例。

一、"光明影院"：保障视力残疾人文化权利的创新实践

（一）"光明影院"七年化茧成蝶

缘起高校师生打造"文化盲道"的助残初心。"我们大家齐心协力做这个项目的初衷，就是希望能够发挥新闻人的力量，为视力残疾人群体尽绵薄之力。"回想起2017年"光明影院"公益项目初创时的情景，中国传媒大学电视学院志愿者团队的师生们依旧满腔热忱。主创团队师生经过认真研讨，在纪录片拍摄、电影短片制作等多个方案中反复考量比较，综合视力残疾人群体接受能力、院校专业能力、社会资源支持程度，最终策划实施了"为视力残疾人讲述电影"的"光明影院"公益项目。根据主创团队介绍，"光明影院"无障碍电影是在电影对白和音响的间隙，插入对于电影画面内容及其背后情感、意义的声音描述，制成可复制、可传播的标准化无障碍电影。"光明影院"项目坚持"用声音传递色彩，用聆听感知艺术"，从创始之初即确立了每周为视力残疾人群体提供2部无障碍电影、每年104部的目标，并将这一为视力残疾人打造"文化盲道"的初心延续至今，助力我国无障碍信息传播事业不断向前发展。

探索无障碍电影标准化制作模式。"会拉片，懂视听。""光明影院"不仅是一个公益行动，更是一项专业行为。对视听语言的理解，视

听修辞的转换，以及配音、剪辑和对整部影片的把握，都对师生专业能力提出极大考验。

"光明影院"项目创始成员、中国传媒大学无障碍信息传播研究院执行院长付海钲介绍，从摸着石头过河到形成标准化制作模式，"光明影院"的创作经历了从稚嫩到蜕变、从成长到成熟的艰辛探索。"团队采用标准化制作流程，具体环节包括选片－撰稿－审核－校对－录制，每一个环节都坚持'三审三校'、精益求精，保证讲述内容真实还原电影画面，努力做到最好。"项目组成员、中国传媒大学教师志愿者赵希婧说。

选片环节，"光明影院"突破了以往无障碍电影题材的局限，涉及动画题材、现实题材、科幻题材、历史题材等众多类型，力求满足不同年龄段视障群体的需求。为了帮助视力残疾人群体关注时事动态、更好参与社会，团队在重要时间节点精心制作系列反映国家、社会、时代发展的影片。

"撰稿和录制环节，要站在视力残疾人群体的视角，用他们可感知的语言生动表现出来。举例来说，红色是什么颜色？是温暖的、太阳一般的颜色。""光明影院"项目创始成员、中国传媒大学博士研究生蔡雨如是说。团队成员对文字、录制的把握，力求做到真实、精准还原，以实现对电影的可信解读。如在战争类题材影片中，对各军兵种、武器、作战区域的描述都通过反复查询资料确保一一精准对应，尽最大努力还原影片信息，努力让视力残疾人感受到真实的影视战争场景。

"光明影院"团队建立起科学高效的运作机制，项目团队中的每个小组都针对自身的工作内容制作标准化手册，从撰稿、审看、配音到监听、合成，涵盖无障碍电影的制作全流程，并延伸到项目的宣传推广，保证不断更新的志愿者团队，能够始终如一地保持工作水准和电影品质。

7年来，800多名师生志愿者参与其中，共制作了600多部无障碍影视作品，类型风格多样、配音声情并茂，凝结着"光明影院"项目团队对实现视力残疾人群体基本权利的热心投入，以及服务国家残疾人事业的责任和信念。

推动无障碍文化服务落地生根。"光明影院"的初心不仅是一年完成百部无障碍电影，更是在全社会范围内积极倡导保障残障人士的文化权利。在媒介技术重塑信息获取方式的当下，"光明影院"帮助视力残疾人以平等的地位和均等的机会充分参与社会文化生活，共享当代物质文明和精神文明成果。

"不仅仅是影片制作，'光明影院'项目甚至延伸到了电影放映环节。"项目组成员、中国传媒大学学生志愿者李超鹏介绍，从发布放映信息、协调影院公益放映，再到志愿者帮助视障朋友入场、现场互动解答、维护观影秩序、解说以及散场疏导等，"光明影院"在放映环节经过严谨周密的思考、设计和演练，力求给视力残疾人观影带来最安全、最佳的体验。

经过7年探索，"光明影院"现已形成进盲协、进影院、进盲校、进图书馆和进社区的"五进模式"，努力打通视力残疾人观影的"最后一公里"。不仅于此，北京国际电影节、中国长春电影节、海南岛国际电影节、丝绸之路国际电影节等还专门设立了固定公益放映单元，让视力残疾人共享文化盛事，在吸引更多人关注视力残疾人群体，关注中国残疾人事业发展新动向、新经验、新思考、新成就的同时，也立足国际舞台，讲好中国的公益故事、人权故事、精神文明建设故事，对于推进全球信息无障碍传播事业，同样发挥了积极作用。

截至目前，"光明影院"项目成果已落地31个省（区、市）及澳门特别行政区，实现2244所特殊教育学校全覆盖，浙江嘉兴、绍兴以及江苏苏州等地文明实践阵地全面推广，20余个"光明影院"固定放映厅在北京等地挂牌，5个电影节设立"光明影院"公益放映单元，上线中国广电"光明影院"公益点播专区，覆盖超 2 亿户家庭，800 万视力残疾人受益……随着一个个数字的增长，"光明影院"依托声影世界所构筑的"文化盲道"不断延伸拓宽，辐射面更加广阔，惠及更多视力残疾人，使以无障碍文化服务助推残疾人事业发展的公益信念，在全国乃至世界范围内产生积极影响。

（二）"光明影院"有效提升视力残疾人的幸福感获得感

法国电影艺术家安德烈·巴赞曾在著作《电影是什么》中提出，人类拥有用逼真的临摹物替代外部世界的心理愿望。他说，电影这个概念与完整无缺地再现现实是等同的，他们所想象的就是再现一个声音、色彩、立体感等一应俱全的外部世界的幻景。"光明影院"项目让视力残疾人获取信息的同时，对于表达的"信、达、雅"及其起到的美育效果，有了更高追求。

弥补了视力残疾人观影信息和艺术审美缺失。 "光明影院"项目受访师生表示，在确保所观电影基本信息准确、真实的基础上，团队在内涵阐释和技术保障上也苦下功夫，不断提升影片质感和传播效果。从内涵阐释层面看，"光明影院"侧重对影片意义的深刻挖掘，在讲清楚故事的基础上，还注重对影片内涵进行整体性诠释，让观众既理解影片的基本内容，还能对影片有更丰富的想象和思考。

项目启动后，中国传媒大学师生与北京市盲人学校等建立起密切联系，每个月都会派出专门的放映团队为学生放映无障碍电影。北京市盲人学校学生王正等表示，以前"看"电影，遇到背景音乐、风景画面甚至是人物对话，一些通过眼神等肢体语言表达的情节无法感知，常常出现"看不懂"的情形，更难以感受到电影之美。"光明影院"项目在学校礼堂固定放映后，生活多了一份期待和快乐的同时，"听得懂"的影片也让同学们更好地学习知识，感受外部世界和生活之美。

北京市盲人学校党委书记王小垂表示，"光明影院"项目以美的追求和美的表达，为学生等受众群体营造了美的空间、美的想象，激发了受众对美的想象、向往和追求，提高了受众的审美能力，也有助于受众陶冶性情、完善人格，具有较好的美育价值。

拓宽了视力残疾人参与社会的渠道。2021年，"光明影院"走进北京市昌平区。区盲协有关负责人介绍，与聋哑等残疾人群体不同，视力残疾人由于视力限制，以及一系列由视力限制带来的沟通交流难题，不愿意、不经常出门。无障碍电影放映活动使这个群体增加了走出家门的机会，和志愿者、其他视障人士有了更多交流，这对于提升他们的生活质量、丰富他们的文化生活具有积极意义。北京市盲人学校部分受访教师表示，"光明影院"项目让孩子们有了了解、感知、参与社会的机会，一些孩子还有机会参与到北京国际电影节、影视作品录制、座谈交流等工作中，在吸引更多社会力量关注、支持这一群体的同时，也让他们对丰富多彩的世界和自己的未来人生有了更多的思考和追求。一些家长甚至希望在有条件的情况下，能够支持孩子突破视力残疾人传统的按摩、音乐等专业和特殊教育学校的选择，到普通学校接受融合教育，勇敢追求自己的人生。可以说，"光明影院"为视障孩子们打造了一条"梦想盲道"。

激发了视力残疾人追求幸福生活的内生动力。对于幸福的追求，常常源于"看见"。视觉作为感知世界最重要、最直接的感觉之一，是人们能够认识世界、了解世界的基础性感官功能。"光明影院"项目以观影活动为载体，为视障群体积极搭建社会活动和交往平台，有效提升其社交能力，精神面貌有明显改观。"好的电影会让我们在某一个时间段去体验各种人生的感觉，所以电影的力量是无穷的。"北京市盲人学校中学老师茹甜子说。电影以动人的故事传递生活的感悟与深刻的思想，电影这扇窗也应该为每个视力残疾人敞开。

文化生活如同阳光、空气，是个体生活和发展中不可或缺的基本要素。对视力残疾人而言，"光明影院"无障碍电影可以增加其人生体验，帮助其获取知识，滋养心灵，丰富精神世界，提升文化水平和素养，对于其平等融入社会，具有重要赋能作用。北京市盲人学校部分受访学生表示，"光明影院"让他们同步感知国家的发展进步、时代的变革、社会的变迁，这不仅给他们带来精神上的愉悦，更拓展了他们想象的空间和思维的边界，激发他们勇敢探索外部世界、追寻内心梦想、追求幸福美好生活。

（三）"光明影院"保障视力残疾人文化权利的经验范式

以高校学生为重要参与力量，发挥其澎湃活力。 中国传媒大学电视学院受访者认为，"高校青年作为'光明影院'志愿团队的主体力量，在创作过程中既有专业支撑，又有澎湃活力，为中国无障碍电影的制作、传播探索注入了青春动力"。培养青年学生家国情怀和社会责任感是高校教育的应有之义，也是"光明影院"项目的创始动力。"光明影院"项目鼓励青年学生积极投身光影制作和人权发展鲜活实践，有效增强了他们尊重和保障人权的意识，既体现了中国传媒大学的办学宗旨，也强化了学生对新闻传播学专业的价值坚守，避免陷入精致的利己主义者思维，实现了个体与时代、青春与公益、初心与奋斗的"双向奔赴"。

以高校为依托，发挥其专业、技术、人才优势。 高校教师团队为学生提供整体指导、专业支持和业务把关，成为项目团队的坚实后盾。中国传媒大学的老师将"光明影院"项目定义为"公益＋教学＋科研＋实验"，引导青年学生学以致用、知行合一、教育报国，用专业知识服务国家和社会。"光明影院"团队学生志愿者温莫寒表示，从项目的整体策划，到每一部影片的选取、文稿的撰写、配音、后期制作以及放映、传播等，都由师生群策群力完成，专业精神、社会经验、青春热情结合在一起，创作过程顺畅、温馨，也让学生有了更多的获得感、成就感。从最初仅 5 名志愿者，到如今数百名志愿者共同支撑着这个辐射全国的公益项目，作为核心指导者的赵淑萍老师深有感触地说："充分放手，相信学生。"学校的大力支持、老师的精心指导，是项目行稳致远的不竭动力。

推进无障碍信息传播研究与合作，提升国际影响力。"光明影院"始终坚持答好"文化扶贫"的新答卷，走进喧嚣城市，走进偏远山区，足迹遍布全国。2023 年 11 月 1 日，在由中国国际扶贫中心、联合国粮食及农业组织、联合国国际农业发展基金、联合国世界粮食计划署和中国互联网新闻中心等联合主办的 2023 全球减贫伙伴研讨会上，中国传媒大学《以文化帮扶促乡村振兴——校企合作"光明影院"无障碍电影制作与传播公益项目案例》荣获"第四届全球减贫案例征集活动"最佳减贫案例，并被收入南南合作减贫案例库。2023 年 12 月 1 日，在第 32个"国际残疾人日"到来之际，由中国人权发展基金会、中国残疾人联合会指导，中国传媒大学与联合国教科文组织联合主办的"无障碍信息传播与人权保障"国际研讨会在北京召开。来自中国、法国、蒙古国、马来西亚等十余个国家的代表共同探讨提升社会的残障包容性、推进信息无障碍传播赋能残障人士的路径方法，分享了无障碍信息传播领域的中国经验，获得国内国际、业界学界的高度评价。

"光明影院"项目还为中国批准加入国际上唯一一部版权领域人权条约——《关于为盲人、视力障碍者或其他印刷品阅读障碍者获得已出版作品提供便利的马拉喀什条约》（简称《马拉喀什条约》）提供了智力支持与实践经验。2021 年，"光明影院"项目承担国家版权管理部门"视听作品与《马拉喀什条约》实施"课题研究任务，围绕中国实施该条约过程中提供视听作品无障碍格式版的必要性、可行性及被授权实体的具体操作等问题进行深入研究，为条约在中国的实施发挥了积极作用。

二、中国保障视力残疾人文化权利的举措和成就

文化权利是一项基本人权。中国传媒大学"光明影院"项目，正是中国保障视力残疾人平等享有文化权利、满足其更高需求的一个缩影。近年来，从完善政策法律体系到狠抓具体落实，从提升无障碍设施理念标准到提供丰富多元的无障碍产品和服务，中国以实际行动，推动视力残疾人文化权利不断得到更好保障。

越来越多的视力残疾人通过普通高考步入大学校园，通过阅读和参与文化活动习得知识文化、提高就业技能、拓宽职业道路、实现人生价值，在共享社会文化成果的同时也为社会奉献着自己的光和热。

（一）中国保障视力残疾人文化权利的政策法律体系不断健全

国家发展规划对于各项事业发展具有战略导向作用。在各类政策规划的制定中，中国始终统筹考虑视力残疾人文化权利保障。国务院先后发布 8 个残疾人事业五年发展规划，并发布实施《国务院关于加快推进残疾人小康进程的意见》《"十三五"加快残疾人小康进程规划纲要》等一批专项规划，细化具体化残疾人事业发展的工作任务和责任清单。

其中，盲文规范普及工作扎实推进。盲文是视力残疾人欣赏文化产品的重要途径，自 2009 年起先后实施的四期国家人权行动计划均规定了盲文推广等相关任务要求和完成指标。设立视力残疾人阅览室，扩大视力残疾人读物出版规模等项目发展目标伴随着经济社会发展得到不断提升，为视力残疾人和健全人同等享受不断繁荣的文化成果铺平了道路。

法律法规的制定和执行，是视力残疾人平等充分享受文化权利的有力保障。1990 年颁布并经 2008 年、2018 年两次修改的《中华人民共和国残疾人保障法》，是国家保障残疾人权益的专门立法，规定了残疾

人文化权利保障的基本原则和视力残疾人文化权利保障的具体措施。该法设立"文化生活"专章，承诺"国家保障残疾人享有平等参与文化生活的权利"；强调"残疾人文化、体育、娱乐活动应当面向基层，融于社会公共文化生活，适应各类残疾人的不同特点和需要，使残疾人广泛参与"；要求政府和社会采取措施，"组织和扶持盲文读物、盲人有声读物及其他残疾人读物的编写和出版，根据盲人的实际需要，在公共图书馆设立盲文读物、盲人有声读物图书室"。

2023 年颁布实施的《中华人民共和国无障碍环境建设法》，为视力残疾人更加充分便捷地享有文化权利提供了进一步支撑。该法设有"无障碍信息交流"专章，规定了一些保障视力残疾人无障碍享有文化权利的条款，例如，"国家鼓励公开出版发行的图书、报刊配备有声、大字、盲文、电子等无障碍格式版本，方便残疾人、老年人阅读"；"国家鼓励教材编写、出版单位根据不同教育阶段实际，编写、出版盲文版、低视力版教学用书，满足盲人和其他有视力障碍的学生的学习需求"；"音视频以及多媒体设备、移动智能终端设备、电信终端设备制造者提供的产品，应当逐步具备语音、大字等无障碍功能"等。此外，《中华人民共和国著作权法》《中华人民共和国公共文化服务保障法》《中华人民共和国公共图书馆法》等法律中，也有与视力残疾人文化权利保障相关的条款。

中国还积极推动本国政策法律与国际条约接轨，不断扩大视力残疾人文化产品供给范围，提升产品质量，促进视力残疾人文化事业领域的国际交流。2021 年 10 月 23 日，中国正式批准《马拉喀什条约》。根据该条约规定，中国可以为包括视力残疾人在内的阅读障碍者提供无障碍格式版作品，包括利用其他相关国家作品提供无障碍格式版，可以不经著作权人许可，不向其支付报酬等。中国视力残疾人可以获取的作品资源进一步丰富，获取作品的成本进一步降低。

（二）中国保障视力残疾人文化权利的举措不断加强

近年来，为保障视力残疾人更便捷地阅读，以及欣赏电视、电影、戏剧等文化作品，各项行政举措接连出台。

盲人数字阅读推广工程是中国各级政府推出的服务视力残疾人享受文化产品和服务的典型举措之一。为破解传统盲文书籍出版存在的制作成本高、印制工艺和校对过程繁琐、耗时长等难题，2017年起，国家有关部门和中国残疾人联合会携手实施盲人数字阅读推广工程。这一工程旨在利用数字出版传播平台和盲用阅读设备，向视力残疾人提供数字有声读物、电子盲文和定制化、持续性知识文化服务。"虽然一个个的盲文点字摸上去涩涩的，但是在我心中它们像是跳动的音符。"谈起阅读带给自己的喜悦，视障女孩王雅祺的脸上满是灿烂的笑容。截至2024年10月，该工程已有353家公共图书馆激活智能听书机设备146575台，激活率81.24%。智能听书机登录用户62281个，在线交互累计10224万次3583万小时，总平均单次使用时长约20分钟，单台产品单日使用时长更存在超过14小时的情形。

视力残疾人艺术活动快速发展。1987年，中国成立中国残疾人艺术团，视力残疾人约占团员总数的三分之一。艺术团赴上百个国家和地区进行交流演出，被联合国教科文组织授予"联合国教科文组织和平艺术家"称号。当前，全国各类残疾人艺术团体已有226个，一大批优秀的视力残疾人乐手、视力残疾人演唱者脱颖而出。中国残疾人联合会、教育部、民政部、文化和旅游部、国家广播电视总局等部门自2001年以来每四年联合举办一届全国残疾人艺术汇演。在2021年举办的第十届全国残疾人艺术汇演中，有约2400名残疾人参加，其中不乏视力残疾人，演出内容涵盖声乐、器乐、舞蹈和戏曲四大类艺术。

视力残疾人文化周活动走向常态。文化和旅游部、国家新闻出版署与中国残疾人联合会连续多年在全国开展残疾人文化周活动。仅2023

年文化周期间就开展相关活动 13459 场次。其中，盲童公益诵读活动、无障碍观影活动等备受视力残疾人喜爱。

视力残疾人参与文化产品创作的渠道不断拓展。中国残疾人联合会联合相关部门多次举办残疾人文学创作研修班，视力残疾人作家参与其中，不断提升文学创作能力。残疾人作品杂志专刊和视力残疾人作家撰写的书籍大量出版，彰显中国视力残疾人丰富多彩的精神世界。

（三）中国保障视力残疾人文化权利的无障碍环境建设不断完善

无障碍是残疾人等特殊群体全面参与社会生活、共享经济社会发展成果的基础和前提。对于视力残疾人而言，帮助他们在文化生活领域进行听、嗅、触、摸等感知的无障碍设施犹如一条条"文化盲道"。

中国政府和社会越来越认识到，一旦"有障"转变为"无障"，视力残疾人就能更加积极地参与文化生活，为社会创造文化财富。伴随着认识水平的不断提升，无障碍设施标准设定理念更加清晰，标准体系建设日益完善。

《中华人民共和国无障碍环境建设法》作为中国无障碍环境建设领域首部专门性法律，明确提出"国家推广通用设计理念"。这一设计理念和着眼点不再强调为残疾人群体专门建造便利设施，而是在设计的过程中就自然地将残疾人群体的需求平等地纳入了设计范围内。该法还着眼于个案中的合理便利，要求在通用设计的前提下，针对不同类型的残疾人进行必要和适当的改造和修正，以确保残疾人在具备平等地位和机会的前提下，享有或行使一切人权和基本自由。

无障碍设施标准是确保无障碍设施"管用""好用"的重要举措。近年来，中国已出台多个保障视力残疾人文化权利的无障碍设施国家标准。2012 年，中国首个公共图书馆服务领域的国家标准《公共图书馆服务规范》正式实施，明确公共图书馆服务对象包括所有公众，应努力满足残疾人等群体的特殊需求，规定视障阅览室宜设置在图书馆本体建筑与社会公共通道之间的平行层。2019 年，中国图书馆标准化领域专门服务于残疾人群体的国家标准《图书馆视障人士服务规范》正式实施，对服务对象、服务资源、服务内容与形式、服务要求、服务监督与评价等予以规范。目前，中国图书馆视障服务标准规范体系框架初步形成。在国家标准指导下，各地图书馆视障文化服务致力于提量扩面、提质增效，常态化服务有效开展，专业化水平大幅提升。

随着数字时代的到来，互联网信息无障碍标准逐步建立。2020 年 3 月 1 日，中国互联网信息无障碍领域首个国家标准《信息技术 互联网内容无障碍可访问性技术要求与测试方法》正式实施，提出提供语音验证码、增加语义描述准确的网页标题等 58 项具体指标，标志着互联网"盲道"铺设取得实质进展。中国开展政务网站和 APP 无障碍及适老化改造专项行动，2021 年以来共对 2726 家网站和 APP 进行改造，为视力残疾人获取信息、进行交流、获得公共服务、实现网上办事创造了更好条件。

中国政府还鼓励发展具有引领性的团体标准、企业标准等，并致力于加强标准之间的衔接和贯通，逐步构建起科学规范、系统配套的无障碍环境建设标准体系。

（四）中国保障视力残疾人文化权利的无障碍产品和服务不断丰富

随着中国经济社会的快速发展，针对视力残疾人的无障碍产品日益丰富，产业规模持续扩大，供给能力不断增强，服务质量稳步提升。

基于触觉的文化产品种类繁多。触觉是视力残疾人精确感知社会的重要渠道，盲文书籍是视力残疾人最常用的文化产品之一。2021 年以来，中国每年出版新版盲文书 500 余种（含明盲对照本 100 余种），重印盲文书 400 余种，最多时达到每年 1200 个品种，3000 万印张。丰富的盲文书籍资源为视力残疾人同享"书香"提供坚实支撑。此外，为了让盲文书籍惠及更多有需要的视力残疾人，中国大力发展盲文图书馆。目前，全国各级公共图书馆共有视力残疾人阅览室座席约 3.52 万个，盲文图书 1.466 亿册。随着科学技术发展，视力残疾人通过触觉通道获取信息的方式更为多元，盲文显示器、盲用电脑等产品陆续进入视力残疾人生活，成为其获取文化产品和服务的重要方式。

基于听觉的文化产品极大丰富。有声读物是视力残疾人最主要、最便捷的阅读载体。当前，由中国盲文出版社制作的盲用有声读物已涵盖大、中、小学教材，涉及文学、医学、评书、音乐等多个领域。此外，一些专注于音频内容制作与传播的互联网平台快速发展，大量用于读屏、听书的信息化辅助产品相继面世，让视力残疾人拥有更多选择。

新型文化产品方兴未艾。近年来，口述影像得到越来越多关注，国家出版基金支持盲文出版社的可供视障人士和听障人士观看且拥有版权的无障碍影视作品已经有 870 部；中国盲文图书馆新馆开馆至今 13 年，每周在馆内放映 1 部影片，均由馆员现场讲述，累计开展观影活动 700 余场，服务 3 万人次，完成脚本创作已达 300 余部，总字数约 240 万字；各级公共图书馆、文化机构、残联部门、社会组织经常组织视障人士观影活动。除"光明影院"项目外，中国一些互联网视频平台专门开设无障碍专区，通过读屏形式进入网站的用户将被直接导航进入该专区"阅读"完整影像，受到视力残疾人广泛欢迎。此外，在科技助力下，一些博物馆、展览馆向视力残疾人张开怀抱，在无障碍 NFC 展馆信息激活、导览音频、可触摸展品、在线云展厅等多样态产品支持下，视力残疾人获得前所未有的无障碍游览体验。

三、中国保障视力残疾人文化权利的经验和启示

中国保障视力残疾人文化权利的实践，充分反映了中国坚持以人民

为中心，积极履行国际人权条约义务，践行"平等、参与、共享"的残疾人事业发展理念，不断提升视力残疾人权利保障水平的积极作为，也为其他国家提供了经验和启示。

（一）坚持发挥国家主导作用

尊重和保障残疾人的人格尊严和各项权利，使他们能以平等的地位和均等的机会充分参与社会生活，共享物质文明和精神文明成果，彰显着一个国家的责任和担当。

中国作为《残疾人权利公约》缔约国，认真履行《公约》义务，无论是在制定与残疾人有关的法律、法规和政策，还是在促进和保障残疾人权利实现方面，都秉持《公约》精神，采取了务实而有力的举措，通过为残疾人提供通用设计的产品、环境、方案和服务，提供合理便利及特别辅助用具和支助服务，积极回应残疾人对美好精神文化生活的期盼和需求，推动残疾人事业高质量发展。

中国注重加强以残疾人为主体的法律法规建设，已形成以《中华人民共和国残疾人保障法》为主干，以《中华人民共和国无障碍环境建设法》《残疾预防和残疾人康复条例》《残疾人教育条例》《残疾人就业条例》等为重要支撑的残疾人权益保障法律法规体系。

中国积极将残疾人事务纳入国家经济社会发展总体规划和国家人权行动计划，多部门联合制定《"十四五"提升残疾人文化服务能力实施方案》，扶持有条件的省、市、县三级公共图书馆建立盲人阅览室（区），增加盲文图书和视听文献资源，配备盲文图书及有关阅读设备，为盲人提供盲文读物、有声读物、大字读物、无障碍版本的电影、电视剧等产品，切实做好盲人阅读服务。扶持全国 50 个地市级公共图书馆、200 个县级公共图书馆的盲人阅览室建设。持续实施盲人读物出版工程、盲人数字阅读推广工程，重点支持出版 50 种残疾人题材或残疾人作者的图书、音像制品；扶持优秀残疾人作家的作品翻译对外出版；鼓励残疾人题材优秀影片、纪录片、公益广告、网络视听节目制作播出；鼓励电影院线、有线电视提供无障碍影视服务。推动线上无障碍影视作品制作与播放。国家电影事业发展专项资金对"光明影院"项目予以资助，发挥了相应引导作用。

（二）坚持引导民间力量参与

残疾人事业是一个浩繁的系统工程，国家鼓励企事业单位、社会组织和个人为残疾人提供捐助和服务。

视力残疾人文化权利的保障离不开民间力量的广泛参与。民间力量不仅能弥补政府力量所覆盖不到的空白，同时也可增进全社会对残疾人的理解和尊重，消除对残疾人的偏见和歧视，推动残疾人更好融入社会，保障残疾人平等享有各项权利和自由。经过不懈努力，中国保障视力残疾人人权的社会基础更加坚实，社会各方面力量的参与更加广泛，各类社会组织、经营主体和志愿者积极投身视力残疾人事业，有力促进了视力残疾人文化权利保障的专业化、常态化和可持续性。平安公益基金会连续三年每年给予100万元，支持"光明影院"项目，正是中国民间力量参与残疾人事业的典型案例。

（三）坚持立足本国国情实际

中国残疾人事业扎根于本国历史文化传统和经济社会发展条件，同时注重学习借鉴国际先进经验，成功走出了一条适合本国国情的残疾人权益保障道路。在保障残疾人康复、就业、教育等权利的同时，中国致力于协调增进残疾人其他各项权利，使残疾人权利保障真正成为公正、包容、惠及每一个体的可持续发展战略的重要组成部分。

鉴于视力残疾人群体的特殊性，整个社会更加重视将其法定文化权利转化为实有文化权利。截至 2023 年底，全国共设有省级残疾人专题广播节目 24 个，地市级残疾人专题广播节目 184 个，全国各级公共图书馆共有 1541 个盲文及盲文有声读物阅览室开展视力残疾人文化服务，全国各类残疾人艺术团体通过组织全国残疾人艺术汇演、开展文化进残疾人家庭"五个一"活动，让视力残疾人共享精神文明建设成果。

（四）坚持技术驱动赋能

科技改变了我们的生活，更改变了残疾人的命运。随着信息技术、人工智能、生命科学等的不断突破，科技进步正在给残疾人生活带来新的希望。《"十四五"残疾人保障和发展规划》对科技助残提出明确要求。2024 年政府工作报告指出，要加强健康、养老、助残等民生科技研发应用。中国残疾人联合会发布的《中国残疾人发展与社会进步年度纵览（2023）》显示，中国已经催生了一大批现代科技助残企业，充分发挥高科技助残优势，不断提升广大残疾人的福祉，为残疾人提供更多自主、便利和平等的社会参与机会。

以提升视力残疾人的精神文化生活为例，触觉反馈无障碍技术将手机、平板电脑等终端设备的震动时长、频率和强度进行组合，向视障用户传递差异化信息。腾讯视频开通"无障碍剧场"专区，自动识别通过"语音读屏"进入的用户，将剧场入口置于其页面显著位置。此外，一批专为视障人群设计的游戏产品，通过 AI 技术综合处理玩家信息并进行实时反馈，不仅能满足玩家的操作需求，更提供了社群交流的平台。科技之光，不仅成为视力残疾人的"眼"，更照亮他们的内心世界，让他们有机会和健全人一样参与社会生活，感受大千世界的美好。

（五）坚持强化主体意识

在发展残疾人事业中，中国始终强调尊重残疾人意愿，注重残疾人的参与，激发残疾人的积极性、主动性、创造性，培树自尊、自信、自强、自立精神，推动残疾人由被动的受助者真正转变为权利主体，成为经济社会发展的参与者、贡献者和享有者。中国首位视障播音专业硕士毕业生董丽娜，通过自身努力改变命运，用声音为更多视力残疾人描绘世界的美好；视力残疾人作家陈光炅的作品关注残疾人的生活、工作、情感，书写视力残疾人的精彩故事；视力残疾人企业家曹军长期致力于助盲软件开发，帮助视力残疾人更好地了解世界、融入社会……

"我看不见世界，但希望世界看见我"，一名参加北京 2022 年冬残奥会比赛的中国视力残疾运动员说出了广大视力残疾人的心声。中国努力提升视力残疾人的主体意识，引导全社会平等对待视力残疾人，正视视力残疾人的价值和贡献，注重向视力残疾人赋能，以多种形式促进视力残疾人学知识、强本领，为视力残疾人平等接受教育、实现就业、参与文化活动和全面融入社会创造条件，让视力残疾人迸发出更加丰富多样的生命光彩。

编写说明与致谢

《中国视力残疾人文化权利保障的实践与启示——从"光明影院"公益项目谈起》智库报告于 2024 年 12 月 3 日第 33 个国际残疾人日，由中国人权发展基金会、新华社国家高端智库联合发布。新华社课题组由新华社副总编辑、新华社国家高端智库学术委员会执行副主任任卫东任组长，成员包括刘刚、崔峰、杨柳、刘明霞、熊琳、高蕾、谢彬彬、鲍晓菁、闫睿等。

课题自 2023 年 10 月启动以来，历时一年多采访、调研、撰写、修改、审校完成。

在报告写作和发布过程中，中国传媒大学新闻传播学部学部长、电视学院院长高晓虹、中国传媒大学电视学院无障碍信息传播研究院执行院长付海钲、中国传媒大学电视学院副研究员赵希婧；全国政协委员、中国残联理事、中国盲人协会主席李庆忠、中国视障文化资讯服务中心副主任何川、北京市盲人学校党委书记王小垂；外交学院人权研究中心主任张爱宁、中央党校（国家行政学院）国际战略研究院教授李云龙、中国政法大学人权研究院常务副院长张伟、中国社会科学院国际法研究所副所长柳华文、中国人民大学人权研究中心执行主任陆海娜、中国政法大学人权研究院副教授徐爽、首都师范大学管理学院副教授廖娟、清华大学未来实验室助理研究员、盲人用计算机项目核心骨干焦阳、清华大学未来实验室专业研究人员高媛、北京青少年法律援助与研究中心国际交流部负责人甘露等专家学者给予了多方面的帮助和指导，在此一并表示诚挚谢意。

中国游：让世界认识更加真实的中国 [①]

前　言

　　旅游是人类对美好生活向往与追求的一种表达方式，是认识新鲜事物和未知世界的重要途径。进入新时代以来，中国着力完善现代旅游业体系，加快建设旅游强国，旅游业日益成为新兴的战略支柱产业。旅游业在服务美好生活、促进经济发展、构筑精神家园、展示中国形象、增进文明互鉴等方面，发挥出越来越大的作用。

　　2024 年以来，中国进一步扩大免签入境国家名单，为入境旅游者提供更加便利的支付、语言、出行环境，外国来华旅游人数实现大幅增长，"中国游"潮流在海外社交平台不断升温。中国实施的一系列便利外国人来华旅游的举措，不仅推动着文化和旅游业更好更快地发展，更成为中国坚定不移推进高水平对外开放的生动写照。

[①] 2024 年 12 月 4 日发布于在海南博鳌举行的 2024 新华中经智库年会。

来自世界各地的数千万游客亲眼见证了开放、自信、文明、安全的中国，切身感受到中国式现代化取得的巨大成就，扭转了美西方国家强加于中国的刻板片面形象，推动了不同文明之间相互认知、交流互鉴。

"中国游"让世界认识了一个可信可爱可敬、更加真实的中国。

一、"中国游"火遍全球

2024 年以来，中国针对外籍人员来华旅游出台了一系列便利措施，持续优化外籍人员来华的各类渠道。随着政策红利的不断释放，外国人来华旅游持续升温，入境游客数量快速增长，"中国游"成为海外社交媒体的热议话题，相关内容的浏览量连续攀升。与此同时，外国人来华旅游呈现出新变化：从单纯的"走马观花"式短期旅游，转向更加个性化的"深度体验"式旅游。外国游客既感受中华优秀传统文化的魅力，又体验中国式现代化的风貌，对中国的认知更加全面、真实、立体。中国将外国人入境旅游作为展现国家形象、增进人文交流的重要契机，努力解决外国人来华的难点和堵点，提升旅游服务水平，讲好新时代中国故事，更好赋能高水平对外开放和高质量发展。

（一）来华外国游客数量大幅增长

随着中国旅游领域的进一步对外开放，中国入境游市场正在迅速复苏，越来越多外国旅客选择将中国作为旅行目的地，亲身体验生动真实的中国。国家移民局最新数据显示，2024 年上半年，中国各口岸入境外国人达到 1463.5 万人次，同比增长 152.7%。其中，通过免签入境的外国人达 854.2 万人次，同比增长 190.1%。2024 年第三季度，中国各口岸入境外国人 818.6 万人次，同比上升 48.8%；其中，通过免签入境 488.5 万人次，同比上升 78.6%。这些数据均显示出中国入境游的强劲复苏势头。随着政策持续优化和市场进一步开放，预计未来中国的入境游市场将继续保持强劲增长态势，为全球经济的复苏与发展贡献更多力量。

通过来华旅游，外国游客感受到中国在交通、支付、预约等服务方面的诸多新变化：在交通领域，我国执行的国际客运定期航班快速恢复，铁路部门优化 12306 网站，并推出外国护照在线身份核验服务；在支付领域，"大额刷卡、小额扫码、现金兜底"等便捷支付方式逐步落实；在预约方面，上海、北京、南京、长沙等地纷纷宣布，除少数特殊场所外，大多数旅游景区全面取消预约要求。这些便利的服务，让外国游客的旅行体验更加舒心。

有些西方媒体曾报道中国的环境脏乱差，人身安全堪忧，但实际上，中国的街道干净整洁，路人热情友好，夜晚的城市也充满活力且安全。很多来华旅游的外国人将自己的旅行经历拍成短视频，并发布到社交媒体上，无论是中国的美景美食，还是便捷的公共交通、安全的生活环境、热情的中国人，都让许多尚未到访中国的外国人心生向往。根据海外社交媒体的数据，"China Travel"（中国游）已成为热门搜索词，相关话题的浏览量突破 7 亿次。在外国友人一句句"好 City 啊！"的震撼与赞叹声中，"中国游"的独特魅力不断展现。

（二）便利化措施红利不断释放

为了吸引并更好地服务国际游客，中国旅游业在产品和服务上进行了诸多创新和升级，特别是在优化签证和通关政策、提升支付便利性、加强数字化旅游服务等方面。这些举措不仅简化了入境手续，降低了"中国游"的门槛，优化了国际游客来华的体验，也推动了旅游业整体服务水平的提升。

来华签证方面，截至 2024 年 11 月末，中国已同 25 个国家实现了全面免签，先后对法国、德国等 38 个国家实行单方面免签政策。国家移民管理局出台了 110 余项便利外籍人员来华政策措施，持续优化区域性入境免签、过境免签、口岸签证政策，推动外籍人员来华数量不断攀升。其中，144 小时过境免签政策，适用范围已增至 35 个口岸、54 个国家。

移动支付方面，文化和旅游部将国家星级以上旅游景区、省级以上旅游度假区、国家级旅游休闲街区、全国乡村旅游重点村镇等四类旅游场所列为重点场所，推动完善外籍人员证件和支付方式的预约验证，让入境游客可以灵活选择银行卡、现金、移动支付等多样化的方式，帮助入境游客"畅游中国"。中国人民银行、国家外汇管理局指导全国主要支付机构，简化身份验证流程，提高绑卡效率，将单笔交易限额提高至5000 美元，年累计限额提升至 5 万美元，便利外籍人员扫码支付进行日常消费。同时，扩大优质商户"白名单"覆盖范围，确保外籍人员在住宿、教育、医疗等关键场景中的支付需求得到保障。此外，线上外卡收单业务稳步推进，进一步丰富外籍人员在境内网购的支付渠道。

中国各地政府根据当地的地域特点和城市特质，积极推动外籍人士来华便利化措施的延伸和完善，这些措施也有效提升了入境旅游的吸引力。

作为正在建设自由贸易港的海岛省份，海南省实行的免签入境政策允许 59 个国家人士因旅游、商贸、探亲、访问、医疗、会展、体育竞技等短期事由免签停留 30 天。自 2024 年 5 月起，外国旅游团乘坐邮轮入境免签政策正式实施，即通过包括海口和三亚在内的 13 个沿海城市的邮轮口岸入境的外国游客，可以免签停留 15 天。7 月 30 日起，港澳地区外国旅游团入境海南 144 小时免签政策正式实施。为进一步提升游客体验，海南还持续扩容旅客查验通道，提升通关效率，并提供多语言服务，确保外籍游客获得高效、便利的出入境服务。

作为中国重要的对俄边境旅游区，黑龙江在"一带一路"倡议背景下积极发展边境旅游。目前，在黑河等边境城市，相继开发了多条康养、休闲等特色旅游线路。数据显示，2024年前10个月入境俄罗斯游客数量已超9万人，显示了中俄边境旅游的活力与成果。

在成渝地区，四川省与重庆市通过建立口岸签证协作机制，实现了"川渝通办"。这一机制通过信息共享与资质互认，进一步优化了入境旅游团的行程管理，将"渝进渝出"调整为"渝进或渝出"，使外国游客的出入境方式更加灵活多样，为两地的旅游合作提供了更为有力的政策保障。

（三）"中国游"市场前景广阔

旅游是综合性产业。在中国，发展旅游业是推动高质量发展的关键着力点，也是拉动各地区经济发展的重要动力。在打造旅游强国的大背景下，"中国游"市场潜力巨大，对带动世界经济发展具有重要作用。

中国是一个旅游资源丰富的大国。从旅游资源样态来看，从北方的冰雪世界到南方的热带海滨，从东部的繁华都市到西部的高原山川，中国的旅游资源在全球范围内都具有独特的吸引力；从旅游理念来看，随着旅游成为世界人民美好生活的刚性需求，中国突出自然绿色、文化保护、科技创新等旅游元素，提供了让境外游客放心、舒心、开心的旅行体验；从旅游产品的创新角度来看，旅游需求和细分市场不断涌现，推动旅游场景、产品和服务的创造性提升和创新性发展；从旅游推动国际贸易合作的角度看，入境旅行商业务逐步恢复，部分企业入境游客接待量接近2019年水平；从旅游宣发与推广的角度看，各类国际交流活动和与国际旅游组织的合作，极大提升了"中国游"在全球的知名度与影响力。

旅游业的发展，有助于提高旅游服务贸易的开放程度，提高旅游服务贸易的竞争力，逐步消除国际贸易壁垒，创造更加自由、便利的投资环境，从而吸引外资进入中国旅游市场。改革开放初期，中国通过"旅游搭台，经贸唱戏"，利用入境游作为契机，向世界展示中国的社会与营商环境。如今，免签政策的不断优化，将进一步吸引更多外国人来华旅行、经商、工作、学习、生活，推动经贸、人文合作，促进各类要素跨国流动。

中国国际经济交流中心首席研究员张燕生表示，单方面免签对促进人员往来非常重要，对促进利用外资作用明显，将为货物和服务贸易、运输、资金、数据和信息往来等活动带来更高水平、更高效率的自由便利。

中欧数字协会主席路易吉·甘巴尔代拉表示，免签政策使欧洲中小企业前往中国参加商务、展览等活动更加便利，在全球经济复苏乏力、保护主义倾向抬头的当下，中国持续优化签证政策让更多外国投资者实地考察、产生兴趣，减少投资的不确定性，无疑为提振世界经济、推进经济全球化注入更大信心和动能。

根据世界旅游及旅行理事会发布的《2024年旅行与旅游经济影响：全球趋势》报告，中国已经成为全球第二大旅游市场，在未来十年，中国有望超过美国，成为全球最大的旅游市场。推动高水平"中国游"发展，能够加快推进旅游业供给侧结构性改革，加大优质旅游产品供给力度，不断完善旅游产品供给体系，推进文化和旅游深度融合，带动文化娱乐、住宿餐饮、交通运输等旅游相关产业发展，同时持续健全旅游服务质量监管体系和旅游市场综合监管机制，大力提升旅游市场治理能力和治理水平。新时代中国形象将以更加多姿多彩、具体可感的方式呈现在全世界人民眼前。

二、"中国游"让世界直观感知中国式现代化发展成果

2024年7月，中国共产党二十届三中全会通过的《中共中央关于

进一步全面深化改革、推进中国式现代化的决定》明确提出，推动走出去、请进来管理便利化，扩大国际人文交流合作。中国政府坚持全面深化改革主基调，不断释放免签入境政策红利，张开双臂欢迎海外友人走进中国、畅游中国，推动中国与世界相知相交。中国拥有悠久历史、灿烂文化、壮美山川、多样风情，来华境外游客在深度游览体验中，对中华文化的博大精深、中国式现代化的发展成果有了直观感受，从内心深处为中国发展的奇迹点赞叫好。

（一）感受古今交融的中华文化魅力

中国旅游研究院入境游客满意度专项调查显示，超六成的受访者将体验中国文化作为来华旅行的主要目的。中华文明历史悠久，是世界上唯一没有中断、发展至今的文明。当代中国重视对历史文化遗产的传承保护，重视对中华优秀传统文化的创造性转化、创新性发展，来华的境外游客在中国时时处处都能享受到传统与当代交融汇聚的文化盛宴。中华文化的独特魅力正成为中国作为国际旅游目的地的核心吸引力。

在丝绸之路重镇敦煌，多元文明在此交汇。2024 年 10 月，由 1000 余名境外游客组成的"美丽中国行·千人入境游甘肃"观光团走进甘肃敦煌，开启了一场精彩纷呈的文化与自然探索之旅。在世界文化遗产莫高窟，他们领略了多元文明交流孕育的石窟艺术瑰宝，每一幅壁画、每一尊雕塑仿佛都在诉说着千年文化的故事。游客们不仅被这些精美的艺术品所震撼，更对敦煌文化的璀璨绚丽、中华文明的博大精深有了最直观的感受。

从展现古丝绸之路文明交流的敦煌莫高窟，到代表中华民族精神的万里长城，从体现明清宫廷文化的故宫博物院，到展示古代士大夫隐逸文化的苏州园林……目前，中国有 59 项世界遗产，其中文化遗产 40 项、自然与文化双遗产 4 项。这些类型众多、内涵丰富的文化遗产都让远道而来的外国游客赞不绝口。

中国传统文化的经典名著，在数字化时代再创作后，以生动的形式传递着中国文化和中国人的价值观。在山西铁佛寺、玉皇庙、延庆寺，来自意大利的"洋悟空"阿雷带着一根定制版金箍棒时而挥舞、时而定格，留下自己矫健的身影。随着首款国产3A游戏《黑神话：悟空》成为中国文化对外传播的名片，越来越多外国人"跟着悟空游山西"。阿雷说，感觉自己就像游戏中的"天命人"，跋山涉水、克服困难，最后得到的"宝藏"就是看到这些宏伟的中华传统建筑。

不仅有形的物质文化遗产让外国游客魂牵梦绕，根植于中华文明并传承至今的非物质文化遗产同样给他们留下深刻印象，非物质文化遗产亦能绽放时代芳华。

2024年9月，黑龙江省黑河市五大连池风景区的工人疗养院迎来一批俄罗斯游客。他们在这里观火山、品矿泉、晒日光浴，享受悠闲的度假时光，还特意体验中医药非物质文化遗产。针灸、推拿等项目吸引了瓦莉亚前来排队体验。她的同胞拉莉萨已经沉浸在拔罐治疗带来的愉悦中，"我感觉效果非常好，这次打算在黑河待14天，深度体验中医疗养，附带旅游。"五大连池工人疗养院康复医院院长许飙介绍，越来越多俄罗斯人对中医感兴趣，回头客也越来越多，高峰期疗养院一天接待俄罗斯游客约1500人。

2024年3月，在深圳一家掐丝珐琅非遗体验工坊，来自澳大利亚的视频博主蒂姆聚精会神地将蓝色矿物颜料填充到一件金属挂件的镂空部分，他想把这款亲手制作的掐丝珐琅工艺品带回国送给母亲。

如今，越来越多外国游客对富有中华文化韵味的中医、茶艺、泥塑、彩绘等非遗技艺流露出浓厚兴趣，并且愿意亲自体验制作过程，感受其丰富而独特的内涵。人们在旅途中感悟文化、增进了解，中国经济社会发展的蓬勃活力与文化魅力也得以充分彰显。

（二）体验科技改变生活的新场景

在这轮"中国游"热潮中，无数外国游客心怀对中国历史古迹和传统文化的向往踏足这片土地，也被当代中国高速发展的壮丽画卷和随处可见的科技成果所震撼。

交通是旅游的重要载体，"坐着高铁看中国"已成为越来越多外国游客选择的出行方式。中国"八纵八横"高铁网逐渐加密成型，从北国雪域到南方水乡，从东部沿海到西部高原，高铁网络覆盖了中国的广袤大地，畅通了旅客游玩之路，使得游客能够轻松到达目的地。来华外国游客可以乘坐高铁快速穿梭于不同的景点之间，欣赏窗外山川美景，体验中国先进高铁技术的智能便捷。

"一部手机游中国"让所有的旅行变得更加轻松和高效。2024年，来自英国的环球旅行博主克里斯·哈钦森带着家人到中国旅游，经历了从现金支付到手机支付的转变。哈钦森表示："学会使用微信和支付宝后，一切都变得轻松简单了许多。一切都能用手机完成，连街边小吃摊都能扫码支付，真是太不可思议了！"行至深圳，哈钦森夫妇体验到了由无人机配送的外卖服务。在上海的外滩，哈钦森夫妇漫步在夜幕下，欣赏着璀璨的城市光影，他们描述道："整个城市都被科技环绕，我们看到了如同火箭般直插云霄的高楼，就连桥上都有不断变幻的全息投影。"

另一对来自英国的旅行博主泰兹和莉比，则更深入地体验了高科技支付方式。他们在深圳开通了刷脸乘车的免密支付功能，体验到"一秒进站"的便捷。泰兹表示："我们从来没有在其他地方体验过将自己的脸作为地铁票，感觉像是穿越到了2050年。"

中国城市的现代感和科技感深深打动了游客。在深圳岗厦北地铁站，一对外国情侣惊讶于其内部极富设计感和科技感的建筑。他们以第一视角拍摄的短视频在TikTok上广受欢迎，评论区满是饱含赞美的留言："它就像星际驿站一样美！""这是通往未来世界的列车！"

黄山通过"国际化友好景区"共建计划，让数字化更好地服务旅游体验。外国游客只需扫描二维码进入小程序，即可查看详细的旅游攻略，通过支付宝内置的"翻译服务"，还可将导览内容一键翻译成英语、法语、德语、西班牙语、马来语、阿拉伯语、意大利语等 16 种语言。手机端优化服务既助力全球游客轻松游玩黄山，又帮助游客加深对徽派文化的理解。

2024 年，新西兰游客阿尔内·赫尔曼时隔 28 年再访上海，连连感叹这座城市翻天覆地的变化："当年从外滩往浦东看，对岸的高楼只有东方明珠广播电视塔。现在在东方明珠周围，陆家嘴地区已高楼成群了。"这一切都体现了上海作为全球科技与经济中心的飞速发展。

（三）走入中国城乡居民的美好生活

在"中国游"热潮中，外国游客不仅被中国城市各具特色的自然景观、历史建筑、民俗文化所吸引，还热衷走进菜市场、街角公园、晨练广场等市井生活场所，感受当代中国城乡居民的日常生活之变，市井生活场景正在成为外国游客"新宠"。

近年来，中国城乡居民的文化消费呈现多元化、个性化、精品化趋势，从阅读、听音乐，到追剧、看电影；从逛展览、看演出，到游览名胜古迹，丰富多彩的文化产品和服务充实了中国城乡居民的精神文化生活。城乡居民的美好生活，正是游客眼中的美好风景。中外游客正在加速进入城乡居民的日常生活场景，"菜市场游"与博物馆、美术馆和戏剧场同时受到游客追捧。

2024 年前 8 个月，上海接待外国游客 290.86 万人次，较 2023 年同期增长 1.4 倍。那些展示着上海市民当下幸福生活的旅游线路和产品深受入境游客青睐。瑞士游客菲利普游览了外滩摩登都市的繁华锦绣之后，步入江南水乡朱家角古镇，走访古色古香的老街，品尝阿婆粽子、小笼包等美食，静享美好时光。

美国姑娘劳伦·加斯特参加了一项特别的上海"跟团游"——探访曹杨新村。短暂的一天内，她和伙伴们跟着上海阿姨学习制作菜肉馄饨等沪上美食，在社区活动中心和当地居民"对战"乒乓球，还逛了充满"烟火气"的菜市场，体验一把"上海人"的感觉。

在位于重庆中心城区的解放碑美食街，琳琅满目的美食汇集于此，闪烁的霓虹与扑鼻的香味相互交融，展现着浓浓的烟火气。来自印度尼西亚的游客贾贾尔温·塞蒂亚布迪对这里的烧烤和甜品情有独钟，他表示，自己去过不少中国的大城市，重庆不仅有丰富的街边美食，更让游客充满"松弛感"。

在几千公里外的中国北疆，越来越多的俄罗斯人选择到黑龙江省黑河市体验异国风情、参与文化活动，包括逛早市、品尝当地美食、购买特色小商品等。黑河市文化广电和旅游局相关负责人介绍，2024 年前 10 个月，黑河接待出入境游客 65.94 万人次，同比增长 160.12%。

随着乡村振兴战略实施和城乡一体化发展，中国乡村焕发出古老乡土文明与现代生活方式交融辉映的无穷魅力。越来越多外国游客把目光从东部一线城市转向广袤的中西部农村，深度打卡乡土中国，沉浸式感受这片古老土地上的风土人情，体验更加立体多元的中国形象。美国摄影师亚当·克莱顿对中国传统古村落情有独钟，这几年他一直辗转在乡土中国，寻访古色古香的传统民居。位于山西省晋城市的皇城相府，气势恢宏、结构精巧，是他最喜欢的中国传统村落之一。

田园采摘、布艺扎染、插秧割麦……携程针对外籍游客推出的"住度假农庄，当一天中国农民"特色农文旅体验项目备受市场欢迎。越来越多的外籍游客走进恬静美好的乡村景观，沉浸式感受这片古老土地上的风土人情，连中国网友都感慨"这届'老外'更会玩了"。

（四）欣赏生态文明建设的美丽画卷

中国，不仅以其深厚的文化底蕴吸引着世界的目光，更以其壮丽多姿的自然景色，让无数外国游客为之倾倒。从壮丽的天山山脉到秀美的江南水乡，从雄伟的黄河之畔到神秘的雪域高原，每一寸土地都蕴藏着大自然的无尽魅力。新时代以来，中国生态文明建设实现了历史性、转折性、全局性变化，美丽中国建设步伐不断加快，促进人与自然和谐共生的现代化蓬勃发展，中国天更蓝、山更绿、水更清，万里河山更加多姿多彩。

用镜头捕捉奇观，海外博主频频点赞中华美景。在湖南张家界，韩国游客望着眼前起伏连绵的千山万峰，发出"这是只有神才能创造出的人间仙境"的由衷赞美，比利时博主一吉徒步四川九寨沟拍摄美轮美奂的湖光山色，英国摄影师深入新疆腹地用镜头捕捉天山脚下的林海雪原……在海外社交平台上，一条条展示中国山水秘境的视频获赞无数。

哈尔滨，作为中国最北部的省会城市，被誉为"冰城"。每年冬季，凭借冰雕雪景、冰雪运动等独特文旅资源，这里吸引海内外游客纷至沓来。2024年2月，加拿大博主史蒂夫和妻子伊凡娜走进哈尔滨冰雪大世界，映入眼帘的中式古建楼阁、西方城堡、摩天轮、拱门、城墙、滑梯皆由冰块雕砌而成。夜幕降临，这些造型华丽、构思精巧的"冰建筑"被灯光点亮，整个景区瞬间变成流光溢彩的童话世界。游客们在冰雪中溜冰、滑雪、打陀螺、骑自行车，享受着冰雪带来的乐趣。史蒂夫感叹道："太酷了，即使我来自加拿大，也从未见过如此奇妙的冰雪世界。到这里的人只有两个选择，要么惊叹于前所未见的景观，要么全程不停地拍照录像。"

作为世界上拥有最多世界自然遗产、文化与自然双遗产的国家之一，中国一直致力于文化遗产和生态资源的保护工作，坚持文化引领、生态优先，创新资源保护利用模式，把文化内涵、"绿水青山就是金山银山"

重要理念融入旅游业发展全过程。许多来华外国友人纷纷用镜头捕捉旅行中的美丽自然景色，他们拍摄的一张张照片、一段段视频，让中国生态治理与绿色发展的辉煌成果生动地呈现在世人眼前。

在浙江省安吉县的余村，翠竹摇曳、溪水流淌，层层叠叠的绿意令人心旷神怡。作为"绿水青山就是金山银山"理念的发源地，余村于2005年深入实施"千村示范、万村整治"工程，淘汰重污染企业，开展村庄整治，转型发展农家乐休闲旅游。2021年，余村入选联合国世界旅游组织评选的首批"最佳旅游乡村"。2023年，余村接待游客115多万人次，村集体经济总收入达2247万元。

云南省西双版纳傣族自治州立足生物多样性资源禀赋，厚植"有林才有水、有水才有田、有田才有粮、有粮才有人"的传统生态理念，以旅游行业"无废景区"建设为抓手，推动旅游产业绿色"无废"转型升级，将"无废景区"建设与4A级景区西双版纳傣族园相结合，全面发展绿色旅游，2024年前10个月接待游客197万人次，比2023年同期增加20%。

三、"中国游"传播可信可爱可敬的中国形象

中国发展高质量、高水平的入境游，让更多外国游客可以来、希望来、愿意来，使他们通过亲身体验、亲自考察爱上了可信可爱可敬的中国，形成对中国的准确理解，进一步参与和共享中国的发展机遇。

（一）有效扭转刻板片面印象

入境游是国际游客直接、深入了解中国的重要渠道，也是以民间交流塑造国家形象的有效方式。许多外国人通过媒体了解中国，但一些西方媒体出于各种目的对中国的报道要么失声失语，要么有失客观公正，

导致外国人不能了解全面、真实的中国。相比之下，基于个人实地体验和互动交流的入境游，为更多外国游客提供了身临其境体验广袤中国的机会，比媒体传达更为直观可触，更有助于塑造一个真实、立体、全面的中国形象。

火爆的"中国游"打开了世界了解认知中国的新窗口、新通道，快乐的"中国行"成为不少外国人的"破除偏见"之旅，"反差感"是很多外国游客在饱览中国大好河山、呼吸中国文化空气之后最直观的感受。大地之上的城市风光和悠久建筑，建筑之下流动的历史底蕴和市民生活，眼见为实有助于刷新认知，置身其中能更好认识和感受真实，一些外国旅游博主甚至直呼"被西方媒体骗了"，越来越多入境游客真切感受到"中国并不像我们原来想象的那样""看到了一个西方媒体永远不会展现的中国"。

美国博主克里斯就是其中典型的例子。来到北京进行为期三天的旅行，彻底改变了他对中国的看法。他感受到了中国的热情友好、高科技的便利和人民生活质量的提高，甚至萌生了长期居住的想法。

日本无限合同会社首席经济学家田代秀敏近日访问上海后表示，他完全没有看到西方媒体所描述的"萧条景象"，反而目睹了中国城市中燃油车与电动车并行行驶、基础设施更新的新变化。他还感受到，中国的各个领域正在实现数字化，从无现金支付到智能交通引导系统，整个社会都在朝着现代化、数字化的方向快速发展。他深刻感受到，中国正逐步向世界领先的地位迈进。

（二）展示中国对外开放决心

开放是当代中国的鲜明标识，也是中国向世界释放的巨大红利。国际旅游是在第二次世界大战后，尤其在全球化进程的推动下，迅速发展成为全球经济中的重要组成部分。2019 年，旅游业为全球 GDP 贡献了

9.6 万亿美元，占比高达 10.3%；还为全球劳动力市场创造了 10% 的就业机会；国际游客支出也达到 1.8 万亿美元，占出口总额的 6.8%。经过新冠疫情的冲击，2023 年全球旅游业的出口收入已恢复到疫情前水平的 96%。然而，相较于欧洲、美洲、非洲等地区，亚太地区的旅游业的恢复速度仍相对较慢。

作为全球旅游业不可或缺的重要组成部分，中国为国际游客提供独特且多元的旅游产品。中国旅游业正以一种开放的姿态，不仅向世界讲述充满活力和机遇的中国故事，还为提升全球旅游业整体服务水平提供中国经验与方案。"中国游"的蓬勃发展，将为全球旅游业的繁荣贡献中国智慧和中国力量。

为了更好地迎接外籍游客，广东省部分旅行社推出了多条入境旅游线路。例如，广之旅国际旅行社推出的旅游线路，从半天到六天不等，涵盖广州快速经典游、步行探索之旅、慢享城市之旅、科技民俗游以及文化体验之旅等多种产品，行程广度涵盖城市生活、周边玩乐、展会商贸等；覆盖区域既有广州本地深度游览，也有"广州 + 湾区城市"联游线路。广之旅国际旅行社相关负责人介绍，预计在广州的春交会、秋交会等境外客商来穗高峰期间，相关旅游产品将成为参展客商"在穗生活方式"的一部分。

在长三角地区，上海与周边城市如杭州、苏州等地合作，推出"144 小时过境免签 + 城市游"的区域游模式。这一模式被专家认为突破了单一城市的限制，有效促进长三角地区入境旅游市场的复苏与发展。自 2024 年 6 月起，上海 3000 余家文化场所取消预约限制，支持外国游客凭护照等有效证件入馆参观，有效提升了外国游客的游览体验。

北京推出境外银行卡非接触式过闸乘车服务，外籍乘客可使用万事达卡和维萨卡直接在地铁站刷卡进站，无需单独购买车票，不区分乘客国籍，实行资费统一。上海则推动公交乘车码外卡刷码改造，外籍乘客只需绑定外卡，并通过腾讯微信小程序开通乘车码，即可在上海公交、地铁、轮渡、磁悬浮等多种场景中使用，为境外人士提供了更便捷的数字化公交出行服务。

在 2024 中国国际旅游交易会上，中外客商交流互动，展现彼此最具吸引力的文化旅游资源。与会者听宣讲、看项目、谈合作，感受中国高水平对外开放为世界旅游经济注入的强劲动力，也进一步体会到中国始终坚定不移扩大对外开放的决心。

（三）共享中国市场发展机遇

以利相交，利尽则散；以势相交，势去则倾……惟以心相交，方成其久远。中国始终秉承"天下大同""天下一家"的观念，始终保持开放包容的态度，接纳吸收不同文化，求同存异、相互尊重，欢迎更多外国朋友来到中国，谱写更多热气腾腾的中外往来佳话，发现更多活力满满的互利合作机遇。入境游受益于中国坚定不移扩大对外开放的政策，与中国发展同频共进。

从繁华的都市景观到古老的乡村风情，从充满活力的产业园区到科技感十足的创新中心，中国展现出的多元面貌让不断涌入的外籍人士着迷。随着对中国了解的加深，一些外国游客从中嗅到发展良机，决定投身这片热土，融入当地的生活，找到事业发展的平台，成为多元文化社会的一部分。

1984 年，美国人布莱恩·林登第一次来到中国。他被中国的风土人情和文化深深吸引，特别是对中国的农村产生了深厚的感情。2008 年，他选择到云南大理经营民宿，搭建起了一个传播中国传统文化的交流平台。在这里，他见证了中国的飞速发展，并表示："40 年前，我对中国一无所知，现在我已经能写毛笔字了。中国也成了我的家。"

十多年前，法国人热雷米·格里尼安受朋友之邀来到海南旅行，被当地的迷人风光所吸引，决定留下来。老街深处的小吃店、公园里的椰林与落日、海上的冲浪爱好者……格里尼安用镜头记录下这里的生活日常，并慢慢找到自己热爱的事业。从拍摄照片到拍摄视频，再到导演电影，格里尼安在海南这片充满机遇的热土上，不断追逐并实现着自己的梦想。

9年前，瓷器爱好者"泥的明"从纽约来到景德镇，深深感受到了这里陶瓷文化的魅力，并在这里找到了一片属于自己的事业天地。从2015年起，景德镇陶溪川国际工作室启动了"候鸟计划"，每年邀请来自50多个国家和地区的艺术家在这里创作并留下作品。泥的明表示："景德镇无处不在的陶瓷艺术气息令我着迷，我喜欢这里亲切、精致、自由的生活环境，我会在这里继续工作、生活下去。"

2024年以来，多个国家的驻华使节和外交官到黑龙江、上海、甘肃等地实地考察，深入了解当地的经济发展、文化特色和社会状况，以期发现新的机遇，共同书写合作发展的新篇章。斯洛伐克驻华大使利扎克在黑龙江考察时说，"雪乡成功将冰雪资源转化为消费现象，这里的环境和氛围让我想起了家乡，我们也有很多这样的小镇，可以利用它们发展冬季旅游，这有很大的潜力。"

2024年6月，来自22个国家的30位驻华使节和高级外交官到甘肃省兰州市和敦煌市，考察调研当地的绿色产业发展。外交官一行来到位于戈壁滩上的敦煌光电产业园区，感受这里蓬勃发展的绿色新动能。佛得角驻华大使阿林多·多罗萨里奥对这个"超级镜子发电站"感到震撼，并赞叹道："戈壁滩上原本寸草不生，但中国用自然和科技的力量，让戈壁滩充满生命气息，创造了不可能的奇迹。"

2024年8月，一个由政府官员、企业家、专家组成的印尼参访团来到能源大省山西，走访参观了多家能源企业和低碳产业园区，近距离探寻了煤炭资源型地区的转型之路，并表示希望未来能有机会与中国山西省的企业合作。

作为一个蓬勃发展的国家，中国拥有充满活力的市场环境、丰富的自然和文化资源、多样的政府扶持政策，不仅为外国人才提供了多元化的职业选择和广阔的发展空间，也为与中国合作的外国企业提供了事业飞跃发展的平台，为推动全球经济的共同繁荣作出了积极贡献。

四、中国游"推动文明交流互鉴

旅游是传播文明、交流文化、增进友谊的桥梁，也是增强人们亲近感的重要方式。伴随着中国旅游业发展日新月异、蓬勃向上，入境旅游在增进不同文明包容理解、丰富世界文明百花园、促进世界和平与稳定等方面发挥着越来越显著的作用。

（一）增进不同文明包容理解

国之交在于民相亲，民相亲在于心相通。国际旅游作为一种全球性的文化交流现象，极大促进了世界各国不同文明的交流交融。旅游为不同国家、民族和信仰的人提供了面对面接触的机会，外来游客通过身临其境的走访和体验对旅游地产生真实感知，当地居民通过与游客的接触互动而对客源国形成初步印象。旅游观光搭建起民心相通的桥梁，有利于提升不同文明间的共情能力，使人们以更加包容的视角看待国家之间的差异和分歧，从而以文明多样性的审美欣赏不同社会的活力与精彩。

1980 年通过的《马尼拉世界旅游宣言》指出，旅游应在促进和平、解决争端、维护国际经济秩序等全球性重大社会问题中发挥作用。各国文化背景不同，在不同文化的碰撞与交流中，各国人民可以相互了解彼此的生活、习俗、价值观念与行为方式，减少误解、消除隔阂，增进理解、建立友谊，为国际合作奠定民意基础。通过真实的旅游接触，主客双方可以增进彼此的文化联系，建构起对异国文化和民众的认知，日益密切的人文交流如涓涓细流，汇聚成友好交往的奔涌长河。

"中国游"为中外民众提供了直接的交流互动平台，这不仅增加中国与世界文化的理解与尊重，还促进了中外民众之间的融合与包容。通过体验和互动，外国游客能够更加深入地了解和欣赏中国的文化背景和社会习俗，不断加强跨文化交流与理解。同时，外国游客亲身体验中国的生活方式和社会环境，能够更真实地感受到中国的发展和变化。同时，社交媒体的发展也让外国游客将他们的中国之旅分享到世界各地，进一步促进不同文化之间的相互理解和欣赏。

近年来，中国与多个国家的文化旅游合作不断深化，中俄、中意等双边合作机制不断发展，中国与法国、哈萨克斯坦、坦桑尼亚、赞比亚、马来西亚等国家互办文化旅游年，与多米尼加、萨尔瓦多等新建（复）交国家开展文旅交流……这些对外文化和旅游交流合作成为中国推动构建人类命运共同体的生动注脚。

2024年5月，以"旅游促进中美人文交流"为主题的第14届中美旅游高层对话在西安举办，时隔5年"重启"的这次交流活动有力促进了两国业界合作。多个美国旅行商踩线团随后陆续走进北京、西安、重庆、上海，观名胜、品美食、扫码付，沉浸式体验"中国游"，两国业界的交流互动助力"旧金山愿景"化为实景。

（二）丰富世界文明百花园

旅游不仅是文化的载体，更是一种文化习得方式。中国古人将"行万里路"和"读万卷书"并列为同等重要的修身之法。在旅游活动中，游客基于"求新""求异""求知""求美""求乐"等旅游动机形成的旅游行为，实质上也是感知文化、体验文化、乐享文化和传播文化的过程。文化产业和旅游产业密不可分，坚持以文塑旅、以旅彰文，推动文化和旅游融合发展，才能更好地让人们在领略自然之美中，感悟文化之美、陶冶心灵之美。

中国文化源远流长，中华文明博大精深。通过到中国入境旅游，世界友人感悟中华文化，深入了解中华文明历史，从中更加深切地感受中华文明突出的连续性、创新性、统一性、包容性、和平性。

亲眼看见气势恢宏、形态各异的秦始皇兵马俑，更能感受到秦统一六国的龙威虎势；亲耳聆听声调柔和、意境古雅的纳西古乐，更能感受到"中华古乐之活化石"的神奇。曲径通幽的苏州园林和华丽婉转的昆曲唱腔，可以让人领略到江南风情和吴侬软语；巍峨高耸的布达拉宫和庄严肃穆的大昭寺，能够令人体会到藏地文化的独特魅力。

近年来，地方政府灵活运用本地旅游资源，坚持弘扬中华优秀传统文化和社会主义先进文化，加快推动文化和旅游深度融合发展，精心打造出诸多体现文化内涵、人文精神的特色文化和旅游产品。北京大兴机场、港珠澳大桥、中国天眼……一批代表性的工程，让旅游成为展示新时代建设成就的重要窗口。164 个国家级旅游休闲街区、142 个国家工业旅游示范基地，丰富社会主义先进文化的传播阵地，让中外游客在旅途中感受城市现代美、工业美、科技美。

新时代"中国游"，向外国游客充分展示中华优秀传统文化的历史渊源、发展脉络、基本走向，充分体现中华文化的独特创造、价值理念、鲜明特色，彰显中国当代文化的独特魅力，使中国文化和中国旅游进一步走向世界，丰富世界文明百花园。

（三）促进世界和平与稳定

旅游是人与人最直接、最自然的交流方式，是开放的窗口、友谊的纽带、和平的使者。"旅游让人们团结在一起。"联合国秘书长安东尼奥·古特雷斯在 2024 年世界旅游日寄语中表示，要思考旅游与和平之间的深刻联系。

　　"以旅游促和平"的理念由来已久。古希腊时期，著名的"奥林匹克休战"是君主们为保障运动员和观众安全的旅行（从遥远的家到赛场）而进行的"和平壮举"。很多希腊城邦在除奥运会之外的日子几乎一直处于战争状态，战争各方约定，奥运会开闭幕的前后7天为休战日，各国要为参会者提供保护，这使得外交、旅行、和平三者之间产生了关联。

　　许多世界名人对国际旅游的作用寄予了很高期待，认为旅行是推动国际合作、国际理解和国际和平的重要方式。"二战"后，尤其是20世纪80年代以来，随着跨国旅游的蓬勃发展，"以旅游促和平"的理念引起越来越多人的关注。圣雄甘地曾说："我看到天南海北的文化飘绕我的庭院，清风吹来了和平的种子，因为旅行是和平的语言。"回顾中国外交史，带有不同目的的和平之旅是中国古代对外交往的一种特殊方式，鉴真东渡、玄奘西行、郑和七下西洋，在今天看虽属宗教之旅、政务之旅，但其旅行的形式和外交的效果流传百世。

　　当前，世界百年未有之大变局加速演进，世界之变、时代之变、历史之变正以前所未有的方式展开，不同文化之间的冲突时有发生。而旅游业被誉为"和平的使者""友谊的桥梁"，能够在紧张局势下起到"稳定剂""润滑剂"的作用。面对逆全球化浪潮和民粹主义思潮，和平与发展依然是绝大多数国家以及国际社会积极努力的方向，也为推动人类共同应对各种严峻挑战和困难注入持续动力。中国旅游外交作为大国外交的一部分，时时把握并放大时代主旋律，通过入境游讲好中国故事，展示"美丽中国"形象。

　　在实践层面，中国入境游从人类长远利益出发，逐步形成了"和平旅游""绿色旅游"等涉旅议题。中国入境游在尊重文化多样性和社会价值观的基础上，充分发挥自身的旅游发展优势，高举构建人类命运共同体的鲜明旗帜，把旅游发展视为人类社会的共同利益，从减少国家间偏见、增进国家间共识、实现国际社会互利共赢的目标出发，在服务国家利益的同时，发挥并突出旅游连接客源地与目的地的媒介作用，进一步缩小国家间利益差距，摆脱客源依赖，促进优势互补和共同进步，努力将其打造成为推动人类进步和实现全人类共同价值的"公共产品"，为构建人类命运共同体宏伟目标的实现开辟新的渠道。

结　语

中国人自古就有旅游的文化传统，先贤们"读万卷书，行万里路"，留下了无数脍炙人口的旅游名篇佳作。

三百多年前，中国明代著名学者徐霞客游历四方，"达人所之未达，探人所之未知"，经 30 多年旅行撰写的《徐霞客游记》，既是系统观察和记述自然的世界地理名著，又是描绘中国大好山河的旅游巨篇，有着广泛而深远的影响。《徐霞客游记》的开篇之日，即 5 月 19 日，被定为中国旅游日。

七百多年前，威尼斯旅行家马可·波罗跨越万里来到中国，打开了东西方相识相知的大门，把个人的非凡之旅转化成了欧亚大陆各国的共同记忆，架起了东西方文明交流的桥梁。一代代使者接续谱写丝绸之路上文明交流的友好篇章，树立了世界不同文明平等对话、共同发展的典范。

随着全球化进程的加快，入境游已不仅仅是经济活动的组成部分，更成为文化交流与民间外交的重要载体，是衡量一个国家文化软实力、国际吸引力的重要指标。改革开放四十多年以来，入境游不仅促进了中国的经济发展，还增进了中国与世界各国之间的交流与合作，加强了地区间的友好往来，为世界文明交融作出贡献。

未来中国开放的大门会越开越大，"中国游"便利化水平会不断提升，将有更多外国友人来到中国、看见中国、享受中国、爱上中国。新时代的"中国游"将带给世界更多的中国故事，也将凝聚更多全球共识，促进世界各国共同开创人文交流、文化交融、民心相通新局面，让世界文明百花园姹紫嫣红、生机盎然。

诚挚地欢迎更多外国朋友来华旅游，欣赏中国美丽的山河，感受中国独特的魅力，携手开启人文交流的新篇章！

参考文献

1.《习近平向第 14 届中美旅游高层对话开幕致信》，新华社，2024 年 5 月 22 日。

2.《习近平对旅游工作作出重要指示 强调着力完善现代旅游业体系 加快建设旅游强国推动旅游业高质量发展行稳致远》，新华社，2024 年 5 月 17 日。

3.《习近平同意大利总统马塔雷拉分别向"意大利之源——古罗马文明展"开幕式致贺信》，新华社，2022 年 7 月 10 日。

4.《习近平在教育文化卫生体育领域专家代表座谈会上的讲话》，新华社，2020 年 9 月 22 日。

5.《习近平在亚洲文明对话大会开幕式上的主旨演讲》，新华社，2019 年 5 月 15 日。

6.《习近平在联合国教科文组织总部的演讲》，新华社，2014 年 3 月 27 日。

7.《习近平在俄罗斯"中国旅游年"开幕式上的致辞》，人民日报，2013 年 3 月 22 日。

8. 刘中才、谢正发：《全球化视域下提升中国旅游外交话语权》，《群言》，2024 年第 8 期，第 36—39 页。

9. 张振鹏：《面向中国式现代化的文化和旅游融合发展方略》，《国家治理》，2024 年第 12 期，第 46—51 页。

10. 徐彤、张毓利、石培华：《中国旅游发展格局的历史演化与现实研判》，《发展研究》，2024 年第 6 期，第 42—48 页。

11. 孙盼盼、黎晓颖：《入境旅游助力建设世界旅游强国：效应机制与优化策略》，《价格理论与实践》，2024 年第 5 期，第 32—38 页。

12. 宋瑞：《论独具特色的中国旅游发展道路》，《价格理论与实践》，2024 年第 7 期，第 50—58 页。

13. 刘民坤、邓小桂：《边境旅游增进文化认同的路径研究——基于讲好中国故事的视角》，《广西社会科学》，2024 年第 2 期，第 21—27 页。

14. 戴斌、阳玉平：《新质生产力视域下我国旅游的理论建构与实践研究——中国旅游研究院院长、博士生导师戴斌教授访谈》，《社会科学家》，2024 年第 3 期，第 3—9 页。

15. 《坚定走好独具特色的中国旅游发展之路》，《新华每日电讯》，2024 年 5 月 18 日，第 002 版。

16. 谢朝武、章坤、陈岩英：《中国入境旅游恢复发展的支撑体系与行动方向》，《旅游学刊》，2024 年第 4 期，第 4—6 页。

17. 陈晔、王璐琪：《中国入境旅游市场的恢复与营销创新》，《旅游学刊》，2024 年第 4 期，第 9—10 页。

18. 黄松山、朱海：《中国入境旅游恢复发展与产品体系升级》，《旅游学刊》，2024 年第 4 期，第 10—12 页。

19. 岳晓燕、孙业红：《遗产旅游：构建入境旅游跨文化交流的重要桥梁》，《旅游学刊》，2024 年第 4 期，第 12—14 页。

20. 韵江、易慧玲、梁春媚：《断裂、变革与创造：入境旅游恢复与发展中的企业响应》，《旅游学刊》，2024 年第 4 期，第 7—9 页。

21. 厉新建、曾博伟、张辉、宋子千、杨勇、马波、王宁：《新质生产力与旅游业高质量发展》，《旅游学刊》，2024 年第 5 期，第 15—29 页。

22. 蔡礼彬、张子彧：《"指日可待"还是"道阻且长"？——目的地居民对中国入境旅游恢复的感知形成研究》，《旅游科学》，2024 年第 2 期，第 35—57 页。

23. 郭子腾：《增进文明交流互鉴 加快发展入境旅游》，《中国旅游报》，2024 年 1 月 3 日，第 001 版。

24. 田里、刘岚、陈军：《聚集与扩散：区位因素驱动的中国入境旅游产业空间变迁》，《经济问题探索》，2024 年第 1 期，第 76—91 页。

25. 孙九霞、李菲、王学基：《"旅游中国"：四十年旅游发展与当代社会变迁》，《中国社会科学》，2023 年第 11 期，第 84—104 页。

26. 郑鹏、刘壮、王洁沺、陈家怡、席建超：《"因商而游"亦或"寻文而至"？——"一带一路"倡议与中国入境旅游业》，《中国人口·资源与环境》，2023 年第 3 期，第 181—193 页。

27. 宋瑞、刘倩倩：《中国式现代化进程中的旅游发展：意义、挑战与路径》，《旅游论坛》，2023 年第 1 期，第 1—11 页。

28. 杨劲松、宋子千：《我国入境旅游政策的历史演变与时代选择》，《旅游学刊》，

2024 年第 4 期，第 1—4 页。

29.沈涵、杨一江、陈庆阳：《数字化时代入境旅游为提升国家形象带来新机遇》，《新华智库研究》，2024 年。

编写说明与致谢

《中国游：让世界认识更加真实的中国》智库报告课题组由新华通讯社党组成员、副总编辑任卫东任组长，新华社研究院院长刘刚任副组长，新华社研究院副院长崔峰任执行副组长，课题组成员包括傅琰、秦彦洋、冯候、任沁沁、徐壮、乌梦达、周慧敏、杨思琪、丁怡全、刘恩黎、解园、郎兵兵、陈爱平、刘锴、冯启迪、李骥志、崇大海等。课题组成员从新华社总社部门、国内分社、驻外分社抽调，均为从事新闻报道和研究工作的骨干力量。课题自 2024 年 7 月立项启动以来，历时 5 个月学习、调研、撰写、修改、审校完成。

在报告写作和发布过程中，中国旅游研究院院长戴斌、中央文化和旅游管理干部学院副院长毕绪龙、中山大学旅游学院教授保继刚、中山大学马克思主义学院教授林进平、中央文化和旅游管理干部学院国际交流部副主任苗宾、北京市社会科学院国际问题研究所助理研究员马鑫等专家学者给予了多方面的帮助指导，中国社会科学院大学博士生闵方正、沈锐、杨豪哲在文献和数据收集方面作出贡献，在此一并表示诚挚谢意。

后 记

新华社国家高端智库是中国国家高端智库方阵中唯一媒体型智库，以政策研究为主攻方向，近年来围绕国内外重大问题开展前瞻性、战略性、储备性研究，形成了众多有影响的智库研究成果。

本书辑录的4篇智库报告包括《更好赋能中国繁荣世界——新质生产力的理论贡献和实践价值》《为了全人类共同的价值和尊严——中国参与全球人权治理的实践与贡献》《中国视力残疾人文化权利保障的实践与启示——从"光明影院"公益项目谈起》《中国游：让世界认识更加真实的中国》。这些报告从不同领域、不同侧面反映中国式现代化的新探索、新经验，反映了中国新发展理念在各领域取得的新成就，为世界各国深入了解中国发展方式、发展道路提供了重要的参考资料。

承担本书编辑工作的是新华社研究院传播战略研究室的文建、陈怡、李成、陈谊娜、何小凡等同志。欢迎各位读者批评指正。

本书编写组

2025 年 5 月

FOSTERING A GLOBAL COMMUNITY OF SHARED FUTURE: CONTEMPORARY SIGNIFICANCE AND TANGIBLE ACHIEVEMENTS

（ENGLISH VERSION）

构建人类命运共同体的
时代价值和实践成就

XINHUA INSTITUTE
新华社国家高端智库课题组　著

XINHUA PUBLISHING HOUSE
新华出版社

图书在版编目（CIP）数据

构建人类命运共同体的时代价值和实践成就 : 英文 / 新华社国家高端智库课题组著 .
北京 : 新华出版社 , 2025. 6.
ISBN 978-7-5166-8006-3

Ⅰ . D81

中国国家版本馆 CIP 数据核字第 20257JW002 号

构建人类命运共同体的时代价值和实践成就（英文版）
著者： 新华社国家高端智库课题组
出版发行： 新华出版社有限责任公司
　　　　　　（北京市石景山区京原路 8 号　邮编：100040）
印刷： 捷鹰印刷（天津）有限公司

成品尺寸： 170mm×240mm　1/16　　　**印张：** 18.5　　**字数：** 250 千字
版次： 2025 年 6 月第 1 版　　　　　　**印次：** 2025 年 6 月第 1 次印刷
书号： ISBN 978-7-5166-8006-3　　　　**定价：** 98.00 元（中英文版）

微店　　视频号小店　　抖店　　京东旗舰店　　　请加我的企业微信

微信公众号　　喜马拉雅　　小红书　　淘宝旗舰店　　　扫码添加专属客服

Contents

Fostering a Global Community of Shared Future: Contemporary Significance and Tangible Achievements[①]

Throughout its development and progress, human society has given rise to diverse civilizations and systems. In light of this, how can we coexist and forge ahead as we collectively inhabit planet Earth, the sole abode of humanity?

In March 2013, Chinese President Xi Jinping put forward the concept of a global community of shared future.[②] As explicitly stated in the Report to the 20th National Congress of the Communist Party of China, a global community of shared future represents the path ahead for all the people of the world. It envisions a world where "all things flourish and nourish each other without harm; paths run parallel and coexist without conflict." It is only when all nations follow the Great Way—living in harmony and engaging in cooperation for mutual benefit—that sustained prosperity and guaranteed security can be achieved.[③]

Over the past 11 years, the concept of a global community of shared future has undergone continuous enrichment and development, with its theoretical framework

---

① Released in Belgrade on April 30, 2024, China-Serbia Media Think Tank Seminar.

② https://www.gov.cn/ldhd/2013-03-24/content_2360829.htm

③ https://www.gov.cn/xinwen/2022-10/25/content_5721685.htm

growing increasingly robust. Its contemporary significance and timeless values have radiated brightly, serving as an inexhaustible wellspring of thoughts that guide the advancement of our era.

Over the past 11 years, the endeavor to build a global community of shared future has evolved from a Chinese initiative to an international consensus. Increasingly, countries and peoples have recognized that this concept resonates with the common interests and values of all humanity, and has the potential to catalyze the greatest synergy among nations in creating a better world. As a testament to its visionary nature, this concept has been repeatedly incorporated into the documents of the United Nations and other international organizations, garnering deep appreciationand support from leaders of numerous countries and international organizations.

Over the past 11 years, the pursuit of a global community of shared future has been translated into concrete practices, yielding fruitful outcomes. International cooperation, exemplified by initiatives like the Belt and Road Initiative, has flourished. The building of bilateral and multilateral communities of shared future has witnessed steady progress. Through the advancement of various initiatives such as a global community of health for all, a community with a shared future in cyberspace, a community of shared future for nuclear security, a maritime community with a shared future, a community of life for humanity and nature, a community of all life on Earth, a global community of development, and a global community of security for all, a multifaceted framework and tangible strategies have been put in place to drive the construction of a global community of shared future.

A global community of shared future is the core tenet of Xi Jinping Thought on Diplomacy. It encapsulates the worldview, life philosophy, and value system upheld by the Communist Party of China, while shedding light on the trajectory of global civilization. It represents the evolution and application of the Marxist notion of a "real community" (die wirkliche Gemeinschaft) and the continuation of the rich traditional Chinese culture and resonates with the wisdom of ancient times and the shared aspirations of diverse civilizations across the globe.

A global community of shared future stands as an inherent imperative for China's path to modernization. With nearly one-fifth of the world's population, China is intricately interconnected with the global community. In its pursuit of modernization, China actively contributes to a future that encompasses lasting peace, universal security, shared prosperity, openness, inclusiveness, and environmental sustainability. The belief that "China can only do well when the world is doing well; when China does well, the world will get even better"①underscores the conviction that China's progress is intertwined with the well-being of the entire world. The vision of a global community of shared future not only aligns with China's own development aspirations but also exemplifies its sense of responsibility as a major country.

"In this world, countries are interconnected and interdependent to an unprecedented degree. Humanity, by living in the same global village in the same time and space where history and reality meet, has increasingly emerged as a community of shared future in which all people have in themselves a little bit of others."② Fostering a global community of shared future is intricately tied to the future of all individuals, nations, and peoples. It represents a concrete endeavor for the ultimate future of humanity and serves as a profound moral compass for the preservation of civilization.

I. Improving Global Governance: A Chinese Initiative Responding to Common Challenges

In the present-day world, human society grapples not only with weighty historical issues but also with significant contemporary challenges. Building a global community of shared future emerges as a governance approach for nations to tackle these challenges, resolve conflicts, and bridge differences. It represents a Chinese proposition aimed at propelling human society towards enduring peace, universal security, shared prosperity, openness, inclusiveness, and the creation of a clean and beautiful world.

1. A Resounding Call to Address Global Challenges

Since the Age of Discovery in the 15th century, Western developed countries have gradually established an unequal international division of labor and an unjust global political and economic order through forceful conquest and exploitative practices. Consequently, the majority of developing countries continue to confront formidable

---

① http://www.beltandroadforum.org/n101/2023/1018/c132-1174.html

② https://www.gov.cn/ldhd/2013-03-24/content_2360829.htm

developmental obstacles, struggling to fully emancipate themselves from the constraints imposed by multinational capital and ideological manipulation. Simultaneously, the profit-oriented capitalist system prevalent in Western developed countries faces its own set of challenges, including excessive financialization, industrial decline, social polarization, and political extremism. These countries find themselves embroiled in political turmoil, grappling with economic stagnation, and experiencing societal fragmentation, leaving their citizens bewildered, perplexed, and frustrated.

Throughout history, especially since the Industrial Revolution in the 18th century, humanity has extracted and exploited natural resources on an unprecedented scale, resulting in severe environmental degradation and detrimental effects on the sustainable development of society. Global warming and climate change have triggered a surge in extreme weather events, diminished agricultural productivity, and contributed to the spread of certain diseases, leading to substantial human casualties and economic losses. The obstacles to achieving economic and social sustainability are indeed formidable.

The ongoing new technological revolution is advancing at a rapid pace, bringing about profound societal transformations that test the adaptability and governance capacities of the countries ofthe world. The emergence of new technologies also gives rise to fresh forms of inequality, as technological disparities and the digital divide create new divisions within societies. Novel forms of injustice, such as oligarchy and manipulative practices by technological giants, come to the forefront. Humanity must not only confront the potential harms arising from technological hegemony but also wrestle with unpredictable technological risks that can have unpredictable consequences.

In addition to the growing prominence of non-conventional threats, various conventional threats have not diminished. While the ongoing Ukraine crisis persists, conflicts in the Middle East have resurfaced, contributing to a deteriorating regional security landscape with repercussions felt globally. Some influential powers lack the willingness to reach consensus on cooperation, leading to a resurgence of a confrontational atmosphere between blocs. The global economy is grappling with a sluggish recovery, accompanied by protectionist measures and zero-sum mindset that disrupt global supply and industrial chains. The current state of the world is marked by deficits in peace, security, development, and governance, presenting formidable challenges to the multilateral governance system.

On top of new and old issues that intertwine and clash, complex problems brew and simmer, making instability and uncertainty the prevailing norm in the world. As UN Secretary-General António Guterres emphasized at the BRICS-Africa Outreach and BRICS Plus Dialogue in August 2023, "we cannot afford a world with a divided global economy and financial system; with diverging strategies on technology including artificial intelligence; and with conflicting security frameworks."[1] Humanity is once again standing at a crossroads, facing the question of which path to take.

Faced with a multitude of risks and challenges in the contemporary world, and in recognition of the crucial question of "what kind of a world we should build and how to build it," which is pivotal for the collective future of humanity, China has presented a distinct proposition: Building a global community of shared future.

2. A Global Aspiration for a Brighter Future

Throughout the extensive course of social development, diverse ethnic groups, histories, and cultures have emerged. From the Chinese standpoint, the world can be likened to a garden, where countries with distinct social systems and rich historical and cultural backgrounds are akin to flowers, each vying to showcase its unique beauty. Despite the divergent paths we have taken, we all share a common yearning for a future that encompasses peace and prosperity. Fostering a global community of shared future can serve as the unified vision for all nations in their collective endeavor to build a better world.

Fostering a global community of shared future places great emphasis on the principle of "sharing." This concept is not aimed at replacing one system or civilization with another. Instead, it revolves around the idea of sharing among nations encompassing diverse social systems, ideologies, history and cultures, and levels of development. It calls for the sharing of benefits, as well as rights and responsibilities in international affairs.

Fostering a global community of shared future promotes the idea of "integration." Throughout history, even in ancient times when means of transportation was limited, various means such as camel caravans along the Silk Road, merchant ships crossing vast oceans, intrepid travelers, and daring explorers played a role in facilitating exchanges, fostering mutual learning,and propelling the advancement of human civilization. The

---

[1] https://news.un.org/zh/story/2023/08/1120907

Age of Discovery further accelerated the global flow of resources, while advancements in science and technology expanded the collective knowledge of humanity. As the grand tapestry of globalization continues to unfold, humanity increasingly becomes an interconnected community, where every individual has a stake in the future of others.

Fostering a global community of shared future underscores the principle of "inclusiveness." President Xi Jinping has emphasized that "on the road to the well-being of all mankind, no country or nation should be left behind."[1] Fostering a global community of shared future aligns with the collective interests of humanity. It embodies the aspirations of people worldwide for peace, development, equity, justice, democracy, and freedom. It signifies the right direction for progress and has garnered growing recognition and support from nations and individuals globally, fostering a collaborative force of cooperation among civilizations.

Since President Xi Jinping first proposed the concept of a global community of shared future in 2013, it has undergone continuous evolution and enrichment, and has been implemented through tangible actions. It has now become a significant approach put forth by China to tackle global challenges and shape a better future during this critical transformation of the world. The concept helps to dissipate the haze in the turbulent world, providing a clear direction for global development.

3. An Intrinsic Requirement of Chinese Modernization

In the new era, rejuvenating the Chinese nation on all fronts through a Chinese path to modernization is the historic mission of the Communist Party of China. Promoting a global community of shared future is not only an integral part of this mission but also one of its intrinsic requirements.

China has never adopted an isolationist stance towards the world. In his keynote speech at the Third Belt and Road Forum for International Cooperation, President Xi Jinping characterized China's relationship with the world as follows: "China can only do well when the world is doing well. When China does well, the world will get even better."[2]

---

① http://www.xinhuanet.com/politics/leaders/2021-07/07/c_1127628998.htm
② http://www.beltandroadforum.org/n101/2023/1018/c132-1174.html

"China cannot be separated from the world in achieving development, and the world also needs China for prosperity."[1] China relies on imports of advanced equipment, raw materials, and critical supplies from over 200 countries and regions spanning six continents. Conversely, the immense market demand in China presents a wide array of cooperation opportunities for enterprises from various nations.[2] China has diligently absorbed outstanding achievements and advanced experiences from civilizations worldwide, which have, in turn, sparked new ideas and insights infused with Chinese characteristics. As the world's second-largest economy, largest manufacturer, and largest trader in goods, China actively contributes to global peace, stability, and economic development. China stands as the second-largest contributor to the United Nations budget[3] and has become "a crucial element and key force in peacekeeping operations."[4] Over the past decade, China has accounted for over one-third of the world's economic growth. China draws its developmental impetus from the world, and its progress undeniably benefits the global community.

Building a global community of shared future represents a natural extension of China's path to modernization. China's path to modernization encompasses a vast population and aims to achieve common prosperity, coordinated material and cultural-ethical advancement, harmony between humanity and nature, and peaceful development. As China pursues peaceful development, it stands as a staunch advocate for world peace, striving to "build a world of lasting peace." Embracing the vision of common, comprehensive, cooperative, and sustainable security, China commits to "building a world of common security." With a focus on prosperity for all, China endeavors to "build a world of common prosperity" through win-win cooperation. Upholding the concept of "coordinated material and cultural-ethical advancement," China advocates for the "building of an open and inclusive world" through communication and mutual learning. In its dedication to ecological conservation and promoting harmony between humanity and nature, China aspires to "build a clean and beautiful world." The goals of China's

---

① http://www.xinhuanet.com/politics/2020-11/10/c_ 1126723118.htm

② https://www.gov.cn/lianbo/fabu/202401/content_6925700. htm

③ https://www.gov.cn/xinwen/2018-12/24/content_5351537. htm

④ http://www.mod.gov.cn/gfbw/jsxd/wh/4839681.html

modernization align harmoniously with those of building a global community of shared future. Both sets of goals reflect China's Five-sphere Integrated Plan, which promotes political, economic, social, cultural, and ecological development. These goals embody the values of respecting individuals, equity, peace, development, and reverence for nature. They exemplify China's wisdom and efforts in effectively managing relationships among people and between humanity and nature.

Chinese modernization is intricately linked to and inseparable from the construction of a global community of shared future. The process of China's modernization will establish a strong foundation for a global community of shared future. With a population accounting for nearly one-fifth of the world's total, China's own modernization efforts contribute significantly to the modernization of human society as a whole. Furthermore, China's modernization can serve as a reference and offer a new path for the modernization of other developing countries, thereby facilitating global common development and the modernization of all humankind. This, in turn, creates more favorable conditions for the establishment of a global community of shared future. The concept of a global community of shared future is an intrinsic requirement of China's modernization. This requirement stems not only from the mission of the Communist Party of China but also from the necessity of an external environment that supports China's modernization endeavors. The Communist Party of China is committed not only to pursuing the well-being of the Chinese people but also to promoting progress for humanity and striving for a harmonious world. A supportive external environment that fosters the common and peaceful development of humanity undoubtedly provides favorable conditions for the modernization of China.

China endeavors to advance the construction of global community of shared future while modernizing itself. This approach sets it apart from Western countries in terms of their respective modernization processes. Western modernization has often been accompanied by aggression, exploitation, conflicts, and inequality. In contrast, China is committed to forging a different path, one that avoids the pitfalls of past Western modernization and does not jeopardize the interests of other nations in the process of its own development. China upholds the concept of a shared future and adheres to principles such as equal consultation, win-win cooperation, and common development. China's development endeavors also provide opportunities for other countries to benefit from its progress and advancements.

"To establish oneself, one must first help others to establish themselves first." Through the construction of a global community of shared future during the course of China's modernization, the Chinese people will collaborate with people worldwide to forge a brighter future together.

II. Standing for Mutual Appreciation: A Chinese Proposition Resonating Globally

The concept of a global community of shared future recognizes the interconnectivity of the future of all nations. It promotes collaboration, harmonious coexistence, and mutual benefits among diverse groups. This concept provides a guiding light for interactions between countries, resonating with the international community and generating hopeful anticipation. It also showcases China's sense of responsibility and commitment as a major global player.

1. The Essence of a Global Community of Shared Future

The concept of a global community of shared future embodies a rich set of ideas and principles, including openness and inclusiveness, equity and justice, harmonious coexistence, diversity and mutual learning, and solidarity and cooperation.

"Openness and inclusiveness" mean not drawing ideological boundaries, not targeting specific entities, not forming exclusive "cliques," and embracing diversity with open arms.

"Equity and justice" entail upholding the international order based on international law, maintaining the authority of international law, ensuring equal and uniform application of international law, and avoiding double standards and selective adherence.

"Harmonious coexistence" involves achieving peaceful coexistence and common development among nations while seeking common ground and reserving differences. The vitality of global development lies precisely in the coexistence of diversity.

"Diversity and mutual learning" recognize that the diversity of civilizations is a fundamental characteristic of the world, and the exchange and mutual learning among different civilizations are crucial drivers of human progress.

"Solidarity and cooperation" emphasize that one should consider the interests of the entire world. Addressing global development challenges requires cooperation among nations, as unilateral efforts are insufficient.

During his visit to Russia in March 2013, President Xi Jinping first put forward the vision of a global community of shared future, urging the international community to embrace the concept of an interconnected and interdependent global community with shared future.[①]

On the occasion of the 70th anniversary of the United Nations and the victory of the World Anti-Fascist War in September 2015, President Xi advocated the establishment of a new type of international relations characterized by win-win cooperation. He outlined a five-point proposal for building a global community of shared future. Firstly, he emphasized the importance of building partnerships based on equality, extensive consultation, and mutual understanding among nations. Secondly, he called for the creation of a security environment that is fair, just, cooperative, and beneficial to all. Thirdly, he emphasized the promotion of open, innovative, and inclusive development that benefits everyone. Fourthly, he highlighted the significance of fostering inter-civilization exchanges to promote harmony, inclusiveness, and respect for differences. Lastly, he emphasized the need to build an ecosystem that prioritizes the well-being of Mother Nature and promotes green development.[②]

In January 2017, during his speech at the United Nations Office at Geneva, President Xi put forth five goals for the world.[③] These goals aim to enhance and broaden the concept of a global community of shared future, providing a more distinct vision for the future of humanity. The five goals are as follows: building a world of lasting peace through dialogue and consultation; ensuring security for all in the world through joint efforts; realizing common prosperity globally through win-win cooperation; embracing an open and inclusive world through exchanges and mutual learning; and making the world clean and beautiful by pursuing green and low-carbon development.

The five-point proposal and the five goals for the world have expanded and enhanced the concept of a global community of shared future, offering crucial principles for the advancement of politics, security, economy, culture, and ecology.

---

① https://www.gov.cn/ldhd/2013-03/24/content_2360829.htm

② http://www.xinhuanet.com/world/2015-09/29/c_1116703645.htm

③ http://www.xinhuanet.com/world/2017-01/19/c_1120340081.htm

In line with the concept of a global community of shared future, China has put forward the notion of building a new type of international relations that embraces a fresh approach to state-to-state interactions. This approach is characterized by principles such as mutual respect, equity and justice, and win-win cooperation. China upholds true multilateralism and encourages all nations to engage as participants in, contributors to, and beneficiaries of global peace and development. Furthermore, China advocates the common values of peace, development, equity, justice, democracy, and freedom for humanity. These values are deeply rooted in the pursuit of a global community of shared future.

2. The Cultural Origins of a Global Community of Shared Future

The concept of building a global community of shared future embodies a profoundly scientific ideology. It encompasses the quintessence of Marxism and builds upon the foundation of traditional Chinese culture by harmoniously merging the two. Furthermore, it reflects the enduring accomplishments of civilizations and the shared values embraced by diversenations.

The concept of a global community of shared future represents a significant theoretical advancement in adapting Marxism to the Chinese context. It is founded on solid theoretical principles and follows the inherent logic of Marxism, aligning with its core essence.

In the Economic and Philosophic Manuscripts of 1844, Karl Marx stated that "man is a social being." He further pointed out in the Theses On Feuerbach that "the essence of man is no abstraction inherent in each single individual. In reality, it is the ensemble of the social relations." Therefore, the flourishing of human social life can only be achieved within a community. In The German Ideology, Marx and Friedrich Engels propose that "only within the community has each individual the means of cultivating his gifts in all directions; hence personal freedom becomes possible only within the community." The concept of community aligns with the inherent requirements of human social nature and represents the natural and necessary expression of our collective essence.

According to Marxism, the development of human community has undergone a historical progression. In the pre-capitalist era, society was organized around the "natural common body" based on kinship and familialties. With the advent of capitalism, an "imagined community" emerged, characterized by individuals gaining the ability to produce and exchange goods. While this development may initially appear as a path toward freedom, it actually signifies a shift from dependence on the community to reliance on "objects" such as property or currency. However, the "imagined community" fails to truly represent the interests of the majority, and it is inevitable that it will be replaced by a "real community." In this real community, individuals will eventually become the masters of their own destiny. They will be embedded in specific social relations and freely or consciously engage in production and life. Through their collective efforts, they will pursue freedom as a unified entity, ultimately achieving genuine freedom in the process.

The notion of a global community of shared future exemplifies the evolution of the Marxist concept of "community" within contemporary contexts, thereby expanding the frontiers and domains of scientific socialist theory.

The concept of a global community of shared future adopts the principles derived from traditional Chinese culture. It encompasses the worldview of fostering harmony among nations and promoting universal peace, the social values of tranquility and coexistence, the moral values of prioritizing the common good and seeking a balanced approach to moral obligations and economic interests, as well as the ecological principles of recognizing the unity of humanity and nature and adhering to the laws of nature.

The principle of fostering harmony among nations and promoting universal peace can be translated into promoting equality and cooperation in the modern world. During the first plenary session of the 8th G20 Summit in 2013, President Xi delivered a speech emphasizing the importance of countries embracing the vision of a global community of shared future and recognizing the interconnectedness of success and loss among nations. That necessitates cooperation amid competition and striving for mutually beneficial outcomes. While pursuing its national interests, a country should also consider the interests of other nations, leading to cascading effects and positive spillovers of its development on others.[①]

The concept of tranquility and coexistence encapsulates the principles of mutual respect and appreciation. As stated in The Doctrine of the Mean, "All things flourish and nurture without causing harm to one another; paths run parallel and coexist

---

① http://www.xinhuanet.com//politics/2013-09/06/c_117249618.htm

without conflicting with one another." China has consistently advocated approaching differences among civilizations and countries with a peaceful mindset and fostering inclusiveness in understanding political systems and values. Within the framework of a global community of shared future, the notion of coexistence and shared prosperity underscores the significance of respecting cultural diversity and acknowledging each country's right to independently determine its own development path.

The principle of prioritizing the common good and seeking a balanced approach to moral obligations and interests serves as the theoretical foundation for pursuing equity, justice, shared benefits, and win-win outcomes. During the 70th Session of the UN General Assembly, President Xi expounded on the core essence of a global community of shared future. He emphasized the need to establish global partnerships at both international and regional levels, advocating a new approach to state-to-state relations based on dialogue rather than confrontation, and seeking partnerships instead of alliances. In managing their relationships, major countries should adhere to the principles of no conflict, no confrontation, mutual respect, and win-win cooperation. Furthermore, large countries should treat small countries as equals and adopt the right approach to moral obligations and economic interests, with a priority on moral obligations.[1]

Recognizing the unity of humanity and nature and adhering to the laws of nature embody the idea of respecting, accommodating, and preserving nature, which reflects the concept of harmonious coexistence between human and nature in Chinese culture. President Xi has emphasized that nature is the source of all life, and humanity and nature form a community. It is imperative that we protect the environment with the same care as we protect our own eyes and cherish it as we cherish our own lives. This approach is crucial in addressing the issue of harmonious coexistence between humanity and nature.

The concept of a global community of shared future concerns the collective future of humanity. It promotes a value system centered on mutual benefits and achieving win-win outcomes for all nations worldwide. It strives to create a more equitable, just, united, and cooperative world, emphasizing the Communist Party of China's dedication

---

[1] http://www.xinhuanet.com/world/2015-09/29/c_1116703645.htm

to peace and development for humanity. This vision aligns with the shared aspirations, beliefs, and ideals of other nations and communities. The concept of a global community of shared future encapsulates the shared vision of diverse civilizations and the collective pursuit of all societies. Across history, humanity hasfostereda multitude of distinct andcoexistingcivilizations. Despite the variations in languages, cognitiveframeworks, and belief systems among these civilizations, the shared objectives ofpursuing peace and development remain the same. The aspiration to establish a fair and equitable order is also shared, as is the pursuit of democracy and freedom.

Numerous civilizations share cultural values that resonate with the concept of a global community of shared future. The dome of the Swiss Parliament Building of the Federal Assembly bears the inscription of a motto, Unus pro omnibus, omnes pro uno (one for all, all for one).[1] The Upanishads, ancient philosophical texts from India, propose the idea of Vasudhaiva Kutumbakam (The world is a big family).[2] In many African regions, the Ubuntu philosophy is embraced, emphasizing the interconnectedness of individuals with the phrase "I am because we are." Similarly, at Fisher Lake in the U.S. state of Utah, there existsatree called Pando, Latin for "I spread", that consists of over 40,000 stems connected by a single root system. This tree, which has survived for 80,000 years, embodies the spirit of interconnectivity. Despite the seemingly separate nature of its individual stems, they are deeply connected and support each other. Through the nourishment provided by each stem, the tree has withstood numerous challenges such as floods, droughts, wildfires, and pests. The story of Pando serves as a powerful inspiration, illustrating that seemingly insignificant individuals are intricately linked and that their collective strength enables survival in the face of adversity.

The concept of a global community of shared future is rooted in inclusiveness. It draws upon the remarkable accomplishments of diverse civilizations around the world, reflecting the universal aspirations of all humanity. It encompasses the shared values of differentethnic groups, faiths, and cultures, showcasing the governance experiences and wisdom derived from various regions, nations, and communities.

---

[1] https://blog.nationalmuseum.ch/en/2020/04/one-for-all-all-for-one/

[2] https://pib.gov.in/PressReleasePage.aspx?PRID=1591742

3. The Contemporary Significance of a Global Community of Shared Future

The path to progress lies in staying in step with the times. The concept of a global community of shared future embodies the shared values and aspirations of people from all nations, who seek peace, development, and stability. It represents the broadest consensus among countries with diverse cultural backgrounds and varying stages of development. It goes beyond outdated mindsets like zero-sum game, power politics, and Cold War confrontations. This concept has emerged as a prominent guiding principle, leading the way in the current era and directing human progress. It serves as China's proposition to collectively address global challenges and forge a better future for humanity, particularly at a crucial juncture in the evolving global landscape.

Promoting a global community of shared future is essential for establishing an international governance system that is characterized by greater equity and justice. The international community recognizes the need to break away from the antiquated mindset of the law of the jungle or zero-sum game. However, there is still a lack of consensus on how to enhance the international governance system, how to make it fairer and more equitable, and how to actively involve all countries in the process. At this crucial juncture in history, the concept provides a clear direction for shaping the international governance system towards equity and democracy.

Promoting a global community of shared future entails upholding equality among all countries, regardless of their size, rejecting hegemony and power politics, and opposing any attempt by a few countries to monopolize international affairs. The concept respects the right of all nations to choose their own development paths and social systems, advocating inclusive consultation among all countries in global affairs. No single country has the authority to dominate global affairs, dictate the future of others, or monopolize developmental advantages.

Promoting a global community of shared future is in line with the current trend of economic globalization. From a historical perspective, today's global economic interactions are deeper and more extensive than ever before, and all countries are more interconnected and interdependent than at any previous time. Embracing openness and integration has become an inevitable choice for all nations.

Promoting a global community of shared future involves upholding the proper course of economic globalization, rejecting technological blockades and decoupling, and collectively expanding the global economic pie.It also entails embracing win-win cooperation and effectively distributing the benefits of growth to ensure fairness among countries and various populations, preventing any nation or individual from being left behind.

Promoting a global community of shared future aligns with the world's pursuit of lasting peace and collective security. In today's interconnected world, certain nations have instigated conflicts and confrontations globally in their pursuit of absolute security.

The concept of a global community of shared future envisions transforming weapons of war into tools of peace. It is dedicated to resolving differences and disputes between nations through dialogue and consultation, while taking into account the legitimate security concerns of all countries. It advocates safeguarding against all forms of security risks, opposing the unlimited expansion of military alliances, and respecting the security space of other nations. It strives to build a new model of international relations characterized by no-conflict, no-confrontation, mutual respect, and win-win cooperation.

Promoting a global community of shared future heralds a fresh vision of openness, inclusiveness, exchange, and mutual learning for the advancement of all civilizations. The concept embodies the transcendence of cultural barriers through exchanges, the avoidance of conflicts through mutual understanding, and the embrace of inclusiveness rather than cultural superiority. It strives for a world characterized by mutual appreciation and coexistence. The concept acknowledges the existence of diverse paths toward modernization and encourages each country to explore a path commensurate with its national conditions. It fosters the creative transformation and development of the rich traditional cultures of various nations amidst the process of modernization. Additionally, it facilitates mutual understanding and friendship among people from all corners of the globe.

No civilization in the world can be deemed superior to others; each civilization is unique and regional in nature. Therefore, cultural differences should not be the cause of conflicts around the world. Promoting a global community of shared future has anticipated the future forms of civilization and embodies the overarching trajectory of human advancement. It provides guidance for different countries, nations, andcivilizations, pointing the way towards progress. This vision is destined to garner growing consensus and promote human society towards a more promising future.

Promoting a global community of shared future facilitates humanity's response to ecological challenges and the attainment of sustainable development. The Earth stands as our singular and exclusive abode. The longing for a harmonious homeland is a shared aspiration among all humanity. In face of environmental challenges, our destinies are interconnected, and no nation can remain impervious.

A global community of shared future promotes the collaborative establishment of a stronger partnership in green development. It emphasizes the pursuit of modernization that fosters harmony between humanity and nature, and calls for collective action in response to climate change to safeguard our planet, the cherished home of humanity.

III. Benefiting the World: A Chinese Practice Serving the Well-being of All Humanity

Since 2013, propelled by China's unwavering commitment, the building of a global community of shared future has made steady progress, transitioning from a "led chorus" to a "group singing" approach. The concept of a global community of shared future has taken root and gained extensive recognition and support from the international community, yielding significant dividends for the world and delivering tangible benefits to people across the world.

1. Steady Progress in Building a Global Community of Shared Future at Various Levels and in Multiple Areas

China has played a constructive role in promoting a global community of shared future at various levels and in multiple areas through multilateral and bilateral cooperation, contributing to global peace and development.

At the multilateral level, the China-Africa community of shared future stands as the earliest of regional communities of shared future, tightly linking the destinies of the largest developing country and the continent with the highest number of developing nations. Upon assuming the presidency, Xi Jinping put forward China's Africa policy principles during his visit to Africa. These principles include sincerity, real results, amity, good faith, and the pursuit of the greater good and shared interests. He proclaimed that China and Africa will be enduring, trustworthy friends and genuine partners, underscoring that "China and Africa have always shared a common destiny." Over the past decade, guided by the leadership and strategic planning of the heads of state from both sides, China and Africa have consistently deepened their cooperation through mechanisms and platforms such as the Belt and Road Initiative and the Forum on China-Africa Cooperation. The outcomes of this collaboration have spanned various domains, including economy, trade, infrastructure, and the well-being of the people. The ongoing development of a China-Africa community of shared future in the new era continues to bring benefits to the people on both sides and serves as a commendable model for China and other regional countries to build their own communities of shared future.

Since then, China has made steady advancements in building regional communities of shared future, including with the Arab States, Latin America, Pacific Island countries, ASEAN, Central Asia, and the Shanghai Cooperation Organization (SCO) member countries. Through unwavering solidarity and mutually beneficial cooperation among the participating nations, the vision of a global community of shared future has gained increasing international recognition and has continued to expand in terms of its depth and substance.

At the bilateral level, China has formulated action plans, issued joint statements, and reached significant consensus with various countries to build bilateral communities of shared future. These countries include Laos, Cambodia, Myanmar, Indonesia, Thailand, Malaysia, Pakistan, Mongolia, Cuba, South Africa, and Vietnam. The building of a global community of shared future at the bilateral level has encompassed all five Central Asian countries, serving as amodel for relations between nations in the new era.

China has actively promoted international cooperation in multiple areas, translating the concept of a global community of shared future into tangible actions. In response to pressing global challenges, China has put forth proposals aimed at building specific communities that reflect the shared future vision. Amidst the rampant COVID-19 pandemic, China proposed the establishment of a global community of health for all. Recognizing the need for orderly cyberspace governance, China has advocated the creation of a community with a shared future in cyberspace. In light of mounting security concerns, China has called for the formation of a community of shared future for nuclear security. Addressing the complexities of maritime issues, China has emphasized the importance of building a maritime community with a shared future. Additionally, in the face of the escalating challenges posed by climate change, China has sought to foster a community of life for humanity and nature, as well as a community of all life on Earth.

A global community of shared future is not only multifaceted but also vibrant, playing a crucial role in addressing urgent global challenges and fostering sustainable development for human society in the long run.

2. The Belt and Road Initiative (BRI) as a Platform for Implementing the Global Community of Shared Future

The BRI proposed by China is a significant international public good and cooperation platform. It focuses on promoting connectivity and adheres to the principles of planning together, building together, and benefiting together. Emphasizing open, green, and clean cooperation, the BRI aims to achieve high standards, sustainability, and improved livelihoods, thereby advancing high-quality collaboration. The BRI facilitates physical and institutional connectivity in various fields, including infrastructure, rules and standards, and people-to-people exchanges. As a result, partner countries are more closely linked in terms of infrastructure, policies, trade, investment, and people-to-people interactions. This promotes coordinated development and contributes to common prosperity. Over the past 11 years, Belt and Road cooperation has expanded from Eurasia to Africa and Latin America, with more than 150 countries and 30 international organizations signing cooperation agreements. The third Belt and Road Forum for International Cooperation was successfully conducted, and over 20 specialized multilateral cooperation platforms havebeen established under the BRI.

The BRI has emerged as a pathway for cooperation, opportunity, and prosperity for China and its partner countries. From 2013 to 2022, the total import and export volume reached an impressive $19.1 trillion, with an annual growth rate of 6.4 percent. Two-way investment between China and partner countries has exceeded $380 billion.[1] In 2023, the imports and exports between China and partner countries reached a record high, accounting for a significant proportion of China's foreign trade.[2] Significant progress has been made in the construction of economic corridors and international routes. Cooperation in port construction, shipping, the Air Silk Road, and the development of

---

[1] http://www.scio.gov.cn/zfbps/zfbps_2279/202310/t20231010_773682.html

[2] https://www.gov.cn/lianbo/fabu/202401/content_6925700. htm

international multi-modal transportation passages in partner countries has continued to expand. Belt and Road cooperation plays a pivotal role in enhancing the poverty reduction efforts of partner countries. According to the World Bank's forecast, by 2030, investments related to the BRI are expected to lift 7.6 million people out of extreme poverty and 32 million people out of moderate poverty in participating countries. Furthermore, China and partner countries are actively expanding cooperation in such areas as culture and tourism, education, media, and think tanks, fostering robust people-to-people exchanges. Progress has also been made in health, green development, innovation, and the establishment of the Digital Silk Road, creating even more opportunities for international cooperation.[1]

The BRI has ushered in a new era of extensive cooperation and development in the 21st century, emerging as a significant endeavor in constructing a global community of shared future. Participating countries are dedicated to coordinated development and mutually beneficial cooperation, leading to the upgrading of industrial structures and optimization of industrial chains. The establishment of the Land Silk Road, Maritime Silk Road, and Air Silk Road networks has significantly enhanced the infrastructure of numerous countries. Through equal consultation and dialogue, policy obstacles have been eliminated for participating nations. The flourishing trade has facilitated international exchanges of goods and services. Facilitation measures have accelerated the flow of capital between partner countries. The win-win economic exchanges have fostered robust people-to-people exchanges among partner countries. This unprecedented mega-scale collaboration, involving an exceptional number of countries, individuals, and diverse fields, has no parallel in history. Belt and Road cooperation has brought forth immense development opportunities in the 21st century. It serves as a vital practice in promoting the common development of all societies and constructing a global community of shared future, bearing historic significance.

3. Three Global Initiatives As Strategic Guidance for a Global Community of Shared Future

Since 2021, President Xi Jinping has introduced the Global Development Initiative,

---

[1] http://www.scio.gov.cn/zfbps/zfbps_2279/202310/t20231010_773682.html

Global Security Initiative, and Global Civilization Initiative. These initiatives serve as guiding principles for China's efforts in upholding global peace, advancing global development, and promoting exchanges and mutual understanding among civilizations.

The Global Development Initiative (GDI) has been an effective response to the strong aspirations and urgent requirements of the international community, especially developing nations, to accelerate economic growth and achieve sustainable development. Its objective is to tackle the imbalances and deficiencies in development, at both the national and international levels. By providing a roadmap for development through cooperation, the initiative has garnered widespread recognition from the international community.

The GDI was introduced by President Xi Jinping in September 2021 during the general debate of the 76th Session of the United Nations General Assembly. President Xi called for accelerated implementation of the United Nations 2030 Agenda for Sustainable Development and the building of a global community of shared future for development.[①] The GDI places people at the center and emphasizes the creation of unified, equal, balanced, and inclusive global development partnerships. It advocates action-oriented measures to promote stronger, greener, and healthier global development.

Currently, the Global Development Promotion Center is operating smoothly, and the GDI project pool is expanding, encompassing over 200 projects that have yielded fruitful outcomes. More than 100 countries and international organizations have voiced their support for the GDI, with over 70 countries actively participating in the GDI Group of Friends established at the United Nations.

China has long been committed to global development and the promotion of an open global economy. It has emerged as the main trading partner for over 140 countries and regions, while also signing more than 20 free trade agreements with 28 countries and regions. As the largest developing country and a member of the Global South, China has been actively assisting other developing and recipient countries in expanding their development capacities. China has collaborated with nearly 20 international organizations, including the World Food Programme, and implemented over 130 projects in nearly 60 countries, such as Ethiopia, Pakistan, and Nigeria. These projects cover various areas, including poverty reduction, food security, COVID-19 response, and climate change, benefiting more than 30

---

① https://www.gov.cn/xinwen/2021-09/22/content_5638597. htm

million individuals. China has played a significant role in assisting Africa with debt relief efforts. It has actively supported and advocated for the adoption and implementation of the G20 Group's Debt Service Suspension Initiative. China has signed agreements or reached understandings with 19 African countries regarding the suspension of debt repayments, making the most substantial contribution among all G20 members to the initiative's implementation.[1]

The Global Security Initiative (GSI) is founded on the principle of indivisible security, emphasizing the interconnectedness between the security of individual countries and common security, as well as the interlinkage between conventional security and non-conventional security, rights and obligations, and security and development. It urges the international community to adopt a more comprehensive approach to addressing global security issues and to uphold the common security of the international community with a heightened sense of responsibility and mission. The GSI provides a pathway for resolving international disputes and safeguarding common security.

The GSI was initially proposed by President Xi Jinping during the Boao Forum for Asia annual conference in April 2022. President Xi emphasized the crucial link between security and development, highlighting that humanity is a community that shares indivisible security.[2] In February 2023, China released The GSI Concept Paper, which outlines the core concepts, principles, cooperation priorities, and cooperation platforms and mechanisms. The paper introduces the Six Commitments that further elucidate the guiding principles of the initiative. According to the paper, the vision of "common, comprehensive, cooperative, and sustainable security" serves as the conceptual guidance. Respecting the sovereignty and territorial integrity of all countries is considered a fundamental premise. Adhering to the purposes and principles of the United Nations Charter is a primary benchmark. Taking the legitimate security concerns of all countries seriously is an important principle. Peacefully resolving differences and disputes through dialogue and consultation is deemed necessary. Lastly, maintaining security in both conventional and non-conventional domains is an inherent requirement.[3]

The GSI has received wide welcome and positive responsefrom the international

---

[1] https://www.gov.cn/zhengce/202309/content_6906335.htm

[2] https://www.gov.cn/xinwen/2022-04/21/content_5686424. htm

[3] https://www.fmprc.gov.cn/wjbxw_new/202302/t20230221_11028322.shtml

community since it was brought up. It has received support and appreciation from over 100 countries and international organizations, and has been written into numerous bilateral and multilateral documents related to China's interactions and cooperation with other countries and international organizations. Some collaborative actions are steadily progressing. Within the initiative framework, 20 key areas of cooperation have been proposed, covering traditional military security fields such as international and regional hot-button issues, peacekeeping operations, as well as non-traditional security fields including climate change, information, biological security, outerspace, artificial intelligence, and public health. These efforts address the most pressing security concerns of the international community today.

China has consistently demonstrated its dedication to becoming an essential constructive force in upholding global peace and tranquility. It has actively pursued political resolutions for the Korean Peninsula nuclear issue and the Iranian nuclear issue. China has also played a successful mediation role in facilitating the reestablishment of diplomatic relations between Saudi Arabia and Iran. Additionally, China has voiced its position on the Ukraine crisis and the recent conflict between Palestine and Israel through official documents, aiming to promote peace and bring an end to the conflicts. China's unwavering sincerity and commitment to safeguarding global security have remained steadfast.

The Global Civilization Initiative (GCI) embodies China's recognition of the diversity and equality of human civilizations, as well as its dedication to fostering exchanges and mutual learning among Chinese and foreign civilizations for the sake of shared prosperity.

The GCI was introduced by President Xi Jinping in March 2023 during the CPC in Dialogue with World Political Parties High-level Meeting. He said that as the future of all countries are closely connected, tolerance, coexistence, exchanges and mutual learning among different civilizations play an irreplaceable role in advancing humanity's modernization process and making the garden of world civilizations flourish.[①] Xi said civilizations have become richer and more colorful with exchanges and mutual learning. No civilization in the world is superior to others; every civilization is special and unique to its own region. Diversity of civilizations

---

① https://www.gov.cn/xinwen/2023-03/15/content_5746950. htm

should not be a source of global conflict; rather, it should be an engine driving the advance of human civilizations. The GCI emphasizes the importance of following the objective laws of progress and highlights the correct attitude and approach towards inter-civilizational relationships. It underscores the significance of enhancing one's own civilization while creating conducive conditions for the development of other civilizations. As a result, the GCI serves as a crucial guiding principle for promoting mutual assistance, harmonious coexistence, and mutual respect and understanding among civilizations.

China has successfully hosted several significant events, including the CPC in Dialogue with World Political Parties High-level Meeting, the CPC and World Political Parties Summit, and the Conference on Dialogue of Asian Civilizations. These gatherings have facilitated extensive bilateral and multilateral exchanges and cooperation among political parties, fostering various forms of people-to-people diplomacy, city diplomacy, and public diplomacy. China has actively collaborated with numerous countries to co-organize bilateral and multilateral cultural exchange activities, such as the Year of Culture and Tourism and the International Arts Festival. Additionally, it has established and cultivated sister city *(province and state)* relationships with multiple counterparts. Through the establishment of new platforms, the mobilization of new forces, and the promotion of new consensus, China has made commendable efforts to encourage exchanges among civilizations. These endeavors have garnered appreciation and support from the international community.

Today, the changes of the world, the timesand history are unfolding in an unprecedented way. The unstoppable trend of peace, development, and win-win cooperation is evident. Faced with a crossroads laden with challenges, China has put forward the vision of building a global community of shared future. This vision aims to draw upon rational global consensus to guide the path forward and inspire collective efforts to advance society amid trials and tribulations.

China's proposition to build a global community of shared future is aligned with the course of history, serving the common interests of the majority of nations and promoting human progress. China has consistently upheld its commitment to being a builder of world peace, a contributor to global development, and a defender of the international order.

The establishment of a global community of shared future is gaining recognition and support from an increasing number of nations and people. It is regarded as the correct trajectory for the world to pursue sustainable development and work towards a shared future for all humanity on our planet.

Jointly Promoting High-Quality Development and Building an Asia-Pacific Community with a Shared Future—Achievements of Future-Oriented APEC Development and China's Actions[①]

Over 400 years ago, Chinese merchants opened a trade route across the vast Pacific Ocean, establishing the maritime Silk Road that connected Asia, the Pacific Islands, and the Americas, laying a foundation for friendly exchanges across the Pacific. For centuries, the spirit of the maritime Silk Road has shone brightly over the boundless waves of the Pacific, illuminating the historical journey of humanity in overcoming obstacles and fostering civilizational exchanges and mutual learning.

Thirty-five years ago, leaders from the Asia-Pacific region, following the trend toward peace and development, agreed unanimously to rise above the outdated mentality of bloc confrontation and zero-sum game by establishing the Asia-Pacific Economic Cooperation (APEC). Since then, regional cooperation in the Asia-Pacific has embarked on a fast track of growth, turning the region into a powerhouse for world economic growth, an anchor of stability for global development, a pacesetter for international cooperation, and a key force for promoting high-quality and sustainable development.

---

① Released in Lima, Peru, on November 8, 2024.

The maritime Silk Road, which connects the East and the West, symbolizes openness and inclusiveness, as well as cooperation and mutual benefit. It aligns with the founding aspiration of APEC and stands as a valuable common asset for humanity. It will enable the Asia-Pacific region in the 21st century to continue to serve as a model for innovative cooperation, assisting the global community in addressing major challenges. It inspires us to work hand in hand to promote high-quality development and to build an Asia-Pacific community with a shared future that supports each other.

I. Focusing on Development: Creating a Remarkable "Asia-Pacific Miracle" Together

"Development is an eternal theme in the Asia-Pacific region. We have stayed focused on development and continually deepened economic and technical cooperation, thus strengthening the ability of developing members to achieve self-development. We jointly developed 'the APEC Approach' based on the principles of voluntarism, consensus-building and incremental progress, and we respect the right to development of all members."[1]

—Xi Jinping, President of the People's Republic of China

Since its establishment in 1989, the Asia-Pacific Economic Cooperation (APEC) has adhered to the principles of openness, cooperation, and mutual benefit, dedicated to promoting economic integration and trade liberalization in the Asia-Pacific region

The value of APEC lies in its commitment to "open regionalism" and the "broad trans-Pacific regionalism" of its members, which have fostered peace and development in the Asia-Pacific for 35 years. APEC has achieved remarkable success in promoting regional economic growth and deepening regional cooperation, significantly promoting trade and investment liberalization and facilitation in the region. As a result, the Asia-Pacific has become the most dynamic geo-economic area with the greatest growth potential in the world.

---

[1] Xi Jinping, "Meeting Challenges with Unity of Purpose To Write a New Chapter for Asia-Pacific Cooperation", written speech delivered at the APEC CEO Summit, November 16, 2023.

1. The Engine of Global Economic Growth

APEC has made significant contributions to global economic development. By strengthening multilateral cooperation and connectivity, APEC economies have maintained long-term stability in their overall economic growth momentum, becoming an important force driving global economic growth.

In 2023, the total GDP of the 21 APEC economies reached USD 64.45 trillion, accounting for over 60% of global GDP. The GDP growth rate was 3.5%, surpassing the global average of 3.2%.[1] The number of people living in extreme poverty in the Asia-Pacific region has decreased from 1.5 billion in 1990 to 260 million in 2015.[2] According to the International Monetary Fund (IMF), the region's economic growth rate is forecasted to reach 4.2% in 2024, higher than the expected global growth rate of 2.9%. These statistics clearly illustrate that the Asia-Pacific is a region with considerable economic vitality and resilience.

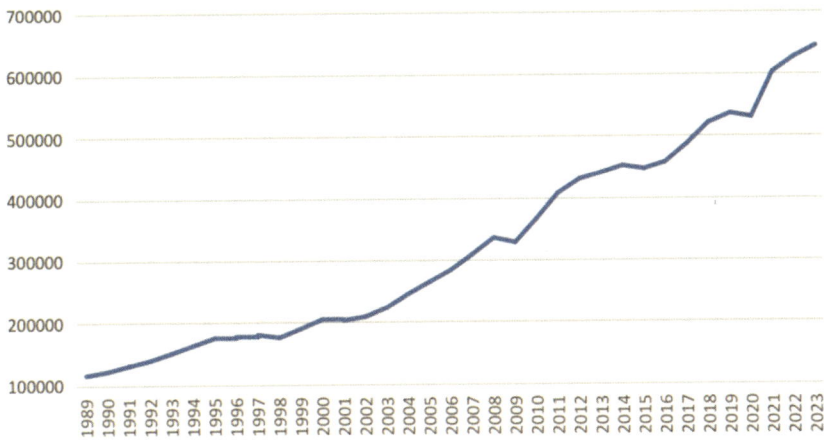

Figure 1: Total GDP of APEC Economies (Unit: USD 100 million)
Source: World Bank, IMF, and OECD.

The higher economic growth rate of APEC economies is primarily driven by increasing internal demand and mutual trade. In 2023, consumption in APEC economies

---

① Source: IMF.

② Source: Asian Development Bank.

accounted for an average of 65.6% of GDP, while the value added by the service sector exceeded 62% of GDP. The growth of the service sector injected new impetus into regional economic recovery. The ratio of trade in goods within and outside APEC economies to GDP has consistently remained above 70%, fluctuating around 90% since 2018.[1] The economies in the Asia-Pacific region exhibit significant complementarities in terms of economic development levels, factor endowments, and policies, which fosters closer value-added trade and value chain connections within the region, laying the groundwork for inclusive and win-win development.

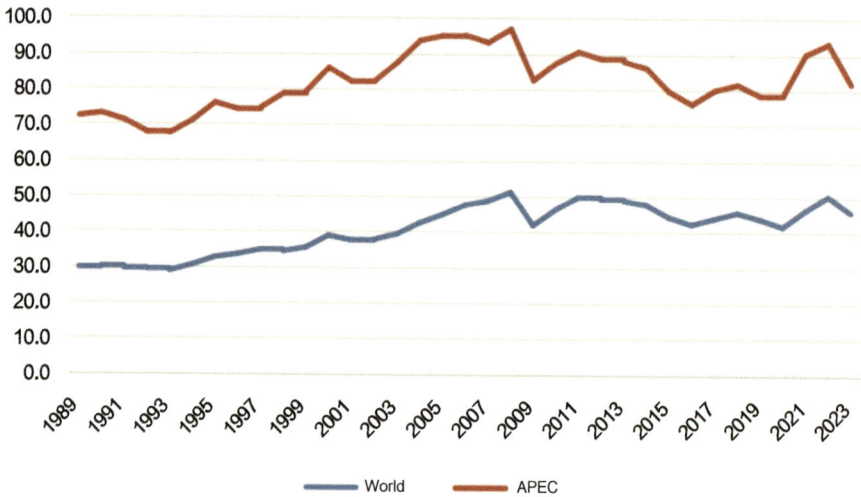

Figure 2: Annual Change in the Share of Merchandise Trade in GDP (Unit: %)
Source: World Bank, and WTO.

Strong trade demand and a secure, stable environment have propelled the rapid development of international shipping, trade, and finance in the Asia-Pacific region. According to the Xinhua Baltic International Shipping Center Development Index (2023), 13 of the top 20 global shipping center cities by overall strength are located in APEC economies. Singapore and Shanghai rank first and third, respectively, leading global shipping development. Additionally, the center of gravity for global finance is shifting

---

[1] Source: Asian Development Bank, and OECD.

toward the Asia-Pacific region. The IFCD Index (2023) indicates that six of the top 10 international financial center cities are in Asia, with Shanghai, Hong Kong, Singapore, Tokyo, Beijing, and Shenzhen driving the rapid growth of Asian finance.

China continues to play a role in APEC economic cooperation as a propeller. China's economy, characterized by high resilience, substantial potential and vitality, supports sustained development and prosperity in the Asia-Pacific region. China has become the largest trading partner for 13 APEC economies.[1] In 2022, the total import and export volume between China and APEC members reached USD 3,739.08 billion, accounting for 59.7% of China's total trade. Investments from APEC economies constituted 86.6% of China's actual foreign capital utilization, while 73.3% of China's outbound investment flowed into APEC economies.[2] Notably, half of China's top 10 sources of foreign investment and top 10 destinations for outbound direct investment are APEC members.

2. Contributor to Trade and Investment Liberalization

Trade and investment liberalization and facilitation within the APEC framework have made the Asia-Pacific region an exemplary model of regional economic integration. In the spirit of APEC community, relevant countries have collaborated to promote trade and investment liberalization and facilitation, advance economic and technological cooperation, advocate for "open regionalism", and adopt the APEC approach of voluntarism, consensus-building, flexibility, pragmatism, and incremental progress. These efforts have made significant contributions to promoting economic integration in the Asia-Pacific region and have injected inexhaustible momentum into building an Asia-Pacific community with a shared future.

In 1994, APEC established the Bogor Goals in Indonesia, i.e. achieving free and open trade and investment in the Asia-Pacific by 2010 for developed economies and by 2020 for developing economies. This initiative has become a "beacon" for APEC cooperation. The two core components of the APEC process are Trade and Investment Liberalization and Facilitation (TILF) and Economic and Technical Cooperation (ECOTECH), often

---

[1] The statistical data for China mentioned here and in this report do not include data from Hong Kong and Taipei of China.

[2] Source: Ministry of Commerce of China.

referred to as the "two wheels" of APEC. Regarding trade and investment liberalization and facilitation, the Bogor Goals have largely been achieved. In terms of economic and technical cooperation, nearly all cooperation initiatives outlined in the *Manila Framework* have been successfully implemented.

Tariff and non-tariff barriers have been significantly reduced. Over the past 30 years, the average tariffs in the Asia-Pacific region fell from 17% to 5% [1], contributing 70% to global economic growth. Meanwhile, from 1989 to 2022, the total trade in goods and services within the APEC region surged from USD 3.1 trillion to USD 30 trillion, with an average annual growth rate of about 7.4%, substantially outpacing trade growth in other parts of the world. The APEC Trade Facilitation Action Plan, implemented from 2001 to 2010, and the APEC Ease of Doing Business Action Plan, launched in 2009, stand out as key trade facilitation measures. Through diverse cooperation in priority areas such as customs procedures, standards harmonization, e-commerce, and business personnel flow, APEC has effectively lowered transaction costs among its members and improved the business environment in the Asia-Pacific region. With APEC's support, the investment climate in the region has continually improved, significantly boosting inflows of foreign direct investment (FDI).

Free trade agreements effectively expand cooperation networks. Through the implementation of Collective Action Plans (CAPs) and Individual Action Plans (IAPs), APEC continues to encourage members to take practical steps toward trade and investment liberalization. This approach not only respects the autonomy of each member but also facilitates intra-regional trade and investment.

As of July 2022, APEC members had signed a total of 207 free trade agreements, of which 196 have entered into force. The signing and implementation of these agreements have further promoted the liberalization of trade and investment among members, providing an institutional framework to advance regional economic integration.

On November 15, 2020, the Regional Comprehensive Economic Partnership (RCEP) was signed. After eight years of negotiations, the world's largest free trade area was established and officially launched. With the implementation of RCEP, the benefits of

---

[1] APEC's official website https://www.apec.org/About-Us/About-APEC/Achievements-and-Benefits

trade policies have been continuously realized, leading to a significant increase in inter-regional economic and trade exchanges. According to the RCEP Regional Cooperation Development Report 2024, global foreign direct investment flows declined by 12.4% in 2022, while the RCEP region attracted foreign direct investment of USD 531.11 billion, reflecting a 13.9% increase. This accounted for 41.0% of the global share, a rise of 9.5 percentage points compared to 2021[①]. RCEP provides a crucial pathway for advancing the Free Trade Area of the Asia-Pacific (FTAAP) process, further enhancing the Asia-Pacific region's significance in the global development landscape.

China advocates for multilateralism and adheres to open regionalism, with its ideas and proposals widely recognized by APEC members. As a key economy in the Asia-Pacific region, China has actively engaged in APEC cooperation. From the high-quality implementation of RCEP and the negotiations for Version 3.0 of the China-ASEAN Free Trade Area to the active promotion of its accession to the Comprehensive and Progressive Agreement for Trans-Pacific Partnership (CPTPP) and the Digital Economy Partnership Agreement (DEPA), China is committed to practicing open regionalism and fostering new systems for a higher-standard open economy.

3. A Model of Innovative Cooperation

The development philosophy is guided by innovation. In response to the 2008 international financial crisis, APEC adopted A New Growth Paradigm for a Connected Asia-Pacific in the 21st Century in 2009 and the APEC Leaders' Growth Strategy in 2010. The leaders' statement emphasized the need for new growth models and specific action plans to implement these strategies. This new growth model, supported by innovation and knowledge, is characterized as "balanced, inclusive, and sustainable". It can be termed "APEC's New Development View", distinguishing it from the traditional view focused on reducing tariffs, expanding trade, and promoting growth.

In recent years, amidst the new scientific and technological revolution and industrial transformation, APEC has broadened discussions and cooperation on the "New Development View". Promoting "innovative growth" in the Asia-Pacific region through

---

① Source: United Nations Conference on Trade and Development, World Investment Report 2023.

cooperation in scientific and technological innovation has become a key focus for APEC. Asia-Pacific economies have prioritized digital economy cooperation and intelligent transformation in their innovative efforts. The APEC Putrajaya Vision 2040, adopted at the 2020 APEC Economic Leaders' Meeting in Kuala Lumpur, emphasizes "leveraging the digital economy and technology to promote economic inclusion" and "promoting innovative sustainable development", aiming to achieve APEC's goals in the "post-Bogor era".

Connectivity drives coordinated regional development. The blueprint for connectivity in the Asia-Pacific meets the needs of countries in the region to strengthen economic and trade exchanges, advance industrialization, and deepen international cooperation. It aims to expand investment and domestic demand in the Asia-Pacific, increase employment, reduce poverty, curb extremism, and inject new impetus into economic growth in the region and beyond.

In 2014, at the 22nd APEC Economic Leaders' Meeting held in Beijing, members approved the APEC Connectivity Blueprint (2015-2025) and committed to completing the jointly established initiatives and targets by 2025. Guided by this blueprint, institutional connectivity cooperation within the APEC framework has made varying degrees of progress and achieved results in key areas such as customs and border management, supply chains, trade facilitation, structural reform, and regulatory cooperation.

In the area of customs and border management measures, for example, some members have modernized their customs and border management agencies and improved customs clearance efficiency by streamlining procedures and promoting the application of new technologies. Notable measures include the Customs Electronic Single Window System and the Authorized Economic Operator (AEO) program. As a result, trade facilitation and logistics efficiency have gradually improved. According to the 2020 World Bank Logistics Performance Index (LPI), the lead time for exports in the APEC region fell from an average of 2.4 days to 2.3 days between 2015 and 2017, which is lower than the average for the Organization for Economic Cooperation and Development (OECD) countries.

The digital economy is paving the way forward. Strengthening digital infrastructure and capacity building to bridge the digital divide has become a consensus and priority area for cooperation among APEC members. In 2014 and 2017, APEC adopted the

APEC Initiative of Cooperation to Promote Internet Economy and the APEC Internet and Digital Economy Roadmap, respectively. In 2018, the 26th APEC Economic Leaders' Meeting held in Papua New Guinea, themed "Harnessing Inclusive Opportunities, Embracing the Digital Future", received positive support from all parties.

With project construction as the focal point, APEC countries have steadily advanced cooperation in major areas such as "smart cities", "smart hospitals", and "smart infrastructure" to assist regional countries in their intelligent transformation and development. In this process, China has played an active role. To date, China has signed intergovernmental science and technology cooperation agreements with over 80 countries, supported more than 1,100 joint research projects, and co-established over 50 joint laboratories and 70 overseas industrial parks under the Belt and Road Initiative.[1] Multiple transnational technology transfer platforms have been developed for countries in ASEAN, South Asia, Latin America, and other APEC countries to effectively promote innovation and cooperation in science and technology among APEC nations. Furthermore, China has established bilateral cooperation mechanisms[2] for "Silk Road E-commerce" with 23 countries and has deepened cross-border e-commerce projects and electronic commerce cooperation with Singapore, Indonesia, Malaysia, and others, becoming a model for APEC countries to share the dividends of the digital economy.

4. An Advocate of Green Development

Green development is one of the important areas for APEC's future development cooperation. As early as 2010 and 2011, the themes of the APEC Economic Leaders' Meetings emphasized the importance of green growth. "Inclusive growth" and "sustainable growth" have been the core topics discussed at various APEC events over the past decade. APEC members have joined hands to explore and practice green development, promoting carbon reduction, pollution reduction, green expansion, and economic growth collaboratively. This not only effectively protects the ecological environment and contributes to climate change response but also positions the green economy as a significant growth driver, making important contributions to development

---

① Source: Ministry of Science and Technology of China.

② Source: Ministry of Commerce of China.

in the Asia-Pacific region and beyond.

Multi-dimensional forest protection and innovation have led to remarkable achievements in forest conservation. As a regional international organization initiated under the APEC mechanism, the Asia-Pacific Network for Sustainable Forest Management and Rehabilitation on Forests (APFNet) has carried out multi-level and multi-type cooperation projects over the past decade to build ecological barriers in the Asia-Pacific region. As of August 2023, a total of 53 projects in various types of sustainable forest management and rehabilitation have been funded, with a funding amount of approximately 43 million US dollars.[1] According to data from the Food and Agriculture Organization of the United Nations, global forest area has decreased by 1.2% over the past decade, but forest area in the Asia-Pacific region has experienced significant growth[2], mainly contributed by China, Vietnam, and Chile, with China's forest area increasing by 9.53%. Over the past decade, China has contributed about a quarter of the world's newly added green area, ranking first globally[3]. As the country with the fastest-growing forest resources, China has created an impressive green miracle.

APEC economies are jointly promoting marine protection and sustainable marine development. In recent years, APEC economies have actively implemented the APEC Roadmap on Marine Debris (2019), the Roadmap to Combat Illegal, Unreported, and Unregulated (IUU) Fishing (2019), and the Road Map on Small-scale Fisheries and Aquaculture (2022). In 2011, the APEC Marine Sustainable Development Center was established in Xiamen, China. The APEC Blue Economy Forum, as a regular project of the APEC Marine Sustainable Development Center, had successfully held seven sessions by December 2023, providing a platform for representatives of various economies to share practical experiences and suggestions on the cooperation framework of the blue economy. In February 2024, the 22nd APEC Ocean and Fisheries Working Group (OFWG) Plenary Meeting was held in Lima, Peru, where the economies reported on the

---

[1] China Green Times, October 2023.

[2] Source: World Bank Database (Food and Agriculture Organization of the United Nations), 2024.

[3] Latest Achievements in Building a Beautiful China, National Forestry and Grassland Administration, August 2023.

completion of the roadmaps and discussed future planning for oceans and fisheries.

The Asia-Pacific new energy vehicle market has demonstrated strong performance and a clear growth trend. In recent years, the region has made significant strides in developing a green economy, achieving carbon reduction goals in response to climate change while also leveraging emerging industries for economic growth. The new energy vehicle industry has emerged as a typical example of this effort. From 2012 to 2022, economies in the Asia-Pacific region actively promoted the adoption of new energy vehicles, leading to a remarkable 142-fold increase in annual sales of battery electric vehicles, which in turn has significantly stimulated the development of related industries.

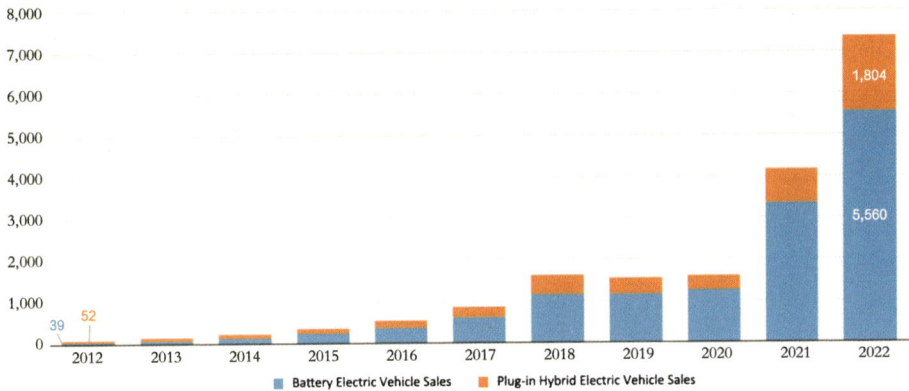

Figure 3: Electric Vehicle Sales in APEC (2012-2022, 1,000 vehicles)①
Source: Official Report of APEC.

With the further strengthening of the global trend of low-carbon travel, cooperation in the field of new energy vehicles will become an important direction for the development of the green economy in the Asia-Pacific. For example, a joint venture between China's SAIC Motor and Thailand's CP Group holds a leading market share in Thailand for two models of battery electric vehicles, while BYD has opened more than 100 stores in the country.

Energy cooperation has promising prospects, focusing on structural optimization and upgrading. APEC economies are committed to promoting the optimization and

---

① APEC in Charts 2023, APEC Policy Support Unit, November 2023.

adjustment of the energy mix, vigorously developing wind, solar, and other renewable energy sources, reducing dependence on fossil fuels, and accelerating the pace of energy transformation. APEC's renewable energy generation increased from 1,384 TWh in 2000 to 4,709 TWh in 2021, with an average annual growth rate of 6%. The share of renewable energy generation rose from 16% in 2010 to 25% in 2021, with hydropower accounting for more than half of APEC's renewable energy generation in 2021, followed by wind (25%) and solar (15%). From 2010 to 2021, wind power grew by an average of 19.2% per year, and solar power grew by an average of 47.3% per year[1].

China has provided strong leadership and support for the green transformation in the Asia-Pacific region. China's installed capacity of wind power and photovoltaic power generation ranked first in the world for 14 consecutive years and 9 years respectively, and the cumulative installed capacity exceeded 1 billion kilowatts by the end of 2023. In 2023, China contributed more than half of the world's new installed renewable energy capacity. In July 2024, the CEME1 project, Chile's largest single photovoltaic project undertaken by PowerChina, officially commenced commercial operation. This project can provide clean energy for approximately 500,000 households and reduce carbon dioxide emissions by about 280,000 tons annually. Luis Felipe Ramos, Chile's Undersecretary of Energy, stated that the project will help Chile increase its share of clean energy generation and take an important step toward achieving decarbonization goals.

Building green Belt and Road resonates with the green development of the Asia-Pacific region. Green is a common feature of cooperation in the Asia-Pacific and Belt and Road cooperation. APEC and the Belt and Road Initiative have been mutually integrated and mutually reinforcing, with the cooperation mechanism for green development gradually improving and the results of cooperation becoming increasingly visible.

By August 2023, China had signed environmental protection cooperation agreements with more than 30 countries and international organizations, established the BRI International Green Development Coalition with over 150 partners from more than 40 countries, and formed Belt and Road Energy Partnerships with 32 countries[2]. In

---

① APEC in Charts 2023, APEC Policy Support Unit, November 2023.

② Source: White paper titled "The Belt and Road Initiative: A Key Pillar of the Global Community of Shared Future", State Council Information Office.

2018, the Green Finance Committee of the China Society for Finance and Banking and the City of London jointly launched the Belt and Road Green Investment Principles (GIP) to encourage vigorous development of green finance cooperation in the Belt and Road region. As of September 2024, there are 49 signatories, 20 supporting organizations, and 2 observing organizations from 17 countries and regions[①].

The BRI International Green Development Coalition strongly supports member countries in investing in renewable energy. In October 2023, at the third Belt and Road Forum for International Cooperation, Indonesia's PLN struck deals worth more than USD 54 billion with Chinese partners. Trina Solar, representing Chinese enterprises, signed the China-Indonesia cooperation document with Indonesia to establish the first photovoltaic cell and module production base in the country. China is ready to collaborate with its partners to build a "Green Silk Road" and promote a steady and sustained path for green development in the Asia-Pacific region.

II. Facing Challenges: Meeting the Era's Responsibilities

"The story of Asia-Pacific prosperity and development shows that development is only possible with cooperation, absence of cooperation is the biggest risk, and that decoupling and supply-chain disruption are not in anyone's interests."[②]

—Xi Jinping, President of the People's Republic of China

Development and security are like the two wheels of a cart and the two wings of a bird; they are interdependent and mutually reinforcing, each essential to the other. Security is a precondition for development, and development is a guarantee for security.

The world today is undergoing major changes unseen in a century. Major-country rivalry, geopolitical conflicts, and bloc confrontation hinder international cooperation and mutual

---

① Source: Green Finance Committee of the China Society for Finance and Banking Work Report for 2023/24 and Outlook for 2024/25.

② Xi Jinping, "Meeting Challenges with Unity of Purpose To Write a New Chapter for Asia-Pacific Cooperation", written speech delivered at the APEC CEO Summit, November 16, 2023.

trust, creating internal and external shocks to the security environment for development in the Asia-Pacific region. Some countries have expanded the concept of national security to the economic sphere, adopting protectionism, "decoupling", and "small yards with high fences" which have exacerbated the already sluggish global economic recovery and negatively impacted the Asia-Pacific region. Uneven economic development and widening wealth disparities within economies challenge regional cooperation. Additionally, climate change has resulted in frequent extreme weather events and natural disasters, seriously threatening the safety and well-being of people in the Asia-Pacific region.

1. Geopolitical Risks Bring Multiple Challenges

At present, some countries cling to a "Cold War mentality" and a "zero-sum game", seeking to rally allies and engage in bloc confrontation. This has led to a tightening geopolitical situation, posing multiple challenges to the Asia-Pacific region.

Geopolitical tensions and conflicts impact the security environment both within and outside the Asia-Pacific region. Regional cooperation and development are inevitably influenced by the regional security situation. The turbulence and conflicts in the current global geopolitical landscape not only threaten the security and stability of the Asia-Pacific region but also adversely affect regional trade and investment activities, posing challenges to regional economic cooperation.

Externally, geopolitical conflicts are intensifying tensions in regions such as Europe and the Middle East, disrupting transportation from the Asia-Pacific to Europe. Many flights connecting the Asia-Pacific to Europe have been suspended or diverted due to airspace closures by relevant countries. Some routes of the "China-Europe Railway Express", a major transport artery between China and Europe, have been suspended or rerouted due to sanctions. Additionally, the sea route from the Red Sea to the Suez Canal has seen increased security risks due to the spillover effects of the conflict, forcing many ships to divert their courses.

European Commissioner for Economic and Financial Affairs Paolo Gentiloni stated in February that shipping times on the Eurasian sea route have increased by 10 to 15 days and transport costs have risen by approximately 400% due to the rerouting of shipping through the Red Sea. The decrease in transport efficiency and the rise in costs have negatively affected the Asia-Pacific economies, which are generally highly reliant on foreign trade.

Internally, some countries promote "major-power rivalry" to pursue geo-strategic self-interests, exploit differences among regional nations to sow discord, and rally certain countries to suppress and contain rivals, engaging in bloc confrontation. This not only undermines the political foundation for dialogue and cooperation among regional countries but also escalates certain regional hotspot issues, which is detrimental to the overall peace and stability of the Asia-Pacific region, further worsening the security environment for Asia-Pacific economies.

Geopolitical conflicts have triggered food and energy crises, causing knock-on effects on the economic and social security of the Asia-Pacific region. This region is already highly sensitive to food-related risks. According to a report by the Food and Agriculture Organization (FAO) of the United Nations, half of the world's undernourished population resides in the Asia-Pacific, with women being particularly vulnerable to food insecurity[1]. Although the incidence of malnutrition in APEC economies has decreased from 3.6% to 2.3%[2] between 2010 and 2023, food security continues to be a significant constraint on development in the Asia-Pacific region.

In terms of energy, energy consumption in the Asia-Pacific region has grown rapidly in recent years. According to the "APEC Energy Outlook 2024" report, electricity has experienced the fastest growth in final energy consumption among energy products, reaching 7.2% and accounting for 33.6% of total final energy consumption. Oil holds the second largest share at 32.9%, with a growth rate of 6.2%. Natural gas grew by 3%, accounting for 18%[3] of final energy consumption.

In this context, the turbulence in international energy and food markets, along with the surge in energy and food prices caused by geopolitical conflicts, has significantly impacted the economic and social stability of economies in the Asia-Pacific region, particularly developing economies. The rise in energy and food prices has also contributed to inflation in some economies, affecting their foreign exchange and other financial markets, and even leading to economic and social unrest in certain countries.

---

① "Food Security and Nutrition in Asia and the Pacific 2023", Food and Agriculture Organization of the United Nations, December 11, 2023.

② "APEC in Charts 2023", APEC Policy Support Unit, November 2023.

③ "APEC Energy Outlook 2024", APEC, August 2024.

2. Trade Protectionism Threatens Supply Chain Security

In recent years, with the rise of backlash against globalization, some countries in the region have turned trade and investment issues into security ones and practiced trade protectionism in the name of safeguarding national security. This has hindered international economic cooperation, disrupted global industrial and supply chains, and significantly impacted cooperation in the Asia-Pacific region.

The momentum of cross-border investment has declined, hitting developing economies particularly hard. According to the "World Investment Report 2024" released by the United Nations Conference on Trade and Development, the global scale of foreign direct investment (FDI) in 2023 reached USD 1.3 trillion, representing a 2% year-on-year decrease, with investment flowing to developing economies dropping by 7%. In Asia, FDI in developing economies fell by approximately 8.4%, while in Oceania, the decline was as steep as 64%. For decades, FDI in the manufacturing sector has been a crucial economic driver for many developing economies in the Asia-Pacific region and a key source of financing for building regional and even global industrial and supply chains. However, the current downward trend in investment is likely to significantly delay the industrialization and upgrading progress of some developing economies in the Asia-Pacific region, undermining the foundation of regional production and supply chain security.

Some countries engage in "decoupling and severing chains" and "small yards with high fences", endangering regional industrial development. For political reasons and trade protection motives, certain countries attempt to exclude their perceived "competitors" from industrial and supply chains. This practice not only contradicts the original aspiration and objectives of APEC, but also seriously hinders international economic and technological cooperation, significantly increases production costs, and harms regional industrial development.

For example, some countries in the region impose sanctions on foreign telecommunications technology companies, forcibly prohibiting the use of such equipment in their own network construction on the grounds of "security risks". These unilateral sanctions have caused massive economic losses to their own telecommunications companies, delayed the upgrading process of their communications industry, and will only backfire on themselves.

Additionally, some countries have introduced large-scale exclusive and discriminatory industrial policies that disrupt the reasonable division of labor in global industries, attempting to forcibly promote the "return" of manufacturing to their own territories. As a result, their manufacturing sectors have not shown improvement, while the reverse effects of "decoupling and severing chains" have become increasingly evident, leading to severe inflation in recent years. This has significantly impacted the lives of domestic populations, especially low-income groups.

3. Imbalanced Development Restricts Long-term Economic Growth

The Asia-Pacific region is the most dynamic area in the world, with significant potential for economic growth, yet it continues to face notable development imbalances. The polarization among countries and the widening wealth gap among different groups have become critical factors that restrict the long-term economic growth of the Asia-Pacific region.

The economic development levels among countries in the Asia-Pacific region vary significantly, creating a clear phenomenon of polarization. This region includes highly developed economies like Japan, South Korea, and Singapore, alongside some economies situated in the Pacific islands and inland areas. Due to factors such as remote geographical locations, resource scarcity, and weak economic foundations, these economies have experienced prolonged developmental lag. This trend of polarization has intensified in recent years. According to data from the International Monetary Fund (IMF), the gap between the countries with the highest and lowest per capita GDP in the Asia-Pacific region has exceeded several tens of times[1], which not only limits the overall development potential of the region but also exacerbates internal instability.

The wealth gap between different groups continues to widen. In some economies within the Asia-Pacific region, rapid urbanization and industrialization have significantly benefited certain groups, while others, particularly those residing in rural and remote areas, have not enjoyed the full fruits of economic development. Data released by the World Bank shows that the Gini coefficient in several Asia-Pacific countries has remained persistently high, and in some cases, has even increased. Despite overall economic growth, social wealth has not been equitably distributed, resulting in a substantial number of people living below the poverty line. This widening gap between the rich and the poor not only impacts social stability but also undermines the

---

[1] "Global Economic Outlook", International Monetary Fund, April 16, 2024.

sustainability of economic growth.

According to the Asia-Pacific Population and Development Report 2023, the Asia-Pacific region accounts for 56% of the world's youth population (aged 15-24) in 2023, with a total exceeding 700 million individuals. In this region, 24.8% of young people are not engaged in education, employment, or training, with a significantly higher proportion of women compared to men in this group.

Unbalanced development is a significant challenge facing Asia-Pacific economic cooperation. APEC member economies should enhance communication and coordination, and collaboratively formulate and implement policies and measures to promote balanced regional development and reduce the wealth gap. Through collective efforts, they can drive comprehensive and balanced long-term development in the Asia-Pacific region.

4. Climate Change Poses Risks to Sustainable Security

The economies of the Asia-Pacific region have diverse natural conditions, but they are largely impacted by climate change. This change has intensified extreme weather events and increased the frequency of natural disasters, presenting increasingly severe challenges to sustainable development in the region.

Frequent natural disasters result in significant economic losses. In 2023, economic losses due to natural disasters in the Asia-Pacific region reached USD 65 billion. There were a total of 79 disasters related to hydrometeorological hazards, over 80% of which were associated with floods and storms. These events led to more than 2,000 fatalities and directly affected 9 million people[1].

Analysis by NASA Sea Level Change Team indicates that sea levels in the Pacific island nations of Tuvalu, Kiribati, and Fiji are expected to rise by at least 15 centimeters over the next 30 years. Additionally, the frequency and severity of coastal flooding in these Pacific island countries are likely to increase in the coming decades[2].

Due to a relatively weak economic system, some developing economies in the Asia-

---

[1] Source: United Nations Economic and Social Commission for Asia and the Pacific, "Asia-Pacific Disaster Report 2023".

[2] NASA, "Analysis Shows Sea Level Rise in Pacific Islands is Irreversible", September 27, 2024.

Pacific region lack sufficient capacity to prevent and mitigate natural disasters, making them significantly vulnerable to their impacts. In particular, losses from natural disasters in the Pacific Small Island Developing States approach 8% of GDP, nearly double the rate seen in other economies in the region. In Southeast Asia, this loss reaches at least 5% of GDP[1].

The Asia-Pacific region is still grappling with a worsening problem of environmental pollution. During the processes of industrialization and urbanization, some developing economies in the region often overlook environmental protection, leading to increasingly severe pollution issues and making it difficult to control carbon emissions. In 2020, all 148 of the world's most polluted cities were located in the Asia-Pacific region. By 2050, approximately 70% of the region's population is expected to live in urban areas. Meeting the needs of these new urban residents will require substantial investment in infrastructure, which could further increase reliance on clean water and energy, potentially resulting in higher greenhouse gas emissions[2].

Marine pollution poses an equally serious threat. Due to high population density and relatively inadequate waste disposal capabilities, the Asia-Pacific region faces various types of marine pollution challenges. For instance, in 2022, the total direct economic losses from marine plastic pollution to the fishing and shipping industries in the Asia-Pacific region reached USD 10.8 billion, nearly a tenfold increase compared to 2009. Consequently, managing marine plastic waste in the Asia-Pacific region has become a crucial component of global efforts to combat marine plastic pollution[3].

Land desertification intensifies pressure on sustainable development. Desertification is becoming an increasingly serious issue in the Asia-Pacific region, particularly in inland and arid or semi-arid areas. According to the report by the United Nations Convention to Combat Desertification, as of 2019, some countries in the region have experienced a shift toward desert climates due to rising temperatures and other

---

[1] United Nations Economic and Social Commission for Asia and the Pacific, "Asia-Pacific Disaster Report 2023", July 25, 2023.

[2] United Nations Economic and Social Commission for Asia and the Pacific, "Asia-Pacific Futures in 2040: Raising Ambitions for a Healthy Environment", September 26, 2021.

[3] United Nations Environment Programme, "From Pollution to Solution: A Global Assessment of Marine Litter and Plastic Pollution", October 21, 2021.

factors. Additionally, changes in precipitation patterns resulting from climate change, water shortages, and irrational land use practices, such as overgrazing, deforestation, and certain agricultural activities, have accelerated soil erosion and land degradation. This further deteriorates fragile ecosystems and expands desertification, which not only directly threatens local agricultural production and livelihoods but also affects food security, water supply, and social stability, posing long-term challenges to sustainable development.

In addition, against the backdrop of global climate change, the Asia-Pacific region is experiencing an increase in the frequency and intensity of extreme weather events such as heat waves, droughts, floods, and typhoons. Extreme heat exacerbates the evaporation of surface water and reduces soil moisture, thereby intensifying the desertification process. Moreover, extreme precipitation events, particularly heavy rainfall over a short duration, can lead to severe soil erosion and degradation, further damaging land resources.

III. Continuing the Glory: Achieving Common Prosperity Through Joint Efforts

"We should strengthen the sense of community with a shared future, contribute to other's development with that of one's own, tap fully into our respective strengths through coordination and interconnection, pass on positive energy and achieve sound interactions and coordinated development among all economies."[1]

—Xi Jinping, President of the People's Republic of China

In the world today, changes on a scale unseen in a century are unfolding at an accelerating pace. The world economy faces multiple risks and challenges. The Asia-Pacific region, which is an engine of global growth, thus has greater responsibility in these times. Where should Asia-Pacific cooperation be heading? The answer bears on the development of the region, the well-being of the people, and the future of the world

---

[1] Xi Jinping, "Fostering a New Development Paradigm and Pursuing Mutual Benefit and Win-win Cooperation", keynote speech delivered at the APEC CEO Dialogues, November 19, 2020.

at large.

Against this backdrop, it is the prevailing trend to build an Asia-Pacific community with a shared future featuring openness, inclusiveness, innovation-driven growth, greater connectivity and mutually beneficial cooperation, which should be the common goal of APEC members. APEC members should uphold the original aspiration of cooperation, reaffirm the APEC spirit, work together to promote high-quality development in the region, and strive to build an open, dynamic, resilient, and peaceful Asia-Pacific community, jointly ushering in and sharing another "golden 30 years" of Asia-Pacific development.

1. Working Hand in Hand: Cooperation and Development as the Main Theme of the Asia-Pacific

Thirty-one years ago, where humanity should be headed in the post-Cold War era was the question of the world, of history and of the times in front of Asia-Pacific leaders. In response, they followed the trend toward peace and development, and convened the inaugural APEC Economic Leaders' Meeting. They agreed unanimously to rise above the outdated mentality of bloc confrontation and zero-sum game, deepen economic cooperation and integration in the region, and build a dynamic, harmonious and prosperous Asia-Pacific community. This major decision enabled Asia-Pacific development and economic globalization to embark on a fast track of growth, turning the region into a powerhouse for world economic growth, an anchor of stability for global development, and a pacesetter for international cooperation.

Today, although the Asia-Pacific region is facing new disputes and frictions due to various factors, and signs of unilateralism and bloc confrontation have emerged in certain countries and regions, it is undeniable that Asia-Pacific economic cooperation has never been a zero-sum political game in which one gains at the expense of the other. Rather, the cooperation has provided regional countries with a development platform to ensure what they each do can be mutually reinforcing and beneficial to all. Seeking common ground by setting aside differences and jointly promoting economic development are still the defining feature of the Asia-Pacific region. As New Zealand international trade expert Chris Lipscombe stated, the practice in the Asia-Pacific region demonstrates that countries and economies can achieve greater benefits by cooperating rather than opposing each other. As a New Zealand proverb goes, "With your basket and my basket, the people will thrive."

In further deepening regional cooperation, APEC can enhance its role as the main channel by fully leveraging the diversity of APEC economies. APEC members include both developed and developing economies, each with unique geographical, industrial, social, and cultural characteristics. This diversity provides strong complementarity, further enhancing the significance and potential of cooperation.

Stephen Jacobi, former executive director of the APEC Business Advisory Council (ABAC), stated that the APEC should unite the region's economies to find solutions, regardless of their economic size, and geopolitical, or political differences.

In the future, APEC should continue to focus on development, promote the spirit of partnership featuring harmony without uniformity, and solidarity and mutual assistance, adhere to the APEC approach of voluntarism, consensus-building, flexibility, pragmatism and incremental progress, respect each member's right to development and their chosen development path, strive to enhance the capacity of developing members for independent development, and continuously transform the diversity of APEC members into a driving force for cooperation.

2. Harmony and Inclusiveness: Building an Asia-Pacific Community with a Shared Future

Reaffirming the APEC spirit, APEC will continue to serve as a key mechanism for regional cooperation. The highly complementary development and deeply integrated interests of all members of the Asia-Pacific community reflect a shared future. Renewing the spirit of the "Asia-Pacific community" and enhancing APEC's role as the primary mechanism in regional cooperation are crucial for the sustainable development of the Asia-Pacific region.

Putrajaya Vision is to build an open, dynamic, resilient and peaceful Asia-Pacific community by 2040. APEC encompasses both developed and developing economies, and this diversity enhances the significance and potential of cooperation. To prevent obstacles in addressing green and digital technologies, APEC should implement "open regionalism", actively promote cooperative innovation, and serve as a vital platform for advancing technological development.

In the future, member economies should focus on development, enhance the capacity of members of the "Asia-Pacific community" for independent development, and respect the APEC approach of voluntarism, consensus-building, and incremental progress. By strengthening connectivity and mutually beneficial cooperation, APEC should promote the spirit of partnership featuring harmony without uniformity, and solidarity and mutual assistance, continually transforming the diversity of our members into a driving force for long-term cooperation.

Harmony and inclusiveness are the common aspirations of the Asia-Pacific. As UN Secretary-General António Guterres has said, "No peace is secure without inclusive and sustainable development that leaves no one behind."[1]

To address the ongoing issue of unbalanced development among Asia-Pacific economies, particularly in key areas such as poverty reduction, food security, industrialization, and financing for development, active multilateral cooperation is essential to tackle the global development deficit. This will ensure that all member economies, especially developing ones, can participate equitably and reap the benefits. Regardless of economic size, population, geographical characteristics, or political systems, under the original aspiration of APEC, all member economies can work together to explore solutions and find effective pathways forward.

Development and cooperation remain the eternal themes of the Asia-Pacific region, and the building of an Asia-Pacific community with a shared future aligns with the trends of the times. Within the context of this community-building, both the Belt and Road Initiative and agreements such as the Regional Comprehensive Economic Partnership (RCEP) and the Comprehensive and Progressive Agreement for Trans-Pacific Partnership (CPTPP) can discover new avenues for cooperation. To advance the development of the Asia-Pacific into a new stage, it is essential to accelerate the implementation of the APEC Putrajaya Vision 2040, thereby promoting global economic recovery and maintaining stable development across the world.

With the strengthening of the multilateral trading system, all members should steadfastly advance the building of a Free Trade Area of the Asia-Pacific, respect laws governing economic development, leverage their comparative advantages, and make their economies more interconnected. They should strengthen synergy between relevant regional trade agreements and development strategies, facilitate trade and investment

---

[1] Statement by UN Secretary-General António Guterres at the UN Security Council Open Debate on Promoting Sustainable Peace through Common Development, November 2023.

liberalization, improve trade facilitation, and enhance the integration of supply chains among members. This will, in turn, increase the level of diversification in the upstream and downstream segments of supply chains within APEC members. At the same time, it is essential to enhance project guidance, improve the phased evaluation of cooperation mechanisms and action plans, and encourage greater participation from the business community and social groups.

3. Vibrant: "China's Actions" Empowering Asia-Pacific Development

Looking ahead to 2035, China will basically realize socialist modernization, and Chinese modernization will offer new opportunities for advancing high-quality development in the Asia-Pacific.

China's economy remains the largest engine for global growth and the biggest driving force for the takeoff of the Asia-Pacific region. China enjoys distinct strengths such as a supersize market in terms of demand, a full-fledged industrial system in terms of supply, and abundant, high-caliber labor forces and entrepreneurs in terms of human resources. China's economic development is self-generative, and also provides impetus to the economic development of the Asia-Pacific region.

"China's economy is so large that a 5% increase is equivalent to the total economic output of a small European country," said Craig Allen, president of the US-China Business Council. He noted that China is expected to contribute about 30% of global GDP growth in 2024, with this trend likely continuing into 2025 and 2026.

Renato Reyes, Peru's APEC Senior Official, stated that China, as a key member of APEC, continues to play a positive role in promoting regional economic cooperation and leading the economic growth of the Asia-Pacific region. To a certain extent, this role is decisive and has a significant strategic impact on driving exports, aligning with Peru's economic development strategy.

China attaches great importance to developing its relations with Latin America and the Caribbean, viewing these countries as key partners in uniting developing nations and promoting South-South cooperation. By December 2023, China had signed memoranda of understanding on Belt and Road cooperation with 22 Latin American and Caribbean countries, established free trade agreements with five Latin American countries[①], and implemented over 200 infrastructure projects in the region.

In the face of common challenges, "China's Actions" continue to empower the development of the Asia-Pacific. China serves as an active advocate, promoter, and supporter of Asia-Pacific cooperation, with the dreams of the Chinese people closely linked to those of other nations.

Chinese modernization is the modernization of peaceful development. China follows an independent foreign policy of peace, urges all parties to work together to build a community with a shared future for mankind, practices the common values of humanity, implements the Global Development Initiative, Global Security Initiative, and Global Civilization Initiative, advocates for an equal and orderly multipolar world, and upholds the vision of common, comprehensive, cooperative, and sustainable security, aligning with the development trends of the Asia-Pacific.

By upholding harmony between man and nature, China is accelerating and leading the transition to green and low-carbon development. China is working with all parties to ensure that reducing carbon emissions and mitigating pollution operate in parallel with expanding the green transition and promoting economic growth, making "green" a defining feature of Asia-Pacific growth while implementing the Bangkok Goals on Bio-Circular-Green Economy. At the same time, the rapid growth of China's exports of new energy vehicles, lithium batteries, and photovoltaic products will assist regional members in further achieving their emission reduction targets. Additionally, the upcoming launch of China's exchange of voluntary greenhouse gas emission reduction will create significant green market opportunities.

By boosting innovation and market application of scientific and technological advances, China pushes forward the full integration of digital and physical economies to unleash vitality in the Asia-Pacific. China is committed to jointly implementing the Internet and Digital Economy Roadmap, strengthening the construction of digital infrastructure, facilitating the dissemination and application of new technologies,

---

① National Development and Reform Commission: China-Latin America Cooperation under the Belt and Road Initiative Shows Strong Development Momentum, Belt and Road Portal, December 15, 2023.

and creating an open, fair, and non-discriminatory digital business environment. Additionally, China will improve global governance of science and technology, bolster the role of scientific and technological innovation in green digital transformation and sustainable development, and foster an open, fair, equitable, and non-discriminatory environment for scientific and technological progress.

By promoting high-standard opening-up, China stimulates trade vitality to create more new opportunities for Asia-Pacific partners. China has improved its trade and investment facilitation policies, opened its service sector wider to the outside world, and safeguarded the legitimate rights and interests of foreign investors. The aim is to create a market-oriented, law-based and world-class business environment, providing high-quality services for foreign investment. This includes enhancing the mechanism for protecting foreign businesses' investment rights and interests, shortening the negative list on foreign investment, guaranteeing the national treatment for foreign-invested enterprises, and continuously strengthening intellectual property rights protection. Additionally, barriers that restrain the flow of innovation factors will be dismantled, and the orderly and free flow of data will be promoted in accordance with the law. China's wider, deeper, and broader opening-up will surely benefit the entire Asia-Pacific region.

China is an active advocate and promoter of connectivity and interconnected development in the Asia-Pacific. The principles of "extensive consultation, joint contribution and shared benefits" and a five-pronged approach (policy coordination, infrastructure connectivity, unimpeded trade, financial integration, and strengthened people-to-people ties) contained in the Belt and Road Initiative are highly consistent with the needs and goals of Asia-Pacific economic cooperation. In October 2023, President Xi Jinping announced at the opening ceremony of the third Belt and Road Forum for International Cooperation that an additional RMB 80 billion will be injected into the Silk Road Fund. Together, they will support BRI projects on the basis of market and business operations. Following this capital increase, the total fund size will reach over USD 40 billion plus RMB 180 billion.[1] The continued advancement of Belt and Road cooperation is expected to contribute significantly to the steady progress in building connectivity in the Asia-Pacific region.

---

[1] Source: Belt and Road Portal.

In the future, the Asia-Pacific economy will continue to lead the global economy and play a vital role in helping the world address major challenges and achieve sustainable development for humanity. To relaunch the Asia-Pacific coopeation, ensuring that high-quality development benefits all people in the Asia-Pacific will remain the common goal of all APEC members. We must remain steadfast in our commitment to APEC's founding mission. We must respond to the calls of our times actively and meet global challenges together. We must build an open, dynamic, resilient and peaceful Asia-Pacific community for the prosperity of all our people and future generations.

IV. Conclusions

A Peruvian proverb says, "The voice of the people is the voice of heaven."

The history of exchanges in the Asia-Pacific region has proven that the vast ocean is not a barrier but a connection for sincere cooperative partners. It is precisely because of this connection that economies in the Asia-Pacific have formed a big community with intertwined interests and a shared future.

Since the establishment of the economic leaders' regular meeting mechanism, APEC has always stood at the global forefront of openness and development. Driven by the spirit of the "Asia-Pacific community", cooperation has deepened through multilateral frameworks such as the Belt and Road Initiative and RCEP. The Asia-Pacific region has seen rapid development in international shipping, trade, and finance, with trade and investment liberalization and facilitation serving as excellent examples of regional economic integration. "Innovative growth" has been advanced through cooperation in scientific and technological innovation, while joint efforts to develop a green economy have made significant contributions to global sustainable development. Our multifaceted cooperation has yielded fruitful results, creating the "Asia-Pacific miracle" that has staggered the world.

At the same time, in the world today, changes on a scale unseen in a century are unfolding at an accelerating pace. The world economy faces multiple risks and challenges. Major-power rivalry, geopolitical conflicts, and bloc confrontations hinder international cooperation and mutual trust, leading to internal and external shocks to the security environment for development in the Asia-Pacific region. The Asia-Pacific region, which is an engine of global growth, thus has greater responsibility in these times.

Looking ahead from the remarkable journey of Asia-Pacific cooperation, we believe that reinvigorating the APEC spirit and building an Asia-Pacific community with a shared future characterized by openness, inclusiveness, innovative growth, connectivity, and win-win cooperation is the prevailing trend of the times and should become the common goal of APEC members.

The future-oriented development of the Asia-Pacific provides profound inspiration and a clear path for practice: cooperation and development is the main theme of the region, innovation serves as a vital driving force for development, openness is a sure path toward common prosperity, green growth is the defining feature of Asia-Pacific development, and inclusiveness is crucial for bridging the development gap.

Looking ahead, in a world full of uncertainties, the Asia-Pacific community must continue to uphold the APEC spirit of openness, inclusiveness, practical cooperation, and mutual benefit. By fully utilizing APEC's function of equal communication, consultation, and cooperation, we can jointly build an innovative, open, green, and shared pattern of regional cooperation and development. Only through these efforts can we achieve common prosperity for all members of the Asia-Pacific community and future generations. Together, we will create a brighter future of global peace, stability, and development, and make greater efforts to build an Asia-Pacific community with a shared future and a community with a shared future for mankind.

V. References

[1] Li Xiangyang et al. Analysis and Outlook on the Situation in the Asia-Pacific Region 2023-2024. International Situation Report of the Chinese Academy of Social Sciences, International Research Department. (2024). Beijing: Social Sciences Academic Press, March 2024.

[2] Yang Zerui. APEC 30 Years: Mechanisms, Processes, and Prospects. World Affairs Press, May 2021.

[3] Sun Zhuangzhi et al. High-Quality Development of the Belt and Road Initiative: Understanding, Practice, and Prospects. People's Press, December 2023.

[4] Su Ge et al. Current Status and Future of Asia-Pacific Connectivity. World Affairs Press, November 2021.

[5] Wang Lei. Global Development Initiative: People-centered Promotion of the 2030

Agenda Implementation. Social Sciences Academic Press, June 2023.

[6] Jiang Ling et al. Research on International Regional Economic Integration and Contemporary North-South Economic Relations. People's Press, December 2019.

[7] Lin Xueping. Supply Chain Offensive and Defensive Battles: The Strength Struggle from Enterprises to Nations. CITIC Press, December 2023.

[8] Wang Wei and Li Hanqing. Super Link: Building High-Quality Trade Corridors under the Belt and Road Initiative. China Machine Press, June 2023.

[9] Zhang Yunling and Li Xuewei. Building a Community with a Shared Future and Peaceful Development in Northeast Asia. World Affairs Press, December 2019.

[10] Wang Shiyu. The Third Wave of Globalization. China Democracy Legal System Publishing House, February 2020.

[11] Wang Huiyao. Globalization: Standing at a New Crossroads. SDX Joint Publishing Company, April 2021.

[12] Wang, Yiwei. Community with a Shared Future for Mankind: The Values of a New Type of Globalization. Foreign Languages Press, December 2021.

[13] Zhang Zhiming. China in the Asia-Pacific Value Chain. People's Press, February 2021.

[14] APEC Policy Support Unit. APEC in Charts 2023, November 2023.

[15] State of the Climate in Asia 2023, World Meteorological Organization, April 23, 2024.

VI. Writing Instructions and Acknowledgments

The research team for the think tank report "Jointly Promoting High-Quality Development and Building an Asia-Pacific Community with a Shared Future" is led by Fu Hua, President of Xinhua News Agency and President of the Academic Committee of the National High-end Think Tank. The team includes Lyu Yansong, Editor-in-Chief of Xinhua News Agency, as the Deputy Leader, and Ren Weidong, Deputy Editor-in-Chief of Xinhua News Agency, as the Executive Deputy Leader. The team members include Liu Gang, Pan Haiping, Cao Wenzhong, Xue Ying, Cui Feng, Li Yue, Yang Mu, Chen Xiaobin, Cao Zhanzhong, Zhang Wenjuan, Xu Haijing, Liu Hua, Li Huimin, Li Tao, Liu Zan, Gao Jie, Qi Fangfang, Li Zhilan, Chang Jialu, Zhou Xiaomiao, Huang Xin, Shi Ang, Pan Yuxin, Jin Xuan, Chang Xuchan, Zhao Yixuan, Liang Qiawen, Zhu Yubo, Hao Yunfu, Ouyang Dina, Li Ting, Li Xiaoyu, Lu Huaqian, and others.

Since the research commenced in the first half of 2024, it has taken over six months to complete through interviews, research, writing, revisions, and proofreading.

During the writing and publication process of this report, several experts and scholars provided valuable assistance and guidance, including Li Xiangyang, a member of the Chinese Academy of Social Sciences and director of the National Institute of International Strategy; Wang Honggang, vice president of the China Institutes of Contemporary International Relations; Liu Chenyang, director of the APEC Study Center of Nankai University; Song Zhiyong, former director of the Asia Research Institute of Chinese Academy of International Trade and Economic Cooperation at the Ministry of Commerce; Liu Junhong, former director of the Globalization Research Center at the China Institutes of Contemporary International Relations; Gao Lingyun, director of the International Investment Office at the Institute of World Economics and Politics, Chinese Academy of Social Sciences; Xie Laihui, executive director of the Belt and Road Research Office at the National Institute of International Strategy, Chinese Academy of Social Sciences; Jing Ran, head of the School of International Trade Department at the University of International Business and Economics; Huang Youxing, associate professor at the School of Economics, Ocean University of China; and Jin Xiangdong, assistant professor at the School of International Relations, Xiamen University. Sincere thanks are extended to all of them.

The Practical Achievements and Global Contributions of the Global Development Initiative[①]

Development is the eternal pursuit of human society. For the people of all countries, it embodies survival and hope and symbolizes dignity and rights.

The United Nations Declaration on the Right to Development passed 37 years ago has constantly emphasized that everyone and the people of all countries are "entitled to participate in, contribute to, and enjoy economic, social, cultural and political development."

However, since the start of the third decade of the 21st century, the changes unseen in a century, coupled with the pandemic, have profoundly transformed human society, pushing the world into a new period of turbulence and change. Standing at the crossroads ofthe future and destiny of humanity, President Xi Jinping proposed the Global Development Initiative (GDI) at the 76th session of the United Nations General Assembly on September 21, 2021. It is another significant public good that China provides to the international community in the new era and an essential practice of the

---

① Released at the United Nations Headquarters in New York on September 19, 2023, during the High-Level Meeting on the Global Development Initiative Cooperation Outcomes.

concept of a human community with a shared future in global development.

The GDI emphasizes development as a priority and closely aligns with the central task of implementing the 2030 Agenda for Sustainable Development of the United Nations (referred to as the UN's 2030 Agenda for short). It aims to deepen cooperation and, through specific projects, promote policy dialogues, experience sharing, capability building, practical cooperation in various fields, and participation by all parties. The GDI expresses the earnest expectations of the international community, especially the developing countries, for advancing the cause of global development, thereby guiding shared development globally. Since its proposal two years ago, the initiative has garnered widespread international response and achieved positive progress and many early accomplishments.

The recently released Progress Report on the Global Development Initiative indicates that the content of the initiative concept has been continuously enriched, the implementation mechanism has constantly been improved, the promotion path has become more apparent, and practical cooperation has been gradually implemented, effectively motivating the international community to refocus on development issues, strengthen international development cooperation, and jointly identify and solve problems in development. The GDI has injected new impetus into accelerating the implementation of the UN's 2030 Agenda.

This report outlines the achievements of GDI cooperation over the past two years. China has collaborated with various partners to advance the GDI, making it more profound and substantial and delivering tangible benefits to countries worldwide: protecting the most vulnerable populations to make the world more compassionate, building the homeland into a cozy one to make the world more habitable, tackling common development crises to make the world more secure, facilitating sustainable development to make the world greener, and achieving strong growth to make the world more prosperous.

This report believes that the Global Development Initiative has led to the promotion of a new paradigm of international development cooperation, which is characterized by building a shared development space with a more inclusive cooperation concept, gathering high-quality development resources through more diversified cooperation channels, and fostering endogenous development momentum through a more sustainable way ofcooperation.

This report calls for the revitalization of economic recovery through technological innovation, the improvement of a just and equitable global governance system, and collective action to build a shared future for human development. It emphasizes the need to integrate the GDI more organically with the UN's 2030 Agenda and align the initiative more closely with the development strategies of developing countries. Together, we aim to create a new era of global development featuring benefits for all, balance, coordination, inclusiveness, win-win cooperation and common prosperity, ultimately building a shared future for humanity.

I. China's Initiative to Promote Global Development

At a time when global development is facing headwinds, Chinese President Xi Jinping proposed the GDI as an effective response to global challenges and developing countries' needs for growth and received positive responses from all parties. Positive progress has been made in the two years since the initiative was proposed.

1. The origin and goals of the Global Development Initiative

Since the third decade of the 21st century, the changes in the world unseen in a century have accelerated while global economic recovery has weakened. The global North-South divide continues to widen, especially under the influence of the COVID-19 pandemic, and multiple challenges, such as geopolitical conflicts, climate change, and food and energy crises, are intertwined. As a result, 800 million people live in hunger, the human development index has declined for two consecutive years, and the global development process is facing unprecedentedly severe tests. Implementing the UN's 2030 Agenda has fallen behind expectations.

At the same time,some countries disregard the most pressing needs of developing nations, which are evident in their failure to fulfill financial commitments in the development sector, provocation of ideological conflicts, marginalization of development issues by emphasizing human rights and democracy topics, formation of exclusive groups, and attempts at "decoupling" and investing significant human and financial resources in geopolitical power games.

Unitedn Nations Secretary-General António Guterres warns that the world has reached a "decisive moment."

Simultaneously, as the largest developing country in the world, China has always placed its own development within the coordinates of human development. China has made remarkable development achievements, especially over the past decade of the new era. While promoting its own growth, China has always cared about developing countries and tried its best to help them achieve joint development through trade, investment, aid, and sharing knowledge of development.

Against this background, President Xi Jinping proposed the GDI at the general debate of the 76th session of the United Nations General Assembly in September 2021, aimed at promoting global development to a new stage of balance, coordination, and inclusiveness.

The GDI focuses on poverty reduction, food security, anti-epidemic and vaccines, financing for development, climate change and green development, industrialization, digital economy, and connectivity in the digital age. It is highly consistent with the UN's 2030 Agenda to promote stronger, greener, and healthier global development.

In June 2022, President Xi Jinping chaired a high-level dialogue on global development with leaders from 18 major developing and emerging-market countries gathering online. This meeting also released an outcome list containing 32 measures, covering eight key areas of cooperation within the initiative, providing clear guidance for the GDI.

The GDI has sounded the "rallying call" to focus on development and paved a "fast lane" to promote it. The GDI has helped bring development issues back to the international core agenda, providing an effective platform for aligning development policies and deepening practical cooperation among all parties.

2. The concept and principle of the Global Development Initiative

Xi Jinping points out that only when countries develop together can there be true development; only when countries prosper together can there be true prosperity. The core idea of the Global Development Initiative is to adhere to the people-centered approach, with its primary purpose being to overcome the challenges posed by the pandemic and accelerate the implementation of the UN's 2030 Agenda. The most fundamental pursuit is to meet the yearning of people worldwide for a better life to realize the common value of all humanity. Such value pursuits determine the GDI's unique core concepts and value principles.

The GDI calls for adhering to the concepts and principles of prioritizing development, putting the people at the center, leaving no country or person behind, coexisting harmoniously with nature, using innovation as a driving force, building partnerships globally, taking action-oriented approaches, and improving synergic productivity. Based on its adherence to such principles and values, the GDI, as an international public good, has become increasingly prominent in its openness and emphasis on "small yet helpful projects that benefit people's livelihoods."

The GDI creates a globally open platform. Though proposed by China, the GDI belongs to the entire international community. From the perspective of participating countries, over 70 have participated in the Group of Friends of the Global Development Initiative initiated by China at the United Nations and opened to the developed countries. From the perspective of cooperation approaches, there are both cooperation created through the United Nations system and tripartite collaboration in which China directly participates. From the perspective of platform alignment, the GDI advocates for complete alignment between the GDI and the African Union's Agenda 2063, the New Partnership for Africa's Development (NEPAD), and supporting initiatives for African development partners, among others, with the UN's 2030 Agenda. It aims to facilitate a powerful convergence of development efforts among the United Nations, the G20, the Asia-Pacific Economic Cooperation (APEC), the BRICS countries, the China-ASEAN (10+1), and other multilateral cooperation processes.

The GDI creates an international public good. Xi Jinping points out that the GDI is "a public good open to the entire world." From an ideological perspective, the GDI adheres to the people-centered core concept and the principles of greenness and innovation, charts the course for global development, and injects ideological impetus into it. From the perspective of action, the GDI clarifies key areas, specifies priority options for promoting the international development process, and adds material strength. As an international public good that combines ideas, principles, and actions, the GDI provides a systematic and holistic solution to global development problems.

The GDI emphasizes "small and helpful projects that benefit people's livelihoods." Under the GDI framework, several "small and helpful" projects have taken root, such as the Smiling Children (for food distribution) project in Nepal and the cervical cancer screening and prevention project in Sierra Leone.

The GDI is rooted in the fine traditional Chinese culture. The Chinese nation pursues the goal of "a just cause for the common good," upholds the principles of "seeking goodwill with neighbors and harmony with all nations," and advocates the idea of "standing together with mutual assistance." These values and cultural genes are the traditional source of contemporary China's effort to develop international development cooperation. They are also its unwavering principle in its initiative for global development cooperation.

3. Early achievements of the Global Development Initiative

The GDI has received extensive and positive responses from the international community in the past two years. With the collective efforts of all parties, the cooperation path of the initiative has become clearer, the cooperation mechanisms have steadily improved, cooperation in the eight key areas has progressed in an orderly manner, the project portfolio continues to grow, development resources are gradually coming together, and a positive trend characterized by focused priorities and comprehensive progress has emerged. The initiative has effectively consolidated international development consensus, mobilized development cooperation actions, and achieved several early accomplishments.

The international development agenda has been revitalized. China convened a high-level dialogue on global development and a ministerial meeting of the Group of Friends of the Global Development Initiative to push development issues back to the center of the international agenda. Pragmatic cooperation in the eight critical areas of the initiative fully covers all 17 sustainable development goals and positively contributes to the UN's 2030 Agenda's implementation.

Many cooperation projects have been carried out. More than half of the 32 practical measures announced by China on the implementation of the GDI have been completed. A global development promotion center and its network have been established. Over 30 counterpart departments of countries and regional organizations have officially joined, providing a platform and support for idea exchanges on development cooperation, planning alignment, and resource coordination.

In September 2022, China set up the GDI project pool and released the first list of global development projects. The initial list of 50 practical cooperation projects covers multiple areas: poverty reduction, food security, industrialization, and more. Over ten of these projects have already been completed, while the remaining projects are progressing vigorously. Furthermore, the project pool continues to expand, and the total number of projects has now approached nearly 200.

The mobilization of development resources is being promoted. China has integrated and established the Global Development and South-South Cooperation Fund, increasing its capital to US$4billion. China has also actively participated in the capital increase of the International Development Association and the Global Environment Facility and has officially launched the third China-FAO South-South Cooperation Trust Fund.

The establishment of abroad cooperative network is being promoted. At present, over 100 countries and international organizations stand behind the GDI, and more than 70 countries have joined the Group of Friends of the Global Development Initiative. China has also signed cooperation memorandums of understanding with more than 20countries and international organizations. The formation of a global development partnership featuring unity, equality, balance, and mutual benefit is accelerating.

The improvement of people's livelihoods in all countries is being promoted. The GDI is bringing substantial changes and tangible hope to the people of all countries, such as providing technical assistance in mycorrhizal fungi and upland rice to the Eastern Highlands Province of Papua New Guinea, a South Pacific island nation; implementing the "East Asia Poverty Reduction Demonstration Cooperation Project" in six impoverished villages in Laos, Myanmar, and Cambodia; and distributing food packages to children in poor communities in Nepal... The efforts to improve people's livelihoods also range from providing the "kits of love" during the pandemic and performing cataract surgeries for patients to constructing elementary and secondary schools and collaborating on research and technology.

Conforming to the historical trend, the GDI has effectively built the international community's consensus on solidarity and cooperation, thus speeding up development, raising the global profile of development issues, and garnering widespread support and response from the international community, particularly from many developing countries.

UN Secretary-General Guterres stated that China-proposed Global Development Initiative aligns with the UN's 2030 Agenda and that China's efforts in assisting developing countries in their common development goals are unparalleled.

Pakistani Prime Minister Muhammad Shahbaz Sharif believes that the Global Development Initiative calls on the international community to prioritize development, responds to the international community's concerns about people's livelihood and development, and provides a realistic path for countries to coexist harmoniously and seek common development.

Thailand's Deputy Prime Minister and Foreign Minister Don Pramudwinai said that China's Global Development Initiative aims to establish an international community of development and provides an excellent opportunity to accelerate the realization of the United Nations' sustainable development agenda.

Currently, the GDI has achieved a leap from "laying the foundation" and "building the framework" to "strengthening cooperation" and "demonstrating tangible results." China has actively united the international community, promoted essential initiatives in a down-to-earth manner, and achieved significant early results. The GDI is taking on a wholesome aspect of joint participation by multiple countries, sectors, and fields.

GDI cooperation facilitating the achievement of all 17 SDGs

GDI	SDG
Poverty reduction	1,2,3,4,5,6,7,8,9,10,11,16,17
Food security	1,2,3,5,6,8,9,10,12,13,17
Pandemic response and vaccines	3,5,6,8,10,16,17
Financing for development	1,2,3,4,5,6,7,8,9,10,11,12,13,14,15,16,17
Climate change and green development	1,3,5,6,7,8,9,10,11,12,13,14,15,17
Industrialization	1,2,4,5,7,8,9,10,11,12,13,17
Digital economy	1,3,4,5,8,9,10,11,12,16,17
Connectivity in the digital era	1,2,5,7,8,9,10,11,17

SDG 1 No poverty

SDG 2 Zero hunger

SDG 3 Good health and wellbeing

SDG 4 Quality education

SDG 5 Gender equality

SDG 6 Clean water and sanitation

SDG 7 Affordable and clean energy

SDG 8 Decent work and economic growth

SDG 9 Industry, innovation and infrastructure

SDG17Partnerships for the Goals

SDG 10 Reduced inequalities

SDG 11 Sustainable cities andcommunities

SDG 12 Responsible consumption and production

SDG 13 Climate action

SDG 14 Life below water

SDG 15 Life on land

SDG 16 Peace, justiceandstronginstitutions

SDG 17 Partnerships for the Goals

II. Practical Achievements of the Global Development Initiative

Since Xi Jinping proposed the GDI two years ago, various parties have expressed their support and approval for it through bilateral and multilateral mechanisms, focusing on its eight key cooperation areas: poverty reduction, food security, pandemic response and vaccines, development financing, climate change and green development, industrialization, digital economy, and digital connectivity in the digital age.

Even more striking is the accelerated cooperation practice and remarkable results under the GDI framework. From individuals to families, communities to natural and human environments, the GDI transforms from blueprints into practical cooperation results: "small but helpful projects that benefit people's livelihoods."

1. Protecting the most vulnerable populations to make the world more compassionate

Building a "safety net" for vulnerable populations is one of the essential missions of the GDI. In pursuit of this mission, the initiative reaches deep into the world's most underdeveloped and remote rural areas, and its practical efforts extend into regions facing turmoil to provide nutritious meals for impoverished children, offer skills training to disadvantaged women, and deliver humanitarian relief and essential supplies to war refugees and displaced individuals. Besides improving their living conditions, it also creates opportunities for them to receive education and participate in economic activities.

Tanorn in Doung commune of Bati district in Takeo province, 60 kilometers south of Phnom Penh, the capital of Cambodia, is a demonstration village for Sino-Cambodian friendship and poverty alleviation. The Sino-Cambodian "Kit of Love" project was kicked off here in August 2022, with masks, lunch boxes, water bottles, rice, and canned food in the kits. Two hundred fifty-seven students from the Angkanha Primary School were the first to receive the gifts from China. Sesuokeuna, a sixth-grader, said excitedly, "This kit of love is handy. We sincerely thank China for its generous aid and always remember the kindness." Cambodia has suffered dramatically from the COVID-19 pandemic as one of the UN-recognized least-developed countries in the world. Unemployment and the number of people living in poverty rose, and some children were at risk of dropping out of school. The "Kit of Love" project provided basic meals and COVID-19 protection for 10,000 children in impoverished areas of Cambodia, alleviating concerns for their families and enabling them to return to work and production with greater peace of mind.

The Nepal Smiling Children Project and Lao National School Meals Program also received strong support from the Global Development and South-South Cooperation Fund. So far, the former project has provided 3,000 Nepalese children with food kits containing rice, beans, and cooking oil. At the same time, the latter has helped the Lao government continue the National School Meals Program that provides nutritious meals to over 130,000 students in more than 1,400 schools in its remote areas. Providing meals to school students is considered an essential social safety net component and a rational investment in the future generation. These projects have reduced malnutrition among impoverished students. In the long run, they also contribute to accumulating human resources to propel poverty-stricken nations toward sustainable development. According to a cost-benefit analysis by the UN's WFP, every USD1 invested in a school lunch program in Laos generates an additional US$5 per beneficiary over a lifetime.

The world's poorest and most vulnerable groups face the most severe impact of unprecedented global challenges, including women, refugees, and those struggling below the poverty line, who require special protection. The grim reality cannot be ignored: according to UN data, global hunger levels have reached their highest since 2005, with approximately 670 million people in extreme poverty. Achieving equal representation for women in positions of power and leadership in the workplace is estimated to take another 140 years. By the end of 2022, the global population of forcibly displaced persons had risen to 108.4 million, 2.5 times that of a decade before.

There is an urgent need for the international community to take practical action, even if it is just a small or partial change. Under the GDI framework, China continues to cooperate with the Women's Congress of Kyrgyzstan to organize the "Knowledgeable Women, Knowledgeable Nation" training course project, offering information technology, sewing technology, speech training, business planning, network marketing, and other courses for local women to help them improve vocational skills and increase employment opportunities. In cooperation with the UN Development Program, China distributes protective materials, family emergency kits, livelihood kits, and roof construction kits to 5,300 displaced families in Cabo Delgado Province, Mozambique, helping refugees resettle and resume production and livelihood. Villagers in Finitugu Village, Eastern Highlands Province, Papua New Guinea, an island country in the

South Pacific, have become beneficiaries of the Juncao and Upland Rice Cooperation Project. Incidentally, Juncao refers to the herbaceous plant that can be used as the culture substrate for growing edible and medicinal fungi. They used to be deeply involved in tribal disputes and suffered from poverty for a long time. Today, under the guidance of Chinese experts, they are learning how to level the land and cultivate rice, experiencing the taste of a bountiful harvest. Tony, the head of Finitugu Village, exclaimed, "Cultivating upland rice has given everyone hope for economic development and prompted them to set aside their conflicts, thus bringing peace and tranquility to the village."

The world population reached a new record of 8 billion on November 15, 2022.

It is a new milestone in human development history and a new moment for the international community to contemplate its shared responsibility towards the Earth. Population growth is increasingly concentrated in poverty-stricken countries. For example, during the transition period from 7 billion to 8 billion global population, approximately 70% of the new population emerged in low-income and lower-middle-income countries. According to projections, these two groups of countries will account for over 90% of the newly increased population in the growth range from 8 to 9 billion. Whether we can help the vast number of vulnerable and marginalized people break free from conflict, hunger, disease, and poverty, enabling them to lead stable and nourished lives, is a test of human conscience. Focusing on every living individual worldwide, the actions undertaken by the Global Development Initiative are of profound importance.

2. Building the homeland into a cozy one to make the world more livable

"How I wish I could have ten thousand houses / So I can provide shelter for all who need it!" The grand aspiration, envisioned by Du Fu, a Chinese Tang-dynasty poet, 1,200 years ago, is now being realized as international cooperation through China's GDI.

The initiative aims to afford individuals and families a safer and more stable haven. In the key cooperation areas it focuses on, such as poverty reduction and industrialization, some collaborative projects are dedicated to creating a more welcoming home desirable to live in for the global population of 8 billion people.

Construction of eight residential buildings comprising a total of 1,008 housing units is currently being accelerated in the Sukhbaatar District of Ulaanbaatar, Mongolia. This shanty area renovation project is funded by the Chinese government, with construction facilitated by the northern Chinese city of Baotou. Upon completion in 2024, the project will benefit over 700 households in Ulaanbaatar awaiting relocation due to building demolition and another 200-odd families temporarily residing in shanty areas of the city. They total approximately 5,000 individual residents. The related projects contribute to improving the living conditions of residents in shanty divisions and support the local achievement of sustainable development goals.

Building welcoming homes is not only reflected in housing improvements. The GDI seeks to improve the human living environment universally. Through global cooperation and solidarity, the initiative strives to enhance the quality of life for every family in developing countries as much as possible. It includes providing sanitary water sources, affordable clean energy, and sustainable community support. Aligning closely with the UN's 2030 Agenda, these are specific actions in implementing the initiative.

From sinking water wells to opening up water sources, from establishing water supply systems to setting up brand-new wastewater treatment plants in regions spanning Southeast Asia and multiple African nations, the Chinese government, businesses, and social organizations coordinate with various cooperating parties as they go to their local communities to develop clean water sources and provide related technologies to benefit the residents.

Water for residents and irrigation in the Siwa Oasis of Egypt comes entirely from groundwater. Previously, the wells sunk in this region were mainly as shallow as 500 meters or less. After long-term drilling for water, it is hard in quality and bitter in taste. With the local government's and residents ' support, a team of Chinese experts participated in the survey and started sinking wells more than 800 meters deep. These deep wells have considerably freed the Siwa Oasis from their drinking and irrigation water shortage.

With its rich experience in infrastructure development, China has brought higher-quality, more sustainable, and cleaner energy to the local areas through "small and helpful" cooperative brand-name projects ranging from water-well projects to street-lighting projects and to wind-power projects in some regions of the country and created new jobs at the same time.

The Abay wind power project in Kazakhstan alone can generate an expected annual electricity output of 510 million kilowatt-hours, meeting the daily electricity needs of 1.4 million households. The project has also provided over 500 temporary job positions and 50 permanent positions for the local community while training more than 20 new energy engineering construction and operation technicians in high demand.

The undertakings show full respect for the locals ' human rights. They will also help make the dividends of common development more balanced and more universally beneficial globally, thus conducive to accelerating the realization of relevant, sustainable development goals.

3. Tackling common crises to make the world safer

In today's world, threats and challenges from non-traditional security fields are increasing. Major infectious diseases, food and energy crises, and sudden natural disasters all threaten human survival and development.

All parties work together to deal with the crises and challenges under the GDI framework.

When the COVID-19 pandemic was rampant, the global vaccine supply was short. Hundreds of thousands of Palestinian refugees in Jordan, Syria, and Lebanon urgently needed vaccines. The Chinese government delivered 200,000 doses of COVID-19 vaccines in batches to the United Nations Relief and Works Agency for Palestine Refugees in the Near East (UNRWA) to assist the Palestinian refugees in those countries.

The severe impact of the COVID-19 pandemic has strained the healthcare systems of many developing countries, including numerous African member states of the Organization of Islamic Cooperation (OIC). These countries were grappling with medical facilities, personnel, and supplies shortages. In response, China helped the organization implement projects under its "Africa Plan" to enhance the public health capabilities of its least developed African member countries. The assistance included conducting health knowledge dissemination and awareness-raising efforts, strengthening healthcare levels in critical areas, and building public health systems. Additionally, China provided centralized assistance services to countries with inadequate medical conditions to enhance disease control and prevention capabilities.

The COVID-19 pandemic will not be humanity's last public health crisis, and global crises require cooperation among nations. Tanzania is one of the countries in Africa with the most severe malaria prevalence. To help Tanzania control and eliminate this infectious disease, China, Switzerland, and Tanzania are exploring a trilateral cooperation project, leveraging their respective strengths and experiences, exploring new collaboration models, and advancing Tanzania's malaria control and elimination process.

Food security is another significant challenge facing the world. According to the 2023 World Food Security and Nutrition report, approximately 735 million people suffer from hunger worldwide, an increase of over 122 million since 2019. If this trend is allowed to continue, by 2030, countries worldwide will be unable to achieve the Sustainable Development Goal oferadicating hunger on schedule.

In the East African country of Burundi, where the local agricultural population constitutes over 90%, agriculture plays a decisive role in the national economy. Chinese rice experts are promoting hybrid rice technology here, helping the local people achieve the goal of "everyone having enough to eat and everyone having savings in the bank." "With the support and assistance of the Chinese agricultural expert team, we have achieved a bountiful harvest in the hybrid rice we grow. Our lives have significantly improved, and we've built new houses and are even supporting seven children," says Charles Ngendakumana, a 43-year-old farmer from Village 4 of Nyingain Gihanga County, Burundi.

In July 2023, the "Burundi Hybrid Rice Technology Poverty Reduction Demonstration Project," jointly initiated by the China Foundation for Rural Development and the Chinese Senior Agricultural Expert Group, was officially launched in Gihanga County, Bubanza Province, Burundi. The project aims to support local farmers in acquiring the necessary inputs, such as hybrid rice seeds, fertilizers, pesticides, and more. It also operates on a revolving fund mechanism to expand the number of beneficiary farmers continuously. Additionally, the project will collaborate with local cooperatives to enhance their management capabilities, jointly assisting the local villagers in escaping poverty.

The impact of the COVID-19 pandemic, geopolitical security conflicts, and the rise of unilateralism and protectionism have seriously hindered the global development process, highlighting the importance and urgency of implementing the GDI and deepening practical cooperation.

4. Facilitating sustainable development to make the world greener

In recent years, several Pacific island nations in the Southern Hemisphere have been facing the threat of large amounts of floating plastic waste in the sea. These island nations cannot manage this plastic waste, and the accumulated piles have even become the "highest peaks" on their islands. The South Pacific Regional Environment Program has repeatedly expressed concerns about this issue.

"Bamboo for Plastic," an environmental initiative and action plan launched jointly by China and the International Bamboo and Rattan Organization in 2022, aimed at the global community. The initiative calls for deeper worldwide cooperation and better utilization of bamboo in reducing plastic pollution and replacing plastic products. It provides nature-based solutions for high-energy consumption and non-biodegradable plastic products.

According to experts from many countries, bamboo and rattan products have great potential and are expected to replace a large number of plastic products to develop the green economy better and create a healthier world. Brazilian economist Ronnie Lins pointed out that implementing the "Bamboo for Plastic" initiative will help promote investment and innovation in the plastics industry and reduce the impact of plastic pollution on the environment.

Plastic reduction and water conservation are two major problems facing the world. Knowledge of water is discussed enthusiastically in classrooms; sewage filters are made by hand, and students are sent to neighborhoods to collect local water conditions and challenges... Through vivid and intuitive learning, teachers and students at Brook Hill School in Nairobi, Kenya, have a deeper understanding of water in their daily lives and a more scientific sense of the community and the natural environment in which they live.

In 2022, following the successful release of the English version of Water Education for Kids, compiled and published in collaboration with UNESCO, the China Institute of Water Resources and Hydropower Research initiated a series of activities to promote water science education in African schools. Students and teachers from institutions such as Brook Hill School in Nairobi, Queen of Peace Education Center in Ruiru, and Bulla Iftin Primary School in Kenya actively participated.

For people living in vast developing countries, especially those in the least developed nations, improving their quality of life while making their lifestyles as "green" as possible is challenging. Therefore, balancing the relationship between economic development and ecological/environmental protection requires even greater support and assistance from the international community.

In the West African country of Mali, there is a shortage of electrical resources, and the rural electrification rate is less than 20%. In 2023, the China-aided solar energy demonstration village project in Mali will pass the completion inspection in the villages of Kourouba and Karang. The project installed a total of 1,195 off-grid solar home systems, 200 solar street lighting systems, 17 solar water pump systems, and 2 centralized solar power supply systems. It directly benefits tens of thousands of local residents.

Today, the pitch-dark villages at night not only have streetlights but also benefit from free solar-powered automatic water towers. "Without the generous assistance from China, we can't imagine when we would have been able to equip our homes with such advanced new energy devices," said a villager named Diop.

More emphasis is given to the "Global South" countries when implementing similar projects, even including places like the Pacific island of Fiji. Over the past year, more than 30,000 villagers in Fiji have started using solar lighting systems, ensuring safe nighttime travel and providing sufficient illumination and network connectivity for children studying at night. Additionally, by utilizing solar energy, the project reduces fossil fuel consumption and contributes positively to carbon emissions reduction, thereby significantly contributing to addressing climate change collectively.

These are a series of practical measures to share clean energy and green development experiences for people' s well-being under the GDI framework. Small but helpful, the projects not only meet the immediate needs of improving rural infrastructure in countries like Fiji and Mali but also respond to the residents ' long-standing aspirations for a better life.

Scorching heat, droughts, wildfires, heavy rainfall, floods—extreme weather events closely linked to climate change in today's world are becoming more frequent in many parts of the globe. They significantly impact various aspects of human life such as health, ecosystems, economy, agriculture, energy, and water supply, with even prolonged threats.

In recent years, extreme weather events accompanied by unprecedented high temperatures worldwide have given people a more direct and keen awareness of the cumulative effects of climate change. "The era of global warming has ended; the era of global boiling has arrived." UN Secretary-General Guterres renewed his warning on the global climate crisis by emphasizing "boiling."

Frequent natural disasters caused by global extreme weather, an accelerated loss of biodiversity, and the challenges of maintaining a harmonious human-nature relationship are becoming increasingly grave. How can we enhance the ability of developing countries to adapt to climate change? How can we promote the formation of an international consensus on protecting the natural environment and biodiversity?

The GDI adheres to the action-oriented idea of harmonious coexistence between man and nature to promote strengthened international cooperation, build communication and dialogue platforms, change production modes and lifestyles, and bolster global development that is stronger, greener, and healthier.

5. Achieving strong growth to make the world more prosperous

In recent years, global industrial and supply chains saw accelerated restructuring. Developing countries, each at different stages of development and with distinct national conditions, must, in line with their own realities, develop industries with comparative advantages and better integrate into global and regional industrial and supply chains for more development opportunities and momentum. At the same time, with the inclusion of more developing countries, the global and regional industrial and supply chains will become more resilient to enhance the stability and sustainability of the world economy.

After putting forward the GDI, China set an example by actively helping other developing countries with industrialization. In December 2021, at the Eighth Ministerial Conference of the Forum on China-Africa Cooperation, China announced that it would encourage its enterprises to invest no less than US$10 billion in Africa in the coming three years and establish a platform for China-Africa private investment promotion to assist Africa in implementing ten industrialization and job promotion projects. In the China-CELAC (Community of Latin American and Caribbean States) Joint Action Plan for Cooperation in Key Areas (2022-2024), China and CELAC have agreed to enhance the exchange in industrial policies, deepen cooperation in areas such as raw materials, equipment manufacturing, green and low-carbon industries, and industrial and supply chains, and promote intelligent, digital, and green development of industries in China and the CELAC countries.

How can we inject more new momentum into global growth? All parties responding to the GDI believe that multilateral coordination is indispensable and that only concrete actions can enhance the resilience of industrial and supply chains, promote direct investment, and bridge the "digital divide."

The United Nations Industrial Development Organization (UNIDO), the German International Cooperation Agency, the China National Textile and Apparel Council, and the Ethiopian Textile and Apparel Industry Research and Development Center have collaborated to assist Ethiopia's textile and apparel industry in enhancing its capacity to meet the environmental, social, and corporate governance (ESG) standards for market access and raise the industry's ESG awareness to promote business partnerships. The experiences gained from this initiative have been replicated and extended to other regions in Africa and in Asia. The project was selected by the United Nations Office for South-South Cooperation as a case of "Sustainable South-South Cooperation and Triangular Cooperation Good Practices" for 2022.

Currently, the "digital divide" continues to widen between the North and the South. The GDI has actively established communication platforms and supported digital capacity building in developing countries.

In collaboration with certain regional international organizations, China is making efforts to remove digital "barriers" and promote the concept of "Digital plus" in many countries and regions of the "Global South." This concept spans various sectors such as precision agriculture, smart fisheries, e-commerce, and online skills training, directly empowering economic development in the "Global South" through the benefits of digitalization. Take coffee beans as an example. China has been importing coffee beans from African and Central and South American markets before distributing them through its robust e-commerce network in recent years. The move has brought international bulk orders to coffee farmers in Rwanda, Timor-Leste, and Costa Rica, significantly improving these coffee growers ' working and living conditions.

Take the highly regarded "cross-border e-commerce" capability training as another example. The online training project jointly launched by the Chinese government and the United Nations Office for South-South Cooperation, namely Cross-Border E-commerce Capacity Building Project for Youth in Developing Countries for Poverty Reduction and Sustainable Development, has attracted active participation from 1,090 students in 93 countries. During the training period, more than 1,000 people simultaneously engaged in online learning daily. These training programs not only provide insights into the latest developments in worldwide related industries but also share experiences from China and other developing countries.

They bring effective methods of using e-commerce for poverty reduction to young people in various countries who urgently need to enhance their digital skills.

Another example is Huawei Egypt's collaboration with the Ministry of

Communications and Information Technology and the Ministry of Higher Education and Scientific Research of Egypt. They carry out a continuous capacity building project, the ITB (ICT Talent Bank Program) . It focuses on artificial intelligence, cloud computing, the Internet of Things, and such cutting-edge technologies as big data and 5G to train professionals for Egypt and help local digital transformation. Through establishing colleges and developing technical courses, Huawei has trained over 35,000 local college students, more than 8,000 of whom have obtained certification. The training has also promoted youth employment, thus starting a virtuous circle. The Communications and Information Technology, Higher Education and Scientific Research, and Labor ministries of Egypt spoke highly of the cooperation with Huawei on the ITB project and appreciated the project's contribution to the construction of the "Digital Egypt."

Under the GDI framework, multiple stakeholders collaborate to facilitate global cooperation in applying digital technology through establishing exchange platforms. They are strengthening digital capacity building to bridge the "digital divide" and conforming to the trend of digitalization to promote the use of big data. All of these efforts will accelerate the realization of the vision for the UN's 2030 Agenda and empower developing countries to gain more information technology dividends, making a shift from "lagging behind" to "running alongside," ultimately promoting shared global prosperity.

III. Contributions of the Global Development Initiative to the World

By steadfastly prioritizing development as its "top task," China has created an astonishing development miracle that has amazed the world, ushering in a new era when China and the world integrate in development and help each other to succeed. In this new era, China is committed to promoting common prosperity domestically while also striving to advance joint development globally. It not only unwaveringly pursues Chinese modernization on all fronts to achieve the great rejuvenation of the Chinese nation but also shoulders its responsibilities as a major country to keep making new and greater contributions to global development. The GDI's proposal, implementation, and promotion represent a vibrant chapter in this new era.

The GDI is an international public good provided by China, combining visionary thinking and actionable measures when the UN's 2030 Agenda faced obstacles.Over the past two years, it has delivered tangible benefits to countless individuals and families, offered hope for stability and growth to various countries, and presented a new model of international development cooperation that is more inclusive, diverse, and sustainable to the international community. It has paved a new path and provided new inspiration for humanity to break free from development challenges and jointly embark on a brighter future of shared development.

1. Shaping anew: Pioneering a new model of international development cooperation

We believe that the new type of international development cooperation led and promoted by the GDI exhibits the following distinctive features:

The Whole World Is One Family: Building a Shared Development Space with a More Inclusive Cooperation Concept

The GDI is global, regardless of North and South. It neither has any interest in bloc politics nor draws ideological boundaries. While adhering to the principle of North-South cooperation as the main channel, it continuously explores new fields and approaches for South-South cooperation, revitalizes global development partnerships, and works together with all parties to create an open and interconnected global development environment, allowing various countries and their people to share development opportunities and achievements. It does not interfere in the domestic affairs of other nations nor attaches any political conditions, firmly supporting each country's right to choose its own path. It upholds the principles of consultation, joint construction, and shared benefits, welcoming all countries and all proactive forces dedicated to global development to contribute their wisdom and strength. So far, over 100 countries and international organizations support the GDI, and more than 70 countries have joined the Group of Friends ofthe Global Development Initiative. China has also signed cooperation memorandums of understanding with more than 20 countries and international organizations. At the First High-level Conference of the Forum on Global Action for Shared Development held in July this year, China announced collaborations with Switzerland in malaria prevention and control in Tanzania and with Germany in agricultural cooperation in Nigeria, serving as new examples of the open and inclusive nature of the GDI.

A Journey with Many Companions Gets Far: Aggregating High-quality Development Resources with More Diversified Cooperation Channels

The GDI emphasizes the full engagement of governments, private sectors, civil society organizations, and international institutions from all countries. It actively mobilizes the business community, academia, and civil society forces from various countries; establishes a broad cooperation network; pools resources such as funds, technology, talents, and data; and allocates them to the most urgently needed areas to achieve maximum benefits. With the support of the Global Development and South-South Cooperation Fund, the United Nations Food and Agriculture Organization (FAO), and the World Food Programme (WFP), among others, nearly 50 triangular cooperation projects have been implemented. These projects have assisted relevant developing countries in improving their food security and overall agricultural production capacity. China has also signed a memorandum of understanding with the Gates Foundation to carry out practical cooperation in healthcare, capacity building, and development financing, jointly advancing the implementation of the GDI and accelerating progress toward the goals of the UN' s 2030 Agenda.

Teaching People How to Fish: Fostering Endogenous Development Momentum Through More Sustainable Forms of Cooperation

The GDI emphasizes the combination of both hard and soft assistance, blending development aid with mutually beneficial cooperation, aiming not only to give people fish but also to teach them how to fish. In the teaching process, the initiative goes beyond narrow economic rationality and advocates for a steadfast commitment to the right balance between morality and self-interest, prioritizing the moral aspect. It encourages all parties to share development experience and industry technologies with developing countries in various ways, helping them cultivate their capacity for independent development. China actively promotes the construction of a global development knowledge network, establishes comprehensive cooperation network platforms, and facilitates international exchanges and sharing of development experience. The "China-ASEAN Development Knowledge Network Secretariat" has been established. In the future, China will explore establishing regional core networks such as the "China-Central Asia Development Knowledge Network" and the "China-Africa Development Knowledge Network," as well as thematic networks focusing on poverty reduction, clean energy development, and more.

2. Setting off again: Embarking on a new journey toward the go alsof sustainabledevelopment

On September 25, 2015, at the United Nations Headquarters in New York, 193 United Nations member states jointly launched the UN's 2030 Agenda at the historic development summit. Halfway through the timeframe for implementing the agenda, only about 12% of the sustainable development goals are expected to be achieved on schedule. According to the Sustainable Development Goals Report 2023: Special Edition, half of the approximately 140 specific goals that can be assessed show moderate or severe signs of falling short of expectations. More than 30% of these goals have made no progress or even gone into reverse compared to the 2015 baseline.

Although the reality is worrying and even depressing, the UN's 2030 Agenda is still the broadest consensus on development issues in the current international community and the most explicit blueprint for human vision. The Special Edition report notes, "As historians write about the 21st century, they will judge our era by whether we turn this blueprint into reality." At present, the most urgent task is to take action to create a more hopeful new reality. In this sense, the GDI points the way for action:

Embrace technological change to boost the vitality of economic recovery

The worldwide electrification rate was 87% in 2015 and increased to 91% in 2021. Global internet users have grown by 65% since 2015, reaching 5.3 billion in 2022. While global manufacturing growth has slowed, medium and high-end technology industries have shown strong growth momentum. The significant progress achieved in the global development sector, particularly in the digital economy and high-end manufacturing industries, indicates that the international community may still be able to make substantive breakthroughs for the betterment of all by seizing the historical opportunities of the new technological revolution and industrial transformation.

Green and digital transformations can be a new way out of development challenges. For example, in regions with high-quality internet services, 44% of businesses are exporters, while in areas with weaker internet services, only 19% are exporters. This is also why the GDI considers innovation-driven approaches one of the fundamental principles and actively engages with various stakeholders to strengthen cooperation in the Internet, big data, 5G, and artificial intelligence.

Improving global governance and building a just and reasonable world order

More encouraging is the eye-catching rise of the "Global South" countries on the world stage. The strong call for "restoring development as the centerpiece on the international agenda" issued by the GDI, and the heightened enthusiasm for cooperation and solidarity shown in the process of promoting the implementation of the agenda have injected strong impetus into international development cooperation.

Currently, wealth inequality among nations is exacerbating, and a fundamental reason for this is the global economic governance system's failure to address the development aspirations ofthe "Global South fairly." For example, during the COVID-19 pandemic, the Group of Seven (G7), representing developed countries, received a total of US$280 billion in funding from the International Monetary Fund. In comparison, some of the least developed countries received only around US$8 billion in assistance. The G7 countries have a total population of approximately 770 million, while the combined population of the least developed countries mentioned above is about 1.1 billion. Therefore, United Nations Secretary-General António Guterres strongly calls for a change in the "bias and inequities ingrained in the existing international financial architecture" and a thorough reform of the International Monetary Fund and the World Bank.

Constructing a more just and equitable global development governance system and institutional framework through a series of practical actions and bold reforms is an urgent priority. It means we must uphold genuine multilateralism and support the United Nations in playing its coordinating role; build an open world economy and establish secure, stable, open, and inclusive supply chains; advance reforms of multilateral development institutions to enhance the representation and voice of emerging market economies and developing countries; and create a united, equal, balanced, and inclusive global development partnership and urge developed countries to fulfill their official development assistance commitments to developing countries, including providing funding, technology, and capacity-building, in a timely and complete manner.

China, as the largest developing country in the world, is a natural member of the "Global South." China will work with other emerging market economies and developing countries to enhance the voice and representation of "Global South" countries in reforming the global governance system, and safeguard their common interests. We will jointly defend the right to development, take on responsibilities for world peace, and contribute to common development.

Taking collective action to build a community of shared future for human development

In today's world, if not pursuing development is the biggest insecurity, not cooperating is the greatest risk, and disunity is the biggest challenge. Economists from the International Monetary Fund have warned that a divided world may become poorer. They particularly pointed out the potential maximum damage that the rise of "friend-shoring" could cause to underdeveloped markets because they are more dependent on investments from countries further afield geopolitically.

The international community's strong consensus is that the development agenda's politicization should be avoided, and geopolitical conflicts and group confrontations will lead the world in the wrong direction, which will cause immeasurable losses to the cause of global development. Development is the key and foundation for addressing all human problems, and it is a challenge faced by all countries and regions worldwide. All parties, including the United Nations, countries from the Global South and North, the poor and the wealthy, and the regional and sub-regional organizations, should unite, shoulder shared responsibilities, and take collective actions.

In this regard, heads of state and government of all countries should demonstrate leadership and take seven years of accelerated, sustained, and transformative actions at the national and international levels. Member states of the United Nations should seize the opportunity of this Sustainable Development Goals Summit to build consensus on development, pool development resources, integrate the GDI more closely with the UN's 2030 Agenda, align it with the development strategies of developing countries, and coordinate with the United Nations development agencies and multilateral development organizations to jointly create a new era of global development that is inclusive, balanced, cooperative, and commonly prosperous.

Looking ahead, the joint construction of a community of shared future for humanity relies on the following principles: eliminating conflicts and jointly building peace, injecting vitality and collectively promoting development, being open and inclusive, seeking common progress, uniting as one, and working together through consultation.

As a member of the big family of the "Global South" and a responsible member of the global village, China maintains that development should be placed at the center of the international agenda, an international consensus on promoting development should be further built, and the legitimate rights of developing countries to develop be safeguarded. We also advocate reinvigorating the global development partnership, cultivating a new driving force for growth, and encouraging developed countries to fulfill their commitments earnestly so that the fruits of development can benefit the people of all nations.

President Xi Jinping pointed out that development is a timeless theme for humanity, and development for the benefit of all is the important path to building a beautiful world. The GDI is not a solo performed by China but a symphony of all parties involved. Global development efforts should be a collective endeavor involving people from all countries, shared by all, without leaving behind any country or individual.

Turning the blueprint into reality starts right now.

Writing Explanation and Acknowledgments

The think tank report "The Practical Achievements and Global Contributions of the Global Development Initiative" was released at the high-level meeting on Global Development Initiative (GDI) Cooperation Outcomes hosted by China at the UN headquarters on Sept.19, 2023. Vice President Han Zheng attended the meeting and introduced the think tank report in his speech.

The think tank is under the guidance of the The Department of International Economic Affairs of the Ministry of Foreign Affairs, and is led by Fu Hua, President of Xinhua News Agency and Chairman of the Academic Committee of Xinhua Institute, with Lyu Yansong, Editorin-Chief of Xinhua News Agency, as the deputy head. Other members of the project team include Ren Weidong, Liu Gang, Ban Wei, Cui Feng, Hao Weiwei, Liu Hua, Yang Liu, Zheng Mingda, Xu Xiaoqing, Liu Mingxia, etc.

Since the initiation in the March 2023, the research team has taken more than 6 months for concentrated study sessions, in-depth investigations, writing, revision and proofreading.

The research group earnestly studied important discourses related to Xi Jinping's diplomatic thought, conducted research on institutions such as China International Development Cooperation Agency, Center for International Knowledge on Development, and United Nations Association of China, and held multiple expert seminars; Conduct on-site research in over 20 state-owned enterprises, including State

Power Investment Corporation, China Energy Investment, China Merchants Group, and China National Offshore Oil Corporation; Through the collection of progress cases of the Global Development Initiative in various countries by multiple foreign embassies and consulates of the Ministry of Foreign Affairs, and in cooperation with the National Governance Research Institute of Huazhong University of Science and Technology, more than 130 excellent case collections of the Global Development Initiative from over 50 countries have been compiled. Among them, more than 30 typical cooperation projects are presented in the report, which effectively demonstrates the contribution of the initiative to the international development cause.

Responsibility and Mission of News Media in AI Era [1]

Media intelligence is developing rapidly around the world. With a stronger sense of mission and urgency in bolstering our capability to guide public opinion, we need to make breakthroughs in the independent innovation of key technologies, exploring the application of AI in news gathering, generating, distribution, reception and feedback. The use of algorithms must be aligned with mainstream values for better guidance of public opinion. [2]

———President Xi Jinping

I. Introduction

The rapid development and wide application of generative AI technology have triggered an AI boom sweeping the world, with news media once again embracing opportunities for transformation and development. The mysterious "technological

---

[1] Released on October 14, 2024, at the Sixth World Media

[2] Part of the speech at the 12th group study session of the Political Bureau of the 19th CPC Central Committee, January 25, 2019.

singularity" in science fiction is moving from imagination to reality, leading mankind into a new space-time full of unknowns. The era of "smart media" seems to have arrived.

How AI will reshape the news media industry is still an unknown mystery as the development of this technology is still fraught with uncertainty. Just like the previous revolutions in communication technology, the development of AI cannot escape from the "Collingridge dilemma". The pros and cons of the emerging technology are still in the "black box" until they are tested in practice.

There is broad consensus within the international community on building an effective governance mechanism to promote AI for the benefit of mankind. In October 2023, Chinese President Xi Jinping put forward the Global AI Governance Initiative at the Third Belt and Road Forum for International Cooperation. The Initiative states that AI governance is a matter of shared future for humankind and a common issue for all countries. World peace and development are facing diverse challenges. Against this backdrop, all countries should be committed to the principle of equal emphasis on development and security, and forge consensus through dialogue and cooperation; they should build an open, fair and effective governance mechanism, promoting AI for the benefit of humankind, and contributing to the building of a community with a shared future for humanity. Focusing on the development, safety and governance of AI, the Initiative sets forth basic principles such as "putting people first" and "intelligence for good", offering a Chinese perspective fortackling the challenges of AI governance.

What opportunities and challenges do news media face in the era of AI? How should news media fulfill their duties and missions to promote intelligence for good? To explore these questions, the research team at New China Research (NCR), the think tank of Xinhua News Agency, conducted a questionnaire survey in Chinese, English and French for global news media organizations in 2024, gathering 1,094 valid questionnaires. Participants from 53 countries and regions, including newspapers, periodicals, broadcasting and television stations, news agencies, websites and mobile application service providers. Additionally, the team visited major mainstream media outlets, technology companies and research institutes around the world to conduct in-depth investigations into the opportunities, challenges, responsibilities and missions of news media in the AI era. Based on the research data and interview results, the group conducted a rigorous qualitative and quantitative analysis and, after extensive discussions, produced the report titled "The Responsibility and Mission of News Media in the Era of Artificial Intelligence".

The report found that the majority of global news media (66%) held a positive view on the impact of generative AI on the industry. Most respondents (67.6%) had already experienced changes brought about by AI and more than half of (51.2%) of them had begun to implement AI technologies. Media organizations primarily expected generative AI to enhance the timeliness (74.6%) and productivity (74.4%) of news reporting. However, they also expressed concerns about the credibility risk brought about by AI, particularly regarding the "distortion and inaccuracy of news clues and materials" (76.4%). Additionally, a significant majority of news media (85.6%) believed that the application of generative AI required better regulation.

According to the report, AI is driving a new wave of productivity in news mediacreating advanced productive forces across content collection, production, distribution, and evaluation. It empowers both media organizations and consumers with enhanced experiences that transcend time and space, integrating virtual and real-world interactions, and facilitating human-machine communication. Additionally, AI is creating new forms of businesses models, including a media-centric approach for everything, platform-based media, and digitalized and intelligent industry.

The report suggests that the uncertainty of AI and its misuse have given rise to multiple risks and challenges. False information has escalated in scale, form and distribution, triggering a global crisis of authenticity. Additionally, the technology's limitations and the users' private interests have created a "collusion" effect, polluting the public opinion and negatively affecting individual perceptions and societal discourse. This situation has intensified international confrontations of information. Furthermore, widespread value disputes and ethical dilemmas have put AI in a dilemma between development and governance. The "intelligence divide" may further widen the gap between people, urban and rural areas, and between the North and the South, promoting technological hegemony and exacerbating global development imbalances.

The report proposes that news media, by shouldering social responsibilities and committing to a "people-first" approach while promoting "intelligence for good", will fulfil its duties in the era of AI in four aspects: accelerating intelligent initiatives to enhance media value, prioritizing ethical use to establish robust standards, shouldering social responsibilities to optimize the cognitive environment, and fostering dialogue and cooperation to improve global governance. In this way, powerful media forces will unite to build a community with a shared future and contribute to a better world.

II. Opportunities: AI Empowers Media Development

We need to seize the opportunities that arise from the integrated digital, networked, and smart development.Artificial intelligence should be utilized in reforms to enhance quality, efficiency, and growth drivers, ultimately boosting the total factor productivity.[1]

——President Xi Jinping

A new generation of artificial intelligence is thriving worldwide, injecting new momentum into economic and social development and profoundly changing people's work and life[2]. In the news media sector, the emergence of intelligence, along with technologies such as 5G, big data, cloud computing, the Internet of Things, and blockchain, has ignited a new wave of media revolution. As the transformation brought about by AI gradually unfolds, the news media sector is presented with opportunities for new production drivers, enhanced user experiences, and promising prospects for industries.

1. New Drivers of Production Capacity

At present, AI is experiencing an explosive growth, with continuous breakthroughs in the application of algorithm recommendations, voice interaction, knowledge Q&A, and image generation. The wave of generative AI is spreading globally. At the end of 2022, OpenAI's generative AI ChatGPT made its debut. In 2024, the text-to-video model Sora once again captivated the world. Meanwhile, multi-modal and vertical domain large models emerged around the globe, signaling an accelerated trend of AI development worldwide.

---

[1] Speech at the ninth group study session of the Political Bureau of the 19th CPC Central Committee (October 31, 2018).

[2] Xi Jinping's congratulatory message to the 2018 World Artificial Intelligence Conference(September 17, 2018)

The booming surge of AI technology offers a new driver of production for news media. Media outlets, both at home and abroad, are seizing this technological opportunity, striving to become "early adopters" of AI. A study conducted by a research team from Xinhua News Agency shows that 10.2% of media organizations worldwide have fully embraced AI, implementing institutional mechanisms to integrate AI into their production processes from the top down. Additionally, 41.0% of media organizations are actively exploring the application of AI technologies, encouraging some news segments to try AI. AI has gradually become a vital enhancer for the news media sector, fostering new productive forces and enabling high-quality development.

The Application of Generative Artificial Intelligence (Large Language Models) in the Media Organizations Interviewed

- 10.2% Fully embrace AI, with institutional-level mechanisms in place, integrating AI into production processes from the top down.
- 41% Explore actively, and encourage some news segments to try AI.
- 36% Only individual editors occasionally use AI and the organization does not oppose the use.
- 12.8% Very few people use AI, or the organization prohibits the use.

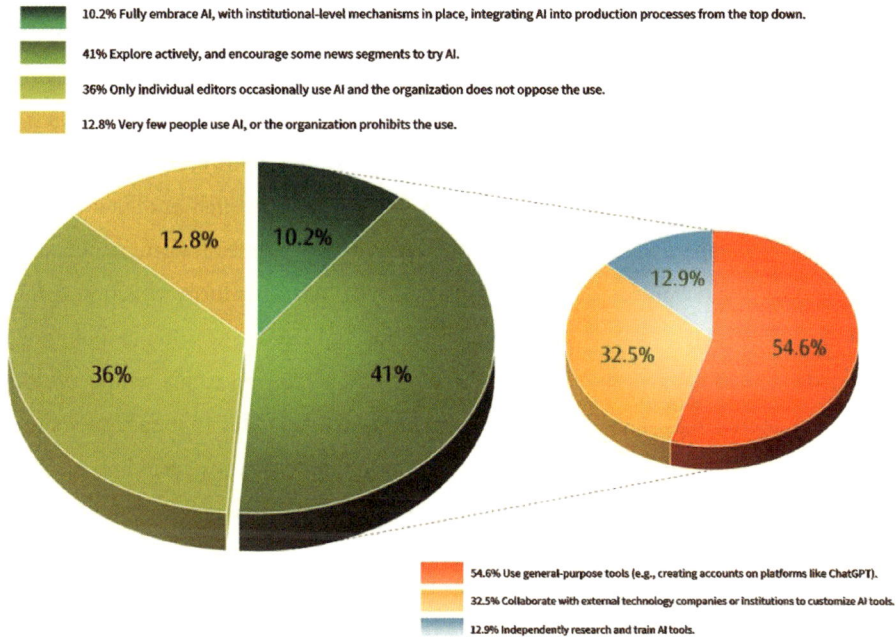

- 54.6% Use general-purpose tools (e.g., creating accounts on platforms like ChatGPT).
- 32.5% Collaborate with external technology companies or institutions to customize AI tools.
- 12.9% Independently research and train AI tools.

Aggregating Information and Enriching Sources

The new generation AI technology automatically gathers background information, recommends news sources and contacts, and verifies them through precise search engines, analytical engines, and visualization tools, providing editors with more valuable news leads and diverse perspectives.

"Juicer", a news aggregation and content extraction system developed by the BBC, automatically collects content from various free news websites around the world.

AI categorizes and tags news to provide journalists with news materials and topic suggestions. "NewsRadar", developed by the Xinhua News Agency, automatically issues early warnings for breaking news and predicts an event's popularity based on its nature and scale. "Blossomblot", a data analysis bot developed by the New York Times, forecasts the most suitable information to share on social media by analyzing articles on social platforms, assisting in the creation of "viral" contents.

Assisting Creation and Improving Quality

In the news creation process, intelligent creation platforms offer media professionals enhanced knowledge support with "Knowledge Services + AI" model. Technologies such as writing bots and AI creative assistants can perform tasks like voice-to-text transcription, automatic editing, subtitle generation, intelligent music matching, automatic translation, and converting text or images into videos. The in-depth application of AI frees media workers from repetitive and tedious tasks, allowing them to focus on content innovation and ingenuity.

Xinhua News Agency's "Yuanmao" metaverse system, powered by AIGC (AI-Generated Content), includes several production-assisting tools such as digital humans, Meta Cube, the Jimu AIGC video production system and an immersive offline interactive space. The People's Daily launched the "Creative Brain AI+" platform, which integrates nearly 20 intelligent tools, enabling the timely creation and rapid generation of multimodal new media products. This platform delivers a one-stop solution to the whole working procedure, including interviews, filming, live broadcasting, editing, and publishing. Additionally, the holographic recording glasses offer multiple features, including real-time facial recognition, AI voice interaction, and initiating live streaming in real time.

According to the study conducted by the research team, the top three application scenarios that media organizations explored are as follows:

1. Editing assistance, such as fact-checking, speech-to-text conversion, adding subtitles, and translation;

2. Content creation, such as generating summaries, creating infographic posters, and providing voiceovers for digital anchors;

3. Topic planning or outline drafting.

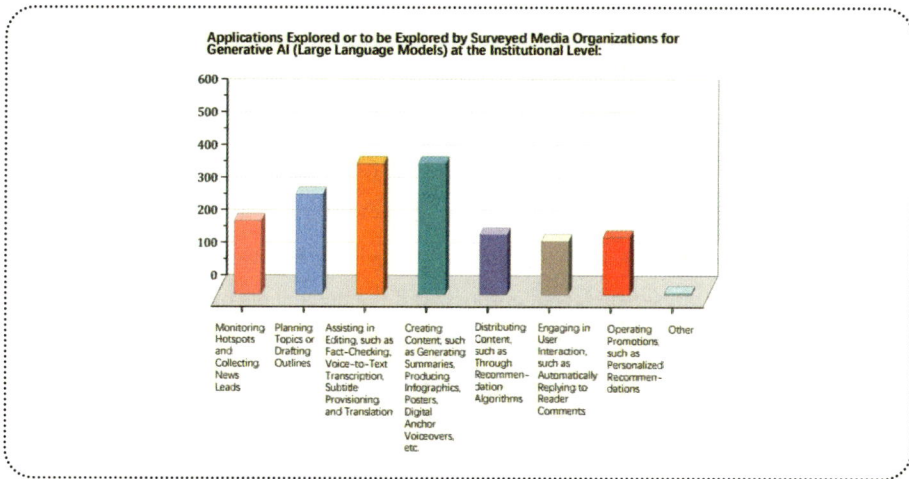

Applications Explored or to be Explored by Surveyed Media Organizations for Generative AI (Large Language Models) at the Institutional Level:

Precise Profiling and Personalized Distribution

In content distribution, AI extensively leverages interconnected data to help media organizations gain deep insights, outline user profiles, and establish closer connections with users to achieve more accurate content delivery.

Today, personalized recommendations, powered by AI technology, have become the mainstream method of news distribution. Media recommendation algorithms rely not only on historical browsing records, but also on more precise data. The American news aggregation site BuzzFeed and the globally popular short-video platform TikTok have perfected user data analysis by considering metrics such as click frequency, time spent, and preferred content to guide content planning, operations, and promotion.

Furthermore, generative AI enables "point-to-point" information dissemination, allowing users to access specific content tailored to their needs in different scenarios. This is facilitated by the personalized "information assistant" embedded in various search engines and applications. The "point-to-point" distribution ensures intelligent delivery even without centralized platforms. Currently, companies like Microsoft, Google, and Baidu have already integrated generative AI into their search engines. The fusion of large language models with search engines may become a new source of traffic and a new channel for news distribution.

Scientific Evaluation and Efficient Management

AI technology evaluates communication effectiveness and precisely assesses data, thereby enhancing the management efficiency of media organizations. For example, by analyzing data such as user viewing time, click-through rates, and the number of shares,

AI can quantify and evaluate content appeal. Sentiment analysis tools capture users' emotional responses during their interactions and monitor discussions on social media to gauge content impact. Observing user interactions, such as the number of comments, likes, dislikes, and reports, can evaluate the level of user engagement.

In the Washington Post's "Arc Publishing" newsroom, TV screens display real-time visualized data charts, showing the number of site logins, ranking of articles by readership, ranking of user-preferred authors, and the percentage of article types favored by readers. The UK Financial Times uses robots to check whether the sources cited in their reports are disproportionately represented by specific groups.

According to the study conducted by the research team, 74.6% of the surveyed media expected generative AI to help improve the timeliness of news reporting; 74.4% of respondents believed that generative AI would enhance the efficiency of news production; 66.7% of the surveyed media anticipated that generative AI would help improve the accuracy of news distribution, and 63.3% believed AI would enhance content creativity.

Media organizations' estimation of the influence of generative AI in news reporting

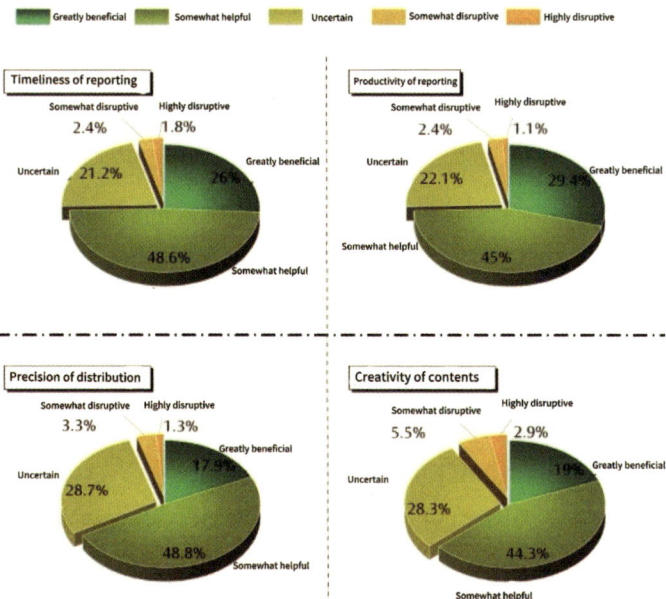

Greatly beneficial   Somewhat helpful   Uncertain   Somewhat disruptive   Highly disruptive

Timeliness of reporting

Somewhat disruptive 2.4%   Highly disruptive 1.8%
Uncertain 21.2%   Greatly beneficial 26%
48.6%   Somewhat helpful

Productivity of reporting

Somewhat disruptive 2.4%   Highly disruptive 1.1%
Uncertain 22.1%   Greatly beneficial 29.4%
Somewhat helpful 45%

Precision of distribution

Somewhat disruptive 3.3%   Highly disruptive 1.3%
Greatly beneficial 17.9%
Uncertain 28.7%
48.8%   Somewhat helpful

Creativity of contents

Somewhat disruptive 5.5%   Highly disruptive 2.9%
Greatly beneficial 19%
Uncertain 28.3%
44.3%
Somewhat helpful

2. Enhanced User Experience

The deep integration of AI with news media empowers news dissemination and brings exciting experiences for consumers. Media consumption in the age of artificial intelligence will be a human-centered and all-connected new experience. The prospects of full-process media, holographic media, all-accessible media, and full-effect media are becoming more evident, revealing vast opportunities on the horizon.

Transcending Time and Space and Reaching Users Anytime, Anywhere

The wide spread application of artificial intelligence technology allows communication to transcend the limitations of time and space. News can reach users anytime, anywhere, and in any situation.

Intelligent media systems can capture users' immediate needs instantly by tracking the dynamic changes in user behavior, stance, and interests. When major news events occur, these systems can quickly identify and forward relevant information. Large models can supplement information based on known facts. They simulate the course of events and restore the news scene, representing news events concretely, offering users accurate and comprehensive information during the "golden time" (the critical period for information dissemination).

Intelligence-driven, context-aware, and personalized services can identify users' geographical locations and deliver content relevant to their daily lives. During the Paris Olympics, NBC Universal launched Virtual Kiosk, a novel e-commerce advertising platform. This tool dynamically tailors advertising services to viewers based on their consumption habits while watching the games. In the future, increasingly sophisticated algorithms will be able to perceive users' diverse needs for information, products and services anytime and anywhere. Enhanced services will be available and properly presented to users anywhere.

Blending Reality and Virtuality for Immersive Experiences

AI combines with Virtual Reality (VR), Augmented Reality (AR), and Mixed Reality (MR), forming comprehensive, multi-sensory, and multi-dimensional communication scenarios. Immersive experiences are becoming more intelligent.

Holographic communication, enhanced by powerful algorithms and computing power, offers real-time presentation of high-fidelity digital images. Users can create virtual avatars that are proportional to themselves and realize real-time interaction in the virtual world through their digital twins. This not only creates more authentic emotional bonds between people but also allows users to create real-life experiences that are otherwise difficult to obtain firsthand. With AR, the New York Times simulated NASA's Mars mission, providing a more direct experience. The Times enabled audiences to review the whole Apollo 11 mission. Time magazine used AR panoramic technology to showcase the changes in the Amazon rainforest for users. China Central Television (CCTV) used Virtual Engine + XR + Virtual Studio Technology to achieve seamless transitions between indoor and outdoor scenes in reporting Typhoon Capricorn, enhancing the artistic expressiveness of the report and the effectiveness of information delivery.

The integration of AI with multimodal technology also enables the digital transformation of culture, region, tradition, and aesthetics, extensively applied in the dissemination of historical, cultural, and artistic information. By tapping the screen, users can simulate striking a virtual replica of the Marquis Yi of Zeng's Bianzhong, an ancient Chinese instrument, to appreciate the charm of the national treasure firsthand. Users can immerse themselves in the virtual Notre Dame Cathedral, where each brick, mural, and carving have been meticulously recreated, experiencing the historical echoes and artistic essence of this world-class cultural heritage in a holographic and multi-sensory way.

Human-machine Communication for Meaningful Interactions

Media outlets use large models to provide information via human-like conversations. This breaks the traditional one-way communication model between media and audiences and enables two-way communication and interaction. Users can have a greater sense of participation in information acquisition. As machines continue to enhance their understanding of human psychology and emotional perception, AI will further drive the transition of media from physical media to psychological media, giving users emotional comfort and fulfillment during information acquisition.

Generative AI, as an intelligent agent, already exhibits a certain degree of personality in news activities. AI-based vertical applications, such as "News Butler" and "Information Companion", will possess stronger social intelligence and be able to customize functions based on defined roles, individual information, and personalized needs. As conversations progress, users will find that generative AI tools are becoming increasingly proactive in the interactions, AI may introduce new topics and provide unexpected additional information and emotional support, and users can refute or question AI responses, prompting AI to improve its answer. Through interactions, AI has transcended its role as a tool and acts as a copilot.

3. New Prospects for Business Forms

AI is a strategic technology that leads this round of technological revolution and industrial transformation, exhibitinga strong spillover effect as a "leading goose".[1] Driven by AI, the media industries in some countries and regions are gradually upgrading from a simple "plus AI" (AI as an auxiliary tool) to a new level of "AI plus" (AI as the core driver). In future, with the support of AI, the media industry is likely to accelerate toward a promising prospect of extensive mediatization, media platformization, and digitized and intelligent industries.

Extensive Mediatization

Emerging technologies represented by information technology and artificial intelligence are developing by leaps and bounds. It has greatly expanded the dimensions of time, space, and human cognition. Humanity is entering an era of human-machine-thing tripartite fusion that intelligently connects everything.[2] AI technology, along with 5G, the Internet of Things (IoT), big data, and cloud computing, is making extensive mediatization a reality. Information dissemination will break free from human limitations, achieving ubiquitous connections between people, people and objects, and among objects.

In the intelligence age of extensive mediatization, media are not only channels of communication, but also generators of expression. In the past, the evolution of communication technologies and the expansion of communication channels have ushered us into an era of mass media where everyone has a voice, yet media remains predominantly human-dominated. With the empowerment of AI, information

---

[1] Speech by Xi Jinping at the ninth group study session of the Political Bureau of the 19th CPC Central Committee , October 31, 2018.

[2] Speech by Xi Jinping at the joint session of the 20th Meeting of the Members of the Chinese Academy of Sciences, the 15th Meeting of the Members of the Chinese Academy of Engineering and the 10th National Congress of the China Association for Science and Technology , May 28, 2021.

dissemination breaks free from human limitations, achieving ubiquitous connections between people, between people and objects, and among objects. Applications such as drones, cameras, and sensors enhance human perception by enabling information acquisition from remote distances. Generative AI and other technologies resemble human by possessing the ability to generate content. These intelligent agents, endowed with pan-media attributes, can effectively collaborate with humans.

In the current era of extensive mediatization, almost all intelligent devices serve as both content distribution and reception terminals and proactive entities for human-machine interaction, collaboration, and companionship. The communication potential of intelligent home appliances, intelligent vehicles, smart speakers, and smart watches is becoming increasingly prominent. Controlling and utilizing intelligent terminals and the data they collect will become a new competitive edge in the media industry and media ecosystem. In the future, human-machine integration and brain-computer interface technologies will further expand the breadth and depth of information dissemination and spiritual communication.

Media Platformization

Platforms, functioning as digital infrastructure, possess powerful technologies, extensiveuser bases, and the ability to connect different communities. Platforms have become a significant force in rebuilding communication power. With AI technologies, the possibilities and potential of media platformization are further expanded.

Media platformization means that technological innovation and user participation allow news media to rapidly disseminate information, deliver personalized recommendations, and offer diverse forms of expression. Information dissemination has become more convenient and interactive. By integrating the strengths of traditional and new media, multi-channel distribution, and comprehensive services, media platforms are reshaping their reach, content, business models and operational mechanisms.

The People's Daily app has undergone multiple revisions, evolving from a platform primarily focused on disseminating official and authoritative news into a comprehensive hub that offers a wide range of information and government services. The "People's Channel" ("Renmin Hao") hosts tens of thousands of accounts representing government agencies, media outlets, and independent creators. The platform uses amainstream algorithm to aggregate and distribute a sea of information, ensuring that diverse and rich content reaches users directly.

In the process of media platformization, news media serve as a communication medium (content creation and operation organizations) and a technological solution (exerting influence on social relationships through data, algorithms, AI technology, etc.). News media also possess the attributes of commercial capital. They can distribute and redistribute market resources by aggregating and connecting these resources. In this way, intelligent media platforms can take more initiative in new communication scenarios, becoming the forefront of social information dissemination and a service carrier for various communities.

Digitized and Intelligent Industries

AI brings immense industrial opportunities and vast market prospects. China's New Generation Artificial Intelligence Development Plan proposes that by 2030, the scale of the AI core industry in China will exceed 1 trillion yuan, driving the related industry to exceed 10 trillion yuan. More and more news media are taking the lead in embracing, upholding, and seeking transformation and breakthroughs by adopting digital and intelligent technologies, transforming from traditional media into intelligent media.

Digital transformation signifies a shift in the media industry from a content-driven model to one that is driven by technology, capital, and content, among other factors. This transformation and upgrade can be seen in the close integration of content and technology, as well as in the reconstruction of the entire industrial chain. AI has profoundly reshaped the entire media industry chain and its relationships. The upstream content creators collaborate throughout the entire creative process, leading to more convenient and efficient content creation. The midstream media platforms strengthen partnerships with technology companies to build "intelligent middleware" platforms. This enhances overall production efficiency, connects broader social resources, and provides scientific and efficient technical solutions for media product creativity, content review, and more. The downstream terminal end prioritizes content distribution and promotion strategies, precisely targeting content to specific user groups to enhance dissemination effectiveness and user loyalty.

The upgrade and evolution of the media industry chain will further adjust and optimize the media industry structure, providing more possibilities for the traditional media industry to break through development bottlenecks and achieve higher-quality development. Beijing News, leveraging spatial roaming technology, has launched a visual product called Immersive Central Axis (AR+VR): A Panoramic Journey Through the Axis of the Capital. This product vividly recreates 15 heritage sites along Beijing's central axis, supporting cultural heritage preservation and the application for World Heritage status while unlocking commercial value through the development of derivative cultural and creative products. Using virtual design, AI digital humans, optical motion capture filming, and other technologies, Qilu Evening News launched the metaverse platform "Yi Dian Tian Yuan", the Online memorial ceremony for the Confucius metaverse release conference, the Qilu International Auto Show metaverse exhibition hall, the metaverse hospital, and the comprehensive metaverse cultural community to explore new business models.[1] The future will see artificial intelligence technology unlock new possibilities, enabling AI-driven collaborations between media and other sectors to boost productivity and revenue.

III. Challenges: AI Creates Multiple Risks

The development of artificial intelligence, like any other technological advancement, is a "double-edged sword."[2]

— President Xi Jinping

All technologies possess a dual nature, offering both potential benefits and harms. Renowned physicist Stephen Hawking cautioned that powerful artificial intelligence could be "either the best, or the worst thing, ever to happen to humanity". Given the inherent uncertainties and extensive applications of AI, its evolution not only empowers the news media, but also introduces a multitude of new risks.

---

[1] Feng Wenlu: The Practice of Digital Intelligence Transformation of Mainstream Media - An Analysis Based on the Collected Cases of China Media Intelligence, The Press, April 2024.

[2] Xi Jinping's speech at the ninth group study session of the Political Bureau of the 19th CPC Central Committee , October 31, 2018.

1. Misinformation Triggers a Crisis of Trust

Trustworthiness is the lifeblood of journalism, facts its foundation, and falsehoods its nemesis.[1] The misuse and abuse of AI have led to the widespread and viral production and dissemination of misinformation. This phenomenon undermines the social trust essential tonews organizations and has sparked a global crisis in the credibility of the information environment.

Unprecedented Scale of Misinformation Production

The technical intervention of AI has lowered the barriers and costs associated with creating and spreading false information, leading to its rapid proliferation and generating multiple layers of "informational fog" that distort the perceptions of reality.

In a study focusing on a large AI language model, researchers prompted ChatGPT with conspiracy theories and fabricated narratives. Within seconds, it generated a substantial volume of seemingly convincing content, ranging from news articles and essays to television scripts, all entirely devoid of factual basis. As industry experts noted, "It could become the most powerful misinformation-spreading tool the internet has ever seen."

A recent study found that generative AI has already triggered disruptions in the media industry. However, different media organizations perceive the impact with varying levels of urgency. While 32.4% of respondents reported that the influence of generative AI on their work remained "not yet apparent," 67.6% observed significant transformations underway. The top three areas of concern are:

1. Production Process Needs Overhaul: The work patterns of editors and journalists are undergoing rapid changes.

2. Heightened Competition from Other Media Outlets: Particularly from self—media and other independent content creators.

---

[1] Xi Jinping's speech at the Party's meeting on news and public opinion work (February 19, 2016).

3. Increased Effort Needed to Combat Misinformation: More resources needed to distinguish genuine news from fabricated content, including fake images.

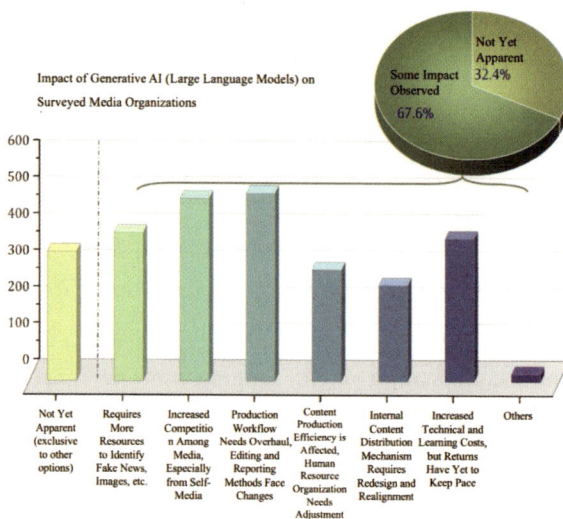

Impact of Generative AI (Large Language Models) on Surveyed Media Organizations

Survey data from various countries indicates that AI has become a potent driver of misinformation proliferation. A report titled Demystifying AI Rumors: A Comprehensive Analysis of Dissemination Paths and Governance Strategies, published by Tsinghua University's New Media Research Center in April 2024, highlights the rapid growth of AI-generated rumors due to the improper use of AI tools. Over the past six months, the volume of AI misinformation surged by 65%, with economic and business-related rumors witnessing an alarming growth rate of 99.91%. Similarly, a report released by a U.S. news credibility assessment and research organization at the end of 2023 revealed a dramatic rise in AI-driven fake news websites which had jumped from 49 to over 600 in just seven months. "AI is fast becoming the next 'super-spreader' of misinformation," the report warned.

The survey also found that most media organizations are adopting a cautious approach to generative AI, primarily concerned that it could undermine their credibility. When asked "What challenges related to generative AI has your media organization encountered or is expected to face?" a significant 76.4% of respondents expressed concern about the "distortion and inaccuracy of news leads and materials", which far exceeded the second most cited issue, "copyright and liability concerns" (61.1%).

Issues Encountered or Expected by Surveyed Media
Organizations When Using Generative AI:

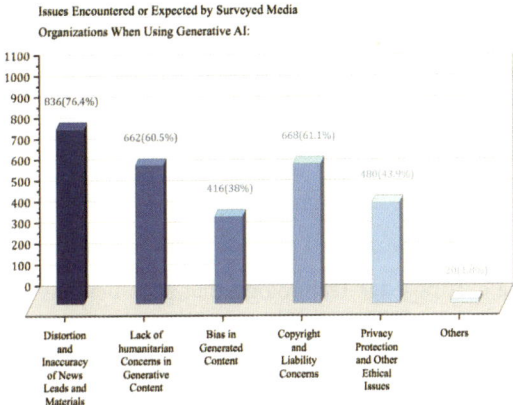

Additionally, regarding the question of whether the integration of generative AI into the media industry will enhance the credibility and reliability of the information environment over the next 3 to 5 years, 36.4% of respondents held a pessimistic outlook, which is 12.3 percentage points higher than the 24.1% who held an optimistic view. 39.5% respondents remained neutral.

Trust and authenticity are the cornerstones of journalism. Therefore, it can be inferred that, in the short term, most media organizations may permit generative AI to play only a limited, auxiliary role in content production.

As generative AI integrates with the media industry, surveyed media organizations' predictions for the credibility and reliability of the information environment over the next 3-5 years:

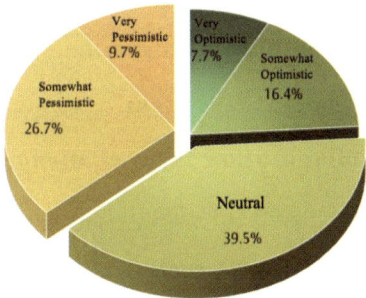

The rise of AI-fueled misinformation has raised global concern and awareness. Both Merriam-Webster and the Cambridge Dictionary selected "Authentic" and "Hallucinate" as their Words of the Year for 2023, respectively, reflecting the broader authenticity crisis sparked by AI. In the World Economic Forum's Global Risks Report 2024, AI-generated disinformation and misinformation ranks as the top short-term global risk, outpacing critical challenges such as climate change, warfare, and economic stagnation.

"Deepfakes" A More Deceptive Threat

AI's multimodal capabilities have significantly diversified the forms of misinformation, making it more difficult for the general public to detect. One prominent example is the rise of "deepfakes," a cutting-edge technology that goes beyond traditional text-based disinformation. Deepfakes can manipulate or fabricate images, voices, and videos to produce highly realistic yet misleading multimedia content.

With deepfake technology maturing and becoming more accessible, scenarios that were once only seen in blockbuster films can now be generated with just a few clicks. Some fabricated content goes beyond mere "misattribution" or "exaggeration," creating entirely fabricated events from scratch. This extreme deceptiveness has fueled social crimes such as telecom fraud and the creation of synthetic pornographic videos, making it increasingly difficult to discern real news from fake. In recent years, various deepfake videos targeting public figures have repeatedly triggered public outcries. At the end of 2023, criminals used deepfake technology to alter the videos of Singapore's former Prime Minister Lee Hsien Loong, including his National Day Rally speech and an interview with a CGTN host, to promote a cryptocurrency investment scam.

The survey found that among media organizations still hesitant to fully embrace generative AI, the top three hindrances were:

AI has its own shortcomings, such as failing to meet expectations for accuracy and reliability in content generation.

Human-machine collaboration faces challenges, particularly due to a shortage of comprehensive talent for effective integration.

The high costs associated with technical investments.

The main reasons why surveyed media organizations that have not yet adopted generative AI at the institutional level are still hesitant:

600	
500	
400	
300	
200	
100	
0	

Internal organizational culture resists automated content production over human creations.

The primary audience of the organization is resistant to AI-generated content.

Imperfection of AI in meeting expectations and requirements for accuracy, reliability, and timeliness.

AI is not suitable for the organization's production characteristics and is currently unnecessary.

Integrating AI into existing editorial systems and production workflows is challenging.

High technical investment costs.

Difficulties in human-machine collaboration due to a lack of cross-functional talent.

Potential regulatory or legal risks associated with AI implementation.

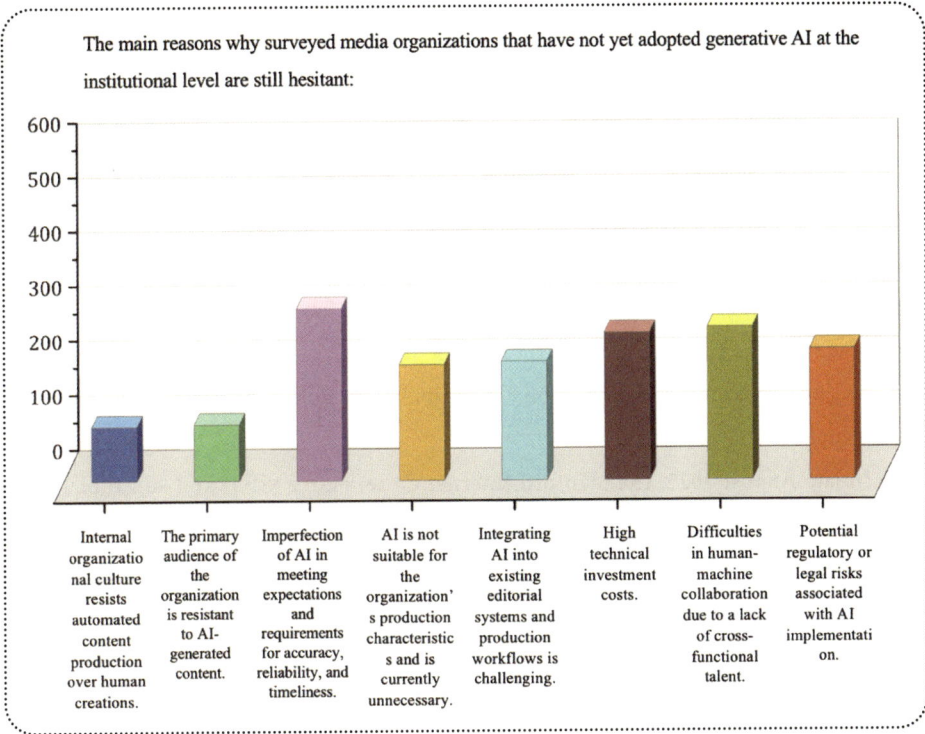

Growing concerns over deepfake technology have also heightened public awareness of the risks posed by misinformation. This, in turn, has led to increased skepticism toward all information sources, including traditional news outlets, thereby further eroding overall social trust. According to Reuters' 2023 Digital News Report, only 40% of respondents indicated trust in news reports, a decline partially attributed to the spread of deepfakes and similar technologies.

"Simulated Dissemination" — Enhanced Concealment

AI has not only accelerated the proliferation of misinformation at the production level, but also provides more powerful tools for its dissemination. Represented by "social bots," a new generation of "internet trolls" has infiltrated major social media platforms worldwide, becoming omnipresent "invisible viruses" on the web.

"On the internet, nobody knows you're a dog." This phrase from The New Yorker years ago became widely known as the internet expanded. In the AI era, an increasing number of intelligent large models have passed the Turing Test, a benchmark designed to distinguish human behavior from machine activity. As a result, it is becoming increasingly difficult to discern whether one is interacting with a human or a machine online, leaving people unable to identify the true entities or motives behind each piece of information.

As an intelligent agent operating on social media platforms, "social bots" can automatically generate content based on the intentions of their operators, mimicking the status and behavior of real human users to engage in interactions. These bots can create "fake popularity" and "artificial consensus." Unlike traditional "internet trolls" who rely on human manipulation through anonymous accounts, "bot armies" composed of social bots can generate personalized viewpoints and operate continuously 24/7, consistently building and reinforcing their "persona." This makes the spread of misinformation more covert and difficult to detect.

In late August 2022, the Stanford Internet Observatory (SIO) and social platform analysis firm Graphika jointly released a report, revealing how the U.S. had leveraged social media to manipulate global narratives related to Xinjiang. Social bots played a key role in this effort by using tactics such as generating AI-created profile pictures, posing as "independent" news organizations and creating trending hashtags to spark discussions.

2. Technology Misuse Disrupts Public Opinion

Establishing a sound public opinion environment is crucial for effective governance and national stability.[①] A secure, peaceful, and transparent international public opinion space is also vital for fostering global cooperation and development. The pervasive application of artificial intelligence in information dissemination has introduced significant variables into the global public opinion landscape, generating new risks and challenges across individual, societal, and international dimensions.

Algorithmic Bias and Its Influence on Individual Cognition

As the primary actors within the public opinion framework, individuals play a key role in shaping this environment. However, the inherent biases embedded in data and algorithms, along with the phenomenon known as the "filter bubble," pose challenges to independent, rational, and healthy cognitive development and value formation.

---

① Xi Jinping's speech during his meeting with representatives of the 9th Council of the All-China Journalists Association and winners of the China Journalism Award and the Changjiang Taofen Award (November 7, 2016).

Due to the characteristics of deep learning, large language models inevitably inherit stereotypes and value biases present in their training data and the designs of their human creators. Without appropriate checks, these overt and covert biases could result in scenarios where AI systems exert significant control over human thought. As illustrated in Liu Cixin's The Three-Body Problem, advanced civilizations imprint beliefs into individual consciousness through technology. While artificial intelligence cannot directly influence the human brain yet, it has already permeated various aspects of social information flow. By leveraging the sheer volume of data and the accumulation of time, AI can gradually dominate social consciousness, ultimately facilitating value transmission to users and even eroding their cognitive frameworks.

Even when AI systems operate under the principle of serving humanity, their reliance on personalized content delivery can limit users' cognitive horizons, exacerbating issues such ascognitive narrowing, rigid thinking, and group polarization. Particularly in the media landscape, where attention is the object of fierce contest, users often gravitate toward content that is visually striking or emotionally resonant. To cater to these preferences, AI may prioritize such content, thereby sidelining more substantive and valuable information.

Machine Posters Manipulating Social Opinion

With the support of artificial intelligence technology, the methods of opinion manipulation are constantly emerging and tools are continuously upgrading, leading to a more complex and murky public opinion ecosystem. This has significantly increased the real-world risks of social fragmentation, disorder, and psychological turmoil, posing a serious threat to the normal and stable operation of society.

"Public opinion is the skin of society." When the public forms sharp and rational opinions about public affairs, society gains a healthy skin that can sense public sentiment. Public opinion is a crucial foundation for the sustained and stable operation of modern democratic societies, yet its powerful social influence attracts attention from various parties. The emergence of advanced artificial intelligence has facilitated the influence or even control of public opinion, casting shadows over the necessary transparency and fairness of social discourse.

In the political realm, artificial intelligence has long been used to influence the value judgments and political stances of target individuals or to undermine the public opinion environment and social image of adversarial forces. In 2016, Cambridge Analytica unlawfully collected personal information from tens of millions of Facebook users for voter analysis, delivering political ads for Donald Trump's presidential campaign, marking a significant event of technological intervention in political elections. As AI technology evolves, various "manipulation tools" are increasingly accessible, with greatly enhanced deception and subtlety. In the so-called "global election year" of 2024, concerns about using AI to interfere with voters, manipulate elections, and disrupt stability are escalating. In the social sphere, malicious actors have exploited AI tools to release large amounts of emotional content, exacerbating social conflicts around sensitive topics such as race, immigration, and wealth disparity. In the commercial realm, AI is also widely used for "data, rating and sales manipulation" to distort and obscure real evaluations, promote products, or discredit competitors, severely damaging the market order.

Intelligent Weapons Intensifies Information Warfare

In a context of frequent social conflicts and tense geopolitical situations, artificial intelligence is widely used in "intelligence warfare," "public opinion warfare," and "cognitive warfare," worsening tensions in international public opinion and significantly increasing the risks of escalation and conflict.

Artificial intelligence provides great convenience for conducting network intrusions, intelligence gathering, and public opinion attacks. Through differentiated data delivery, AI can instantaneously create waves of public opinion that influence group cognition. By tracking data and employing algorithmic strategies, AI can predict the cognitive dynamics of different regions and groups, assisting in planning and promoting core narratives and topics.

On social media, the fabrication of false information, incitement of group antagonism, and ideological infiltration through AI has become commonplace. In 2022, a fake video purportedly showing Ukrainian President Zelensky calling for his troops to surrender and Russian President Putin declaring the end of the war circulated widely. Since the outbreak of the recent Israel-Palestine conflict, social media has also seen a surge of false content, including manipulating realistic video game footage to depict Hamas attacks and faking images of internationally renowned figures waving Palestinian flags. Amidst the fog of war information disseminated by AI, truth and falsehood have become blurred, and suspicion and division has grown, fundamentally altering the nature, means, and methods of modern warfare.

3. Rapid Development Exacerbating Governance Concerns

As new types of artificial intelligence rapidly emerge, discussions about the potential of these technologies to disrupt human values are intensifying, sparking concerns of varying degrees. Disputes over values and governance challenges raised by AI are beginning to surface.

The Debate over Development Paths

AI, characterized by its programmatic capacity for self-learning and self-control, presents a "black box" challenge, as even its developers often struggle to predict how it processes data after self-optimization. This uncertainty, far exceeding what is known, has fueled a widespread debate over AI's development trajectory.

Should AI development be "accelerated" or "aligned"? As researchers explore the future of AI, two camps have emerged. Proponents of acceleration argue that societal progress depends on technological innovation. Thus, pushing AI forward should be an ongoing pursuit for mankind. The alignment camp, however, advocates prioritizing the ethical impacts and social consequences of AI to ensure that technology advances in line with human values. In March 2023, thousands of entrepreneurs, scholars and executives in the field of AI—including Yoshua Bengio and Tesla CEO Elon Musk—signed an open letter titled "Pause Giant AI Experiments," voicing concerns about super-intelligent AI and calling for joint development and implementation of a safety protocol shared by mankind as a whole. Yet, even as this discussion grows, major tech companies worldwide are ramping up research and development, launching a continuous stream of new products and applications.

For the foreseeable future, AI's progress will likely be influenced by this ideological tug-of-war. As AI becomes a key strategic resource, stakeholders may encounter even deeper divisions. Ethical issues surrounding AI could become politicized, with tech giants engagedin a technology race and nations competing in an arms race, complicating future global legislative and governance efforts.

The survey conducted by this research team reveals that most media organizations currently on the fence do not reject or underestimate generative artificial intelligence; rather, they plan to adopt it once the key conditions are met. Their top three priorities are:

Clearly identifying areas where AI can significantly enhance productivity and reduce labor costs; Achieving significant improvements in AI performance, particularly in accuracy and reliability; Ensuring absence of ethical controversies, regulatory challenges, and legal disputes related to journalism.

Only 6.4% of respondents stated that they would never consider using generative AI tools under any circumstances.

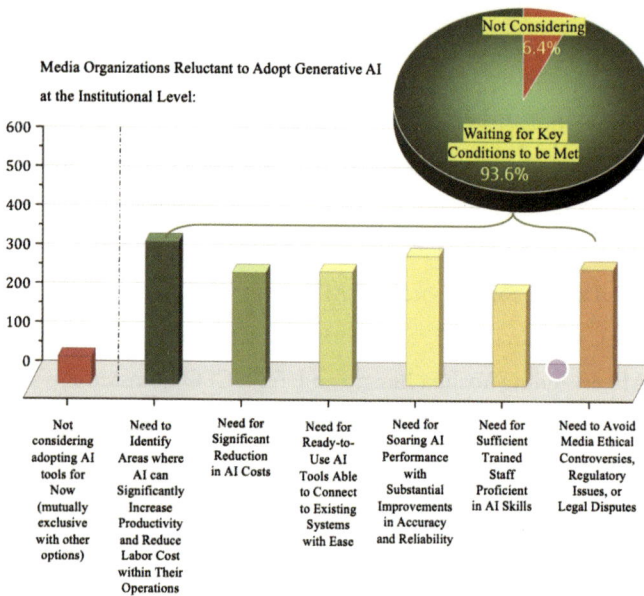

Media Organizations Reluctant to Adopt Generative AI at the Institutional Level:

The Dilemma of Value Alignment

As concerns about threats posed by AI intensify, value alignment has become one of the most fundamental and challenging aspects in AI governance, facing multiple obstacles in practice.

The goal of value alignment is to ensure that AI operates in accordance with ethical principles, moral norms, and values of human so that it functions in a socially benign way. However, in the context of global cultural diversity, questions like "Whose values should AI be aligned with?" and "How should AI be aligned?" remain difficult to answer. In the media sector, discrepancies in news value judgments, professional identities, and editorial practices across countries make it challenging to establish consistent standards for AI's application. Even fundamental journalistic principles like truth, fairness, and equality face risks of misinterpretation when translated into AI systems through abstracting, quantifying, and alignment. For example, when Amazon attempted to use AI to screen job applicants, the algorithm was soon found to disproportionately filter out female candidates. Similar biases such as gender and racial discrimination are equally challenging to remove from AI applications in newsrooms.

As artificial intelligence becomes increasingly integrated into news production, its operational standards and logic will significantly impact how editors and journalists define what constitutes news, good news, and valuable news, leading to a necessary re-evaluation and evolution of the news value system. If news production becomes overly reliant on technical rules to regulate journalists' behavior, traffic data to assess news quality, and algorithms to determine news value, it risks shifting from a value-driven approach to a purely utilitarian one. This could lead to a divergence between news value and public interest, distancing media outlets from societal priorities and undermining their positive role in serving the public good.

Regulatory Gaps

The rapid development of AI and other new technologies has given rise to new industries and forms of business, but there remain significant gaps and delays in regulatory frameworks[1]. Issues like privacy and copyright require a greater sense of urgency for consensus and prompt development of regulatory frameworks.

A fundamental conflict exists between privacy protection and AI development as AI relies on extensive human behavioral data and knowledge to improve, develop and be applied to different scenarios, such high dependence on data making privacy "nowhere to hide". In 2023, Italy temporarily banned ChatGPT due to privacy concerns and restricted OpenAI from processing data from Italian users. Similarly, the UK, Ireland, and other countries launched investigations into potential privacy violations linked to large AI models. In the media sector, user data help news outlets provide more convenient, accurate, and efficient services, but also increase the possibility of privacy breaches. As guardians of public interest, media organizations are held to higher ethical

---

[1] Xi Jinping's speech at the central conference on work related to law-based governance , November 16, 2020.

standards in defining privacy boundaries and balancing data use with privacy protection, a challenge highlighted by the use of AI.

With the decentralization of rights related to information production, processing, publication, and redistribution, copyright disputes arising from the use of AI are gaining prominence. High-quality, professional news content serves as a crucial training dataset for AI. However, the content generated by these systems often closely resembles the raw data, potentially violating the copyrights of some media organizations. In December 2023, The New York Times filed a lawsuit against OpenAI and its investor Microsoft, accusing them of using millions of its articles without permission to train AI, the first case where an AI company has been sued for its copyright infringement by a major media organization, epitomizing the copyright issues faced by the media in the AI era. Furthermore, issues around the copyright ownership and profit-sharing of AI-assisted news products remain unresolved. As a result, it has become a priority for lawmakers worldwide to protect the legal rights of all parties and establish a fair and transparent copyright system.

4. Intelligent Applications Widen the Development Gap

Like other transformative technological breakthroughs, the widespread application of next-generation AI will inevitably lead to shifts in social wealth and power, triggering a range of socio-political and economic issues and ensuing discussions around income inequality, urban-rural divide, and disparity between the Global North and Global South. At the heart of these issues lies the question of how to equitably distribute the benefits of technological advancement, ensuring that the fruits of progress are shared by all of humanity.

Individual Differences and Vulnerable Groups

There is no doubt that those with access to AI technology will be more competitive and advantaged in the future. However, due to disparities in cognitive ability, resource availability, and AI literacy, certain groups—such as the elderly, the poorly educated and low-income populations—will be increasingly marginalized as AI applications continue to evolve, becoming the new disadvantaged groups in the AI era.

Take the elderly as an example. Nicholas Negroponte, the author of Being Digital, once asserted that "each generation will become more digital than the preceding one". With global aging and rapid AI development advancing simultaneously, senior citizens, often limited by lower information skills, declining learning abilities, and physical deterioration, struggle to reap the benefits of AI advancements. They are likely to fall into one of two extremes: resistance or overdependence. On the one hand, many elderly individuals tend to resist new technologies, finding it difficult to accept and grasp. On the other hand, some are highly susceptible to digital addiction and vulnerable to misinformation, algorithmic manipulation, and echo chambers.

Urban-rural Disparities and Digital Deserts

The "intelligence gap" between urban and rural areas is a widespread issue globally, not only as a technological challenge, but also as a social and economic one. This disparity exists across various dimensions, including social development, resource allocation, education levels, and infrastructure, as well as in individual income, cultural literacy, information technology skills, and notions of knowledge.

In China, urban users have largely accessed 5G and gigabit fiber networks while rural areas still lag in network speed and stability. A majority of new AI technology companies are located in regions like Beijing, the Yangtze River Delta, and the Pearl River Delta, with very few in the western regions. Widespread AI backwater or and even desertsalso exist in the United States. In anews report published in June 2024, The Washington Post noted that rural areas in the United States have long been waiting for broadband services, with most relying on slow internet transmitted via copper lines which cannot handle large data transfers; some areas don't even have access to internet. The issue of disconnection is particularly acute in rural areas inhabited by minorities and indigenous populations.

Problems such as the imbalance of educational resources in the AI age are also gaining prominence. Children in urban areas can engage with technology first-hand, appreciating the novelty and convenience AI offers while grasping the scientific principles behind it. In contrast, for most rural children, AI remains an abstract term, with no practical experience or understanding. This pervasive existence of "AI deserts" will contribute to further social division and fragmentation, making equitable access to technological benefits a distant goal.

The North-South Divide and the "AI Divide"

In his speech on strengthening international cooperation in the capacity building of AI at the UN General Assembly, China's Permanent Representative to the United Nations Fu Cong highlighted that the rapid advancement of global AI technology profoundly impacts economic and social development across countries and human civilization. However, most people in developing countries have yet to engage with or benefit from AI, and the global digital divide continues to widen. As the global economy shifts toward AI-driven growth, underdeveloped nations risk falling further behind, deepening the economic and social divide between them and developed countries. The uneven adoption of AI technology has become a pressing concern, outpacing the overall rate of economic development.

Currently, the economic and social benefits of AI are geographically concentrated in the Global North. The fourth edition of the Global AI Index 2023, published by UK media company Tortoise, ranks the U.S. first, followed by China and Singapore in terms of AI investment, innovation, and implementation. Among the top 20 countries, eleven are from Europe. While advanced AI technologies are widespread in leading countries, many in Africa and Latin America still rely on 2G networks for phone calls and texting, some completely offline. As society increasingly adopts intelligent production, disparities in productivity, economic growth, education, digital literacy, and research between the Global North and South are expected to widen. In areas such as large language model development, talent recruitment, and the creation of AI infrastructure—communication networks, big data platforms, and computing centers—significant capital investment is required. This creates an "AI divide" that developing countries will struggle to bridge in the near term.

A report by the International Labour Organization in 2024, titled "Mind the AI Divide: Shaping a Global Perspective on the Future of Work," warns that while AI technology brings immense opportunities for innovation and development, the uneven investment and deployment among countries may exacerbate disparities in income levels and quality of life. The current emergence of an "AI divide" means that high-income countries benefit from technological development and application while middle-and low-income countries, particularly those in Africa, lag behind. The impact of AI on labor markets also varies by country and region. In developed countries, many jobs are increasingly subject to automation and AI integration, but these countries can also better leverage AI technology to enhance productivity. In contrast, developing countries, while temporarily shielded from automation risks due to insufficient digital infrastructure, may face long-term productivity bottlenecks. The report warns that without measures to strengthen international cooperation and support for developing countries, this divide will only widen, potentially negating the socio-economic benefits that AI technology could otherwise provide.

Additionally, some developed countries are found to leverage their first-mover advantage in AI technology to seek technological hegemony, forming exclusive groups that hinder other countries' progress and deliberately creating technological barriers to disrupt global AI supply chain. This "small courtyard with high walls" phenomenon will deepen the AI development gap between the Global North and Global South, exacerbating the situation where "the strong gets stronger, and the weak gets weaker".

IV. Mission: Putting People First and Promoting AI for Good

Media bears important social responsibilities in seeking correct answers to the major questions of our times and building wide consensus around the world.[①]

——President Xi Jinping

It has become a global consensus to strengthen the regulation of AI usage. In the Global Artificial Intelligence Governance Initiative, Chinese President Xi Jinping proposed fundamental principles including "Putting People First" and "AI for Good", providing China's solution to the challenges of AI governance. Amid the transformative wave brought about by AI, the global media need to share opportunities and risks together. By leveraging their professional strengths, they can foster a positive information environment and ecosystem of public opinion, thereby contributing to an open, fair, and effective mechanism of global AI governance, building a community with a shared future for humanity, and creating a better world by harnessing the powerful influence of the media.

1. Accelerating AI-Driven Industry to Enhance the Value of Media

News media should fully leverage the instrumental value of AI, exploring its all-inclusive application through the process of news collection, production, distribution, reception and feedback, harnessing AI as a new quality productive force, and offering better news products and services to the public.

Enhancing Systemic Efficiency Through Intelligentization

To address the challenges posed by a decentralized environment where anyone

---

① Xi's Congratulatory Letter to the Fourth World Media Summit, November 22, 2021.

can act as media, news media practitioners need to focus more on empowering themselves with technology, transforming from traditional "information processors" to "intelligent information producers". By building systems for production and dissemination, data technology, organization and management, and reception feedback driven and supported by AI, practitioners can significantly improve their media penetration, influence, and credibility. Relying on AI technology, they can enhance the speed, depth, breadth, and accuracy of news dissemination, thereby strengthening their role in connecting society and building consensus.

The survey conducted by the research group shows that most media organizations have recognized that generative AI is infiltrating the media industry with unstoppable momentum. Whether they choose to actively engage or wait and see, media are facing pressures of self–transformation to adapt to the changing landscape of the industry.

Regarding how to transform themselves to cope with these changes, the interviewed media organizations mainly identified the following three approaches:

1. Enhancing the adaptability of editorial teams;

2. Increasing investment in technology;

3. Revamping the processes of news collection, editing, and distribution.

The Self-Transforming Paths Recognized by the Media Organizations Interviewed:

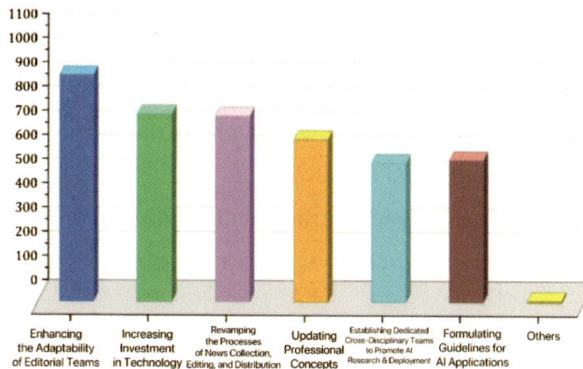

Ensuring Safety and Reliability through Standardization

In response to the features of changes in business forms in the era of AI, the media should continue to upgrade standards for news production and dissemination. AI technology should be fully utilized to empower the whole processes—collection, production, distribution, and dissemination—while minimizing associated risks. A risk assessment and prevention framework for AI in the media sector should be established. News media should further improve mechanisms for verifying the authenticity of news content, particularly regarding deepfake content, automatically generated writing, and algorithm-driven content, and should use AI technology to verify leads and materials, ensuring the trustworthiness and reliability of information. The investment in fact-checking technologies and the training of specialized professionals should be increased. Public participation in fact-checking efforts should be encouraged.

Enhancing News Quality through Professionalization

The depth and professionalism of reporting have become more valuable amid "information overload" and "information cocoon". These qualities are significant reflections of media's social responsibilities and credibility. News organizations should, on the one hand, strengthen the expertise of their editorial teams in niche areas while, on the other hand, fully leverage AI technology to mine, filter, verify, correlate, and analyze information, thereby enabling more in-depth and high-quality reporting to cater to the demands of the audience and contribute to social progress.

2. Establishing Ethical Standards based on Good Use

In the AI age, the media not only disseminate news and information, but also shape and safeguard social values. While enhancing the application of technology, global media must uphold journalistic ethics and fulfill social responsibilities. Mainstream values of humanity should guide "machine algorithm", embedding journalistic ethics all-inclusivelyin theuse of AI in the media. A people-oriented ethical framework must be established.

The survey shows that, regarding the potential negative impacts of generative artificial intelligence in the media industry, only 14.4% of respondents believed that "the existing regulatory framework is sufficiently binding". Meanwhile, 85.6% of respondents supportedcertain forms of strengthened regulation and governance.

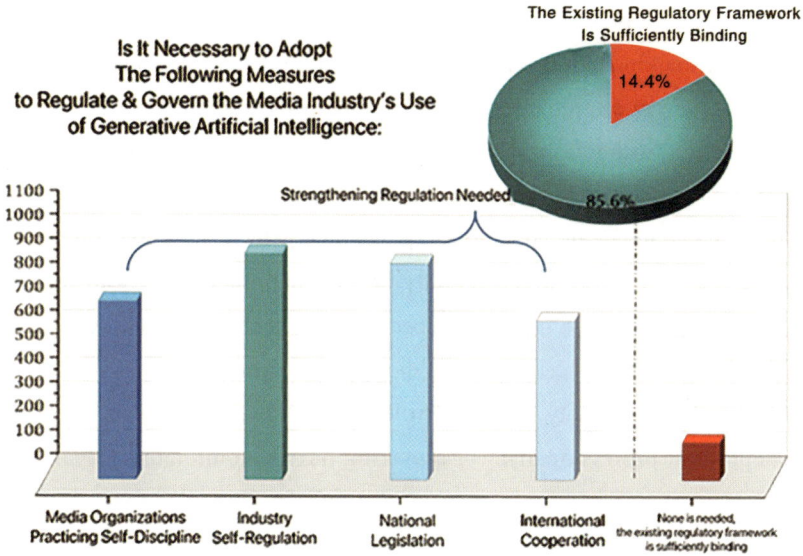

The Existing Regulatory Framework Is Sufficiently Binding — 14.4%

Is It Necessary to Adopt The Following Measures to Regulate & Govern the Media Industry's Use of Generative Artificial Intelligence:

Strengthening Regulation Needed — 85.6%

Media Organizations Practicing Self-Discipline | Industry Self-Regulation | National Legislation | International Cooperation | None is needed, the existing regulatory framework is sufficiently binding

Dispelling the Information Fog with News Authenticity

News authenticity is the cornerstone of a media outlet's credibility and influence. Any technological innovation that departs from the truth in news is putting the cart before the horse. The media must use the truthfulness of news as the ultimate standard for applying AI technologies, constructing a reliable cognitive space for the public through authentic reporting. By combining the expertise of journalism with the technological edge of AI, the media can provide audiences with authentic, impartial, comprehensive, and timely information, eliminating misinformation, information pollution, information silos, and misleading information. Media must lead by avoiding "cognitive warfare," refraining from producing false information, and steering clear of manipulating public opinion to interfere in other nations' internal affairs. They should strive to be the "night watchmen" and "breakwaters" against the spread of misinformation.

Guiding Instrumental Rationality with Journalistic Ethics

As direct users of AI, media practitioners bear ethical responsibilities that directly impact the social effects of technology use. Media organizations should enhance the ethical education of their employees in the use of AI through continuous training and learning, improving their ethical awareness and technical proficiency to ensure the regulated and reasonable use of AI in practice. In using AI technology for data collection, algorithm design, and R&D of technologies and products, media practitioners should pay special attention to potential distortions and biases in the products, ensure the diversity, fairness, and inclusiveness of information, and proactively identify and eliminate what may contradict the principles of fairness and non-discrimination, to reduce public misunderstandings, divisions, and hostility. Media should uphold shared human values as gatekeepers of news and leaders of social values. They must actively counteract extreme and harmful information online, working together to prevent the spread of extremism and terrorist content. Media must uphold journalistic ethics and enhance social responsibilities.They need to foster a cognitive environment and ecosystem of public opinion that is rooted in truth, rational communication, inclusiveness, and a healthy, positive atmosphere. This will promote the effective dissemination of knowledge and the equitable sharing of technological dividends, injecting positive energy for human welfare and social progress.

Protecting Data Privacy through Regulatory Mechanisms

Media should pay more attention to the potential risks posed by AI, including those against technological safety, cybersecurity, and socioeconomic development. They should monitor and address concerns about AI models' "black box" of non-transparent algorithms, including risks of personal privacy breaches, national security leaks, deepfake threats, copyright disputes. Media practitioners need to understand the importance of data security and user protection, particularly for minors, and to establish robust mechanisms to ensure that user information is fully protected in the processes of collection, storage, handling, and transmission. Following the principle of "data minimization", media organizations should try their best to limit the collection and storage of personal data. When analyzing data with AI technologies, they should strictly control data access. In designing and using AI algorithms, they should adhere to a mechanism of moderate transparency to ensure users' right to be informed and foster self-regulatory mechanisms within the industry to elevate its operation standards and norms. Additionally, they should prevent data breaches and cyberattacks through encryption and security protocols. Through risk monitoring and fact-checking, they can safeguard the cognitive spaces and promote trust and communication among countries.

3. Strengthening Dialogue and Cooperation to Improve Global Governance

The media worldwide should build consensus through dialogue and cooperation, creating an open, effective, and fair global mechanism for AI governance that ensures benefits forthe human race.

Bridging the Intelligence Divide for Fairness and Inclusivity

The media should work together to bridge the digital and intelligence divides between different social groups and regions. By leveraging AI for multi-lingual and diversified content, they can ensure the outreach of knowledge to all segments of society, raising overall cognitive levels. There should be a focus on addressing the North-South divide in the use of AI, promoting collaboration in areas including technology development, content production, data analysis, rule-setting, and talent cultivation. Sharing experiences and resources will foster joint progress, opposing the "small yard, high fence" mentality and technological hegemony in AI use. The media in Global South countries should actively participate in the formulation of AI-related rules and standards within the global media landscape, enhancing their representation and voice in international policy-making. Through concrete actions, they can advocate equal rights, opportunities, and rules in the development and governance of AI for all countries.

Enhancing Collaboration to Promote Practical Cooperation

Media organizations should work together with professionals to strengthen information exchange and technological cooperation, sharing the latest development and knowledge outcomes. Open-source technology should be encouraged and the exploration of standards for the use of AI in the media prioritized. In high-consensus areas such as natural language processing, image recognition, and user behavior analysis, AI tools and systems could be developed to avoid redundant research and resource waste. Key issues such as the "black box effect" and "information cocoons" can be addressed collaboratively through risk assessment and experience-sharing. Resources need to be pooled toestablishlong-term joint verification projects or mechanisms to improve the use of AI in detecting and combating misinformation. A multilateral media dialogue mechanism should be explored, building a long-term platform for communication to lay the groundwork for joint communication and cooperative research.

Aligning Values for Better Global Governance

Media worldwide not only serve as conduits for information, but also play a key role in cultural transmission and exchange between civilizations. Peace, development, fairness, justice, democracy, and freedom—shared values of mankind—form the foundation for consensus among different civilizations globally. These values are a critical intellectual sourcefor promoting global governance and the "golden key" to overcoming challenges in the value alignment of AI. The media around the world should engage in multi-level and multi-form discussions on global AI governance, encouraging rational dialogue and advocating shared values. This will drive public attention, understanding, and participation in the governance, creating a conducive social environment for international consensus. Based on the principles of broad participation, consensus-building, and gradual progress, dialogue and exchanges should be deepened while respecting the differences in national policies, regulations, and practices. By promoting the integration of national laws and industry standards and adhering to a people-centered approach, media organizations should champion AI for good and strive to establish ethical guidelines and global governance frameworks based on shared values, steering the development of AI in a direction that supports the construction of a global community of shared future. The media around the world should harness the dual empowerment of "culture+technology" to enhance the discourse power and influence of different civilizations in international communication. They should create a platform for "digital diplomacy" in the international community, deepening intercultural exchange, eliminating misunderstandings, and fostering mutual understanding, thereby promoting the construction of a global community of shared future in the AI era.

V. A Survey on the Perception and Use of Artificial Intelligence in Global News Media

In 2024, New China Research, a national high-end think tank under Xinhua News Agency, launched a global survey targeting news media organizations regarding their perception and use of AI. The research team conducted the survey in three languages—Chinese, English, and French—covering media organizations from 53 countries and regions, including newspapers, broadcasting stations, news agencies, websites, and mobile service providers. A total of 1,207 questionnaires were collected, with 1,094 valid responses.

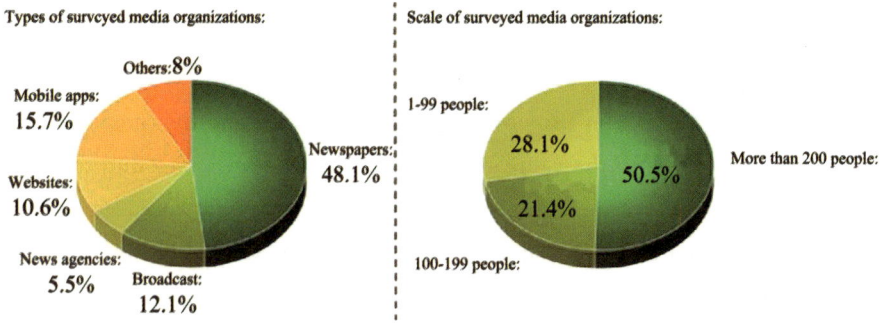

Types of surveyed media organizations:

Others:8%
Mobile apps: 15.7%
Newspapers: 48.1%
Websites: 10.6%
News agencies: 5.5%
Broadcast: 12.1%

Scale of surveyed media organizations:

1-99 people: 28.1%
More than 200 people: 50.5%
100-199 people: 21.4%

Given that generative AI, represented by ChatGPT, has had a significant impact on media organizations whose main business is the production of texts, images, and video content, the survey was designed to provide insights into the new shifts and dynamics AI is bringing to this industry. An analysis of the valid responses revealed the following:

1. A majority of media organizations (66%) have a positive attitude toward generative AI

As with any new phenomenon, generative AI has triggered both controversies and doubts. It is praised as a type of new quality productive force, but also frequently questioned for issues such as hallucinations, bias, stereotypes, and "political correctness". The survey results indicate that media organizations generally have a positive outlook regarding AI's impact on the industry.

The data show that 20.3% and 45.7% of respondents highly agree or somewhat agree with the statement that "The opportunities brought by generative AI outweigh the challenges, and its benefits outweigh the drawbacks". Only 2.8% and 1.6% disagree or strongly disagree with this view while 29.6% believe the pros and cons are still uncertain.

This suggests that, generally speaking, global media organizations are highly attentive to technological changes affecting the entire industry and are optimistic about AI becoming a "game-changer" in media.

Regarding the statement "The opportunities brought by generative AI (large language models) to the media industry outweigh the challenges, and the benefits outweigh the drawbacks," the attitudes of the surveyed media organizations:

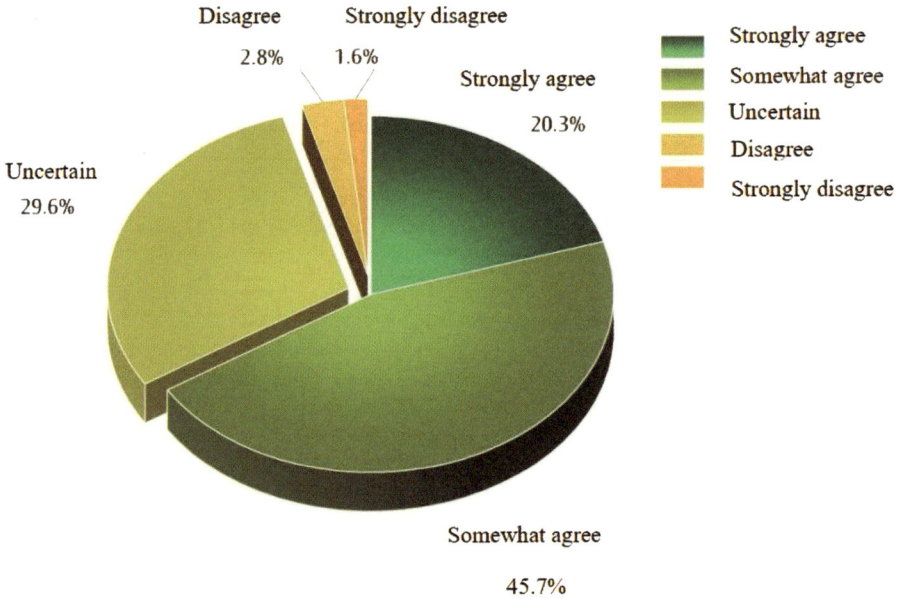

2. A majority of media organizations (67.6%) have already experienced changes brought by generative ai

Generative AI has already triggered a shift in the media industry. However, different media organizations have varying levels of awareness of these changes. 32.4% of media respondents state that the impact of generative AI is "not yet obvious". Meanwhile, 67.6% have already noticed significant changes. The three changes mentioned most frequently are:

1.Production processes require restructuring, and the working methods of editors and reporters are transforming;

2.Competition among media outlets, especially from social media platforms, is intensifying;

3.More effort is needed to identify fake news, fake photos, and other forms of disinformation.

The Impact of Generative AI (Large Language Models) on Surveyed Media Organizations

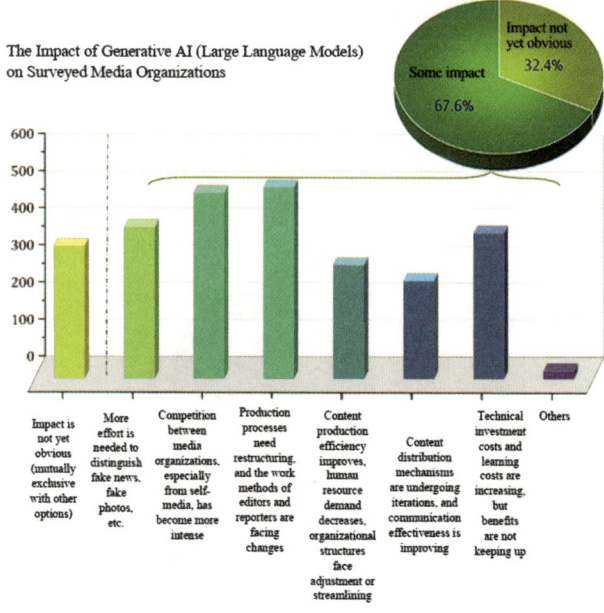

This shows that most media organizations recognize that generative AI is penetrating the industry with unstoppable momentum and they will face the pressure to adapt whether they choose to dive in or stand back and wait.

To cope with the changes, the top three recommended strategies by respondents are:

1.Enhancing the adaptability of editorial teams;

2.Increasing technological investments;

3.Reforming news gathering, editorial, and publication processes.

Self-Transformation Paths Recognized by Surveyed Media Organizations:

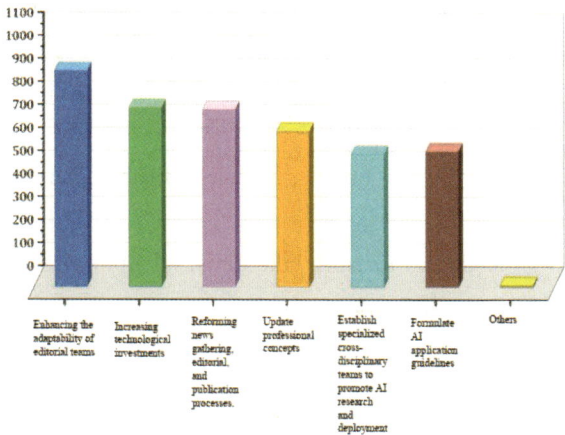

3. More than half of the media organizations (51.2%) have begun using generative AI

2024 is the year organizations began large-scale application of generative AI. As leaders in content production, many media organizations are striving to be "early birds". Globally, 10.2% of media organizations have fully embraced AI, establishing institutional mechanisms to integrate AI into their workflows from the top down. Meanwhile, 41.0% of organizations are actively exploring AI applications, encouraging and supporting certain sections to experiment with AI. Another 36% of respondents have not adopted AI through a top-down approach, but individual staff members are experimenting with AI at a personal level with the tacit approval of their organizations. Only 12.8% of media organizations report minimal use of AI, some banning its use entirely.

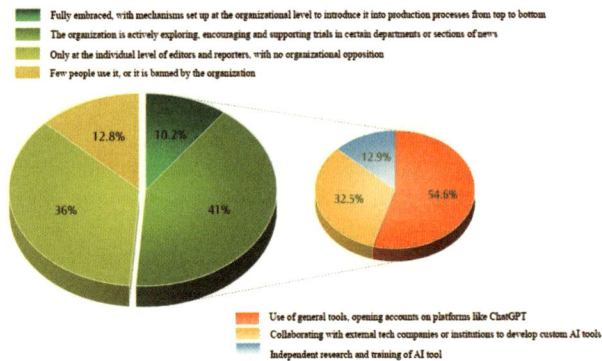

The Application Level of Generative AI (Large Language Models) in Surveyed Media Organizations:

- Fully embraced, with mechanisms set up at the organizational level to introduce it into production processes from top to bottom
- The organization is actively exploring, encouraging and supporting trials in certain departments or sections of news
- Only at the individual level of editors and reporters, with no organizational opposition
- Few people use it, or it is banned by the organization

- Use of general tools, opening accounts on platforms like ChatGPT
- Collaborating with external tech companies or institutions to develop custom AI tools
- Independent research and training of AI tool

Among the organizations actively promoting AI at an institutional level, the most common approach (54.6%) is using publicly available tools like ChatGPT. Additionally, 32.5% are collaborating with third parties to develop and customize AI tools, while 12.9% are developing their own AI systems. This suggests that there is still considerable growth potential for privately deployed large language models in vertical applications within the media industry.

The top three AI application scenarios being explored by media organizations are:

1.Assisting with editing tasks, such as fact-checking, speech-to-text conversion, adding subtitles, and translation;

2.Content creation, such as generating summaries, creating graphic posters, and providing voiceovers for digital anchors;

3.Planning topics or drafting outlines.

Applications Explored or to be Explored by Surveyed Media Organizations for Generative AI (Large Language Models) at the Institutional Level:

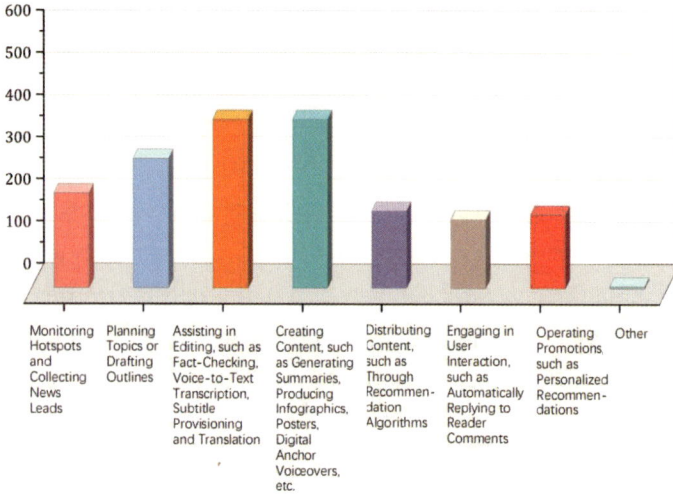

For media organizations that are currently hesitant, the top three barriers to fully embracing generative AI are:

1.AI's not yet where it needs to be, with content accuracy and reliability falling short of what's required;

2.Challenges in human-machine collaboration, compounded by a scarcity of talent skilled in integrating AI;

3.The steep cost of investing in the technology.

Main Reasons for Hesitancy in Adopting Generative AI at the Institutional Level:

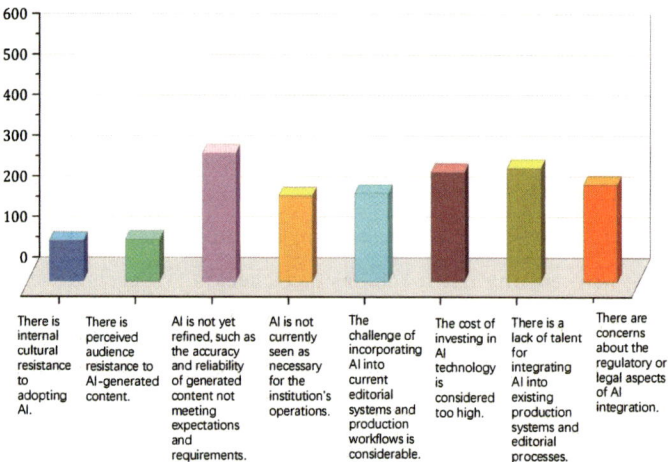

That said, the majority of media organizations taking a wait-and-see approach are not dismissing generative AI. They're strategizing to adopt it at the right time, with these top three considerations:

1.Pinpointing areas in their business where AI could markedly boost productivity and cut down on manpower;

2.Seeing a quantum leap in AI capabilities, especially in terms of accuracy and reliability;

3.Making sure that the integration won't bring out ethical disputes, regulatory hurdles, or legal issues.

A mere 6.4% of the media organizations surveyed are currently not considering the adoption of generative AI tools at all.

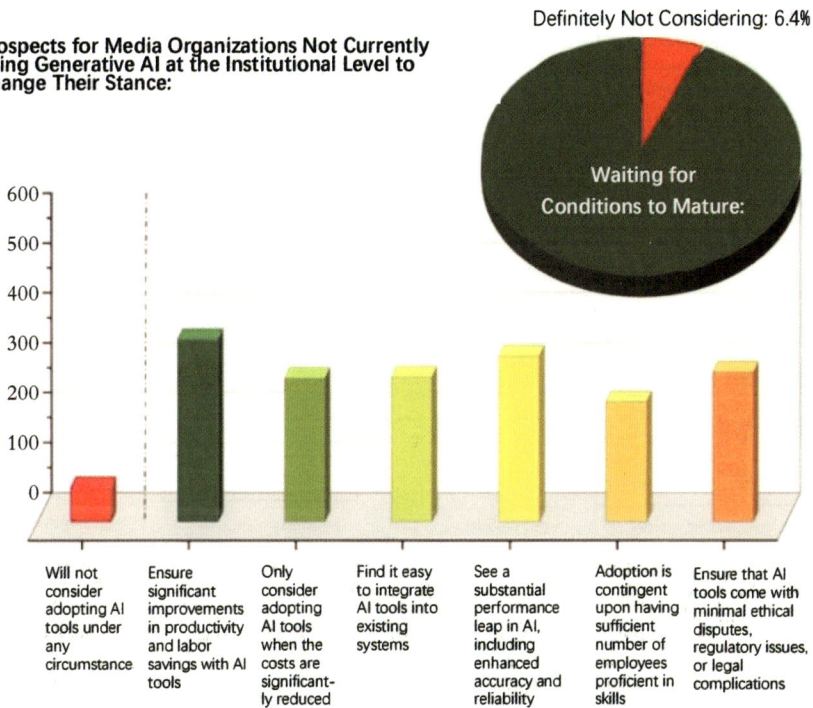

Prospects for Media Organizations Not Currently Using Generative AI at the Institutional Level to Change Their Stance:

Definitely Not Considering: 6.4%

Waiting for Conditions to Mature:

4. News Media's Anticipation of Generative AI Centers on Speed and Efficiency

The media outlets surveyed, whether they have adopted generative AI at the institutional level or not, generally harbor a positive outlook on the potential of this novel technology to contribute to the industry. They anticipate that generative AI will be a driving force in enhancing both the "speed" and "efficiency" of news reporting, bringing it to new heights.

74.6% of the media organizations surveyed anticipate that generative AI will contribute to the timeliness of news reporting. Similarly, 74.4% believe it will boost the efficiency of news production. Additionally, 66.7% expect improvements in the precision of news distribution while 63.3% look forward to enhancements in the creativity of content presentation.

Estimated Effectiveness of Generative AI in News Reporting by Surveyed Media Organizations:

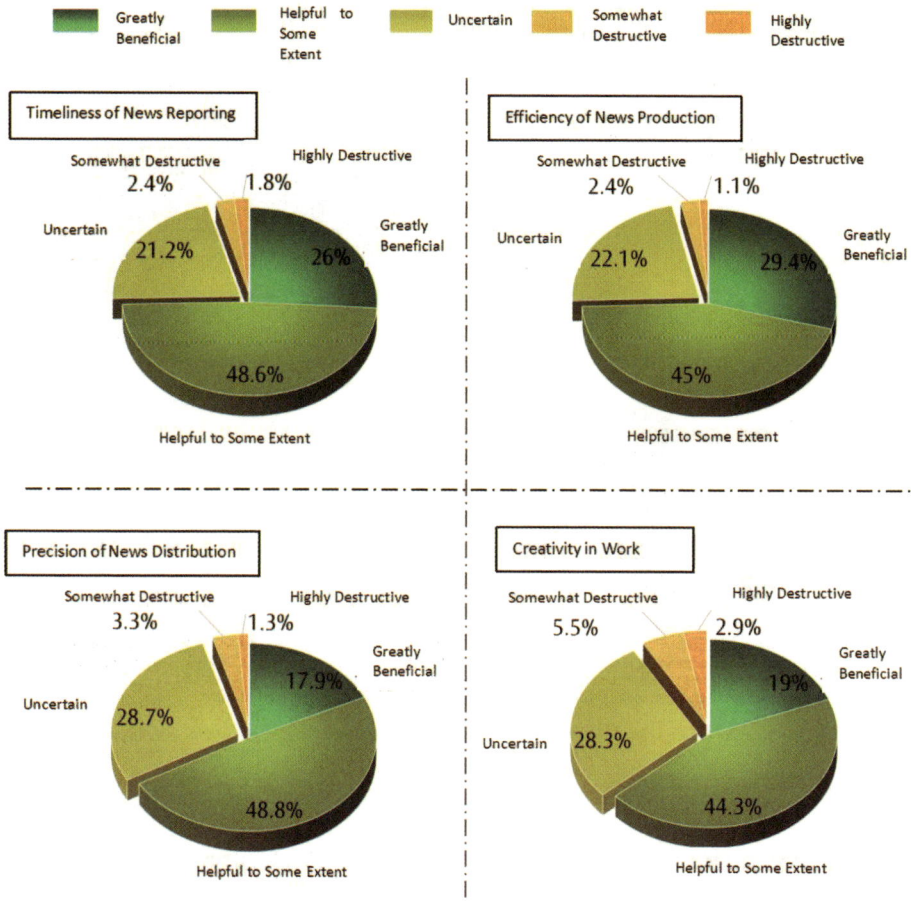

The top three areas where media organizations value the empowerment of generative artificial intelligence are:

1.Intelligent proofreading and fact-checking;

2.Intelligent creation of charts, videos, and music;

3.Text generation/robotic writing/translation.

Areas of Generative AI Empowerment Valued by Surveyed Media Organizations:

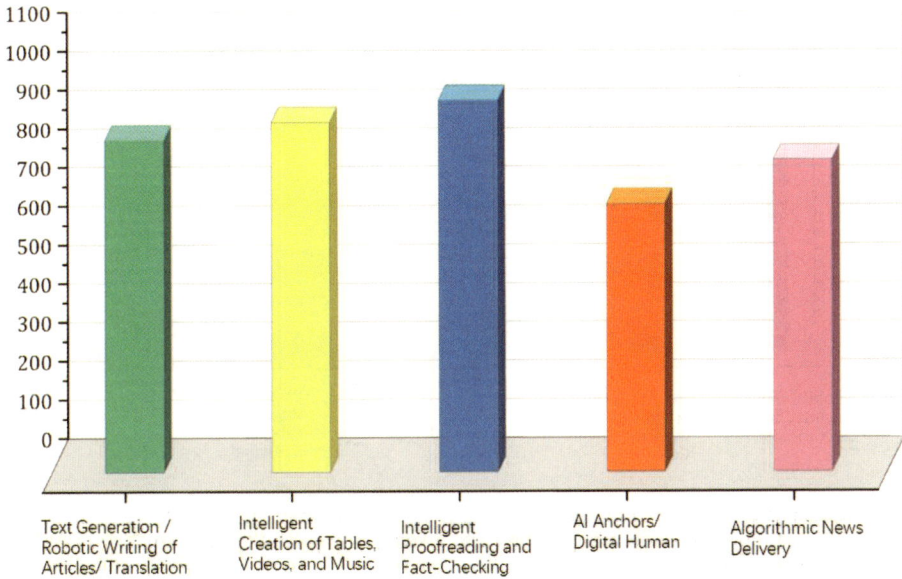

5. Media's Wariness of Generative AI Centers on Trustworthiness

The majority of media agencies approach the deployment of generative AI with a healthy dose of skepticism. When asked about the issues they have encountered or anticipate with generative AI, a staggering 76.4% of respondents voice concerns over the potential for "distortion and misalignment of news leads and materials", which far exceeds the 61.1% who point to "copyright and liability issues" as the second most pressing concern.

Moreover, when considering the impact of generative AI integration into the media industry over the next 3 to 5 years on the trustworthiness of the information environment, 36.4% of those surveyed are pessimistic, a notable 12.3 percentage points above the 24.1% who are optimistic. A significant portion, 39.5%, remain neutral in their expectations.

Trustworthiness and authenticity are the cornerstones of journalism. It is thus inferred that, in the immediate term, most media organizations will likely restrict generative AI to a minor supportive role in content production.

Problems Encountered or Expected by Surveyed Media Organizations When Utilizing Generative AI:

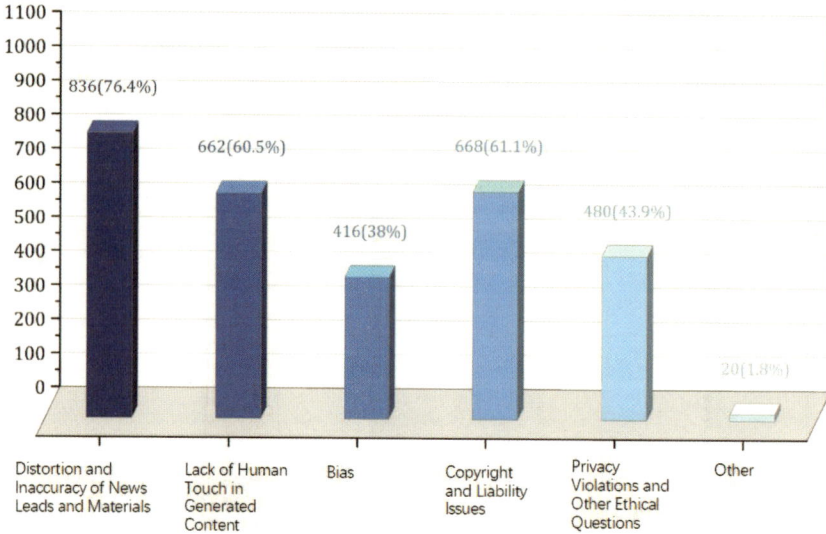

Surveyed Media Organizations' Predictions for the Credibility and Reliability of the Information Environment in the Next 3 to 5 Years with the Integration of Generative AI:

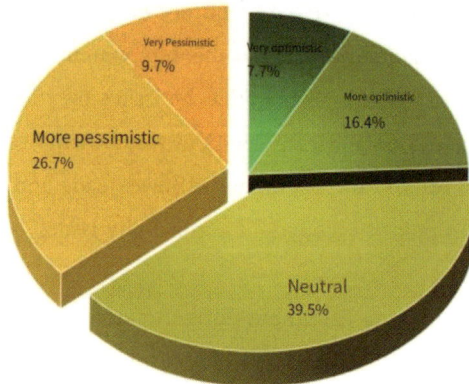

6. A Majority of Media Organizations (85.6%) Call for Enhanced Oversight of Generative AI

Regarding the potential adverse effects of generative AI within the media sector, a mere 14.4% of respondents feel that "current regulatory frameworks are sufficiently binding". An overwhelming 85.6% are in favor of bolstering regulation and governance measures, with a strong inclination towards "industry self-discipline", "enactment of national laws", and "internal media organization regulation".

This indicates that media organizations are not only wary of the inherent technical issues with generative AI, but also vigilant about the risks associated with its unintentional misuse or deliberate abuse, which can lead to the proliferation of false information. Such risks cannot be curbed merely by dealing with one's own problems in isolation.

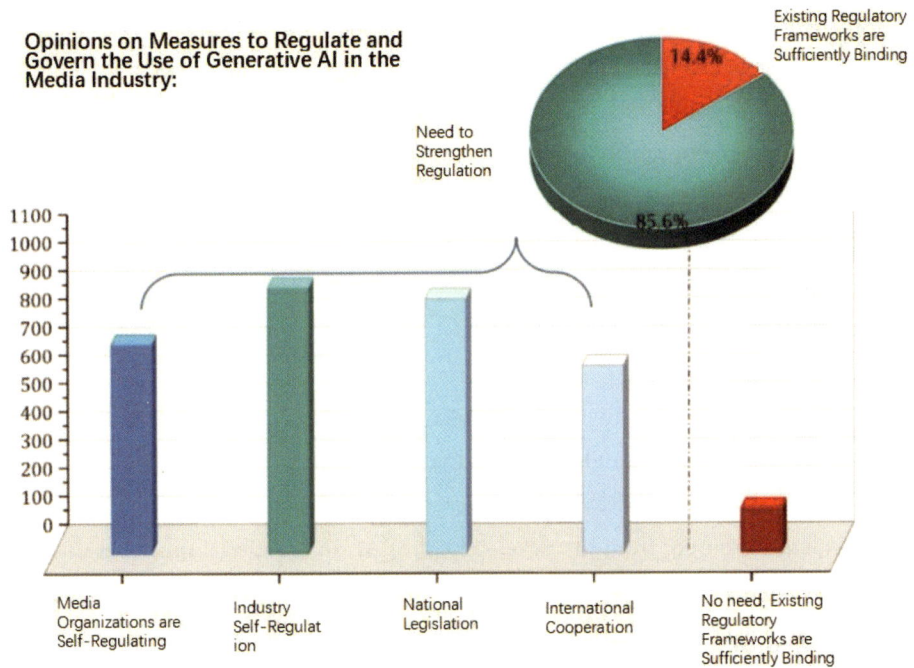

Opinions on Measures to Regulate and Govern the Use of Generative AI in the Media Industry:

Existing Regulatory Frameworks are Sufficiently Binding

Need to Strengthen Regulation

14.4%

85.6%

| | Media Organizations are Self-Regulating | Industry Self-Regulation | National Legislation | International Cooperation | No need, Existing Regulatory Frameworks are Sufficiently Binding |

It should be noted that the survey was conducted using a mix of online questionnaires and in-person interviews. Participants were invited representatives from various organizations, primarily consisting of Xinhua News Agency's global media clients. The respondents were all institutional media outlets, with each permitted to submit only one response. The collected valid responses demonstrated a wide range of representation across different types, sizes, nationalities, and audience demographics, providing a comprehensive reflection of the global media industry's understanding and approach to generative AI.

Generative AI was used to assist in certain stages of data analysis and interpretation for this report. All AI-generated content included in this report has been manually checked and verified to ensure accuracy.

VI. Conclusion

Everything about humanity is being reshaped by AI. After years of evolution, AI, entering an explosive period, has become an important driving force for the technological revolution, industrial transformation, and even social change. In the past two years, generative AI technology represented by ChatGPT, Sora, etc. has triggered a new wave of global AI technology and industry.

The future is here, but what we don't know outweighs what we do know. AI is challenging people's cognitive and ethical boundaries while humans are caught off guard by the "new species" they have created. People don't even know whether they have created AI as a "tool" or whether they are just "acting as an unconscious tool of history" in the evolution of AI.

Humans are amazed, delighted, anxious and worried, in a state of "culture shock" brought about by AI.

Fortunately, the rationality of human beings is also awakening at the same time as they are starting to explore and contemplate new forms of human-machine integration. Faced with a series of novel challenges in areas of regulation, law, security, ethics and employment stemming from the development of AI, international organizations and numerous countries have embarked on exploring viable pathways for AI governance and have achieved some consensus, endeavoring to seek a balance between progress and security. By now, hundreds of laws and regulations, administrative instructions, and ethical norms on AI governance have been issued by countries and regions.

The information environment in the AI era is undergoing crucial changes, with the boundaries between virtuality and reality disappearing and the online and offline highly integrated. In this media ecosystem, the "pseudo-environment" created by information dissemination has become more decisive in building human cognition, influencing subject decision-making and guiding the direction of civilization. The evolution of AI from "tool" to "subject" undoubtedly complicates further the information environment.

In this context, the traditional social role of news media in shaping the information and cognitive environments is being reconstructed. From the height of human civilization, global news media should jointly consider their new roles, missions and responsibilities in the AI era, to better defend the common values of humankind and inject more positive energy into building a community with a shared future for humanity.

Notes and Acknowledgments

The expert group of this think tank report on "The Responsibility and Mission of News Media in the Era of Artificial Intelligence" is led by Fu Hua, President of Xinhua News Agency and Chairman of the Academic Committee of Xinhua Institute, with Ren Weidong, Deputy Editor-in-Chief of Xinhua News Agency, as the deputy head. Members of the group include Liu Gang, Wen Jian, Liu Hua, Chen Yi, Li Feihu, He Huiyuan, Li Cheng, Chen Yi'na, He Xiaofan, Li Tao, Shen Li, Zhao Yixuan, Dou Shuqi, Zhou Yu, Li Lijun, Liu Rongrong, Guo Xinfeng, Li Xuedi, Zhu Junqing, Huang Xinchuan, Wang Zhonghao, Chen Guoquan, and Liang Qiawen.

After the launch of the project, the group visited many media outlets, technology companies, and research institutes and it distributed questionnaires to global media organizations in Chinese, English and French before completing the writing, revision, proofreading and translation.

Professor Hu Zhengrong of the Chinese Academy of Social Sciences, Professor Shen Yang of Tsinghua University, Professor Guo Quanzhong of the Minzu University of China, and experts from the Chinese Academy of Cyberspace, the China Center for Information Industry Development (CCID), Tencent, Baidu, and Alibaba, etc. have provided assistance and guidance in the preparation of this report. The questionnaires have been received by more than 1,000 media organizations, including newspapers and periodicals, broadcasting and television stations, news agencies, and websites, in 53 countries and regions. We would like to registerour sincere thanks for the support we have received throughout this project.

Errors or omissions might exist in this report given the limited scope of materials available and the authors' limited expertise. We welcome any constructive criticism and suggestions for improvement.

Empower China, Benefit the World — An Analysis of the Theoretical Contribution and Value Orientation of New Quality Productive Forces[①]

The notion of "new quality productive forces" was first introduced by General Secretary Xi Jinping during his inspection tour in Heilongjiang province in September 2023. Since then, he has addressed major issues concerning the essence, purpose, and formation of new quality productive forces at the Central Economic Work Conference, the collective study of the Political Bureau of the Central Committee of the Communist Party of China, the annual "two sessions", and during his local inspection tours, offering methodical explanations of this key concept and crafted significant plans for its implementation.

His expositions represent an innovative evolution of the Marxist theory on productive forces, further enriching the connotation of Xi Jinping Thought on the Economy. These perspectives provide a fundamental guideline and practical roadmap for China to embark on a new journey to further emancipate and develop productive forces, achieve high-quality development, and propel and expand Chinese modernization in the new era. These expositions will also inject fresh input and impetus into the prosperity of

---

① Released in Brussels, Belgium, on June 19, 2024.

China and the world.

I. Innovative Development of Marxist Theory on Productive Forces

"In conclusion, the new quality productive forces are primarily driven by innovation, and break free from the development paths of traditional economic growth models and productive forces; they feature high technology, high efficiency, and high quality, and are advanced productive forces required by the new development philosophy."[1]

— President Xi Jinping

1. Theoretical Contributions of New Quality Productive Forces
Basic Connotations of New Quality Productive Forces

On January 31, 2024, the Political Bureau of the CPC Central Committee held a collective study session regarding advancing high-quality development with solid steps. General Secretary Xi Jinping delivered an important speech in which he gave an in-depth explanation of the brand-new concept of "new quality productive forces".

"In conclusion, the new quality productive forces are primarily driven by innovation, and break free from the development paths of traditional economic growth models and productive forces; they feature high technology, high efficiency, and high quality, and are advanced productive forces required by the new development philosophy. They are fostered by revolutionary technological breakthroughs, innovative allocation of production factors, and deep industrial transformation and upgrading, with the improvement of labor forces, means of labor, subjects of labor and their optimal combination as underlying elements, and a substantial increase in total factor

---

① Xi Jinping emphasizes at the eleventh collective study of the Political Bureau of the CPC Central Committee the importance of accelerating the development of new quality productive forces and solidly promoting high-quality development, Xinhua News Agency, Feb 1, 2024.

productivity as a core hallmark. Marked by innovation, and with high quality as the key, new quality productive forces are advanced productivity inessence."

High-quality development stands as the unyielding principle of the new era. Since China entered a new era, the CPC Central Committee has made a series of vital decisions and arrangements, making high-quality development a widespread consensus and a shared consciousness across the whole Party andsociety,and putting it front and center in economic and social progress. Over the past few years, China has accomplished a great deal in scientific and technological innovation, and the efficacy of innovation-driven development is increasingly evident. Development has become much more coordinated and balanced between urban and rural areas as well as between regions. Reform and opening up have been deepened across the board, spurring a strong momentum and vitality of development. The country has made notable progress in green, low-carbon transformation, accelerated the shift in its development mode, and achieved remarkable results in high-quality development. At the same time, there remains an abundance of constraints hindering high-quality development, which must be taken seriously and addressed effectively.

General Secretary Xi Jinping emphasizes that high-quality development has to be supported by a new quality productive forces theory. Since new quality productive forces have emerged in practice and exhibited their strong role in driving and supporting high-quality development, they should be theorized systematically to guide further development.[1]

New quality productive forces are innovation-driven. Innovation, particularly original and disruptive sci-tech innovation, is crucial for fostering new quality productive forces. A review of the successive industrial revolutions reveals that new scientific theories laid the groundwork to usherin new production tools, significant adjustments in economic structures and development models, and vital transformations in the ways of production and life in society. Revolutionary breakthroughs in technology will propel a leap in the laborers, labor materials, and labor objects, along with their

---

[1] Xi Jinping emphasizes at the eleventh collective study of the Political Bureau of the CPC Central Committee the importance of accelerating the development of new quality productive forces and solidly promoting high-quality development, Xinhua News Agency, Feb 1, 2024.

optimal combination, thereby achieving a substantial leap in productiveforces.

New quality productive forces represent a transformation in the growth model. Economic growth driven by traditional productivity is characterized by a reliance on quantitative, replicative expansion through substantial inputs of labor materials, labor objects, and laborers, heavily dependent on factor inputs. In contrast, new quality productive forces focus on enhancing the caliber of laborers and labor productivity and refining production methods and tools. This transformation is akin to the establishment of a new "production function," which redefines the correspondence between the "independent variable" of factor inputs and the "dependent variable" of outputs, leading to a notable increase in total factor productivity.

New quality productive forces are applied across industries. New quality productive forces, committed to high-quality supply, satisfy and generate new demands, which in turn catalyze the emergence of new products, services, and industries, thereby transforming the industrial structure. From the perspective of industrial development ladders, sci-tech innovation results, when applied to specific industries and industrial chains, can transform and upgrade traditional industries, cultivate and grow emerging industries, as well as foster and strengthen future industries, continuously driving industrial evolution and upgrading.

New quality productive forces are a pathway to green development. They represent adeparture from traditional growth models, which were excessively reliant on conventional resources and energy. As advanced productive forces, they embody the philosophy of green development. These forces are inherently green, environmentally friendly, and conducive to sustainable development. The cultivation of new quality productive forces necessitates an accelerated transition towards a development path that prioritizes environment al conservation and green development.

Innovative Development of the Marxist Theory on Productive Forces

Productive forces represent the capacity of humanity to transform and harness the forces of nature, constituting the most dynamic and revolutionary elements in propelling societal progress.

Prior to Marxist theory on productive forces, Western economists such as Adam Smith, David Ricardo, and Friedrich List had already researched and expounded on the subject.

Karl Marx and Friedrich Engels provided systematic analysis and deep insights into productive forces. In *Capital*, Marx noted, "Productive forces, i.e., the development of productive capacity and its factors," [1]"Labor productivity is determined by various circumstances, amongst others, by the average amount of skill of the workmen, the state of science, and the degree of its practical application, the social organization of production, the extentand capabilities of the means of production, and by physical conditions." [2] Engels regarded the origin of productive forces as the ability to transform nature formed by the combination of human labor power and means of production.[3] In *Manifesto of the Communist Party*, Marx and Engels pointed out that after the proletariat took political power, it was imperative to "increase the total productive forces as quickly as possible."[4]

The theory on productive forces stands as a classical tenet of Marxism. The Communist Party of China has consistently integrated and advanced the Marxist theory on productive forces through practical application. Comrade Mao Zedong distinctly stated, "The aim of the socialist revolution is to liberate the productive forces." [5]Comrade Deng Xiaoping proposed that "Among socialism's many tasks, the fundamental one is to develop the productiveforces."[6]

Since the 18th CPC National Congress, General Secretary Xi Jinping has placed great emphasis on the role of productive forces and has delivered a series of significant statements. He underscored, "To complete the building of a moderately prosperous society in all respects, achieve socialist modernization and the great renewal of the Chinese nation, the most essential and urgent task is to further release and develop the productive forces."[7]"We must regard science and technology as our primary productive

---

[1] Collected Works of Karl Marx and Friedrich Engels, Vol. 7, People's Publishing House, Dec. 2009.

[2] Capital: Volume One, People's Publishing House, April2018.

[3] Contemporary Chinese Marxism Review Vol. 2, Social Sciences Academic Press,April 2018.

[4] Manifesto of the Communist Party, People's Publishing House, Jan.2015.

[5] Selected Works of Mao Zedong , Volume 7 People's Publishing House , Jun. 1999.

[6] Selected Works of Deng Xiaoping, Volume 3, People's Publishing House, April 2001

[7] XiJinping: UnitethoughtsontheguidingprinciplesoftheThirdPlenarySessionofthe 18 thCPCCentral Committee, Xinhua News Agency, Dec.31, 2013.

force, talent as our primary resource, and innovation as our primary driver of growth. We will fully implement the strategy for invigorating China through science and education, the workforce development strategy, and the innovation-driven development strategy. We will open up new areas and new arenas in development and steadily foster new growth drivers and new strengths." [1] "Upholding and developing socialism with Chinese characteristics necessitates continuously balancing the relations of production to align with the development of social productive forces."[2]

Facing swift changes both domestically and internationally, clinging to old conventions and rigid thinking, combined with a lack of courage for theoretical innovation, will fail to scientifically answer the questions posed by China, the world, the people, and the era.General Secretary Xi Jinping, by coordinating the great rejuvenation of the Chinese nation and global changes of a magnitude not seen in a century, and accurately perceiving and grasping the global trends of sci-tech development, has creatively introduced the major theory of developing newquality productive forces. He pointed out, "Developing new quality productive forces is an inherent requirement and an important focus for promoting high-quality development. It is essential to keep prioritizing innovation to propel the accelerated cultivation of new quality productive forces."[3] His significant discourses systematically clarify the rich connotation, essential elements, practice pathways and scientific methodologies of the new quality productive forces. They provide profound answers to such major theoretical and practical questions as "What are new quality productive forces? Why should they be developed? How should they be developed?" These contributions have enrichedand advanced the Marxist theory on productive forces, elevating the CPC's understanding of the laws of productivity

---

[1] Xi Jinping underscores science and technology as the primary productive force, talent as the primary resource, and innovation as the primary driver of growth, Xinhua News Agency, Oct. 16, 2022.

[2] Xi Jinping stresses that the entire party should study and master historical materialism to better understand the laws and advance work more proactively, Xinhua News Agency, Dec. 4, 2013.

[3] Xi Jinping emphasizes accelerating the development of new quality productive forces to solidly promote high-quality development during the eleventh collective study session of the Political Bureau of the CPC Central Committee, Xinhua News Agency, Feb 1, 2024.

development.

Augmentation of Xi Jinping's Thought on Economy

Marx observed, "The realization of theory in a country always depends on the extent to which it meets the needs of that country."[①]

Xi Jinping's Thought on Economy, rooted in China's development stage and direction, has progressively enriched and matured within the country's significant modernization drive. It has charted the right course and provided fundamental guidance for China's high-quality economic development. The pivotal discourses on new quality productive forces, as the latest achievements of Xi Jinping's Thought on Economy, hold profound practical and historical significance for propelling high-quality development and advancing Chinese modernization in the new era.

Since the 18th CPC National Congress, General Secretary Xi Jinping has articulated a suite of innovative concepts, ideologies, and strategies that are guiding China's economic development with a coherent and unified logic. The "new normal in economic development" has served as the general context for China's economic growth, while the pursuit of "high-quality development" has charted the country's future course. The concepts of a "new development stage," "new development philosophy," and "new development pattern" have delineated China's historical development position, provided guiding principles for its modernization drive, and defined the trajectory for its economic modernization. The "new quality productive forces", an embodiment of advanced productive forces, have unveiled the evolutionary laws of productive forces, and are designed to inject new impetus into high-quality development.

Currently, the world is entering a period of technological innovation with unprecedented and intensive vitality. General Secretary Xi Jinping, with a firm grasp on the overall development trend of productive forces, has guided China to seize the opportunities presented by the latest round of technological revolutions and industrial transformation. Under this leadership, production relations evolve to meet the changing needs of productive forces, ensuring China's economy remains resilient amidst adversity.

The concept of new quality productive forces underpins Xi Jinping's Thought on the Economy. General Secretary Xi Jinping has underscored that "innovation is the

---

① Marx and Engels Collected Works, Volume 3, People's Publishing House, Oct. 2002.

primary driver of growth," pinpointing innovation as the linchpin of economic and social advancement. In deepening supply-side structural reforms, the pivotal aim is to catalyze industry innovation through scientific and technological innovation. Enhancing the technological sophistication of products and services through innovation serves to meet people's material and psychological demands, and facilitates a more refined alignment between supply and demand. General Secretary Xi Jinping advocates for pursuing "high-quality development," delineates a vision for a"moderneconomic system" and urges the accelerated building of a "modern industrial system." Innovation-driven development is spearheaded by new quality productive forces. The essential feature of the modern industrial system and the core competitiveness of the modern economic system are the cultivation and growth of new quality productive forces. The introduction of new quality productive forces indeed has provided a solid foundation for innovation-driven development and development empowered by advanced productivity, and has enriched and extended Xi Jinping's Thought on Economy. These forces,with substantial theoretica linsights and practical significance, have further answered the key questions in the economic development under socialism with Chinese characteristics in the new era, pushing forward the frontiers of Marxist political economy.

Cultivating new quality productive forces is a vividpractice of pursuing Chinese modernization and establishing a socialist economy. These forces exemplify the great advantages and dynamic vitality of the socialist system with Chinese characteristics. They represent the core mission of socialism in the new era, and on the new journey, and constitute an imperative to advance high-quality development through advanced productive forces. Furthermore, they reflect China's greater resolve to pursue an innovation-driven development path aimed at forging new competitive edges and taking the initiative in development.

2. Dynamics Essential for Grasping New Quality Productive Forces

Interaction Between Productive Forces and Relations of Production

Marxist political economy posits that when productive forces develop to a certain stage, contradictions inevitably arise with the existing relations of production. When the current relations of production become a constraint on the development of productive forces, the transformation of these relations becomes inevitable, which, in turn, promotes the further development of productive forces.

In his important speech at the conference commemorating the 200th anniversary of Karl Marx's birth, General Secretary Xi Jinping emphasized, "To study Marx is to study and practice Marxist thoughts on productive forces and relations of production." "We must courageously deepen reform across the board, consciously stimulate the vitality of social productive forces through adjusting relations of production, and consciously adapt to the developmental requirements of the economic base by improving the superstructure, thereby enabling socialism with Chinese characteristics to develop more in line with objective laws."[①]

Since the 18th CPC National Congress, the country has undertaken a series of explorations and practices in ownership of the means of production, income distribution, and the socialist market economy. These efforts have expanded the Marxist political economy theory on relations of production and have propelled the development of productive forces.

Likewise, fostering new quality productive forces requires developing compatible, new types of relations of production. This imperative is essential for advancing high-quality development in the new era. It necessitates continuously deepening reforms in economic and technological systems and other fields to remove bottlenecks and obstacles that constrain the growth of these new forces, thereby enabling the smooth flow and efficient allocation of various advanced, high-quality production factors, all in service of nurturing new quality productive forces.

Interplay Between Supply and Demand

New quality productive forces areaimed at balancing supply and demand. In economic development, supply and demand are interdependent,with a relative balance and an absolute imbalance. Meeting people's ever-growing aspiration for a better life through high-quality supply is an inherent requirement in developing new quality productive forces.

The report to the 20th CPC National Congress proposed to "make sure that our implementation of the strategy to expand domestic demand is integrated with our efforts

---

① "Xi Jinping's Speech at the Commemoration of the 200th Anniversary of Karl Marx's Birth," Xinhua News Agency, May 4th, 2018.

to deepen supply-side structural reform." [1] The new products, services, and industries formed by new quality productive forces continuously not only satisfy the people's growing needs for a better life, but also create, stimulate, and fulfill emerging demands. Concurrently, productive forces cannot exist in isolation from demand; the supply of products or services by enterprises is only meaningful when transformed into consumption through exchange. The cultivation of new-quality productive forces must be oriented towards meeting the needs of people's all-round development, giving full play to demand in driving the advancement of productive forces.

In the current and upcoming period, constraints on China's economic development are present on both the supply and demand sides, with the primary contradiction on the supply side. Therefore, to develop new-quality productive forces, we must harness innovation as the primary driver of growth, breaking down supply-side bottlenecks, and satisfying andcreating demand through high-quality and effective supply. As we keep expanding domestic demand and satisfying the people's growing aspirations for a better life, it is imperative to drive ongoing supply-side improvements and innovation. This will catalyze the emergence of new industries, technologies, products, and business models, establishing a more sophisticated dynamic equilibrium, where demand and supply mutually reinforce each other.

Balance Between Inheritance and Innovation

Marxism holds that everything in the world is in perpetual motion and flux, with labor productivity ever-evolving. New quality productive forces are not static, but are dynamically generated and constantly developing.

As an ancient Chinese adage advises, "If one can make things better for one day, he should make them better every day." The relentless march of science and technology will spawn birth to new forms of productive forces and industrial patterns. To seize the initiative in fostering new quality productive forces, it is imperative to stay abreast of the cutting edge of science and technology, grasp technological development trends, and encourage the emergence of original and disruptive scientific and technological

---

[1] "Xi Jinping: Hold High the Great Banner of Socialism with Chinese Characteristics and Strive in Unity to Build a Modern Socialist Country in All Respects—Report to the 20th National Congress of the Communist Party of China", Xinhua News Agency, Oct 25, 2022.

innovations. This approach will ensure a continuous infusion of new impetus into developing new quality productive forces.

The development of new quality productive forces must follow a pragmatic approach, ensuring that new systems are established before abolishing the old ones and strategies are tailored to local conditions. In technological innovation, developing practical productive forces should be taken as the fundamental goal to steer clear of any impractical approaches or blind imitation. In industrial development, vigilance is needed to prevent both reckless expansion and economic bubbles, while also ensuring that valuable traditional industries are not forsaken in the pursuit of new ones. General Secretary Xi Jinping aptly illustrated this point: "We cannot throw away our current means of sustenance before securing new ones." As localities enthusiastically nurture strategic emerging industries and incubate future industries, they must not neglect or abandon traditional sectors. Instead, they must integrate the transformation and upgrading of traditional industries with the cultivation and growth of emerging industries and the layout of future industries, advancing these efforts in a well-considered and coordinated manner. Currently, alongside supporting the development of strategic emerging industries and future industries, it is equally important to apply new technologies to transform and upgrade traditional industries to become higher-end, smarter, and greener.

Synergy Between Material and Civilization

The evolution of socio-economic forms and civilizations is marked by advancements in productive forces and production tools. Throughout human history, from the Stone Age through the Bronze, Iron, and Steel Ages, and then to the eras defined by steam, electricity, and information technologies, we have witnessed not only the development of tools but also the cultural advancement and civilizational progress brought about by the growth of productive forces.

The creation and cultivation of new quality productive forces serve as a crucial force and indicator of cultural and civilizational progress. Culture is the dynamic manifestation of civilization, while civilization is the cumulative heritage of culture. The essence of civilization lies in a state of progress, and it is through continuously mastering new technological means that we drive the evolution of civilization forward. At present, the world is transitioning into an era where information technologies fully lead innovation and serve as the foundation for building national core competitiveness. Countries that can better understand and harness this trend, better adapt to and steer the development of new quality productive forces, and promote the transformation of relations of production and superstructure,will be poised to strengthen their comprehensive national strength. The emergence of new quality productive forces coincides with an era marked by the burgeoning and relentless evolution of mobile internet, big data, and artificial intelligence. It is imperative to recognize the boundless potential of disruptive innovations and their applications, and to contemplate the development of civilization and the progress of our times from this vantagepoint.

3. Contemporary Significance of Developing New Quality Productive Forces

Requirements for Building a Strong Country and Achieving National Rejuvenation

Fostering new quality productive forces is an inevitable choice for advancing Chinese-style modernization and the great rejuvenation of the Chinese nation. It is both an inherent requirement and a key focus for driving high-quality development, as well as a practical necessity to continuously fulfill the people's aspirations for a better life.

At present, profound changes unseen in a century are unfolding at an accelerated pace. Nurturing new quality productive forces is in line with the current trend and is essential for development, helping to tackle the challenge of adapting, generating new opportunities, and opening new possibilities while maintaining leadership in development and historical progress.

After 75 years of swift advancement since the founding of the People's Republic of China, and particularly over 40 years of reform and opening-up, China's economic aggregate has steadily remained the world's second-largest. However, there remains a considerable gap with leading global levels in areas such as technological innovation and core industrial competitiveness. To basically realize socialist modernization by 2035 and build China into a great modern socialist country that is prosperous, strong, democratic, culturally advanced, harmonious, and beautiful by the middle of this century, it is an objective necessity to catalyze qualitative, efficiency, and dynamic transformation in economic development,to enhance total factor productivity, and to expedite the formation of new quality productive forces.

China has compressed the industrialization process that took Western developed countries centuries into just a few decades. It has established the world's most complete and largest industrial system and has become an innovative country, laying a solid foundation for cultivating new quality productive forces. As it embarks on a new journey, China will prioritize innovation, reinforce greendevelopment, take proactive reform measures and build a strong talent pool, with a view to consistently breaking newground, bolstering new momentum, shaping new advantages and exploring more potential for propelling high-quality development to new heights.

Answering the Call for Global Sustainable Development

At present, the global economic rebound remains arduous, lacking effective new growth drivers. The International Monetary Fund (IMF) has forecasted a 3.2% global economic growth for 2024 in their April 2024 report, an upward revision of 0.3 percentage points from the October 2023 forecast. However, this forecast remains well below the historical average growth rate of 3.8% between 2000 and 2019.

For many years, China has been a powerhouse of global growth, contributing approximately 30% to annual global economic growth. Its acceleration in developing new quality productive forces, spearheaded by technological innovation ,is set to provide a robust impetus to the global economy.

China's development of new quality productive forces will significantly propel global technological transformation. In 2023, China's annual expenditure on research and experimental development reached 3.3 trillion yuan, an 8.1% increase year-on-year[1], ranking second globally in absolute terms. By the end of 2023, China's domestic (excluding Hong Kong, Macao, and Taiwan) invention patent ownership reached 4.015 million, a 22.4% increase year-on-year, making it the first country to surpass 4 million valid domestic invention patents. China has become a veritable intellectual property powerhouse, making consistent and significant contributions to global innovative development.

As China's new quality productive forces extend globally, they are positioned to stimulate world economic development. China's 5G technology underpins communications and mobile internet in many countries. China has long topped the

---

[1] National Bureau of Statistics of China: Statistical Communique of the People's Republic of China on the 2023 National Economic and Social Development, Feb 2024.

world in producing desktop computers, laptops, and mobile phones. Additionally, innovative Chinese models are also gaining global traction, with Chinese apps like Temu emerging as some of the fastest-growing shopping applications in globa markets, offering more people cost-effective goods and services from Chinese enterprises.

China is a crucial supporter of global green and low-carbon transition. Its highly efficient production and manufacturing systems for solar energy equipment and electric vehicles have significantly lowered the costs associated with this transition. In 2023, despite weak global trade conditions, China's exports of the "new trio"—new energy vehicles, lithium-ion batteries, and solar cells—surpassed one trillion yuan, marking a 29.9% year-on-year growth.

China's commitment to building a community with a shared future for mankind is reflected in its ongoing efforts to expand high-level opening-up and advance the high-quality development of the Belt and Road Initiative. This approach creates more opportunities for other countries to participate in emerging industries and benefit from the dividends of new quality productive forces, which is conducive to advancinginternational economic cooperation and promoting regional sustainable development.

II. Developing New Quality Productive Forces with Sci-tech Innovation as Core Element

"Scientific and technological innovation can generate new industries, new models and new momentum, and is the core element for developing new quality productive forces."[1]

——President Xi Jinping

---

[1] Xi Jinping emphasizes at the eleventh collective study of the Political Bureau of the CPC Central Committee the importance of accelerating the development of new quality productive forces and solidly promoting high-quality development, Xinhua News Agency, Feb 1, 2024.

1. Strengthening Sci-tech Innovation, Particularly Original and Disruptive Innovation

Sci-tech innovation stands a sapivotal engine of productivity. The Marxist perspective on the key role of science and technology in fostering productive forces has evolved through theoretical and practical explorations, from "production includes science"[1] to "science and technology are the primary productive force"[2] and now to "scientific and technological innovation is the core element for developing new quality productiveforces."[3]

The conversion of sci-tech achievements into tangible productive forces is achieved by incubating new industries and driving deep industrial transformation and upgrading. Currently, sci-tech innovation is fueling socio-economic progress with its pervasive influence, ability to spread, and its driving force. China possesses unique advantages in nurturing new quality productive forces. In recent years, China's overall strength in sci-tech innovation has steadily improved and its basic research capabilities have been strengthened, with investment in basic research a ccounting for 6.65% of its total R&D spending in 2023. The country is also seeing benefits from its growing pool of mid- to high-end talent. China's vast domestic market offers diverse application scenarios. With a comprehensive and extensive industrial chain, China's manufacturing sector has consistently ranked first globally for 14 consecutive years.

The introduction of new quality productive forces signals China's stronger resolve and endeavors to drive sci-tech innovation. It means China will accelerate its pursuit of high-level sci-tech self-reliance and self-strength, intensify efforts to overcome challenges in keycore technologies, and produce more original and disruptive innovations so as to inject new momentum into China's socio-economic development.

---

[1] Collected Works of Karl Marx and Friedrich Engels, Vol. 7, People's Publishing House, Dec. 2009.

[2] Selected Works of Deng Xiaoping, Volume 3, People's Publishing House, April 2001.

[3] Xi Jinping calls on Hunan to stay committed to reform and innovation and follow a realistic and pragmatic approach to write its own chapter in advancing Chinese modernization during his inspection tour in Hunan, accompanied by Cai Qi, Xinhua News Agency, March 21, 2024.

Mastering Essential Technologies in Crucial Areas

At the heart of the industrial tech ecosystem, key core technologies are pivotal to strengthening the leading role of sci-tech innovation and the guarantee to achieve high-level self-reliance and self-strength in science and technology.

General Secretary Xi Jinping emphasized: "China cannot ask for, buy, or beg for core technologies in key fields from other countries." [1] Only by achieving breakthroughs in core technologies in key fields at a faster pace can we keep the initiative for innovation and development securely in our own hands.

To win the battle for key core technologies, we must focus on breaking through the key difficulties. Weshould direct full efforts towards areas essential to both the urgent and long-term needs of the country, including basic materials, advanced chips, and industrial software. By targeting innovation in key generic technologies, cutting-edge frontier technologies, modern engineering technologies, and disruptive technologies, we must adopt forward-looking plans for strategic and reserve technological R&D projects and deliver important national scientific initiatives and projects. It's essential to refine the allocation of fiscal resources in science and technology, encourage enterprises and society to boost R&D investment, and reinforce intellectual property rights protection. We must also improve tax policies that stimulate corporate technological innovation, increase capital market support for tech enterprises, and actively cultivate venture capital and expand patient capital.

To win the battle for key core technologies, we must leverage the unique strength of our socialist system to rally efforts to accomplish sizable tasks, reinforce the leadership of the Party and the state in significant scientific and technological innovations and refine the new system for mobilizing nationwide resources. By aligning with national strategic needs, we will enhance top-level design, allocate innovation resources strategically, and better define the roles of national research institutes, advanced-level research universities, and leading high-tech enterprises to improve their layout. We aim to create a powerful synergy for sci-tech breakthroughs by integrating the efforts of government,

---

[1] Xi Jinping's address at the 19th Meeting of the Academicians of the Chinese Academy of Sciences and the 14th Meeting of the Academicians of the Chinese Academy of Engineering, Xinhua News Agency, May 28, 2018.

market, andsociety.

Consistently Reinforcing Basic Research

Basic research is the foundation of the scientific research chain, from research to application and production. A solid foundation is essential for building a robust scientific and technological edifice. Today, with rapid changes in scientific research paradigms and shortened global basic research cycles, there's an urgent need to bolster basic research to address key technological challenges at their source and core.

On February 21, 2023, the Political Bureau of the CPC Central Committee conducted a collective study session on strengthening basic research. General Secretary Xi Jinping highlighted that bolstering basic research is imperative for achieving high-level self-reliance in science and technology and is crucial for building China into a world leader in science and technology.[1]

With its ever-increasing capacity for zero-to-one innovation over recent years, China has incubated a string of major innovations that command international influence, with the completion of heavyweight projects including the Five-hundred-meter Aperture Spherical Radio Telescope (FAST), the Steady High Magnetic Field Facility (SHMFF), the China Spallation Neutron Source (CSNS), as well as breakthroughs in such fields as quantum computing, synthetic starch, nano-confined catalysis.

Basic research is the wellspring of scientific and technological self-reliance and self-strength. Only through basic research can we transform uncertainties into certainties and unknowns into knowns. As we enter the era of mega-science, basic research is organized in an increasingly sophisticated way, and its output is increasingly influenced by institutional support and policy guidance.

To advance basic research, we must first optimize the structure of basic disciplines. By supporting the growth of key subjects, emerging subjects, less popular subjects, and underdeveloped subjects, we will foster a high-quality disciplinary system to underpin basic research and original innovation. Second, we must diversify funding for basicresearch to cater to its various forms, and ensure financial support for the

---

[1] Xi Jinping emphasizes strengthening basic research to solidify the foundation for self-reliance and self-strength in science and technology at the third collective study session of the Political Bureau of the CPC Central Committee, Xinhua News Agency, Feb 22, 2023.

continuous emergence of groundbreaking, frontier achievements.

Regarding major scientific issues and strategic needs, we must make systematic and visionary plans and layouts by coordinating strategy-oriented systematic basicresearch, frontier-oriented exploratory basic research, and market-oriented applied basic research. To secure leadership in cutting-edge technologies and protect it with institutional innovations, we will enhance comprehensive planning and integrated deployment across the entire spectrum, from basic research to key technologies, equipment development, and application of scientific advancements.

Empowering Enterprises to Drive Innovation

Enterprises are the principal organizers and participants in sci-tech innovation, and are vital for nurturing new high quality productive forces. Enhancing their role as the main innovators is crucial for achieving high-level self-reliance and continuous sci-tech advancements.

By the end of 2023, China had 427,000 enterprises with valid invention patents, an increase of 72,000 from the previous year. Enterprises possessed 2.909 million valid invention patents, accounting for 71.2% of the total, surpassing the 70% mark for the first time.The share of corporate R&D investment in the total society R&D input has exceeded 75% for consecutive years, which underscores the growing prominence of enterprises as the backbone of innovation.

As part of its efforts to accelerate the development of new quality productive forces, China has implemented multiple measures to reinforce the principal role of enterprises in sci-tech innovation, including enhancing enterprises' principal role in innovation decision-making by supporting their broader and deeper participation in national sci-technology innovation policies; bolstering their leading role in R&D investment by stepping up the implementation of policies such as additional deductions for R&D expenses and integrating science, technology, industry, and finance; and strengthening their central role in scientific research organizations by allowing them to lead in key technological breakthrough projects, includingmajor special projects and engineering initiatives.

The key to bridging the "last mile" in the application of sci-tech advances lies with enterprises. China will continue to improve laws and regulations on the application of sci-tech advances, and remove policy barriers related to the rights to use, disposal, and benefit from sci-tech achievements. We will enhance mechanisms for synergizing industry-academia-research outcomes with industrialization, support enterprises in building pilot verification platforms, and improve their ability to commercialize sci-tech achievements. By leveraging the driving force of leading enterprises and the supporting role of SMEs, we aim to foster a comprehensive industrial ecosystem where the entire industrial chain is interlinked and integrated.

The advancement of new quality productive forces necessitates a surge of high-caliber, multi-disciplinary entrepreneurs in science and technology. They should have an innovative spirit and scientific acumen to recognize the value of new scientific discoveries, and have the ability to mobilize production factors around innovation, coordinating effortsacross industry, academia, and research. China is fostering a favorable environment for entrepreneurs skilled in scientific innovation, business models, and management methods to standout.

2. Sci-tech Innovation as a Driving Force for Industrial Innovation

Throughout the course of modern history, every leap-frog development in productivity has been fueled by scientific and industrial revolution. However, only under adequate socioeconomic conditions can scientific advancements spur industrial upgrades.

Currently, we are embracing a new wave of scientific innovations, including artificial intelligence, clean energy, and biotechnology. Countries are boosting new growth drivers via industrial revolution strategies, including USA's Advanced Manufacturing Partnership (AMP), Germany's Plattform Industrie 4.0, Japan's "JAPAN is BACK", France's "Nouvelle France Industrielle", and UK's High Value Manufacturing Catapult (HVMC).

During the process of Chinese modernization, the establishment of a modern industrial system has become the prerequisite for accelerating the cultivation of new quality productive forces.

Upgrading Traditional Industries

China's relatively comprehensive industrial system has placed the country in an important position in global labor division as well as industrial and supply chain. It is important to sustain and fully leverage our advantages in our world-leading industries.

Traditional manufacturing forms a crucial cornerstone in advancing the national economy and satisfying the everyday needs of the population. Giving traditional industries a "new" and "quality" dimension means prioritizing high-end, intelligent, and green approaches. This includes accelerating structural upgrades, innovating technological pathways, and optimizing development models to effectively enhance quality and foster balanced growth in quantity.

To prioritize high-end approaches entails accelerating the R&Dandwiderapplica tionofadvancedpracticaltechnologiesin traditional industries so as to further solidify their existing strengths. To bridge gaps in the industry chain, enhance synergy between upstream and downstream sectors, and expand in both directions, enterprises are encouraged to delve deeply into specialized niches, incubate new technologies, seek new domains, and foster new industries. By thoroughlyimplementing an industrial foundation reconstruction project, we aim to strengthen the support system for the traditional manufacturing industry.

To prioritize intelligent approaches necessitatesaccelerating the adoption of digital technology to empower enterprises in innovating connectivity solutions, and integrating AI, big data, cloud computing, 5G, IoT, and other technologies deeply into the manufacturing process and all aspects. Collaborative networking within industrial and supply chains will be facilitated to advancing the overall transformation and upgrade of industrial parks and clusters.

To prioritize green approaches calls for accelerated innovation and wide application of green technologies, so as to strengthen green manufacturing, service, and energy industries. Green and low-carbon industries and supply chains should be cultivated to establish a sustainable, recycling economic system and increase the share of eco-friendly industrial growth.

According to the joint Guiding Opinions by the Ministry of Industry and Information Technology, the National Development and Reform Commission, the Ministry of Education, the Ministry of Finance, the People's Bank of China, State Taxation Administration, National Financial Regulatory Administration, and China Securities Regulatory Commission, by 2027, the level of high-end, intelligent, green, and integrated development in traditional manufacturing industries will significantly improve. This advancement will effectively support the manufacturing industry's share, maintaining a basic stability and further consolidating and enhancing its position and competitiveness in the global industrial division of labor. The popularity rates of digital research and development tools in industrial enterprises will exceed 90%, while the rates of key process digitization will reach around 70%. Industrial energy consumption intensity and carbon dioxide emissions intensity will continue to decrease. Water consumption per 10,000 yuan of industrial added value will decrease by about 13% compared with 2023.The comprehensive utilization rate of bulk industrial solid waste will exceed 57%.

Currently, China is forwarding a new round of large-scale equipment renewals and trade-in of old consumer goods. According to the action plan issued by the State Council, priority industries include petrochemicals, steel, non-ferrous metals, building materials, machinery, automobiles, light industry, textiles, and electronics. Efforts will be made to advance the update of advanced equipment, digital transformation,promotion of green equipment, and enhancement of safetylevels.

Comprehensive efforts will be made to promote equipment upgrading and technological transformation, laying a solid foundation for the transformation and upgrading of traditional industries.

Fostering Emerging Industries

Emerging industries of strategic importance are at the forefront of technological and economic development. They play a leading role in the long-term socioeconomic development, and, to a large extent, determine the comprehensive strength, especially the core competitiveness, of a country or region.

Emerging industries of strategic importance are important vehicles for new quality productive forces. In September 2023, General Secretary Xi Jinping pointed out at a meeting on promoting the fullrevitalization of northeast China in the new era that: "It is necessary to foster strategic emerging industries including new energy, new materials, advanced manufacturing and electronic information, and nurture industries of the future, in a bid to create new quality productive forces boosters and new growth impetus."[1]

Emerging industries of strategic importance are industrial leaders, featuring a novel growth pattern of integration and clustering. Such strategic industrial clusters within a certain geographic space enable the organic integration of talents, technology, and capital to maximize benefits, thereby becoming an important trend in China's industrial development.

---

[1] Xi Jinping presides over a meeting on promoting the full revitalization of northeast China in the new era and stresses firmly grasping the important mission of northeast China, so a stowriteanew chapter for the full revitalization of northeast China, Xinhua News Agency, Sept 9, 2023.

In March 2024, 18 AI application scenario are presented in Nanjing, China, with focuses on "AI+Industry", "AI+Electricity", "AI+Transportation", "AI+Medicine", and "AI+Information Consumption". These scenarios serve as pioneer projects for the coordination between underlying technologies and their application, so as to explore and implement more promising artificial intelligence innovation models and product directions.

China is seizing the opportunity to develop emerging industries of strategic importance. It is building a number of internationally competitive advanced industrial clusters in fields such as new information technology, artificial intelligence, biotechnology, new energy, new materials, high-end equipment, and environmental protection, so as to construct a set of distinctive, complementary, and structurally sound engines of growth with their own advantages.

In order to promote the integrated development of strategic emerging industry cluster, it is also necessary to take a series of measures, including the deployment of the innovation chain based on the industrial chain, the refinement of the construction of an ecological civilization, the expansion of application of new technologies, and optimization of digital platforms.

To align the innovation chain with the industrial chain, it is crucial to fully leverage the advantages of leading enterprises, platform effects, and demonstration effect, promotingintegration and coordinated development throughout the industry chain.

To refine the construction of an ecological civilization, and expand the application of new technologies, government investment should further drive investment society-wide. The government should support localities to fully leverage their endowments for future development and establish their trademark market segments, so as to fuel development in education, science & technology, and human resources by industrialdemands.

Building digital platforms will accelerate the integration of digital technologies with the real economy. Digitalization necessitates integrating companies in the industrial chain, research institutions, and the public sector to achieve comprehensive system integration and resource sharing.

Laying the Groundwork for Future-oriented Industries

Future-oriented industries are pioneers of reshaping global innovation and economic landscapes. They are the key to keeping China well-positioned for pursuing future development.

General Secretary Xi Jinping attributes great importance to the growth of future-oriented industries and has provided a series of important instructions, decisions and plans accordingly. The Outline for the 14th Five-Year Plan for Economic and Social Development and Long-Range Objectives through to the Year 2035 of the People's Republic of China stated that, "In brain-like intelligence, quantum information, genetic technology, future network, deep-sea and aerospace exploration, hydrogen energy and energy storage, and other areas of cutting-edge technology and industrial transformation,we will organize and implement the plan for incubating and accelerating industries of the future, and plan and create a layout for such industries of the future." China's future-oriented industries are embarking on a clear path of development, and the blueprint for the development of key areas is gradually unfolding.

Currently, future-oriented industries are becoming the key to new growth engines at the central and local levels. They aim to create new pillar industries and industrial clusters of hundreds of billions or even trillions of RMB. Moreover, by promoting the transformation and upgrading of traditional advantaged industries through extensive empowerment, they can greatly contribute to the enhancement, supplement, and extension of industrial and supply chains.

In November 2022, the Ministry of Science and Technology and the Ministry of Education approved the Pilot and Cultivation List of Future-Oriented Industry Science Parks, establishing 10 pilot SCI-TECH parks in Beijing, Shanghai, Jiangsu, Hubei, Guangdong, Sichuan, Shanxi, and Heilongjiang. In August 2023, General Office of the Ministry of Industry and Information Technology issued the Notification to Open the Bidding for Selecting the Best Candidates for Innovation Tasks of Future Industries in 2023. The Notification Stated that in order to accelerate the application of new technologies and products, the bidding and selection focuses on four key areas: the metaverse, humanoid robots, brain-computer interfaces, and general artificial intelligence.

Based on their scientific and technological capacities as well as industrial foundations, regions are actively investing in future industries. Places such as Beijing, Shanghai, Zhejiang, Guangdong, and Shenzhen have taken the lead in issuing development plans, action plans, implementation schemes, and supporting policies for future industries. They consider the forward-looking layout of future industries as a key strategy for long-term economic development.

China's future-oriented industries are experiencing a critical phase featuring drastic enhancements in innovation, coverage, and comprehensive strengths. It is vital to adopt new ideas and measures to adapt to such industrial development. Temporal and special layouts should also be planned for these industries. Currently the technology roadmaps of future industries are yet to be clarified and their business models remain immature. Therefore, instead of a deluge of stimuli, future industries require delicately regulated supporting measures—focus should be given to consolidating the foundation of development, supporting the newly established and more vulnerable entities, stepping up original innovation, and supporting scene marketing. It is also crucial to innovate regulatory models, increase institutional supply, and create an environment that encourages innovation as well as trials and errors.

3. Developing New Quality Productive Forces According to Local Conditions

Whether in scientific and technological innovation or industrial innovation, the key is to be practical, build on a strong scientific and technological foundation, and effectively leverage one's own advantages.

At the second session of the 14th National People's Congress (NPC) held in March 2024, General Secretary Xi joined a deliberation with fellow deputies from the delegation of Jiangsu province, during which he stressed, "We must firmly adhere to the top priority of high-quality development and develop new quality productive forces according to local conditions." "Developing new quality productive forces does not mean neglecting or abandoning traditional industries." He said, "It is necessary to prevent a headlong rush into projects and the formation of industry bubbles, and avoid adopting just a single model of development."[1]

His emphasis on "adapting to local conditions" embodies Marxist epistemology and methodology, and points the way for different regions of China to develop new quality productive forces in line with their own strengths.

"Adapting measures to local conditions" not only accurately grasps the Chinese context but also demonstrates a profound understanding of the laws of innovation.

---

[1] Xi Jinping emphasizes developing new quality productive forces according to local conditions at the Deliberation Session of the Jiangsu Delegation, Xinhua News Agency, March 5, 2024.

The development of new quality productive forces involves multiple aspects such as technological innovation, industrial upgrading, organizational management, and talent cultivation. Different regions have variations in resource endowment, functional capabilities, industrial foundations, and research conditions. Therefore, the approaches to developing new quality productive forces may differ. It is essential not to overlook the laws of innovation, industrial dynamics, and specific conditions while taking action. It is necessary to adhere to practicality, seek truth from facts, and explore a path for the development of new quality productive forces that is in line with actualcircumstances.

The success of new quality productive forces hinges not only on being new, but primarily on maintaining high quality.

Drawing insights from past experience and the current context, when it comes to using technological advancement to fuel industrial innovation, the course of history is never precisely the same. Henceforth, there have never been a one-size-fits-all shortcut for one to mindlessly imitate. It is essential to focus on the national regional innovation layout, drawing from local distinctive advantages and grassroots explorations, to find a reasonable path for innovative development, while avoiding homogenous models.

To develop new quality productive forces, it is important to emphasize the application and commercialization of innovative achievements. Innovations should not be kept within laboratories, but rather should be transformed into industrial products and market commodities. When accelerating the commercialization of scientific and technological achievements, it is vital to pay greater attention to the practical problems regarding local socioeconomic development. The industrial chain and the innovation chain should be integrated, so as to speed up the transformation of innovation into productive forces and to strengthen the internal momentum of the localities.

To develop new quality productive forces, it is crucial to refrain from involution and homogenous competition. Planning and implementing industrial upgrades need not be all-encompassing, nor should they focus solely on certain domains or products. Instead, localities should tap into their comparative strengths to ensure complementarity.

To develop new quality productive forces, it is vital to step up cooperation among departments and the integration among the sci-tech chain, industrial chain, policy chain, human resource chain, and financial chain, so as to avoid problems triggered by localities working in isolation. It is therefore crucial to ensure a coordinated nationwide approach, so as to properly arrange and showcase each region's strengths, highlighting the overall advantages of the country.

Scientific and technological advancements require urgency but cannot be rushed. To properly fuel development with innovation, China must adhere to the core element of scientific and technological innovation and the pillar of industrial innovation. Only by adhering to overall planning and taking into account various factors can we unleash a torrent of technological innovation achievements and strengthen the consistent and potent growth of new quality productive forces.

III. Forging a New Type of Relations of Production Compatible With New Quality Productive Forces

"The relations of production must meet the requirements for developing productive forces. To develop new productive forces, it is imperative to deepen reform across the board so as to create a new type of relations of production that is compatible with the development of new productive forces."[1]

——President Xi Jinping

Developing new quality productive forces is not just a proposition for development, but also one for reform.

General Secretary Xi Jinping pointed out,"Reform is the key to unleashing and developing productive forces, it is what stimulates the development of our country"[2], "To develop new quality productive forces, it is imperative to deepen reform across the board to create a new type of relations of production that is compatible with the development of new quality productive forces."

When referring to the history of industrial development, it is evident that any country aiming to lead the global technological and industrial revolution must establish a new

---

① Xi Jinping stresses development of new productive forces, high-quality development at the 11th group study session of the CPC Central Committee, Feb 1, 2024.

② Excerpt from Xi Jinping's speech at a meeting with experts from economic and social sectors, Xinhua News Agency, Aug 24, 2020.

institutional system that can better stimulate and protect innovation compared to its counterparts. This new system constitutes the vehicle for core national competitiveness. Therefore, the competition among nations in terms of new quality productive forces appears to be a competition of new technologies and industries, but essentially, it is a competition of institutional systems between countries. The country that can first provide market mechanisms, industrial regulations, financial systems, and industrial policies that match the latest technological and industrial trends will be able to emerge victorious in the global competition of new quality productive forces.

1. Advancing Comprehensive Reforms to Enhance the Efficient and Synergistic Allocation of New Quality Production Factors

The development of new quality productive forces requires both proactive guidance and appropriate policy support from the government, as well as innovation from micro-level entities such as market mechanisms and enterprises. It is formed and driven by the combined efforts of the government's "visible hand" and the market's "invisible hand".

Since the launch of the reform and opening up, the CPC, through continuous theoretical explorations and practices, has proposed the theoretical innovation of the development of a market economy under socialism, and has established and refined China's socialist market economy. Since the 18th CPC National Congress, China has, centered on the drive to build a high-level socialist market economy, accelerated the effort to improve basic systems underpinning the market economy, such as those for property rights protection, market access, fair competition, and social credit, as well as to work unswervingly both to consolidate and develop the public sector and to encourage, support, and guide development of the non-public sector, laying an institutional foundation for the efficient and synergistic allocation of various factors of production.

Ensuring a Solid Understanding of the Emerging Traits in New Quality Production Factors

Compared with traditional productive forces, new quality productive forces are ones that incorporate new quality factors of production. Fueled by the new wave of technological advancement, laborer, instruments of labor, and objects of labor have been through major upgrades, combinational optimization, and innovative allocation. It is imperative to sustain a vigilant awareness of the evolving qualities in new quality production factors.

A workforce of a higher caliber is the primary factor of new quality productive forces.The new type of labor is the most active and the most determinant factor of new quality productive forces. Unlike traditional workers who primarily engage in simple repetitive labor, the new type of labor represents the transformation of modern workforce. They are innovative strategic talents capable of creating new quality productive forces and adept at mastering new productive materials. These workers are better educated, with stronger learning abilities, and command traditional occupational skills alongside proficiency in digitalized and intelligent work settings. They also possess comprehensive inter-disciplinary abilities.

The new workforce includes the following types of personnel: top-notch technological talents who lead the world's technological frontier and innovate to create new types of production tools, especially those who make significant scientific and technological breakthroughs; technological leaders who make outstanding contributions in the fields of fundamental research and core technologies; engineering and technical talents, including outstanding engineers and skilled craftsmen; daring and proactive entrepreneurs with strategic thinking, adept at seizing cutting-edge technologies and industry trends. They persistently invest in innovative projects, propelling industrial innovation through technological advancements.

Advanced instruments of labor are the power source of new quality productive forces. The integration and application of new generation information technology, advanced manufacturing technology, new materials technology, and others have given birth to a large number of smarter, more efficient, lower-carbon, and safer instruments of production.Fundamental transformation has taken place regarding instruments of production, which used to be dominated by traditional machinery. The wide application of advanced tools such as the industrial internet and industrial software has drastically enlarged the pool of production instruments. Laboring process is currently transitioning into production and collaboration featuring platform-orientation, ecological friendliness, sharing, and online occupation. This promotes the organic integration of the digital economy and the real economy, greatly enhancing productivity and economic efficiency.

As an important component of instruments of labor, new infrastructure is the foundation and pillar of new quality productive forces. The new type of infrastructure, with information network infrastructure at its core, is characterized by digitization, networking, and intelligence. It includes high-speed networks, big data centers, and intelligent logistics systems. China is accelerating the construction of a comprehensive, efficient, practical, intelligent, green, safe, and reliable modern infrastructure system. This will provide the necessary conditions for the emergence of new types of labor objects and the application of new labor tools.

A broader range of objects of labor is the material foundation of new quality productive forces. Sci-tech developments have brought radical changes to objects of labor. On the one hand, humans have developed more advanced means to acquire materials and energy from the natural world, expanding the scope of utilization and transformation of nature to include deep space, deep sea, deep underground, etc.; on the other hand, material resources have been created via labor and transformed into objects of labor, thereby drastically enhancing productivity. The extensive integration of new objects of labor such as data across industries will unlock significant productivity gains.

Under a new round of technological revolution and industrial transformation, laborers, labor instruments, labor objects, and production methods are undergoing transformative adjustments. This promotes the convenient flow, networked sharing, systematic integration, collaborative development, and efficient utilization of factors such as labor, capital, land, knowledge, technology, management, and data, thereby accelerating the formation of new quality productive forces.

Adopting New Means to Allocate Factors of Production

On 31 January 2024, when hosting the Group Study Session of the Political Bureau of the CPC Central Committee, General Secretary Xi stressed that it is vital to focus on clearing hindrances to the development of new quality productive forces, establish a unified market that adheres to high standards, adopt new means to allocate factors of production, and ensure the smooth translation from advanced high-quality factors of production to new quality productive forces.[1]

Deepening reform lies at the core of the drive for innovative allocation of factors of production.

——Deepening the reform for the market-based allocation of production factors.

The 19th CPC National Congress clearly identified the market-based allocation of

---

[1] Xi Jinping stresses development of new productive forces, high-quality development at the 11th group study session of the CPC Central Committee, Feb 1, 2024.

production factors as one of the key focuses of economic reform. The Fourth Plenary Session of the 19th CPC Central Committee further stressed that China should promote market rules for production factors, and ensure market-oriented pricing for factors, free and orderly flow of factors, and efficient and fair allocation of factors. Issued in 2020, the Opinions of the CPC Central Committee and the State Council on Improving the Systems and Mechanisms for Market-based Allocation of Factors of Production listed five areas for the reform of production factor, namely land, labor, capital, technology, and data.

China is continuously deepening the reform for the market-based allocation of production factors. At the beginning of 2024, China issued the Three-Year Action Plan (2024-2026) for "Data Elements X" which stressed the necessity of "maximizing the amplification, superposition and multiplication role of data elements". Compared to the previous campaign of "InternetPlus", "Data Elements X" fully considered the innovative allocation of production factors.

——Speeding up the creation of a national unified market.

Market has become the world's scarcest resource. China's large market possesses the advantages of abundant application scenarios and amplified innovation income. Accelerating the construction of a unified national market can promote the orderly flow and rational allocation of innovative factors, supporting the transformation from technological innovation to industrial innovation. It can also better leverage economies of scale and agglomeration effects, further reducing market transaction costs. Moreover, it allows higher-quality goods and services to standout in market competition, creating favorable conditions for the continuous emergence of new quality productive forces.

Recent years have seen a series of accomplishments in the construction of China's unified national market, including the rolling out of registration-based IPO rules across all market, the pilot program of the marketization of rural collectively-owned commercial construction land, the construction of a national unified electricity market and carbon market. At the same time, a number of policies and measures that impede the unified market and fair competition have been abolished, revised, or rectified. Complementary policies have been introduced to improve property rights, market access, fair competition, credit, among other aspects.

In the next step, China will continue to dismantle local protectionism and regional barriers, aiming to create a favorable environment for business entities. The country will optimize the allocation of resource and industries. It will establish a multi-level cultivation and development system featuring provincial-level, national-level, and world-level clusters, so as to promote the orderly transfer of domestic manufacturing industries.

——Building a high-standard market system.

To clear the impediment to the development of new quality productive forces, it is fundamental to provide institutional support for the innovative optimization of resource allocation.

The establishment of China's high-standard market system constitutes a fundamental reform, featuring unification, inclusiveness, orderly competition, well-founded system, and fine governance. The system includes high-standard institutions, high-standard factor market system, high-standard market environment and quality, high-standard market infrastructure, high-standard market openness, and high-standard modern market regulatory mechanisms.

With regard to the underlying mechanism of the high-standard market system, strict protection of property rights is the fundamental driving force to stimulate the vitality of business entities. The implementation of negative list for market access is the prerequisite for the formulation of a unified national market. Fair competition is an effective mechanism for market operation that promotes full competition among business entities and facilitates the survival of the fittest.

The construction of a high-standard market system places greater emphasis on the completeness of institutions, fair competition, and the importance of government intervention to rectify market failures and maintain market order. In summary, it is crucial to ensure the market's decisive role in resource allocation with effective government intervention, so as to foster optimal synergy between an efficient market and a well-functioning government.

Enhancing Factor Participation in Income Distribution Mechanism

Ensuring broader factor participation in income distribution mechanisms is of great theoretical and practical significance to the construction of a vibrant environment that stimulates the proactiveness, initiative, and creativity of various factors of production.

New quality productive forces place higher requirements on the innovative allocation of traditional quantity-based factors such as land, capital, and labor. New forms of factors such as artificial intelligence, green energy, data, aerospace, deep sea, and frequency are emerging at an accelerated pace. Quality-based factors including knowledge, technology, and management are playing increasingly important roles. Enhancing such factors' participation in the income distribution mechanism is an integral part of the efforts to adapt to the relations of productions deriving from the new quality productiveforces.

The Fourth Plenary Session of the 19th CPC Central Committee identifies "the system of multiple modes of distribution with 'to each according to his contribution' as its principal form" as a key component of the socialist market economy. The 20th CPC National Congress highlighted the need to improve policies and institutions for distribution based on factors of production.

China is working to improve the distribution mechanism for the following areas: 1) labor: China is working to give more weight to work remuneration in primary distribution, so as to keep distribution according to work as the mainstay; 2) capital: China is promoting the reform and development of capital markets and improving a mechanism where risks match with gains; 3) land: the country is undertaking more targeted and more effective approaches to allocate land resources, establishing and optimizing a mechanism for the distribution of incremental benefits from land; 4) knowledge: a virtuous cycle is being established in society where knowledge creation generates value, and the creators of value receive fair rewards; 5) technology: a sound mechanism to implement equity, stock options, and profit-sharing incentives for researchers is being established; 6) management: mid-to-long-term incentives such as employee stock ownership, equity incentives, and stock dividend measures are being utilized in a coordinated manner; 7) data: China is establishing and improving rules regarding data ownership, openness, sharing, and transactions, enabling data owners to obtain rightful benefits from datautilization.

Ensuring a Smooth Virtuous Cycle of Education, Science and Technology and Talents

President Xi emphasized that "in accordance with the requirements of developing new quality productive forces, the virtuous cycle of education, science and technology and talents should be smooth". [1]He also highlighted the importance of "deepening

---

[1] Xi Jinping stressed development of new productive forces, high-quality development at the 11th group study session of the CPC Central Committee, Feb 1,2024.

reforms in systems including sci-tech, education and talent management".[①]

Education is a crucial foundation for developing new quality productive forces; science and technology serve as its core components; and talents is its primary resource. China prioritizes education, self-reliance in science and technology, and talent cultivation to drive pioneering development, strengthen resource allocation, and activate key engines for new dynamics and advantages.

It is imperative to deepen structural scientific and technological reform. To boost innovation, it is vital to deepen reforms in the science and technology management system, giving research institutions more autonomy and scientists increased authority in making decisions on technical directions and funding use. In response to the questions of "Who to innovate for?" "Who should innovate?" "What to innovate?", and "How to innovate?", comprehensive deployment should be made for the entire chain of technology innovation, including decision-making on technological innovation, research and development investment, scientific research organization, and outcome commercialization. In addition, it is essential to strategically plan key innovation resources such as policies, funding, projects, platforms, and talent.

It is also imperative to deepen structural educational reform. To fully unleash the potential of human resources and boost innovation development, it is crucial to promote collaborative innovation in vocational education, higher education, and continuing education and promote integration between vocational education and general education, between industry and education, and between science and education. It is vital to align closely with national strategies and industry demands and make adjustments and optimizations to the discipline layout, structure, and program offerings in universities. Whether it is in basic education, higher education, or vocational education, emphasis should be placed on stimulating the innovative thinking and creative abilities of talents.

It is also imperative to deepen the reform of the institutional mechanism for talent development. We should expedite the formation of mechanisms that foster talent development, mechanisms that maximize talent utilization, incentive structures that promote growth competition, and competitive mechanisms that encourage diverse

---

① Xi Jinping stressed development of new productive forces, high-quality development at the 11th group study session of the CPC Central Committee, Feb 1,2024

talent emergence. It is important to refrain from "one-size-fits-all" standards and to accelerate the construction of a talent evaluation system oriented to innovation value, ability and contribution. Proactive measures should be taken to lighten the load for talents, offering them sufficient trust and an open environment for their development. Especially for long-term research and development projects in fundamental science and technological applications, it is import ant to maintain strategic patience. Mechanisms such as "open bidding for selecting the best candidates" and "open competition for selecting the top candidates to lead key research projects" should be properly implemented. It is crucial to implement a more open and inclusive international strategy for cooperation in science and technology, thereby facilitating the cross-regional circulation channels for education, science and technology, and talent factors, so as to welcome talents from all over the world to help booster China's development.

2. Adhering to the Path of High-standard Opening up to Foster a World Class Business Environment

China's economic development achievements have been realized in an environment of openness. Therefore, the development of new quality productive forces and the high-quality development of China's economy will also be based on broader opening-up.

General Secretary Xi stressed, "high-level opening up must be expanded to create a sound international environment for the development of new quality productive forces". [1] Facing an increasingly complex international environment and exacerbating uncertainties, China continues to promote high-standard opening up and foster a world-class business environment that is market-oriented, law-based, and internationalized, providing solid support for the development of new quality productive forces.

Optimizing the Allocation of Global Resources

High-quality capital, key resources, advanced technology, and top-notch talent are crucial for the development of new quality productive forces. The allocation of global resources is taking on a new momentum. While persistently advancing high-level

---

[1] Xi Jinping stresses development of new productive forces, high-quality development at the 11th group study session of the CPC Central Committee, Feb 1, 2024.

opening up, China is leveraging the strength of its enormous market, attracting global resources and production factors with a strong domestic economy, and amplifying the interplay between domestic and international markets and resources, thus creating an innovation ecosystem with global competitiveness.

Since the launch of the reform and opening up, China has played three vital roles in economic globalization: 1) deeply-engaged participant: China is deeply involved in division of labor along the global value chain in manufacturing; 2) proactive promoter: China has made tremendous contribution to world economic growth; 3) collaborative innovator: China is working with countries around the world to promote a new round of technological revolution and industrial transformation.

According to foreign press, China is actively promoting the formation of a global technology ecosystem and gradually emerging as an irreplaceable participant in international scientific and technological cooperation. It has become a magnet for global innovation resources and elements.

China's position in the global division of labor has been steadily rising, building a solid foundation for the country to engage at a higher level in the global economy and attract global resources and production factors. Faced with a complex international environment, China is releasing stronger signals of openness with a series of proactive measures.

China has initiated pilot programs for market access in value-added telecommunications and other sectors, and has fully lifted restrictions on foreign investment in the manufacturing industry. China issued the Action Plan for Steadily Advancing High-level Opening up and Making Greater Efforts to Attract and Utilize Foreign Investment, rolled out national and pilot free trade zone (FTZ) versions of negative lists for cross-border trade in services, and published Provisions on Promoting and Regulating Cross-border Data Flow. An implementation plan for Pudong's pilot comprehensive reform between 2023 and 2027 proposed a series of measures including exploring the implementation of capital account convertibility and the pilot use of digital RMB in trade settlement, e-commerce payment, carbon trading, green power trading, etc. Other measures include hosting major events such as China International Import Expo, Canton Fair, the China International Fair for Trade in Services, Global Digital Trade Expo, China International Consumer Products Expo, as well as establishing two-way opening-up platforms.

China is opening its door wider, optimizing the allocation of resource factors on a global scale, so as to create a better environment for the development of new quality productive forces.

Expanding Institutional Opening Up

Compared with opening up based on flows of goods and factors of production, institutional opening up is the opening up of a higher level. Removing institutional and regulatory barriers can effectively amplify the interplay between domestic and international markets and resources, giving full play to the advantages in bringing together innovative factors on a global scale.

General Secretary Xi stressed that centering around fostering a new development pattern, institutional opening up should be the focus when it comes to further reform of systems and mechanisms in such key areas for international exchange and opening up as investment, trade, finance, and innovation, so as to improve supporting policies and measures, and proactively elevate the country's opening up to a higher level.[1]

China is further expanding its institutional opening up. Through continued integration opening up efforts of coastal and inland regions, it is exploring institutional rules appropriate to their linkage development; through continued integration of "bring in" and "go global" strategies, it is creating a new platform for international cooperation; through continued integration of manufacturing and services sectors' opening up efforts, it is crafting new rules and standards to promote opening up in areas such as education, medical care, finance; through continued integration of multilateral opening up and regional opening up, it is participating in the push for global institutional opening up.

At present, China is advancing opening up, with institutional guarantees in the areas of management, standards, rules, and norms. It has increased the number of pilot free trade zones to 22, and improved the quality of existing pilot free trade zone. Pilot projects of comprehensively connecting with international high-standard economic and trade rules are being implemented in pilot free trade zones in Shanghai, Guangdong, Tianjin, Fujian, and Beijing, as well as Hainan Free Trade Port. The country

---

[1] Xi stresses establishing new systems for higher-level open economy and establishing and implementing the system for controlling both the total amount and intensity of carbon emissions when presiding over 2nd meeting of central committee for deepening overall reform, Xinhua News Agency, July 11, 2023.

is continuing to open up the modern services sector, establishing 11 Integrated National Demonstration Zones for Opening up the Services Sector. China is comprehensively and effectively implementing Regional Comprehensive Economic Partnership (RCEP), taking active steps to join the Comprehensive and Progressive Agreement for Trans-Pacific Partnership (CPTPP) and Digital Economy Partnership Agreement (DEPA). China is contributing to the creation of an open innovation ecosystem with global competitiveness.

Deepening International Cooperation

Advancing new quality productive forces is in line with China's vision of achieving high-quality development and the world's expectation of impetus from China. Particularly, in green development and digital reforms, there is tremendous potential for cooperation between China and its international partners. Deepening international cooperation in new quality productive forces is conducive to leveling up global industrial and supply chains, which will optimize the allocation of global resources to share opportunities for upgraded industries and high-quality development with all partner countries.

China is striving to deepen international cooperation, laying a solid foundation for fostering new quality productive forces. Specifically, China continues to promote high-quality cooperation under the Belt and Road Initiative (BRI) and achieve win-win cooperation based on extensive consultation, joint contribution, and shared benefits; China speeds up the construction of grand channels for international trade and logistics, such as the China-Europe Railway Express and the new western land-sea corridor, elevating connectivity to a next level; in firm support of the multilateral trade system, the country proactively engages in and build momentum for necessary WTO reforms, aiming to improve the globally-oriented free trade zone network with high standards.

In 2023, China made $130.1 billion in non-financial outbound direct investment with an 11.4% year-on-year growth, maintaining its position among the world's top three for 11 consecutive years. Foreign direct investment (FDI) from China to over 190 countries and regions across the world totaled $2.8 trillion, securing China's top-three position for six years in a row. By the end of 2023, China had directly invested over $300 billion in BRI partner countries and set up more than 100 overseas economic and trade cooperation zones, with the turnover of China's overseas contracted projects in BRI partners approaching$2 trillion. These numbers witnessed profound and concrete achievements in BRI investment and cooperation. In pursuit of deepening cooperation in green development, digital economy, and blue economy, China has signed 64 MOUs for investment and cooperation with 38 countries in related fields, established 70 bilateral investment and cooperation working groups with 60 countries, and founded 150 chambers of commerce for overseas Chinese enterprises in over 120 countries and regions.

General Secretary Xi Jinping pointed out that China can only do well when the world is doing well. When China does well, the world will get even better.[1]

To create opportunities with an open world economy and solve problems with cooperation is a precious experience that China gained in the expansion of opening up. The international cooperation driven by the new quality productive forces will deliver more extensive potential and beneficial practices.

IV. New Quality Productive Forces: Global Implications

"The world today is not peaceful. Withthe future of humankind and the well-being of its people in mind, China, as always, endeavors to contribute its wisdom and solutions to the cause of peace and development of mankind, advocate an equal and orderly multi-polar world and a universally beneficial and inclusive economic globalization."[2]

—President Xi Jinping

The development of productive forces is a common characteristic of achieving modernization in all countries. Since the industrial revolution, two centuries have witnessed a leap in the productive forces of a few modernized countries to varying degrees. However, by and large, the process of modernization in the world is never smooth sailing and still grappling with multiple challenges, including sluggish economic

---

[1] Keynote Speech at the Opening Ceremony of the Third Belt and Road Forum for International Cooperation by Xi Jinping, Xinhua News Agency, Oct 18, 2023.

[2] Xi Jinping Accepts Credentials of New Ambassadors to China, Xinhua News Agency, Jan 30, 2024

recovery, geopolitical tensions, trade protectionism, and deglobalization.

Against such a backdrop, the development of new quality productive forces illustrates not only China's focus and initiative on the great rejuvenation of the Chinese nation, but also its sense of responsibility to facilitate world peace, development, mutually beneficiary cooperation, and shared prosperity with China's modernization practices.

1. Boosting Global Economic Recovery and Sharing Opportunities for Development

China is playing a never more crucial role as the engine and cornerstone of the global economy. According to Bloomberg calculations using International Monetary Fund (IMF) forecasts, in total, 75% of global growth is expected to be concentrated in 20 countries over the next five years, and China will be the top contributor. Meanwhile, China will account for about 21% of the world's new economic activity from 2024 through 2029, compared with 20% for the G7.[①]

Playing a New Role as the Economic Engine

What factors allow China to stay as an engine foreconomic growth despite the world's struggles with economic transition?

A significant reason lies in China's optimism in embracing a new round of technological and industrial revolutions. Driven by developing new quality productive forces, China endeavors to leverage revolutionary breakthroughs in technology and innovative allocations of production factors to fuel industrial innovation, while exploring new areas, advantages, and arenas to foster new impetus.

Currently, new quality productive forces are motivating vitality and potential within the Chinese market, enhancing the resilience of China as an engine for the world economy. In 2023, the combined output of biomedicines, artificial intelligence, and nanotechnology applications, China's three major industries, exceeded $55 billion. And its digital economy is expected to achieve a gross value of $15.7 trillion in 2027. Additionally, China's endeavors to achieve carbon peaking and carbon neutrality are

---

① Bloomberg: China Outweighs G-7 as the Top Contributor to Global Economic Growth over the Next Five Years, Xinhua News Agency, April 20, 2024.

leading the building of a brand-new zero-carbon industrial system, while drawing substantial investments and generating numerous industrial opportunities. In renewable energy, China has become a veritable global leader. As outlined in the Global Wind Report 2024 released by the Global Wind Energy Council (GWEC), in 2023, a record-high 117 GW of new wind power was installed worldwide, representing a 50% hike from the previous year. However, if excluding China's contribution, the global wind power industry is caught in a stagnant growth.[1]

According to IMF analysis, China's economic growth has positive spillover effects on other regions across the world. A one percentage point increase in Chinese growth leads to a 0.3 percentage point increase over the medium-term to other economies in the region. [2] With the upgrading of traditional industries and prosperous emerging industries, new quality productive forces, while injecting new impetus into China's high-quality economic development, will bolster the expansion of the middle-income and the progress and upgrading of China's consumer markets. It is anticipated that China, as an economic engine, will yield more dividends for the world.

Creating Opportunities for Win-win Development

Expediting the development of new quality productive forces will pump up the unique advantages of China's market, creating more development opportunities for its international partners.

First, the development of new quality productive forces will bring an upswing in labor productivity, value added by industry, income of laborers, and welfare.By 2035, China's middle-income population is projected to reach 800 million, giving rise to stronger purchasing power. With new quality productive forces making headway, the production and lifestyles of the Chinese people move faster to digital and green transformation, which will generate new consumer demands for various and high-end products, diversifying the consumption scenarios in China. Driven by both purchasing power and consumer demands, a larger scale of imports in China will take shape, making the development opportunities in China's big market more accessible to its trade

---

① Foreign Media: Hyping China's "Green Overcapacity" Complicating the Global Energy Transition, Xinhua News Agency, April 22, 2024.

② China's Economic Fundamentals in the World Coordinate, Xinhua News Agency, Feb 8, 2024

partners.

Second, accelerating the development of new quality productive forces enables China to play a more essential role in the global innovation chain. A growing number of foreign-funded enterprises, engaged in crafting China's advanced industrial chain and updating its innovation chain, are concentrated on innovation, highlighting the R&D and exploration of high-value-added innovation technologies and services. For many multinational corporations (MNCs), China, beyond an important market, serves as a multiplier for innovation revenues.

Many MNCs are investing more in China, a vote of confidence in its innovative development. AstraZeneca, a biopharmaceutical company doing business in China for over three decades, will pour $475 million into building a small molecule drug factory in Wuxi and $700 million U.S. for an inhaled aerosol manufacturing site in Qingdao. Valeo, a French automotive supplier, has unveiled its Comfort and Driving Assistance Systems R&D Center in Shanghai. GE HealthCare China, a leading medical technology innovator,has committed to doubling its R&D spending over the next three years. Globally, it is hard to find another investment highland like China with such a massive scale and extensive potential. As new quality productive forces pick up steam, more foreign businesses will endorse that the "next China" is still China.

The irreplaceable role of China is proven by the MNCs' financial reports. In fiscal year 2023, Bosch, a German engineering and technology company, achieved a growth of over 5% year-on-year in its sales in China, with smart mobility serving as a major driver for its business in China. Apple's earnings in Greater China accounted for a fifth of its total revenue. Gigafactory Shanghai, with its efficiency topping the auto industry, has become a major global export hub for Tesla. In late April 2024, Elon Musk, CEO of Tesla, paid his second visit to China in less than 12 months. In addition, a large group of visionary foreign entrepreneurs, with their business acumen, have projected new opportunities sprouting from China's new quality productive forces.

2. Forming a New Type of Relations of Production and Expanding New Practices in Economic Governance

New quality productive forces, with enormous revolutionary energy, embody CPC's development and innovation to the Marxian Political Economy, while posing a new test for China's economic governance.

Currently, China is focusing on improving its own economic systems and enhancing economic governance capacity. Such a strategic initiative, demonstrating China's confidence in its systems, offers precious experience and examples for other developing countries in economic governance.

Responding to Global Challenges of Frontier Technology with Strategic Initiative

At present, China is veering away from the "trap of comparative advantages", which has become commonplace in developing countries. It indicates that China, though taking a leading position in the technological R&D and applications of many nascent fields, is wrestling with the challenges resulting from technological development. Therefore, China vigorously improves its policy planning, fills in the gaps in its systems, and explores the advantages of its systems and mechanisms, aiming to open up new horizons on a shifting landscape and seize the strategic initiative.

China has made a remarkable development in exploring systems for driving the digital economy. Since the 18th CPC National Congress, the Party Central Committee with Comrade Xi Jinping at its core has placed a great value on the digital economy, making data a fundamental strategic resource for China. In April 2020, the Party Central Committee and the State Council jointly issued the Guidelines on Improving the Market-based Allocation Mechanism of Production Factor, which marked the first time data was recorded in a central government's paper asa new production factor. Moreover, China has become the first country in the world to identify data as a factor of production in terms of national policy.

Since 2022, China's data factor market has been on the fast track of development. In December 2022, the Party Central Committee and the State Council jointly issued the Measures to Build Basic Systems for Data to Put Data Resources to Better Use, painting a blueprint for the prospect of the digital factor market. A year later, they released the Plan for the Overall Layout of Building a Digital China, mapping out goals and tasks for different stages with an overarching objective that China needs to top the world in digital development by 2035. Then, in March 2023, the Plan on Reforming Party and State Institutions was unveiled in a bid to establish the National Data Administration.

China's elevation of data to the status of a new type of production factor is in line with the trend of digital economy development. China is working hard to strengthen the foundation driven by data factors, maintain data sovereignty, and propel the digital economy, in order to build new strengths in digital competition. Meanwhile, China is engaged in international cooperation and rule-making on the digital economy, benefiting more countries and people with its achievements and experience gained in digital development.

China is a pioneer in responding to deficits in global digital governance and governance challenges in emerging digital fields. In 2020, China proposed the Global Initiative on Data Security to specify the government code of conduct and encourage enterprises to shoulder their responsibilities and cooperate to address data security risks. In 2023, the Interim Measures for the Management of Generative Artificial Intelligence Services released by China was the first specialized legislation for generative AI in the world. Also, China's Positions on Global Digital Governance submitted to the United Nations called on countries to narrow down the digital capacity gap and stand against technological monopoly.

China's initiatives and measures for data, the new factor of production, show case its resolve and efforts in enhancing China's economic governance capability to stimulate global economic governance reforms and unleash the potential and vitality of the global economy.

Inspiring the World with New Practices in Economic Governance

China motivates the new quality productive forces to galvanize systemic innovation and the reforms of production relations, which has struck a chord across the world.

The core of China's economic reforms lies in a proper government-market relationship. As put forward by General Secretary Xi Jinping, China will "let the market play the decisive role in allocating resources and let the government play its role better", stimulating innovation and breakthroughs in the theories and practices of the socialist market economy.

In terms of basic research and core technologies in key fields, China gathers strengths to improve the system with unified leadership of the Party Central Committee for science and technology work and the new system for mobilizing resources nationwide to make key technological breakthroughs. China will enhance its strategic science and technology with better allocation of innovation resources. In terms of the commercialization of technological results, China underscores the role of the market and encourages enterprises to engage in innovation, imbuing benefits and inspiration in both "the invisible hand" and "the visible hand".

With China's comprehensive deepening of reforms and improvement of economic governance, the methodology within Xi Jinping's Thoughts on Economy, such as "establishing the new before abolishing the old, seeking progress while maintaining stability, and promoting stability through progress", is drawing even more international attention.

Professor Anna Malindog-Uy, vice president of External Affairs at the Asian Century Philippines Strategic Studies Institute, spoke highly of President Xi Jinping's proposal of making industries "higher-end, smarter, and more eco-friendly". She regarded it as a forward-looking deployment that emphasizes both economic developments empowered by sci-tech achievements, digital economy, and green technology and the balance between economic growth, technological progress, and sustainable development.[1]

In the views of the international community, China has placed it in a crucial position to form a new type of production relations that is compatible with the new quality productive forces, guiding its economy toward maturity. With new quality productive forces taking shape and growing strong, China shows the tremendous strength and vitality of the socialistsystem with Chinese characteristics, offering China's plan for exploring better economic governance.

3. Empowering Chinese Modernization and Creating a New Form of Human Advancement

Every leap in human civilization has been driven by advancements in production forces. As China embarks on a new journey toward the great rejuvenation of the Chinese nation on all fronts through its unique path to modernization, it is fostering new quality productive forces to enhance its culture and civilization.

Fostering a Community of Life for Humanity and Nature

Industrialization, while creating an unprecedented amount of wealth and possessions, has caused indelible trauma to the ecosystems, adding to the conflict between people's unlimited wants and limited resources. Climate change has become one of the most severe challenges facing humanity. The traditional productive forces,

---

[1] Building a "New" Strength for China's Economy and a Better World for Prosperity—General Secretary Xi Jinping's Speech on Developing New Quality Productive Forces Arousing Heated Discussions among People Overseas, Xinhua News Agency, March 6, 2024

featuring reliance on investment inproduction factors and an extensive growth model with low efficiency and high pollution, can barely support economic sustainability.

Compared with traditional productive forces, new quality productive forces emphasize the innovation-driven inclusive growth of productive forces.A key part is to leverage knowledge, information, data, and computing power to advance industrial iteration and upgrading, thus reducing dependency on finite and depleting natural resources. Boosting a new round of productive forces, beyond technological innovation, is more about an in-depth understanding of a community of shared life for humanity and nature.

It has become a consensus across China that environment and civilization share weal and woe. The Chinese path to modernization features harmony between humanity and Nature. In this context, new quality productive forces are conducive to fostering green and low-carbon industries and promoting a thorough green transition in socio-economic development. As the development models of "treatment after pollution" and "to control and exploit the nature" fade into the past, an eco-cultural journey featuring harmony between humanity and Nature toward sustainable development is unfolding.

Highlighting a Caring and Humane Modernization Process

Chinese modernization is a new type of modernization oriented toward the people and the future. As stated by General Secretary Xi Jinping, "The ultimate goal of modernization is people's free and well-rounded development. For a modernization path to work and work well, it must put the people first."[1]

China's development of new quality productive forces aims to make the fruits of modernization benefit more people in a fairer way to advance their all-round development. Therefore, promoting new quality productive forces is integral to China's efforts to advance further progress in human rights.

New quality productive forces place more value onbuilding a high-caliber workforce and cultivating competent laborers, which steers the economic growth to a model driven by investment in people, instead of assets. China believes that only by achieving people's high-quality development in a more advanced and more extensive way can it lay a more solid foundation for continuously nurturing new quality productive forces.

---

[1] Keynote Address by President Xi Jinping at the CPC in Dialogue with World Political Parties High-level Meeting, Xinhua News Agency, March 15, 2023

Chinese modernization pursues common prosperity for all. As a populous country, China needs to create a large amount of social wealth for its huge population. Developing new quality productive forcesis beneficial to fostering new areas of economic growth and growth poles, thus sustaining economic increase and expanding social wealth. With a focus on motivating newquality productive forces, China improves its income distribution mechanism, which helps to narrow down the wealth gap and provides firm support for realizing common prosperity.

The development of new quality productive forces will bring new economic forms to human society, serving "the modernization of people". In that way, people present more engagement, creativity, and competence in modern production and life. The progress of new quality productive forces provides more possibilities for an all-round development of the people, underscoring a caring and humane modernization.

Boosting Developmental Confidence in the Global South and Fostering Mutual Learning Among Civilizations

Science and technology serve the progress of our era and the world at large. Empowered by new quality productive forces, the Chinese path to modernization is good news for the Global South. China's technological innovation, upgraded industries, and reform experience will help other developing countries to break new grounds in modernization, pushing the world economy toward a more diversified and balanced future.

China pursues not a self-centered modernization, but a common modernization jointly achieved by all developing countries. This vision is beckoning, yet challenging. For one thing, some countries, dominated by capital and resorting to financial expansion from industrial expansion, suffer from sluggish real economy and a widening wealth gap. A few countries even restrict the flow of innovation factors, such as knowledge, technology, and talent, and suppress the industries where other countries find their competitive advantages, impeding world development. For another, developing countries have long been trapped in their comparative advantages and find it difficult to break through the bottleneck of "dependent modernization" and impossible to advance their productive forces in an equal and independent manner.

If a country fails to become a key player and contributor in the new round of adjustments in the global economic governance system and global economic and trade rules, then it will lose its say and initiative in the new areas of the global economy and industrial development, which is a pressing issue for developing countries. In shaping the international innovation environment, China is committed to cheering for other developing countries to collectively promote the global flow of innovation factors and seek economic growth impetus. Also, China advocates that technological results should be a benefit to all people rather than a tool of restriction or containment to other countries' development. That's why China has published the International Science and Technology Cooperation Initiative to advocate implementing the concept of open, fair, just, and non-discriminatory international cooperation in science and technology, joining hands tobuild a global community of science and technology. Also, China has introduced the Global AI Governance Initiative to call on all countries to enhance information exchanges and technological cooperation, in order to develop AI governance frameworks, norms, and standards based on broad consensus.

China is also devoted to making BRI a road for innovation and building a technological innovation alliance and base with and for the BRI partner countries, so as to create new opportunities and platforms for the common development of all countries. China proposes capitalizing on the APEC mechanism for SMEs, with the APEC Forum on Promoting Specialized and Innovative Development of SMEs, to keep building consensuson the specialized and innovative development of SMEs.

Confronted with deglobalization and anti-globalization, China has always been propelling high-level institutional opening-up and technological innovation and advocating opening-up, communication, and integration among countries at deeper levels to collectively advance productive forces. Standing at a new crossroads of human development and facing unprecedented changes and dynamics, China remains an active player and determined supporter of economic globalization. China's motivation for new quality productive forces will unleash abundant new opportunities for the world. In pulling together to build a global community of shared future, China firmly believes that the international community can blaze a trail for win-win cooperation in advancing productive forces, thus opening a new chapter for sustainable prosperity and harmony among countries.

V. Mobilizing New Quality Productive Forces: Local Exploration and Practice

"Local governments should continue to proceed on a basis of reality, establish the new before abolishing the old, consider actual conditions, provide targeted guidance, and promote new industries, new models and new impetus in a selective way, in light of local resources, industrial basis, and research conditions, thus transforming traditional industries with new technologies and advancing high-end, smart and green industries."[1]

———President Xi Jinping

According to General Secretary Xi Jinping's important instructions and the decisions and plans of the Party Central Committee on developing new quality productive forces, all local governments in China, aligned with national development goals, are committed to practical, targeted measures to accelerate the cultivation and formation of new quality productive forces and ensure continual progress. Many typical cases have sprung up, providing new inspiration and opportunities for China's high-quality development.

1. Domestic Shipbuilding Industry Picks Up Speed

China's shipbuilding industry celebrated another milestone with the advancementof large cruiseships, its jewel in the crown. The second domestically-built large cruise ship started its final assembly, construction picking up speed.

On April 20, 2024, China's second homegrown large cruise ship, measuring 341 m in length, 37.2 m in width, and weighing over 142,000 tons, docked at the No.2 dock of Shanghai Waigaoqiao Shipbuilding Co., Ltd. (SWS), a subsidiary of China State Shipbuilding Corporation Limited (CSSC). This event marked a significant achievement in China's cruise ship mass design and construction capabilities.

In November 2023, the Adora Magic City, the first domestically-built large cruise ship, was named and delivered. Since then, China has secured its position in the global cruiseship industry. Adora Magic City completed its maiden commercial voyage in January 2024, becoming a part of people's lives.

Globally, China's large cruise ships have disrupted the long-standing monopoly held by the U.S. and European countries. Today, with China's vast consumer market

---

[1] Xi Jinping Underscoring the Development of New Quality Productive Forces Based on Local Conditions when Participating in the Deliberation of the Jiangsu Delegation, Xinhua News Agency, March 5, 2024.

and diverse application scenarios, these cruise ships are poised for significant industrial opportunities.

As "great pillars of the great country", these cruise ships feature a large volume, comprising millions or tens of millions of components. Their comprehensive development and integrated innovation processes are complex and challenging. In addition, the breakthroughs in their key technologies and industrial upgrading offer great motivation to the shipping industry.

So far, China has successfully built its own large cruiseships, large LNG carriers, and aircraft carriers, collectively known as the "three diamonds" shining bright in China's shipbuilding. These landmark achievements of advanced manufacturing, high-end equipment, and technological innovation highlight that China's high-end manufacturing industry is ascending and scaling new heights. There are three main factors contributing to this success.

First, exceptional capability in engineering and execution. Millions of large ships, built by SWS, have entered the global shipping market, including ultra-large container shipsand offshore oil drilling vessels. They are the leading projects in China's new industrialization progress. Designing and building large cruise ships represents that China'sshipbuilding capabilities have been taken to a new height. Domestically-built cruise ships, gathering over 1,500 suppliers across the world, have created a global supply chain for cruise ships, laying the groundwork for mass production.

Second, robust capacity to spearhead innovation. High-end equipment serves as an arena for national innovation capacity. Based on its large cruise ship projects, China has established the first national team for cruise ship design and cultivated a group of core and backbone professionals in R&D and design. Through the interplay between fundamental scientific research and ship projects and construction, the team has navigated the overall layout, aesthetic design, safe return to port, alternative design, and other key technologies.

A ship is an innovation platform, an industrial chain, and a window to opening up. In 2023, China achieved growth in the three main indicators of shipbuilding, with its share in the international market exceeding 50% for the first time. China's three major shipbuilding indicators all increased, with their international market shares all exceeding 50% for the first time.

Statistics showed that among the 18 major ship types in the world, China had 14 types with new orders ranking first globally.

Third, powerful leadership in fostering industry chain development. Large cruise ships, owing to the complicated integration and sophisticated techniques of its "mega-system" engineering, represent the pinnacle of high-end equipment in the shipbuilding industry, as high-end equipment encapsulates national innovation capabilities. With mass production, China's domestically-built large cruise ships are increasingly focusing on domestic companies. SWS, while enhancing international cooperation, keeps building a domestic network, aiming to promote the local cruise ship supporting industry clusters in China for a complete domestic cruise ship industry chain.

Currently, apart from the second domestically-built cruise ship, SWS is pushing its research on the design and R&D for ultra-large, medium, and small cruise ships, pursuing a comprehensive and large-scale development of cruise ship series and building a fleet of homegrown cruise ships. With rich experience and expertise gained from cruise ship projects, China is more capable of building an industrial innovation system integrated with technological requirements, product development, technological innovation, technology demonstration, and industrialization.

2. Quantum Science and Technology Innovation Advances in Anhui Province

In recent years, quantum science and technology has developed by leaps and bounds. Anhui, dedicated to building a scientific and innovative highland of quantum information, has seen its quantum industry burgeoning. At present, Anhui hosts over 60 quantum technology enterprises in the industrial chain, making it one of the top provinces in China for quantum industry.

Yunfei Road, located in the High-tech District of Hefei and home to the the Institute of Advanced Technology in University of Science and Technology of China (USTC), is known as "quantum street" for its concentration of quantum science enterprises dedicated to the industrial chain. This area is the birthplace of the Beijing-Shanghai Trunk Line, the world's first 1,000-km quantum confidential communication line, the world's first quantum science experimental satellite "Mozi", and the "Jiuzhang" quantum computer prototype achieving the landmark superiority of quantum computing.

In 2023, the first national quantum information future industry science and technology park was unveiled in the same District. From laboratory results to application on the "quantum street" and the complete industrial chain in the park, the three-pronged industrial chain of quantum communication, quantum computing, and quantum precision measurement is accelerating its technological industrialization and improving its productivity for applications.

What enabled a landlocked province in central China to rapidly advance in quantum information?

The key lies in technological innovation. Anhui has developed a comprehensive quantum information research system that includes multiple institutions. In recent years, it has successfully built the "Jiuzhang 3.0" quantum computer prototype with 255 detected photons and the 62-qubit programmable superconducting quantum processor "Zuchongzhi 2.0". Additionally, it's establishing a mechanism to commercialize the phrased achievements of frontier scientific research and creating application platforms for sci-tech results from China's universities, colleges, and research institutions, which fosters rapid development in quantum technology in China.

Scenario innovation is critical in efficiently transforming basic innovation into applications. Anhui, providing access to companies and governments, allows sci-tech enterprises to apply and demonstrate their new technologies, products, and innovative solutions, aiming to expedite the applications and iteration of relevant technological results.

Thanks to the access to governments, in 2012, QuantumCTek, a quantum information technology start-up based at USTC, completed the Hefei municipal quantum communication experimental demonstration network, the world's first large-scale quantum communication network. This milestone marked QuantumCTek's transition from laboratory research to engineering of quantum communication technology. As of today, the Hefei quantum municipal network is fully operational, with 1,147 km of network fiber, covering 8 core sites and 159 user nodes and providing quantum secure access and data transmission services.

Enterprises are the primary drivers of innovation, which is essential for their survival and growth. Hefei's emphasis on key technological projects, innovation platforms, and talent acquisition for local quantum enterprises has propelled it to the forefront of quantum patent applications in China.

CIQTEK, a developer and manufacturer of high-precision instruments, invested nearly 30% of its budget in R&D in 2023, with 70% of its 600 employees in R&D.

Supported by the key R&D projects and human resource policies, CIQTEK, committed to original innovation, has made breakthroughs in core technologies in key fields. Today, CIQTEK's quantum measurement technology has been applied in oil exploration, life sciences, aerospace, and other fields. Last year, its turnover surpassed 500 million yuan.

3. Hangzhou West Sci-tech Innovation Corridor Fosters a New Engine for Growth

Stretching 39 kilometers from the Zijinggang campus of Zhejiang University to Zhejiang A&F University, the Hangzhou West Sci-tech Innovation Corridor traverses key tech zones like the Zijinggang Technology City, Future Technology City, and Qingshanhu Lake Technology City, covering about 416 square meters.

Viewed from above, the Corridor appears futuristic, hosting 3,354 national high-tech enterprises, 91 national science and technology platforms, and 580,000 professional technical talents. The super gravity experimental field, resembling a spaceship with outspread wings, adds to its advanced look. Five provincial laboratories, including Zhejiang Lab and Westlake Laboratory, are strategically distributed along the Corridor. Since 2023, an average of 80 new enterprises have been established in the corridor each workday, consistently injecting vitality into local high-quality economic development.

Among the high-tech products from the Corridor are the "smart bionic arm" wornby the final torchbearer at the Hangzhou Asian Para Games opening ceremony, and the four-legged robotic dogs patrolling 8 meters underground in the Asian Games Village.

Also located in the Corridor is BrainCo, China's one-and-only brain-computer interface unicorn company. One of its flagship products is the smart prosthetic hand. At an exhibition, Ni Mincheng, Chief Experience Officer of BrainCo who lost both hands, wore the robotic hand to write beautiful calligraphy of "good fortune and happiness" in Chinese.

At present, the Corridor is dedicated to building a world-class digital technology industrial cluster and a strategic emerging industry cluster. According to industry experts, with years of supportive policies, the Corridor has attracted talent, advanced technological R&D, and encouraged market applications, laying a solid market foundation for industrial development and creating a favorable business environment.

Fang Yi, CEO of Merit Interactive Co., Ltd., a big data mobile internet integrated service provider, remarked that the Corridor features an ecosystem for innovation and entrepreneurship consisting of five elements, namely, capable government, renowned colleges and universities, leading enterprises, and diverse investors and entrepreneurs. These elements ensure industrial development through sustainable policy support, talent inflow, technological information, capital support, and entrepreneurship projects.

To better serve companies and promote high-quality development, Hangzhou has introduced specialized policies for the Corridor's industries, talent, and technologies. Since last year, officials from over 30 departments directly under the Hangzhou municipal government have visited the Corridor for service coordination. In talent pool building, public infrastructure, and general smart governance, the Corridor has achieved impressive results.

In April 2023, Mu Haowen, a 26-year-old entrepreneur, led his team to establish their startup in Hangzhou Dream Town and won first prize in a high-profile cyber securitycompetition within three days. Mu and his colleagues were amazed by how much the Corridor staff knew about the team and their projects, and they were convinced to settle down by the alluring entrepreneurial environment, supporting infrastructure, and warm services.

Currently, the Corridor is leveraging its innovation-based advantages to foster a new engine for economic growth. In 2023, the value added of the Corridor's industries stood at 350 billion yuan, with the high-tech industry contributing to 85% of it.

4. Beijing "Star Valley" Facilitates China's Journey Towards a Strong Space Presence

In Beijing Zhongguancun, located north of Houchangcun and south of Dongyu River, lies the Beiqing Road. Along this road situates an area known as the "Star Valley" where a multitude of commercial satellite and industry chain companies are scattered. From here, a fleet of commercial satellites takes flight into space, creating multiple highlights in the field of commercial aerospace.

"3...2...1...Ignition!" On April 28, 2024, in the "Star Valley" located in Beijing, AoTian Technology Co., Ltd. conducted an ignition test of its customized krypton gas electric propulsion engines designed specifically for space satellites in their smart manufacturing workshop.

According to Liu Tongbo, the R&D director of AoTian Technology, this independently developed new energy engine specialized for satellites achieves 90%

reduction in propellant consumption, a 40% decrease in satellite mass, and facilitates rapid orbit insertion of satellites in a reliable, efficient, and cost-effective manner.

AoTian Technology, established merely six years ago, has swiftly emerged as a leader within the industry, distinguished by its prowess in on-orbit orders, product delivery, application volume, and technological sophistication. Yet, this company merely offers a glimpse into the ambitious pursuits of Beijing "Star Valley" in the realm of space exploration.

Beijing stands as one of the cradles for China's space industry. In the Haidian District, where the "Star Valley" resides, a group of institutions, including the China Aerospace Science and Technology Corporation, China Aerospace Science and Industry Corporation Limited, and the Chinese Academy of Sciences have transformed the valley into a prominent component of the "North Star" in Beijing's industrial layout, known as the "South Rocket,North Star" constellation.With nearly 200 commercial aerospace industry chain companies and organizations, the region has preliminarily established a whole-industry-chain ecosystem, encompassing satellite manufacturing, satellite telemetry and control, and satellite operations.

The region has been upholding its commitment to cutting-edge technology, focusing on fields with bottleneck issues and industry gaps. By fostering core competitiveness through technological innovation, the "Star Valley" has forged a distinct set of advantages.

Jiang Ke, Chairman of ZhongGuanCun eValley (Beijing) Technology Service Co., Ltd, the operating company of the "Star Valley", underscored the impressive strides achieved by various enterprises within the valley. Despite their recent establishment, they have made huge leaps from "Zhongguancun-level high-tech company" to "National-level high-tech company" within a short period of time.

Teemsun Technology Co., Ltd. has garnered the rewards of independent R&D with its soaring performance, generating an annual revenue of over 500 million yuan. Recently, the company's self-developed infrared components have gained recognition for their exceptional cost-performance ratio. This heightened demand has fueled a surge of urgent orders in the overseas market.

The product's surge in demand is closely related with the company'sin-depthexploration in the optoelectronic field and its emphasis on independent R&D. As Luo Juedian, chairperson of Teemsun Technology Co., Ltd. has remarked, the journey of innovation resembles an endless marathon, wherein each successive breakthrough is hard-won only through steady and measured strides.

The innovative mechanisms of pioneering trials and proactive services have not only fostered an environment that allows innovation pioneers to wholeheartedly focus on their pursuits but have also instilled a sense of confidence and reassurance in their developmental endeavors. In 2024, Beijing issued the Action Plan for Accelerating the Innovation and Development of the Commercial Space Industry (2024-2028), while Haidian District released the Action Plan for Building a Commercial Space Innovation Highland (2024-2028). These plans aim to coordinate resources at both the municipal and district levels, with the goal of enhancing the quality of the industrial value chain, promoting open application scenarios, and optimizing the innovation ecosystem.

With a strategic focus on pivotal domains such as satellite networking and communication, as well as space remote sensing and monitoring, Beijing has established collaborative fund under the Beijing Natural Science Foundation to bolster original innovation with acumulative fund size reaching 380 million yuan. Currently, a total of seven districts in Beijing, along with 39 companies, have actively participated in this fund.

The growing influence of "Stary Valley" further bolsters and solidifies new advantages for regional development. Haidian District is now steadfastly pursuing the "Double Hundred and Double Thousand" objective, which encompass constructing 1 million square meters of industrial space, nurturing 100 specialized and innovative enterprises, launching over 1,000 satellites into orbit, and surpassing a commercial aerospace industry scale of 100 billion yuan by 2028. These endeavors are set to contribute significant impetus to innovation breakthroughs in the domain of aerospace information technology and the aspiration to build China into a strong space presence.

5. The Unique "Optics Valley of China" in the Optoelectronic Information Industry

Founded in 1988, Wuhan East Lake High-tech Development Zone earned the distinction of being named China's National Optoelectronic Information Industrial Base, where the country's first optical fiber was manufactured. It has emerged as the "Optics Valley of China" for its remarkable scale and innovation capacity. The valley now accommodates 16,000 optoelectronic information enterprises, encompassing the entire industry chain of optical core screen end network extended from the application of optical fiber. The Valley has generated a GDP of over 270 billion yuan.

It is the birthplace of China's first 400G coherent commercial silicon optical transceiver chip, the world-leading 232-layer three-dimensional flash memory chip, andthecountry's inaugural industrial fiber laser boasting an impressive power output of 100,000 watts, among many other notable accomplishments.

The manufacture of optical fiber has given rise to a world-class optoelectronic information industry base. "Optics Valley of China" centers around optics industry whilecontinuously striving for breakthroughs in chip technology, screens, and end networks. A series of plans have been implemented to fortify the supply chain, bridge gaps, and expand the value chain, with the goal of creating an internationally competitive industrial cluster.

With a focus on core technologies, a cluster of optoelectronic information enterprises situated in the "Optics Valley of China" has been strengthening their dedication to independentinnovation. By developing industry standards, they are not only leading the domestic market but also achieving remarkable strides in international markets, firmly establishing their significance over the industry's development.

Wuhan Accelink Technologies Co.,Ltd. is one of the leading suppliers of optical communication device in China. As a high-tech enterprise, it specializes in systematic and strategic research and development of optoelectronic device systems. Capitalizing on the trend of fiber optic communication bandwidth evolving towards the C++ band, the company's research and development team successfully developed fiber optic amplifier products in 2020 and further established international standard in this field.

China Information Communication Technologies Group Corporation (CICT) has demonstrated its unwavering commitment to independent research and development by accumulating a portfolio of over 20,000 patents, with 90% of them being invention patents. In addition, CICT has taken a leading role in establishing over 80 relevant international standards, nurturing a team of talented professionals with a global vision and exceptional technical proficiency.

The "Optics Valley of China" is committed to developing a range of scientific research infrastructure, attracting talents from around the world, fostering an ecosystem for innovation, and building open and sharing research centers. One such example is the Hubei Jiufengshan Laboratory.

According to Ding Qichao, director of Hubei Jiufengshan Laboratory, "the path of scientific and technological innovation involves progressing from 0 to 1, and subsequently achieving breakthroughs from 1 to 10." In this context, they have successfully built an industry-leading infrastructure for compound semiconductors, boasting a 9,000-square-meter clean room and cutting-edge facilities dedicated to compound semiconductor processes, testing, and materials.

Hundreds of projects are concurrently operating, emphasizing not only the joint efforts of academia and industry to explore cutting-edge advancements and tackle bottlenecks in key common technologies but also the integration of the entire industry chain to bridge gaps and drive collaborative development among academia, industry, and research.

An incubation, acceleration, and manufacturing base has also been established here. Construction has begun to the south of Hubei Jiufengshan Laboratory, encompassing research and development office buildings, pilot workshops, clean rooms, conference centers, and talent apartments. The establishment of an innovative community that integrates government, industry, academia, research, and financial services is expected to yield remarkable results.

6. "Universities Without Walls" by Western China Science and Technology Innovation Harbor

Located at the Western China Science and Technology Innovation Harbor of Xi'an Jiaotong University, the Research Center of Novel Energy Storage and Energy Conversion Nanomaterials is conducting experiments on diverse energy storage and energy conversion materials. Since its inception, this collaborative technology platform has not only achieved multiple technological breakthroughs but has also incubated five new energy enterprises operating in fields such as lithium-ion batteries, sodium-ion batteries,hydrogen production, and hydrogen storage.

Among the enterprises is Xi'an 1908 New Energy Technology Co.,Ltd., a high-tech company that emerged through the transformation of original technological achievements from Xi'an Jiaotong University. The company has successfully developed a series of new high-density solid hydrogen storage materials to address challenges in the hydrogen energy storage and transportation industry. These materials find extensive applications in industrial hydrogen supply, electric power energy, mobile applications, and other fields. Their technology is at the forefront of the global stage.

"Emerging field enterprises cannot thrive in their early stages of development without the support of universities," said Cheng Yonghong, founder of the company and professor at Xi'an Jiaotong University, emphasized that prior to the establishment and operation of the pilot workshop, the company had been working in an adjacent community, just a wall away from the Innovation Harbor. This close proximity facilitated seamless coordination of personnel, information, and other essential factors. Xi'an Jiaotong University plays a vital role in providing crucial support in these areas.

The Western China Science and Technology Innovation Harbor is a significant platform for Shaanxi Province and Xi'an Jiaotong University to actively participate in the joint construction of the Belt and Road Initiative, as well as to pursue innovation-driven development and promote large-scale development of western China. Located in the first phase of the Xi'an Xixian New Area, the Harbor comprises the Platform Zone, College Zone, and Incubation Zone. The Platform Zone has established eight major platforms, 30 research institutes, and over 300 scientific research platforms in the fields of science, engineering, medicine, and humanities, attracting over 30,000 scientific and technological talents.

The China Western Science and Technology Innovation Harbor serves as a powerful embodiment of Xi'an Jiaotong University's vision of "Building a university without boundary walls." It actively explores a new model of deep integration among industry, academia, and research, focusing on the principles of "one center, one incubation, two orientations, and one sharing." The harbor endeavors to attract global innovation resources, align with national development strategies, meet local industry demands, and attract diverse forms of financial capital. By fostering a favorable innovation ecosystem and nurturing exceptional innovative talents, the harbor has already established practical partnerships with over 170 leading enterprises and research institutions.

Continued exploration is underway to advance a systematic and task-oriented innovation consortium, with a strong emphasis on aligning with major objectives and fostering closer collaboration between the academic and industrial sectors. The introduction of financial capital facilitates the establishment of technology transfer incubators led by prominent enterprises, with the aim of incubating new technologies while the matured ones are available for market. Leveraging the attractiveness of "Double First-Class" universities, mechanisms have been established to attract, train, and utilize high-end overseas talents through university-industry partnerships, striving to achieve a synergy where universities enroll, enterprises provide, governments support, and all parties benefit.

"Within the innovation consortium, universities and enterprises are forming" scientist+engineer" teams,moving away from the conventional model of collaboration defined by singular bilateral agreements, limited to one project, contract, and funding allocation at a time. This approach accelerates the deep integration of industry, academia, and research, with enterprises taking the lead." explained Lu Jianjun, secretary of the CPC of Xi'an Jiaotong University.

Since 2021, Xi'an Jiaotong University has carefully examined over 30,000 existing technological achievements and identified 1,300 results that are highly suitable for commercialization. The university has successfully transferred and licensed more than 1,000 patents, giving rise to 204 scientific and technological enterprises.

7. Shandong Province Accelerates the Integration of Digital Technology in the Real Economy to Promote Industry Digitalization

Inside Weichai Power Co., Ltd's No. 1 Factory assembly workshop, located in the Weifang Hi-Tech Industrial Development Zone, industrial robots and automated guided vehicles (AGVs) diligently perform various tasks. From material handling to online inspections and even production cycle optimization, everything is monitored and adjusted in real-time. The automation rate of the equipment has reached 99%. Electronic displays are positioned throughout the factory, providing real-time updates on the production progress. On average, one diesel engine is completed every 85 seconds.

As the first batch of intelligent manufacturing pilot demonstration projects of China, Weichai Power is expediting the integration of next-generation information technology and manufacturing. Visual recognition, online inspection, robotics, and a wide range of intelligent manufacturing technologies are extensively utilized by the company throughout the production process. The information support platform acts as a "digital brain" that encompasses the entire product life cycle, not only facilitating intelligent, automated, and digitized production but also extending its benefits to the overall operation of the company.

Weichai Power stands as a prominent representative in Shandong province, spearheading the integration of digital technology into the real economy, the transformation and upgrading of traditional manufacturing industries, and the development of new quality productive forces.

In recent years, Shandong has implemented a series of policies, including the "Opinions on Accelerating the High-Quality Development of the Digital Economy" and the "Action Plan for the Digital Transformation of the Manufacturing Industry in Shandong Province

(2022-2025)". The province has established China's first SME Digital Transformation Promotion Center, launched the "Ten Major Projects" for digital industrialization, and initiated the "Eight Major Actions" for industrial digitalization. The province has also prioritized the development of digital talent pools. At the provincial level, a special fund of 10 billion yuan has been established. Shandong ranks at the forefront across China in terms of the number of national-level industrial internet platforms, the digitalization index of industries, the digital transformation index of manufacturing industries, and the digital-real economy index.

Constructing industrial internet platforms plays a crucial role in advancing industrial digitalization. Shandong province has been steadfast in its implementation of the "Empowering Shandong through Industries" special initiative, which seeks to accelerate the wide-scale adoption of the industrial internet. By setting up models in this regard, Shandong is committed to catalyzing the digital transformation on a larger scale.

In the city of Linqing, known as the "Hometown of Chinese Bearings," leveraging the industrial Internet platform, the local bearing industry has embraced the era of digitalization. Over 400 bearing enterprises and more than 5,000 sets of equipment have been integrated into the cloud-based system. As a result, these companies have witnessed an average reduction of 20% in labor and energy consumption, leading to a significant enhancement in their competitiveness.

Shandong province now boasts 47 national-level industrial Internet platforms, with over 10 million industrial devices connected to platforms at the provincial level and above. These platforms serve more than 3 million enterprises across the country.

To facilitate efficient data integration, exchange, and utilization across the government, industries, and enterprises, Shandong has made significant efforts in the development of "Industrial Brain" initiatives. So far, the province has cultivated 32 provincial-level "Industrial Brain" centers. These centers have gathered 957 "compact, rapidly-developing, lightweight, and targeted" products and solutions, benefiting 49,500 small and micro enterprises. One notable example is the Shandong special whole vehicle "Industrial Brain" developed in collaboration with Inspur Yunzhou. This initiative has reduced the matching time for industry raw material supply and demand by 70% and decreased production costs for various specialized vehicle components by nearly 25%.

Meanwhile, Shandong is continuously advancing its digital infrastructure. By the end of 2023, the province has constructed and activated 202,000 5G base stations and a deterministic network covering 11,800 kilometers. Furthermore, the province has connected to 29 national top-level nodes for industrial internet, with 230 million registered internet of things terminals in operation.

In 2023, the digital transformation coverage rate of industrial enterprises above designated size in Shandong province reached 87.3%. The adoption rate of industrial Internet applications in small and medium-sized enterprises within specialized industry clusters reached 50%. By 2024, Shandong aims to achieve a digital transformation coverage rate of approximately 90% among industrial enterprises above a designated sizewhile boosting the digitaleconomy's contribution to the provincial GDP to over 50%.

8. New Energy Vehicle Industry in Chongqing

In mid-April 2024, German Chancellor Olaf Scholz paid an official visit to China. His first destination was Chongqing, a municipality located in southwest China. Together with executives from automobile enterprises such as Mercedes-Benz and BMW, Chancellor Scholz visited Bosch Hydrogen Powertrain Systems (Chongqing) Co., Ltd.

As a prominent hub of the Chinese automotive industry, Chongqing has seized the opportunity in the new energy vehicle sector in recent years with a focus on building an innovation highland for new energy vehicles. Chongqing has now established a whole industry chain "blueprint" based on 16 new energy whole-vehicle enterprises and around 200 enterprises above designated size. This blueprint encompasses all technological routes, including pure electric, extended-range, hybrid, and hydrogen-powered vehicles, while integrating advanced technologies such as intelligent networking and autonomous driving.

In 2023, Bosch Hydrogen Power Systems (Chongqing) Co., Ltd. has delivered over 1,000 units of hydrogen assembly products, ranked at the forefront of the domestic market. Building on these accomplishments, Qingling Motors Co., Ltd., one of its parent companies, subsequently launched a range of hydrogen-powered commercial vehicles with different specifications, ranging from 4.5 tons to 18 tons. This pioneering initiative has positioned Qingling Motors as a frontrunner in advancing the industrialization of cutting-edgy technologies.

Stepping into the global research and development center of Changan Automobile, a series of technologically advanced and aesthetically appealing new energy vehicles are lined up, accompanied by displays showcasing the latest technological achievements such as the all-electric digital platform and high-performance central computing platform. Zhu Huarong, the Chairman of Changan Automobile, remarked that the company has been continuously investing in research and development for years, mastering over 600 technologies in areas such as intelligent connectivity and autonomous driving.

In its quest to establish a new energy automobile innovation hub, Chongqing recognizes the necessity for meticulous efforts and strategic shifts from vehicle and supporting enterprises, alongside crucial support from ICT and Internet companies. It also demands participation from ICT and internet companies. Embracing the trend of cross-industry collaboration, Chongqing has attracted companies like Huawei and Baidu in recent years. This collaboration has sparked pioneering technology trials and pilot demonstrations, effectively propelling the development of industries.

With a simple tap on the smartphone app, an autonomous vehicle promptly arrives to drive passengers to their destinations and then departs automatically. This scene of smart transportation unfolds every day in Yongchuan District, Chongqing. In 2022, Baidu took the lead in launching fully autonomous commercial operations in Yongchuan, driving industrial implementation through scenario-based applications. This initiative has further attracted more than ten companies, including Anhui Kuwa Robot Co., Ltd. and Juspeed Millimeter.

Technological innovation has enhanced the competitiveness of products. In the first quarter of 2024, Chongqing's production of new energy vehicles witnessed a year-on-year growth rate exceeding 100%, with an estimated annual output of one million vehicles. Notably, Chongqing Seres Group Co., Ltd. achieved a quarterly profit of 220 million yuan for the first time. Benefiting from the collaboration with Huawei in creating the high-end brand called AITO, the automotive software and hardware technologies developed by Huawei have flourished in Seres Automobile. The cumulative sales of AITO have reached nearly 300,000 units, including over 120,000 deliveries of the new M7 model.

"Chongqing is currently making continuous efforts across various domains, including whole-vehicle research and manufacturing, supporting key components and application scenarios, and the construction of charging and battery swapping infrastructure. The aim is to build a trillion-yuan level industrial cluster for intelligent connected new energy vehicles," a spokesperson from Chongqing Municipal Commission of Economy and Information Technology said. Chongqing is also actively driving innovation and application in autonomous driving and innovative application of vehicle connectivity. The city is accelerating the deep integration of software, artificial intelligence, and the automotive industry, laying a solid foundation for the future development of the automotive industry.

9. Building a Vibrant Technology Cluster in the Guangdong-Hong Kong-Macao Greater Bay Area

Thanks to the Guangzhou "Tianhe-2" supercomputer and advanced algorithmic analysis techniques, Associate Professor Lin Zanyu from the University of Hong Kong can now efficiently track the origins, transmission, and evolution of important pathogens withinvast volumes of pathogen genomic data, as well as other epidemiological and ecological data.

With the assistance of the Guangzhou supercomputer, Professor Gan Jianping and his team from the Ocean Dynamics and Modeling Research Group at the Hong Kong University of Science and Technology have successfully developed a new three-dimensional and high-resolution China Sea Multi-Scale Ocean Modeling System, a significant scientifc breakthrough.

"During the past five years, over 200 teachers from the Hong Kong University of Science and Technology have leveraged the power of the Guangzhou supercomputer.The platform offered by the Guangzhou Supercomputing Center enables us to accomplish tasks that were previously unattainable." said Gao Min, dean of HKUST Fok Ying Tung Research Institute.

The Guangdong-Hong Kong-Macao Greater Bay Area is a hub of scientific and technological resources with a vibrant atmosphere for innovation and entrepreneurship. In recent years, the three regions have collaborated to advance the development of an international science and technology innovation center and a comprehensive national science center in the Greater Bay Area. This collaborative effort aims to facilitate efficient connectivity of innovation elements, enhance the effectiveness of innovation, and promote the flourishing growth of innovative industries, thereby unleashing the full potential of technological innovation within the "Bay Area powerhouse."

Collaboration is underway between the marine industry and science industry within Southern Marine Science and Engineering Guangdong Laboratory (Guangzhou). This laboratory, headquartered in Nansha, Guangzhou, has established branches in Hong Kong and Shenzhen, with an allocation of 38 million yuan to its Hong Kong branch.

"The exchange of science and technology between Hong Kong and the mainland has been expanding, and efforts are being made to create favorable conditions that encourage Hong Kong scientists to participate in mainland science and technology initiatives," said Qian Peiyuan, founding director of the Department of Ocean Science of the Hong Kong University of Science and Technology.

The collaboration in talent attraction is also on a fast track. In the Hengqin Guangdong-

Macao In-depth Cooperation Zone, the combined institutional and resource advantages of Hengqin and Macao are being harnessed to explore new models of collaborative talent attraction. The University of Macau and Macau University of Science and Technology give full play to their role as "talent reservoirs" to attract and gather a group of highly skilled professionals who possess exceptional expertise, an intimate understanding of international market operations, and a robust drive for innovation and entrepreneurship.

Each city within the Guangdong-Hong Kong-Macao Greater Bay Area boasts its own unique advantages. Guangzhou serves as a hub for universities and research institutions with remarkable capabilities in basic scientific research. The city is equipped with national laboratories, comprehensive national technology innovation centers, and major national-level infrastructure for science and technology. Shenzhen stands out for its robust corporate sector, which contributes 94% of the total investment in research and development. Hong Kong is home to five universities ranked among the top 100 universities. The SAR government has introduced the "Hong Kong I&T Development Blueprint," investing over HKD 200 billion in recent years to accelerate the vibrant growth of the innovation ecosystem.

Benefiting from the complementary advantages across cities, the Guangdong-Hong Kong-Macao Greater Bay Area continues to unleash its immense potential for the development of technology clusters. In the 2023 edition of the Global Innovation Index (GII) released by the World Intellectual Property Organization in September 2023, the Shenzhen-Hong Kong-Guangzhou cluster was ranked at the second place in the "Science and Technology Clusters" category, marking the fourth consecutive year that the cluster has held the second position globally.

Currently, the alignment and coordination of innovation rules and mechanisms across Guangdong-Hong Kong-Macao are deepening, actively promoting cross-border capital flow, people-to-people exchanges, balanced taxation, and seamless logistics, with the aim of better aggregating innovation elements. This also signifies the drive to facilitate interaction and openness between different systems and frameworks under "One Country, Two Systems", thereby generating more significant chemical reactions and fostering better integration in areas such as basic scientific research and applied technology within the Greater Bay Area.

10. Chengdu-Chongqing Jointly Construct the Western Science City to Form Innovation Highland

"Currently, the platform has launched 272 sets of equipment and instruments, and published a list of 232 technical services, offering thousands of professional services to over 100 integrated circuit design companies from Chengdu, Chongqing, and other parts of the country," said the head of the Tianfu New Area Integrated Circuit Design Innovation PublicPlatform.

Situated within the Western (Chengdu) Science City, this public platform is widely recognized as the "Chip Hospital," providing solutions to address technical challenges in concept verification, product development, and pilot production for enterprises. It significantly reduces research and development costs and shortens the development cycle for chip companies in the Chengdu-Chongqing region, enabling them to achieve substantial cost savings and accelerate their innovation processes.

Over the past four years, the Chengdu-Chongqing Economic Circle has placed great emphasis on the establishment of a nationally influential science and technology innovationcenter to jointly build a high-level Western Science City.

In recent years, the Western (Chengdu) Science City has adopted a spatial layout strategy of "one core, four districts, and multiple bases." This strategy aims to establish a high-level laboratory system comprising "national laboratories, provincial laboratories, and key laboratories." The city has made accelerated progress in constructing the first national laboratory in the western region and creating a cluster of large-scale facilities that are interconnected in terms of disciplinary directions and mutually supportive in terms of functionality. The Western (Chongqing) Science City has focused on building four major highlands for scientific and technological innovation, namely digital and smart technology, life sciences and health, new materials, and green and low-carbon technologies. It has made significant strides in the development of 16 key areas, including artificial intelligence, blockchain, cloud computing, and big data.

In the joint construction of the Western Science City, Chengdu and Chongqing are working in tandem, with a focus on enhancing the City's core functions of transforming innovation source and strategies while fostering the growth of a modern industrial system. Throughout the process, a new pattern is beginning to take shape, characterized by the continuous aggregation of innovative resources and the active emergence of innovation vitality.

First, establishing a coordinated layout of major innovation platforms. As of the end of March this year, the number of national key laboratories in Sichuan and Chongqing has reached 27, including 319 major scientific and technological platforms, 22 newly established national science and technology innovation bases, and 316 national-level innovation platforms. Currently, tens of thousands of large-scale instruments and equipment in the Western Science City have been made available for open sharing. Sichuan and Chongqing have jointly implemented over 160 core technology breakthrough projects and successfully tackled a number of challenging problems.

Second, enhancing collaboration between industry and research to leverage their complementary strengths. Enterprises from Sichuan Tianfu New Area collaborated with scientific research institutions from Chongqing on nine research projects. Among them, Chengdu Aerospace Science and Technology Big Data Research Institute Co., Ltd.and Invant Future have received support from the Chengdu Regional Collaborative Science and Technology Project. The National Supercomputing Center in Chengdu has established cooperative relationships with more than 50 users, including the Chongqing Institute of Green and Intelligent Technology of Chinese Academy of Sciences and the Chongqing Seres Group.

Third, emphasizing strong efforts in providing scientific and technological services. Chengdu and Chongqing regard scientific and technological services as a crucial means to promote technological innovation and the commercialization of research outcomes. For instance, the Tianfu International Technology Transfer Center has collaborated with the Mingyue Collaborative Innovation Zone in the Liangjiang New Area to further innovate and explore new approaches in connecting resources between the two regions and facilitating the exchange of innovation elements.

Driven by the joint construction of the Western Science City, the conversion of scientific and technological achievements in Sichuan and Chongqing is being fully unleashed.The two regions have gathered nearly 70,000 scientific and technological enterprises and 21,000 high-tech enterprises. The transaction volume of registered technical contracts has surpassed 280 billion yuan.

VI. Epilogue

Since its founding, the Communist Party of China has represented the development requirements of China's advanced productive forces and has shouldered the historic mission of transforming old relations of production and establishing new ones.

The development of new quality productive forces is an intrinsic requirement and a crucial focus for promoting high-quality development. Since the 18th National

Congress of the CPC, the Party Central Committee with Comrade Xi Jinping at its core has regarded the further liberation and development of social productive forces as the fundamental and most pressing task in realizing the great rejuvenation of the Chinese nation. This has guided China's economy into a stage of high-quality development. In the logical progression of developing new quality productive forces, achieving high-quality development, and building a socialist modernized country, the formation and development of new quality productive forces will enable China to adapt to the trends of the new round of technological revolution and industrial transformation. It will strive to achieve sustainable leapfrog development of social productive forces and provide important support for shaping Chinese path to modernization and building a modern socialist country in all respects.

Productive forces are the fundamental driving force behind the development of human society. Faced with common challenges in global development, the emergence of new productive forces will open up new ideas and possibilities for the development of human society's productive forces. It will not only propel China's own modernization process but also benefit developing countries at large and contribute to the modernization of the entire human society.

VII. Glossaries

1. National Laboratory System

A platform system that revolves around national laboratories, with state key laboratories as the support, aims at fostering collaborative and interactive relationships among various types of scientific and technological innovation bases. The construction of a well-structured and efficient national laboratory system entails two aspects. Firstly, it should be guided by national goals and strategic demands, accelerating the development of national laboratories and establishing interdisciplinary, highly collaborative research organization models. Secondly, it should optimize and integrate existing state key laboratories by meansof adjustments, enrichment, integration, and closures, thereby enhancing the support capabilities for innovation chains and industrial chains.

2. Future-oriented Industry

Forward-looking emerging industries that are driven by cutting-edge technological innovation and are currently in their nascent or early stages of industrialization. These industries possess tremendous development potential and have the capacity to become leading and foundational industries. They play a significant role in guiding and transforming future economic and social development.

3. Modern Infrastructure System

A comprehensive infrastructure system that is developed around the goals of promoting Chinese modernization, ensuring overall national security, and building new competitive advantages in the international arena. This system is built upon the foundation of infrastructure development in various fields. It involves improving the layout, optimizing the structure, expanding functionality, and integrating systems to create a well-connected network of facilities, strong hub nodes, advanced equipment and technology, and efficient management services. The main components of this infrastructure system include transportation, energy, water resources, information (digital), as well as ecological, environmental, scientific and technological, and financial infrastructure.

4. New Infrastructure

Infrastructure based on information networks and driven by technological innovation, providing fundamental and public services related to digital transformation, intelligent upgrading, and integrated innovation. Its connotation continues to expand with the mature application of new technologies. Currently, it mainly includes three categories. First, information infrastructure. This mainly refers to the infrastructure generated by the evolution of new generation information technologies, including 5G networks, data centers, and other infrastructure. Second, converged infrastructure. This mainly refers to the new form of infrastructure formed by the deep application of information technology, promoting the transformation and upgrading of traditional infrastructure, including intelligent transportation and logistics facilities. Third, innovative infrastructure. This mainly refers to the infrastructure that supports scientific research, technological development, and the research and development of products and services, including scientific research facilities.

5. Industrial Innovation Project

Projects that serve as an important lever for promoting the development of emerging industries and future industries by focusing on the practical needs of major engineering project construction, strategic product development, and application scenario expansion. It effectively organizes and implements key core technology breakthroughs, pilot verification capabilities, and application demonstrations of independent innovative products. By integrating innovative resources such as projects, bases, talents, and funds, it facilitates integrated innovation across the upstream, midstream, and downstream of the industrial chain, as well as among large, medium, and small enterprises. The ultimate goal is to foster the creation of emerging industrial clusters with global competitiveness and to genuinely implement innovation, thereby generating new growth points

6. National Strategic Emerging Industry Cluster Development Project

A systematic project deployed and promoted by the government to seize the commanding heights of the new round of technological revolution and industrial transformation, as wellas to build new international competitive advantages. The projects aim to cultivate several strategically significant emerging industry bases with global influence, establish a number of internationally competitive strategic emerging industry clusters, and guide local areas in constructing and developing distinctive strategic emerging industry ecosystems. It drives the integrated, clustered, and ecological development of strategic emerging industries, promotes the nurturing and growth of new growth points and growth poles, and constructs a hierarchical development system for strategic emerging industry clusters that are distinctive, complementary in advantages, and structurally sound.

7. "AI+" Action

The "AI+" action aims to promote the deep integration of AI technology with various sectors of the economy and society. It supports innovative applications in all industries, empowers intelligent transformation and upgrading across industries, improves production efficiency, stimulates innovation vitality, reshapes industrial ecology, nurtures new driving forces for economic development, and fosters a broader new form of economic and social development where artificial intelligence serves as a key innovation element.

8. East-to-West Computing Resource Transfer Project

In 2022, in accordance with the deployment of the Communist Party of China Central

Committee and the State Council, and in line with the implementation of China's major regional development strategies, national computing hub nodes were established and data center clusters were developed in the Beijing-Tianjin-Hebei region, the Yangtze River Delta, the Guangdong-Hong Kong-Macao Greater Bay Area, the Chengdu-Chongqing region, as well as in Inner Mongolia, Guizhou, Gansu, and Ningxia, based on factors such as energy structure, industrial layout, market development, climate, and environment. The east-data-west-computing project aims to coordinate the construction of computing infrastructure across the country, leveraging the advantages of the institutional mechanism, optimizing the allocation of computing resources, and deepening the collaboration of computing capabilities between the eastern and western regions.

9. "Data Elements X" Action

The action emphasizes focusing on key industries and sectors to synergistically integrate data elements with labor, capital, technology, and other factors. It aims to facilitate the multi-scenario application and multi-party reuse of data, accelerate the integration of diverse data sources, enhance total factor productivity, create new opportunities for economic growth, and foster new driving forces for economic development.

10. Market Access for Sea-Land-Air All-space Unmanned System

The sea-land-air all-space unmanned system is a new type of logistics and transportation system that operates and supervises a variety of unmanned equipment and its supporting infrastructure by sea, land and air, such as unmanned aircraft, unmannedvehicles,unmanned ships and electric vertical take-off and landing vehicles. It improves market access rules, systematically builds unmanned system policies and regulations, standards, testing and certification, data management, operation and supervision, and other institutional mechanisms, optimizes the allocation of airspace resources, data arithmetic, communication frequency, right-of-way allocation, land space and other elemental resources, and forms a new kinetic energy for the integrated development of low-altitude economy, logistics and transportation, and vehicle-road coordination. In January 2022, with the consent of the Central Committee of the Communist Party of China and the State Council, the National Development and Reform Commission (NDRC) promoted the construction of a sea-land-air all-space unmanned system in the form of special measures for market access. In September

2023, the world's first city-level application demonstration project of an all-space unmanned system was completed in Hefei City, Anhui Province. In accordance with the relevant working arrangements, in 2024, a number of technical standards for all-space unmanned systems for sea, land and air will be released, a testing and certification platform will be constructed, and demonstration experiences will be promoted in the Guangdong-Macao In-Depth Cooperation Zone in Hengqin and the Nansha New Areain Guangzhou City.

VIII. References

1. Han Wenxiu. Consolidate and Strengthen the Momentum of Economic Recovery. Peoples' Daily, January 2024.

2. National Development and Reform Commission. Accelerating the Construction of a Nationally Unified Large Market to Provide Strong Support for the Construction of a New Development Pattern. Qiushi, June 2022.

3. Huai Jinpeng. Accelerating the Construction of a Powerful Educational State. Peoples' Daily, December 2022.

4. Xi Jinping Thought on Economy Study Center. Internal Characteristics and Development Priorities of New Qualitative Productive Forces. Peoples' Daily, March 2024.

5. Sun Xugong and Rong Chen. Chinas' New Quality Productive Forces Injects New Momentum into Global Development, Guangming Daily. March 2024.

6. Lu Yanchun. Compacting the Data Factor-Driven Foundation and Cultivating the Price Chain of Data Assets, Price: Theory & Practice. Vol. 3, 2023.

7. Hu Yongjun. Forward-Looking Layout of Future Industries: Advantageous Conditions, Practical Exploration and Policy Orientation, Reform. Vol. 9, 2023.

8. Zhang Yuczhe. Accelerating the Integrated Development of Strategic Emerging Industry Cluster. Economic Daily, June 2024.

9. He Jun. The Economics Essence and Core Propositions of New Quality Productive Forces. Peoples' Tribune, 2024.

10. Yan Lianfu. Integrating Education, Science and Technology Talents to Promote the Development of New Quality Productive Forces, Guangming Daily. April 2024.

11. Chen Qiqing. Improving and Perfecting the Participation of Factors of Production in the Distribution Mechanism, Peoples' Daily Online. March 2020.

12. Liu Zhibiao. Developing New Quality Productive Forces to Inject New Vitality into the World Economy. Guangming Daily, April 2024.

13. Wu Wen. Accelerating the Formation of New Quality Productive Forces is a Matter of China' Modernization, Beijing Daily. October 2023.

14. Xi Weijian. New Quality Productive Forces Will Change Geopolitical Landscape. Huanqiu, December 2023.

Editor's Note and Acknowledgments

The research team for the think tank report titled "Empower China, Benefit the World — An Analysis of the Theoretical Contribution and Value Orientation of New Quality Productive Forces" is led by Fu Hua, president of Xinhua News Agency, and chairman of the Academic Committee of Xinhua News Agency's National High-end Think Tank. Lyu Yansong, editor-in-chief of Xinhua News Agency, serves as the Deputy Team Leader, and Ren Weidong, deputy editor-in-chief of Xinhua News Agency, serves as the Executive Deputy Team Leader. The team members include Liu Gang, Zhang Xudong, Zou Wei, An Bei, Fu Yan, Cheng Yunjie, Yuan Junbao, Shang Yiying, Zhang Ziyun, Hu Zhe, Zhang Xinxin, Dai Xiaohe, Chen Weiwei, Li Yanxia, He Huiyuan, Liang Jin, Chen Yongrong, Jia Yuankun, Zhang Manzi, Ma Xiaocheng, Wang Zichen, Zheng Xin, Huang Xing, Yang Siqi, Li Like, and others. The team members were selected from various departments of Xinhua News Agency's headquarters and domestic branches, and they are all key professionals engaged in news reporting and research work.

Since its initiation in September 2023, the project has spanned a period of 9 months, during which the team has dedicated their time to learning, conducting research, writing, revising, and proofreading. All members from the project team have thoroughly studied General Secretary Xi Jinping's important speeches on the subject of new quality productive forces. They have also conducted extensive interviews with authoritative departments, institutions, experts, scholars, business professionals, and researchers, aiming at comprehending the theoretical framework and practical pathways of the new quality productive forces and uncovering exemplary case studies and captivating stories. The team has meticulously conducted research and writing. After a series of versions and revisions, the report draft was completed in April 2024. After seeking opinions from authoritative departments and relevant experts and scholars, the draft was further refined, improved, and finally completed.

For the Common Value and Dignity of All Humanity—China's Practice of and Contribution to Global Human Rights Governance[①]

Human rights are the fruits and symbols of the progress of human civilization. Respecting and protecting human rights is a fundamental spirit of modern civilization. Seventy-five years ago, the Universal Declaration of Human Rights (UDHR), born in the ashes of World War II, affirmed the respect and protection of basic human rights. Thirty years ago, the Vienna Declaration and Program of Action clarified the close relationships among various types of human rights. As a result, the concept of promoting human rights through development and cooperation has taken root in people's hearts.

Since the founding of the People's Republic of China (PRC), especially since the 18th National Congress of the Communist Party of China (CPC), under the guidance of Xi Jinping Thought on Socialism with Chinese Characteristics for a New Era, China has continuously summarized the experience of human society development and pursued a people-centered approach in the great practice of building socialism with Chinese characteristics. In the great practice of building socialism with Chinese characteristics, China adheres to the people-centered human rights concept, combines the universal principles of human rights with China's reality, and has successfully embarked on a path of human rights development that conforms to the trends of the times and is suitable for

---

① Released in Beijing on September 19, 2023.

China's national conditions under the CPC's strong leadership. China has historically addressed the issue of absolute poverty, built a moderately prosperous society in all respects, and established the world's most extensive education system, social security system, and healthcare system. The rights of specific groups such as ethnic minorities, women, children, elderly people, and people with disabilities are fully protected. The human rights of the Chinese people have received unprecedented levels of protection, and China has made enormous contributions to the development of global human rights cause.

While continuing to advance its human rights cause, China has actively supported the just cause of developing countries in breaking free from colonial rules, achieving national independence, and eliminating racial segregation. China has made significant contributions to assisting developing countries in their development, providing humanitarian aid, maintaining world peace and development, and promoting the progress of international human rights endeavors. China has always adhered to the concepts of equality, mutual trust, inclusiveness and mutual learning, win-win cooperation, and joint development. China actively participated in United Nations human rights affairs, conscientiously fulfilled its international human rights obligations, carried out extensive international human rights cooperation. It has taken concrete actions to promote global human rights governance toward a more fair, just, equitable, and inclusive direction, providing China's wisdom and solutions to international human rights governance.

Currently, humanity stands at another historical crossroads, and global human rights governance faces severe challenges. China advocates safeguarding human rights through safeguarding international security environment, respecting national sovereignty and territorial integrity, pursuing peaceful development with the rest of the world, and implementing the Global Security Initiative to create a peaceful environment for human rights. China also promotes human rights through development, implements the Global Development Initiative, enhances the inclusiveness, universality, and sustainability of growth, and ensures that people in all countries enjoy human rights fairly through their distinctive paths to modernization. Furthermore, China advocates promoting human rights through cooperation, mutual respecting, treating each other as equals, implementing the Global Civilization Initiatives, strengthening exchanges and mutual appreciation among civilizations, and building consensus through dialogue to jointly advance the development and progress of human rights civilization.

China practices genuine multilateralism, upholds the shared values of peace, development, fairness, justice, democracy, and freedom for all humankind, promotes the building of a global community of a shared future, and provides new ideas, new solutions, and new opportunities for global governance, including human rights governance. It demonstrates the responsibility and commitment of a major country.

I. China's Practice of Participating in Global Human Rights Governance

China has been elected multiple times as a member of the United Nations (UN) Human Rights Council. It has consistently participated in UN human rights affairs with a responsible attitude, actively engaged in global human rights governance, and made efforts to promote the healthy development of international human rights. China has deepened its involvement over time, expanded its scope of participation, and continued to grow its influence.

In March 2023, at the 52nd session of the United Nations Human Rights Council, China first made a joint speech on behalf of more than 70 countries on the 75th anniversary of adopting the Universal Declaration of Human Rights (UDHR), putting forward clear proposals for implementing the Declaration. Soon after, on behalf of nearly 80 countries, including Brazil and South Africa, China made a joint speech on the 30th anniversary of adopting the Vienna Declaration and Program of Action, calling for strengthening international cooperation, reviving the spirit of the UDHR, and promoting high-quality development. On the global human rights governance stage, China is playing an increasingly important role, making greater and greater contributions and gaining more and more international recognition.

1. "In-depth participant" in international mechanisms

As early as the 1950s, China proposed the Five Principles of Peaceful Coexistence and got the Bandung Conference to adopt the 10 principles of Bandung Declaration based on the Five Principles of Peaceful Coexistence. In May 1955, Chinese Premier Zhou Enlai pointed out at an enlarged meeting of the Standing Committee of the National People's Congress that the ten principles of the Bandung Declaration also stipulate respect for basic human rights and respect for the purposes and principles of the Charter of the United Nations. These have been the views advocated by the Chinese people and the principles China has always adhered to.

Human rights are essential part of China's participation in United Nations affairs and global governance. After restoring its lawful seat in the UN, China began to participate in the work of its human rights bodies, including sending delegations to attend relevant meetings, participating in the review of relevant human rights issues, and maintaining constructive, cooperative relations with the UN human rights bodies. Since the reform and opening up, China has taken a more active stance on human rights.

Since 1979, China attended meetings of the United Nations Commission on Human Rights as an observer for three consecutive years. In 1981, China was elected a member state of the Commission on Human Rights. The United Nations Human Rights Council replaced the Commission on Human Rights in 2006 and China was elected to the newly established Human Rights Council. Since then, China has actively participated in elections and has been successfully elected every time, thus becoming one of the few countries to have been elected five times since the UN Human Rights Council's establishment.

China participates in the work of UN human rights mechanisms such as the Human Rights Council constructively, increasing its appearance in various UN human rights institutions. Many Chinese experts serve as members of several human rights treaty bodies, including the UN Committee on Economic, Social and Cultural Rights, the Committee against Torture, the Committee on the Elimination of Racial Discrimination, the Committee on the Elimination of Discrimination against Women, and the Committee on the Rights of Persons with Disabilities.

China adheres to the principles of international law and conscientiously fulfills its international human rights obligations. As of July 2022, China has ratified or acceded to 29 international human rights instruments, including six core United Nations human rights treaties. China has comprehensively fulfilled its treaty obligations, submitted timely implementation reports, and participated in the deliberations of various treaty bodies, demonstrating its openness and confidence on human rights issues.

In February 2009, China participated in its first Universal Periodic Review (UPR) by the United Nations Human Rights Council. At the meeting, the Chinese representative first introduced the development of China's human rights cause. In the subsequent interactive dialogue, representatives from 60 countries spoke one after another. Most of the country representatives believed that China's human rights report was "constructive transparent and open," praising China for its "huge and shocking" achievements in the field of human rights. So far, China has successfully undergone three rounds of UPRs by the United Nations Human Rights Council.

China has also actively expanded cooperation with the UN High Commissioner for Human Rights and its office, and the special mechanisms of the Human Rights Council, prompting them to carry out their work fairly and objectively and to engage in constructive dialogue with various countries. China has invited envoys from some countries stationed in Geneva and UN officials to visit Xinjiang over the past years. We comprehensively deepened their understanding and recognition of China's human rights development path through meetings, discussions, exchanges, on-site visits, and other methods. We exposed them to first-hand experience of a real Xinjiang with social security and stability, sustained development, and a situation where people live and work in peace and contentment.

2. "Co-constructor" of governance rules

The concept and norms of human rights are important expressions of the common values shared by all humanity in contemporary times. The acceptance and implementation of human rights treaties by countries worldwide are essential means to promote and protect human rights. China has continuously striven to promote contemporary human rights concepts and norms, promote and improve the human rights governance rules system, and uphold the shared values of humanity.

China has often sent representatives to participate in drafting international human rights legal instruments. It has successively participated in formulating significant international human rights instruments such as the Convention against Torture and Other Cruel, Inhuman or Degrading Treatment or Punishment, the Convention on the Rights of the Child, and the Convention on the Rights of Persons with Disabilities. China's opinions and amendments have been valued by all parties and made significant contributions to drafting, revising, and improving these rules. As the world's largest developing country, China firmly regards the rights to subsistence and development as the most fundamental human rights. China represents on the international stage the most basic human rights needs of the vast developing countries. As one of the leading promoters, China participated in the drafting of the Declaration on the Right to Development and has successively urged the UN Human Rights Commission and the Human Rights Council to hold consultations on the realization of the right to development, dedicated to promoting mechanisms for the implementation of the right to development.

In 1993, China participated in the World Conference on Human Rights in Vienna and participated in the discussion and drafting of the Vienna Declaration and Program of Action. China put forth many constructive suggestions, contributing to drafting and adopting the Declaration. China actively engages in developing international documents related to human rights, including labor protection and etc.

3. "Active advocate" of exchanges and cooperation

For a long time, China has actively advocated and vigorously promoted foreign exchanges and cooperation in human rights and is committed to carrying out human rights exchanges and cooperation based on equality and mutual respect. Since the 1990s, China has successively established human rights dialogue or consultation mechanisms with more than 20 countries; conducted human rights dialogues or exchanges with such Western countries and regional organizations as Germany, Switzerland, Hungary, Greece, and the European Union; and conducted human rights consultations with developing countries and regional organizations, including Russia, Egypt, South Africa, Brazil, Malaysia, Pakistan, Belarus, Cuba, and the African Union. Human rights non-governmental organizations like the China Society for Human Rights Studies have become increasingly active on the international stage, arranging for delegations to go overseas for exchange visits while inviting officials, experts, and scholars from many countries in the field of human rights to come to China for exchange visits. From March to April 2023, during the 52nd session of the UN Human Rights Council, several Chinese civil society organizations actively participated in the conference, gave speeches online and offline, and held thematic side events covering the topics of "Protecting the Rights of Ethnic Minorities in the New Era," "Empowering Women from a Sustainable Development Perspective," and "China's Human Rights Philosophy and Practices." They aimed to introduce China's perspective on human rights, its specific practices, and achievements while addressing severe human rights violations committed by certain Western countries. These events gave Chinese civil society a voice at the Human Rights Council.

China has actively created platforms and avenues to promote exchanges and cooperation in human rights. It has successfully organized various international conferences such as the Beijing Forum on Human Rights, the South-South Human Rights Forum, the "China-EU Human Rights Seminar, the International Human Rights

Cultural Expo, and the International Seminar on the 30th Anniversary of the Adoption of the UN Declaration on the Right to Development. These conferences have facilitated consensus-building, reduced differences, and enhanced mutual understanding among all parties on human rights issues. These external exchanges and collaborations have expanded channels for communication and facilitated mutual learning between China and other relevant countries in the field of human rights.

The Forum on Global Human Rights Governance was held in Beijing from June 14 to 15, 2023. More than 300 guests from nearly 100 countries and international organizations, including UN agencies, attended the forum.

During their visit, foreign participants explored sites in Beijing's Dongcheng District, including the Sanlihe Park and the Pigment Guild Hall on Qianmen Street. They highly praised the historical heritage preservation, environmental improvement, and the enhancement of living conditions in the Sanlihe area. They learned about cultural innovations, such as the revitalization through the usage of traditional guild halls in Dongcheng District, and enjoyed a Beijing opera performance. "People not only enjoy civil and political rights but also economic, social, and cultural rights. China's preservation and inheritance of its historical culture have left a deep impression on me," Patricia Narsu Ndanema, Commissioner of the Human Rights Commission of Sierra Leone, said that "Apart from cultural preservation, one thing that has deeply impressed me is how clean it is here. Having a clean, healthy, and sustainable environment is a fundamental human right."

The forum's attending guests spoke freely about their views on global human rights governance, giving full recognition to China's achievements in the field of human rights practice and its contributions to the development of international human rights endeavors. Abdoulaye Mar Dieye, Vice Chairperson and Rapporteur of the United Nations Committee on Economic, Social, and Cultural Rights, expressed that China has achieved numerous accomplishments in protecting human rights, such as poverty alleviation. He stated, "It not only is a major achievement for China but also represents a significant victory for humanity." William Jones, Washington bureau chief of the American magazine Executive Intelligence Review, said that China's role in protecting the human rights of its citizens deserves high praise. More importantly, China's call to consider development as a human right has received widespread recognition from the international community. Robert Coon, Chairman of the Kuhn Foundation in the

United States, praised the event as "a relevant and forward-looking gathering."

4. "Essential promoter" of governance change

In March 2017, China, representing 140 countries, made a joint statement titled "Promoting and Protecting Human Rights, Building a Community of Shared Future for Humanity" at the 34th session of the UN Human Rights Council, which resonated widely among diplomats present. Aftab Khurashi, the Permanent Deputy Representative of Pakistan to the United Nations, said, "Given the many challenges facing the world today, we should especially appreciate the concept China has offered to our global village."

While advancing its own human rights development, China has consistently attached importance to participating in reforming the global human rights governance system to steer global human rights governance toward greater fairness, equity, and inclusiveness.

China has actively participated in the reform of the United Nations human rights institutions, played an active role in the consultation and final voting process for establishing the United Nations Human Rights Council, and put forward a series of propositions that the vast majority of countries have recognized. China also supports establishing thematic special mechanisms by the United Nations Human Rights Council on issues such as the right to development and food and unilateral coercive measures. It advocates convening special meetings on food security and the international financial crisis and actively promotes the improvement of international human rights mechanisms.

On June 18, 2007, the Human Rights Council agreed on a package plan to establish a charter and system for the Human Rights Council. The Chinese delegation actively participated in relevant negotiations and consultations with a constructive attitude, particularly on issues involving the primary interests of the developing countries, adhering to principles and daring to speak out boldly to uphold justice. For that, it was widely praised by the developing countries. Public opinion generally believed that the Chinese delegation displayed the demeanor of a major country during the negotiations, acted flexibly, helped all parties reach a consensus, and demonstrated the image of a responsible major country.

Over the years, based on its own human rights practices, China has put forward a series of constructive ideas and initiatives that align with the trend of the times and echo the international community's concerns, which have been widely accepted.

In response to the difficulties in improving the level of global human rights protection, impediments in human rights cooperation, and challenges in protecting economic, social, and cultural rights during post-epidemic recovery, China has repeatedly pushed the UN Human Rights Council to adopt a resolution on Promoting the International Human Rights Cause through Win-Win Cooperation, and called on all parties to carry out constructive dialogue and cooperation and strengthen human rights technical assistance;

China has repeatedly urged the passage of the resolution on The Contribution of Development to the Enjoyment of All Human Rights, calling on all countries to achieve people-centered development;

China has advocated for the adoption of resolutions addressing the negative impact of the legacies of colonialism on the enjoyment of human rights, calling for the elimination of all forms of colonialism and the resolution of issues stemming from colonial legacies;

China has pushed for the adoption of resolutions aimed at promoting and protecting economic, social, and cultural rights and eliminating inequalities in the context of the pandemic. These resolutions call on all countries to promote and protect economic, social, and cultural rights and to take inclusive measures to address the pandemic and advance post-pandemic recovery;

Since 2017, with China's promotion, the idea of building a community of shared future for humanity has been incorporated into more than ten UN Human Rights Council resolutions, becoming an integral part of the international discourse on human rights.

II. China's Contribution to Promoting the Development of World Human Rights

Human rights are concrete, historical, and practical. Respecting and safeguarding human rights requires proactively creating conditions for their realization. Necessary prerequisites for the sustainable advancement of human rights include a secure and peaceful environment, the driving force of development and progress, and a fair and just order. China actively promotes the shared values of peace, development, fairness, justice, democracy, and freedom for all humanity. While advancing its own human rights cause, China contributes to the world's human rights endeavors with a sense of benefiting both oneself and others. China remains committed to being a builder of world peace, a contributor to global development, a defender of international order, and a promoter of human civilization progress.

1. Laying a solid foundation for developing global human rights protection

Development is the master key to solving all problems, the foundation of human rights protection, and the crux of achieving people's happiness. China has long been committed to promoting the realization of the right to life and the right to development for the people of developing countries. China provides support and assistance to developing countries and regions in areas such as infrastructure, education, healthcare, and agriculture. Through international cooperation under the "Belt and Road Initiative" (BRI), China will accelerate the advancement of the UN 2030 Agenda for Sustainable Development and contribute to further solidifying the development foundation for global human rights protection.

In the capital of the Solomon Islands, Honiara, there is often a long queue outside the National Referral Hospital's physiotherapy room. Patients are there to see the acupuncture physicians of the Chinese medical team assisting the Solomon Islands. A resident named Rex Faulkner, who often came for medical treatment, mentioned that he used to have severe headaches that lasted for several hours at a time, and the only relief was through medication. However, after receiving a ten-session acupuncture treatment prescribed by the acupuncture physician, he felt relieved after merely six sessions.

The Solomon Islands is one of the least developed countries, and its medical and healthcare conditions are relatively backward. At the primary and regional clinics, medical services are often provided only by nurses and nurse assistants, while doctors are available only in hospitals at and above the provincial level. After China established diplomatic relations with the Solomon Islands in 2019, a medical assistance team was sent to the Solomon Islands in early 2022. Currently, the second batch of eight team members are working there. With the assistance of the Chinese medical team, several medical milestones have been achieved at local hospitals, including cases of the first dual endoscopic urethral rupture repair surgery, the first ureteroscopy-assisted stone extraction surgery, the first urethral incision combined with prostate resection surgery, the first thrombolysis treatment using third-generation drugs, and the first temporary pacemaker implantation etc.

2023 marks the 60th anniversary of China's dispatch of medical teams abroad. Since the first medical team for foreign aid was dispatched to Algeria in 1963, China has sent a total of 30,000 medical personnel to 76 countries and regions worldwide, providing medical treatment to 290 million patients. This year, President Umaro Sissoco Embaló of Guinea-Bissau awarded the "National Medal of Honor for Cooperation and Development" to the Chinese medical team in Guinea-Bissau. The Ministry of National Defense of Laos awarded the Medal of Valor of Lao People's Army to the 8th Chinese military medical experts team to Laos. The Ministry of Health of Cambodia also presented the "Night Class" honorable medals to the traditional Chinese medicine (TCM) team aiding in Cambodia's fight against COVID-19.

Beginning from the early days of the People's Republic of China, despite full-scale reconstruction with financial constraints, China started to assist relevant countries, providing strong support to developing countries in their struggle for national independence and people's liberation and their endeavor to promote economic and social development. The people of Tanzania and Zambia have never forgotten the support they received from China during the 1960s and 1970s when the two countries were committed to developing their national economies and supporting the national liberation movements of countries in the region after independence. They remember that China overcame numerous difficulties, provided interest-free loans, and sent tens of thousands of experts and railway workers to Africa to assist in the construction of the Tanzania-Zambia Railway. This "Freedom Road" running through East Africa and Central and South Africa has effectively promoted local economic and social development and improved the livelihoods of the people there.

Since the reform and opening up in 1978, China's foreign aid has become richer in content and more diverse in form. In the new era, China has steadily increased its foreign aid funding, expanding the scope of assistance. It has increasingly focused on Asia and Africa's least developed and developing countries. The various forms of China's foreign aid include grants, interest-free loans, loans on favorable terms, and the provision of complete sets of equipment. Over the years, China has established channels such as the Global Development and South-South Cooperation Fund and the China-UN Peace and Development Fund. Through these channels, China has collaborated with nearly

20 international institutions and non-governmental organizations, including the UN Development Program (UNDP), the World Food Program (WFP), the World Health Organization (WHO), and United Nations International Children's Emergency Fund (UNICEF), to implement aid projects jointly, benefiting tens of millions of people in more than 100 countries in Asia, Africa, Latin America, and other regions.

While giving "fish" to others, China also teaches them how to "fish."

From Africa to Oceania, Chinese Prof. Lin Zhanxi and his team, the inventors of the Juncao technology, which in Chinese means breeding mushroom with herbaceous plants, have brought it to countries like Fiji, Lesotho, Nigeria, Rwanda, and Eritrea. They have actively engaged in international poverty alleviation cooperation, helping the people of those countries escape poverty and become prosperous. People in Papua New Guinea called the technology "Lincao" to express gratitude to the Chinese poverty alleviation experts led by Lin Zhanxi. A ballad goes in Lesotho, "Some call it weed; some call it life. But it is food and medicine. It is a symbol of hope..." Juncao technology has helped some countries address long-standing agricultural development bottlenecks and created green job opportunities for over 100 countries worldwide, earning the approval of María Fernanda Espinosa Garcés, President of the 73rd session of the UN General Assembly.

China helps those in need and those in poverty.

China continues to increase its assistance in technology and human resource development cooperation. It helps developing countries improve their governance, planning, and industrial development capabilities and train their management talents and technological experts. For example, China helped Grenada formulate a national development strategic plan, worked with Cuba to jointly compile medium to long-term industrial development planning recommendations, provided policy advice to Zimbabwe on special economic zones and state-owned enterprise reform, and helped Cambodia work out plans for a national road network and modern agricultural development. It has signed memorandums of understanding on human resources development cooperation with 36 countries, including Rwanda, Kyrgyzstan, El Salvador, Papua New Guinea, and Trinidad and Tobago. It provides targeted capacity-building support based on the actual needs of different countries. China has established a trust fund with the UN to provide training for nearly 900 government statisticians in 59 developing countries.

China helps developing countries enhance technological innovation capabilities and industrial production skills by sharing technological achievements, promoting technology transfer, and improving vocational skills. For example, China has implemented over a thousand intergovernmental science and technology exchange projects and invited 755 young scientists from Egypt, Pakistan, Myanmar, and India to conduct research in China through the International Young Scientists Program. It trained over 7,700 students from over 100 developing countries and regions. China's Juncao technology has taken root in over 100 countries worldwide, creating hundreds of thousands of green job opportunities there. With the support of the Global Development and South-South Cooperation Fund, the UN Food and Agriculture Organization (FAO) and the World Food Program have implemented nearly 50 trilateral cooperation projects to help relevant developing countries improve their food security and comprehensive agricultural production capabilities.

As a responsible major country, China provides essential public goods to the world in global development and international cooperation, offering an action guide for countries to focus on development, unite for development, and achieve joint development. In 2013, Chinese President Xi Jinping proposed the Belt and Road Initiative (BRI) to integrate China's development into global development, drive common development among countries worldwide, and promote the realization of people's right to development in all countries.

In December 2021, the China-Laos Railway, a landmark project of the BRI, officially went into operation, realizing the Lao people's dream of turning a landlocked country into a "land-linked country." During the inauguration ceremony, the Vice Chairman of the Lao National Assembly, Sommad Pholsena, who once served as Minister of Public Works and Transport, said emotionally, "China may not be the first to say they will come to Laos to build railways, but it is the only one that has come and built one." Similar projects can be found within the Belt and Road cooperations, such as the Maldives-China Friendship Bridge, Croatia's Peljesac Bridge, Mozambique's Maputo-Catembe Bridge, the Mongolia-Russia Railway, the Addis Ababa-Djibouti Railway, the Jakarta-Bandung High-Speed Railway, etc. These projects have become national landmarks, livelihood projects, and symbols of cooperation, paving the way for common development. Former Japanese Prime Minister Yukio Hatoyama believes that co-building the BRI can prevent conflicts by promoting economic development in neighboring regions.

Over the past decade, the BRI has become a highly welcomed international public good and global platform for international cooperation, attracting participation from more than three-quarters of the world's countries. For ten years, the BRI has attracted nearly trillions of USD in investment, developing over 3,000 cooperative projects and creating 420,000 job opportunities for countries along the route.

In September 2021, Chinese President Xi Jinping put forward the Global Development Initiative (GDI), emphasizing the importance of prioritizing development, focusing on people-centered approaches, promoting inclusiveness and innovation-driven development, fostering harmonious coexistence between humans and nature, persisting in action-oriented approaches, advocating for a global development community. The GDI has become another essential public good that China offers to the world. UN Secretary-General Antonio Guterres praised the GDI, highlighting its great positive significance in promoting global equality and balanced, sustainable development.

This significant initiative responds to the real needs of people worldwide for peaceful development, fairness and justice, and win-win cooperation. Upon its proposal, it received responses from international organizations like the UN and numerous countries. It has already achieved a series of early accomplishments: First, it has garnered broad international consensus for advancing cooperation under the initiative and accelerating the implementation of the UN 2030 Agenda. Over 100 countries and international organizations, including the UN, have supported the GDI, and more than 70 countries have joined the Group of Friends of Global Development Initiative established within the framework of the UN. The initiative has been incorporated into cooperation documents with ASEAN, Central Asia, Africa, Latin America, and Pacific Island countries. Second, financial measures are gradually being put into action. The Global Development and South-South Cooperation Fund, with a total of 4 billion USD, has been implemented. The third phase of China-FAO South-South Cooperation Trust Fund has officially launched. Third, collaboration platforms have been established, including the Global Development Promotion Center Network, the World Alliance for Vocational and Technical Education Development, and the International Civil Poverty Reduction Cooperation Network. These platforms have built a cooperation network among all parties regarding agriculture, education, anti-epidemic, and response to climate change to drive the construction of cooperation mechanisms in various fields.

Currently, the construction of GDI project database is proceeding in an orderly manner. The first batch lists 50 practical cooperation projects and 1,000 capacity-building projects. They are progressing proactively, covering poverty alleviation, food security, and industrialization. Fourth, the GDI has enhanced knowledge sharing for development. China has published the Global Development Report and is rapidly building a global development knowledge network, actively exchanging governance and development experiences among different countries.

2. Guarding a secure environment for global human rights protection

Everyone has the right to enjoy peace so that all human rights can be promoted and protected and full development can be realized. In 2016, the 71st UN General Assembly adopted the Declaration on the Right to Peace, solemnly declaring that everyone has the right to enjoy peace, further affirming and developing the right to peace.

China has always been a steadfast force in safeguarding world peace.

On May 31, 2016, the camp in the Gao UN mission area in Mali, where the 4th batch of the Chinese peacekeeping engineering unit was located, was suddenly attacked by a terrorist vehicle loaded with explosives. At that time, Shen Liangliang was on duty and quickly reported the situation, sounded the alarm with gunshots, and pushed his comrades away in a moment of life and death, sacrificing himself heroically at the age of 29.

In January 2015, the Chinese military dispatched a 700-strong infantry battalion to the UN Mission in South Sudan, marking the first time that a Chinese military sent an infantry battalion to perform overseas peacekeeping missions in an organized manner. One day in July 2016, fierce fighting broke out in South Sudan, China's second peacekeeping infantry battalion lost two soldiers, the 33-year-old Master Sergeant Yang Shupeng and 22-year-old corporal Li Lei.

China has participated in United Nations peacekeeping operations since 1990. Over the past 30 years, the Chinese military has sent over 50,000 officers and soldiers to more than 20 countries and regions to participate in United Nations peacekeeping operations. Twenty-five peacekeepers have sacrificed their precious lives.

Currently, China is the country that sends the largest number of peacekeepers among the permanent members of the United Nations Security Council and is also the second largest contributor to United Nations peacekeeping operations. On May 29, 2023, the United Nations International Day of United Nations Peacekeepers and also the 75th anniversary of United Nations peacekeeping operations, Jean-Pierre Lacroix, the Under-Secretary-General for Peace Operations, praised China for playing a significant role in the United Nations peacekeeping efforts. He acknowledged China's unwavering support for United Nations peacekeeping and noted the "extremely valuable contributions."

On the eve of International Children's Day in 2023, 12-year-old Bangladeshi girl Alifa Chin received an exceptional holiday gift, the Chinese President Xi Jinping wrote back to her, encouraging her to study hard, pursue her dreams, and inherit the traditional friendship between China and Bangladesh.

Back on November 9, 2010, the Chinese naval hospital ship "Peace Ark" arrived at Chittagong, a port city in southeastern Bangladesh, and began a week-long medical service to Bangladesh.

At that time, a local pregnant woman faced a life-threatening situation due to a long-term heart condition as she was about to give birth. Bangladesh urgently sought assistance from the "Peace Ark." Despite tremendous pressure, Chinese doctors performed a cesarean section for them. After the child was born, Chinese doctors remained in the ward, watching over the mother and daughter for two days. They did not leave until the mother and daughter's condition stabilized. The father, Anwar Hossen, named his daughter "Chin," which means "China" in Bengali, hoping his daughter would remember China.

In 2013, the "Peace Ark" hospital ship visited Bangladesh for the second time, where doctors conducted a comprehensive medical examination of Chin. In 2017, the anesthesiologist who had been part of the surgical team during the operation, Sheng Ruifang, accompanied a Chinese Navy fleet on a friendly visit to Bangladesh. While at the port, Sheng Ruifang met Chin, and it was the first time Chin called her "Chinese mom." In December 2019, Chin and her family came to China and boarded the "Peace Ark" at a military port in Zhoushan. Since Chin's birth, the care from China has never ceased, and her story with China continues to unfold.

As of June 2023, the Chinese naval hospital ship "Peace Ark" has embarked on ten overseas missions, covering more than 260,000 nautical miles, providing medical services to 43 countries and regions, and serving over 250,000 individuals, with over 1,400 surgeries performed. Today, this big white ship filled with the spirit of international humanitarianism, sows the seeds of peace and friendship worldwide. It has indeed become a vessel of life, peace, and friendship.

The Chinese nation is a peace-loving nation, and the Chinese people are a peace-loving people. The confidence and consciousness of pursuing peaceful development rooted in China's peace-oriented cultural genes. As early as the 1950s, China jointly advocated the Five Principles of Peaceful Coexistence with India and Myanmar. In recent years, China has contributed Chinese wisdom, proposed Chinese solutions, and played a constructive role in resolving the nuclear issues of North Korea and Iran and the problems in Syria. China actively pursues the idea of peaceful diplomacy, emphasizes peaceful coexistence with all countries, advocates a common, comprehensive, cooperative, and sustainable security concept, is committed to promoting South-South cooperation and North-South dialogue, strives to narrow the North-South gap, and proposes global security initiatives. China will continue to contribute its strength to lasting peace and development in the world and to safeguarding the right to peace of people worldwide.

China actively participates in international law enforcement and security cooperation, strengthening collaboration within global and regional organizations such as the UN, the International Criminal Police Organization, and the Shanghai Cooperation Organization. This cooperation aims to combat all forms of terrorism, separatism, extremism, and drug-related crimes. China is also actively engaged in international arms control and disarmament processes, having acceded to dozens of global arms control treaties and mechanisms, including the Treaty on the Non-Proliferation of Nuclear Weapons (NPT). Regarding the Ukraine crisis, China decides its position and policy based on the merits of the matter concerned, upholds objectivity and fairness, and actively promotes peace talks.

Peace is an essential prerequisite for the development of human rights. A continuously growing China remains a significant guardian of world peace. In April 2022, Chinese President Xi Jinping, at the Boao Forum for Asia, solemnly put forward the Global Security Initiative (GSI), systematically elucidating China's stance and propositions for promoting security for all worldwide and maintaining global peace and stability. President Xi emphasized that We, humanity, are living in an indivisible security community, advocated a concept guided by the principles of common, comprehensive, cooperative, and sustainable security, with mutual respect as the guide for action, inseparability of security as the essential principle, and security community building as the long-term goal. It paves the way for a new type of security characterized by dialogue rather than confrontation, partnership rather than alliance, and win-win cooperation rather than zero-sum competition. Former Slovenia President Danilo Türk believes the

GSI was proposed at the right time and provides a robust conceptual framework for global security dialogues and cooperation.

Over the past year, the content of the GSI has continued to evolve and has gained recognition and acceptance from more and more members of the international community. It has contributed Chinese wisdom and solutions to addressing international security challenges and filled the deficit in global peace. In February 2023, China released the Concept Paper on the Global Security Initiative, further elaborating on the core concepts and principles, key areas of cooperation, and cooperation platforms and mechanisms of the GSI. China actively engaged in diplomatic mediation efforts and successively issued documents such as China's Position on the Political Settlement of the Ukraine Crisis, and China's Position on the Afghan Issue, firmly standing on the side of peace. On March 10, 2023, China, Saudi Arabia, and Iran signed and issued a joint statement announcing the agreement between Saudi Arabia and Iran to restore diplomatic relations. It marks a successful practice of China's vigorous implementation of the GSI. It sets an example for regional countries to resolve conflicts and differences through dialogue and negotiation and promote neighborly and friendly relations. As a result, a wave of reconciliation has swept through the Middle East. Saeed Abu Ali, assistant Secretary-General of the Arab League, expressed that Arab countries looked forward to China's significant role in maintaining peace in the Middle East and the world.

China actively promotes international security dialogue and exchanges. For instance, it facilitated the hosting of the first Horn of Africa Peace Conference for countries in the African region and successfully hosted two rounds of the Middle East Security Forum. Additionally, China actively promotes security-related exchanges and cooperation among various parties through multilateral platforms, such as the Shanghai Cooperation Organization, the Conference on Interaction and Confidence-Building Measures in Asia, and the East Asia Cooperation Mechanism. China is committed to cooperating with various parties in non-traditional security areas such as pandemic response, counter-terrorism, biological security, cybersecurity, food security, and climate change. Within the framework of the G20, China proposed initiatives for international food security cooperation and promoted the BRICS Country Food Security Cooperation Strategy. The China-Pacific Island Countries Disaster Risk Reduction and Management Center officially commenced operations in February 2023, representing another robust action by China under the GSI framework to assist developing countries in addressing non-traditional security challenges. Belarusian President Alexander Lukashenko remarked that China is a mainstay in safeguarding world peace.

3. Defending fairness and justice in global human rights governance

Developing countries account for more than 80% of the population in today's world. The development of global human rights cannot be achieved without the joint efforts of developing countries. After the end of the Cold War, faced with Western countries' scheme to interfere in other countries' internal affairs under the pretext of human rights, developing countries actively participated in international human rights dialogues, hoping to eliminate confrontation in international human rights activities through international cooperation.

Developing countries emphasize the universality, objectivity, and non-selectivity of human rights. They advocate for promoting human rights through cooperation and negotiation, considering the diverse political, economic, social, and cultural realities of the world when advancing human rights governance. They believe that human rights are indivisible, encompassing both civil and political rights, as well as economic, social, and cultural rights, and including both individual and collective rights. In 1993, the Second World Conference on Human Rights adopted the Vienna Declaration and Programme of Action, which to some extent reflected many developing countries' human rights views and propositions. It resulted from continuous efforts by developing countries, including China, in the struggle for fairness and justice.

Declaration and Programme of Action, which, to some extent, reflected many developing countries' human rights views and propositions. It resulted from continuous efforts by developing countries, including China, in the struggle for fairness and justice.

On June 14, 2023, during his visit, Palestinian President Abbas, in a meeting with President Xi Jinping, said, "I sincerely thank China on behalf of the Palestinian people for its strong support and selfless assistance to the Palestinian people in their just cause of restoring their legitimate national rights." President Abbas's statement, "China is a trusted friend and partner for the Palestinian side," expresses deep recognition of China's long-standing commitment to speaking up and upholding justice for the Palestinian people in multilateral forums.

In history, China shares a similar fate and experiences with many developing countries. Today, there are common demands for economic development, improving people's livelihoods, and enhancing fundamental human rights such as the rights to life and development. All of these factors determine that China and many developing countries have similar or identical concepts and positions on human rights issues. China has consistently upheld justice and made unremitting efforts to defend third-world countries' national self-determination rights and prevent large-scale human rights violations. China's persistent efforts over the years in seeking a just and equitable resolution to issues such as Cambodia, Afghanistan, Palestine, and occupied Arab territories are well-known.

On July 5, 2023, during the 53rd session of the UN Human Rights Council, the Chinese representative spoke about the issue of Syria, stating that peace and stability are the greatest guarantees of human rights and that advancing a political solution is the only way out for Syria. The Chinese representative emphasized that when discussing the issue of Syria, the Human Rights Council should not forget the responsibilities that countries like the United States and the United Kingdom bear for the suffering of the Syrian people. China urged these countries to cease their illegal presence and military operations in Syria, halt unilateral sanctions against Syria, and restore genuine human rights, wealth, freedom, and dignity to the Syrian people. As a permanent member of the UN Security Council, China has exercised its veto power in several Security Council votes related chiefly to the Syrian issue. China consistently bases its decisions on principles of right and wrong, safeguarding the interests of the Syrian people, speaking up for the fair treatment of Syria, and acting fairly, thereby upholding international equity and justice.

Sovereign equality is the foundation of global human rights governance. In global human rights governance, we must respect sovereignty and oppose hegemony to safeguard human rights. We must resolutely oppose the politicization of human rights. We must insist that all countries, big or small, strong or weak, rich or poor, are equal and participate in global human rights exchanges and dialogue as equal partners, striving to achieve win-win cooperation and jointly contributing to global human rights governance. As an essential member of the international community, China upholds fairness and justice and has made joint statements on behalf of countries with similar views at the UN Human Rights Council on many occasions. In response to unwarranted smears from Western countries, China courageously fights back and tells the true stories of human rights in China. It has exposed Western countries' racism, gun violence, forced labor, violations of indigenous rights, and other human rights abuses, firmly opposing the bullying behavior of some countries that frequently impose unilateral sanctions and blockades against other countries... These concrete actions not only steadfastly defend international fairness and justice and safeguard the sovereignty and dignity of developing countries but also effectively promote international human rights exchanges, cooperation, and the healthy and orderly development of global human rights governance.

4. Promoting exchanges and mutual appreciation among different human rights civilizations

Human rights are the fruits and symbols of the progress of human civilization. Respecting and safeguarding human rights is the fundamental spirit of modern civilization. Through long and arduous efforts, China has successfully embarked on a human rights development path that conforms to the trends of the times and suits its national conditions. China's human rights development path is a significant manifestation of the path of socialism with Chinese characteristics in the field of human rights. It has enriched and advanced human rights civilization, contributing Chinese strength, wisdom, and solutions to the cause of human progress.

Chinese modernization is deeply rooted in China's fine traditional culture and infused with the vitality of Chinese civilization. Its practical path is based on the realization of human freedom and comprehensive development, contains profound and rich human rights thoughts, and injects the power of Chinese civilization into the development of the world's human rights cause and conceptual innovation. In the modernization practice characterized by a vast population, China can perceive the people-oriented thinking of "people being the foundation of the country, and a consolidated foundation determining the country's stability. In the unremitting pursuit of "common prosperity for all the people," China can find the governance philosophy of "a prosperous nation being built on the well-being of its people." In the coordinated development of material and spiritual civilization, China can appreciate the moral character of "virtues promoting growth" and "improving oneself with unceasing efforts." In the solid actions of "harmoniously coexisting with nature," China can realize the development philosophy of "following the natural order and achieving unity between man and nature." In the determined choice of "pursuing a path of peaceful development," China can understand the social ideal of "emphasizing trustworthiness and seeking harmony" and "all people under heaven being of one family." The profound and extensive Chinese civilization benefits not only the Chinese people but also provides valuable insights for the world.

In the "world history" process initiated during the Age of Exploration, debates regarding the paths to modernization and the diversity and singularity of civilizations have never ceased. Unlike those who embraced "civilization superiority" and "clash of civilizations" theories, China has consistently advocated for the coexistence and exchange of different civilizations, always with the genuine well-being of people worldwide as the starting point. "The contributions made by a country or a nation to the world and humanity are not only measured by material creations but also by the ideas it puts forward." The former Greek president Prokopis Pavlopoulos sincerely appreciated China's view on civilization.

On March 27, 2014, President Xi Jinping delivered a speech at the UNESCO headquarters, clearly expounding China's cultural perspective in the new era. He pointed out, "Intercultural exchange and mutual learning are important impetuses for the progress of human civilization and world peace and development." His speech received enthusiastic applause and strong endorsement from the audience. "The vision of Chinese leader aligns with the mission of UNESCO," commented the then Director-General of UNESCO, Irina Bokova.

In May 2019, the Conference on Dialogue of Asian Civilizations (CDAC), initiated by China, was held in Beijing. The conference produced a document endorsed by more than 1,000 representatives from 47 Asian countries and other countries worldwide, as well as international organizations. The document emphasized the principles of diversity and coexistence transcending claims of civilization superiority, harmony and symbiosis transcending civilization conflicts, integration and sharing transcending civilization divides, and prosperity and progress transcending the stagnation of civilizations. China has consistently been committed to providing a platform for equal dialogue and mutual learning among different civilizations.

In March 2023, President Xi Jinping introduced the Global Civilization Initiative (GCI), issuing a heartfelt call to all countries worldwide, urging them to "fully harness the relevance of histories and cultures to the present times, and push for creative transformation and innovative development of all fine traditional cultures in the process of modernization." The GCI aims to promote cultural exchange and mutual learning among civilizations, fostering the progress of human civilization. It represents China's new and significant contribution to improving global governance and advancing the building of a human community with a shared future. It reflects China's firm commitment to upholding lasting world peace and development and promoting the continuous progress of human civilization.

III. Chinese Wisdom that Enriches the Form of Human Rights Civilization

Respecting and safeguarding human rights at home is the foundation of China's participation in global human rights governance. Since the 18th National Congress of the CPC, the Chinese government has regarded respecting and safeguarding human rights as an important task in its governance. It has promoted historic achievements in the field of human rights, accomplished the first centenary goal, and built a moderately prosperous society in all respects. China has historically solved the issue of absolute poverty, contributing to over 70% of global poverty reduction, achieving the UN 2030 Sustainable Development Agenda's poverty reduction goals ten years ahead of schedule, directly accelerating international poverty reduction efforts, and making significant contributions to the progress of human rights worldwide. This success has laid a more solid material foundation for the development of China's human rights cause.

China has continuously developed a whole-process people's democracy, promoted the rule of law to safeguard human rights, and firmly upheld social fairness and justice. The Chinese people enjoy broader, more extensive, and more comprehensive democratic rights. China has strived to achieve fuller and higher-quality employment; established the world's most extensive education system, social security system, and healthcare system; vigorously improved the quality of the living environment; and made continuous progress in areas such as childcare, education, employment, healthcare, elderly care, housing, and support for the vulnerable. China upholds the principle of people first and the sanctity of life, and it has effectively responded to the COVID-19 pandemic, maximizing the protection of people's lives and health... China's human rights practices, achieved through independent exploration of development paths, have been highly successful. The underlying logic of this success stems from a commitment to putting people first, a practical and truth-seeking approach, and self-confidence in open and inclusive human rights.

From a moral perspective, people are the core concern of human rights development. Taking the aspirations of the people to live a better life as the focus of our efforts, adhering to the basic principle of developing and safeguarding the fundamental interests of the vastest majority of the people, and constantly enhancing the sense of gain, happiness, and security among the people are the core values of the CPC's governance. Upholding the people's central role in the human rights cause, prioritizing the people's interests before anything else, promising a good life for the people, ensuring that the fruits of development offer greater benefits to all the people in a fair way, and enabling every person to enjoy opportunities for self-development and a good life is the essence of China's efforts to ensure that everyone enjoys more comprehensive human rights. In the over 70 years since the founding of the People's Republic of China, tremendous achievements have been made in China's human rights endeavors, vividly demonstrating the people-centered human rights philosophy, which is the moral essence of China's human rights path.

From a practical perspective, human rights are a product of specific historical conditions, and as history progresses, they will exhibit gradual and diverse changes. Different countries, at various stages of development, with varying levels of economic growth, cultural traditions, and social structures, face different human rights development tasks and must adopt different approaches to human rights protection. China has not mindlessly copied the practices of other countries but has, based on its own experiences, proposed that the rights to survival and development are fundamental human rights. China adheres to the principle of the universality of human rights while integrating it with its own reality, thus pursuing a human rights development path that aligns with its national conditions.

From an open perspective, China has developed a systematic concept of human rights centered on the people, based on more than 70 years of achievements in human rights. It also engages in human rights cooperation and exchanges with countries worldwide, learning from each other and sharing experiences. Emphasizing the common values of peace, development, fairness, justice, democracy, and freedom cherished by humanity, China seeks common ground in international human rights cooperation. China has put forward significant concepts, such as building a community with a shared future for humanity. These ideas contribute Chinese wisdom and solutions to developing international human rights efforts, significantly promoting global human rights governance toward greater fairness, equity, justice, and inclusiveness.

1. The people-centered nature of human rights endeavors

The people-centered set of principles is the most prominent characteristic of China's path to human rights development. "A country's human rights condition is essentially gauged by whether its people's interests are protected and whether they enjoy a growing sense of fulfillment, happiness, and security. It is the most important criterion for evaluating a country's human rights situation." China ensures the democratic rights of its people, fully stimulates their enthusiasm, initiative, and creativity, and allows them to become the main participants, promoters, and beneficiaries of human rights development. This approach effectively advances comprehensive human development and achieves more significant substantive progress in shared prosperity for all people. The human rights that China aims to achieve are not abstract concepts but tangible, happy livelihoods for its people. They are not privileges enjoyed by a few but inclusive human rights accessible to the vast majority of the population. Over the years, China has adhered to the people-centered development philosophy, making it a starting point and focus of development to improve people's well-being, safeguard their rights to self-governance, and promote comprehensive human development. This approach effectively protects the rights and interests of the people. China regards the happiness of its people as the most significant human right, making human rights construction more tangible and practical. The "goal-practice" logic it has established is clear and aligns with a new era of development, representing a fresh perspective on human rights.

2. Autonomy in human rights practice

The autonomy of China's human rights practices is reflected in the insistence on proceeding from reality, integrating the principle of universality of human rights with China's specific conditions, promoting the development of human rights from the perspective of China's national conditions and people's demands, and ensuring that the people enjoy a wide range of rights which are genuine, specific, and effective in accordance with the law. Countries have different national conditions, histories, cultures, social systems, and economic and social development levels. They must and can only explore a human rights development path that suits them based on their own realities and the needs of their people. Only the wearer knows best if a pair of shoes fits. Departing from reality and mindlessly adopting foreign institutional models not only leads to dysfunction and failure of implementation but also brings disastrous consequences, ultimately harming the interests of the vast majority of the people.

3. Comprehensiveness in human rights promotion

Over the years, China has consistently combined the principle of universality of human rights with its own realities, continuously promoting economic and social development, enhancing the well-being of its people, fostering social fairness and justice, strengthening the rule of law for human rights, and striving to promote the comprehensive and coordinated development of economic, social, cultural rights, as well as civil and political rights. These efforts have significantly improved the guarantee level of the people's rights to survival and development, charting a path for human rights development suitable for China's national conditions. Human rights cover a wide range, and various human rights are interdependent. Economic, social, cultural, civil, and political rights are inseparable components of the human rights system. The Vienna Declaration and Programme of Action reaffirms the fundamental view and position that "all human rights are universal, indivisible, interdependent, and interrelated." The connotation of human rights is complete and rich, requiring comprehensive and systematic measures to advance. Based on its own historical traditions, specific national conditions, and institutional characteristics, China plans its human rights development goals systematically, recognizing both the progressive nature of the human rights cause and the comprehensiveness and coordination of human rights construction. For a large society with a population of 1.4 billion, China adheres to the concept of "food is the priority for the people," striving to eliminate poverty, "the biggest obstacle to the realization of human rights," and protecting people's rights to survival and development. At the same time, in line with the people's expectations for a high-quality and better life, China continuously meets the growing and diverse rights demands of the people. It coordinates promoting economic development, democracy and the rule of law, ideology and culture, fairness and justice, social governance, and environmental protection. China comprehensively improves employment, income distribution, education, social security, medical care, housing, elderly care, and child support, among other aspects.

In the coordinated development of material, political, spiritual, social, and ecological civilizations, China enhances human rights protection in all aspects. It has embarked on a progressive, coordinated, and comprehensive path of human rights development, allowing every individual to enjoy their human rights more thoroughly, thus creating the Chinese model of respecting and safeguarding human rights.

4. Sustainability in human rights development

Sustainable development of human rights means not only providing a sustainable development impetus and material foundation for human rights but also institutionalizing and legalizing successful experiences in human rights progress to form a stable mechanism for respecting and safeguarding human rights. China attaches great importance to the sustainability of human rights development, adheres to the principle of people-centered development, and regards development as the top priority, laying a solid foundation for sustainable human rights development. China entirely, accurately, and comprehensively implements the new development concept; adheres to the idea of people-centered development; ensures that development is for the people, relies on the people, and benefits the people; focuses on addressing the most concerning and immediate issues of the people; and works to address the problems related to imbalances and inadequacies in development. Efforts are made to achieve higher-quality, more efficient, fairer, more sustainable, and safer development, ensuring that the general population experiences greater fulfillment, security, and sustainability regarding their sense of gain, happiness, and safety within the context of development. At the same time, China adheres to the rule of law, exercises law-based governance, and builds the rule of law in China to provide institutional guarantees for promoting sustainable human rights development. "The rule of law is the most effective safeguard for human rights." In advancing comprehensive law-based governance, China integrates human rights protection into various aspects such as sound legislation, strict law enforcement, impartial administration of justice, and social-wide observance of the law. Respecting and safeguarding human rights has become an essential principle in legislation, and the socialist legal system with Chinese characteristics with the Constitution as the core has been continuously improved; law-based government administration has been further promoted, making exercising administrative power more standardized. Judicial reform has been deepened, with efforts to ensure that the people feel fairness and justice in every judicial case. The construction of a law-based society has advanced in depth, and the society's awareness of the rule of law and the legal protection of human rights has been significantly enhanced. Since the 18th National Congress of the CPC, its Central Committee, with Xi Jinping at its core, has made a major strategic deployment for law-based governance in all respects. It places a greater emphasis on respecting and safeguarding human rights in building a socialist, law-based country, ushering in a new era of human rights rule of law construction in China from the perspective of advancing the modernization of the national governance system and capacity. From compiling the Civil Code to the comprehensive implementation of the Outline for Building a Law-Based Government (2015-2020), from the unwavering promotion of judicial system reform to the advancement of building a society based on the rule of law in all areas... China has achieved significant accomplishments in the legal guarantee of human rights. The fundamental rights and freedoms of the Chinese people are effectively safeguarded, and the foundation for the sustainable development of human rights in China is even more solid.

IV. China's Plan to Improve Global Human Rights Governance

Human rights civilization continues to evolve. Temporarily, the breadth and depth of human understanding of their rights expand with technological innovation, economic development, and social progress. Spatially, differences in historical culture, social systems, and development stages result in distinct human rights forms in different countries. The diversity of human rights civilization keeps enriching itself.

In today's world, economic globalization is further deepening, and despite headwinds, the historical trend cannot be reversed. Humanity is increasingly becoming an interconnected global community where "your interests are mine, and mine are yours." The rise of groups and the political awakening in developing countries drive international power structures and political landscapes toward multi-polarity. The demand for autonomous development and an enhanced voice in global governance continues to grow. This historical trend significantly impacts international human rights governance and presents new needs for our time. The holistic nature of human society is increasingly prominent, highlighting the need for a holistic human perspective in global human rights governance. The alignment of development with human rights progress is becoming increasingly crucial to meeting developing countries' realistic demands. Raising developing countries' voices in human rights discussions and practicing genuine multilateralism have become urgent tasks in constructing a new vision for global human rights governance in the context of the new era. China has made outstanding historic achievements in human rights practice and opened up a path for developing human rights with Chinese characteristics. At the same time, China has also contributed its ideas and plans to promote the development of global human rights causes and improve global human rights governance.

1. Unity and cooperation

Humanity living together on the earth has a shared destiny. Global human rights governance based on human integrity is the right direction for human rights civilization's evolution. From the Renaissance, the Enlightenment, and the bourgeois revolution to the national independence and liberation movements after World War II and then to the rapid advancement of globalization that integrates the global village, the importance of collective human rights in the international human rights governance structure has become increasingly evident. The primary forms of collective human rights, such as those pertaining to ethnic groups, individual nations, or all of humanity, also take a more significant place in international human rights. In today's world, the situation unseen in a century is evolving faster, and the world has entered a new period of instability and transformation. Traditional security risks intertwined with non-traditional ones and external challenges combined with internal ones pose profound challenges to human rights protection in individual countries and global human rights governance. Challenges such as hunger, poverty, conflict, terrorism, environmental pollution, climate change, and emerging issues in the realm of the internet get intertwined, especially with the global outbreak of the COVID-19 pandemic and various countries' response philosophies and strategies. While demonstrating the global nature of modernization risks, they also call for a holistic and cooperative approach to address common challenges. Promoting global human rights governance with a holistic perspective has become an inevitable trend in the evolution of human rights civilization in the context of globalization.

In the "engagement" philosophy of traditional Chinese culture, individuals do not live in abstract or isolation" but rather "coexistent" with one another based on interactive relationships. It is only within the context of these "coexistent" relationships with others that individuals derive value and meaning in their existence. This "coexistence and sharing" mindset shapes the way Chinese people perceive interpersonal relationships and, at the same time, profoundly influences China's interactions with the world.

When attending the "Work Together to Build a Community of Shared Future for Humanity" high-level meeting in Geneva on January 18, 2017, President Xi Jinping delivered a keynote speech entitled "Work Together to Build a Community with a Shared Future for Humanity," explaining the concept of a community with a shared future for humanity to the world. To elucidate China's perspective on human rights governance through the idea of a "a community with a shared future for humanity" means taking the diversity of global human rights governance and the diversity of interest demands as the practical context, taking the fact that "in today's world, the degree of interconnection and interdependence between countries has increased to an unprecedented level" as the logical starting point, taking shared risks in globalization and "shared destiny of humanity" as the basic awareness, and taking the cooperative development and rights protection of all human beings as the goal. Such an approach presents a distinct feature of holism. China's perspective on human rights governance guided by this significant concept emphasizes the pursuit of the times: common prosperity, mutual benefit, joint development, shared results, balanced and inclusive growth, and peaceful coexistence. It encompasses not only the shared values of peace, development, fairness, justice, democracy, and freedom for all of humanity but also underscores the holistic nature of global human rights protection efforts, representing a significant advancement beyond previous human rights concepts. It greatly enriches the content of human rights in the new era and has important guiding significance for building a fair and equitable international human rights governance system.

On March 1, 2017, on behalf of 140 countries, China issued a joint statement entitled "Work Together to Promote and Protect Human Rights and Build a Community of Shared Future for Humanity." It elaborated on the essential concept of a human community with a shared future and its significance in promoting the development of international human rights, thus receiving recognition and support from all parties. The two resolutions passed at this meeting on "economic, social, and cultural rights" and "food rights" clearly stated the need to "build a community with a shared future for humanity." Since then, building a community with a shared future for humanity has been written into multiple UN human rights documents and has become an essential part of the international human rights discourse system. Under the guidance of this concept, China advocates that all countries should collectively discuss global human rights governance, and the fruits of human rights development should be shared by the people of all nations, thus promoting the development of international human rights governance toward a more equitable, just, fair, and inclusive direction.

2. Development drive

It is an ideal pursuit of human society to have equal opportunities for development and share the benefits of development so that every individual achieves comprehensive growth and enjoys the full right to development. The right to development, along with the right to life, is a fundamental and primary human right. It represents the successful experience derived from China's own human rights practices and reflects the practical aspirations of many developing countries in their independent exploration of human rights paths. It aligns with the contemporary need to improve global human rights governance.

Most developing countries have experienced a long history of being colonized or semi-colonized. Dominated in the imperialist colonial system, they have long suffered economic exploitation and political slavery. After World War II, the independence and liberation movements in Asia, Africa, and Latin America flourished, and most developing countries gained sovereignty and independence. However, these countries continue to grapple with profound challenges such as hunger, poverty, educational deficiencies, stalled development, and governance inefficiencies. The collective psychological experiences shaped by their specific political histories and social memories often make it the most pressing human rights needs for developing countries to eliminate hunger and poverty and gradually realize the right to development based on ensuring the right to life. As developing countries increase their awareness of self-reliant development, more and more of them are attracted to and supportive of the "development-based human rights path." In 1986, the UN General Assembly adopted Resolution 41/128, formally recognizing the Declaration on the Right to Development and establishing the right to development as an "inalienable human right." This move represents the natural evolution of global human rights governance in response to the changing times.

Since China initiated its reform and opening-up policy, China's human rights cause has continued to develop and progress. A fundamental experience China has gained in the continuous development and advancement of its human rights cause is that it has steadfastly committed itself to development as something of paramount importance, consistently based its growth on its realities, and unswervingly laid a solid foundation for advancing human rights cause in all respects through development. In the new era, the CPC, based on the latest development stage, has implemented the new development philosophy and constructed a new development pattern, thus promoting high-quality development and leading people to achieve the first centenary goal. It has then embarked on a new journey toward building a socialist modernized country in all respects and advancing toward its second centenary goal. China's development and progress in its human rights cause promote and complement each other, exhibiting an explicit, logical relationship, namely, "the effective safeguarding of the right to subsistence is a prerequisite and foundation for enjoying and developing other human rights" and "only through development can the root causes of global challenges be eliminated; only through development can the basic rights of the people be guaranteed; only through development can human society progress." President Xi Jinping pointed out when meeting with the then UN High Commissioner for Human Rights Michelle Bachelet Jeria in May 2022, "For developing countries, the rights to subsistence and development are their primary and basic human rights. They must ensure higher-quality and more efficient, equitable, sustainable, and secure development of their economy and human rights."

The world economy faces high inflation, weakening demand, geopolitical conflicts, and energy and food security issues. Many countries, especially developing ones, are grappling with multiple development predicaments. The obstruction of the right to development has become a significant obstacle in global human rights governance. UN Secretary-General Guterres warned during the opening of the 2023 Development Financing Forum that the UN's 2030 Agenda for Sustainable Development is at risk of becoming a "mirage." Based on its development-driven approach to realizing human rights, China advocates "promoting development through cooperation and advancing human rights through development." It has also put forward the GDI, which is particularly significant in the current global development challenges. To fully protect their people's rights to human rights, countries cannot stay aloof from the interconnectedness of joint development. They should promote human rights development through cooperative development. They must form a development community for economic growth and adopt an open attitude to learn from each other's development experiences. For countries facing development difficulties, all other nations should offer assistance and extend a helping hand proactively. The China-proposed GDI advocates action-oriented approaches, focusing on developing countries' urgent livelihood needs. It urges practical cooperation in critical areas such as poverty reduction, food security, pandemic response, development financing, climate change, and the digital economy. The initiative is committed to advancing human rights progress through joint development and has received positive responses from members of the international community.

3. Multilateral governance

Changes in the global balance of power will inevitably promote the democratization of international relations. Developing countries will actively participate in global human rights governance, and their demands for enhanced representation and voice in human rights governance will be significantly improved. In this context, practicing genuine multilateralism and promoting multilateral co-governance led by the United Nations is the future of global human rights governance.

Equity deficit is a critical issue facing current global human rights governance. For a long time, Western countries have dominated the global governance mechanism and often adopted double standards in the global governance process based on their national interests. The "center-periphery" structure of the international power system remains clearly defined, and unilateralism and hegemonism continue to erode the effectiveness and fairness of the global human rights governance system. Against this background, it is difficult for developing countries to participate in global human rights governance on an equal footing and enjoy a voice commensurate with their rising international influence.

In recent years, the international community has increasingly called for a change in Western countries' monopoly control of global governance mechanisms. In this context, China advocates that the global human rights governance structure should reflect the multi-polarity of international politics, the globalization of the world economy, the democratization of international relations, and the diversity of world civilizations. To this end, China supports the structural reform of global human rights governance to ensure the active participation of developing countries. It aims to enhance the democracy and inclusivity of international human rights institutions, uphold the principle of cultural diversity, further strengthen the principle of equitable geographical distribution of members in international human rights institutions, and increase the representation and discourse power of developing countries in global human rights governance. This approach is intended to ensure that all nations share the benefits of global human rights governance and that the international human rights order is established on the basis of fairness and equity.

Multilateralism is an important foundation for promoting the development of human rights in the world, and the UN is the leading force in global multilateral cooperation and governance of human rights. President Xi Jinping pointed out: "In the world, there is only one international system, the one with the international system with the United Nations at its core. There is only one international order, the one with the international order underpinned by international law. And there is only one set of rules, the one with the basic norms governing international relations underpinned by the purposes and principles of the UN Charter." The global human rights governance system and order must be based on firmly safeguarding the authority and status of the UN as a necessary condition. China proposes to champion the banner of multilateralism, adhere to genuine multilateralism, defend international law and norms of international relations, practice the concept of global governance through consultation, joint contribution, and shared benefits, promote the common values of all humanity, address human rights issues in a just, objective, and non-selective manner, resolve human rights disputes through equal dialogue, advocate for UN-led multilateral governance, push for the evolution of global human rights governance toward greater fairness and equity, and build a community with a shared future for humanity.

Enhancing global human rights governance cannot be achieved without active engagement from civil society. While maintaining or even strengthening national responsibilities, it is essential to involve other actors from the market and society in the collective effort to advance global human rights governance. Civil society organizations also play a crucial role in promoting human rights and development, contributing significantly to mutual development, human rights advancement, dialogue and exchange, and cultural mutual learning. For example, during the 47th UN Human Rights Council session, the China International Exchange Promotion Association for Civil Society organized a thematic side event on "The Contribution of Civil Society to the Right to Development in Times of Great Changes." Experts, scholars, and leaders of civil society organizations from China, Pakistan, India, Bulgaria, Sri Lanka, Kazakhstan, and other countries participated in the discussion. During the 49th session of the UN Human Rights Council, several social organizations and human rights research institutions in China, including the China Society for Human Rights Studies, the China Association for NGO Cooperation, and the UN Association of China, organized multiple online side events. Leaders of civil society organizations, experts, and scholars from China, Pakistan, Cambodia, Argentina, the United Kingdom, and other countries engaged in extensive and in-depth discussions and exchanges on 12 topics, including "Human Rights Progress in Xinjiang and the Well-being of People of All Ethnic Groups," "Experience Sharing on Whole-process People's Democracy and Development," and "American View of Human Rights and Its Harm to Global Human Rights Governance."

4. Tolerance and mutual appreciation

In terms of both conceptual ideas and practical content, human rights civilization is an evolving and open system, and the historical trajectory of human rights development fully confirms this. In scope, human rights have gradually expanded, reaching out to the entire world and ultimately becoming a mainstream international discourse. The universality of human rights is widely recognized and acknowledged. In addition, more and more developing countries combine the universality and particularity of human rights based on their specific national conditions. They independently explore human rights development paths that suit their particular situations. The diversity in human rights continues to grow, showcasing each country's unique and independent human rights civilization values. It shows that the development of human rights progresses alongside human society's development and progress. Human rights have unlimited potential for development and are rich in diversity. Viewing human rights from a Western-centric perspective will only hinder human rights civilization's progress. Approaching human rights development with an open and evolving mindset, fostering a spirit of inclusiveness and mutual learning, and adopting a developmental and innovative attitude to enhance global human rights governance is the direction for advancing human rights civilization.

The cause of human rights is an integral part of the socio-economic development of all countries and must be promoted according to their national conditions and people's needs. The richness and variety of human rights development concepts and practices in various countries should become the source of the prosperity of the international human rights cause rather than the source of confrontation and opposition among all parties. The Universal Declaration of Human Rights advocates openness, inclusiveness, and mutual learning among civilizations. One of the fundamental principles of international human rights is "that of non-discrimination." Some countries, however, neither recognize cultural diversity nor respect the right of all nations to choose their particular development paths, and incite color revolutions and forcefully promote regime change under the guise of human rights and humanitarianism, resulting in conflicts, turmoil, and a series of humanitarian crises and becoming a significant source of the current chaos in the world.

Modernizing human rights civilization does not necessarily mean the universalization of Western-centrism; the modernization of global human rights governance does not necessarily mean the Westernization of international human rights governance. As some Western scholars have pointed out: "Modernization is different from Westernization in that it has neither produced any meaningful universal civilization nor produced the Westernization of non-Western societies. President Xi Jinping emphasized that there is no one-size-fits-all path for human rights development in the world. "When it comes to human rights issues, there is no such a thing as an 'ideally perfect country.' We do not need patronizing lecturers, still less should human rights issues be politicized or used as a tool. Double standards and using them as an excuse to interfere in other countries' affairs should be rejected."

Inclusion and mutual learning are the driving forces for promoting and safeguarding human rights. The Chinese concept of human rights takes the pluralism of human rights civilizations as the theoretical context, advocates the diversity of human rights theoretical systems and development paths, and opposes unilateralism and hegemonism in international human rights governance. In the last analysis, this is because the diversity of human rights theoretical systems, discourse systems, and human rights paths is an essential part of the diversity of human civilization, and respecting diversity is the foundation for the sustainable development and vitality of human civilization. Human rights can be interpreted as "insubstantial" or "substantial." The so-called "insubstantial human rights" refers to those expressed in abstract concepts with which all countries may agree easily. It simply talks about whether human rights exist and if they are good or bad. Whereas the "substantial human rights" refers to the rich-contented human rights rooted in each society's history, culture, and particular conditions. It is easier for various countries to reach a consensus on "unsubstantial human rights," but where "substantial human rights" are concerned, mutual learning and appreciation rather than forced uniformity are needed.

V. Conclusion: Improving Global Human Rights Governance and Building A Community with a Shared Future for Humanity

"Everyone can enjoy human rights" is the lofty goal that humankind strives for. After "humans twice experienced the unspeakable scourge of war," they learned from the painful experience and established the UN to "promote social progress and improve people's livelihood in greater freedom." The international human rights cause has since opened a new chapter. For over 70 years, the world has experienced relative peace and stability, with most countries and regions spared from the impacts of war and conflict. The rights to peace and life have been generally protected, and significant achievements have been made in the rights to survival and development. The mainstreaming of human rights has continued to evolve, and international cooperation on human rights has thrived, with principles of fairness, objectivity, and non-selectivity serving as the foundation and guiding principles of United Nations human rights work. At the same time, injustice, intolerance, and unrest persist in the world. Imbalances, disparities, and unsustainability in development continue to be prominent, especially with persistent issues like hunger, poverty, refugees, pandemics, terrorism, racial discrimination, protectionism, and climate change, severely affecting human social development. The tendencies toward politicizing human rights and double standards remain prevalent, and a significant "governance deficit" still exists in the international human rights arena.

Respecting and safeguarding human rights mirrors humanity's long-standing pursuit of justice against tyranny and oppression, the struggle for freedom and equality, and the aspiration for peace and happiness throughout history. It reflects humankind's deepening understanding of the meaning and value of its existence and its beautiful vision for the future. China's human rights dream is one of national prosperity and people's happiness. It is also a dream of promoting world peace, development, and win-win cooperation. In the process of advancing the development of the global human rights cause, China has never stood by. Instead, it has always been taking earnest actions, playing an increasingly important role in promoting the construction of a community with a shared future for humanity. China has become a significant force influencing and driving the development of the global human rights cause, contributing Chinese wisdom and providing Chinese solutions to promote the development of human rights worldwide.

Under the strong leadership of the CPC, the Chinese people are working hard to embark on a new journey of building a socialist modernized country in all respects and marching toward the second centenary goal. In this new journey of grand scale, China will uphold the principle of placing people first, adhere to the path of human rights development aligning with the trends of the times and suitable for its own national conditions, continuously enhance the level of human rights protection, and promote the free and comprehensive development of individuals during the process of advancing Chinese modernization. China is willing to work together with the international community to uphold the spirit of the Universal Declaration of Human Rights and the Vienna Declaration and Program of Action, promote the development of global human rights governance toward greater fairness, justice, and inclusiveness, and strive to build a community with a shared future for humanity and create a better world together.

Writing Explanation and Acknowledgments

The think tank report "For the Common Value and Dignity of All Humanity—China's Practice of and Contribution to Global Human Rights Governance" was released by China Society for Human Rights Studies and the National High-level Think Tank of Xinhua News Agency jointly on Sep. 19 2023.

The think tank report is led by Fu Hua, President of Xinhua News Agency and Chairman of the Academic Committee of Xinhua Institute, with Lyu Yansong, Editorin-Chief of Xinhua News Agency, as the deputy head. Other members of the project team include Yuan Bingzhong, Ni Siyi, Xue Ying, Ye Shuhong, Qiao Jihong, Xie Binbin, Li Jie, etc.

Since the initiation in the April 2023, the research team has taken more than half a year for concentrated study sessions, in-depth investigations, writing, revision and proofreading.

During the process of writing and releasing the report, experts and scholars have provided valuable assistance and guidance. These include Liu Huawen, Deputy Director of the Institute of International Law, Chinese Academy of Social Sciences, Chang Jian, Director of the Human Rights Research Center at Nankai University, Mao Junxiang, Executive Director of the Human Rights Research Center at Central South University, He Liping, Professor of the School of Economics and Business Administration, Beijing Normal University, Shang Haiming, Associate Professor of the Human Rights Research Institute of Southwest University of Political Science and Law. We extend our heartfelt gratitude to all of them.

China's Efforts to Safeguard Cultural Rights for the Visually Impaired: Insights from the "Cinema of Light" Public Welfare Initiative[①]

Since the founding of the People's Republic of China, and particularly since the 18th National Congress of the Communist Party of China (CPC), historic achievements have been made under the strong leadership of the CPC Central Committee with Xi Jinping at its core. The basic rights of people with disabilities, including the right to survival and the right to development, have been comprehensively safeguarded, significantly enhancing their sense of well-being, happiness, andsecurity.

As China's economy and society continue to develop rapidly, meeting the growing cultural and spiritual needs of people with disabilities and ensuring their cultural rights are now of critical importance. These efforts not only enhance the quality of life for people with disabilities but also contribute to building a more equal, just, inclusive, and harmonious society.

Among people with disabilities, those with visual impairments face unique challenges. Limited access to cultural products and services leaves them with fewer opportunities for cultural enrichment. According to the World Health Organization's World Report on Vision (2019), over 2.2 billion people globally experience vision

---

① Released in Beijing on December 3, 2024.

impairment or blindness. China, with the largest population of visually impaired individuals in the world, is home to approximately 17.31 million people with visual disabilities. Their desire to engage with the richness of the world and pursue a fulfilling life underscores the urgent need to protect and enhance their cultural rights.

To address this, China has established a robust support system and mobilized widespread social participation, achieving notable results. A prominent example is the "Cinema of Light" public welfare project led by the Communication University of China. By producing accessible films, creating barrier-free cinemas, and promoting cultural inclusivity, this initiative exemplifies China's commitment to safeguarding the cultural rights of people with visual impairments.

I. "Cinema of Light": An Innovative Approach to Protecting Cultural Rights for the VisuallyImpaired

1. A Seven-year Journey: The Evolution of "Cinema of Light" from Infancy to Maturity

The "Cinema of Light" stemmed from our college students and faculty's commit menttobuildinga"CulturalPathwayfortheVisuallyImpaired." "Our original goal was to combine our efforts as media professionals to make a meaningful contribution to the lives of people with visual impairments," recalled the students and teachers from the Communication University of China's Television School, who launched the "Cinema of Light" public welfare initiative with enthusiasm in 2017. After extensive discussions and evaluations of various project options, including documentary filmmaking and short film production, the team settled on a project to "tell the story of movies for the visually impaired," taking into account the needs of visually impaired audiences, the university's resources, and community support. According to the founding team, "Cinema of Light" produces accessible films by inserting descriptive narration between dialogue and sound effects, explaining the visual scenes and the emotions and meanings behind them, creating a replicable and distributable model for accessible films. The project follows the mission "to convey color through sound and let listeners experience art." Since its inception, the initiative has aimed to provide two accessible films per week for visually impaired audiences, totaling 104 films annually, and this commitment to building an "inclusive cultural pathway" for people with visual impairments continues to this day, supporting the ongoing development of accessible media in China.

We Have Developed a Standardized Model for Accessible Film Production.

Proficiency in film analysis and audiovisual language has been essential. "Cinema of Light" is more than just a charitable initiative; it is a professional endeavor. The project challenges the students and faculty to apply their understanding of audiovisual language, transform visual cues into descriptive audio, and manage voiceovers, editing, and the overall narrative flow of each film. This process tests their skills to the fullest, requiring both technical and creative expertise.

Fu Haizheng, a founding member of the "Cinema of Light" project and Executive Director of the Institute for Accessible Media Communication at the Communication University of China, explains that the journey from trial and error to a standardized production model has been one of growth and transformation. "The team adopted a standardized production process, with specific steps including film selection, scriptwriting, review, proofreading, and recording," says Zhao Xijing, a faculty volunteer on the project team. "Each step adheres to a 'three-stage review and three-stage proofreading' process to ensure that the narration authentically reflects the film's visuals and maintains the highest quality possible."

In the film selection stage, "Cinema of Light" has broadened the scope of accessible films beyond traditional genres, incorporating a variety of types, including animation, drama, science fiction, and historical films, to meet the needs of visually impaired audiences across different age groups. To help individuals with visual impairments stay informed and engaged with current events, the team carefully producesaseriesoffilmsrefl ectingnational,social,andcontemporarydevelopments around key events and milestones.

"In the scriptwriting and recording stages, we aim to capture the perspective of visually impaired audiences, using language they can vividly perceive. For instance, how do we describe the color red? It's a warm, sun-like color," explains Cai Yu, a founding member of the "Cinema of Light" project and a doctoral candidate at the Communication University of China. The team meticulously crafts each word and recording to ensure an authentic, accurate portrayal, offering a reliable interpretation of the film. In war films, for example, descriptions of military branches, weapons, and combat zones are cross-referenced with extensive research to ensure precise details, striving to immerse visually impaired audiences in a realistic cinematic war experience.

The "Cinema of Light" team has established a scientific and efficient operating mechanism. Each group within the project team has developed standardized manuals specific to their tasks, covering every step of accessible film production—from scriptwriting, reviewing, and voiceover to audio monitoring and final editing. This comprehensive approach even extends to project promotion, ensuring that the continuously evolving team of volunteers maintains consistent quality and standards in both their operations and the produced films.

Over the past seven years, more than 800 student and faculty volunteers have contributed to the project, producing over 600 accessible films in a broader range of genres and styles, each with expressive and heartfelt narration. These films embody the Cinema of Light team's dedication to securing fundamental rights for people with visual impairments and reflect their commitment to supporting China's initiatives for people with disabilities.

We Have Promoted the deep-rooted establishment of accessible cultural services.

The mission of "Cinema of Light" goes beyond producing a hundred accessible films each year; it actively advocates for protecting cultural rights for people with disabilities across society. In an era where media technology is reshaping how information is accessed, Cinema of Light empowers individuals with visual impairments to fully engage in social and cultural life on equal footing, allowing them to share in the achievements of contemporary material and cultural development.

"'Cinema of Light' extends beyond film production; it even reaches into the screening phase," explains Li Chaopeng, a student volunteer at the Communication University of China and a member of the project team. From publicizing screening information and coordinating charity screenings in theaters to helping visually impaired attendees find their seats, engaging in on-site Q&A, maintaining order, providing live descriptions, and assisting with post-film exit, "Cinema of Light" has carefully planned and rehearsed every detail of the screening experience to ensure the safest and most enjoyable viewing experience for visually impaired audiences.

After seven years of exploration, "Cinema of Light" has established a"Five-Assess Model" that brings accessible film screenings to associations for the blind, cinemas, schools for the visually impaired, libraries, and community centers, effectively bridging the "last mile" for visually impaired audiences. Beyond these efforts, prominent film festivals, such as the Beijing International Film Festival, Changchun Film Festival, Hainan International Film Festival, and Silk Road International Film Festival, have dedicated public welfare screening sessions, allowing visually impaired individuals to participate in these global cultural events. While drawing greater attention to the needs of people with visual impairments and new developments, experiences, insights, and achievements in China's disability support initiatives, these screenings also provide a platform to share China's stories of public welfare, human rights, and cultural-ethical development on the international stage, advancing global efforts toward accessible information.

To date, the "Cinema of Light" initiative has extended its achievements to 31 provinces, autonomous regions, and municipalities across China, as well as the Macao Special Administrative Region, ensuring full coverage of 2,244 special education schools. Its practices have been widely promoted in cultural hubs like Jiaxing and Shaoxing in Zhejiang Province, as well as Suzhou in Jiangsu Province. More than 20 dedicated "Cinema of Light" screening halls have been established in cities such as Beijing, and five major film festivals now feature "Cinema of Light" public welfare screening units. Additionally, a "Cinema of Light" on-demand channel has been launched through China Broadcasting Network, reaching over 200 million households and benefiting eight million visually impaired individuals. As these figures grow, the "Cinema of Light" initiative continues to expand the "inclusive cultural pathway" it has built through the medium of sound and visual narration, reaching an increasingly broad audience and benefiting more visually impaired individuals. This public welfare initiative, driven by the mission of promoting inclusive cultural services to empower disability development, is generating positive impacts not only across China but also on a global scale.

2. "Cinema of Light" Enhances Well-being and Fulfillment for the Visually Impaired

French film artist André Bazin once noted in his work "What is Cinema?" that "humankind has a psychological desire to substitute the external world with realistic replicas." He explained that "the concept of cinema is equivalent to the complete reproduction of reality, an imagined illusion of a world filled with sound, color, and depth." Through "Cinema of Light," visually impaired audiences not only gain access to information but also experience an elevated aesthetic and expressive quality that aligns with the principles of faithfulness, clarity, and elegance, achieving an enriched cultural and educational impact.

We Have Fulfilled the Gaps in Information and Artistic Appreciation for Visually Impaired Audiences.

Students and faculty involved in "Cinema of Light" explain that, while ensuring the accuracy and authenticity of basic information in each film, the team has also dedicated significant efforts to enhancing both the interpretive depth and technical quality of their productions. On the interpretive level, "Cinema of Light" emphasizes a deep exploration of each film's meaning. Beyond simply telling the story, the team strives to offer a comprehensive interpretation, allowing audiences not only to grasp the fundamental storyline but also to develop a richer understanding, encouraging imagination and reflection on the film's broader themes.

After the launch of the "Cinema of Light" project, faculty and students from the Communication University of China established close connections with schools for the visually impaired, such as Beijing School for the Blind. Each month, a dedicated screening team is dispatched to show accessible films to students. Wang Zheng, a student at Beijing School for the Blind, shares that previously, "watching" a film often meant missing key details, such as background music, scenic visuals, or character interactions conveyed through gestures and expressions, leading to confusion and only a partial understanding of the story.Now, with regular screenings in the school's auditorium, the "Cinema of Light" project has brought not only new joy and anticipation to daily life but also "comprehensible" films that help students gain knowledge and experience the beauty of the world andlife.

Wang Xiaochui, Party Secretary of Beijing School for the Blind, remarks that the "Cinema of Light" project cultivates a sense of beauty and appreciation for students and other audiences, creating a space filled with aesthetic expression and imaginative possibilities. With its thoughtful selection of positive films and poetic interpretations, the project offers an environment where audiences can experience beauty, inspiring a sense of wonder and aspiration. This approach not only enhances the audience's aesthetic sensibilities but also helps nurture the students' character and enrich their personal growth, providing meaningful value in aesthetic education.

We Have Broadened Social Engagement Opportunities for the Visually Impaired.

In 2021, "Cinema of Light" extended its reach to Changping District in Beijing. A representative from the district's association for the blind explained that, unlike individuals with other disabilities, such as hearing impairment, visually impaired people often face significant barriers to communication due to their limited vision, making them less likely to venture outside. The accessible film screenings have provided this community with more opportunities to leave their homes and connect with volunteers and other visually impaired individuals, positively impacting their quality of life and enriching their cultural experiences. Teachers interviewed from Beijing School for the Blind noted that "Cinema of Light" has given students opportunities to engage with and participate in society. Some students have even joined activities like the Beijing International Film Festival, film production, and discussion panels, inspiring more community support for this group and broadening their perspectives on the world and their future aspirations. Some parents now hope that, given the right support, their children can pursue broader educational and career options beyond traditional paths such as massage therapy or music, even advancing to mainstream schools to pursue their dreams boldly. In many ways, "Cinema of Light" has built a "pathway of dreams" for visually impaired children.

We Have Inspired a Drive for a Happy Life among the Visually Impaired.

The pursuit of happiness often begins with the ability to "see." As one of the most essential and immediate senses for perceiving the world, vision forms the foundation of how people understand and engage with their surroundings. "A good film allows us to experience different lives in a short time, and the power of cinema is limitless," says Ru Tianzi, a teacher at Beijing School for the Blind. Through moving stories, films convey life's insights and profound ideas, and this window to the world should be open to everyone, including those with visual impairments.

Like sunlight and air, cultural life is an essential element of individual growth and development. For people with visual impairments, the "Cinema of Light" initiative provides accessible films that enrich their life experiences, help them acquire knowledge, nurture their spirit, broaden their horizons, and enhance their cultural literacy and competence. This initiative plays a vital role in empowering them to achieve equal social inclusion. Some students from Beijing School for the Blind commented that "Cinema of Light" enables them to perceive the nation's development simultaneously, the changes of the times, and the transformations of society. It not only brings them spiritual joy but also expands their imagination and pushes the boundaries of their thinking, inspiring them to courageously explore the external world, pursue their inner dreams, and strive for a happy and fulfilling life.

3. "Cinema of Light" as a Model for Safeguarding Cultural Rights for the Visually Impaired

We Have Infused the Energy and Vitality of University Students by Empowering Them as Key Contributors.

"With university students serving as the backbone of the 'Cinema of Light' volunteer team, the initiative combines professional expertise with youthful energy, injecting fresh momentum into the production and dissemination of accessible films in China," remarks a representative from the Television School at the Communication University of China. Cultivating a sense of patriotism and social responsibility among young students is both an essential mission of higher education and the original driving force behind the "Cinema of Light" project. The initiative encourages students to actively engage in film production and real-world human rights practices, effectively enhancing their awareness of the importance of respecting and safeguarding human rights. This approach not only embodies the educational philosophy of the Communication University of China but also strengthens students' commitment to the core values of journalism and communication studies. It helps them avoid a narrow, self-serving mindset, guiding them instead toward integrating their personal aspirations with societal needs. By fostering a dual alignment of individual growth with social contribution, the "Cinema of Light" project exemplifies the synergy between youthful enthusiasm and the pursuit of public welfare. It harmonizes ideals with action, intertwining the spirit of youth with dedication to social good and uniting foundational values with purposeful efforts.

We Have Given Full Play to Universities' Expertise, Technology, and Talent.

Teachers provide comprehensive guidance, professional support, and quality control, serving as a strong backbone for the project team. The faculty at the Communication University of China defines the initiative as a blend of "public welfare, teaching, research, and experimentation," guiding students to apply their knowledge in service of the country and society, embodying the principle of integrating knowledge and action. Wen Mohan, a student volunteer with "Cinema of Light", explains that every aspect of the project—from planning, film selection, scriptwriting, and voiceover to post-production, screening, and distribution—is a collaborative effort between faculty and students. The synergy of professionalism, social experience, and youthful enthusiasm creates a smooth and inspiring creative process, giving students a strong sense of fulfillment and achievement. From just five initial volunteers, the team has grown to include hundreds, supporting a nationwide initiative. Reflecting on this growth, Zhao Shuping, the project's primary advisor, shared her insights, saying, "Giving students free rein and trusting them make all the difference." The university's strong backing and teachers' dedicated guidance remain the project's unwavering source of momentum, ensuring its sustainable impact.

We Have Advanced Research and Collaboration in Accessible Information Dissemination to Enhance the Project's Global Impact.

"Cinema of Light" has consistently committed to addressing the challenge of "cultural poverty alleviation," extending its reach from bustling urban centers to remote rural areas, with footprints spanning the entire nation. On November 1, 2023, at the 2023 International Seminar on Global Poverty Reduction Partnerships—jointly organized by the International Poverty Reduction Center in China, the United Nations Food and Agriculture Organization, the United Nations International Fund for Agricultural Development, the United Nations World Food Programme, and the China Internet Information Center—the Communication University of China's case study, *Promoting Rural Revitalization through Cultural Support: A Case of University-Enterprise Collaboration on Accessible Film Production and Dissemination with "Cinema of Light"*, was awarded the "Best Poverty Reduction Case" in the "4th Global Poverty Reduction Case Collection." This project has since been included in the South-South Cooperation Poverty Reduction Case Library, serving as a distinctive example of poverty alleviation through cultural initiatives and providing valuable insights for global poverty reduction and rural development. On December 1, 2023, in observance of the 32nd International Day of Persons with Disabilities, the Communication University of China and UNESCO co-hosted the International Symposium on Accessible Information Dissemination and Human Rights Protection in Beijing, under the guidance of the China Foundation for Human Rights Development and the China Disabled Persons' Federation. The symposium gathered representatives from over ten countries, including China, France, Mongolia, and Malaysia. Participants explored strategies for enhancing social inclusion and empowering people with disabilities through accessible information dissemination. China's practices in accessible media were highly praised by domestic and international attendees, as well as by experts from both industry and academia.

The "Cinema of Light" project has also played a significant role in supporting China's ratification of the Marrakesh Treaty to Facilitate Access to Published Works for Persons Who Are Blind, Visually Impaired, or Otherwise Print Disabled (Marrakesh VIP Treaty)—the only international human rights treaty in the copyright domain aimed at enabling equitable access to published works for visually impaired individuals. In 2021, the project undertook a research initiative commissioned by China's copyright authorities titled *Audiovisual Works and the Implementation of the Marrakesh VIP Treaty*. This research provided an in-depth analysis of the necessity, feasibility, and operational procedures for authorized entities to produce accessible versions of audiovisual works. By offering intellectual and practical contributions, the "Cinema of Light" project has significantly advanced the implementation of the treaty in China.

II. China's Initiatives and Achievements in Protecting Cultural Rights for the Visually Impaired

Cultural rights are fundamental human rights, and the "Cinema of Light" project at the Communication University of China embodies China's efforts to ensure that the visually impaired enjoy equal access to cultural resources and meet their needs for enriched cultural engagement. In recent years, China has implemented a series of measures to strengthen the protection of cultural rights for the visually impaired. These actions range from enhancing policy and legal frameworks to rigorous on-the-ground implementation and from elevating standards for accessibility facilities to providing diverse, accessible products and services.

Growing numbers of visually impaired individuals are gaining access to higher education through the general college entrance examination. Through reading and cultural engagement, they acquire knowledge, develop employable skills, expand their career paths, and realize personal ambitions. In sharing the cultural achievements of society, they also made their contributions, adding warmth and value to the community.

1. Continuous Improvement of China's Policy and Legal Framework to Protect the Cultural Rights of the Visually Impaired

National development plans play a guiding role in shaping various fields of progress, and in formulating these policies, China consistently prioritizes the protection of cultural rights for the visually impaired. The State Council has issued eight consecutive five-year development plans focused on disability affairs. Additionally, specialized frameworks such as the *Opinions of the State Council on Accelerating the Process of Building a Moderately Prosperous Society for People with Disabilities* and the *Outline of the 13th Five-Year Plan to Accelerate the Well-off Process for People with Disabilities* have been enacted and implemented. These documents specify concrete tasks and detailed responsibilities to advance initiatives supporting the well-being of people with disabilities.

Efforts to standardize and expand Braille usage have made solid progress. As a crucial medium for accessing cultural content, Braille provides an essential gateway for the visually impaired. Since 2009, four successive National Human Rights Action Plans have outlined specific tasks and measurable targets for promoting Braille, ensuring steady advancement in this area. Initiatives such as establishing reading rooms for the visually impaired and increasing the publication of accessible reading materials have continuously evolved alongside economic and social development, paving the way for visually impaired individuals to enjoy the same flourishing cultural achievements as others.

The establishment and enforcement of laws provide robust support for the visually impaired to fully and equally enjoy cultural rights. The Law of the *People's Republic of China on the Protection of Disabled Persons*, initially enacted in 1990 and amended in 2008 and 2018, serves as the country's specialized legislation for protecting the rights of individuals with disabilities. This law outlines the basic principles of safeguarding cultural rights for people with disabilities, including specific measures for the visually impaired. A dedicated chapter on "Cultural Life" affirms the state's commitment to ensuring that people with disabilities have equal rights to participate in cultural activities. It underscores that cultural, sports, and recreational activities for people with disabilities should be community-focused, integrated into public cultural life, and tailored to meet the diverse needs of various disabilities, encouraging widespread participation. Additionally, it mandates that the government and society take steps to support the creation and publication of Braille and audio materials for the visually impaired and establish designated sections in public libraries to provide these resources according to their specific needs.

The Law of the People's Republic of China on the Construction of Barrier-Free Environments, which came into effect in 2023, provides further support for visually impaired individuals to enjoy cultural rights more fully and conveniently. This law includes a dedicated chapter on "Barrier-Free Information Exchange," outlining provisions to ensure accessible cultural rights for the visually impaired. For instance, it encourages the publication of books, newspapers, and periodicals in accessible formats such as audio, large print, Braille, and digital versions to facilitate reading for individuals with disabilities and senior citizens. It also promotes the creation and publication of Braille and low-vision textbooks tailored to the needs of students at different educational stages, ensuring learning resources are accessible to the visually impaired and others with visual challenges. The law further requires that manufacturers of audiovisual, multimedia, mobile smart devices, and telecommunications terminal equipment gradually incorporate accessibility features, such as voice guidance and large text options. Moreover, related laws, including the *Copyright Law*, the *Law on the Guarantee of Public Cultural Services*, and the *Public Library Law of the People's Republic of China*, also contain related provisions to protect and enhance the cultural rights of visually impaired individuals.

China is also actively aligning its domestic policies and laws with international treaties to broaden the availability of cultural products for the visually impaired, enhance their quality, and foster international cultural exchange. On October 23, 2021, China officially ratified the *Marrakesh VIP Treaty*. Under this treaty, China can provide accessible-format versions of works for individuals with reading disabilities, including the visually impaired, and can also utilize works from other treaty-member countries to create these formats without requiring permission from, or payment to, copyright holders. This ratification significantly expands the range of resources available to China's visually impaired population while reducing the cost of accessing suchworks.

2. Strengthening Measures to Protect the Cultural Rights of the Visually Impaired in China

In recent years, a series of administrative measures have been introduced to enable the visually impaired to read more easily and enjoy cultural works, such as television, films, and theater productions.

The "Digital Reading Promotion Project for the Visually Impaired" is a flagship initiative launched by various levels of government in China to enhance cultural access for the visually impaired. Since 2017, the project has addressed key challenges in traditional Braille book publishing, such as high production costs, complex printing processes, and lengthy proofreading times. In collaboration with relevant government agencies, the China Disabled Persons' Federation has implemented this project to provide digital audiobooks, electronic Braille, and customized, continuous cultural services through digital publishing platforms and specialized reading devices. "Although each Braille dot feels a bit rough to the touch, to me, they are like vibrant musical notes," said Wang Yaqi, a visually impaired young woman, her face lighting up with joy as she described the pleasure of reading. As of October 2024, the project has activated 146,575 smart listening devices across 353 public libraries, achieving an activation rate of 81.24%. The devices support 62,281 registered users, facilitating a cumulative total of 102.24 million online interactions spanning 35.83 million hours. The average duration of a single use is 20 minutes, with some devices logging over 14 hours of use perday.

Artistic activities for the visually impaired have seen rapid development in China. Established in 1987, the China Disabled People's Performing Art Troupe includes visually impaired members, who make up roughly one-third of the troupe. This group has performed in over 100 countries and regions and has been recognized as a UNESCO Artist for Peace by the United Nations Educational, Scientific, and Cultural Organization. Currently, there are 226 disability arts troupes across the country, with more people with disabilities working in cultural and arts professions. Many talented visually impaired musicians and vocalists have emerged from these initiatives. Every four years, the China Disabled Persons' Federation, in cooperation with the Ministry of Education, Ministry of Civil Affairs, Ministry of Culture and Tourism, and the National Radio and Television Administration, organizes the National Disability Art Festival. The 10th festival, held in 2021, featured around 2,400 performers with disabilities, including visually impaired artists, showcasing a wide range of talents in vocal music, instrumental music, dance, and traditional Chinese opera.

The "Cultural Week for the Visually Impaired" has become a regular event. For several consecutive years, the Ministry of Culture and Tourism, the National Press and Publication Administration, together with the China Disabled Persons' Federation, have organized this cultural week across the country. In 2023 alone, over 13,459 activities were held, including public reading sessions for blind children and accessible movie screenings, both of which were particularly popular among visually impaired participants.

Opportunities for visually impaired individuals to contribute to cultural creation continue to expand. The China Disabled Persons' Federation, in collaboration with relevant departments, has organized numerous literary workshops for writers with disabilities, offering visually impaired authors the chance to develop their skills in creative writing. An array of scholarly journals dedicated to disability literature and books authored by visually impaired writers have been published, offering a glimpse into the rich inner world of China's visually impaired community.

3. Continuous Improvement in Accessible Environment for Protecting the Cultural Rights of the Visually Impaired in China

Accessibility is foundational to enabling individuals with disabilities and other special groups to fully participate in society and share in the benefits of social and economic development. For the visually impaired, accessible facilities that support sensory engagement—through sound, smell, touch, and tactile surfaces—function as "Cultural Pathways for the Visually Impaired," similar to a tactile guide for cultural experiences.

The Chinese government and society increasingly recognize that transforming "barriers" into "accessibility" empowers the visually impaired to engage more actively in cultural life and contribute to society's cultural wealth. With this growing awareness, standards for accessible facilities are becoming more refined, and the framework for accessibility standards continues to evolve and improve.

The *Law of the People's Republic of China on the Construction of Barrier-free Environments*, the country's first dedicated legislation on accessibility, introduces the concept of "universal design." Unlike traditional approaches that focus on building facilities specifically for people with disabilities, universal design incorporates the needs of people with disabilities equally into the design process from the outset. The law also emphasizes reasonable accommodation in specific cases, requiring modifications and adjustments tailored to various types of disabilities, all within the framework of universal design. These provisions ensure that people with disabilities can enjoy or exercise all human rights and fundamental freedoms on an equal footing.

Standards for accessible facilities are essential to ensure they are functional and effective. In recent years, China has introduced several national standards to protect the cultural rights of the visually impaired. In 2012, China's first national standard in public library services, the *Public Library Service Specifications*, was implemented. This standard specifies that public libraries serve all members of the public and should make efforts to address the specific needs of groups such as people with disabilities. It recommends that reading rooms for the visually impaired be situated on accessible levels, ideally between the main library building and public walkways. In 2019, the *Library Services Specification for the Visually Impaired* became China's first national standard tailored to services for people with disabilities in libraries. This standard provides guidelines on the target audience, resources, service content and delivery, requirements, and oversight and evaluation of these services. A structured framework for library services for the visually impaired has since emerged across China. Guided by national standards, libraries nationwide are focused on expanding service reach, improving service quality, and building efficient, ongoing, and increasingly professionalized services for the visually impaired.

With the advent of the digital era, standards for internet accessibility have gradually been established. On March 1, 2020, China implemented its first national standard for accessible internet content, *Technical Requirements, and Testing Methods for Accessibility of Internet Content in Information Technology*. This standard outlines 58 specific measures, including providing audio-based CAPTCHA codes and adding accurately descriptive web page titles, marking substantial progress in creating an "information pathway" for the visually impaired online. China has launched a special initiative to improve the accessibility and age-friendliness of government websites and apps. Since 2021, a total of 2,726 websites and apps have been upgraded, creating better conditions for visually impaired individuals to access information, communicate, obtain public services, and conduct online transactions.

The Chinese government also encourages the development of pioneering group and corporate standards and is committed to strengthening the coherence and integration of these standards. This approach aims to build a scientifically sound and systematically integrated framework for accessibility standards across various domains.

4. Expanding Accessible Products and Services to Protect the Cultural Rights of the Visually Impaired in China

With China's rapid social and economic growth, the range of accessible products for the visually impaired has steadily expanded, industry capacity has continued to grow, and the ability to supply these products has strengthened, with service quality also improving steadily.

A diverse range of tactile cultural products is available. Tactile sensation serves as a crucial channel for visually impaired individuals to accurately perceive and engage with society. Braille books remain one of the most commonly used cultural resources for this community. Since 2021, China has annually published over 500 new Braille book titles, including more than 100 editions with combined Braille and standard text formats, and reprinted over 400 Braille book titles, with production peaking at 1,200 titles and 30 million printed pages in a single year. This rich repository of Braille books provides a solid foundation for visually impaired individuals to share in the tangible "fragrance" of books. To further expand the reach of Braille books to those in need, China has heavily invested in the development of Braille libraries. Currently, public libraries across the country feature approximately 35,200 reading seats for the visually impaired and house a collection of around 146.6 million Braille books. With advancements in technology, the methods for visually impaired individuals to access information through touch have become increasingly diverse. Products such as Braille displays, and computers designed for the visually impaired are now integral tools for accessing cultural resources and services.

Auditory-based cultural products have significantly expanded. Audiobooks serve as the primary and most convenient reading medium for the visually impaired. Audiobooks produced by the China Braille Press have covered a wide range of subjects, including textbooks for primary, secondary, and higher education, as well as literature, medicine, storytelling, and music. Additionally, audio-focused internet platforms have rapidly developed, introducing numerous screen-reader-compatible products for book listening and other information needs, offering the visually impaired a wealth of choices.

New forms of cultural products are on the rise. In recent years, audio-described films have gained increasing attention as a growing cultural product category. Supported by the National Publishing Fund, the Braille Press has produced 870 accessible films with copyright permissions, making them available to both visually and hearing-impaired audiences. The new building of the China Braille Library, which has been in operation for 13 years, screens one film per week with live narration by librarians. To date, over 700 film screenings have been held, serving approximately 30,000 attendees. Additionally, more than 300 film scripts with a total word count of approximately 2.4 million characters have been created for these activities. Public libraries, cultural institutions, disability organizations, and social groups across various levels frequently organize film-watching activities for visually impaired individuals. In addition to the Cinema of Light project, several video streaming platforms in China have established dedicated accessibility sections. These platforms automatically direct visually impaired users using screen-reader technology to curated collections of fully audio-described films, which have become immensely popular within the visually impaired community. Technology has also played a crucial role in enhancing accessibility in museums and exhibition centers. Features such as NFC-activated information, audio guides, tactile exhibits, and online virtual tours have provided visually impaired visitors with unprecedented opportunities for immersive, barrier-free cultural experiences. These innovations demonstrate a commitment to creating inclusive environments where visually impaired individuals can explore art and culture in new and meaningful ways.

III. Experiences and Insights from China's Efforts to Protect the Cultural Rights of the Visually Impaired

China's initiatives to protect the cultural rights of the visually impaired fully reflect the nation's adherence to a people-centered approach, its active fulfillment of international human rights treaty obligations, and its commitment to the principle of "equality, participation, and sharing" in the development of disability services. Through these efforts, China has continuously enhanced its protections for the visually impaired, offering valuable insights and inspiration to other countries.

1. Emphasizing the Leading Role of the State

Respecting and safeguarding the dignity and rights of people with disabilities, enabling them to fully participate in society on equal footing and with equal opportunity, and ensuring they share in both material and cultural-ethical achievements reflect a nation's sense of responsibility and commitment.

As a signatory of the *Convention on the Rights of Persons with Disabilities (CRPD)*, China has fulfilled its obligations under the Convention. In formulating laws, regulations, and policies related to people with disabilities—and in promoting and protecting their rights—China adheres to the spirit of the Convention. Practical, robust measures have been implemented, including "universal design" products, environments, programs, and services, along with "reasonable accommodations" and specialized assistive devices and support services. These initiatives address the aspirations and cultural needs of people with disabilities, supporting high-quality development in disability services.

China has focused on strengthening a legal framework centered around individuals with disabilities, establishing a comprehensive system led by the *Law of the People's Republic of China on the Protection of Disabled Persons*. This system is further supported by key legislation, including the *Law on the Construction of Barrier-Free Environments, Regulations on Disability Prevention and Rehabilitation, Regulations on Disability Education*, and *Regulations on Employment for People with Disabilities*, creating a solid foundation for the protection of disability rights.

China actively integrates disability affairs into its overall national economic and social development plans as well as its National Human Rights Action Plan. Multiple departments have jointly formulated the *14th Five-year Plan for Enhancing Cultural Services for Persons with Disabilities*. This plan supports eligible public libraries at the provincial, municipal, and county levels in establishing reading rooms or areas for the visually impaired, increasing resources such as Braille books and audiovisual materials, and equipping these facilities with Braille books and related reading devices. The initiative aims to provide visually impaired individuals with Braille books, audiobooks, large-print books, and accessible versions of movies and TV shows, ensuring comprehensive reading services for this community. Support has also been allocated to construct reading rooms for the visually impaired in 50 city-level and 200 county-level public libraries nationwide. Ongoing initiatives include the Visually Impaired Publications Project and the Digital Reading Promotion Project for the Visually Impaired, with a focus on publishing 50 disability-related works or works by disabled authors. Efforts are also being made to promote the translation and international publication of outstanding works by disabled writers. Additionally, the scheme encourages the production and broadcast of disability-themed films, documentaries, public service ads, and online audiovisual programs. It promotes accessible film services in cinemas and cable television networks alongside the production and streaming of accessible online films. The National Film Fund has provided financial support for the "Cinema of Light" project, playing a guiding role in its development.

2. Encouraging Civil SocietyParticipation

Disability services represent a vast and complex undertaking, and the state actively encourages enterprises, social organizations, and individuals to contribute donations and services for people with disabilities.

The protection of cultural rights for the visually impaired requires extensive involvement from civil society. Such involvement not only complements areas that government resources may not reach but also promotes a deeper understanding and respect for people with disabilities throughout society, reducing prejudice and discrimination. This broad support helps visually impaired individuals integrate more fully into society, ensuring equal enjoyment of all rights and freedoms. Through sustained efforts, China has built a strong social foundation for human rights protection for the visually impaired, with diverse social organizations, market players, and volunteers actively supporting initiatives that professionalize, normalize, and sustain these protections. The Ping An Public Welfare Foundation has contributed 1 million yuan annually for three consecutive years to support the "Cinema of Light," serving as a prime example of grassroots participation in disability initiatives in China.

3. Tailoring Approaches to National Conditions

China's disability services are rooted in the nation's historical and cultural traditions as well as its social and economic conditions. At the same time, China draws on international best practices, successfully creating a disability rights protection model suited to its unique context. Alongside the rights to rehabilitation, employment, and education, China is committed to advancing the full spectrum of disability rights, making the protection of these rights an integral part of a fair, inclusive, and sustainable development strategy that benefits every individual.

Given the unique needs of the visually impaired community, society has placed increasing importance on transforming their legal and cultural rights into tangible cultural benefits. By the end of 2023, China had established 24 provincial and 184 city-level radio programs dedicated to disability topics. Additionally, 1,541 public library reading rooms nationwide provide access to Braille and Braille audiobooks, and art troupes have been formed to serve individuals with disabilities. Through initiatives such as the National Disabled Art Festival and the "Five Ones" program, which brings cultural activities into the homes of individuals with disabilities, visually impaired individuals are included in the nation's cultural and ethical development efforts.

4. Empowering through Technology

Technology has reshaped daily life and profoundly transformed the prospects of people with disabilities. With ongoing breakthroughs in information technology, artificial intelligence, and life sciences, technological advancements are bringing renewed hope to individuals with disabilities. *The 14th Five-year Plan for Disability Protection and Development* sets specific goals for leveraging technology to support people with disabilities. The 2024 State Council Government Work Report emphasizes the importance of advancing technological research and applications for health, elderly care, and disability support. *The 2023 Overview of Disability Development and Social Progress in China*, published by the China Disabled Persons' Federation, reveals a growing number of high-tech enterprises dedicated to disability support. These companies are maximizing the benefits of cutting-edge technologies to enhance the well-being of people with disabilities, providing them with greater independence, convenience, and equal opportunities for social participation.

To enhance the cultural and spiritual life of the visually impaired, haptic feedback accessibility technology customizes the vibration duration, frequency, and intensity of mobile devices like phones and tablets to convey distinct information to visually impaired users. Tencent Video, for instance, has launched an Accessible Theater section that automatically recognizes users entering through "voice screen readers," placing the theater entrance prominently on their homepage. Additionally, a new range of games designed for visually impaired players uses AI to process player information and provide real-time feedback, meeting operational needs while creating a platform for community interaction. This "light of technology" serves not only as the eyes of visually impaired individuals but also illuminates their inner world, offering them the same opportunities as others to participate in society and experience the beauty of the world.

5. Strengthening the Sense of Agency

In advancing services for people with disabilities, China consistently emphasizes respecting their wishes, prioritizing their participation, and inspiring their enthusiasm, initiative, and creativity. The aim is to foster a sense of self-respect, confidence, resilience, and independence, encouraging a shift from viewing people with disabilities as passive recipients of aid to recognizing them as rights holders and active contributors to economic and social development. Dong Lina, China's first visually impaired broadcasting master's degree graduate, has transformed her life through her efforts, using her voice to convey the beauty of the world to other visually impaired individuals. Chen Guangjiong, a visually impaired author, focuses his work on the lives, work, and emotions of people with disabilities, portraying the richness of visually impaired experiences. Entrepreneur Cao Jun, who is visually impaired, has long been committed to developing assistive software for blind people, helping them better understand and integrate into society.

"I cannot see the world, but I hope the world sees me," remarked a visually impaired Chinese athlete during the Beijing 2022 Winter Paralympics, capturing the sentiment of many in the visually impaired community. China is dedicated to strengthening the agency of visually impaired individuals, guiding society to treat them with equality and recognize their value and contributions. Efforts are focused on empowering them in multiple ways, facilitating learning and skills development, and creating conditions for equal access to education, employment, cultural activities, and full social integration, allowing them to realize the vibrant potential of their lives.

Writing Explanation and Acknowledgments

The think tank report " 'China's Efforts to Safeguard Cultural Rights for the Visually Impaired: Insights from the 'Cinema of Light' Public Welfare Initiative " was released by The China Foundation for Human Rights Development and the National High-level Think Tank of Xinhua News Agency jointly on Dec. 3 2024, the 33rd International Day of Persons with Disabilities.

The think tank report is led by Ren Weidong, Deputy Editor-in-Chief of Xinhua News Agency. Other members of the project team include Liu Gang, Cui Feng, Yang Liu, Liu Mingxia, Xiong Lin, Gao Lei, Xie Binbin, Bao Xiaojing, Yan Rui, etc.

Since the initiation in the Oct. 2023, the research team has taken more than 1 year for concentrated study sessions, in-depth investigations, writing, revision and proofreading.

During the process of writing and releasing the report, experts and scholars have provided valuable assistance and guidance. These include Gao Xiaohong, Minister of the Department of Journalism and Communication and Dean of the School of Television at Communication University of China, Fu Haizheng, Executive Dean of the Institute of Accessible Information Communication at the School of Television, Communication University of China, Zhao Xijing, Associate Researcher at the School of Television, Communication University of China, Li Qingzhong, member of the National Committee of the Chinese People's Political Consultative Conference, director of the China Disabled Persons' Federation, and chairman of the China Blind Association, He Chuan, Deputy Director of China Visually Impaired Cultural Information Service Center, Wang Xiaochui, Secretary of the Party Committee of Beijing School for the Blind, Zhang Aining, Director of the Human Rights Research Center at the Foreign Affairs College, Li Yunlong, Professor of the International Strategic Research Institute of the Central Party School (National School of Administration), Zhang Wei, Executive Vice President of the Institute of Human Rights at China University of Political Science and Law, Liu Huawen, Deputy Director of the Institute of International Law, Chinese Academy of Social Sciences, Lu Haina, Executive Director of Human Rights Research Center of Renmin University of China, Xu Shuang, Associate Professor of the Institute of Human Rights at China University of Political Science and Law, Liao Juan, Associate Professor of the School of Management, Capital Normal University, Jiao Yang, Assistant Researcher at Tsinghua University's Future Laboratory and Core Backbone of the Blind Computer Project, Gao Yuan, a professional researcher at Tsinghua University's Future Laboratory, Gan Lu, Head of International Exchange Department at Beijing Youth Legal Aid and Research Center. We extend our heartfelt gratitude to all of them.

China Travel—Inviting the World to Experience a Real China[①]

Travel reflects humanity's hope and pursuit of a beautiful life and serves as a vital pathway to discovering the novel and the unexplored. Since entering the new era, China has focused its efforts on improving its modern tourism industry system and accelerating the construction of a strong tourism nation. Its tourism industry is becoming an emerging strategic pillar that is playing an ever-greater role in, among others, improving life quality, stimulating economic growth, nurturing a spiritual home, projecting China's image, and fostering inter-civilizational learning.

Since the beginning of 2024, China has further expanded its list of visa-free entry countries and made payment, communication, and travel more convenient for inbound tourists. This has led to a substantial surge in the number of international visitors to China, the "China Travel" trend gaining momentum on global social media platforms. The array of measures China has adopted to facilitate travel for foreigners is not only promoting a better and faster growth of the culture and tourism sectors, but also stands as a living testament to China's steadfast pursuit of high-level international openness.

Tens of millions of tourists hailing from across the globe have witnessed China's

---

① Released on December 4, 2024, at the Xinhua CEIS Think Tank Annual Conference 2024 held in Boao, Hainan.

openness, confidence, civilization, and security and have experienced firsthand the monumental achievements of China's modernization. This has helped change the one-sided stereotypes of China imposed by the U.S. and some other Western countries, fostering exchanges, mutual recognition, and learning between different civilizations.

China Travel has introduced the world to a country that is trustworthy, endearing, and respectable—a China that is more genuine and closer to reality.

I. "China Travel" Takes the World by Storm

Since the beginning of 2024, China has rolled out an array of measures to facilitate travel for inbound international visitors, continuing to optimize the channels for foreigners to visit the country. Along with the continuing flow of these policy dividends, there is a steady upsurge of tourists from abroad, with a spiraling number of inbound visitors. "China Travel" has become a trending topic on international social media platforms while the number of hits for related content keeps soaring.

Concurrently, there is a noticeable shift in the pattern of China Travel by international tourists: moving from cursory sightseeing trips to more tailored, immersive experiences. International tourists are now not only drawn to the allure of China's fine cultural heritage, but also exposed to the achievements of Chinese modernization, leading to a more holistic, genuine, and multifaceted perception of the nation. China leverages inbound tourism as an important opportunity to display its national image and foster cultural exchanges. It has worked diligently to address the difficulties and pain points for foreign visitors, improve tourism services, and narrate stories of China in the new era to better bolster high-level international openness and drive high-quality development.

1. A Surge in the Number of Foreign Visitors to China

With China's further expansion of its tourism sector to international travelers, the market for inbound tourism is witnessing a swift rebound, attracting more and more foreign visitors eager to immerse themselves in the dynamic and genuine experience of China. The latest figures from the National Immigration Administration (NIA) reveal that in the first half of 2024, the number of foreigners entering China through all ports soared to 14,635,000, a staggering year-on-year increase of 152.7%.

Among those visitors, a significant 8,542,000 individuals availed themselves of visa-free entry, representing a 190.1% year-on-year growth. Continuing this trend, the third quarter of 2024 saw 8,186,000 foreigners arriving in China, which was a 48.8% rise compared with the same period in the previous year; of these, 4,885,000 million entered through visa-free channels, an impressive 78.6% increase year-over-year. These statistics collectively signal a robust resurgence in China's inbound tourism. With continuing policy optimization and further opening of its market, it is expected that China's inbound tourism market will sustain this strong growth trajectory, contributing further to the recovery and development of the global economy.

Traveling in China has allowed foreign visitors to feel firsthand the numerous new developments in China's services such as transportation, payment, and booking. In transportation, China has rapidly resumed its regular international passenger flights and the railway department has optimized the 12306 website, including the introduction of an online identity verification service for foreign passports. In payment, convenient methods like "large transactions by card, small by QR code, and cash as a last resort" have been phased in. In bookings, cities like Shanghai, Beijing, Nanjing, and Changsha have announced that, with few exceptions, reservation requirements in the majority of tourist spots have been lifted across the board. These user-friendly services have greatly enhanced the comfort of travel for international visitors.

Contrary to some Western media portrayals of China as having a poor and dirty environment and serious safety concerns, the reality is that China's streets are clean and well-maintained, its people warm and welcoming, and its cities vibrant and safe at night. Many foreigners who visited China captured their travel experiences in short videos and shared them on social media, showing not only the country's stunning landscapes and culinary delights, but also its efficient public transport, safe living conditions, and warm, friendly citizens. These posts have sparked great interest among many who have yet to visit China. According to data from international social media platforms, "China Travel" has become a trending search term, with related topics garnering over 700 million views. With each exclamation of "What a Super city!" from international friends, the unique allure of China Travel is constantly on display.

2. The Continuing Flow of Dividends from Facilitation Measures

To attract and better service visitors from abroad, China's tourism industry has introduced a myriad of innovations and enhancements in products and services, particularly by way of optimized visa and immigration policies, increased payment convenience, and enhanced digital tourism services. These initiatives have not only streamlined entry procedures and lowered the barriers to China Travel, but also significantly improved the overall experience for foreigners visiting the country and elevated the service standards across the tourism sector.

As for visa policies for entering China, as of the end of November 2024, China had reached full visa exemption agreements with 25 countries and declared, in tranches, its unilateral visa-free entry policy for nationals of 38 countries such as France and Germany. The National Immigration Administration has rolled out over 110 policies aimed at easing the process for foreigners coming to China and has continued to optimize, on a regional basis, policies on visa-free entry or transit and port entry visas. This has resulted in a continuing surge in the number of foreign nationals visiting China. Notably, the 144-hour visa-free transit policy has been extended to apply to 35 ports of call and 54 countries.

In mobile payment, the Ministry of Culture and Tourism has prioritized four types of tourist venues: national star-rated scenic areas, provincial-and-above tourist resorts, national-level tourism leisure streets and blocks, and major national rural tourism towns and villages. The ministry is promoting moves to improve reservation and verification processes for foreign national documents and payment methods, offering international visitors the flexibility of choosing from diverse payment options, from bank cards to cash to mobile payment, thus making their travels through China seamless.

The People's Bank of China and the State Administration of Foreign Exchange (SAFE) have directed major payment institutions nationwide to streamline identity verification procedures, boost the efficiency of card binding, and raise the transaction limits to $5,000 per transaction and $50,000 per year, facilitating daily consumption for foreigners through QR code payment. In addition, the "whitelist" of premium merchants has been expanded to ensure that the payment needs of foreigners in critical areas such as accommodation, education, and healthcare are well catered for. Moreover, the steady advancement of online foreign card-acquiring services has further diversified the payment options available to foreigners shopping online while in China.

Local governments across China, leveraging their regional characteristics and urban identities, have actively promoted the extension and refinement of convenience measures for foreign visitors. These initiatives have effectively increased the appeal of inbound tourism.

In its ongoing effort to build a free trade port, Hainan Province offers a visa-free entry policy to visitors from 59 countries, permitting stays of up to 30 days for short-term purposes such as tourism, trade, family visits, official visits, medical treatment, conferences and exhibitions, and sports events. Since May 2024, a visa-free policy for foreign tourists arriving by cruise ship has been in effect, allowing visitors entering through the cruise ship ports of call of 13 coastal cities, including Haikou and Sanya, to enjoy a 15-day stay without a visa.

Starting from July 30, a 144-hour visa-free policy for foreign tour groups entering Hainan from Hong Kong and Macao officially took effect. To further enhance visitor experience, Hainan is continuing to expand passenger inspection channels, improve customs clearance efficiency, and offer multilingual services to ensure that international tourists receive efficient and convenient immigration entry and exit services.

Heilongjiang Province, an important region of China for border tourism with Russia, has been actively developing border tourism under the Belt and Road Initiative. To date, in border cities like Heihe, several distinctive travel routes focusing on health and leisure have been developed. Statistics show that the number of Russian tourists arriving in China surpassed 90,000 in the first ten months of 2024, highlighting the vibrancy and success of China-Russia border tourism.

In the Chengdu-Chongqing region, Sichuan Province and Chongqing Municipality have implemented a collaborative port visa mechanism, achieving a streamlined process known as "Sichuan-Chongqing Interoperability". By virtue of information sharing and mutual recognition of qualifications, this mechanism has helped improve the management of itineraries for inbound tourist groups. It has adjusted the previous requirement of "entry and exit only through Chongqing" to a more flexible "entry or exit through Chongqing", offering foreign visitors a variety of entry and exit options. This move has beefed up policy support for tourism collaboration between the two areas.

3. Broad Prospects for the China Travel Market

Tourism is an integrated industry. In China, the development of the tourism sector is a critical handle for high-quality development and serves as a vital driver of regional economic growth. Against the backdrop of China's resolve to build itself into a global tourism powerhouse, the China travel market holds vast potential and plays a pivotal role in driving global economic development.

China is a big country that boasts abundant tourism resources. In terms of the diversity of its tourism resources, it offers experiences that span from the icy landscapes of the North to the tropical coastlines of the South, from bustling metropolises in the East to the majestic plateaus, mountains, and rivers in the West. This geographical richness makes China a uniquely captivating destination for international tourists. In tourism philosophy, as travel becomes an essential aspect of a better life for people worldwide, China prioritizes tourism elements such as natural greenery, cultural heritage preservation, and technological innovation, elements that offer a relaxing, comfortable, and enjoyable experience for global visitors. When it comes to innovating tourism products, new demand for emerging trends and niche markets is driving the development of creative tourist venues, facilities, products, and services. From the perspective of tourism's vital role in boosting international trade and cooperation, with the gradual recovery of the inbound travel market, some companies are seeing a return to pre-2019 levels in the number of tourists they serve. For promotion and marketing, China's organization of various international exchange events and its cooperation with the World Tourism Organization has significantly elevated the visibility and appeal of the "China Travel" brand on the world stage.

The development of the tourism industry is conducive to further opening the tourism services trade sector and increasing its competitiveness. By gradually removing international trade barriers, the opening creates a more liberalized and convenient investment environment, thereby attracting foreign capital to China's tourism market. In the early years of reform and opening up, China leveraged inbound tourism as a platform to present to the world China's society and business environment. Today, the continuous optimization of visa-free policies is set to further attract more foreigners to China for travel, business, work, study, or living, thus fostering economic and cultural exchanges and facilitating the cross-border movement of various elements.

According to Zhang Yansheng, Principal Researcher of the China Center for International Economic Exchanges (CCIEE), the unilateral visa-free policies are crucial for promoting cross-border movement and have a noticeable effect on foreign capital utilization. These policies will further the level and efficiency of trade in goods and services, transportation, capital flows, and data and information exchange through liberalization and facilitation.

Luigi Gambardella, President of ChinaEU, pointed out that the visa-free policy makes it easier for small and medium-sized enterprises in Europe to visit China for business and exhibitions, among other activities. In the midst of a sluggish global economic recovery and rising protectionism, China's ongoing efforts to simplify its visa policy allow foreign investors to visit and observe the field, grow in interest, and reduce investment uncertainties. Undoubtedly, this policy has further boosted confidence, providing greater momentum for global economic revitalization and globalization.

According to the report entitled "Travel & Tourism Economic Impact 2024: Global Trends" published by the World Travel & Tourism Council (WTTC), China has emerged as the world's second-largest tourism market and is projected to surpass the United States as the largest within the next decade. Promoting the high-quality development of "China Travel" can accelerate supply-side structural reforms in the tourism industry, enhance the availability of quality tourism products, and continuously improve the tourism product supply system. It also boosts the deep integration of culture and tourism, drives growth in related industries such as cultural entertainment, accommodation, dining, and transportation, and enhances the quality control of travel services and comprehensive market oversight within the industry, thus significantly strengthening the governance capabilities and standards of the tourism industry.

China's image in the new era will be presented in a more colorful, tangible, and relatable manner to people around the world.

II. "China Travel" Offers a Direct Insight into the Achievements of Chinese Modernization

In July 2024, the 20th CPC Central Committee adopted at its third plenary the Resolution of the Central Committee of the Communist Party of China (CPC) on Further Deepening Reform Comprehensively to Advance Chinese Modernization. This resolution explicitly proposes facilitating management for outbound and inbound tourism and expanding international cultural exchanges and cooperation. The Chinese government remains committed to deepening the reform comprehensively and expanding the benefits of the visa-free entry policy to welcome with open arms friends from overseas to enter and tour China extensively, to foster mutual understanding and connections between China and the rest of the world. With its time-honored history, splendid culture, magnificent mountains, long rivers, and diverse customs, China offers foreign visitors a direct, immersive experience of its profound culture and the achievements of its modernization drive, gaining heartfelt acclaim from them for the miracles in the country's development.

1. Experiencing the Charm of Chinese Culture Which Fuses the Past and Present

According to a dedicated survey by the China Tourism Academy on inbound tourist satisfaction, over 60% of respondents cited experiencing Chinese culture as their primary reason for visiting China. Chinese civilization has a long and uninterrupted history, making it the only continuous civilization that has developed to the present day. The China of today places great importance on preserving its historical and cultural heritage while creatively transforming and innovatively developing its outstanding traditional culture. Visitors from abroad can enjoy in China a cultural feast that seamlessly blends tradition and modernity at every turn. The unique charm of Chinese culture is becoming a core attraction for China as an international tourism destination.

Dunhuang, a key hub on the ancient Silk Road, is where diverse cultures converge. In October 2024, a sightseeing group of over 1,000 international tourists embarked on a fully packed eye-dazzling cultural and natural exploration tour of Gansu's Dunhuang as part of the Beautiful China Tour: Thousand-people Inbound Tour to Gansu. At the Mogao Grottoes, a UNESCO World Heritage site, they were introduced to the cave art born of cultural exchanges across civilizations; each mural and sculpture seemed to narrate stories that went back centuries before. The visitors were not only awed by these exquisite artworks, but also gained a direct appreciation of the brilliance of Dunhuang culture and the vastness and depths of Chinese civilization.

From showcasing at Mogao Caves the exchanges between civilizations along the ancient Silk Road to representing the spirit of the Chinese nation on the Great Wall, from reflecting the court culture of the Ming and Qing dynasties at the Palace Museum to displaying a culture of reclusion among ancient scholar-officials in the classical gardens of Suzhou—China boasts 59 UNESCO World Heritage sites today, including 40 cultural heritage sites and four natural-cultural heritage sites. These diverse and cultural riches leave foreign visitors thoroughly impressed and full of praise.

Classic masterpieces of traditional Chinese culture, after being reimaged in the digital age, now vividly convey the values of Chinese culture and its people. In Shanxi's Tiefo Temple, Yuhuang Temple, and Yanqing Temple, Italian "foreign Wukong" artist Ale was wielding a custom-made iron shaft, pausing now and then to pose with a striking silhouette. With China's first domestically produced AAA game Black Myth: Wukong becoming a calling card for the international dissemination of Chinese culture, more foreigners are now following the footsteps of Wukong the Monkey King on a journey through Shanxi. Ale said, "I feel like I'm the 'chosen one' in the game, climbing mountains, crossing rivers, and overcoming challenges until finally finding the 'treasure' —these grand traditional Chinese architectures that lie before my eyes."

Not only do tangible cultural heritage sites captivate foreign visitors, but the intangible cultural heritage deeply rooted in Chinese civilization also leaves a lasting impression. Intangible cultural heritage also radiates with the splendor of the times.

In September 2024, the Workers' Sanatorium at the Wudalianchi Scenic Area in Heihe City, Heilongjiang Province greeted a group of tourists from Russia. Here, they explored the volcanic landscape, sampled mineral spring water, and basked in the sun, enjoying a leisurely vacation. They also sought out experiences of traditional Chinese medicine (TCM), an important component of China's intangible cultural heritage.

Acupuncture and massage therapies attracted Valeria to line up for a try. Larisa, her compatriot, was already relishing the benefits of cupping therapy. "I feel great after the treatment. I plan to stay in Heihe for 14 days this time to have a deeper experience of TCM treatments along with some sightseeing," she said.Xu Biao, director of the rehabilitation hospital at Wudalianchi Workers' Sanatorium, noted that an increasing number of Russians were showing interest in TCM and the number of repeat visitors was on the rise. During peak periods, the facility hosts about 1,500 Russian tourists daily .

In March 2024, Tim, an Australian video blogger, was focused intently on filling a metal pendant with blue mineral pigment at a cloisonné enamel-making intangible cultural heritage workshop in Shenzhen. He wanted to take this self-made cloisonné art piece back home as a gift for his mother.

Today, more and more foreign visitors are showing keen interest in intangible Chinese art techniques such as TCM, tea culture, clay sculpture, and colored painting. They are eager for hands-on experience in the processes and feel the rich and unique meaning behind them. Through travel, people can feel the culture and deepen their understanding while China's vibrant social and economic development and cultural charm are fully shown as a result.

2. Experiencing New Scenes of Life-transforming Technology

Amid the current "China Travel" boom, countless foreign visitors, drawn by China's historical sites and traditional culture, have set foot on this land. They are also amazed by the magnificent tapestry of its rapid development and the omnipresent technological achievements.

Transportation is a vital carrier of tourism. "Traveling through China by high-speed train" has become an increasingly popular choice among foreign visitors. China's extensive high-speed rail network, comprising eight vertical and eight horizontal lines, has gradually formed a tight grid. Stretching from the snowy northern regions to the water towns of the South, from the eastern coast to the western plateaus, this extensive rail network covers vast expanses of China, facilitating easy access for travelers to their destinations. Foreign tourists can swiftly shuttle between different attractions on high-speed trains, enjoying stunning landscapes outside their windows while experiencing the intelligence and convenience of China's advanced rail technology.

"Traveling in China with a smartphone" has made all journeys more relaxing and efficient. In 2024, British global travel blogger Chris Hutchinson took his family on a China tour. They experienced a transition from cash payment to mobile payment. Hutchinson remarked, "Once we had learned how to use WeChat and Alipay, everything became so much simpler. You can do everything with your phone—even pay for street food by scanning a QR code. It's truly incredible!" By the time they got to Shenzhen, the Hutchinsons enjoyed food delivery by a drone. Strolling along the Bund in Shanghai at night, they enjoyed the city's dazzling lights, describing them as follows: "The entire city was surrounded by technology. We saw skyscrapers shooting up like rockets into the clouds. Even the bridges featured ever-changing holographic projections."

Another pair of British travel bloggers Tez and Libby took their high-tech payment exploration a step further. In Shenzhen, they turned on the facial recognition payment function for subway rides without keying in a password and experienced the convenience of "entering the station in a second". Tez said, "We've never experienced using our faces as subway tickets anywhere else. It feels as if we had been transported to 2050!"

The modernity and technological sophistication of Chinese cities deeply impressed tourists. At Gangxia North Subway Station in Shenzhen, a young foreign couple was astonished by its ingenious tech-savvy interior architectural design. Their first-person perspective video on TikTok gained widespread popularity, with comments overflowing with praise: "It's as beautiful as an interstellar station!" "This is a train to the future world!"

Mount Huangshan has embraced digitalization through its "International Visitor-friendly Scenic Spots" immersion initiative to enhance tourism experiences. Foreign visitors simply need to scan a QR code to access a mini-program that offers a detailed travel guide. Through Alipay's built-in translation service, they can have the travel guides translated into 16 languages including English, French, German, Spanish, Malay, Arabic, and Italian with just one click. This mobile optimization service not only helps global tourists enjoy Huangshan with ease, but also deepens their understanding of Huizhou culture.

In 2024, New Zealand tourist Arne Herman revisited Shanghai after 28 years and he kept marveling at the city's dramatic transformation: "When I looked at Pudong from the Bund back then, the Oriental Pearl Tower was the only high riser across the river. Now, it is surrounded by numerous skyscrapers in Lujiazui." This transformation exemplifies Shanghai's rapid development as a global center for technology and economy.

3. Entering the Happy Lives of Chinese Urban and Rural Residents

Amid the China Travel boom, foreign tourists are not only captivated by the diverse natural landscapes, historical architecture, and folk cultures of Chinese cities, but also eager to immerse themselves in the everyday lives of urban and rural residents, exploring local markets, neighborhood parks, and morning exercise squares, experiencing the changes in the life of common folks in China today. These live street scenes are becoming a new favorite among foreign visitors.

In recent years, cultural consumption among urban and rural residents in China has shown a trend toward greater diversification, personalized choices, and high quality. A rich array of cultural products and services from reading and listening to music to binge-watching dramas and movies, from visiting exhibitions and performances to exploring famous landmarks, has enriched the cultural lives of Chinese residents, urban and rural. The beautiful lives that urban and rural dwellers enjoy are seen by visiting tourists as part of the beautiful scenes. Both domestic and international tourists are increasingly entering the daily life scenes, with local markets on apar with museums, galleries, and theaters in terms of popularity.

In the first eight months of 2024, Shanghai welcomed 2,908,600 foreign tourists, a 1.4-fold increase compared with the same period of 2023. Tourism routes and products that showcase the happy contemporary lives of Shanghai's residents have become particularly favored by international visitors. After visiting the bustling Bund, Swiss tourist Philipp ventured into the ancient water town of Zhujiajiao on the riverine outskirts of Shanghai. He explored the quaint old streets, sampled local delicacies like Granny's Zongzi (sticky rice dumplings) and Xiaolongbao (soup dumplings), enjoying the peaceful charm of this traditional town.

Lauren Gassett, an American girl, participated in a unique Companion Tour in Shanghai—a participatory visit to Caoyang New Village. In just one day, she and her groupmates learned how to make local delicacies such as wontons after "Shanghai aunties", had a table tennis "duel" with local residents at a community center, and strolled through a bustling local market, experiencing what it truly felt to be "Shanghai locals".

In the vibrant food street of Jiefangbei CBD in Chongqing, an array of delicious food assembled here dazzled visitors while the flashing neon lights were mixed with enticing aromas, creating a lively local ambience. Indonesian tourist Jajarlwin Setiyabudi is particularly fond of the barbecues and desserts here. He said that while he had been to many major cities in China, Chongqing not only offers a great variety of street food, but also gives visitors a sense of relaxation.

Thousands of kilometers away in northeastern China, an increasing number of Russians are choosing to experience the exotic customs and participate in cultural activities in Heihe City, Heilongjiang Province, including touring morning markets, tasting local cuisine, and shopping for specialty souvenirs. According to the Heihe Municipal Bureau of Culture, Radio, Television and Tourism, the city received 659,400 international and domestic tourists in the first ten months of 2024, marking a year-on-year increase of 160.12%.

With the implementation of the rural revitalization strategy and integrated urban-rural development, China's countryside is showing its infinite charm with a fascinating blend of ancient local traditions and modern lifestyles. More and more foreign tourists are shifting their focus from first-tier cities on the eastern coast to the vast rural areas in central and western China. They go deep into rural China to immerse themselves in the culture and customs of this ancient land to acquire a multifaceted image of the country.

American photographer Adam Clayton, who has a deep love for traditional ancient villages in China, has spent the last few years traveling through rural China searching for charming ancient dwellings. One of his favorite traditional Chinese structures is the Mansion of the Huangcheng Chancellor in Jincheng City, Shanxi Province, known for its commanding grandeur and intricate architecture.

Ctrip, a major Chinese travel agency, launched a unique experience product for foreign tourists called "Stay at a Holiday Farm and Be a Chinese Farmer for a Day", a well-received tourist program that combines farming experience with cultural entertainment, allowing tourists to engage in activities like fruit picking, fabric dyeing, rice planting, wheat harvesting, etc. More and more foreign visitors are entering the peaceful beauty of rural settings and diving into such authentic local culture. Even Chinese netizens proclaimed, "This wave of foreigners knows better how to enjoy themselves!"

4. Enjoying the Beautiful Tapestry of Ecological Advancement

China not only draws the world's attention with its profound cultural heritage, but also mesmerizes countless foreign visitors with its myriad breathtaking natural landscapes. From the majestic Tianshan Mountains to the picturesque water towns south of the Yangtze River, from the banks of the mighty Yellow River to the mysterious Xizang Plateau, every inch of this landis imbued with the infinite charm of nature. Since the advent of the new era, China has achieved a historic, transformative sea change in ecological conservation. The pace of building a beautiful China has accelerated, fostering the vigorous development of a modernization that features the harmonious coexistence of man and nature. In China, the sky is bluer, the mountains greener, the water clearer, and the vast land more vibrant and colorful than ever before.

With their lenses, bloggers from overseas frequently capture and praise the breathtaking beauty of China. At Zhangjiajie, Hunan Province, a Korean tourist gazed at the range of staggered mountain peaks and exclaimed from the bottom his heart, "This is a paradise on earth that only gods could create." Belgian blogger Yiji hiked through Jiuzhaigou in Sichuan to film its breathtaking lakes and mountains while a British photographer ventured deep into Xinjiang to capture the snow-capped forests at the foot of Tianshan Mountains...A stream of videos showcasing China's hidden natural wonders has garnered countless likes on international social media platforms.

Harbin, reputed as an "Ice City", is China's northernmost provincial capital. Each winter, it attracts a huge influx of domestic and international tourists with its unique cultural and tourism resources, including ice sculptures and winter sports. In February 2024, Canadian blogger Steve and his wife Ivanna visited the Harbin Ice and Snow World, where they were greeted by ice sculptures of traditional Chinese architecture, Western castles, Ferris wheels, arches, city walls, and slides, all built and carved with ice blocks.

As night fell, these intricately designed beautiful "ice structures" were illuminated, transforming the entire park into a dazzling fairy-tale world. Visitors enjoyed ice skating, skiing, spinning tops, and cycling in this winter wonderland. Steve remarked, "It's so cool! Even as a Canadian, I've never seen such a magical world of ice and snow. People who come here have only two choices: either be in awe of the sights you've never seen before or keep taking pictures and videos all the time."

As one of the countries with the biggest number of World Natural Heritage and Mixed Heritage sites, China has always been committed to protecting its ecosystems and preserving its natural heritage. By persisting in having culture and ecology as the drivers and innovating resource preservation and utilization models, China has integrated its cultural background and the important "green is gold" concept into the entire process of tourism development. Many international friends who visit China invariably use their cameras or videocams to capture the beautiful landscapes along their journey with the photos and videos they take and vividly present to the world China's achievements in ecological governance and green development.

In Yucun Village, Anji County, Zhejiang Province, the swaying bamboo and flowing streams form layers of green, creating a refreshing and tranquil atmosphere. As the place of origin of the concept that "lucid waters and lush mountains are invaluable assets", Yucun started implementing the Green Rural Revival Program in 2005 to phase out heavy-polluting enterprises while transforming the village into a leisure tourism destination with farm stays. In 2021, Yucun was selected as one of the first Best Tourism Villages by the United Nations World Tourism Organization (UNWTO). In 2023, Yucun entertained over 1,150,000 visitors and achieved a total collective income of 22,470,000 yuan.

The Xishuangbanna Dai Autonomous Prefecture of Yunnan Province has leveraged its rich biodiversity endowment and built itself firmly on the traditional ecological concept that "forests collect water, water brings fields, fields produce food, and food nourishes people". Focusing on building "waste-free tourist destinations" to move forward the green, "no-waste" transformation and upgrading of its tourism industry, Xishuangbanna has integrated the development of green tourism with its 4A-rated scenic area—Dai Minority Park in a bid to develop green tourism in a comprehensive manner. In the first ten months of 2024, the region had hosted 1.97 million visitors, a 20% increase compared with the same period of 2023.

III. "China Travel" Presents China as a Country Worthy of Trust, Love, and Respect

China is advancing high-quality and high-level development of inbound tourism so that more international tourists are able to, hope to, and want to visit the country. Through firsthand experiences and exploration, they will fall in love with a country that is trustworthy, lovable, and respectable, form an accurate understanding of the country, and further engage with and share in China's development opportunities.

1. Effectively Breaking Down Stereotypes and One-sided Impressions

Inbound tourism is an important way for international visitors to gain a direct and deep understanding of China. It is also an effective way to shape a national image through people-to-people exchanges. Many people outside of China learn about the country through the media, but some Western media, for various purposes, either remain silent or fail to report objectively and fairly on China, resulting in an inability for many foreigners to get a full picture of a real China. In contrast, inbound China travel, based on personal experience on the spot and interactive exchanges, offers more international visitors the opportunity to immerse themselves in the vastness of China. This experience is far more direct and tangible than what the media conveys. It is more conducive to forming an accurate, multi-dimensional, and panoramic image of China.

The booming "China Travel" has opened a new window and pathway for the world to learn about and understand China. For many foreign visitors, the joyful "China Travel" has become a "journey to breakdown stereotypes", with a "sense of contrast" being the most immediate impression after experiencing China's stunning landscapes and breathing China's air of vibrant culture. The urban landscapes and time-honored architecture, combined with the rich historical underpinnings and the everyday lives of its people, offer a fresh firsthand perspective that helps overturn the misconceptions. Being there in person enables a better, real understanding. Some international travel vloggers even proclaimed, "We've been deceived by the Western media!" More and more visitors shared what they felt directly, "China is not what we once imagined", asserting that they had "discovered a side of China that Western media rarely show".

American vlogger Chris is a perfect example. A three-day trip to Beijing totally changed his view on China. He experienced the warmth and friendliness of the Chinese people, the convenience of high-tech advancements, and the improvement in people's life quality. These experiences even led to an idea germinating in his mind about residing in China long-term.

Upon his return on a Shanghai visit recently, Hidetoshi Tashiro, Chief Economist of Infinity LLC, Japan, said that he had seen none of the "sights of depression" depicted by Western media but instead, witnessed in the Chinese city gasoline-powered vehicles and electric ones traveling side by side on the streets and observed significant changes in infrastructure updates. He also noticed that various sectors in China are embracing digitalization, from cashless payment to smart traffic systems, with the whole society rapidly moving toward modernization and digitalization. He deeply felt that China is making strides, step by step, toward a leadership position in the world.

2. Demonstrating China's Commitment to Opening up

Opening up is a defining feature of contemporary China and a great dividend that China brings to the world. International tourism, which developed rapidly after WorldWar II, particularly with the propulsion of the globalization process, has become an integral part of the global economy. In 2019, the tourism industry contributed $9.6 trillion to global GDP, accounting for 10.3% of the total; it also created 10% of global jobs. In the same year, international tourist spending reached the $1.8 trillion mark, representing 6.8% of total exports. After experiencing the shocks of the COVID-19 pandemic, by 2023 global tourism export revenue had rebounded to 96% of pre-pandemic levels. However, compared with regions like Europe, the Americas, and Africa, the pace of tourism recovery in the Asia-Pacific region remains relatively low.

As an indispensable part of the global tourism industry, China offers unique and diverse travel products to international visitors. Opening up to the world, the Chinese tourism industry not only shares with the world stories of a dynamic China full of opportunities, but also provides Chinese experience and solutions to raise the overall service standards of global tourism. The thriving development of "China Travel" will contribute Chinese wisdom and strength to the prosperity of the global tourism industry.

To better welcome international tourists, several travel agencies in Guangdong Province have launched new inbound tourism routes. For example, GZL International Travel Service offers tours ranging from half-day to six-day packages, featuring a variety of options such as the Guangzhou Fast Classic Tour, Walking Exploration Tour, Slow-Paced City Tour, Tech and Folk Culture Tour, and Cultural Experience Tour. The itineraries cover everything from city life and suburban leisure activities to exhibitions, commerce, and trade. The routes include both in-depth tours of Guangzhou proper and multi-city packages combining Guangzhou with other cities in the Greater Bay Area. According to an executive of GZL International Travel Service, during peak periods like the Canton Fair in spring and autumn, these tourism products are expected to become an integral part of the "Guangzhou lifestyle" for exhibitors and business people from abroad.

In the Yangtze River Delta region, Shanghai has partnered with surrounding cities like Hangzhou and Suzhou to launch a regional tourism model featuring "144-hour visa-free transit + city tours". Experts believe this model has broken the limitations of a single city and will be effective in promoting the recovery and development of the inbound tourism market in the Yangtze River Delta. Since June 2024, more than 3,000 cultural venues in Shanghai have lifted reservation requirements, allowing foreign tourists to visit with a passport or other valid identification, significantly enhancing their experience.

Beijing has launched a contactless gate entry service for foreign bank cards, allowing international passengers to directly use MasterCard and Visa to get onto subway platforms without the need to purchase a separate ticket. The same fare applies to every passenger, with no distinction based on passengers' nationality. For its part, Shanghai has upgraded its public transport system to support international bank cards through the bus code. International passengers only need to bind their foreign cards and activate the bus code through Tencent's WeChat app. This service is available across multiple modes of transportation in the city, including buses, subways, ferries, and maglev trains, offering a more convenient digital travel experience for international visitors.

At the 2024 China International Travel Mart (CITM), domestic and foreign business representatives were engaged in exchanges and interactions, showcasing to each other their most attractive cultural and tourism resources. The participants listened to presentations, explored various projects, and discussed potential collaborations. They experienced the strong momentum injected into the global tourism economy by China's high-level opening up and came to better appreciate China's unwavering commitment to expanding its opening up.

3. Sharing Development Opportunities of the Chinese Market

"When relationships are built on benefits, they dissipate once the benefits are exhausted; when relationships are built on power, they collapse once the power wanes... Only when relationships are built on the heart can they endure for the long term." China has always adhered to the philosophy of "harmony under heaven" and "one world, one family." Always open and inclusive, it has been absorbing diverse cultures, seeking common ground while putting aside differences, and engaging in mutual respect. China welcomes more international friends to China, to foster exchanges and create more exciting stories about them, and to discover more vibrant and mutually beneficial opportunities for cooperation. Inbound tourism benefits from China's unwavering policy of expanding opening up, advancing in tandem with China's development.

From bustling urban landscapes to ancient rural charm, from dynamic industrial parks to cutting-edge innovation hubs, China's multifaceted image fascinates the ever-growing influx of foreign nationals. As their understanding of China deepens, some international visitors perceive promising opportunities for development and have decided to invest in this land of opportunities, integrate into local life, and find platforms for their career development. They will become an integral part of this multicultural society.

In 1984, Chicago-born Brian Linden first came to China. He was deeply captivated by the local customs and culture, and he developed a profound affection for rural China. In 2008, he chose to open a guesthouse in Dali, Yunnan and thus established a platform to promote traditional Chinese culture. Here, he witnessed China's rapid development. He remarked: "Forty years ago, I knew nothing about China; now I know how to write Chinese calligraphy with a writing brush. China has now become my home."

Invited by a friend, French photographer Jeremy Walter Grinan visited Hainan over a decade ago. Enchanted by the local scenery, he decided to stay. The small eateries in old streets, the coconut palms and sunsets in the park, and surfers on the sea... Grinan used his camera to capture the daily life here and gradually found his passion. From photography to video production and eventually film direction, Grinan continues to pursue and fulfill his dreams in Hainan, a land full of opportunities.

Nine years ago, Allan Denis Naymark came to Jingdezhen from New York. As a ceramic enthusiast, he gave himself a Chinese name Ni Deming. The Chinese character "Ni," which is pronounced similar to the "Nay" in his name, means clay, the main component in ceramics. Ni was deeply drawn to the charm of the local ceramic culture and found his own career here. In 2015, the Taoxichuan International Art Center in Jingdezhen launched the "Migratory Bird Program". Every year, artists from over 50 countries and regions are invited here to create and leave their works here. Ni said, "I am fascinated by the ubiquitous atmosphere of ceramic art at Jingdezhen and the warm, delicate, and liberal living environment here. I will continue to work and live here".

Since the beginning of 2024, foreign envoys and other diplomats from many countries who are stationed in China have made study visits to Heilongjiang, Shanghai, and Gansu, among others. With the aim of discovering new opportunities to write together a new chapter of development through cooperation, they gained a deeper understanding of local economic development, cultural characteristics, and social conditions during these visits. Peter Lizak, Ambassador of Slovakia to China, remarked during a visit to Heilongjiang: "The Snow Town has successfully transformed its ice and snow resources into a consumer phenomenon. The environment and atmosphere here remind me of my hometown. We also have many small towns like this, which can be developed for winter tourism. This has great potential."

In June 2024, 30 foreign envoys and other senior diplomats from 22 countries who were stationed in China visited Lanzhou and Dunhuang in Gansu Province to inspect and learn about the development of local green industries. The diplomatic delegation visited the burgeoning green energy industry at the Dunhuang Photovoltaic Industrial Park, located on the Gobi Desert. Arlindodo Rosario, Ambassador of Cabo Verde to China, was amazed by the "super-mirror powerplant" and proclaimed, "The Gobi Desert was once barren, but China has used the mighty force of nature and technology to breathe life into the Gobi Desert and create an incredible miracle".

In August 2024, an Indonesian delegation composed of government officials, entrepreneurs, and experts visited the energy-rich province of Shanxi. They toured several energy companies and low-carbon industrial parks to explore up close the transformation path for coal-heavy regions and expressed the hope for future collaboration with enterprises in China's Shanxi Province.

As a country undergoing vigorous development, China boasts a dynamic market environment, abundant natural and cultural resources, and a diverse range of government support policies. These factors not only provide foreign talent with diverse career options and a vast space for development, but also offer foreign businesses in cooperation with China a platform for growth and takeoff. In so doing, China is making a positive contribution to the shared prosperity of the global economy.

IV. "China Travel" Promotes Inter-civilizational Exchanges and Learning

Travel is a bridge for civilization dissemination, cultural exchanges, and friendship building. It is also an important way to bring people closer. Along with China's rapid and dynamic development in tourism, inbound tourism is playing an increasingly significant role in enhancing the inclusivity of and coexistence among different civilizations, enriching the garden of civilizations, and promoting world peace and stability.

1. Enhancing the Inclusivity and Coexistence of Civilizations

State-to-state relations thrive when people share bonds, and bonds flourish when hearts are connected. As a global cultural exchange phenomenon, international travel has greatly promoted the exchanges between and integration of different civilizations in the world. Travel provides opportunities for people of different countries, nations, and beliefs to have face-to-face contact. Foreign tourists can learn about the realities of the places covered in their travel through physical visits and firsthand experience. Through their contact and interaction with visitors, local residents form a first impression of the source countries. Tourism builds a bridge to connect people's hearts and minds in a way that is conducive to enhancing the capacity for empathy among civilizations. It enables people to view the differences and divergences between countries from a more inclusive perspective and thus appreciate the vitality and splendor of different societies with the aesthetic lens of civilizational diversity.

The Manila Declaration on the Social Aspects of Tourism adopted in 1980 states that tourism should play its role in addressing major global social issues, including the promotion of peace, settlement of disputes, and the maintenance of the international economic order. Although countries have different cultural backgrounds, through the collision of and exchanges between these cultures, people can better understand each other's lifestyle, customs, values, and behaviors, and thus reduce misunderstandings, break down barriers, increase mutual understanding, and form public opinions that serve as the foundation of international cooperation. Through real contact by way of travel, hosts and guests can enhance their cultural ties and form the cognition of other countries' cultures and populace. The ever-closer cultural exchanges, like trickles and streams, will converge into a mighty river of friendly interaction.

China Travel provides a platform for direct communication and interaction between the Chinese people and foreign visitors, which helps not only increase the understanding of and respect for Chinese and other cultures of the world, but also foster the integration and inclusiveness between them. Through firsthand experience and interaction, foreign tourists can gain a deeper understanding and appreciation of China's cultural background and social customs, which contributes to continuous cross-cultural exchange and understanding. In addition, by experiencing in person China's lifestyle and social environment, international visitors can get a more genuine picture of China's development and changes. At the same time, the well-developed social media also allow foreign tourists to share their China trips with the rest of the world, further promoting mutual understanding and appreciation among different cultures.

In recent years, China has continued deepening cultural and tourism cooperation with many countries: the growing bilateral cooperation mechanisms between China and Russia and between China and Italy, the mutual hosting of the Year of Culture and Tourism between China and France, Kazakhstan, Tanzania, Zambia, Malaysia, and other countries, China's exchanges in culture and tourism with the Dominican Republic, El Salvador, and other countries which have just established or resumed diplomatic relations with China... These external cultural and tourism exchanges and cooperation have become a vivid footnote about China's promotion of a community with a shared future for mankind.

In May 2024, the 14th China-U.S. Tourism Leadership Summit took place in Xi'an under the theme of "Expanding China-U.S. Travel and Tourism and People-to-people Exchanges". This exchange event, "restarted" after a lapse of five years, gave a strong boost to the cooperation between the related industries in China and the United States.

After the event, a number of U.S. travel agent delegations tested the water by following each other to Beijing, Xi'an, Chongqing, and Shanghai to view the scenic spots, taste the food, try cashless payment in an immersive experience of China Travel. Exchanges and interaction between the travel industries of the two countries will help turn the "San Francisco Vision" into reality.

2. Enriching the World Garden of Civilizations

Tourism is not only a carrier of culture, but also a way to absorb it. The ancient Chinese equated "traveling ten thousand miles" with "reading ten thousand books" as a way for self-cultivation. In traveling activities, tourists' behaviors based on motives like seeking a new or different experience, seeking knowledge, beauty, and pleasure are essentially processes of perceiving, experiencing, enjoying, and spreading culture. The cultural and tourism industries are inseparable. Only by being committed to shaping tourism with culture, presenting culture through tourism, and promoting the integrated development of both can we better enable people to appreciate the beauty of culture and cultivate the beauty of the soul through the beauty of nature.

China boasts a time-honored culture and an extensive, profound civilization. Through inbound tourism to China, friends from all over the world can see and experience Chinese culture and gain a deeper understanding of the history of Chinese civilization and thus have a deeper understanding of the outstanding continuity, innovation, unity, inclusivity, and peacefulness of this great civilization.

Seeing with your own eyes Emperor Qin Shi Huang's magnificent Terracotta Warriors and Horses, each with a diverse shape and feature of its own, enables you to feel the power and might of the emperor's unification of the six states into a single country. Listening on the spot to the Naxi ancient music with soft tunes and elegant vibe enables you to feel the magic of the "living fossil of Chinese ancient music". The winding and peaceful paths in the Suzhou gardens and the gorgeous and elegant Kunqu opera expose the visitors to the Jiangnan style south of the Yangtze River and the beauty of the soft Wu dialect. The towering Potala Palace and solemn Dazhao Temple make people realize the unique charm of Xizang's culture.

In recent years, local governments in China have flexibly utilized local tourism resources and continued to develop China's fine traditional culture and advanced socialist culture to accelerate the deep integration and development of culture and tourism by elaborating many distinctive cultural and tourism products embodying cultural underpinnings and humanistic spirit. A number of representative projects like Beijing Daxing International Airport, Hong Kong-Zhuhai-Macao Bridge, and China's Five-hundred-meter Aperture Spherical Radio Telescope (FAST) have helped make tourism an important window to China's achievements in development in the new era. One hundred and sixty-four national tourism and leisure street blocks and 142 national industrial tourist demonstration bases have expanded the outlets for disseminating the rich and advanced socialist culture and bring Chinese and foreign tourists alike the beauty of urban modernity, industry, and technology during their journey.

China Travel in the new era fully demonstrates to foreign tourists the historical origin, development processes, and general direction of progress of the fine traditional Chinese culture. It fully reflects the unique creativity, values, and distinctive features of Chinese culture and highlights the unique charm of contemporary Chinese culture. It ushers Chinese culture and tourism further unto the global stage, enriching the world garden of civilizations.

3. Promoting World Peace and Stability

Travel is the most direct and natural way of people-to-people communication, a window of openness, a bond of friendship, and a channel for peace. "Tourism brings people together," said United Nations Secretary-General António Guterres in his message on World Tourism Day 2024, pointing to the need to reflect on the deep connections between tourism and peace.

The concept of "Travel for Peace" goes back a long way in history. In ancient Greece, the famous "Olympic Truce" was a "feat of peace" undertaken by the monarchs to ensure safe travel for athletes and audiences (from their distant homes to the games). Many Greek city-states were at war practically all the time except for the days during the Olympics. The warring parties agreed to a seven-day truce before and after the opening and closing of the Games, with each country obliged to provide protection for the participants. This created a linkage among diplomacy, travel, and peace.

Many of the world's eminent figures have high expectations of the role of international tourism and consider travel an important means of promoting international cooperation, understanding, and peace. After World War Two, and particularly since the 1980s, with the flourishing of cross-border tourism, the concept of "travel for peace" has attracted more and more attention. Mahatma Gandhi once said: "I have watched the cultures of all lands blow around my house and other winds have blown the seeds of peace, for travel is the language of peace." A review of China's history of diplomacy shows that the journey for peace, different as they were in terms of purposes, was a special way for ancient China to engage in communication and exchanges with the external world. The high monk Jianzhen's voyages to Japan, Xuanzang's journey to India, Zheng He's seven voyages across seas and oceans, though regarded today as journeys of a religious or political nature, have had their forms of travel and diplomatic effect passed down through the centuries.

The world is now going through profound changes unseen in 100 years at an accelerating pace. The changes of the world, the times, and the juncture in history are unfolding in an unprecedented way, with conflicts between different cultures occurring from time to time. Reputed as the "envoy of peace" and "bridge of friendship", tourism can play the role of a "stabilizer" and "lubricant" to ease tensions. In the face of the wave of anti-globalization and populism, peace and development are still the direction that most countries and the international community are actively striving for. They have also injected sustained impetus to strengthening the common efforts of mankind to deal with all kinds of serious challenges and difficulties. As a part of major country diplomacy, China's tourism diplomacy should always be based on the main theme of the times and amplify it by telling China's stories well through inbound tours and showcasing the image of a "Beautiful China".

At the practical level, China's inbound tourism has, in the context of serving the long-term interests of mankind, gradually developed such tourism-related items as "peace tour" and "green tour". Based on respect for cultural diversity and social values, China's inbound tours are organized by leveraging its own advantages in tourism and holding high the distinctive banner of building a community with a shared future for mankind while regarding tourism development as a common interest of human society. By proceeding from the goal of reducing prejudice between countries, promoting consensus among countries and realizing mutual benefit and win-win results for the international community, inbound tourism should play and highlight its role as a medium linking source countries and regions with destinations while serving national interests. Efforts should be made to further narrow the gap between the interests of countries, break away from over-dependence on tourist sources, and increase the complementarity of advantages for common progress, striving to forge tourism as a "public product" that drives human progress and the realization of the common values of humankind and open up new channels for the grand goal of building a community with a shared future.

V. Concluding Remarks

The Chinese have since time immemorial had a cultural tradition of travel. The ancient sages advocated "reading ten thousand books and traveling ten thousand miles", leaving behind countless classic travel essays and travelogues that have resonated throughout history.

Over three hundred years ago, Xu Xiake, a renowned Ming dynasty scholar, traveled extensively up and down China. His travelogue The Travel Diaries of Xu Xiake, which was written over the course of more than 30 years, is not only a world masterpiece on geography that contains his systematic observations and records of nature, but also a monumental work that depicts the beautiful landscapes of China, with a far-reaching and profound effect. May 19, the first day recorded in The Travel Diaries of Xu Xiake, was later designated as China's National Tourism Day.

More than 700 years ago, the Venetian traveler Marco Polo traversed thousands of miles to China and opened the door for the East and the West to meet with and understand each other, turning his extraordinary personal journey into a shared memory among countries across the Eurasian continent and creating a bridge for cultural exchanges between Eastern and Western civilizations. Over generations, other emissaries have continued to write chapters of friendly exchanges among civilizations along the Silk Road in an exemplary role for dialogues on an equal footing and common development among world civilizations.

With the acceleration of globalization, inbound tourism has become not only a component of economic activities, but also a vital vehicle for cultural exchanges and people-to-people diplomacy. It serves as an important indicator of a country's soft cultural power and international appeal. Over the past four decades of reform and opening-up, inbound tourism has not only boosted China's economic development, but also strengthened China's exchanges and cooperation with countries around the world, enhancing friendly interaction between regions and contributing to the blending of world civilizations.

In future, China's door will open even wider and the facilitation of "China Travel" will continue its upward trend. Even more friends will come to China from abroad to see China, enjoy China, and fall in love with China. The China Travel of the new era will share with the world more stories about the ancient and modern country and will foster greater global consensus and promote efforts by all countries to open a new chapter of cultural exchanges and integration as well as the linking of people by the heart. This will make the global garden of civilizations bloom in vibrant colors with full vitality.

We sincerely welcome more international friends to China for travel, to appreciate its beautiful landscapes, feel its unique charm, and join hands to begin a new chapter of cultural exchanges between peoples!

VI. References

1. "Xi Jinping' Letter on the Opening of the 14th China-US High-Level Tourism Dialogue," Xinhua, May 22, 2024.

2. "Xi Jinping Issues Important Instructions on Tourism Work, Emphasizing the Need to Improve the Modern Tourism System and Accelerate the Development of a Strong Tourism Nation," Xinhua, May 17, 2024.

3. "Xi Jinping and Italian President Mattarella Respectively Send Congratulatory Letters on the Opening of The Source of Italy—Ancient Roman Civilization Exhibition", Xinhua, July 10, 2022.

4. "Xi Jinping' Speech at the Symposium of Experts on Education, Culture, Health, and Sports," Xinhua, September 22, 2020.

5. "Xi Jinping' Keynote Speech at the Opening of Conference on Dialogue of Asian Civilizations," Xinhua, May 15, 2019.

6. "Xi Jinping' Speech at UNESCO Headquarters," Xinhua, March 27, 2014.

7. "Xi Jinping' Speech at Opening of the Year of Chinese Tourism in Russia," People' Daily, March 22, 2013.

8. Liu Zhongcai and Xie Zhengfa: "Enhancing China' Tourism Diplomacy in the Context of Globalization," Popular Tribune, Issue 8, 2024, pp. 36-39.

9. Zhang Zhenpeng: "Culture and Tourism Integration Strategies for China' Modernization," Governance, Issue 12, 2024, pp. 46-51.

10. Xu Tong, Zhang Yuli, and Shi Peihua: "Historical Evolution and Current Analysis of

China's Tourism Development Pattern,"Development Research, Issue 6, 2024, pp. 42-48.

11. Sun Panpan and Li Xiaoying."Inbound Tourism and the Building of a World Tourism Powerhouse: Mechanisms and Optimization Strategies,"Price: Theory & Practice, Issue 5, 2024, pp. 32-38.

12. Song Rui."On the Unique Path of China's Tourism Development,"Price: Theory & Practice, Issue 7, 2024, pp. 50-58.

13. Liu Minku and Deng Xiaogui."Study on the Path to Cultural Identity Enhancement through Border Tourism: From the Perspective of Telling China's Story,"Social Sciences in Guangxi, Issue 2, 2024, pp. 21-27.

14. Dai Bin and Yang Yuping."Theoretical Construction of and Practical Research on China's Tourism in the Context of New Productive Forces: An Interview with Professor Dai Bin, Director of China Tourism Research Institute,"Social Scientist, Issue 3, 2024, pp. 3-9.

15."Resolutely Follow China's Unique Path in Tourism Development,"Xinhua Daily Telegraph, May 18, 2024, Issue 002.

16. Xie Chaowu, Zhang Kun, and Chen Yanying."The Support System and Action Direction for the Recovery of China's Inbound Tourism,"Tourism Tribune, Issue 4, 2024, pp. 4-6.

17. Chen Ye and Wang Luqi."The Recovery and Marketing Innovation of China's Inbound Tourism Market,"Tourism Tribune, Issue 4, 2024, pp. 9-10.

18. Huang Songshan and Zhu Hai."The Recovery and Development of China's Inbound Tourism and Product System Upgrade,"Tourism Tribune, Issue 4, 2024, pp. 10-12.

19. Yue Xiaoyan and Sun Yehong."Heritage Tourism: Building an Important Bridge for Cross-Cultural Exchanges in Inbound Tourism,"Tourism Tribune, Issue 4, 2024, pp. 12-14.

20. Yun Jiang, Yi Huiling, and Liang Chunmei."Disruption, Transformation, and Creation: Enterprise Responses in the Recovery and Development of Inbound Tourism,"Tourism Tribune, Issue 4, 2024, pp. 7-9.

21. LiXinjian, Zeng Bowei, Zhang Hui, Song Ziqian, Yang Yong,Ma Bo, and Wang Ning."New Productive Forces and High-Quality Development of Tourism,"Tourism Tribune, Issue 5, 2024, pp. 15-29.

22. Cai Libin and Zhang Ziyu."'Soon to Come'or'a Long Way to Go? Study on the Perceptions of Destination Residents on the Recovery of China's Inbound Tourism,"Tourism Science, Issue 2, 2024, pp. 35-57.

23. Guo Zitong."Enhancing Civilizational Exchanges and Accelerating the Development of

Inbound Tourism,"China Tourism News, January 3, 2024, Issue 001.

24. Tian Li, Liu Lan, and Chen Jun:"Concentration and Diffusion: Spatial Changes in China' Inbound Tourism Industry Driven by Location Factors,"Inquiry into Economic Issues, Issue 1, 2024, pp. 76-91.

25. Sun Jiuxia, Li Fei, and Wang Xueji:"'Tourism in China' Forty Years of Tourism Development and Contemporary Social Changes,"Social Sciences in China, Issue 11, 2023, pp. 84-104.

26. Zheng Peng, Liu Zhuang, Wang Jiejie, Chen Jiayi, and Xi Jianchao:"'Travel for Business' or'Arrival for Culture? The Belt and Road Initiative and China' Inbound Tourism Industry,"China Population·Resources and Environment, Issue 3, 2023, pp. 181-193.

27. Song Rui and Liu Qianqian:"Tourism Development in China' Modernization Process: Significance, Challenges, and Paths,"Tourism Forum, Issue 1, 2023, pp. 1-11.

28. Yang Jinsong and Song Ziqian:"The Historical Evolution and Era Choices of China' Inbound Tourism Policies,"Tourism Tribune, Issue 4, 2024, pp. 1-4.

29. Shen Han, Yang Yijiang, and Chen Qingyang:"Inbound Tourism in Digital Age Brings New Opportunities for Elevating National Image,"Xinhua Institute Research, 2024.

Editorial Note and Acknowledgement

The Xinhua Institute project team for this report titled "China Travel – inviting the world to experience a real China" is headed by Ren Weidong, a member of the Party Leadership Group and Deputy Editor-in-Chief of Xinhua News Agency, with Liu Gang, Director of the Xinhua News Agency Research Institute, serving as the Deputy Leader. Cui Feng, Deputy Director of the Xinhua News Agency Research Institute, is the Executive Deputy Leader. Other team members include Fu Yan, Qin Yanyang, Feng Hou, Ren Qinqin, Xu Zhuang, Wu Mengda, Zhou Huimin, Yang Siqi, DingYiquan, Liu Enli, Xie Yuan, Lang Bingbing, Chen Aiping, Liu Kai, Feng Qidi, LiJizhi, and Chong Dahai. The team members were selected from the headquarters, domestic branches, and overseas bureaus of Xinhua News Agency. All of them are core members of the Agency engaged in news reporting and research. Since the project was authorized and initiated in July 2024, the report has taken five months of study, research, writing, revision, and proofreading before completion.

In the course of writing and publication of the report, valuable guidance and assistance in many areas were provided by experts and scholars including Dai Bin,

Director of the China Tourism Research Institute; Bi Xulong, Vice President of the Central Academy of Culture and Tourism Administration; Bao Jigang, Professor at the School of Tourism Management, Sun Yat-sen University; Lin Jinping, Professor at the School of Marxism, Sun Yat-sen University; Miao Bin, Deputy Director of the International Exchange Department, Central Academy of Culture and Tourism Administration; Ma Xin, Assistant Researcher at the Institute of International Issues, Beijing Academy of Social Sciences. Additionally, PhD students Min Fangzheng, Shen Rui, and Yang Haozhe from the Chinese Academy of Social Sciences University contributed to literature and data collection. We hereby express our sincere gratitude to them.

Postscript

As the only media-based think tank in China's array of national high-end think tanks, the national high-level think tank of Xinhua, with policy research as its main focus, has in recent years carried out forward-looking, strategic and preparatory research concerning major domestic and global issues—producing many influential research outcomes in the process.

This volume compiles four pivotal think tank reports, including Empower China, Benefit the World: An Analysis of the Theoretical Contribution and Value Orientation of New Quality Productive Forces, For the Common Value and Dignity of All Humanity: China's Practices and Contributions of Participating in Global Human Rights Governance, China's Efforts to Safeguard the Cultural Rights of Visually Impaired: Insights from the "Cinema of Light" Public Welfare Initiative, and China Travel: Letting the World Know a More Authentic China. These reports, from diverse fields and perspectives, reflect new explorations and experiences of Chinese modernization comprehensively, providing much valuable reference for countries worldwide to gain a deeper understanding of China.

The editorial team for this publication, comprising Wen Jian, Chen Yi, Li Cheng, Chen Yina, and He Xiaofan from the Strategic Communication Research Center of Xinhua Institute, has diligently curated this collection. We warmly invite readers to share their critiques and suggestions. Any comments and suggestions will be appreciated warmly.

Editorial Committee
May 2025